REGIME CONSOLIDATION AND
TRANSITIONAL JUSTICE

Regime Consolidation and Transitional Justice explores the effect of transitional justice measures on 'regime consolidation', or the means by which a new political system is established in a post-transition context. Focusing on the long-term impact of transitional justice mechanisms in three countries over several decades, the gradual process by which these political systems have been legitimatised is revealed. Through case studies of East and West Germany after World War II, Spain after the end of the Franco dictatorship in 1975 and Turkey's long journey to achieving democratic reform, *Regime Consolidation and Transitional Justice* shows how transitional justice and regime consolidation are intertwined. The interdisciplinary study, which will be of interest to scholars of criminal law, human rights law, political science, democracy, autocracies and transformation theories, demonstrates, importantly, that the political systems in question are not always 'more' democratic than their predecessors and do not always enhance democracy post-regime consolidation.

ANJA MIHR is Programme Director of the Center on Governance through Human Rights, at the Humboldt-Viadrina Governance Platform in Berlin.

REGIME CONSOLIDATION AND TRANSITIONAL JUSTICE

A Comparative Study of Germany, Spain and Turkey

ANJA MIHR

Center on Governance through Human Rights, Humboldt-Viadrina Governance Platform, Berlin

CAMBRIDGE
UNIVERSITY PRESS

CAMBRIDGE
UNIVERSITY PRESS

University Printing House, Cambridge CB2 8BS, United Kingdom

One Liberty Plaza, 20th Floor, New York, NY 10006, USA

477 Williamstown Road, Port Melbourne, VIC 3207, Australia

314–321, 3rd Floor, Plot 3, Splendor Forum, Jasola District Centre, New Delhi – 110025, India

79 Anson Road, #06-04/06, Singapore 079906

Cambridge University Press is part of the University of Cambridge.

It furthers the University's mission by disseminating knowledge in the pursuit of
education, learning, and research at the highest international levels of excellence.

www.cambridge.org
Information on this title: www.cambridge.org/9781108423069
DOI: 10.1017/9781108394895

© Anja Mihr 2018

First published 2018

Printed in the United Kingdom by Clays, St Ives plc

A catalogue record for this publication is available from the British Library.

ISBN 978-1-108-42306-9 Hardback
ISBN 978-1-108-43568-0 Paperback

CONTENTS

ACKNOWLEDGEMENTS

This book is the result of many field trips, archive research, conversations and conference talks for over ten years to find out whether and if and to what extent there is any correlation and inter-linkage between transitional justice measures and the quality or the level of democracy in a modern democracy. During this time friends and colleagues granted me access to data and research funds including valuable time and space to work.

Much of my gratitude therefore goes to the Wissenschaftszentrum Berlin, where I first presented and discussed the idea for this research project, and to the European Inter-University Centre for Human Rights and Democratisation in Venice, where I served as Director of Program and received generous funds to continue with the project. I am particularly grateful to the Netherlands Institute for Human Rights (SIM) at Utrecht University. SIM not only supported this endeavour as part of my academic research work during my time as associate professor, but also granted me generous field research and conference funds to put this book further into progress. The Open Research Area fund I received together with colleagues in London in a similar research area on the impact of transitional justice on democratic institution building until 2016 allowed me to get more comparative insights into the matter. My gratitude also goes to the Centre for Criminology at the Faculty of Law at Oxford University, the Hanse Wissenschaftskolleg, Bremen and to the Transitional Justice Institute of Ulster University in Belfast. They all generously granted me short-term fellowships to continue and discuss my work. Thanks also to The Hague Institute for Global Justice where I served as head of Rule of Law and which kindly supported this project.

Throughout the years, I received valuable research assistance, critical comments, ideas and feedback from Elazar Barkan, Colm Campbell, Jenny Goldschmidt, Marianne Kneuer, Ulrike Liebert, Brianne McGonigle, Wolfgang Merkel, Rory O'Connell, Leigh Payne, Filipa Raimundo, Sandra Rios, Chandra Lekha Sriram, Georg Ulrich and Britta Weiffen. Those and many more colleagues, witnesses, archivists, activists, scholars and interns were all invaluable to my research.

ABBREVIATIONS

AKP	Party for Justice and Progress / *Adalet ve Kalkınma Partisi*
APO	Extra-Parliamentary Opposition / *Außerparlamentarische Opposition*
ARMH	Association for Dealing with the Past / *Asociación para la Recuperación de la Memoria Histórica*
AU	African Union
BTI	Bertelsmann Transformation Index
CDU	Christian Democratic Union
CHP	Atatürk's Republican People's Party / *Cumhuriyet Halk Partisi*
CSCE	Commission on Security and Cooperation in Europe
CSOs	civil society organisations
DP	Democratic Party / *Demokrat Parti*
DTP	Kurdish Democratic Society Party
EC	European Community
ECHR	European Convention on Human Rights
ECtHR	European Court of Human Rights
ETA	Basque Homeland and Freedom Movement / *Euskadi Ta Askatasuna*
EU	European Union
EVZ	*Stiftung Erinnerung, Vernantwortung Zukunft*
GAL	*Grupos Antiterroristas de Liberatión*
GDR	German Democratic Republic
GRAPO	*Grupo de Resistencia Anti-Fascista Primero de Octubre*
HRAA	Turkish Human Rights Agenda Association
IAC	Inter-American Court of Human Rights
ICAD	International Committee Against Disappearances
ICC	International Criminal Court
ICCPR	International Covenant on Civil and Political Rights
ICESCR	International Covenant on Economic, Social and Cultural Rights
ICJ	International Court of Justice
ICTJ	International Center for Transitional Justice
ICTR	International Criminal Tribunal for Rwanda
ICTY	International Criminal Tribunal for the former Yugoslavia
IDEA	(International) Institute for Democracy and Electoral Assistance
IDH	Turkish Human Rights Association / *İnsan HaklariDerneği*
JITEM	*Jandarma İstihbarat ve Terörle Mücadele*
KPD	Communist Party of West Germany / *Kommunistische Partei Deutschlands*

MGK	National Security Council
NATO	North Atlantic Treaty Organization
NCCR	National Centre of Competence in Research
NGOs	non-governmental organisations
NSDAP	*Nationalsozialistische Deutsche Arbeiterpartei*
OHCHR	UN Office of the High Commissioner for Human Rights
OSCE	Organization for Security and Cooperation in Europe
PACE	Parliamentary Assembly of the Council of Europe
PDS	Socialist and Communist Party / *Partei des demokratischen Sozialismus*
PKK	Kurdistan Workers' Party /*Partiya Karkerên Kurdistanê*
PNV	*Partido Nacionalista Vasco*
PP	*Partido Popular*
PSOE	*Partido Socialista Obrero Español*
RAF	Red Army Faction
SED	East German Socialist Unity Party of Germany / *Sozialistische Einheitspartei Deutschlands*
SPD	Social Democratic Party / *Sozialdemokratische Partei Deutschlands*
SS	Schutzstaffel
TAF	Turkish Armed Forces
TARC	Turkish-Armenian Reconciliation Commission
TJ	Transitional Justice
TRC	Truth and Reconciliation Commissions
TRNC	Turkish Cypriot Immovable Property Commission
UCD	Unión de Centro Democrático
UDHR	Universal Declaration of Human Rights
UN	United Nations
US	United States
YARSAV	Judges and Prosecutors' Association

1

Introduction

Transitional Justice (TJ) measures are a driver of regime change and regime consolidation. They can consolidate both democratic and authoritarian regimes. TJ encompasses a number of different legal, political or historical instruments and mechanisms and thus measures that are used by various political and civil actors with different political wills and intentions. Trials, truth commissions, reparations, apologies, vetting procedures, compensations, security sector reforms or amnesties are just a few of these measures. Different political, economic and social civil actors use TJ measures as tools or means for their political or social interests, to strengthen, weaken, enhance or accelerate processes and paths of regime consolidation of both democracy or autocracy. In this book I will focus on regime consolidation and TJ measures that are linked to this long-term process. Furthermore, TJ measures such as commissions of inquiry, trials, lustrations and vetting procedures, or memorials, are instruments for dealing with an unjust past and building a civic and political culture that is the foundation of a consolidated regime. However, the main focus on their possible mutual impact or – as I will further explain – spiral effect, will be that these measures can consolidate not only democratic but also authoritarian and dictatorial regimes. In this book I will test these assumptions on the case studies of the Federal Republic of Germany (West Germany) from 1949 to 1989; the socialist German Democratic Republic (GDR, East Germany) 1949–1989; Spain from 1975 until present; and Turkey from around 1989 until present. I will also look at the multi-causal interlinkage of TJ measures and regime consolidation after the German reunification in 1990 and thus accession of the GDR to the Federal Republic of Germany. To better highlight the differences for the reader between the Federal Republic of Germany (West) and the GDR (East), I will use the short forms of West and East Germany and unified Germany throughout the entire book.

In any regime type, political and civil actors can use TJ measures in political processes to delegitimise the previous regime and at the same time strengthen and legitimise a new political regime or system of whatever type.[1] TJ measures support political actors and help citizens to 'practise' fundamental components of the new – ideally democratic – regime, such as respect for those people who are different because of their gender, ethnicity, and religion or otherwise. If used in an inclusive way to address all relevant victims and victimisers of the past, the measures can contribute to a more pluralistic society, which can be the basis for a democratic regime. TJ measures also allow citizens to become familiar with the rule of law during trials and tribunals, which show that human rights-based constitutions and law is for everyone, not just for the winners. So long as these measures are employed equally *by* and *for* all civil and political actors, victims and victimisers alike, they can be helpful measures for building and strengthening democratic regimes because they leverage the respect of others and the principle of fairness.[2]

After the end of an authoritarian, a dictatorial and violent regime, the society enters a period of regime change through transition. This period lasts until a new political regime is established, usually after a new constitution and its subsequent legal reforms and institutions are in place. If the regime aims to be democratic, this period is also called democratisation. The period of regime change is over and transition has passed when the political regime starts to consolidate and enters the period of long-term transformation.

But whether the new-born political regime turns into an authoritarian or democratic regime type depends on various factors such as economic development, constitutional and institutional setup, political spectrum and parties, political culture and many more – among which TJ measures are only one factor of many. During the short period of regime change political and societal actors determine the future of the subsequent medium and long-term political consolidation of that regime. Generally speaking, regime change takes between one to five or ten years. During these short periods, also called transition, the pathways to authoritarianism or democracy are mostly determined, i.e. by the way the constitution or electoral system is set up. But it also depends on how various actors and parts of society delegitimise the previous regime (from which they aim to be different by all means) and how they aim to legitimise the new political

---

[1] R. Teitel, *Globalizing Transitional Justice* (Oxford: Oxford University Press, 2014), pp. 11–18.
[2] W. Merkel and H. Puhle, *Von der Diktatur zur Demokratie, Transformationen, Erfolgsbedingungen, Entwicklungspfade* (Wiesbaden/Opladen: Westdeutscher Verlag, 1999), p. 167.

regime. This is where in the first years of regime transition TJ measures are influential to set the pathways of consolidation. The subsequent longer period of regime consolidation can be either democratic or authoritarian consolidation.

Authoritarian regimes are those political systems in which pluralism and human rights are limited, ideological claims for nationalism or patriotism are high on the agenda and civil participation is either suppressed or radically restricted by a political elite.[3] Trust in political institutions is low and free civic engagement either top-down organised or non-existent. Juan Linz and Alfred Stepan, however, argue that an authoritarian regime in its latest stage might have a robust civil society, a legal culture supportive of constitutionalism and rule of law – albeit not entirely free, but present and active. Opposed to authoritarian regimes, necessary steps to turn regime change towards democratisation would be the creation of the autonomy, authority, power and legitimacy of democratic institutions firmly based on civic engagement and civil society.[4] In the case of the latter, TJ measures can pave the way when used by civil society actors, because democratic regimes are characterised by constitutionally installed and granted human rights and equity norms, a pluralistic society and institutions that enjoy a high level of trust and civil participation. The political elite does not control all aspects of society and instead reacts and responds to civic engagement and participation in decision-making processes in a timely and adequate manner.[5]

I define consolidation of a regime referring to the general definitions of Linz, Stepan, Wolfgang Merkel and Larry Diamond. Linz and Stepan define a regime as consolidated if five interconnected and mutually reinforcing conditions are met. First, there has to be a free and lively civil society; second, a relatively autonomous and valued political society; third, there must be a rule of law and thus, for example, a constitutional court or other supervising legislative and judicial bodies, to ensure legal guarantees for citizens and human rights; and fourth, a state bureaucracy that is usable and under the mandate of the new democratic government. Last but not least there must be an institutionalised economic society.[6]

---

[3] W. Merkel, *Systemtransformation* (Oplanden: Leske & Budrich UTB, 1999), p. 36.
[4] J.J. Linz and A. Stepan, *Problems of Democratic Transition and Consolidation: Southern Europe, South America, and Post-Communist Europe* (Baltimore, MD: Johns Hopkins University Press, 1996).
[5] W. Merkel, *Systemtransformation*, p. 143.
[6] Ibid., p. 7.

Nevertheless, the authors make clear that a robust civil society is among the most crucial elements among these reinforcing conditions. They also differentiate four different types of autocratic regimes of which an authoritarian regime next to a totalitarian, post-totalitarian or sultanistic one is the most likely one to transit successfully to a democracy because it has stronger roots of civil society than all the other autocratic regimes.[7] In addition to this, Diamond argues that consolidation is most usefully constructed as the process of achieving deep legitimation when all significant political actors on an elite and mass or civil society level agree that the democratic regime is the best one for the society. Legitimation of a democratic regime is thus complete, if the attitude, behaviour and habits of citizens go beyond the normative constitutional commitment to democracy and when all relevant actors regard democratic laws, procedures and institutions as 'the only game in town'.[8]

In response to their definitions, an authoritarian regime lacks strong civil society participation. It is thus an active and free citizen participation that makes most of the difference between modern authoritarian and democratic societies and which can with the help of TJ measures be strengthened. In authoritarian regimes we usually find a segregated society in which ethnic, ideological, religious and social conflicts prevail. These segregations can even be enhanced through selective and exclusive TJ measures such as biased memorials and compensation programmes or show trials. This is due to a political leadership that is incapable of reconciling different social groups in the first years after the regime change. Nevertheless, regime consolidation takes place in two dimensions – the normative and behavioural –for both authoritarian and democratic regimes. These dimensions take place on three levels of society. The highest one is the political elite, the top decision makers, organisational leaders, governments, opinion makers, or economy. The intermediate one is the level of parties, organisations or civil movements; and the third level is that of mass public, and whether or not they believe in the democratic regime or not. At least two-thirds of them should support it, but 66 per cent is a more compelling indicator to show whether a regime is truly consolidated.[9]

---

[7] Ibid., pp. 56ff.
[8] L.J. Diamond, *Developing Democracy: Toward Consolidation* (Baltimore, MD: Johns Hopkins University Press, 1999), p. 65.
[9] Ibid., p. 68.

Merkel elaborates the concept of democratic regime consolidation further and draws fine lines between the different stages of consolidation, to which in this book I will draw back during the case studies. He, for example, confirms that a regime is consolidated when all social groups can fully and freely participate, democratic institutions have been established, and these institutions respond adequately to citizens' claims and needs. The regime is legitimised if the overall majority of citizens believe that the regime's institutions and procedures are better than any alternative regime or political system. But in order to get there, society and institutions have to undergo several stages of constitutional, representative, behavioural and attitudinal and civic consolidation, which I will later explain in more detail.[10] Whatever its defects regime consolidation faces during its consolidation it is legitimised if the majority of people believe it to be.[11] Merkel borrows most of his criteria for system legitimacy from Hannah Arendt, Karl Loewenstein and Otto Brunner and classifies aspects of power and governance into legitimacy of power structures, access to it, the monopoly of power, the structure, the claims and the way this power is executed. These criteria serve as assessment tools to differentiate between fully fledged democracies when moving towards or from defective or deficit democracies or weak regimes as opposed to authoritarian regimes, in which any of the abovementioned logic of democracy is perverted, absent or reversed.[12] Totalitarian regimes, such as the communist ones until 1989, lack any pluralism. Power is in the hands of a political elite and the rule of law is absent, for example.[13] This is a regime type with a power structure that leaves little room for TJ measures claimed by victim groups of the previous regime. My case study on the former East Germany will highlight this relationship also in reference to TJ measures. In an ideal democracy, however, executive, legislative and judicial power needs to be in full but independent control, acting according to general constitutional agreements made during the regime change. In contrast, an authoritarian regime consolidation is based on coercion and lack of free citizen participation. It is possible that the majority of people support the

[10] W. Merkel, *Systemtransformation, Eine Einführung in die Theorie und Empirie der Transformationsforschung*, 2nd edition (Wiesbaden: VS Verlag, 2010), pp. 40–54.
[11] W. Merkel and H.-J. Puhle, *Von der Diktatur zur Demokratie, Transformationen, Erfolgsbedingungen, Entwicklungspfade* (Opladen: Westdeutscher Verlag, 1999), p. 176.
[12] Merkel, *Systemtransformation, Eine Einführung in die Theorie und Empirie der Transformationsforschung*, pp. 22–23.
[13] Ibid., p. 24.

leadership and thus the authoritarian regime, but this is due to coercion and lack of alternatives as the case study of Turkey will show.

Throughout this comparative study, I will explore how the stages and pathways of regime consolidation interact and are intertwined with TJ initiatives, and whether these interactions relate to the civic trust and civic engagement that is eventually key to consolidation as will be shown in the case studies of West Germany, Spain and reunified Germany.

Throughout this book, I view TJ measures as tools, means, instruments or as 'glue' that links different actors with political institutions in a mutually reinforcing and thus spiral way. They link in a spiral way legal and political instruments; politics and mechanisms such as trials, commissions of inquiries and memorials. These measures can be used or abused by actors and their institutions for political purposes or individual interests. They can channel people's voices and claims or they can deny and silence them. As such, the measures themselves have no direct or mono-causal effect on regime consolidation. They stand in a cumulative causal relationship to regimes, and their effects depend on how diverse actors use or abuse them in their power games during regime change and consolidation.

My main hypothesis is that the likelihood in which political and civil actors are using TJ measures in an inclusive manner positively correlates with the quality in which regime consolidation takes place. A more inclusive use of TJ measures, in turn, helps legitimise institution building and regime consolidation in a democratic way. An exclusive and selective (ab)use of these measures leads the regime towards autocracy. Thus, throughout this study, I hypothesise that there is a cumulative causality and spiral inter-linkage between, on the one hand, the institutions put in place during regime change and transition; and, on the other hand, the use of TJ measures by actors. Both affect the degree of legitimacy that political institutions enjoy.

I compare different regime types in three different countries. My sample comprises three countries with three different regime types that moved from autocratic regimes to democratic or semi-democratic or back to authoritarian or totalitarian regimes. Taking Linz's and Stepan's concepts of autocratic regimes into account, one could argue that West and East Germany moved from totalitarian and post-totalitarian regimes after 1945 to a democratic one in West Germany and back to a totalitarian one in the East. Spain moved from an authoritarian one to a democratic one. And Turkey moved first from a sultanistic autocracy to an authoritarian and later to a democratic regime with major democratic flaws or deficits, and due to the lack of free civil society in recent years, it moved back to an authoritarian one.[14] Nevertheless, what they all had in common was the clear commitment to normative democratic reforms at some stage in their development and they all had forms of statehood and state institutions on which they could build on and through which they later introduced TJ measures, such as trials, commissions of inquiry, amnesties, vetting or reparation measures.

The first case study in this book looks at the countries of West and East Germany since 1949 and the unified Germany since 1990; the second case study looks at Spain since 1975; and the third one studies Turkey since 1989. Each case study chronicles the countries' development in the decades since their regime changes after war or dictatorship and their clear formal or *de jure* commitment to democracy, but not yet de facto. I provide evidence that the use of TJ measures as political tools affects both autocratic and democratic regime building as well as those regimes' pathways to consolidation. In these processes, the TJ measures used (for example, commissions of inquiry, memorials, lustration, amnesties or trials) and the existing basic state, non-state and inter-governmental institutions (constitution, courts, parliaments, civil society, memberships in international organisations, etc.) mutually reinforce each other in an upward or downward spiral way.

I use the term 'regime change' to denote the change of relations of power during the transition period, for example through altering norms of institutions. This period is usually completed when a new constitution and the subsequent institutions are in place and start working and first or second election terms have been held. In the early stage of regime change the promise for justice by way of trials, tribunals, reparations, compensations or vetting procedures can be an incentive to set up the necessary legal and political framework, for example providing for truth commissions to come into force in the near future, to allow for domestic or international trials of past perpetrators, etc. It does not mean that all TJ measures ought to be applied in the first two to three years of transition. Most countries opt also for amnesty laws during this period, for reasons of stability and tranquillity, as Spain did. As long as they are not blanket amnesties, but rather conditional, such laws can be changed later but during early transition they can have a positive effect on the later consolidation process. Early regime change is a series of negotiations and compromises between actors such as political parties, victim groups,

---

[14] See examples given by Linz and Stepan, pp. 56ff.

victimisers and international organisations, who often have very different interests and resources. A regime is no longer in 'change' but starts to consolidate when new political rules are in place and widely adhered to. But the term 'consolidation' does not in itself say anything about whether this adherence is achieved by means of terror, pressure or through consent and persuasion.[15]

TJ measures are thus in this study, the independent variables in the hands of actors and society; and regime consolidation is my dependent variable. I argue that the mutual reinforcement between institutions and TJ measures over a longer period of time can lead either to democracy or authoritarianism and even totalitarianism. There is no 'autopilot' determining that dealing with the unjust or atrocious regimes of the past through trials, truth commissions or reparations will automatically lead a regime into democracy. Therefore, there is no mono-causal path from TJ measures to either democracy or authoritarianism nor to any other specific regime type. The difference is grounded in *the way how* powers and institutions use TJ measures for their political goals. If the pathway to consolidation is determined by a rule of law abating manner, by means of pluralism based on the sovereignty of the citizens, the likeliness that the regime becomes democratic is higher than if the pathways are arbitrary, repressive and exclusive towards interest groups or former elites which characterise authoritarian and totalitarian regimes.[16]

In general, I speak of a *multi-causal cumulative process* of mutual reinforcement of institutions and actors based on their attitudes, trust, behaviours and policies that result in regime consolidation of various degrees and kinds. Overall I argue that the main role TJ measures can have in this multi-causal cumulative process is the ability to delegitimise the previous (unjust) regime and to legitimise the new regime, be it democratic or authoritarian as illustrated in Table 1.1.

The spiral relationship between TJ measures and institutions can go in various directions. For example, if a country decides to prosecute crimes committed by the previous regime, and the domestic judiciary proves itself independent and impartial in its judgment of those on trials, citizens will become more positive about the effect that TJ measures can have. In this way, when institutions are strong and a TJ measure such as open and

---

[15] J. Brückner, 'Transitionasansätze' in R. Kollmorgen, W. Merkel and H.-J. Wagner (eds.) *Handbuch Transformationsforschung* (Wiesbaden: Springer VS, 2014), pp. 90–91.

[16] W. Merkel, *Systemtransformation, Eine Einführung in die Theorie und Empirie der Transfor mationsforschung*, p. 23.

Table 1.1 *Multi-causal linkage between independent and dependent variable*

Independent variable	⇨	Dependent variable
Transitional justice measures –*Historical*, apologetic justice and memorials –*Criminal*, punitive, retributive justice – *Political*, restorative and cultural justice –*Silence* and amnesty laws	Multi- and cumulative causal pathways Spiral interlinkages and effect	– *Regime change and consolidation* (constitutional, representative/institutional, behavioural/attitudinal and civic) – *Democratic or authoritarian* regime consolidation

fair trials succeeds, TJ can trigger demands from local actors for more such measures. Thus, it will increase citizen participation for more claims for trials or other measures.

However, TJ measures can also fail. For example, if imposed on a country through winner's justice or by foreign powers, trials have the potential to intimidate domestic claims and thus hamper justice. Alternatively, and as has been the case in many post-conflict societies, countries often pass on perpetrators to international courts and tribunals without aiming to take domestic action. In these cases, when domestic institutions are weak or otherwise incapable of putting perpetrators to justice, international, hybrid or special courts can fill the 'justice gap' for a determined time or for a single case until domestic independent judiciary is in place – ideally. The fact that these determined courts, such as the International Criminal Tribunals for the former Yugoslavia (ICTY) or for Rwanda (ICTR) take decades to close their final cases, also indicate the weakness of domestic political institution building and lack of independence, but not necessarily the imperial character of such international tribunals or courts.

Gunnar Myrdal convincingly described the mutually reinforcing relationship between measures and institutions, as well as the spiral effect already in the 1950s.[17] He showed how external incentives, such as initiative by international organisations, politics and civil society could affect

---

[17] G. Myrdal, *Rich Lands and Poor: The Road to World Prosperity*, World Perspectives Edition (New York: Harper and Brothers, 1957), vol. XVI.

circular and cumulative causation in regime change and consolidation. These causations spiral either upward or downward, having either a positive or negative effect on the development of the regime. Upward would be in his terms towards a democratic regime and downward development would be towards an authoritarian regime. According to Myrdal's concept, TJ measures can thus be seen as external incentives and interference mechanisms, and their effects depend on how actors use or abuse them. TJ measures can either prompt democratic institution building and consolidation or they can impede democratic development and strengthen autocratic and dictatorial government.

With the examples of East, West and reunified Germany, Spain and Turkey, I illustrate how this spiral effect has also been working in the context of TJ and regime consolidation. As I will explain in more detail throughout this book, my approach compares the 'most different' case studies, choosing countries that are most different in their histories, contexts and outcomes and yet all have used or misused TJ measures during the period of regime change and consolidations. The reader will see that there is no mono-causal or automatic link between TJ measures and regime consolidation. At best, TJ is only one factor among many others that have a long-lasting effect on regime transformation.

As mentioned earlier, of relevance to this comparison are the studies by Linz and Stepan because of their profound investigations of regime change and consolidation. They focus on rule of law and civil society in transition countries and identify five main factors that matter for regime consolidation and have remained the same for over decades, namely: (1) the role played by civil society; (2) political society and elites; (3) the rule of law; (4) the state apparatus and institutions; as well as (5) the market economy. And, as indicated earlier, Merkel has specified these different levels and stages of regime consolidation by identifying four stages of consolidation after transition which in addition apply to these case studies: first, the normative-constitutional; second, the representative role of actors that use or abuse the norms set in the constitution; third, the behaviour and attitudinal shift in society when all political and civil actors, private companies as well as civil society organisations (CSOs) adhere to these constitutional norms and play a fair game; and fourth, when civil culture is established because civil society interacts with politics through active participation, which is usually the case one generation after regime change.[18] Throughout this study, I will repetitively come back

---

[18] W. Merkel, *Systemtransformation*, pp. 145–146.

to the stages two to four, in particular, as they apply mostly to my cases studies in relation to TJ.

Subsequent to the abovementioned stages, Merkel and Hans-Jürgen Puhle differentiate between consolidated democratic and authoritarian regimes by how strong and interactive the different 'sub regimes' of the specific political regime are. Both define seven 'sub regimes': stability; the party system; organised society and interest groups; political and societal elites; political institutions; inclusion of 'others' such as minorities; and, last but not least, the attitudes, opinions and behaviour of citizens who either support or oppose the regime.[19] Not surprisingly, they emphasise that the more diffuse and independent citizen groups are, the more they legitimise a democratic regime through their actions and engagement. Pluralism and civic engagement is key to strong democracy. But the more the government organises, controls or represses citizens' engagement, the less likely citizens are to legitimise a regime and thus the regime becomes authoritarian. But relevant for this book is the definition of consolidation, when they and others paraphrase that '[c]onsolidation requires that habituation to the norms and procedures of democratic *conflict* regulation be developed. A high degree of *institutional routinisation* is a key part of such a process. *Intermediation* between state and civil society and the structuring of *compromise* are likewise legitimate and necessary tasks of political society.'[20] Legitimacy is therefore based on the belief that for that particular juncture no other type of regime could assure a more successful pursuit of collective goals, as Linz has explained earlier.[21] For this intermediation, I argue, TJ measures can be useful tools, the 'clue' that glues civil society, political institutions and political and economic elites together in a society.

Authors of democracy and democratisations agree that institutions and TJ mechanisms alone cannot guarantee successful democratic consolidation. Because as explained above, the main difference between democracy and authoritarianism is that the first has an active and plural civil society, while the second has an inactive one and if it has one it is controlled by the government. In authoritarianism, there is little to no free or citizen-driven interaction. Instead, in authoritarian regimes, TJ measures are top-down rituals political elites employ to distance themselves from the previous

---

[19] W. Merkel and H.-J. Puhle, *Von der Diktatur zur Demokratie*, p. 138.

[20] J. Linz and A. Stepan, *Problems of Democratic Transition and Consolidation*, p. 10, italics in original.

[21] J. Linz, *Crisis*, 'Breakdown, and Reequilibration' in: J.J. Linz and A. Stepan (eds.), *The Breakdown of Democratic Regimes* (Baltimore, MD: Johns Hopkins University Press, 1978), p. 18.

regime. TJ measures are not used by citizens to trigger more transparency or accountability of the new regime – but the opposite. Thus authors like Merkel, Puhle, Linz and others conclude that democracy is more than a political regime, it is an interacting system, while authoritarianism is a top-down regime in which free citizen participation is not welcomed.[22] We observe that it is usually only about 20 years – or one generation – after regime change that it becomes clear whether civil society can be active without fear, intimidation and free from want in a regime. This is the '20+ generation', as I will call it throughout this book. It is at this stage that one can see whether political and civil actors respect, incorporate and adhere to rules, norms and regulatory frameworks. Because civil society has such a large impact on the process of regime development and transformation, I will focus mainly on political and civil society and their use and interaction with TJ measures.

This study will also give examples that provide insights into why some countries in post-war or post-autocratic transitions turn back to authoritarianism, become fragile or defective – as Merkel[23] argues – instead of strong and democratic consolidated, whilst their political and civil actors use or misuse the same TJ measures as countries that succeed in consolidating democracy. This study will show that the difference in outcome can be explained by the difference in the ways 'how' political and societal actors use TJ measures.

Furthermore, I argue that the effect of TJ measures on attitudes, trust, behaviour and politics only appears a generation after regime change, at which time the regime is usually on its best way to consolidation. This leads to another argument, namely that while TJ may have the strongest effect in democratic societies, TJ measures thus can only contribute to strengthen such a democratic society but they are not its main or exclusive cause for the creation of democracy.

In addition to this, the reader will see throughout the comparative country studies that in the first ten and even 20 years of regime development, political actors in all regime types mainly use TJ for tactical

---

[22] J. Linz and A. Stepan, *Problems of Democratic Transition and Consolidation*, pp. 13–15.

[23] A defect democratic regime is one in which the rule of law is limited or corrupted, and elections are manipulated with the aim to turn the regime into an authoritarian one, although there is still a plural but yet more and more controlled political spectrum and civil society visible, which is slowly shrinking and democratic aspects of the regime are declining. W. Merkel, *Systemtransformation, Eine Einführung in die Theorie und Empirie der Transformationsforschung*, pp. 40–54.

purposes or because their own political commitments force them to deal with the past.[24] It is only when citizens freely use TJ measures as a tool to change policies and engagement with state institutions that these measures become part of the moral, ethical, political and civil instruments used by politicians, civil society and private enterprises alike.

In order to show the spiral and mutually cumulating nature of the interaction, I use a most different comparative design focusing on the case studies in Europe. I look at Germany during its different stages of development after World War II in 1945 and after new regimes or regime policies had been established: East Germany during the period of 1949–1990; West Germany in 1949–1990; and reunified Germany after 1990. East and West German political and civil actors all used TJ measures after World War II as a catalyst for certain political reforms and to consolidate their respective authoritarian and democratic regimes. Later, unified Germany used TJ measures to deal with the legacy of the communist totalitarian dictatorship in the East. I will also detail the case study of Spain, from 1975 until the present day. This case study illustrates the fact that neither the absence of TJ nor its systematic approach alone is responsible – let alone mono-causal – for democratic regime consolidation, but rather indicates strength or weakness of a regime and its level of legitimacy.

Turkey is the 'test case' in this study, which means that my findings from the other case studies will be applied to the case and stages of regime consolidation and TJ in Turkey. With Turkey as a case I investigate whether TJ measures were introduced after the government sought cooperation with the European Community (EC) and made major commitments to democracy in the late 1980s and through the 1990s, and whether these measures had any effect on regime consolidation and the increase of citizen participation until around 2010 when the decline back to authoritarianism became slowly visible.

I will consider TJ measures during different time periods, divided into decades of transition and regime consolidation in all country cases. The different political regimes of East and West Germany developed in different, diachronic directions between 1949 and 1990. However, after reunification in 1990, the two sides developed more in sync. Spain is a unique

---

[24] N. Deitelhoff and K.D. Wolff, 'Business and Human Rights: How Corporate Norm Violators Become Norm Entrepreneurs' in T. Risse, S.C. Ropp and K. Sikkink (eds.), *The Persisting Power of Human Rights, From Commitment to Compliance* (Cambridge: Cambridge University Press, 2013), pp. 227–230.

case because regime change happened only after the death of its dictator in 1975. There were no major uprisings calling for the dictator General Franco's overthrow and claims for justice after his death. Instead a new head of state was directly in place the day the dictator died, with King Juan Carlos taking the leadership role. There was no power or leadership gap as found in most other transition countries. Neither was there a lack of political infrastructure. Turkey passed a series of democratic reforms in the late 1980s, motivated by its desire to join the EC in 1989 and reflecting the democratic shifts and changes in greater Europe at that time. From then on, Turkey continued to slowly introduce reforms that were the result of painful concessions to international organisations and citizens' claims for TJ, that were partly fulfilled. The country is an example for the struggle between civic actors and their claim for more inclusive TJ and political actors that misused TJ measures for strategic political manoeuvres.

Regardless of whether these countries' histories were marked by hot or cold war, military or communist dictatorships, what these countries have in common is their commitment to political democratic reforms after regime chance took off. They turned into consolidated democracies or strong authoritarian regimes only a decade or more after they made these formal commitments to democracy. That is to say, the effect to which TJ measures contribute to autocratic or democratic types of regimes can only be seen a decade or so after they have been installed.

During the early transition period, the leadership and government of all countries claimed to adhere to international law and human rights standards, making efforts to join international organisations such as the United Nations (UN), the Organisation for Security and Cooperation in Europe (OSCE), the Council of Europe or the EC. Their leadership also made a formal commitment to civil society and their free interaction and participation in politics, although this was soon restricted in East Germany and in Turkey. Regardless of the fact that all four countries (ab)used TJ measures, it is clear that the new regimes developed in very different directions.

In socialist East Germany, for example, TJ measures such as memorials or trials were often used to purge political opponents and to shape the historical narrative to justify and legitimise a newly emerging totalitarian communist dictatorship that lasted until 1989. After its foundation in 1949, the Federal Republic (West Germany) slowly moved towards a market-based consensual democracy, as did Spain after a sharp regime change between 1975 and 1977. In each of these cases, TJ measures played a very different but instrumental role.

In the example of Turkey, regime change happened under external incentives when aiming to join the EC/EU. Until around 1987, Turkey had an almost continuous autocratic past with a massive and repetitive record of human rights violations. But after officially claiming regime shift around the EC talks in 1987 and 1989, the Turkish government made a clear commitment to democratic reforms, to adhere to its own democratic constitution from 1982 that had been a farce until 1989, and to stronger ties with the international community, particularly the Council of Europe and the EC and later the EU. The Turkish government's willingness for democratic transition in 1987 and 1989 cannot be seen independently of the transitions and political shifts in Eastern Europe and the rest of the world at that time. What makes Turkey an interesting 'test case' study for this book is the fact that Turkey used TJ measures as catalysts to trigger major security sector reforms and to please EU claims for more political reform, yet with very different results than those found in Germany and Spain. Moreover, I can only use Turkey as a case study because of the lack of access to sources such as archives in a language that I cannot read.

As I have repetitively argued, while TJ measures are tools, instruments or catalysts for changes and consolidations, there is no direct causal link between TJ and outcomes that can prove for example that one specific trial or a series of trials leads to more adherence of the rule of law, let alone democracy. For example, the Frankfurt Auschwitz trials starting in 1963 in West Germany, never automatically increased the level of trust or the rule of law. There is more to the story of the cumulative or spiral effect TJ has to democratic consolidation, but the trials show some interesting bounds to other citizen engagement and political reforms happening at the same time. It is a two-way flow of causality; a form of circular interaction between politics on the one hand and the way TJ measures are used on the other.[25] TJ measures have always been seen as a bundle of tools that are used for political or individual purposes by political and civil actors that can – but do not always – influence and affect regime consolidation.[26]

Instead, the more democratic a regime becomes, the more TJ measures become ingrained in politics. This is because these measures contribute to reuniting society and making it inclusive – which is a prerequisite for a stable and solid democracy. In return, the more citizens feel encouraged to use TJ to raise their claims or get civil society running, the more they

[25] D.A. Rustow, 'Transition to Democracy: Toward a Dynamic Model', Comparative Politics, 2(3) (1970), 344.
[26] W. Merkel and H.-J. Puhle, Von der Diktatur zur Demokratie, pp. 174–175.

contribute to democracy. Transformation to democracy can endure for decades and generations, prior to measurable results being produced.[27] Generational patterns are seen in transformation and consolidation studies, in which the generational shift that occurs around 15 to 20 years after regime change is a sort of magical point in time, at which it becomes clear whether all the reform efforts of the first post-regime change decade have led to success or not.[28]

Emergence from authoritarian or suppressive rule is often accompanied by sweeping changes in the governance system. Most countries in transition opt for a democratic model, or at least claim to. These countries create new institutional structures such as courts, a parliament and government that are based on fundamental human rights norms. However, this does not say anything about the way in which these institutions actually perform and whether they are efficient. Nevertheless, these new democratic institutions – as fragile as they may be – are put in place to ensure a minimum level of the rule of law, liberty and participation rights, usually in a way that is manifested in their constitutional setups. This was the case for all countries in this study in the initial post-regime change stage, but later most of these countries compromise the human rights to participation or free expression of interests, claims and views of which a TJ process benefits the most.

It is often the general memory and catharsis of a violent and dictatorial past that inspires the content of new constitutions and the mandate of new constitutional courts. The constitution plays a pivotal role in whether and how TJ measures have positive or negative effects on consolidation. TJ measures have their most positive effect if they become tools for civil society, governments and international organisations alike, thus exerting international human rights or criminal justice standards, while also being used domestically. But it is only when actors and institutions on the international, national and civil society level work together that TJ can have an effect on the change of civic culture, and thus on the legitimacy of the new regime. If instead civil society is excluded from this process or if international interference, incentives or human rights norms, are ignored,

---

[27] The long-term aspect of Transitional Justice (hereinafter: TJ) measures has been stressed by the UN Special Rapporteur on the promotion of truth, justice, reparation and guarantees of non-recurrence (Greiff, in his 2013 report to the UN General Assembly). UN Doc A/HRC/24/42 Human Rights Council, Report of the Special Rapporteur on the promotion of truth, justice, reparation and guarantees of non-recurrences, Greiff, Geneva and New York, Twenty-Fourth Session, 28 August 2013.

[28] W. Merkel, *Systemtransformation*, p. 146.

then the likeliness that TJ measures are used for power purposes only, and thus the likelihood of TJ measures enhancing autocratic – instead of democratic – performance, is high.

Methodologically, this study employs an empirical, qualitative and comparative analysis of the incremental correlation between TJ measures and regime change. I compare these most different cases and look at the way TJ measures are used by actors and their institutions (independent variable) and how these interact with regime change and (de)consolidation (dependent variable) over a longer period of time. Generally speaking, the quality and strength of political institutions can be measured by measuring their effectiveness and how the executive, legislative and judicial powers respond and react to demands and needs of victims and victimisers from the past regime. This is where TJ measures are used and can make a difference in regime change and consolidation.

If civic engagement and trust score high we assume a more strongly consolidated democratic regime. If they score low, for example because of a high level of corruption and low independence of judiciary or legislative powers, regimes tend more towards autocracy or non-consolidated democracies. TJ measures can be the means to encourage participation and interaction, such as through fair trials and equal and fair distributions of reparations, and thus can trigger high levels of engagement. Presidents, prime ministers, members of cabinets, parliamentarians, commissioners, judges, etc., on all domestic and local levels, are elites that determine how this process takes place, by their adherence to norms and behaviour. Their adherence or non-adherence also determines the attitudes, trust and behaviour of citizens and civil society. Effective performance can be determined based on whether decision-making processes are inclusive, open to compromise and transparent in the way they take their decisions; and whether the implementation of decisions occurs with accountability and citizens widely agree upon means of enforcement. In other words, the level of transparency, accountability and responsiveness by governmental authorities towards constituencies, may they be the electorate, citizens, non-governmental organisations (NGOs), victim groups, militias or survivors of past atrocities, matters.

Government transparency and accountability is pivotal when illustrating the spiral effect between TJ measures, actors and institutions. It can be assessed by citizen participation and civic engagement with these institutions and whether or not state institutions respond to citizens' claims for TJ, for example, when victim groups ask for forensic investigations about alleged mass graves during the war and whether or not state institutions respond to these claims, become active and later publish a report about their activity and forensic investigations. In other words, the TJ process can trigger acts that contribute to more transparency during the institution-building process. Indicators such as whether or not claims for investigations, for trials, for vetting procedures or commissions of inquiries have led to state responsiveness and triggered further claims and initiatives by victim groups, can be assessed throughout any of these case studies. Therefore, transparency, accountability and in particular responsiveness of state institutions and their representatives, as well as the level of citizen participation, are the foundation of strong democratic regime consolidation. The opposite is of course true for authoritarian consolidation.

On the one hand, TJ measures are able to catalyse the delegitimisation and demystification process of the previous autocratic, violent or wrongful regime and their elites, for example by ensuring that those guilty of grave injustices, atrocities or crimes against humanity are held accountable or by demystifying their 'heroic' claims when installing memorials on mass atrocities.[29] On the other hand, TJ measures serve as a tool for practising democracy and thus legitimising the new – and democratic – regime through rehabilitation, retributive, restorative and reconciliation policies that reunite a divided and mistrustful society and that create active citizens who legitimise new political institutions. This is pivotal for the unity of the society and the country; without it a democratic government cannot govern. TJ measures can shift the rules of the game, that is to say they can change the customs, traditions, cultures and behaviour that were previously manifested in the autocratic or authoritarian regime.

Another way this study will measure the mutual reinforcing effects of TJ measures and consolidation is to conduct an actor-specific assessment, i.e. to look at how some policy makers and representatives of CSOs have put TJ measures on the political agenda. It helps to assess how TJ measures, and in particular international human rights and criminal law-based measures, change the parameters of and transform the legal and political culture of the society, for example in domestic trials. This cultural transformation process, from a rule-by-law to a rule-of-law culture is crucial to democracy. Modernisation theorists argue that this transformational shift can take up to a generation after the regime change, a claim that is

---

[29] M. Nalepa, *Skeletons in the Closet: Transitional Justice in Post-Communist Europe* (Cambridge: Cambridge University Press, 2010).

strongly underlined by the findings in this book.[30] This reiterates that TJ measures can serve as a transmitter of or catalyst for the establishment of civic trust between citizens and institutions, trust that had been lost during past dictatorships or wars.[31] Critical theorists argue that democratic regimes have more inclusive orders than authoritarian ones, that is to say they can be characterised as equal and free societies. Whatever incentives, measures or mechanisms the new political elite chooses to help achieve this order and to overcome old traditional violent and ineffective ways of governance are seen as a contribution to democratic consolidation.[32]

Bearing Myrdal et al.'s theorems in mind, the potential catalytic and spiral effects of TJ tools in regime consolidation can contribute to the downward spiral, if the new political elite uses these measures in a biased and exclusive manner during transition processes, for example if the new political elite uses these tools in an attempt to cleanse itself of former opponents. As stated earlier, I put much weight on the role actors play and how they lead and represent institutions. Thus, a way to measure and assess regime consolidation through TJ measures is by looking at how the political will of elites and citizens translates into institutional performance. Attention for these actors, may they be corporate, political or civil, is important because it is these actors who decide, choose and react to international or domestic pressure. They also represent the majority of any society and thus without them a regime can never be fully legitimised. Institutional performance is thus the result and output of actors' decisions. If the political will to use TJ measures to strengthen democracy is missing or – as we will see in the cases of East Germany or Turkey – only aims to purge political opponents, the positive effect of TJ will fail. TJ measures can also be assessed based on whether they are used to include or exclude societal groups in a pluralistic society. For example, if political elites allow amnesty for one group of perpetrators but not for others and are not willing to place blame for past atrocities on all sides (including their own constituency) this indicates bias. Such use of TJ measures only perpetuates the divisions within society, thus harming democratic regime

---

[30] R. Kollmorgen, 'Mondernisierungstheoretische Ansätze' in R. Kollmorgen, W. Merkel and H.-J. Wagner (eds.), *Handbuch Transformationsforschung*, p. 79.

[31] E. Schniter, R.M. Sheremeta and D. Sznycer, 'Restoring Damaged Trust with Promises, Atonement and Apology', Capman University, University of California, 22 December 2011. ssm.com/abstract=1975976 (last accessed February 2014).

[32] C. Humrich, 'Critical Theory' in S. Schneider and M. Spindler (eds.) *Theories of International Relations* (London: Routledge, 2014), pp. 269–271.

consolidation. After 1949, in East Germany the political elite was willing to punish Nazi perpetrators for the crimes they committed, but not communists for their crimes during the same period of World War II and thereafter; and in Turkey military officials were almost always exempted from punitive actions during transition periods after military coups. This hindered the creation of an inclusive and rule-of-law abating society.[33]

1.1   Research Questions and Spiral Effect

Referring to the abovementioned country case studies, I will examine whether there is any mutually reinforcing effect between regime change, consolidation and the kind of TJ measures employed. Furthermore, I will argue that the sequence of the measures employed is also relevant: it matters whether trials are held two years after regime change or 20 years after the political shift took place. The spiral effect only can be made visible after one generation. I will furthermore examine whether a certain mix or combination of TJ measures are able to succeed in changing the attitude and behaviour of civil and political actors, or whether these measures as such might be counter-productive to or completely ineffective at achieving regime consolidation? Whether the TJ measures leverage the independence of the courts, trigger parliamentary debates or urge political actors to respond to victims' needs and claims depends on the institutional setup as well as the overall political will? Increasing sentiments of revenge; placing blame on only one side or, conversely, assigning no blame to anyone at all; excluding certain groups from the decision-making process or ignoring their claims – such as was the case in relation to the Kurds in Turkey, the Roma in Germany or Franco's 'abducted children' in Spain during the first decades after regime change – can destabilise and thus deconsolidate a regime temporarily or permanently. Such exclusionary TJ measures reinforce the past and lead to acts of vengeance that recreate the past culture of violence and mistrust, undermining the rule of law and adherence to democratic standards and thus providing the soil in which autocracies flourish. For example, Turkey's inability to come to terms with the Armenian Genocide has led to a closure of borders and restrictions of trade with neighbouring Armenia. West Germany's unwillingness to accept the borders of Poland and towards other eastern Communist states after World War II led to a freeze of economic and diplomatic relationships

---

[33] J.L. Gibson, 'The Contribution of Truth to Reconciliation, Lessons from South Africa', *Journal of Conflict Resolution*, 50 (2006), 409–432.

for decades. The Spanish political elite's unwillingness to open up a public debate concerning the Franco regime led to myths about him and his constituency that fuelled separatism, terrorism and instability in the country for decades. But can TJ measures really channel the prospect of regime consolidation?

Myths about the past have provided fertile ground for the separatist terror group ETA (Basque Homeland and Freedom Movement or *Euskadi Ta Askatasuna*) to justify its violence and killings of state officials that seriously affected state security and cost many civilian lives for decades after Franco's death. ETA implicitly justified its terror attacks with the fact that many members of the former Franco elite continued to run important state institutions and permeated the security sector and the judiciary. Such a haunting past is a constant sword of Damocles hanging over attempts at democratic development. TJ measures are one way of confronting, demystifying and delegitimising this past.

I am fully aware of the many failed attempts to prove either a direct or mono-causal effect between TJ and/or democratic institution building and consolidation. There is simply no good evidence of such direct or mono-causal effect. Spain is one good example of this lack of a direct link between TJ measures and democratic regime consolidation. Although Spain is no doubt a consolidated democracy, major TJ measures were never called for or implemented during its period of consolidation. Similarly to Dankwart Rustow, I will thus argue that the relationship between TJ measures and consolidation can best be characterised as a spiral or circular interaction, rather than as a direct causal link between the independent and dependent variables.[34] Alexandra Barahona de Brito, Carmen Gonzaléz-Enríquez and Paloma Aguilar emphasised this in their comparative efforts to examine transitional countries in Europe and Latin America. They could not find any direct correlation or causal effect between TJ and democracy.[35] As discussed earlier, strong support for democratic regimes and their legitimacy depends on many factors, such as economic development, balance of power, inclusion of old and new elites and representatives of CSOs and so on. It is in relation to these many factors that TJ measures can be seen as a tool or a 'learning opportunity'

---

[34] D.A. Rustow, 'Transition to Democracy: Toward a Dynamic Model', 344.
[35] A. Barahona de Brito, C. Gonzaléz-Enríquez and P. Aguilar (eds.), *The Politics of Memory, Transitional Justice in Democratizing Societies* (Oxford: Oxford University Press, 2001), pp. 312–313.

for how to act and behave differently towards others and how to apply fair and human rights-based principles in a democratic context.

I will also look at whether stable institutions can perform even better and more resiliently if certain conditions are met, such as equal participation of all stakeholders involved, adherence to international human rights law and standards, the continuing quest for independent legislative and judicial powers and the comprehensive inclusion of citizens. Can TJ measures really be a catalyst to achieve better institutional performance?

Some TJ measures may be more appropriate during the first five or ten years, while others only after 20 years, depending on the context of the conflict, the level of seriousness of the previous regime's crimes or atrocities, as well as the willingness of political actors and civil society throughout the transitional and transformation periods. It does not matter whether certain measures, such as trials or memorials, precede other measures. Rather, what matters is that several TJ measures are employed parallel to one another and are used by different actors during institution-building periods. Trials can be held later or earlier, but never without other TJ measures running alongside them, such as for example the use of apology or memorials.

This relates closely to the other important factors that affect consolidation, namely the level of civic trust, which was mentioned earlier. Although there is no satisfying conceptual framework to measure civic trust, social science research indicators do allow one to equate the level of civil engagement to levels of trust. So, for example, one could look to the number of civil networks formed by victims or victimisers to claim their rights or compensation vis-à-vis new institutions, such as parliament, courts or other state agencies. Thus, civic trust is defined here by the level of interactive engagements citizens have and the use they make of political institutions such as courts, public administration, parliamentarian delegates, elections or police. Without such engagement by citizens and the responsiveness from institutional actors there is no civic trust.[36] Democracies cannot work without citizens' broad commitment to democratic rules and procedures and thus rely on citizens' trust in institutions.[37] In post-dictatorial societies, citizens often lack trust in public institutions; they believe the institutions to be corrupt and ineffective due to the fact that elites of the previous

---

[36] K.S. Cook, R. Hardin and M. Levi, *Cooperation Without Trust?* (New York: Russell Sage Foundation Series on Trust, 2005), p. 176.

[37] W. Kymlicka, *Contemporary Political Philosophy: An Introduction* (Oxford: Oxford University Press, 2002), p. 285.

regime still govern the country and have not changed their attitudes, habits or behaviour. In order to even start engaging with public and new (democratic) institutions, there has to be a minimum level of pluralistic freedom and human rights assurance for citizens to do so. Such are voting and participation rights, the freedom of media, Internet and press, as well as equal access to social security, health, education facilities and food supplies. If access and rights are denied, it will be hard for trust among citizens, political actors and institutions to flourish. Only once these rights are guaranteed through new civil laws and independent courts can citizens' participation increase and legitimise the new (democratic) regime. Thus, for the best mutual reinforcement of institutional performance and TJ measures, it needs democratic institutions in place.

The term 'quality of democratic regimes' is often used to rank institutional performance per se. Unlike other democracy rankings,[38] it allows us to explain democratic performance in a more multi-dimensional way by focusing on how and why institutions work the way they do. The same is true for arguing that institutions become more resilient when their actors are self-critical. Dealing with an unpleasant past in an open way may contribute to this resilience and quality. Constraints can deconsolidate institutions and can be both informal, such as clientelism, corruption or traditions, as well as formal, such as electoral setups, representations, consensual mechanisms or autonomy rights.

Different surveys that measure trust in institutions have shown an incremental correlation between civic trust and the level of institutional performance.[39] Civic trust implies that the person who trusts freely transfers assets to this institution without controlling their actions or having the possibility to retaliate. This is in fact often not the case in post-dictatorial societies where mistrust is widespread because of past bad experience, as was the case in East and West Germany, Spain and Turkey during regime change. There must be a potential gain or incentive for the 'as yet trust-inexperienced' citizens to engage with institutions and their leaders. Memorials, apologies, vetting processes, commissions of inquiry or trials can break the vicious circle of mistrust. A criminal judgment on past injustice and condemnation of former perpetrators by an international court, tribunal or new domestic civil court based on human rights

---

[38] For example the Global Democracy Ranking – Global Democracy Ranking, democracy-ranking.org/wordpress/ (last accessed July 2016).
[39] M. Naef and J. Schupp, 'Measuring Trust. Experiments and Surveys in Contrast and Combination', *IZA Discussion Papers*, No. 4087 (2009).

standards, aims to give such a positive example and shows that new institutions can work in citizens' favour and not against them. Symbolic acts of reconciliation, such as the joint commemoration of Holocaust victims between Israeli and West German leaders, or the official apology from the Spanish government towards the victims of the Franco regime, can increase civic trust. This is where TJ measures and institutions correlate and form cumulative and spiral causalities that are mutually reinforcing over a longer period of time.[40]

Needless to say, citizens who have spent most of their lives under oppressive regimes and who have experienced nothing but human rights violations, corruption and arbitrariness will need time before they can (again) trust any institution. To re-establish trust in institutions that only committed violence, corruption or fraud in the past, often takes a generation. Change and consolidation are thus endogenous, that is to say that they arise from individuals' rational responses to the performance of political institutions. In new democracies in which the structure and character of the political institutions are still taking shape, political outputs (for example, the reduction of corruption and the protection of human rights) can matter as much as economic or other outputs.[41] But what matters in terms of the link between TJ, institutions and their actors is that the institutions and their actors aim to satisfy the needs and claims of the citizens, and that they deliver and perform what they promise. The higher the level of citizen satisfaction, the higher the level of trust will be. Therefore, institutional performance is an important determinant of civic trust.

Interestingly enough, surveyors in a global survey regarding trust in institutions found that people who have little trust in their domestic institutions also fail to have any trust in international institutions and organisations, such as the European Union (EU) or the UN, due to a lack of any direct positive experience.[42] It appears that the poor performance of one form of, for example, tribunals or courts (whether at the national or international level), leads to a general mistrust in all tribunals or courts. This effect does not appear to be dependent on the regime type.[43]

---

[40] Ibid., p. 3.
[41] T. Ka-ying Wong, W. Po-san and M. Hsiao Hsin-Huang, 'The Bases of Political Trust in Six Asian Societies, 264 and 266.
[42] B. Torgler, 'Trust in International Organizations: An Empirical Investigation Focusing on the United Nations', *Review of International Organizations*, 3 (2008), 65–93.
[43] T. Ka-ying Wong, W. Po-san and M. Hsiao Hsin-Huang, 'The Bases of Political Trust in Six Asian Societies', 273.

We know today that without civic trust and free support of citizens of state institutions, no democracy can survive for a long period of time – let alone be stable, resilient, effective and consolidated. If there is widespread mistrust among citizens and institutions, regimes will face serious troubles, which this book refers to as 'unconsolidated pockets of democracy'. Myrdal's downward spiral would continue to progress in this case. Spain, East and West Germany and Turkey faced many of these unconsolidated pockets both during and after regime change and consolidation. Unconsolidated pockets can be uncontrolled territory within the respective country and/or terror groups such as the PKK (Kurdistan Workers' Party or *Partiya Karkerên Kurdistanê*) in Turkey; the RAF (Red Army Faction, or *Rote Armee Fraktion*) in West Germany; or the ETA in Spain that frustrate governmental efforts to deal openly with the past and perform in a fully democratic way. Many of these terror groups legitimise themselves by pointing directly to the undealt-with past, such as the legacies of the Nazi regime that still played a role in making law in postwar Germany, or the myth that Franco's disciples and followers still held power in Madrid and aimed to install a second Franco regime. Often, these unresolved myths about the past are used to 'justify' violent struggle and vengeance, separatist or neo-Nazi movements and terror against new institutions. Therefore, a silenced past triggers more mistrust and thus political radicalisation as a form of outcry and discontent with a lack of reforms. If TJ measures are used to deal with the past they can contribute to the dismantling of these unconsolidated pockets and lead to more civic and political participation.

To methodologically show how TJ measures can trigger a change in attitude, behaviour and politics that correlate cumulatively into regime consolidation, I will argue as follows:

(1) The spiral correlation and effect between TJ, actors and institutions and their consolidation depends on whether former combatants, political prisoners, victims of violence, perpetrators, bystanders and supporters of the past regime enjoy equal rights as set out in the constitution and thus have access to the same justice and participatory mechanism under the new regime. Everyone, regardless of his or her suffering or responsibility for suffering, ought to have access to the same constitutional and thus normative opportunities to be compensated, punished or (re-)integrated into the post-dictatorial democratic society. The level of integration in divided societies can be measured in two ways: a) in a functional and formal manner based

on how the rule of law is applied and on how perpetrator and victim groups engage with democratic institutions, or b) based on the level of cultural integration, that is to say, whether citizens have developed a political attitude, behaviour and thus culture that embrace the new regime's doctrines and regard this as 'the only game in town'. This in turn indicates a level of civic trust in institutions. As explained with Gabriel Almond and Sidney Verba's words earlier, political or civic culture can be measured by assessing the number of public cultural events, novels, films or debates that confront issues of the past, among other things.

(2) Another way to look at these variables is from a more qualitative perspective. Here, one might determine whether technocrats that served under both the old and the new regime (for example judges and administrators that remain in office after regime change) are a threat to the new regime. Having such technocrats stay in office can contribute to the stability of the new regime, due to their institutional knowledge and skills and the continuity, which they provide. These are much needed in many regime change processes. Elites from the former regime do matter in regime consolidation and are often crucial for peaceful and successful transition; purging them can thus frustrate the process of transition. Yet, at the same time, many of these former elites still adhere to anti-democratic principles; they prefer violence to diplomacy and police actions over civil problem-solving mechanisms. Thus, if too many of them remain in leadership positions, they can weaken democratic processes, in particular if they are not balanced or outnumbered by new elites open to more fundamental democratic reforms. This was an issue when judges who had worked under the Nazi regime remained in office in post-war Germany and later defended a 'militant democracy' (*streitbare Demokratie*), using former Nazi language to defend their positions. Judges in post-Franco Spain successfully frustrated any citizen claim raised to deal with the wrongdoings of Franco's perpetrators. The former supreme court judge, Baltasar Garzón, has often argued that the amnesty laws issued in 1976 and 1977 will never allow for a fully fledged TJ process and were thus a flaw in Spanish democracy. Because of these amnesty laws the political successors – willingly or not – indirectly indicate their loyalty to the previous regime, which many citizens in Spain have considered a betrayal of democracy.

(3) International organisations, external pressure and incentives matter very much in the process of regime consolidation. They are part

of the mutual reinforcing spiral effect because they trigger, install or finance TJ measures. In the case studies presented in this book, the Council of Europe, the UN and/or the EU have played that role and since these are countries located in Europe the European institutions much more than global once, like the UN. International organisations and institutions, such as the Allied forces in the case of East and West Germany after 1945, provide incentives and put pressure on the new regime to increase compliance with international human rights law and to issue, for example, reparations and trials. Yet, occupying foreign powers or international organisations can also frustrate the process, as can be seen in East Germany, when the Soviet Allied Force fostered arbitrary trials against Nazi perpetrators.

Today, international NGOs and CSOs often undertake tasks for implementing TJ policies and receive financial aid and support from foreign donors and international organisations. Since governments have to respond or report to international organisations on how they are performing, the 'side effect' of such external interference is an increase in transparency and accountability, as well as of responsiveness by governments to citizen claims, without which no democracy can survive. Furthermore, international organisations such as the UN or EU often push for international human rights and criminal law standards to be adhered to when applying TJ measures, thus leading to these rights' and standards' slow diffusion in the new legal orders of the political regime, for example through constitutional or penal code reforms. Membership in international organisations and norm compliance had an immense impact on triggering TJ processes for the countries mentioned in this book. These organisations constantly urged their Member States to adhere to human rights norms and to ensure a certain level of accountability during regime change and consolidation. UN treaty body mechanisms, Special Rapporteurs, decisions by the European Court of Human Rights (ECtHR) or resolutions by the European Parliament have called on the respective governments of East, West and reunified Germany, Spain and Turkey to deal with their unjust past and to launch reforms. Such interference and pressure do not go entirely ignored.

Nevertheless, the different political regimes of Germany, Spain and Turkey have shown democratic flaws or deficits on their ways to consolidation, due for example to violent suppression of minorities, detention of protesters, biased and political trials and expulsion of political parties. Some political powers overcame the deficits, others cultivated them, leading to a decline and re-autocratisation of the regime such as in East Germany and Turkey.[44] But they also developed differently over time and reunified Germany and Spain are today consolidated democracies. Democratic flaws are often related to the government's fear that former political elites will return to power without their role in the previous regime having first been delegitimised. If, years after the regime change in West Germany, the wider public still perceives Nazis as 'heroes' of a 'Germanic idea', Francoists as the 'guarantors for law and order', the Stasi as the 'shield and sword' of law and order in former East Germany, and the Turkish military apparatus as the 'guardians of secularism', then the new political regime has failed to delegitimise the former political elites and has failed to legitimise new alternative (democratic) ways of stabilising society.

To conclude this introductory part: it is fundamental in this comparative assessment to assign some dependent variables in terms of regime consolidation to an effective TJ process and the change or difference it may cause. Otherwise the process and the role the TJ measures play remain descriptive, even though TJ measures might have only a minimal influence on institutional progress and regime consolidation.

---

[44] See again clasification of defecit regime types and their decline by W. Merkel, *Systemtransformation, Eine Einführung in die Theorie und Empirie der Transformationsforschung*, pp. 23–24 and 44–54.

2

Methodology

There is not much empirical evidence, let alone any mono-causal one, for TJ measures causing democratic regime consolidation. There is, however, much research done on the assessment of regime consolidation via indices or barometers but without any linkage or reference to TJ. The closest we get to a multi-causal interlinkage between both is that focus on the interaction between regimes and TJ is the light that some authors shed on the link between the rule of law, civic culture and values, as provided by Gabriel Almond and Sidney Verba, for example, and the level of civic trust and legitimacy, as provided by Wolfgang Merkel, Hans-Jürgen Puhle, Juan Linz and Alfred Stepan. They have carved out fundamental elements of regime consolidation, which as I argue can be leveraged by the use of TJ measures. The reader may note that these are not the only elements that play a role in regime consolidation and, in fact, there are many more, such as whether a market economy and constitution have been put in place, the level of independence of the judiciary, etc. None of these factors in themselves can guarantee solid regimes, let alone democracies.

According to the hypothesis outlined above that there is an intertwining cumulative or multi-causal causality and spiral interlinkage between TJ measures and the degree of regime legitimacy and thus consolidation, methodologically one needs to look at actors' and institutions' performance in terms of responsiveness and accountability to the past, as well as citizens' participation and engagement with these institutions. Even though East and West Germany, Spain and Turkey are countries with most different system designs (MDSD) there are also some similarities to highlight. The countries are similar on the criterion of formal democracy (by constitution) and have been chosen based on an explorative comparative assessment because they have all to a greater or lesser extent applied TJ measures over the past decades. Therefore, I apply the mixed method and triangular approach of John Creswell and Vicki Plano Clark.[1] Phuong Pham and Patrick Vinck call this an 'evidence-based transitional justice method' that consists of the initiation of policies and programmes based on evidence derived from the best available data.[2] The data can be quantitative (for example numeric data of measures such as trials or memorials) as well as qualitative (for example semi-structured interviews with stakeholders, media coverage, observations of political elites and participant observation).

The focus in this study will be, nevertheless, on qualitative data and literature review, and in particular on narratives, historical facts, timelines, opinion surveys, historical records and a few semi-structured interviews. I will supplement this with quantitative data, such as numbers of trials, openings of memorials, legal and political reforms, and democracy rankings whenever necessary. I will benchmark these mostly historical and evidence-based data against the performance of institutions and actors in democratic and authoritarian regimes and thus the regime's level of legitimacy. Quantitative data are ideal for answering questions regarding the magnitude of the phenomena or for generalising findings during the long-term process of regime consolidation that can take decades. Hence, there will be stages in this book when I refer to quantitative-based evidence rather than qualitative-based evidence because I believe it is more suited to the nature of what I am trying to illustrate and test, namely the long-term cumulative causation and spiral effect between TJ and regime consolidation. For example, the long time frames of regime development (more than 60 years in the case of Germany or 40 years in the case of Spain) make it impossible to observe individuals and events equally or have the same qualitative data and sources on all of the four countries. It is in these cases when quantitative data are an invaluable addition.

This method applied here has three main advantages that make it most appropriate for the investigation being conducted. In this first place, this method facilitates in-depth study in a case-orientated approach of the countries under investigation. Second, it allows the use of a few variables to test the hypothesis that TJ measures used by political and civil actors as catalysts to legitimise regime consolidation. Third, it allows for the analysis of data and evidence resulting from multiple causes where conditions

---

[1] J.W. Creswell and V.L. Plano Clark, *Designing and Conducting Mixed Methods Research* (London: Sage Publications, 2011).

[2] P. Pham and P. Vinck, 'Empirical Research and the Development and Assessment of Transitional Justice Mechanisms', *International Journal of Transitional Justice*, 1 (2007), 233.

sometimes combine in contradictory ways to produce similar outcomes. The case-orientated strategy helps to interpret specific cases because of their intrinsic values in causal analytical ways, for example, between European institutions and domestic politics. It will help to determine correlations and thus causal generalisation, which are different from purely historical and descriptive interpretation.

The quantitative and qualitative analysis will assess the following factors:

(1) *Qualitative and behavioural data* such as opinion surveys on political participation, narratives and public statements by civil society, judges, reports by NGOs and political actors or international organisations, which underline the interlinkage between TJ and regime consolidation. Individual narratives, personal stories and memories based on semi-structured interviews with victims, perpetrators and actors of civil society, pressure groups and politicians with a key role in the process of dealing with the past. Other interviewees were state bureaucrats, organised lobby groups, lawyers, state prosecutors, NGOs, academics, eye-witnesses and researchers, for example judge Baltasar Garzón and activists and writers Leyla Zana and Murat Bardakci. Specific historical events, the level of the severity of atrocities, the level of totalitarianism or authoritarianism of the previous regime type and other historical context will not be systematically assessed or evaluated in this study. They are seen as (often gruesome and dramatic) facts and have been researched and commented upon extensively by many other authors for each of the cases dealt with in this study.

(2) *Quantitative data* of civil society activities, victim organisations, number of trials and the founding of TJ-related foundations or NGOs, etc.; documentation analysis of government and legislative initiatives such as constitutional and law reforms, public policies, and legislative or court decisions. These data are, for example, historical records from the Archivo de la Guerra Civil-Salamanca; the Fundacion Franco Madrid; the Archivo Nacional Espana Madrid; the Fritz Bauer Institute Frankfurt; and the Federal German Archives (Bundesarchiv) in Koblenz and Berlin. Furthermore, I have used statistics and public opinion polls, such as Eurobarometer; Democracy Barometer, MetroPoll Turkey; Allensbach; Infratest; Eurostat; Bertelesmann Transformation Index; Democracy Index, Democracy Ranking, and the Polity Index.

The triangulation of these data allows for quantitative and qualitative data to be placed on an equal footing and situated in the timeline of regime development after regime change has taken place. It also allows me to benchmark these data jointly against the assumption that TJ is used or misused for regime consolidation. The focus will be less on what TJ measures can directly do to delegitimise or demystify past perpetrators and their regimes, and more on how these measures are generally linked to the legitimisation of the new regime.

In earlier studies on transitions in Europe, researchers have often underestimated the international and other external factors, as well as the influence of citizens and other bottom-up factors. As early as 1991, Philippe Schmitter and others highlighted the fact that more research needs to be done to assess the impact of citizens, international organisations and EU membership on democratic transformation. Only after the observation of democratisation in Southern and Eastern Europe have these factors became more prevalent in democracy research.[3] In addition to external and domestic non-governmental actors who at the end also determine the effectiveness of democracy, Schmitter pointed to the importance of the 'absence of direct responsibility' for past injustice in southern Europe which are somewhat connected to the flaws in democratic consolidation. This lack of direct responsibility, through amnesty and impunity especially in Spain and Turkey, can hamper successful consolidation.[4]

Furthermore (3), the *timeline matters*; the empirical part of this study is divided into country cases, with each country's regime development divided by decades starting from the moment the change of the regime was determined by serious constitutional reforms or a political leadership that made a clear commitment to change and reforms after times of injustice, atrocities, suppression or war. After various attempts to structure the chapters to show and see correlation, it became evident that a linear causality was impossible to draw and therefore the mutual reinforcing causal one over a longer period of time has brought more evidence to light than anticipated at the beginning. The research framework presented here can be characterised as process tracing in the context of qualitative analysis. Process tracing is a systematic examination of diagnostic evidence selected and analysed in light of the abovementioned research questions

---

[3] J.J. Linz and A. Stepan, *Problems of Democratic Transition and Consolidation*.
[4] P.C. Schmitter, 'An Introduction to Southern European Transition' in G. O'Donnell, P.C. Schmitter and L. Whitehead (eds.), *Transition from Authoritarian Rule. Southern Europe* (Baltimore, MD/London: Johns Hopkins University Press, 1991), p. 5.

and hypotheses. It is describing political and social phenomena and aims to evaluate causal and multi-causal claims over a longer period of time as is the case when illustrating the spiral effect in this study.[5]

Yet, after some investigations, a process tracing and narrative approach proved ultimately to be the best way to shed light on whether the assumptions expressed earlier are based on any evidence. Thus, the chapters are written narratively in chronological order, approaching TJ measures as tools and independent variables used by actors and institutions alike for political purposes and consolidation of the regime, the dependent variable.

Data coming from democracy or autocracy measurement methods and indicators, such as the Vanhanen Index, Freedom House Index, the Bertelsmann Transformation Index (BTI), the National Centre of Competence in Research (NCCR) Democracy Barometer or the Polity IV index are helpful sets of data for this book, but are used in a non-systematic way to highlight certain periods of regime consolidation and to illustrate examples given. The number of democracy or authoritarianism 'barometers' has reached a peak in the past few years, as mentioned earlier. These indices measure and compare a large number of democracies and large N-studies. Vanhanen's index is primarily based on the two dimensions of participation, competition and the distribution of resources.[6] Further indices such as Freedom House or the BTI help to quantify and compare the responsiveness of democratic institutions to their citizens per country. The NCCR Democracy Barometer for established democracies aims to directly assess the quality of democracy. The barometer bases its assessment on human rights, but also on the balance between civil liberties, equality and governance. Indices such as the Eurobarometer, the Civil Society Index and the UNDP-Human Development Report on Democracy[7] consider economic effectiveness criteria as an indicator of the level of democracy, as do Ronald Ingelhart and Christian Welzel in their assessments.[8] In line with the most recent indices and barometers, Guillermo O'Donnell, Jorge Vargas Cullell,

[5] D. Collier, 'Understanding Process Tracing', *Political Science and Politics* 44, 4 (2011), 823–830.
[6] T. Vanhanen, *Democratisation. A Comparative Analysis of 170 Countries* (London: Routledge, 2003).
[7] UNDP Human Development Reports: United Nations Development Programme, *UNDP Human Development Reports*.hdr.undp.org/en/reports/global/hdr2002 (last accessed July 2016).
[8] R. Ingelhart and C. Welzel, *Modernization, Cultural Change and Democracy: The Human Development Sequence* (Cambridge: Cambridge University Press, 2005), p. 151 et seq.

Osvaldo Iazzatta, Philippe Schmitter, Hans-Joachim Lauth et al. have been developing more indicators to provide possible definitions for the quality of democracies.[9] O'Donnell et al. focused on the incremental correlation between the degree to which human rights are granted and the functioning level of democracy. Schmitter, on the other hand, examined political leadership's accountability and responsiveness towards citizens' demands. Lauth added the aspect of 'control' to the assessment, looking at who has effective control over the commons. Such an approach can be extended to include the question of who has control over TJ measures, when holding trials or commissions of inquiry, and who does not. It is the aspect of political leadership's responsiveness that remains the pivotal variable in all the measurements and will, therefore, also be used in this book. This measurement defines efficacy as citizens' perceptions of governmental power in the political realm and the performance of political institutions.[10] For example, in the context of TJ, such a measure can be applied to an instance in which the government responds in a non-violent and non-suppressive manner to citizens seeking legal reforms or amnesties. What they all have in common is to show the difference between good and bad democratic performance and the role that civil society plays and citizens' engagement and trust plays in it.

In this respect, Ted R. Gurr et al.'s Polity IV democracy and autocracy scales are important for showing cumulative causal effect because they show that the level of citizen participation, the recruitment of technocrats and political elites, and the constitutional limits on executive powers, correlate with TJ measures, when the measures are used as a catalyst or tool to purge or lustrate technocrats of the former state bureaucracy or when creating public memorials.[11] For example, truth commissions increase

[9] G. O'Donnell, J. Vargas Cullell, and O.M. Iazzetta, *The Quality of Democracy, Theory and Applications* (Notre Dame, IN: University of Notre Dame Press, 2004), pp. 56–69; H.-J. Lauth, 'Die Qualität der Demokratie im interregionalen Vergleich – Probleme und Entwicklungsperspektiven', in G. and S. Pickel (eds.), *Demokratisierung im internationalem Vergleich, Neue Erkenntnisse und Perspektiven* (Wiesbaden: VS Verlag, 2006), pp. 89–110; P.C. Schmitter, *The Quality of Democracy: The Ambiguous Virtues of Accountability* (Florence: European University Institute, 2003) (online published paper); P.C. Schmitter and N. Guilhot, 'From Transition to Consolidation, Extending the Concept of Democratisation and Practice of Democracy', *Geojournal Library: Democratic and Capitalist Transition in Eastern Europe*, 55 (2000), 131–146.

[10] M.E. Morell, 'Survey and Experimental Evidence for a Reliable and Valid Measure of Internal Political Efficacy', *The Public Opinion Quarterly*, 67 (2003), 489.

[11] T.R. Gurr, K. Jagger and W. Moore, 'The Transformation of the Western State: The Growth of Democracy, Autocracy, and State Power since 1800', *Studies in Comparative International Development*, 25, 1 (1990), 73–108.

victims' and victimisers' participation and engagement with new state institutions; vetting and lustration measures determine who can and will be part of the future political or bureaucratic elite. Gurr's political indicators implicitly reveal when TJ measures will help to increase participation or limit the return of corrupt and criminal elites back to political power. Regime change towards autocracy is more likely to happen if TJ measures are used in a biased way, for example if commissions of inquiry, trials or vetting procedures only allow one victim group to testify in front of a commission, as was the case in post-war Germany. Well into the 1950s and 1960s, in West Germany predominantly German refugees from the East or the former German Reich territories were considered victims, and in East Germany only communists who had suffered Nazi suppression and persecution were considered victims. Due to much international and civil society pressure, only much later Jews were seen as primary victims of the Holocaust in West Germany. Only decades later Nazi victims of euthanasia, homosexuals or Sinti and Roma became part of the common narrative of the past. When trials only try one group of perpetrators, or if vetting procedures only purge those who happen to be political opponents of the new political regime, an exclusive and biased TJ process takes place. The latter was the case in East Germany after 1949 when trying only enemies of the new political regime but not all those who had been responsible for Nazi terror, regardless of their political affiliation, and in Turkey after several military coups.

By comparing East, West and reunified Germany, Spain and Turkey, I illustrate patterns in how political and civil elites use TJ measures in the period from regime change to consolidation. Countries such as East and West Germany and Spain faced serious threats to democracy in the first decade after regime change because they failed to delegitimise the previous regime and sufficiently include civil society and victim groups in their consolidation process. Yet, all regimes also experienced a post-dictatorial generation that began to ask questions about the past, about 20 years later. The West German student movement of 1968, as well as the young generation of Spaniards that protested against the 'silence pact' around 2000 in the streets of Madrid and Barcelona, represented a generation 20 years after the regime change. This '20+ generation' represents a generation that was free from personal responsibilities and fear, and thus ready to deal with the past and consequently the acts of their parents.[12] Dankwart

---

[12] Institut für Demoskopie Allensbach, *Demokratie-Verankerung in der Bundesrepublik Deutschland: Eine empirische Untersuchung zum 30 jährigen Bestehen der Bundesrepublik* (Allensbach am Bodensee: Institute für Demoskopie Allensbach, 1979), p. 95.

Rustow had already predicted a similar phenomenon in his earlier studies on transition to democracy. According to him, the first post-regime change generation (the one born towards the end of the previous regime or during the period of regime change) usually values freedom and liberty rights more than older generations.[13] Interestingly enough, the post-war/dictatorial generation always has stronger desires for liberty, even in authoritarian regimes, than the one that directly experienced suppression, as can be seen in East and West Germany around the year 1970. A period that was marked by a generation striving for regime change, a generation that succeeded in the west but failed in the east; and in Spain around the year 2000. In Turkey this was also the case around the year 2013 when the 20+ generation mobilised against the authoritarian turn of the government. Riots and claims for more democracy and coming to terms with the past commenced, suppression against them increased and has now accelerated the downward spiral for Turkey's new authoritarian regime.

The generational shift of 20 or 25 years after regime change cannot be underestimated when understanding regime consolidation and TJ, and is thus an aspect that must be considered. It is the human search for identity and answers about the (unjust) past that drives the members of each generation. Once they reach a certain age, these young people ask about their parents' past which is also their own. Thus it is not surprising that the student movement of 1968 in West Germany (but also in East Germany) had so much in common with the 'Ya basta!' generation in Spain around 2000 and the Turkish youth initiatives to commemorate the Armenian Genocide with candlelight throughout Turkish cities around 2005 and the following years. All these groups belonged to the same generation. It is not only their demands for democratic reforms that they have in common, but also the urge to deal with their country's atrocious past as part of the process of forming their identity and a common narrative.

Wolfgang Zapf and Rustow, along with many others, included this generational approach in their studies. They argue that this first post-regime change generation must first habitualise the regime's new norms, rules and procedures before one can speak of a consolidated regime or a successful transformation.[14] Rustow even goes so far as to state that one generation

---

[13] Herbert Quandt Stiftung, *Allensbach-Studie: Freiheit und bürgerliches Engagement* (Bad Homburg, 3 May 2012), herbert-quandt-stiftung.de, p. 3. (last accessed August 2013).

[14] W. Zapf, 'Mondernisierungstheorien in der Transformationsforschung' in K. von Beyme and C. Offe (eds.), *Politische Theorien in der Ära der Transformation* (Opladen, Wiesbaden: PVS Sonderheft, 1996), No. 26, p. 177.

is probably the minimum period of transition. In countries with few or
no earlier models of democracy, this transition can take even longer.[15]
Although this timespan is contested in transition and consolidation literature, the general consensus is that regime consolidation takes time,
and even more time until democracy is seen as 'the only game in town'.[16]
The change in behaviour and the willingness to practise democracy is
linked to civic trust and, consequently, to the level of citizen participation and engagement with institutions. These factors must be included
if one wishes to measure regime change and consolidation. Like Linz,
Stepan, Merkel, Puhle, Larry Diamond, Schmitter, Laurence Whitehead
and many others, Tatu Vanhanen emphasised civil participation as one
of the two key indicators for distinguishing autocracies from democracies. Civil participation is key to this study, because in all cases it has
been civil society which triggered and called for more TJ measures. And
it is consequently civil society which consolidates a regime. But in order
to participate in decision-making processes, one has to be free. This is
why TJ measures are more often used and implemented in democracies
than in authoritarian regimes. In the light of the rising importance of TJ
measures in democratisation, Freedom House broadened the definition
of participation in order to properly measure it in the context of regime
consolidation.[17] Thus, citizen participation can be participation in elections, but also citizens' participation in NGOs, advocacy, involvement in
media or social media, public debates etc. And if victims and victimisers
alike cannot use these tools to express their desires for compensations,
vetting or fair trials, then such exclusionary TJ measures can contribute
to the deconsolidation of a regime.

My data are nominal, not statistical, which allows for interpretation
of the meanings that different actors and representatives of democratic
institutions connect to their behaviour.[18] The point is not that whichever

---

[15] D.A. Rustow, 'Transition to Democracy: Toward a Dynamic Model', *Comparative Politics*,
2, 3 (1970), 347.

[16] J.J. Linz and A. Stepan, *Problems of Democratic Transition and Consolidation, Southern
Europe, South America, and Post-Communist Europe* (Baltimore, MD/London: Johns
Hopkins University Press, 1996), p. 5.

[17] Freedom House Data set and definition for political and civil rights influence on level
of participation – Freedom House, *Home Page*. https://freedomhouse.org/ (last accessed
July 2016).

[18] Tilburg Institute for Interdisciplinary Studies of Civil Law and Conflict Resolutions
Systems (TISCO) (ed.), *A Handbook for Measuring the Costs and Quality of Access to Justice*
(Apeldoorn, Antwerp, Portland: Tilburg Institute for Interdisciplinary Studies of Civil Law
and Conflict Resolution Systems 2009), p. 47.

regime has more memorials, lustration laws or number of verdicts will be more resilient and stronger or let alone consolidated, but rather that what matters is how these measures are utilised by various actors, political and civil ones, and groups to 'practise democracy' or to 'practise authoritarianism'. The systematic and the inclusive or exclusive use of these TJ measures make the difference between autocracy and democracy, not their numbers. The more self-reflective political and civil actors are about the past, the more likely they are to establish institutions and reforms that consolidate and strengthen the regime. If a regime never learned to deal with unpleasant truths and historic facts, it will also not be able to deal with such things in the present and future. This is where the practical use of TJ measures can make a difference. If governmental institutions and citizens have learned to face unpleasant and hurtful issues in their own past, for example through the acknowledgement of the existence of concentration camps and mass killings of civilians under German, Spanish or Turkish military dictatorship or Stasi surveillance, they will be more likely to try to avoid those hurtful things to be done again. The point is that dealing with one's unpleasant past in a democratic and thus inclusive, that is to say to all sides of the political and societal spectrum, and participatory way, shapes a democratic culture that will be more likely to prevail during times of crisis and thus lead to decisions that might be more resilient and sustainable than those taken by autocratic leadership that suffers from a lack of this kind of citizen-driven legitimacy.

Thus, the proposed comparative analytical framework for this investigation is, on the one hand, the practicality and use of TJ measures (independent variable) by actors and, on the other, the consolidation of political institutions (dependent variable). Practical, empirical, qualitative and quantitative data on TJ measures, combined with the theoretical principles of democracy and authoritarian governance criteria, form this comparative study's framework.

The mutually reinforcing relationship between TJ and institutions can be measured by political actors' and institutions' level of responsiveness towards citizens' claims, as well as by citizens' participation. These measures indicate the extent to which political actors and institutions respect civil rights and include them in decision-making processes, for example by allowing citizens and victim groups to participate in round-tables and negotiations about new penal laws, while at the same time assessing whether citizens themselves react to governmental decrees or decisions in a peaceful manner. The more peaceful and willing to compromise citizens are, the better it is for the consolidation process. Similarly, regime theories

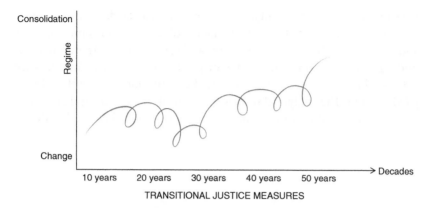

Figure 2.1 Spiral Model Illustration: Regime Consolidation and Transitional Justice

hold that a successful regime consolidation towards democracy has taken place when government and opposition no longer issue claims against each other but compromise and respect each other, when the security sector is under control, a private market economy can flourish, when political and social disputes are solved in a peaceful and consensual manner, and when all political and civil actors are included in the decision-making process and agree on common norms and standards.[19]

Therefore, the upward or downward spiral effect between TJ and regime consolidation can only be seen over a longer period of time and by studying the coherence of institutional, elite and citizen behaviour. It takes at least one decade until a regime is somewhat consolidated. During the first periods of transition and consolidation, spoilers can be present and very active and thus the spiral can go up and down over decades. But the general tendency whether it will eventually move more upwards then downwards is of major significance (Figure 2.1).

I will thus methodologically refrain from the strict application of linear process tracing, as it would require the tracing of all the steps leading to a particular decision.[20] Instead I will look more generally to political and civil behaviour, attitudes, trust and policies that result from using TJ

[19] P.C. Schmädeke, *Politische Regimewechsel, Grundlagen der Transitionsforschung* (Tübingen and Basel: A. Francke Verlag, UTB, 2012), p. 33.
[20] J.K. Ford, N. Schmitt, S.L. Schechtmann, B.M. Hults and M.L. Dohrety, 'Process Tracing Methods: Contributions, Problems and Neglected Research Questions', *Organisational Behaviour and Human Decision Process*, 43 (1989), 76.

measures as tools to consolidate a regime.[21] This can be done in this narrative comparative study due to the variances of actors, diachronic timelines and endogeneity between TJ measures and consolidation. Therefore these findings are based on a correlative or perpetuating circular interlinkage between TJ measures as used by actors, the institutions and level of citizen participation. The analytical (quality), practical (measures) and empirical (country case) dimensions of this study are thus looked at per decades.

---

[21] M. Schulte-Mecklenbeck, A. Kühberger and R. Ranyard, 'The Role of Process Data in the Development and Testing of Process Models of Judgement and Decision Making', *Judgment and Decision Making*, 6(8) (2011), 733–739.

3

The Concept of Regime Change and Consolidation

Although this book concentrates on consolidation, the difference between regime change and consolidation should be briefly illustrated. Change and consolidation differ in stages and levels of regime development. Regime change refers to the point at which democratic institutions are first established and TJ measures are initiated but not yet (necessarily) executed, even if this only happens on paper in the first instance. This period of change starts with the end of a previous, often atrocious, dictatorial or suppressive regime, and usually takes a couple of years. Sometimes even less than a year, sometimes up to five or ten years, and lasts until a constitution is in place and first free and open elections have been held or a shift in government has taken place. During this change period, the political leadership or interim government makes an oral or written commitment to democracy and its norms and rules as well as to the political willingness to come to terms with the past, even if only half-heartedly said or done.

In all the studies shown in this book, the new or interim governments established or reintroduced democratic rules and participatory mechanisms during this period of political change. The fact that often the same governments in later years violate these norms and break the law is another issue. It affects the consolidation process but not the one of regime change.

Regime consolidation follows the period of change and transition.[1] It is a long-term process and can be divided into different phases or levels of consolidation. Such levels are, according to Wolfgang Merkel, the first level of 'constitutional consolidation', when institutions are in place and norms have been agreed on, i.e. through elections; the second level of representative consolidation of the regime through actors, when political parties and civil society support or adhere to the regime type and its rules;

---

[1] Most of these criteria have been explained earlier. A good summary is also found in: W. Merkel, *Systemtransformation, Eine Einführung in die Theorie und Empirie der Transformationsforschung*, pp. 110–111.

the third level is the 'behavioural or attitudinal' consolidation, when all other private actors such as financial or technocratic elites and the military or police support and adhere to the regime type; and the fourth and highest level of consolidation is completed when all civil society actors and citizens at large support the regime type, ideally the democratic one.[2] Consolidation by civil society is the last and most difficult stage of legitimising the regime and can take decades if not generations. Yet, if the majority of civil society freely and without coercion supports the regime, it is fully consolidated with 'no way of return'. Needless to say, some regimes don't make it through the first levels to reach the fourth one, because their political actors and governments or military limit, censor or suppress civil society and therefore the regimes turn downwards towards authoritarianism.

I will not systematically assess or apply the different types of consolidation of Merkel, Juan Linz, Alfred Stepan, Philippe Schmitter and other authors during my case studies, but their established categories are helpful patterns to understand the different steps and phases of regime consolidation when correlating with the use or abuse of TJ measures during this process. Therefore, I will sometimes refer to their concepts when looking at the spiral and mutual reinforcing effect between TJ and regime consolidation, when, for example:

(a) Democratic institutions are in place and the constitution complies with fundamental human rights principles;
(b) a minimum set of TJ measures has been employed or guaranteed by law;
(c) the sequencing of TJ measures takes place;
(d) a societal and citizen-driven demand exists and is growing to redress grievances and to use TJ to respond to the needs expressed by citizens, victim and pressure groups, political parties, NGOs, writers, film makers, media etc. This is known as a process of national catharsis; and
(e) the country in question is a member or seeks membership of international organisations such as the Council of Europe, EU, the North Atlantic Treaty Organization (NATO) or the UN and adheres to some extent to their norms and regulations.

While regime change is a process that changes actors' and institutions' paradigms and behaviour, consolidation is the time during which these

[2] Ibid., pp. 112ff.

paradigms (norms, rules and procedures) are implemented and lived up to. The 'regime' is thus the type of governance – democratic or authoritarian, totalitarian or anarchical – and is generally considered consolidated when the overall majority of societal actors and institutions act according to common norms or laws.[3] Equally to Larry Diamond, Linz and Stepan or Merkel, Laurence Whitehead argued that democratisation and regime change towards democracy is 'complete when all significant political actors accept (with good grace or ill) that the electoral process has become "the only game in town" for reallocating public office', thus emphasising the role of actors and the 'tools' they make use of.[4] He went on to illustrate that after regime change has taken place, the same community that brought about the fall of the dictator must respond to the new possibility for political participation. This is the momentum when TJ measures can be used as tools or catalysts for such participation. The stability of the regime and its progression towards consolidation depends on the way in which citizens respond to this opportunity for participation.[5] I want to add that, for example, the practise of TJ commissions of inquiry, memorials, restitution funds or trials allow civil as well as political actors to learn. Further on, Guillermo O'Donnell and Schmitter differentiated four types of regime change and consolidation, namely the shift (1) towards political democracy; (2) towards authoritarian rule; (3) towards confrontational rule; or (4) towards revolutionary rule or political confusion.[6]

To illustrate these shifts, levels or phases of consolidation with the case studies of this book, I will focus mainly on Gunnar Myrdal's concept of political transition or regime change that can progress in an upward, democratic, and consolidated way, or in a downward, authoritarian and rather 'deconsolidated' way as opposed to democratic consolidation.

Authoritarian regime consolidation is based on coercion by governments against civil society. Exclusion of minorities, political parties or former elites, suppression of civil society and governing through fear and terror are just a few of the 'ways to govern' one can observe in these regimes. Nevertheless, democratic and authoritarian regimes both have to face the challenge of gaining the support of their citizens. Yet, while

---

[3] P.C. Schmädeke, *Politische Regimewechsel*, Grundlagen der Transitionsforschung (Tübingen and Basel: A. Francke Verlag, UTB, 2012) pp. 7–17.

[4] L. Whitehead, *Democratisation, Theory and Experience* (Oxford University Press, 2002), p. 27.

[5] Ibid., p. 65.

[6] G. O'Donnell and P.C. Schmitter (eds.), *Transition from Authoritarian Rule. Prospects for Democracy* (Baltimore, MD: Johns Hopkins University Press, 1986), Parts I–IV.

democracies attempt to win this support in the form of genuine consent (however begrudgingly), authoritarian regimes rely on coercion, fear and terror. These regimes are generally speaking weakly consolidated because they have no free and deliberate support by the overall majority of citizens. Although the durability of such a regime can last for generations, as seen in the case of East Germany or Turkey, they are not sustainable in the long run. The length of an authoritarian regime's survival depends on many factors, which have been explained in great detail by other authors.[7] I will not further elaborate on these issues, but what is interesting for the purposes of this study is that all regimes, regardless of how (un)democratic they may be, employ TJ measures – although they do so to very different extents and with very different intentions. Such authoritarian regimes distinguish themselves from democracies primarily by the fact that their power is concentrated in a few institutions, if not one singular governmental institution, such as an extremely powerful presidency or a politburo. Such regimes do not allow the free participation of civil society. In such regimes, the separation of power in a legislative, executive and judicial branch is a mere farce, used to manipulate citizens' belief and trust. In authoritarian regimes there is no power for citizens, let alone for freely established NGOs or CSOs. Organised and state-controlled 'mass organisations' under constant surveillance by the government are not the same as freely established citizen movements. Authoritarianism is a regime in which no viable channels exist for opposition. In the context of TJ that means, for example, that there are no opportunities for 'non-official' victims, that is to say the unacknowledged victims of the past regime to legally contest the executive power and claim reparations or other forms of restorative justice. These types of regimes often have formal democratic institutions on paper, but these are reduced to a façade in practice.[8]

As opposed to this, TJ measures can accelerate the development of democratic regimes by encouraging victim groups and those concerned about the past to become active citizens, establish CSOs and participate in political agenda setting. Memorials and trials in democratic post-conflict and post-authoritarian regimes are often initiated through former victim groups. Because a consolidated democratic regime needs a diverse and

---

[7] A comprehensive summary of authoritarian regime consolidation is given by: C. Göbel, 'Authoritarian Consolidation', *European Political Science*, 10 (2011), 176–190.

[8] A. Levitsky and L.A. Way, *Competitive Authoritarianism, Hybrid Regimes after the Cold War* (Cambridge: Cambridge University Press, 2010), pp. 6–7.

varied civil society and thus one that is not state-controlled, as Merkel and Hans-Jürgen Puhle have argued, these initiatives are much appreciated. The mutually reinforcing relationship between constitutional normative arrangements (to allow for citizen participation) and the way people's attitudes change (to dare to speak up for one's own interests), how they behave and participate are pivotal for long-term democratic consolidation (become an active citizen).[9] These attitudes and behaviours can be influenced by TJ measures.

In authoritarian regimes, citizens' activities and TJ measures are either centrally organised by the state and/or party for their own interest and purposes, such as the use of massive military parades, show trials and commissions or glorious memorial ceremonies to put the State in the best possible light; or otherwise they are considered hostile claims for justice by opponents and threats to the regime. In such cases, the regime will repress citizen-driven initiatives for TJ, like an attempt to establish a private memorial to commemorate massacres. Claims for compensation or trials will be ignored or denied by political elites. Control over citizens is crucial to autocracies, whereas in democracies citizens initiate TJ measures such as history commissions, memorials and apologies in order to exert control over their governments. In this way, citizens, victims, bystanders and victimisers in a democratic regime legitimise the institutions by which they are governed, while institutions in autocracies aim to legitimise themselves.

Even in existing democracies, such as in post-1990 Germany or in Spain, regime consolidation and transformation of political regimes continue, independently of whether a country is in the process of democratisation or has already achieved democracy. Even if democracy is already consolidated, a regime's political elite and civil society can still use TJ measures to enhance political and democratic performance and to integrate groups and citizens that otherwise would be excluded and thus would pose a threat to the achieved consolidation. Post-1990 reunified Germany had to undertake major reforms and use trials, vetting, memorials and reparations as tools for integrating up to 18 million 'new' citizens from East Germany who joined a country whose system was completely new to them. In Spain, TJ measures were only employed around the year 2000, after pressure from mass demonstrations and citizen-driven demands for repentance of the past. This was well after the regime was

---

[9] W. Merkel and H.-J. Puhle, *Von der Diktatur zur Demokratie*, p. 175.

already democratically consolidated. Indirectly, TJ measures used mostly by civil society also addressed unconsolidated pockets of democracy in Spain, such as separatist movements and other threats to a consolidated democracy that had long opposed the regime in Madrid.

Thus, I will operate on the assumption that TJ measures can enhance democratic institutions' performance and facilitate a more inclusive society, even when the regime is already consolidated for a long time as was the case in West Germany after some decades or in reunified Germany after 1990. Consequently, TJ measures are often applied even within the most democratic countries in the world, such as in Canada, West Germany or Australia, with the aim to improve and leverage existing democratic practice and thus the quality of democracy.

Reunified Germany's late trials of Nazi perpetrators in 2015 and 2016, as much as 70 years after the end of the war, or Spain's compensation and acknowledgement of its Civil War victims around 2009, 60 years after the end of the war in 1939, can positively impact regime development, consolidation or simply the quality of the regime. There is no time limit, no 'Schlussstrichdebatte' or 'punto final'. As Wolfgang Zapf and Dankwart Rustow reminded us, the steady and permanent use of TJ measures is pivotal for regime consolidation and can be necessary more than a generation after the regime change.[10] Rustow, often considered the creator of 'transitology', claimed that successful regime change and consolidation (towards democracy) is a matter of national unity and of how political elites and institutions/rules interact over a longer period of time.[11] This is the same national unity that Linz and Stepan have often emphasised when describing the pathways to democracy. TJ measures can contribute to the political reconciliation of divided societies and can thus contribute to a country's unity, which is a necessity for an effectively functioning state. As Stephen Winter has explained, TJ measures contribute to personal and political reconciliation within a divided society. However, as can be seen in the re-authoritarianisation of post-war and post-genocide Rwandan society, the opposite can also happen. Despite the fact that massive amounts of TJ measures were used, an international tribunal was installed, and compensation and reconciliation programmes between Tutsi and Hutus were on every agenda, the regime is today, 20 years later, an authoritarian one. Despite these TJ measures, democratic regime consolidation never

[10] D.A. Rustow, 'Transition to Democracy: Toward a Dynamic Model', 337–363.
[11] Ibid.

took place, but instead TJ measures were used to reinstall an authoritarian one. Marina Rafti, who followed the case of Rwandan regime change, explicitly blamed the strong top-down use of TJ measures and, in general, the pressure placed on reconciliation that, in the end, was abused to strengthen a new authoritarian regime, instead of a democratic one.[12] That TJ process was entirely government-owned and funded by the international donor community and therefore had difficulties to get through to the people, let alone enhance democracy.

But in Europe, after war, genocide, dictatorship and terror, societies were generally divided in their political views, experiences, morals and values. TJ aims to reconcile and bridge this division, but can only work if blame and responsibility are placed on all sides. Political elites and institutions that aim to redress past violence and human rights violations are essential if TJ is to have any spiral effect. Rustow's assessment of historical and societal context is also relevant in this case study. Although he would probably have only seen its relevance in regime consolidation's third phase, the 'decision phase', which can be years after the conflict has ended, when rules are agreed on, elites are in place and some minimum form of national unity is in place. In the cases of Germany, Spain and Turkey, however, the variable context shows that not all TJ measures should necessarily be applied immediately in the first five or ten years of the early transition, but rather that only those measures are used that have some benefit in achieving political and societal unity and common rules.

Merkel and Puhle have defined this process also as one that is intergenerational. They defined the first level of regime change as a normative one, i.e. when a constitution is in place but yet not fully embraced by citizens; the second level as one of establishing political parties, associations, civil society, media; and the third level a time in which elites must work towards gaining support from citizens and towards creating a civic culture that fully stabilises and legitimises the regime, so that consolidation can take place.[13]

In reference to the abovementioned transformation framework in this study, I use a normative approach to describe the changes and shift of institutions, actors and TJ measures over a longer period of time. These are based on the principles of human rights, rule of law and good governance

---

[12] M. Rafti, 'A Perilous Path to Democracy, Political Transition and Authoritarian Consolidation in Rwanda, Discussion Paper', *Institute of Development Policy and Management*, IOB, University of Antwerp (2008) 2008–3, p. 19.
[13] W. Merkel and H.-J. Puhle, *Von der Diktatur zur Demokratie*, p. 174.

such as equity and liberty rights, access to justice, transparency, account-ability and participation. Respecting these principles is necessary if TJ measures are to have any effect on consolidation at all. As mentioned earlier there needs to be a basic democratic structure (constitutions and a legal framework) that allow for citizens and political actors to use the tools of TJ. Consequently, my conceptual framework consists of actors and institutions that interact on the different levels to achieve effective and high levels of political performance. To operationalise the notion of spiral effect, governmental institutions are seen as duty-bearers that must deliver and respond to citizens in accordance with principles of due dili-gence and accountability. Citizens and civil networks are rights holders and interact and participate with, or sometimes oppose, these institutions.

As briefly indicated earlier, not only the levels or phases, but also the types of consolidated democratic regimes can be differentiated by the level of their quality, as done by, for example, Leonardo Morlino, one of many who coined the phrase 'quality of democracy'. He stated that this quality of a consolidated regime concerns institutions' procedures and outputs, which can be measured along eight dimensions. Four of his eight dimen-sions for measuring quality are directly linked to the politics of the past, which is why his approach is of particular interest to my study. These four dimensions of quality measurement are: (1) the rule of law; (2) electoral accountability; (3) participation; and (4) fundamental freedoms granted to citizens. The other four criteria are more related to constitutional design, such as the emergence of a party system and economic policies.[14] Morlino proposed that quality is enhanced – and thus consolidation strengthened – when a stable set of institutions exists that realises liberty and equality through legitimate and proper functioning, thus respecting these four criteria. What makes the quality of democracy interesting for my country cases studies is the focus on the institutions' responsiveness and interaction with society, which we find also in transformation and regime change and consolidation theories and neo-institutionalism.[15] TJ measures can be a continuous or permanent trigger of such interaction if they aim to change parameters of governance that were not successful in

---

[14] L. Morlino, 'Authoritarian Legacies, Politics of the Past and the Quality of Democracy in Southern Europe: Open Conclusions' in A. Costa Pino and L. Morlino (eds.), *Dealing with the Legacy of Authoritarianism: The 'Politics of the Past' in Southern European Democracies* (New York: Routledge, 2011), p. 169.

[15] P. Hall, 'Political Science and the Three New Institutionalisms', *Political Studies*, 4(55) (1996), 936–957.

the past and did not benefit society at large. This type of governance aims to reduce the level of insecurity, which is particularly high in early times of transition, and to increase the level of trust.[16] Responsiveness and participation are thus regarded as key to the extent to which (new) governments and their formal institutions are able to deliver on their obligations and execute their decisions.

This builds the bridge to Bingham Powell's 2004 study on the *Chain of Responsiveness*. He has also provided some theoretical inspiration for this assessment because in the *Chain of Responsiveness* he highlights the fact that incoherence among citizens' groups in terms of their claims, political intentions or even education, makes defining an 'adequate responsiveness' for institutions a daunting task because interests of citizens differ too much to find a simple common definition. Nevertheless, the difficulty of finding appropriate units should not prevent further investigation of this variable. Powell suggested that comparative cross-national country research could promote understanding of the variances of responsiveness, and thus its interconnectedness to quality.[17] Similarly, Robert Dahl has emphasised the institutional responsiveness to citizen needs, and these needs' subsequent satisfaction, as key characteristics of regime change towards democracy. Thus, in Dahl's view, it is the government's 'continuing responsiveness' to demands from its citizens that is fundamental for democratic regime change.[18] This type of responsiveness simply does not exist in autocracies and is crucial for *democratic* consolidation. This also explains why trials of past perpetrators, compensation of second or third-generation victims, and even memorials that are established decades if not centuries after the tragic happenings are so important, even to the most consolidated democracies like present-day Germany and Spain. According to Voigt, such measures contribute to the paradigm shifts in values and ethics, which turn into the morals that are crucial to regime change and consolidation.[19]

---

[16] M. Dauer and S. Voigt, 'Institutionen' in R. Kollmorgen, W. Merkel and H.-J. Wagner (eds.), *Handbuch Transformationsforschung* (Wiesbaden: Springer VS, 2014), p. 54.

[17] G.B. Powell, 'The Chain of Responsiveness', *Journal of Democracy*, 5(4) (2004), 91–105, at 100.

[18] R. Dahl, *Polyarchy, Participation and Opposition* (New Haven, CT: Yale University Press, 1971), p. 1.

[19] S. Voigt, 'Values, Norms, Institutions and Prospects for Economic Growth in Central and Eastern Europe' in S. Pejovich (ed.), *The Economics of Property Rights II* (Cheltenham: Edward Elgar, 1996), p. 306.

Yet, since it is almost impossible for a government to be responsive to all claims at all times, it must set priorities. Often these priorities become state doctrines in the context of TJ. For example, in Germany diplomatic relations with Israel and the United States are granted high priority, regardless of their actual geo-political importance, due to the status in German politics of atonement for the atrocities of World War II and of the role that the United States played after the war. It follows that the government sees claims by World War II victims as important, and such claims will most likely be fast-tracked. The Turkish government prioritises claims made by victims of Kurdish descent above those of the Armenian diaspora, because Kurds form an important constituency at present in Turkey, while this is not the case for Armenians. In Spain, claims made by victims of the dictatorial Franco regime are prioritised above those related to the Civil War, because many of the victims of Franco's regime are still alive and thus more relevant to the country's integration process. Prioritising is not an uncommon practice, but rather illustrates the effect that TJ policies can have on consolidation. During the first phase of transition, TJ measures are employed tactically only much later, after a generation, when moral and ethical aspects come into play. It is only during the phase of regime consolidation that a moral, empathetic or ethical approach to TJ begins, such as symbolic memorial acts, founding of institutions to deal with the past and invest in the education of the next generation, and so on. During the earlier phase, and that means during the first post-conflict and authoritarian generation, tactical concessions such as reparations, compensations, trials that serve domestic and international politics, are at the top of the agenda.

Nevertheless, even tactical concessions in the early transition and transformation phase impact the further development of democracy because they pave the way to more moral, ethical and value-based, consensus-based decisions later on. Arnd Lijphart's consensus-based democratic model based on fundamental freedoms and equality might is seen as a benchmark responsiveness towards and satisfaction of the needs of all citizens. Both Lijphart and Schmitter have often highlighted the importance of consensual shift, in particular to the creation of a culture of democracy based on respect and compromise.[20] The use of TJ measures is a way to facilitate this consensus-building, without which, as Juan Mendez, David

---

[20] P.A. Schmitter, 'The Quality of Democracy: The Ambiguous Virtues of Accountability', *Journal of Democracy*, 15(4) (2004), 47–90, at 54.

Bloomfield and others have argued earlier, any new democratic political order would be based on the weak foundation of privilege for old elites and perpetrators and the denial of the rule of law.[21]

Old and new elites, all main societal groups, former opponents, victims, survivors, minorities and stakeholders must be included in the process of reconciliation and reintegration of society in order to enhance regime change and to establish solid and effective democratic institutions. For an inclusive society political and civil actors on all sides have to agree on common standards and, for this to take place, a common narrative of the past is helpful. The tactical use of TJ measures such as commissions of inquiry, memorials and truth commissions can facilitate this process.

Nevertheless, the beginning is difficult, both for installing democratic reforms as well as for TJ measures. In her comparative study of democracies in southern Europe, Lauren McLaren showed a number of correlations between, on the one hand, low clarity of rules, procedures and competencies as well as exclusionary arrangements during the early stages of transition and, on the other, a rather bumpy road towards democracy.[22] It is common in the early stages of transition for a lack of democracy to correlate with the exclusion from the regime change process of radical groups and non-democratic forces, descending from former elites or militant groups. The exclusion of such groups often proves problematic and negotiated transition processes, in which former and new elites jointly draft the new constitutional setup, have proven to be the most successful regime changes.[23] The complete replacement of all former elites is least successful in a regime change and leads to what O'Donnell and Schmitter claim to be a violent or confusing regime change.[24] The mix of old and new political elites reduces conflicts, although it is often painful for the many survivors of mass atrocities, war crimes or torture to see those responsible for their suffering joining the new power elite.[25] However, a

[21] J.E. Mendez, 'In Defence of Transitional Justice', in J.A. McAdams (ed.), *Transitional Justice and the Rule of Law in New Democracies* (Notre Dame, IN: University of Notre Dame Press, 2001), p. 4.

[22] L.M. McLaren, *Constructing Democracy in Southern Europe. A Comparative Analysis of Italy, Spain and Turkey* (London/New York: Routledge, 2008), p. 142.

[23] W. Merkel and H.J. Wagener, 'Akteure' in R. Kollmorgen, W. Merkel and H.-J. Wagner (eds.), *Handbuch Transformationsforschung* (Wiesbaden: Springer VS, 2014), p. 67.

[24] G. O'Donnell and P.C. Schmitter, *Transition from Authoritarian Rule. Prospects for Democracy* (Baltimore: John Hopkins University Press, 1986), Part I–IV.

[25] G. O'Donnell, P.C. Schmitter and L. Whitehead (eds.), *Transition from Authoritarian Rule, Comparative Perspectives* (Baltimore: Johns Hopkins University Press, 1986), vol. III, pp. 38–40.

majority of old elites in the new regime can threaten the regime change and consolidation process and can lead to a fragile, violent process and even the return to an autocratic regime, as was often the case in Turkey after the many military coups and autocratic governments and even in 2016. It is thus important to strive for a balance between old and new elites in the new administration.

Thus, successful democratic regime consolidation is also based on criteria that appear today in the context of institutional quality assessment similar to what Morlino or Dahl have been defining.[26] Today, democracies such as Germany and Spain are under scrutiny and are being tested for their levels of resilience to threats in times of crisis. This is why looking at how consolidated democracies make use of TJ measures long after the initial regime change phase, becomes an interesting matter in the following case studies. The level of institutional resilience, robustness or consolidation also depends on how democracies dealt with their past 50 years after a military coup or 70 years after the Holocaust and war crimes.

Elections, for example, although crucial for any democratic regime, are given a different weight today than they were decades ago when testing the quality of democracy. Instead, attention is now shifted towards how citizens participate in decision making and how they legitimise even the most consolidated regime. As Powell described, alternative criteria such as security-sector reform and legal rights for citizens to assemble freely and participate are equally important to citizens' ability to express their political will.[27] Nevertheless, the core aspects of democratic regime consolidation have remained the same for decades. Researchers use basic criteria for assessing democratic performance, such as those provided by Diamond (1999),[28] Huntington (1991),[29] Gunther/Diamandouros/Puhle (1995),[30] Linz and Stepan (1996),[31] Schmitter (2003),[32] Merkel (2008 and

---

[26] R.A. Dahl, *On Democracy* (New Haven, CT: Yale University Press, 1998); M.S. Lipset, 'Some Social Requisites of Democracy: Economic Development and Political Legitimacy', *American Political Science Review,* 53 (1959), 69–105.

[27] G. Bingham Powell, 'The Chain of Responsiveness', pp. 91–105, at p. 97.

[28] L. Diamond, *Developing Democracy, Toward Consolidation* (Baltimore, MD: Johns Hopkins University Press, 1999).

[29] S.P. Huntington, *The Third Wave. Democratisation in the Late Twentieth Century* (Oklahoma: Oklahoma University Press, 1991).

[30] R. Gunther, P.N. Diamandouros and H.-J. Puhle (eds.), *The Politics of Democratic Consolidation. Southern Europe in Comparative Perspective* (London: Johns Hopkins University Press, 1995), p. 7.

[31] J.J. Linz and A. Stepan (eds.), *Problems of Democratic Transition and Consolidation.*

[32] P.C. Schmitter, 'The Quality of Democracy'.

2010),[33] Merkel/Puhle (1999),[34] and O'Donnell et al. (2004),[35] to name but a few.

Diamond, for example, highlights how important democratic belief and behaviour is for any consolidation. It is not a static concept, but a living one and 'norms/beliefs' and citizens' 'societal behaviour' need to be constantly fuelled. This is why TJ can make a difference for democratic stability even in the most consolidated democracies. He emphasises that the first indicator of (democratic) consolidation is that the government or state bureaucracy (the elite level) has to function in a transparent and accountable manner. And I would add that this is where trials and commissions of inquiry can make a difference. Second, a well-functioning intermediate level with collective actors, organisations or interest groups must exist. Finally, at the mass level, public involvement is crucial, and a majority of citizens has to actively participate in the democratic processes. Diamond argues that at least two thirds and thus a large majority of society and of the mass public – approximately 66 to 70 per cent of the population – has to consistently believe in democracy as a concept and support democratic reforms in order for a society to be called democratic, and it is here where memorials, education and even late trials about the past can contribute to consolidation. The level of confidence and trust in the democratic system can alter the functioning of democratic institutions.[36]

Governments' responsiveness depends on horizontal variables such as elections, voter participation, civil society and the level of checks and balances. Horizontal powers monitor both equal competition and participation. In this respect, Robert Putnam and Charles Tilly have long opted for a stronger focus on the dependent variable of 'trust', which – as has been outlined earlier – plays a pivotal role when using TJ measures as tools. Putnam concludes that the greater the public participation, the higher the effectiveness through public or civic trust in a political system.[37] This means that high public participation indicates high civic trust in institution, which then leads to higher effectiveness of these institutions. This coincides with Tilly's additional analysis that in order to establish civic trust in democratic institutions, there needs to be an insulation of

---

[33] W. Merkel, *Systemtransformation* (2008) and W. Merkel, *Systemtransformation, Eine Einführung in die Theorie und Empirie der Transformationsforschung.*
[34] W. Merkel and H.-J. Puhle, *Von der Diktatur zur Demokratie.*
[35] G. O'Donnell, J. Vargas Cullell and O.M. Iazeetta, *The Quality of Democracy.*
[36] L. Diamond, *Developing Democracy: Toward Consolidation.*
[37] R.D. Putnam, *Making Democracy Work, Civic Traditions in Modern Italy* (Princeton, NJ: Princeton University Press, 1993).

categorical inequalities in public politics and a transformation of non-state powers to establish a protective relationship between citizens and the state.[38] TJ measures can be catalysts for such a process. In summary, all authors acknowledge the fact that the high threshold of institutional performance can only be attained if the large majority of citizens engage and participate in the institutions that govern them, leading to higher levels of trust in these institutions and, finally, resulting in legitimisation of these institutions.

With the spiral and mutual reinforcing effect between institutional consolidation and TJ measures, I will highlight how civic trust in political regimes is a matter of attitudinal and behavioural change that can be fostered through TJ measures. Claims by victims, perpetrators or bystanders seek a government response and if no response is given, confidence in institutions decreases. When using trials to deal with past wrongdoing, governments use constitutional frameworks to bring those responsible to justice, according to their relative share of responsibility in the crimes of the past. It is thus claimed that arbitrary vengeance and intimidation must be avoided when using such constitutional frameworks, thus increasing trust in institutions.

As mentioned earlier, Linz and Stepan[39] have long argued democracy can only become 'the only game in town' if citizens participate in public life, thus increasing citizen trust in democratic institutions. That is to say, democracy can only be consolidated if citizens actively and without fear participate and if the government responds with non-violent or suppressive means.[40] A simple majority of citizens who support the regime for whatever reasons and by whatever means is not sufficient to sustain consolidation; two-thirds is a minimum to consolidate it and that supports 'the game', as also highlighted by O'Donnell. These indicators emphasise that 'loyalty' to the democratic regime is one of the factors that contributes to consolidation. Trust and legitimacy have already been indicated by Gabriel Almond and Sidney Verba in their work on civic culture and has often been reiterated when looking at how authoritarian regimes differ from democratic ones. For regime consolidation, according to Merkel, political elites need the support of citizens and civil society in a democratic society, while in an authoritarian one political elites suppress citizens

---

[38] C. Tilly, *Democracy* (Cambridge: Cambridge University Press, 2007), p. 96.
[39] J. Linz and A. Stepan (eds.), *Problems of Democratic Transition and Consolidation*.
[40] Ibid.

and civil society. Without the broad support of civil society, no democratic regime can survive.[41]

To summarise these key factors, this loyalty, however, has to be (re) gained over and over again, through interactions between political elites and civil society. This is where consolidated democracies may differ in quality as Morlino and Dahl have outlined. Political elites, as well as organised civil society groups, have to be accountable for their actions and must adhere to the rule of law at any state of democracy. Trials, memorials or commissions of inquiry can be useful tools in this sense. Such measures help political elites, civil society and individual citizens to distance themselves from dictatorial habits and policies. This is echoed in John Keane's assessment of democratic consolidation, in which he highlighted that it is the citizens who stabilise democratic institutions not political elites (alone).[42]

Coming back to the spiral effect between political institutions, actors and TJ measures, Cynthia Horne has shown that lustration of public officers after the communist regimes, for example, had a positive effect on civic trust over a longer period of time and thus on democratic development in Eastern Europe. She illustrates that lustration and vetting procedures have an indirect effect on citizens' perceptions of institutions and increase the perceived trustworthiness of institutions.[43] This, however, implies not only simple participation via citizen engagement or access to institutions via trials and elections, but also implies that the political system will respond to citizen claims in a non-restrictive and non-violent manner. Consequently, the judiciary and the parliament shall work to diminish inequalities, be they by virtue of birth, gender, and ethnicity or through the legacy that the past authoritarian or dictatorial regime is left behind.[44] Moreover, it is only if citizens make use of public or governmental institutions to seek control that we can really speak of trust in the institutions. 'Control' is regarded as an aspect to assess equality and participation when establishing the political agenda.[45] If democratic institutions and their representatives are corrupt, biased or disregard equality rights, people will simply not utilise them. As a consequence, the level of

---

[41] W. Merkel, *Systemtransformation* (1999), pp. 164–165.
[42] J. Keane, *Life and Death of Democracy* (London: Simon & Schuster, 2009).
[43] C.M. Horne, 'Assessing the Impact of Lustration on Trust in Public Institutions and National Government in Central and Eastern Europe', *Comparative Political Studies*, 45(4) (2001), 439–440.
[44] D. Beetham, *Democracy and Human Rights* (Oxford: Polity Press, 1999), p. 90.
[45] R.A. Dahl, *On Democracy*.

civic trust will decline and citizens will solve their problems and issues in alternative ways that sometimes result in violence or in revenge. Putnam, Susan Pharr and Russell Dalton stressed the importance of this variable throughout their studies as one that defines regime change outcome and thus consolidation. It is normal for citizens to be sceptical of a government, but it is quite different if this cynicism focuses on specific legislative or judicial powers. Such cynicism will dramatically impede a successful transition to democracy.[46]

Many of these abovementioned explanations of and for regime consolidation are mirrored by the plenitude of TJ case studies of countries experiencing transition from autocracy to democracy – and often the subsequent return to autocracy, as illustrated for example by O'Donnell and Schmitter. TJ research has often stressed the importance for more research on whether TJ actually impacts regime change and consolidation, as was illustrated by the 2011 World Development Report on Transitional Justice, Security and Development. In his report, the former UN Special Rapporteur on Transitional Justice, Pablo de Greiff (first appointed in 2012) argued that trust in institutions is shaped through acts of prosecution, truth-telling exercises, material or symbolic reparations and vetting – but without any long-term thorough research and evidence.[47] He argued that these measures promote civic trust by reaffirming the relevance of (human rights) norms that victimisers once violated. Thus, TJ measures enhance human rights awareness and convert people into rights holders, which is fundamental for democracy. Ideally, judicial proceedings guarantee that no one is above the law or human rights norms. Testimonials and truth-telling exercises have a long-term impact on the 'de-legitimation' or demystification of the previous regime. They simply put the facts on the table and leave little room for speculation. Additionally, reparations can foster civic trust by demonstrating the seriousness with which the democratic institutions involved take the violation of personal rights. Finally, vetting induces trust not only by replacing former elites with new faces, but also by demonstrating a commitment to systematic

---

[46] R.D. Putnam, S. J. Pharr and R. J. Dalton (eds.), 'Introduction: What's Troubling the Trilateral Democracies?', in S.J. Pharr and R.D. Putnam (eds.), *Disaffected Democracies, What's Troubling the Trilateral Countries?* (Princeton, NJ: Princeton University Press, 2000), p. 18.
[47] UN Human Rights Council, *Special Rapporteur on the promotion of truth, justice, reparation and guarantees of non-recurrence*, P. de Greiff, Doc. A/HRC/21/46, 9 August 2012.

norms governing employee hiring and retention, disciplinary over-
sight, and prevention of cronyism.[48]

Government institutions that perform well are likely to elicit the confidence of citizens; those that perform badly or ineffectively generate feelings of distrust. The trust variable is thus one that is important to link
to the possible effect TJ measures can have to consolidate democratic
regimes.

But interestingly enough, Karen Cook, Russel Hardin and Margaret
Levi argued against the importance of trust in democratic societies. In
their book *Cooperation Without Trust?* they argue contrary to most civic
trust studies in transformation theories, that trust is no longer the central
pillar of social order. In their view, trust is simply an overrated requirement for democratic regime consolidation, because we often find high
levels of trust also in authoritarian regimes. Although trust is important
in many interpersonal contexts and personal relationships between citizen and institutions, it cannot, according to the authors, carry the weight
of making complex and divided societies function productively and
effectively.[49] However, whether some argue in favour or against civic trust
being the 'glue' that connects citizens to their political regimes, there is
an existing lack thus far of alternative explanations on what otherwise
matters for consolidation. Instead, attempts to argue in favour of trust are
multiple and authors such as Kenneth Newton and Pippa Norris[50] emphasise the role of civic trust because the level of trust or mistrust is an accur-
ate thermometer of public life and democratic culture. If politicians and
political elites are able to deliver on promises to their citizens, the level of
civic trust is enhanced, democratic processes run more efficiently and the
relationship between institutions and citizens is improved, according to
these authors.

Although these are far-reaching assumptions about civic trust and the
role that TJ measures can play in creating it, it would appear that trust and
confidence in political institutions are the product of government performance in much the same way that estimations of trustworthiness of
others on the individual level affect others' behaviour.[51] I will argue that

---

[48] P. de Greiff, 'Transitional Justice, Security, and Development, Security and Justice Thematic
   Paper', Background Paper, World Development Report 2011 (2010).
[49] K.S. Cook, R. Hardin and M. Levi, *Cooperation Without Trust?*, p. 1.
[50] K. Newton and P. Norris, 'Confidence in Public Institutions: Faith, Culture, or
   Performance?', in S.J. Pharr and R.D. Putnam (eds.), *Disaffected Democracies, What's
   Troubling the Trilateral Countries?* (Princeton, NJ: Princeton University Press, 2000).
[51] Ibid., p. 61.

TJ measures such as trials, apologies and reparations for past injustice are tools used by civil and political actors to catalyse different attitudes and behaviours, and can be particularly used to benefit civic trust. Citizens' trust will increase once they see the new government dealing with the past in an adequate manner and in accordance with the rule of law. TJ strengthens political institutions, which in turn increases governmental performance and thus also citizens' trust.

Regardless of whether one sees the trust variable as being overrated or not, one can argue that in post-conflict or post-authoritarian societies, the use of TJ measures can help in the first phase of transition to (re)establish civic trust in institutions and to encourage people to (re)engage with public institutions. If a transition to democracy is succeeding, it is this next generation that has incorporated the values and attitudes that were 'learned', 'practised' and 'tested' through use of the early TJ measures during the first 20 years after regime change.

Thus, with the help of TJ measures, citizens learn and experience to build and enhance their trust in courts and judges, a trust that they did not experience under the former regime. Citizens begin to trust and interact or engage with politicians, parliament and the government, because these institutions have proven to be accountable for their words and deeds. Almost all studies in the context of regime consolidation highlight this relationship, although Cook or Winter only emphasised that trust cannot be more than interpersonal. But how is one to measure citizen engagement and legitimacy and thus social capital or citizens' capacity and behaviour in the context of regime change and consolidation? Putnam, for example, posited that civic trust derives from social capital, which is the combination of norms (such as the constitution) and political and civil networks that are based on reciprocity and civil engagement with institutions. He states that social capital improves the efficiency of societies by facilitating and coordinating actions that create changes.[52] Pierre Hazan argued that the driving force behind such citizens' behaviour in post-authoritarian or post-conflict societies is 'national catharsis' of the traumatised and still fearful society that has little to no experience with peaceful or democratic problem solving. The window of opportunity for national catharsis to take place is the first year or two of the regime change.[53] In this short period, this process must install pathways for regime consolidation and TJ. If

---

[52]   R.D. Putnam, *Making Democracy Work*, p. 167.
[53]   W. Merkel, *Systemtransformation*, p. 137.

such a catharsis takes place among the various actors, a consensus can be built around the sentiment of 'never again' and a common understanding can arise among all citizens and political elites to agree on regime change and further transformation. Although this national catharsis does not last long (sometimes not more than a few months), it indicates the beginning of regime transformation and shows that there is a chance of democracy. In West Germany, this process of national catharsis was often referred to as 'Nie wieder Auschwitz' and in Spain it was known as 'Nunca más', used by different groups often with different intentions as a constant reminder to move on towards democracy.

Hazan suggests that prior to applying any TJ measures, there has to be a common agreement between political and civil actors to adhere to human rights norms and standards and to set up democratic institutions, even if only on paper at first. Without society at large having gone through a catharsis of the past, there will be no common acceptance of the outcomes of TJ measures. According to him, the national catharsis and the common pursuit of truth and justice is the beginning of creating a common narrative about the past, a process that can take decades. Without this narrative, fragile countries in transition often remain divided for decades. Hazan divided regime transition into short-, medium- and long-term post-conflict phases, showing that full consolidation can take up to one generation, that is to say 20 to 25 years after the initial regime change. This is in line with Zapf and Rustow's generational model, explained above. According to Hazan, all TJ measures aim to legitimise the new government and their institutions and delegitimise the previous regime.[54]

If this is the case, then why can the use of TJ measures also lead to authoritarianism? The short answer would be that exclusive, sporadic and only tactical use of TJ measures will not have the effect on free citizen participation as would an inclusive, systematic and morally based use of the same measures. Jeff Spinner-Halev has looked at a number of other country cases around the world to see why some countries have used TJ measures and others not, and he agrees with Hazan's observations by highlighting that if past injustice and harm is not dealt with it becomes enduring injustice, which harms the development of the rule of law in a country and thus in consequence leads to the return to authoritarianism.[55]

---

[54] P. Hazan, 'Measuring the Impact of Punishment and Forgiveness: A Framework for Evaluating Transitional Justice', *International Review of the Red Cross*, 88 (2006), 19–47.

[55] J. Spinner-Halev, 'From Historical to Enduring Injustice', *Political Theory*, 35 (2007), 574–597.

In other words, if political and civil society has not learned to treat past perpetrators and victims in a humane and fair way (according to their own constitutional norms and standards), society will also not be able to treat present and future perpetrators in accordance with the rule of law. Instead, enduring injustice will prevail, people will not gain trust in institutions and the regime risks weak institutions and a downward spiral effect. If injustice prevails in a society – usually because of a failure to delegitimise and demystify the past through legal and political means – the society will return to an authoritarian system.

If used in an inclusive and systematic way, TJ measures can prevent such developments. TJ measures can enhance the respect for the dignity of persons and can feed into the liberalisation process of society, which is one of the fundamentals of an effective democracy. West German Attorney General Fritz Bauer referred to this effect during the Auschwitz Trials of 1963–1965 in Frankfurt. The trials he initiated aimed to deal with the guards and directors at the extermination camps in Auschwitz during World War II. In his press conference a day prior to the trials, Bauer claimed that even 20 years after the atrocities and in the then-democratic West Germany, these trials, during which only a handful of people were convicted, were important for Germans and its future generations and the rest of the world to show that there is a different Germany to be trusted in again. The trials were a test for the West German democracy to see whether it could deal with these atrocities while continuing to respect the rule of law. Bauer, himself a Holocaust survivor, claimed that apart from giving truth and justice to those who suffered and bringing perpetrators to justice, the trials served the purpose of rebuilding trust in the German judiciary; a judiciary that would now adhere to human rights and the rule of law instead of one populated with racist judges acting with hate and prejudice. The trials were far from perfect and would not meet today's human rights or international law standards, but they marked a clear shift in the German judiciary. It was not only about punishing perpetrators, but also about re-educating the wider public to understand that there was a 'new German society' that now adheres to democratic principles and distances itself from totalitarianism. Therefore, as Bauer stated, these trials and how their judges interpreted the law had an educational and catalytic effect on democracy and a delegitimising effect on the Nazi regime.[56] While there is no direct causation, one could say that the trials

---

[56] F. Bauer on 20 December 1963 *Press Conference Auschwitz Trials*, see also D. O'Pendas, *The Frankfurt Auschwitz Trial, 1963–1965: Genocide, History, and the Limits of the Law* (Cambridge: Cambridge University Press, 2006).

and democracy mutually reinforced each other. Eventually, citizens in general must take ownership of the TJ process, feel responsible for the past and present and consequently support and legitimise the democratic regime.[57] The assumption is that if they do so with regard to the past, they will also do so regarding the present and the future and, accordingly, they will effectively engage in democratic procedures. Dealing with the past is the basis for civil trust in institutions as well as the basis for the legitimation of institutions. Without this process of TJ succeeding, the likelihood of facing threats to democracy from myths and assumptions about the past is high. But because of the stabilising effect dealing with the past has, TJ is also used by autocratic regimes, such as those in East Germany and Turkey. These regimes also employed trials, vetting procedures and reparations to rebuild the trust and confidence of former victims and enemies in the new political regime. The difference is that these autocratic regimes used TJ measures in an exclusionary manner and to their own advantage, for example by purging political enemies from positions of power.

I have re-emphasised that going from a post-conflict regime to a consolidated democracy is not a linear process, but rather a bumpy one. In the first phase of transition, there is often a lack of political willingness to reconcile with previous enemies and to face the past. New political elites abuse TJ measures, using them to cleanse themselves of political opponents. Vengeance and mistrust is widespread and often perpetuated. The sense of fear that former elites will 'emerge again' and trigger new outbreaks of violence prevails, leading to coups d'état and other anti-democratic measures, as was the case in Spain and Turkey. Therefore, societies often opt for amnesty and even impunity of perpetrators in the hope that this will bring peace to society.

The irony is that while fear and avoidance of TJ measures is triggering rebellion, revolution and coups and often leads to granting amnesties, it is this very subsequent impunity that can lead to new violence. Either way, to avoid a thorough TJ process for whatever reasons will subsequently lead to unrest, violence and flaws in the consolidation process. The fear of openly dealing with past perpetrators will frustrate national catharsis and thus prevent society from moving towards peace and democracy. Former military elites who feel threatened by TJ measures, unless amnesties are offered to them, threaten with coups and rebellions and violent attacks are the consequence, as one saw in Spain in 1981, six years after it

---

[57] T. Ka-ying Wong, W. Po-san and M. Hsiao Hsin-Huang, 'The Bases of Political Trust in Six Asian Societies', 263–281.

chose the democratic path; in East Germany in 1954, five years after the establishment of the communist regime; as well as several times during Turkey's long transitional phase after 1987/89 where the fact that the past was dealt with in a biased and exclusive way led to rebellion and coups until present times. In turn, during regime change, governments fear that the weak and new democratic institutions cannot withstand the massive pleas for justice while society remains intimidated by the old elites, security forces, the secret service or paramilitary groups that are still in place and whom society has feared for decades. Anne Leebaw explains that the application of TJ measures can contribute to more justice and peace in a society but, if their use is not democratic, they will not automatically lead to more legitimacy of the new system.[58] Thus, the silence pacts of post-Franco Spain, or the repetitive culture of impunity in Turkey after every military coup, may have had a positive impact on 'stability' by preventing society from taking personal vengeance and initiating social turmoil that was feared if trials would have been issued – but it hampered the development of the rule of law at the same time. However, turmoil rose in any case in these societies but under other labels than TJ. One of the root causes was the fact that too many of the old militant elites remained in power untouched both in Spain and in Turkey. Accordingly, some have argued that a period of silence and 'leaving the past alone' might be more important in stabilising a society during regime change but not during consolidation periods. However, others also argue that this depends largely on how political and social elites deal with the past. Silence is not the only alternative. Scholars such as O'Donnell, Schmitter and Laurence Whitehead[59] argue for 'quick trials or no trials', of which others like Hazan would disagree. However, James Gibson's evaluation of South Africa's TJ process reached the conclusion that bringing events of the past to the surface through longer TJ processes and using measures such as Truth and Reconciliation Commissions (TRCs), can lead to the reduction of inter-group conflict, thus stabilising society as well as enhancing the democracy effort.[60]

The majority of researchers in the field of regime consolidation adhere to the assumption that silence, amnesty and impunity will by

---

[58] Bronwyn A. Leebaw, 'The Irreconcilable Goals of Transitional Justice', *Human Rights Quarterly*, 30(1) (2008), 95–118.

[59] G. O'Donnell, P.C. Schmitter and L. Whitehead, *Transition from Authoritarian Rule. Southern Europe*, p. 30.

[60] J.L. Gibson, 'The Contribution of Truth to Reconciliation', p. 415.

no means result in democratic consolidation. After the short period of change, the regime should dedicate itself to facing its unpleasant and painful past. And the best way to do that is through democratic measures, overall a strong and free civil society, which can break the vicious circle of silence, fear, violence and vengeance. Indeed, independently from each other, they argue that amnesty will only encourage further human rights abuses and acts of vengeance. This will lead to an ability to deal with the future and the denial of the rule of law will weaken the foundations of the new democracy.[61] According to these authors, silencing the past, for example by avoiding acknowledgement of or apologising for atrocities carried out by the previous regime, or by passing blanket amnesty laws, cannot prevent a democratically elected government from sooner or later having to carry out its duty to apply international law, human rights and to pursue justice. Often this correlates with the fact that after the new regime has been in place for a period of time, a critical mass of citizens or NGOs gain knowledge concerning their rights and subsequently claim the human right to fair trials and reparations.

According to the findings undertaken at the Michelsen Institute in Bergen, where researchers tried to draw a direct mono-causal link between TJ and democracy by looking at the context, the type of TJ measure, the degree to which they were implemented and the improvement in democracy over a short period of time, such a direct link could not be found. Rather it was posited that there might be parallel developments between respecting and implementing TJ measures on the one hand and democratic development on the other.[62] This is what I call a mutual reinforcing spiral effect. When aiming to assess the cumulative causality or spiral effect, it is the process rather than a singular outcome that is important. Alexandra Barahona de Brito, Carmen Gonzaléz-Enríquez, Paloma Aguilar and Eric Wiebelhaus-Brahm claimed in their case studies that there is no clear evidence for TJ measures having any significant impact on or link with democracies, although they do not deny that democratic setups can leverage the way TJ measures impact a cultural change from violence to peace.[63]

[61] J.E. Mendez, 'In Defence of Transitional Justice'.
[62] E. Skaar and A.J.R. Dahl, *Dealing with Violent Past. The Impact of Transitional Justice* (Bergen: CMI, CHR, Michael Institute, 2012).
[63] A. Barahona de Brito, C. Gonzaléz-Enríquez and P. Aguilar, *The Politics of Memory*; E. Wiebelhaus-Brahm, *Truth Commissions and Transitional Justice: The Impact on Human Rights and Democracy* (New York/London: Routledge, 2010).

Thus, although it remains challenging, and indeed may never be possible to draw direct causal links between TJ measures and consolidation, it is clear that there is some sort of indirect, spiral relationship between the two.

Another assumption to note down here is that some authors such as Jeremy Sarkin and Eric Daly argue that TJ measures such as TRCs or other commissions of inquiry can mitigate inter-group conflicts and help to remedy deficits in justice, yet they can also increase them. That is why many policy makers often opt for silence and amnesty instead. Unfortunately, quantitative and qualitative comparative case studies that analyse the impact of TJ measures on society have not yet added much to this debate.[64] Though the discourses vary, all researchers in the field of TJ deal with the question whether TJ methods lead more to retributive or restorative justice or justice at all.[65] Others are instead attempting to identify more precise criteria and indicators of TJ,[66] or the role and contributions of certain actors in the process.[67] The list of authors and publications can hardly be exhausted; only a few have been mentioned above.[68] International interference and incentives to use TJ measures speed up the process of consolidation if used in the manner previously described.[69]

---

[64] J. Sarkin and E. Daly, 'Too Many Questions, Too Few Answers: Reconciliation in Transitional Societies', *Columbia Human Rights Law Review*, 35 (2004), 101–168; E. Barkan, *The Guilt of Nations, Restitution and Negotiating Historical Injustice* (Baltimore, MD: Johns Hopkins University Press, 2000); R. Teitel, 'Transitional Justice Globalised', *International Journal of Transitional Justice*, 2 (2008), 1–4; P.B. Hayner, *Unspeakable Truths, Facing the Challenges of Truth Commissions* (New York/London: Routledge, 2002); M. Minow, *Between Vengeance and Forgiveness, Facing History after Genocide and Mass Violence* (Boston, MA: Beacon Press, 1998).

[65] R.A. Wilson, 'Anthropological Studies of National Reconciliation Processes', *Anthropological Theory*, 3 (2003), 367–387; M. Ure, 'Post-Traumatic Societies: On Reconciliation, Justice and the Emotion', *European Journal of Social Theory*, 11 (2008), 284.

[66] P. Hazan, 'Measuring the Impact of Punishment and Forgiveness, 19–47.

[67] D. Backer, 'Civil Society and Transitional Justice: Possibilities, Patterns and Prospects', *Journal of Human Rights*, 3 (2003), 297–313.

[68] S.L. Mazzuca, 'Access to Power Versus Exercise of Power, Reconceptualizing the Quality of Democracy in Latin America', *Studies in Comparative International Development*, 45 (2010), 334–357, at 354.

[69] B. Kohler-Koch, T. Conzelmann and M. Knodt, *Europäische Integration – Europäisches Regieren* (Wiesbaden: VS Verlag, 2004); M. Kneuer, *Demokratisierung durch die EU, Süd- und Ostmitteleuropa im Vergleich* (Wiesbaden: VS Verlag, 2007); J. Zielonka, 'The Quality of Democracy after Joining the European Union', *East European Politics and Societies*, 21 (2007), 162–180.

Figure 3.1 Using Transitional Justice Measures for Legitimacy

3.1 Delegitimising and Legitimising Regimes

In the context of change and consolidation of new regimes, TJ measures have the power to delegitimise previous political regimes and legitimise new ones. The more a new political regime distances itself from a previous, atrocious, corrupt or unjust regime, it delegitimises it and can use these policies and tools to legitimise the new regime and consolidate it – as shown in Figure 3.1.[70] Political and civil actors can use TJ measures to delegitimise the previous regime by shedding light on past wrongdoings, corrupt elites or war crimes under the former command and so on. But for authoritarian regime deconsolidation, this means that TJ measures are predominantly used by political elites to purge political opponents and to manipulate public opinion in favour of the newly emerging one-party government.[71] For democratic regime consolidation it means that TJ measures are used by civil society actors and political or other elites to demystify the previous one and strengthen on the basis of non-recurrence and rule of law of the new regime.

Seymour Lipset explains regime legitimacy as 'the capacity of a political system to engender and maintain the belief that existing political institutions are the most appropriate ones for society'.[72] A regime is legitimised if citizens support its rules and behaviour over a long period, regardless of what type of regime the citizens would actually prefer if they had the choice. Merkel and Puhle have added a nuance to this description by emphasising that a regime is legitimised if a large majority of citizens support it, despite the fact that they know alternative regime types exist.[73] It

---

[70] D. Easton, *A Systems Analysis of Political Life* (New York: John Wiley & Sons, 1965).
[71] A. Kästner, 'Autokratieförderung' in R. Kollmorgen, W. Merkel and H.-J. Wagner (eds.), *Handbuch Transformationsforschung* (Wiesbaden: Springer VS, 2014), pp. 493–498.
[72] S.M. Lipset, *Political Man* (Baltimore, MD: Johns Hopkins University Press, 1980), p. 460.
[73] W. Merkel and H. Puhle, *Von der Diktatur zur Demokratie*, p. 176.

is imperative to win citizen support and have public opinion on the side of the regime during the first decade of transition, during which political elites have to make tactical concessions and compromises to (re)stabilise society and the new regime, regardless of whether it turns out to become authoritarian or democratic. Since vetting procedures, amnesty laws, truth commissions and trials of former political elites help change people's perception of the past regime they do not automatically legitimise the new regime.

However, one must not be too idealistic about the early years of regime change in any political context. During the first ten years or so most TJ measures are employed as tactical concessions to international and external pressure, in order to gain financial benefits, international recognition and party support, as outlined earlier. Any sense of a moral obligation to atone for the past is usually absent. It is in this first decade during which TJ measures are most often misused as a way to purge political opponents, to place blame only on former enemies and increase prejudice and resentment. Linz and Stepan referred to this first phase of transition as 'about eight years of breathing space' for new democracies, during which the first two election terms (each four years) and subsequent legislative periods take place. For them, it is this period and the choices made therein that determine whether the regime will follow a path towards democracy or authoritarianism.[74]

A sense of a moral or ethical obligation to use TJ measures is usually experienced later, when the next generation comes into power, a generation that has no personal responsibility for the past. This was the case in West Germany during the 1970s, in Spain around the year 2000 and in Turkey after 2005. Such cases lend great support to Rustow and Zapf's assumption that regime consolidation and the full embrace of new values and norms only take place 20 to 25 years after the initial regime change. Interestingly enough, this 20+ generation shows up on the political scene after regime consolidation is on the way, but not much earlier. It reflects Merkel's fourth level of 'consolidation by civil society' during which the *demos* is the most pivotal actor, and it is the last and most important level in order to complete the consolidation process.[75] Whether the 20+ generation emerges in the public arena as a voice in favour of TJ depends on whether fundamental participatory and freedom rights are somewhat

---

[74] J. Linz and A. Stepan, *Problems of Democratic Transition and Consolidation*, p. 79.
[75] W. Merkel, Systemtransformation, *Eine Einführung in die Theorie und Empirie der Transformationsforschung*, p. 124.

guaranteed (at least formally). In other words, the 20+ generation is able to emerge and push for TJ measures and thus increase democratic performance based on the level freedom rights are guaranteed, a sense of moral and ethical obligation and if an independent judiciary (at least in theory) exists. Thus, whereas during the first decade after regime change TJ measures are mainly applied by the political leadership for tactical reasons and participation is still rare, the institutions that arise out of this period are what determines the rise of a vocal 20+ generation as well as TJ measures that focus on a moral obligation for justice.

There are many definitions of legitimacy in regard to political regimes. I will not deal with all of them here, but will rather highlight those that have been most frequently applied in the field of regime consolidation and TJ. As highlighted many times already, legitimacy of a new political regime depends on citizens accepting the regime's new values and rules, either democratic or autocratic.[76] This is the case, regardless of whether a regime is totalitarian or authoritarian, such as the East GDR and Turkey, or democratic ones such as Spain, West Germany and reunified Germany. What matters is that people accept the new regime's ideas of justice, fairness and its institutional structure. This is true for authoritarian regimes as well; if the regime is to be considered legitimate by its citizens, these citizens must support the idea of, for example, centralistic governments, and exclusive participation of a few, but not all, societal groups and interests.

Leslie Holmes and Richard Rose have analysed the processes of (de)legitimation that occurred after the communist regimes of Eastern Europe declined. They discovered that in these countries regime change was significantly driven by external pressures by old elites but not necessarily revolution by new elites, such as the desire to become a respected member of international organisations, the desire to gain support from external NGOs and the desire to compare well against other 'successful and prosperous' regimes in the west.[77] Despite the fact that strong CSOs existed in Poland, Czechoslovakia or Hungary and East Germany, the transition has mainly been pushed by former elites, by international organisations such as the Council of Europe,

---

[76] D. Lambach, 'Legitimitaet' in R. Kollmorgen, W. Merkel, H.-J. Wagener (eds.) *Handbuch Transformationsforschung* (Wiesbaden: Springer VS, 2014), pp. 599–604.

[77] L. Holmes, *Post Communism, An Introduction* (Durham, NC: Duke University Press, 1997); R. Rose, *Understanding Post-Communist Transformation: A Bottom Up Approach* (London: Routledge, 2009).

the European Community/Union and by external (Soviet or US) forces and occupying powers.

Often, dealing with past injustices increased these countries' chances of gaining membership in international organisations and of becoming a respected member of the international (or European) community. Thus TJ measures, such as commissions of inquiry, trials, memorials and compensations, were used for tactical reasons to achieve these goals. In the years after the regime changes of the 1990s, TJ measures such as vetting, commissions of inquiry, etc. have been seen as tactical concessions for the new political and civil class to finally achieve their goal of international recognition. There was a general consensus that the return to communism was not an alternative, but TJ was not necessarily seen as a way to delegitimise that regime, because the discontent with the regime was with Soviet occupying powers and a bad socialist economy, not so much with their own political elite. One fortunate by-product of using TJ measures in this tactical way was that the previous regime and its leadership had to confront a general public inquiry by means of an open and new free media, but there was little popular consent to put them on trial or systematically investigate their crimes.

Ideally, after a regime change has taken place, democratically elected leaders usually distance themselves from the autocratic political practices of the previous regime and promise to hold accountable those responsible for the crimes of the past. In doing so, they send the message that the new regime adheres to new values and rules, under which such crimes have no place. Based on a comparison of several southern European and Latin American transition and regime change processes, Morlino argued that democratic institution-building practices must have one eye on the country's past authoritarian legacy and one eye on the country's future after transition.[78] Governments that do not want to or cannot come to terms with the past will sooner or later have to deal with problems such as the culture of impunity that arose in Turkey and Spain during their transitions, old elites returning to power and a recurrence of state crimes. These problems that arise from ignoring the past risk entrenching autocratic practices in the new regime.

A government's level of responsiveness to truth commissions' recommendations and their achievement of the allotted objectives indicates whether the government aims to demystify and delegitimise the past, or

---

[78] L. Morlino 'Authoritarian Legacies', p. 166.

whether old loyalties prevent a distancing from the previous regime. The latter was the case in Turkey, when its government ignored the recommendations issued by the ECtHR and by the international history commission on the Armenian Genocide.

If the new elite distances itself from the old regime, it agrees to take a different political direction towards the future. And if the executive and legislative branches pass laws and regulations to exclude people from amnesty and instead grant reparations, this indicates a higher level of political legitimacy. In contrast, if governments refuse or restrict claims without providing reasons, then unrest, civil disobedience and even turmoil may occur. This stems from citizens' lack of satisfaction with the government's failure to respond to their needs and claims, as has been the case many times in Turkey, Spain and East Germany. In other words, regardless of the extent to which injustice has happened in the past, the executive and legislative powers must respond to grievances made in the public sphere that are related to past injustice. In such situations, the matter of transparency is crucial and a claim for TJ can increase the level of transparency. Concealing or silencing claims or the need for retributive justice can have negative consequences on democratic stability, and suppression and unrest are likely to recur.

In order to call for trials that may have a delegitimising effect, citizens must enjoy the human right to free expression and assembly, which requires a minimum level of constitutionalism and rule of law. Once citizens start feeling free to call for more TJ, governments often respond with tactical concessions. Governments may introduce a partial truth commission that deals with a limited number of the past injustice's aspects, as was the case in Spain and Turkey. After some time has passed and it becomes apparent that it is possible to demand more measures, such as reparations or memorials, without fear of repercussions, victim groups begin to call for more. This was the case in the German-Jewish diaspora that started to establish memorials in West German concentration camps in the 1960s but only much later received governmental support and recognition for it. This helped to regain trust in the political institutions and thus legitimised the new regime during the consolidation phase. In these cases one can see the upward spiral relationship between citizen participation and governmental response. Together with the strengthening of this upward spiral relationship, the legitimacy of the new regime increases.

Trials, lustration policies and memorial events can improve power sharing between different groups within society, thus also improving democratic institutions' functioning and effectiveness and improving the new institutions' and elites' legitimacy. Amnesty laws and lack of transparent trials or commissions will intimidate and demotivate civil society to engage with political institutions. Therefore, egalitarian distribution of power is an important ideal that must be espoused in citizens' collective decision-making processes, if effectiveness and legitimacy are to increase.[79] As we will see was the case in East Germany, Spain and Turkey, newly established democracies with weaker institutions will react more carefully and restrictively when utilising the full spectrum of TJ measures than would be the case in stable democracies. The fear of opening 'old wounds' and triggering acts of revenge is a valid argument against using TJ measures in too pervasive a way during the first post-regime change decade. As explained above, this change period is the time for tactical concessions, compromises and slow changes – and not necessarily for deep soul-searching. Consensus-based democracies such as Spain and West Germany are more likely to deal well with the exigencies and tensions of this phase, as this type of regime is most likely to protect the rights and safety of all groups, perpetrators and victims, former and new elites alike. Authoritarian regimes or de facto single-party regimes such as East Germany and Turkey often lack the incentives to make concessions to external or internal pressures, unless they fear destabilisation.[80]

It follows from the arguments mentioned above that the full spectrum of TJ measures are applied more often in regimes with a clear and determined commitment to democracy, the abovementioned 'constitutional' and 'represented' consolidated regime as Merkel referred to them;[81] rather than in those that pretend to be democratic but in fact are headed towards a new authoritarian regime. Nevertheless, what all regime types have in common is that in the early transition period they may focus on only one or two measures and omit others due to the fear that a comprehensive and inclusive TJ process will threaten security and public safety by eliciting acts of revenge, because too many potential spoilers of the democratic shift are still in power.

There is a general assumption that the likelihood of TJ measures being used increases with the level of democracy a society knows, and

---

[79] C.H. Knutsen, 'Measuring Effective Democracy', International Political Science Review, 31 (2010), 109–128.
[80] In the TRC Report introduction of Report 1, Desmond Tutu has some great remarks on this fact.
[81] W. Merkel, Systemtransformation, Eine Einführung in die Theorie und Empirie der Transformationsforschung, p. 112.

vice versa. This is a similar concept that is used for this study. However, the frequency of using TJ measures often has little to do with the level of democracy in a society. In post-war Rwanda, for example, almost all TJ measures were applied top-down, and yet led to a new authoritarian regime. Thus, the difference is whether TJ measures are used bottom-up with top-down support. But if they are only used top-down, they have few legitimising effects.

On the contrary, in post-war West Germany, most of today's known TJ measures were applied within one generation after the end of the war, and therefore mostly for tactical reasons. External pressure from domestic policy makers and bottom-up efforts from citizens, most of whom were World War II victims, drove the application of these measures. These drivers meant that the West German government faced pressure both from the top and bottom, which forced a response from the government. External and international pressure and incentives played an additional role in the successful implementation of TJ measures. A result of this reinforcing circular causation between claims for TJ and responsiveness from government was a more consolidated regime.[82] Nevertheless, it took the country's post-war generation to embrace TJ measures and regard atonement not only as an obligation of holding perpetrators accountable, but also as a catalyst for the whole society to live democracy and 'consolidate by citizens and the demos'.[83] The historian Hans Goschler argued that TJ in West Germany revolved around two separate issues: first, a call from West Germans insisting on more knowledge of what had happened; and second, enough time passing that West Germans had some distance from what had happened. Both moments came about towards the end of the 1950s, 15 years after the war had ended and way into regime consolidation. In East Germany, the opposite was the case. The communist authoritarian regime continued to be a paternalistic, top-down one (similar to the Nazi regime) where individual responsibility and acknowledgement of victims of the whole atrocious spectrum of the Nazi regime played no role.[84] No serious TJ measures, let alone citizen-driven ones based on international human rights law, were ever introduced. In Spain,

---

[82] J. Herf, *Divided Memory: The Nazi Past in the Two Germanys* (Cambridge, MA: Harvard University Press, 1997).

[83] W. Merkel, Systemtransformation, *Eine Einführung in die Theorie und Empirie der Transformationsforschung,* p. 124.

[84] C. Goschler, *Schuld und Schulden, Die Politik der Wiedergutmachung für NS-Verfolgte seit 1945* (Göttingen: Wallstein Verlag, 2005), p. 289, at 407.

very few measures that would qualify as TJ were applied after Franco died in 1975. Yet, ten years after the regime change, the Spanish democracy was already considered a consolidated democracy because it complied with democracy's basic norms, and only started much later to apply a fuller spectrum of TJ measures.[85] Nevertheless, the fact that the Franco regime and its political elites were never delegitimised through trials or vetting procedures led to major flaws in the transition process and Spain had to deal with instances of serious violence decades after the regime change in areas such as the Basque region and the autonomous Catalan regions. These unconsolidated pockets of democracy remained; not surprisingly caused when and where citizens' claims for TJ were ignored and suppressed. The 'victim' pensions granted to Franco's political prisoners by the new political regime was an indirect way to acknowledge past wrongdoings, although it was not part of any official TJ policy. The private and victim-driven instalments of memorials at the local level were appreciated but remained local and were not supported at state level. The delegitimising effect of the Franco regime was rather low. A common, national narrative of what happened during the Franco regime was long missing from schoolbooks and television. The absence of substantial TJ measures alone is not automatically determinative of a failure of democracy, but rather one of the factors that can lead to a low-quality democracy.[86]

Ruptured and rapid regime change, such as in East and West Germany in 1945/9 and in Spain in 1975 through war, revolution or death of the dictator, often leads to more citizen resistance to the new regime than slower changes.[87] In cases of rapid change, the call for TJ measures can lead to massive resistance among political elites and citizens alike, turning back any successful development of democratic transition that had already taken place. But the absence of TJ measures as tools to trigger change and consolidation can also lead to unconsolidated pockets within the state, such as was the case in Italy, France, Czechoslovakia, Ukraine, Spain, Turkey, West Germany and the United Kingdom, countries that all had to face strong and violent separatist or political movements. Most countries that are transitioning towards consolidation share

---

[85] A. Barahona de Brito, C. Gonzaléz-Enríquez and P. Aguilar, *The Politics of Memory*.

[86] A. Mihr, 'Transitional Justice and the Quality of Democracy', *International Journal of Conflict and Violence*, 7(2) (2013), 298–313.

[87] C.R. Mitchell, 'Conflict, Social Change and Conflict Resolution. An Enquiry', in D. Bloomfield, M. Fischer and B. Schmelzle (eds.), *Social Change and Conflict Transformation* (Berlin: Berghof Handbook Dialogue Series, 2010), p. 20.

the experience that vulnerable and underprivileged minority groups seek greater acknowledgement and influence through undemocratic and violent means. These groups see themselves as victims of the previous regime and thus often base their claims for more justice on the 'unresolved issues' of the past.[88] TJ measures can be a tool for channelling these claims and for reintegrating previously excluded groups.

I contest the idea that unconsolidated pockets do not threaten consolidated regimes. They do so because these pockets withhold legitimacy. While separatism, terrorism or radical groups submerge regime consolidation, they may be unavoidable during early transition. But if they continue to exist 20 years or longer into consolidation they are a clear sign of a lack of legitimacy by citizen and civil society of the new regime and thus indicate democratic flaws.[89] They must not be tolerated in consolidated regimes because these pockets undermine the stability of the system. In this case, TJ measures can be used as mediating tools for reintegrating members of these groups into the larger society. This cannot be done without the new regime making concessions.

Unconsolidated pockets are often found in regimes with a high level of clienteles by old elites that is true for most post-authoritarian or conflict-torn societies. Separatist and violent movements are able to remain successful for generations because of the complete disregard for their claims about the past and because past elites have not been delegitimised. For example, the RAF in West Germany, the ETA in Spain and the PKK in Turkey maintained their support with narratives and myths about former elites still being in power, narratives and myths that can thrive in a society that has not fully dealt with and delegitimised its past. Such separatist and violent groups 'ignore' or mistrust the current democratic institutions, thus weakening them. TJ measures such as memorials, apologies or even symbolic trials can overcome this schism and close the gap between the 'myths' of the past and the regime of the present. This was indeed the case in Spain in the late 1980s and in West Germany in the late 1970s when politics changed in such a way that the terror decreased.[90] In Turkey that started with the first dialogues among government and Kurdish victim groups in the late 1990s and eased the tensions among the conflicting parties for some time until violence

---

[88] L.M. McLaren, *Constructing Democracy in Southern Europe.*
[89] W. Merkel, Systemtransformation, *Eine Einführung in die Theorie und Empirie der Transformationsforschung.*
[90] W. Merkel, *Systemtransformation,* pp. 293–297.

re-emerged in 2015. Needless to say, the use of TJ measures to reconcile unconsolidated pockets with the rest of society only affects the outer layers of radical groups. The core often remains resistant to democratic reforms for more than a generation – and for other reasons than because of a past that has not been adequately dealt with. More public dialogue about the past and an active reconciliation process can prevent these groups from gaining further supporters. Such dialogue might come in the form of commissions of inquiry, trials or memorials that recover and identify the facts and truth.

One can only ascertain correlations between democratic institutions and TJ when one compares governments' levels of responsiveness and transparency with levels of citizen engagement. We find many similar cases in Europe and beyond. In the former Yugoslavia, for example, a significant number of citizens rejected both the decisions of the International Criminal Tribunal for the former Yugoslavia (ICTY) as well as the application of the TRC's recommendations.[91] In the eyes of many Croatians, Serbs, Bosnians and Kosovars, the wounds of the past were too deep and the narratives about the war too controversial. The ICTY and the TRCs did not seem to serve the purpose of reconciliation and democratisation. Regardless of these sentiments, the Serbian political leadership and government decided to cooperate – for political and tactical reasons, not moral or ethical ones – with international requests from the ICTY by implementing TJ measures. In this case, as the following case studies will also show, the level at which post-dictatorial governments engage with or depend upon international organisations and their TJ policies is of the utmost importance. It appears that international human rights norms and standards, combined with nationally driven initiatives seeking membership in international organisations, have an impact on the way TJ measures are implemented.[92]

Linz and Stepan's definition of consolidation through legitimacy, namely that 'a democratic transition is complete when sufficient agreement has been reached about political procedures to produce an elected government, [and] when this government de facto has the authority to generate new policies, and when the executive, legislative and judicial power generated by the new democracy does not have to share power with

---

[91] P.C. McMahon and D.P. Forsythe, 'The ICTY's Impact on Serbia: Judicial Romanticism Meets Network Politics', *Human Rights Quarterly*, 30 (2008), 412–435.

[92] L.M. McLaren, *Constructing Democracy in Southern Europe*, p. 240.

other bodies de jure'[93] is a valid one to link to TJ measures. Consolidated regimes ought to enjoy the support of 'all significant groups' and these groups 'regard [the regime's] key political institutions as the only legitimate framework for political contestation, and adhere to democratic rules of the game' regardless of whether they agree with current policies.[94] In the process of consolidation the commitment made by the dominant class, may it be economic or political, is of high importance.[95] Without such commitment, the road to authoritarianism remains open. Thus, during a regime's transition, it is imperative that supporters of the old regime, those of the new regime, and victim groups engage in dialogue and interaction.

However, the more centralised the autocratic regime of the past was, the less likely TJ measures will be applied immediately as a tool for transforming norms, attitudes and behaviour. Transition requires many compromises and one of them can be the silencing of the past, instead of explicitly rejecting it. Silencing the past is a move in the process of transition that is common to all the case studies dealt with in this book. The reader will see that if power remained firmly in the hands of few and citizens had no experience of engaging with democratic institutions, the fear of vengeance and repercussions is omnipresent. Here again, Spain and Turkey are illustrative of a slow development and so is post-war Germany for its reluctance to come to terms with the past at the beginning. Once power is shared, free citizen participation is more likely to happen and political institutions gain more public support. In response policy makers apply TJ measures to which people in general reply positively – if applied in an inclusive manner – and the regime becomes a more legitimate one.[96]

Since TJ measures are tools in the hands of actors, their use or misuse depends on domestic and international dynamics and politics. These tools are nevertheless in part based on principles of accountability and redress. The choice to use a particular TJ measure over

[93] J.J. Linz and A. Stepan, *Problems of Democratic Transition and Consolidation*, p. 3.
[94] R. Gunther, P.N. Diamandouros and H.-J. Puhle (eds.), *The Politics of Democratic Consolidation*, p. 7; H.-J. Lauth and U. Liebert, *Im Schatten demokratischer Legitimität* (Opladen/Wiesbaden: Sozialwissenschaftlicher Verlag, 1999); P.C. Schmitter, 'The Quality of Democracy', online published paper; W. Merkel, *Systemtransformation*; W. Merkel and H.-J. Puhle, *Von der Diktatur zur Demokratie*; G. O' Donnell, J. Vargas Cullell and O.M. Iazeetta, *The Quality of Democracy*.
[95] Barrington Moore, Jr, *Social Origins of Dictatorship and Democracy: Lord and Peasant in the Making of the Modern World* (London: Beacon, 1993).
[96] A. Mihr, 'Transitional Justice and the Quality of Democracy', 298–313.

another available one is context specific. Sometimes it is better to start with measures of acknowledgement, such as historical commissions, while in other cases it is best to begin with trials and under yet other political circumstances it is better to start with lustration and vetting procedures. What matters most is that some type of TJ is employed so that the newly elected government can distance itself from the previous regime and indicate that it is willing to reckon with the past. In the beginning, tactical concessions may be made due to international or domestic pressure. After a while these concessions turn into wilful compliance and eventually a commitment towards TJ can become part of foreign policy, as can be seen in Germany's foreign policy towards Israel. However, these steps in transition are not linear or sequential, but exist along a spiral road, where developments can go back and forth over the course of decades, as will be illustrated throughout this book.

Gerardo Munck argues that follow-up procedures to install TJ policies are a requirement in order to witness the multi-causalities or cumulative causalities based on the high level of correlation between TJ and consolidation data.[97] That means that there have to be institutions in place, such as parliamentarian commissions, courts and CSOs that monitor and observe whether the judgments of courts or reparation policies are actually implemented. Furthermore, Munck and Jay Verkuilen observe that problems of direct causal interference have long overshadowed the equally important factors and multidimensionality of data that contribute to regime consolidation of conceptualisation and measurement.[98] Notwithstanding, democratic norms and thus constitutionalism have to be in place before one even starts with TJ, in order for it to have a leveraging effect on civic culture.

Juan Riado, when observing the Spanish TJ case, explained this by way of the generational effect. He argued that there is a psychological and sociological tendency for grandchildren to feel closer to their grandparents' causes than to those of their parents and that political demands regarding the past occur each time a new generation wishes to assume power.[99] It

---

[97] G. Munck, 'Ten Fallacies About Qualitative Research', *Qualitaive Methods, Newsletter of the American Political Science Association*, 3(1) (2005), 5.

[98] G. Munck and J. Verkuilen, 'Conceptualizing and Measuring Democracy', *Comparative Political Studies*, 35(1) (2002), 29.

[99] J.M. Ridao, 'Democracy and the Past', in *Politorbis, Zeitschrift für Aussenpolitik. Tenth Anniversary of the International Criminal Court: The Challenges of Complementarity* (Bern: Federal Department of Foreign Affairs, 2012), p. 131.

is at this moment that institutional responsiveness depends on horizontal variables such as competition (for example in the form on elections), participation (voters and civil society) and control (checks and balances, institutions, courts, etc.) for an impact on democratic development. This requires not only simple participation, access to power and democratic institutions, but also that the political system will respond to the needs of people and that the judiciary and the parliament assist in diminishing the inequalities that have long been established through the authoritarianism of the previous regime.

Today, over 60 per cent of all states qualify as democracies – although not fully consolidated ones – if one utilises the major democratic indices mentioned earlier in this book. This percentage is rising and the majority of the world's population is seeking ever more justice and democracy. The average citizen desires democratic institutions that promise more justice and equality, particularly in transition countries that arise out of the aftermath of conflict-torn and despotic societies, such as in the Middle East, Southeast Asia and Northern Africa. Another, striking trend runs parallel to the increase in the number of democratic states, namely the increase in the international community's willingness to monitor the development of domestic accountability through TJ measures.[100] This is often achieved through reporting systems at the international level and within international organisations. Many countries in transition are urged to report to external and international donors or to organisations to which they wish to become members, such as the Council of Europe, the EU or the UN. These organisations and donors ask for periodic progress reports and engagement in return, which can lead to further concessions in terms of TJ. In short, with the rise of democracies under international surveillance, the issue of legitimacy and quality of institutional performance becomes more pivotal. Therefore, it is not surprising that TJ measures are seen as one way to reach that better performance.

Turkey, for example, had to revise several of its laws and practices concerning unresolved crimes of the past because the ECtHR ruled that they should do so. Post-war Germany was obliged to report to the Allies and in order to seek membership of the UN it had to make many tactical concessions, including agreeing to employ TJ measures. Thus, the early period of regime change and consolidation often entails radical commitments and reforms in order to please external and international donors. These

---

[100] B.A. Simmons, *Mobilizing for Human Rights, International Law in Domestic Politics* (Cambridge: Cambridge University Press, 2009), p. 26.

external forces often foster the rule of law and democracy in the country, which in turn provides favourable conditions for more TJ in the future.[101] Along with demands for reports, international organisations urge their Member States, democratic or not, to also deal with unresolved issues of the past and to apply TJ measures as a way to increase stability and the rule of law.[102] Hence, a study that shows the circular cumulative causalities between the measures on the one hand, and regime consolidation on the other, could add to these claims by either verifying or falsifying the claims made. Thus far, the simple assumption that TJ measures contribute to democratic institution building and democracy is widely shared, although not necessarily true, because these measures can – if misused – also contribute to authoritarianism.

Keane's concept of monitoring democracy highlights the fact that the effective democratic performance of any regime no longer only depends on governments and courts, but also on actors and institutions that monitor, survey and determine decision-making processes, such as social networks, civil society groups and international organisations.[103] This leads to the second claim made in this book, namely that actors that use TJ measures can legitimate the new regimes.

The sequencing of TJ measures in transition processes has to be taken into account in order to provide an intelligible context for understanding the character of democratic conditions.[104] That means that not all TJ measures have to be applied at once, but over a longer period of time and whenever there is a consensus among bottom-up civil society actors and governmental ones. To put TJ measures on the agenda as soon as possible to delegitimise and to legitimise the new regime ought to be a primary goal for any new government seriously committed to democracy.

Another practical approach to showing the multi-causal interlinkages between (de)legitimisation and legitimisation and TJ was undertaken by International IDEA (Institute for Democracy and Electoral Assistance) some years ago. The Institute's researchers argued that TJ measures could

---

[101] O.N.T. Thoms, J. Ron and R. Paris, 'State-Level Effects of Transitional Justice: What Do We Know?', *International Journal of Transitional Justice, Special Issue: Transitional Justice on Trial –Evaluating Its Impact*, 4 (2010), 329–354, at 329–342.

[102] M. Avello, 'European efforts in Transitional Justice', Working Paper No. 58, FRIDE: Madrid (2008), pp. 1–18.

[103] J. Keane, *Life and Death of Democracy*.

[104] D. Beetham, E. Carvalho, T. Landman and S. Weir, *Assessing the Quality of Democracy, A Practical Guide* (Stockholm: International IDEA, 2008), p. 30.

leverage the 'abilities of democratic actors and institutions to establish a civil society and to secure basic economic rights, living standards, security, and free political processes and to resolve disagreements through peaceful dialogue and negotiations'. In this context IDEA emphasised that a country's specific atrocious or violent history has to be taken into account when defining benchmarks for the evaluation of the quality of democracies, stating that '[t]he process of democracy assessment should begin with a full account of those cultural, political and economic aspects of the country and its history. This has to be taken into account in order to provide an intelligible context for understanding the character of its democratic condition.'[105] Here, the country's historical context and its citizens' experience with an unjust, oppressive or violent past can be converted into important data. However, it must still be determined which point in history is to be selected as a benchmark for evaluation. Thus, the use of TJ measures can be backward looking and forward looking to legitimise the new regime.

In the following paragraphs I will highlight the specific criteria for regime legitimacy, the quality of democracy and consolidation in connection to TJ measures.

3.2   Increase Accountability

During regime change and transition, constitutional reforms are installed, but governments and citizens alike are uncertain and confronted with a political instability that is often connected with an unresolved past and its remaining elites. Executive accountability fosters consolidation and the quality of democracy because when people see that the government takes responsibility for past injustice (even if they are not personally responsible for it), it increases the people's belief that the government will also do so in the present and the future. During the first ten years of regime change, TJ measures allow for many citizens to experience for the first time in their lives some form of fairness and public acknowledgement of wrongdoings. Public acknowledgement by means of memorials, apologies or pensions/financial awards has to be explained well to the public, to prevent such acknowledgement being seen as biased, thus causing even more disparity and tension, as was the case in post-Franco Spain and post-communist East Germany. Envy and mistrust can be a sensible

---

[105] D. Beetham, E. Carvalho, T. Landman and S. Weir, *Assessing the Quality of Democracy.*

response to the new regime and trust can only be won over a long period of time.

As Hazan outlined earlier, the first year of transition acts as a window of opportunity in which TJ measures have to be announced and applied in a prudent way so as to build confidence and trust among the citizens of the new political system. This civic trust leads to political legitimacy and stabilisation of the new system. To measure the responsiveness of a new regime, Schmitter suggested asking the question 'Have there been major incidents in which significant parties, associations or movements have refused to participate in hearings or discussions about law or legislations [sic] reforms – and why?'[106] In other words, to what extent do governments respond to the claims and needs of citizens, victims, bystanders, perpetrators, diaspora, donor community, international stakeholders or former opponents when revealing past injustices by former military dictatorships or totalitarian or authoritarian regimes? Do victims and victimisers participate in commissions of inquiry? Do they form part of the constitution-building process? Do victims and bystanders of the past regime file cases against former elites? Which benchmarks and historical events are included or omitted when coming to terms with the past during the process of regime change or after consolidation has taken place? Is the rule of law applied in any of these contexts? Are former elites, perpetrators, military leaders or others immune from litigation or granted amnesty? And last but not least can the level of accountability by the regime be leveraged through these TJ measures?

The urge for responsiveness by executive and legislative powers is pivotal to reach successful consolidation. It increases accountability and shows how governments balance public versus constitutional interests and respond to citizens' claims. The balancing of legal imperatives, public safety and pragmatic considerations is crucial in any regime consolidation and TJ process.[107] For example:

(1) It is helpful to examine when and how political and civil societies formally acknowledge or respond to past wrongdoings through parliamentarian or public debates. Possible responses include issuing and/or supporting truth commissions and implementing their recommendations, publicly apologising, establishing memorials,

---

[106] P.C. Schmitter, *The Quality of Democracy*, online published paper.
[107] T.D. Olson, L.A. Payne and A.G. Reiter, *Transitional Justice in Balance. Comparing Processes, Weighing Efficacy* (Washington, DC: US Institute of Peace, 2010), pp. 154–155.

introducing memorial days, initiating or reacting to public debates, and opening archives for investigations.[108]

(2) Political society and elites, in particular governments and parliaments, can establish restitution or reparation funds, initiate rehabilitation or compensation for expropriations, imprisonment and loss of family members. They can also set quotas for working relationships amongst former enemies or combatants in public institutions or issue amnesties to political prisoners of the former regime, as well as to old elites. Parliaments can enact laws creating funds to restore and maintain memorials and publicly exhume mass graves. To a large extent, these measures are also seen when restoring buildings and converting them into memorials or in maintaining historical or religious sites with donations or public money. They go beyond state obligations of a humanitarian or restitution-based nature as set out in the 1949 Geneva Conventions. More mechanisms are outlined in the 2006 UN Basic Principles and Guidelines on the Right to a Remedy and Reparation for Victims of Gross Violations of International Human Rights Law and Serious Violations of International Humanitarian Law mentioned earlier.

(3) The same elites and political society can set up a framework for criminal justice by passing necessary legal reforms to support international tribunals and court procedures against perpetrators and victimisers. They can apply international human rights and humanitarian law in order to confront past injustices and perpetrators, to reform national legislation, criminal codes and criminal justice in general, and introduce the vetting of civil servants. These mechanisms not only help to establish a new national court system, but also to improve the judiciary in consolidated democracies. Such measures combat impunity and reform the security system.

(4) Governments and parliaments can introduce amnesty laws according to agreements between old and new political elites and the government. These measures can be issued through pacts, informal agreements, laws or national legislation. However, the culture of impunity that emerges in many post-conflict countries for a non-determined period is counter-productive to the rule of law and, therefore, democracy. It allows former perpetrators to remain unchallenged and

---

[108] N.J. Kritz, 'Policy Implications of Empirical Research on Transitional Justice', in H. Van der Merwe, V. Baxter, and A.R. Chapman (eds.), *Assessing the Impact of Transitional Justice: Challenges for Empirical Research* (Washington, DC: USIP Press, 2009), p. 17.

unaccountable for their wrongdoings, leaving them untouched in their professional and personal capacities.

Some of these procedures and policies can be seen as accountability and/ or responsiveness measures and are part of any transition process, regardless of whether it turns towards authoritarianism or democracy. While many of these procedures and politics are labelled as TJ measures, they still lead to the opposite of what TJ often claims to achieve, namely peace and stability. By increasing levels of accountability and improving the responsiveness of executive and legislative powers, an end can be brought to unfair vetting and lustration processes.[109] Studies compiled by Tricia Olson, Leigh Payne and Andrew Reiter,[110] as well as an earlier one by Neil Kritz, conclude that executives that deal with past injustices can provide rationale and momentum for the new government to reform its institutions and ideologies. These studies find that a broad social discussion model, that is to say one that links responsiveness to citizen participation, helps TJ measures to have better effects.[111]

The way in which executive powers establish TJ mechanisms or policies, support them and respect their outcomes, is essential to whether TJ measures either contribute to the effective functioning of democracy or are counterproductive and perpetuate divisions in society. Hence, the way in which political figures such as the first Chancellor Konrad Adenauer in West Germany, Wilhelm Pieck in East Germany, President Felipe Gonzáles in Spain or Prime Minister Tayyip Erdogan in Turkey comply with the standards they set during the transition period, is crucial data that adds to an understanding of the spiral correlation. Nevertheless, responsiveness is not an independent variable in and of itself. Its presence or absence can be observed when assessing other governmental action, such as government performance and the implementation of truth and history commissions' recommendations, or when the government conducts unfair vetting within societal groups.

3.3   Leverage Transparency

Successful democratic regime consolidation goes hand in hand with a high level of transparency and institutional independence. The functioning of

---

[109] O.N.T. Thoms, J. Ron, and R. Paris, 'State-Level Effects of Transitional Justice', 329–342.
[110] T. Olson, L. Payne and A. Reiter, *Transitional Justice in Balance*.
[111] N.J. Kritz, 'Policy Implications of Empirical Research on Transitional Justice', pp. 13–22

an independent judiciary and the capability to bring perpetrators to justice within one's own country are indicators of the level of the rule of law
and thus reflect Merkel's levels of 'representative' and 'behavioural' consolidation.[112] Transparency is pivotal for change, consolidation and thus
the quality of any democracy, too. The impact that courts, tribunals, parliamentary commissions of inquiry, truth commissions, historical commissions and even traditional, local and customary justice mechanisms
have increases their independent and transparent operation and their use
of international human rights standards. The independence of the judiciary and the rule of law is one of the most, if not the most, difficult hurdle
for young democracies to clear and upholding these principles remains a
struggle for consolidated ones.[113]

The pursuit of retrospective justice is seen as an urgent task of new
political elites for the reasons provided earlier. It highlights the fundamental character of the new order to be established – which again is based
on the rule of law. It takes a great deal of effort to restore truth and justice
where denial and impunity have once reigned. Hence, these processes are
frequently attacked as destabilising and vindictive.[114] Executive and legislative powers have to decide whether to confront the dilemma through
the prosecution of the former regime's leaders, or to leave the past behind
them with silence pacts and blanket amnesty laws.

Countries in transition also face the obstacles related to statutes of
limitations or the prohibition on retroactive application of the law. Thus,
here, international law and courts, such as the ECtHR, the ICTY and
International Criminal Court (ICC) often fill the gap of jurisdiction and
intervene. They have interpreted acts as crimes against humanity, which
allows the court to get around limitations posed by statutes of limitations
and the prohibition on retroactive application of the law.[115] Many times,
interim or new governments opt for a compromise and carefully examine
the type of sanctions and penalties they apply as illustrated by Lijphart's
consensual model. If the rule of law is taken seriously, the prohibition on

---

[112] W. Merkel, Systemtransformation, *Eine Einführung in die Theorie und Empirie der Transformationsforschung*, pp. 118–124.
[113] B. Weiffen, 'Der vergessene Faktor – Zum Einfluss von Transtional Justice auf die Entwicklung von Rechtsstaatlichkeit in Demokratisierungsprozessen', *Zeitscchrift fuer Vergleichende Politikwissenschaft (Comparative Governance and Politics)*, 5 (2011), 51–74.
[114] J.E. Mendez, 'In Defence of Transitional Justice', pp. 1–26, at p. 1.
[115] E. Brems, 'Transitional Justice in the Case Law of the European Court of Human Rights', *International Journal of Transitional Justice, Oxford Journals*, 5(2) (2011), 298.

retroactive application of criminal law will be applied. No one may be prosecuted for an act that was not criminal at the time it was committed.[116] One way to overcome this obstacle without violating the prohibition of retroactivity is to apply international (customary) human rights or criminal law to the case at hand. This body of law and its prohibitions on crimes against humanity and other cruel and inhuman treatment apply regardless of the particular laws of the previous regime.

Citizens, and even more so victims of the past regime, who dare to file claims, particularly when suffering personal threats of vengeance in retaliation, contribute to the establishment of confidence and trust in the (new) judiciary. But overall these acts increase transparency of the new regime. Freedom from fear of telling one's own narrative is the basic requirement for fair and open trials. If this condition is present and there is a minimum sense of the rule of law after regime change, a spiral effect is triggered: TJ contributes to the transparent functioning of institutions, which in turn prompts actors to demand more TJ measures.

Needless to say, transparency is often difficult to attain during periods of regime change when trust in institutions is still low or absent and nepotistic political elites are used to solve problems behind closed doors. In most societies in transition the old judicial elites remain in office, due to a lack of new legal elites to replace them and thus attitudes, behaviour and transparency only changes slowly. This fact, which is the rule not the exception, hinders victims in filing claims against those who are still in office or covered by de facto amnesties. But it is also not easy for judges from the old regime to be independent, even if they wish to be so, because spoilers in society often threaten their lives if they challenge any of the former combatants or 'war heroes'.

Independence and transparency of the judiciary, which is fundamental for democratic consolidation and for an effective use of TJ measures, is probably one of the biggest challenges in the early transition phase. This was the case in post-war Germany in 1945 and in post-Franco Spain after 1975 and continues to be the case in Turkey. Many lawyers and technocrats in transitional societies are supportive and loyal to the previous oppressive regimes, because that was the system that provided them with jobs and power. Under the new regime this legal elite often has few incentives for bringing those responsible for crimes of the past to justice, as

---

[116] N.J. Kritz (ed.), *Transitional Justice, How Emerging Democracies Reckon with Former Regimes* (Washington, DC: United States Institute for Peace, 2004), vol. II Country Studies.

they often still have close bonds or loyalties to them. Moreover, citizens have good reasons not to trust any judiciary, old or new, that all of a sudden claims to be independent even though it has no experience with what that actually means in practice. This is one reason why the rule of law is often not attained in early transitional countries. But trials at international courts and tribunals show the opposite. They are public and transparent and can turn this vicious circle of dependence into a virtuous one of showing how transparency, common rules and independence of the judges can benefit the whole society. Therefore, the new courts and the judiciary have to gain (or possibly regain) the trust of its citizens over a long period of time by applying international law or making reference to cases that took place at the ECtHR or other international tribunals.

International tribunals established under the umbrella of the international community can provide important incentives to solve this dilemma and thus interrupt the common understanding of 'justice' by trials behind closed doors, arbitrary judgments or corrupt judges that bend the law. International or hybrid tribunals bridge the 'old' understanding with new forms of speaking justice based on transparent judiciary. Needless to say, they cannot serve as a permanent replacement for the domestic judiciary and the rule of law in the long term. The Nuremberg Tribunal in post-war Germany, for example, or the decisions by the International Criminal Tribunal for former Yugoslavia (ICTY) and the International Criminal Tribunal for Rwanda (ICTR) for the cases of post-war Yugoslavia and Rwanda, and even the ECtHR's decisions against Turkey, were all intended only to bridge this justice gap. These courts were perceived as filling an absence of the rule of law on the domestic level and once German courts were back in place, judges trained and legal reforms passed, the trials against Nazi perpetrators were meant to pass on to these domestic courts. The relevance of this TJ tool is not to be underestimated, even in the European context. The case law of the ICC, the International Court of Justice (ICJ) in The Hague, the Inter-American Court (IAC) in Costa Rica and the ECtHR in Strasbourg has led to a rising demand among domestic lawyers for more domestic and local trials concerning past wrongdoings.

Nevertheless, domestic trials within firm democratic institutions are always preferred over international or hybrid ones. Trials that took place in West Germany after 1949 contributed more to the public acknowledgement of past wrongdoings than any of the Nuremberg trials and other earlier domestic public trials under Allied powers. In East Germany, where the rule of law was established 'overnight' upon Germany's reunification in 1990, the new political elite did not have to worry about serious spoilers of prosecution or trials. It was an exceptional case in regime change history because the whole legal elite was almost completely replaced immediately with judges from West Germany. The fact that in the overall majority of post-conflict or post-dictatorial societies one cannot replace 100 per cent of the judges and prosecutors by 'new' ones made objective, fair and open trials in other TJ settings precarious and complicated. German reunification was a unique regime change experience, namely an almost de facto 'regime replacement' with new elites, which has never happened elsewhere after a dictatorship. In East Germany, although only a few communist party leaders were ever convicted, the border guard trials from 1991 onwards led to the conviction of two soldiers for killing people who had fled the communist regime.[117] Those soldiers were found guilty of violating international and national human rights law, despite the fact that they were simply following orders. Whether these trials served the purpose of delegitimising the former regime remains an open question because they were hardly publicly discussed.[118] In the case of Spain, old elites are still omnipresent in governmental offices and in courts. Moreover, in addition to the amnesty laws of 1977, which *per forma* impede trials, the lack of political will to try perpetrators is largely related to the fact that 'Franco's shadow' has never been fundamentally removed.

Impunity is one of the most intriguing challenges to regime consolidation. Granting amnesty is a sign of non-transparency and lack of independence of legal institutions. This is a major threat to democracy, as well as to a successful transition. Yet, it is a common phenomenon that countries in transition pass amnesty laws, even though silencing of past injustice can encourage nepotism and corruption, and will reduce social capital in terms of participation and political engagement.

Amnesty laws form their own category of TJ measures and are often seen as a last – but nevertheless effective – resort. They are neither

---

[117] J.A. McAdams, 'Communism on Trial: The East German Past and the German Future' in J.A. McAdams (ed.), *Transitional Justice and the Rule of Law in New Democracies* (Notre Dame, IN: University of Notre Dame Press, 2001), pp. 239–267.

[118] Chile or Argentina were different. In the negotiated transitions of Argentina and Chile, there were military elites waiting in the wings to reassert themselves; a fact that prevented the countries' democratically elected leaders from being able to go far enough in their reckoning with past crimes by means of public trials. Spain has been a similar case to the South American TJ processes. Interestingly, attempts in recent years to convict perpetrators of the Franco regime have been radically opposed by the constitutional courts and large parts of the political elite, despite the fact that Spain is a consolidated democracy. G. Alonso and D. Muro, *The Politics and Memory of Democratic Transition. The Spanish Model* (New York: Routledge, 2011).

increasing the level of accountability nor that of transparency, but nevertheless, they are a fundamental part of any transition process. Amnesty laws are a significant type of TJ measure that aims to achieve peace in the short term, and thus researchers interested in TJ cannot ignore amnesty laws. They affect large numbers of political and military elites, and several thousands of former technocrats, administrators and lawyers. Once amnesty is granted to them, they generally refrain from regaining power through violent means. Thus, amnesties can contribute to easing tensions between conflicting parties for a specific period of time. They are seen as a last and timely determined resort in periods of early and fragile transitions. In this respect, Mark Freeman concludes that more flexibility in international law to utilise amnesty as a flexible tool in TJ processes would be helpful.[119]

It is clear that the 'culture of impunity' that sometimes results from granting permanent amnesties nurtures mistrust and fear in societies, preventing civil society, and in particular victims, from claiming compensation, demanding memorials, and calling for trials. Amnesties hide or mystify the past. They intimidate victims who want to speak up, they nurture terror and acts of vengeance and one has to be careful when and how to apply them. If major segments of society openly agree to forget the crimes of the past and accept victims' silence and perpetrators' impunity, then new democratic institutions cannot function in a fully democratic manner. This brings a risk of past injustice becoming enduring injustice and of the rule of law becoming (or remaining) dysfunctional, let alone the regime becoming a transparent one.[120]

The tension between politics and TJ measures (particularly trials) can be better contextualised by looking at earlier instances of regime change and consolidation in which silencing the past was a main aspect of the political response to the regime change. Examples of this can be seen with the silence agreements or 'pacto de silencio' embraced by the post-Franco regime in Spain, the 'punto final' of the post-Junta regime in Argentina, the Expiry Law in Uruguay, and the widely exercised amnesty laws that led to a culture of impunity after the military coup in Turkey in 1980. In these countries, a chain of amnesty laws led to a culture of impunity for political verdicts, which hampered the development of an independent

---

[119] M. Freeman, *Truth Commissions and Procedural Fairness* (Cambridge: Cambridge University Press, 2006).
[120] J. Spinner-Halev, 'From Historical to Enduring Injustice', 574–597.

and transparent judiciary, let alone the rule of law.[121] As Myrdal and Rustow would phrase it, the lack of balance between redress and amnesty led to a downward spiral effect that paralysed the democratic process to a large extent.[122] Amnesty laws were outnumbering redress. In this way, political actors missed their window of opportunity to redress grievances with TJ measures.

The ECtHR has played a pivotal role in not only increasing accountability but also transparency of emerging democratic regimes in Europe after 1990. After the legacy of World War II, the communist past and authoritarian regimes in the South, the Court and Council of Europe were intended to advise on and amend 'wrong' decisions of domestic legal institutions, thus aiming to prevent a recurrence of the past. The case law of the ECtHR includes hundreds of judgments and decisions dealing with compensation, restitution, prosecution, lustration, memory and truth among its Member States; furthermore some of its case law deals specifically with the transitional regimes in unified Germany, Spain and Turkey. The ECtHR shows how international law and jurisdiction can affect political and democratic culture. This court is a prime example of an international institution that has attempted to foster successful regime change, and thus also has concern for the democratic use of TJ measures.[123]

Turkey's domestic legislation and governmental action have changed in response to the ECtHR's many demands for legal and political change, including open and fair trials in regard to victim compensation, torture and the restriction of the freedom of expression that particularly affected national minorities. The Turkish government has also had to respond to EU demands for more democratic reforms, including the introduction of measures to deal with previous injustices, such as the thousands of disappearances, and claims of restitution in eastern Anatolia. In such ways, the ECtHR and EU play a constructive role in regime consolidation through the call for implementation of TJ measures.

In 2006, the ECtHR issued a general recommendation to all 46 states that were members of the Council of Europe at the time, reminding them

---

[121] C.J. Kerslake, K. Oktem, and P. Robins (eds.), *Turkey's Engagement with Modernity: Conflict and Change in the Twentieth Century* (Basingstoke: Palgrave Macmillan, 2010).

[122] D.A. Rustow, 'Transition to Democracy: Toward a Dynamic Model', 355.

[123] T. Allen, 'Restitution and Transitional Justice in the European Court of Human Rights', *Columbia Journal of European Law*, 13 (2006), 1–46.

that every Member State ought to deal with past injustice, regardless of how much time had since elapsed. The judges stated that every state must ensure that its history is debated openly and passionately and thus in a transparent way. Yet, the Court also justified some restrictions of free speech in the interest of dealing with the past, such as the criminalisation of the denial or defence of the Holocaust in Germany.[124] Although this particular recommendation has been widely debated, it shows how important the Court believes TJ measures are for democratic regime consolidation.

Some citizens see transparent political manoeuvres, for example by courts or parliaments, as a sign that their government will respect a broad range of human rights, many of which are almost synonymous with democracy itself, although they will often be disappointed when they realise that political elites think otherwise.[125] This is one of the reasons why O'Donnell, Jorge Vargas Cullell and Osvaldo Iazzetta argue in favour of a spiral correlation between the degree to which human rights are granted and the functioning of democracy and the degree in which citizen claims are reckoned with.[126] Other human rights, such as freedom of expression, the right to fair trial and truth, the right to participate in decision-making processes, and the freedom of media and communication are implemented with the idea that they increase the efficiency of democratic regime change.[127] But the same is true for authoritarian regimes. Consequently, these states have transferred and implemented these norms and standards into their constitutions and domestic legislation, even though they do not aim to respect and implement, i.e. human rights norms or democratic standards, but just use them for window-dressing a legitimate regime. Schmitter, Marc Bühlmann, Merkel et al. conclude that formal incorporation of these norms in legislation is not enough. In addition to human rights laws on the books, it is imperative to have a political leadership that deals

---

[124] E. Brems, 'Transitional Justice in the Case Law of the European Court of Human Rights', 287–288.

[125] B.A. Simmons, *Mobilizing for Human Rights*, pp. 24–25.

[126] G. O'Donnell, J. Vargas Cullell and O.M. Iazeetta, *The Quality of Democracy*.

[127] Those human rights are legally binding and enshrined in the ICCPR and ICESCR as well as in many other international conventions, treaties and agreements that followed the 1948 Universal Declaration of Human Rights. There is no state in the world that can seriously consider itself democratic that, at the same time, has not ratified at least a number of these international human rights treaties.

with human rights claims in a transparent, accountable and responsive way. Without this, institutions will fail to comply with human rights norms.[128]

Thus in order for TJ to increase transparency of the new regimes, the authorities have to guarantee both human rights, as well as the safety of those who make the claims; for example, before commissions, the parliament or courts.[129] Most of these debates offer the possibility to construct and evaluate what has been referred to as 'evidence-based transitional justice', through which it can be understood to what extent TJ measures reach their anticipated outcome when guaranteeing the basic human rights.[130]

3.4   Enhance Civic Participation

Much has already been said about the participation and role of citizens in the relation between TJ and consolidation. Therefore I will only briefly contextualise participation in the spiral correlation to TJ.[131] Only if citizens, former victims and survivors as well as victimisers of the past regime or civil society are free and independent to participate and engage can regime consolidation be democratic. 'Organised applause', mass ceremonies and commemorations of victimhood or victory and the selective use of TJ often combined with coercion will be negative to consolidation. In the emerging communist regime in East Germany, the Nazi trials held in Waldheim in the early 1950s were biased and far from fair, open or just, but they were part of the TJ process. The trials served the purpose of delegitimising the past elite, which they did, but they were exclusive and politically motivated and thus did not lend support to the newly emerging regime. The communist elite received significant support from the people as a consequence of the national catharsis at that time but not through the trials. The support that initially comes out of a process of national catharsis can vanish quickly if citizens

---

[128] P.C. Schmitter, *The Quality of Democracy*, online published paper; M. Bühlmann, W. Merkel and B. Wessels, 'The Quality of Democracy, Democratic Barometer for Established Democracies', *National Centre of Competence in Research (NCCR) Challenges to Democracy in the 21st Century*, Working Paper No. 10 (2008).

[129] Ibid.

[130] P. Pham and P. Vinck 'Empirical Research and the Development and Assessment of Transitional Justice Mechanisms', *International Journal of Transitional Justice*, 1 (2007), 231–248, at 232.

[131] W. Merkel, Systemtransformation, *Eine Einführung in die Theorie und Empirie der Transformationsforschung*, p. 124.

perceive the new regime as non-responsive or biased in responding to their claims.

Public use of TJ measures can assist in empowering citizens and elites to respect pluralistic aspects of democracy through public dialogue between citizens and political institutions, which is something that authoritarian regimes fear. The contributions of civil actors, NGOs and other civil initiatives determine the relationship between civil society and governmental agencies. Moreover, their reactions and initiatives are a useful barometer for what TJ tools can accomplish and for the direction of political society. Both civil society and political society share the burden of addressing residual needs and their relationship can be symbiotic.[132] The specific nature of the democratic regime change process determines the conditions under which citizens deal with the past and supplement governmental accountability and transparency.[133] Gabriel Almond and Sidney Verba have argued that trust and participation by citizens in institutions shapes the political culture, which is vital for the proper functioning of a democracy.[134] Such trust depends on the level of free participation and engagement with or against public institutions and it can be enhanced if public institutions respond to people's needs for justice and transparency, regardless of whether this is in relation to past or present misconducts. In addition to the earlier definitions of civic trust given in this study, Almond and Verba claim that civic culture is a form of trust that can lead to democratic behaviour, but that in itself cannot be created or imposed. Instead it must develop over time, sometimes even over the course of decades. The creation of a civic culture determines the political culture of any society – the specific political orientation and attitudes citizens have towards the political regime, as well as to one's own role in the system. Without a civic and political culture based on active and free participation, democracy has little hope of survival.

People form groups for various reasons, one of them being the wish to deal with the past, commemorate victims and seek justice for wrongdoings. Therefore, the urge for TJ can trigger civil engagement, which in turn can benefit trust in new institutions. In democracies, this process leads to an increase in trust, in a positive feedback loop.

---

[132] D. Backer, 'Civil Society and Transitional Justice', 306.
[133] P. Hazan, 'Measuring the Impact of Punishment and Forgiveness', 36.
[134] G.A. Almond and S. Verba, *The Civic Culture, Political Attitudes and Democracies in Five Nations* (London/Thousands Oaks, CA: Sage, 1989).

However, in autocracies this process reduces trust because people's calls for justice go unanswered and can be repressed by the government. Intimidation, coercion and negative repercussions towards victims who claim justice are the rule not the exception. The legitimacy gap this causes has to be filled with more suppression and terror, as well as with propaganda campaigns aimed at erasing people's doubts about the regime's legitimacy. Political and legal institutions' constant rejection of people's claims for justice can lead to radicalisation of these groups which are 'silenced through coercion'. It can dramatically increase political cleavages that in turn lead to more undemocratic and radical responses from authorities, as for example was the case in Spain, Germany and Turkey during different periods of regime consolidation or deconsolidation.[135]

Can political culture nonetheless be fostered by the use of TJ measures? Civic trust grows slowly through engagement with democratic institutions and is often influenced by citizens' past experiences with justice and injustice, as seen in the new democracies that have come about since the 1940s, 1970s and 1990s. Civic trust is seen as a reflection of the behaviour of current societies and how this impacts or even predicts future societal conflict resolution and problem solving. Stable and well-functioning democratic institutions are intertwined with 'soft' and informal contacts between institutions and society.[136]

Not surprisingly, in societies where citizens can express their needs without fear of vengeance, the level of civic trust is higher than in countries where citizens are intimidated or feel threatened. Citizens who are able to declare needs freely and without fear are more likely to organise victims and interest groups and initiate memorials or trials. If they can participate in the decision-making process and voting procedures free from fear, they are more likely to demand further TJ measures as a way to attain truth and justice. At the same time, citizens' abilities to act freely and make these claims depend on the creation of legal frameworks, usually based on human rights, by a regime's executive, legislature and judiciary. This is where the spiral effect becomes particularly relevant and we see that conceptualising the relationship between TJ and regime consolidation in a mono-causal way is not sufficient.

---

[135] L.M. McLaren, *Constructing Democracy in Southern Europe*, pp. 106–107.
[136] R. Rohrschneider, 'Institutional Quality and Perceptions of Representation in Advanced Industrial Democracies', *Comparative Political Studies*, 38 (2005), 850–874.

For the matter of regime consolidation, Putnam has explained that 'the greater the participation, the higher the effectiveness and trust in a democratic system'.[137] This premise combines nicely with Tilly's analysis that in order to establish trust in democratic processes, categorical inequalities in public politics must be reduced and non-state powers must be transformed to establish a protective relation between citizens and state.[138] If people trust state institutions, they will utilise these institutions more often for their claims for justice and will engage less in vigilantism than they would if trust was low. Those who seek truth and justice will receive a greater response to their claims in democracies than in authoritarian regimes or oligarchies, thus allowing democratic institutions to increase their legitimacy. Schmitter succinctly highlighted this when he stated that in order to measure the quality of democracy we have to look at the levels, frequencies and timelines of participation or abstentions in society. We also have to look at how, to what extent and when public institutions respond to demands and needs or whether they simply impose decisions.[139]

Citizens also regard TJ measures as a way to achieve more social justice in terms of distribution of social wealth. In West Germany millions of German refugees from the East received privileged access to the labour market; in Spain victims received additional pensions; and in Turkey reconstruction and infrastructural measures for the Kurds were part of the TJ process. Redistribution and reparations are thus crucial for re-establishing trust in the institutions that provided them. Distribution of public resources and access to social and economic wealth is part of both TJ and consolidation and the foundation of sustainable democratic development. Thus, the intertwining principles of power sharing, participation, rule of law and equal distribution of resources have long been regarded as a core element of regime consolidation to which TJ can contribute.[140] Other criteria, such as socio-economic growth, the functioning of democratic institutions, distribution of power resources, human capital and the geographical distance to other democracies also indicate the level of democratic

---

[137] R.D. Putnam, *Making Democracy Work*.
[138] C. Tilly, *Democracy*, p. 96.
[139] P.C. Schmitter, 'The Quality of Democracy', online published paper.
[140] D. Senghaas, *Zum irdischen Frieden* (Frankfurt am Main: Suhrkamp Verlag, 2004), p. 30 et seq.

development, but will not be highlighted in this assessment, unless in close connection to TJ measures.[141]

Before this book continues with the case studies, it will provide a brief overview what the TJ tools and measures are and why they are helpful tools or catalysts in any regime change and consolidation process that occurs.

---

[141] P. Schmidt (ed.), *Kleine Geschichte Spaniens* (Stuttgart: Reclam, 2004).

4

Transitional Justice Measures

Much has already been said about TJ measures, but it is necessary to give a closer overview of how these measures and tools are internationally defined and embedded in the different conceptual and theoretical frameworks.

Today TJ is a discipline of itself that includes social sciences, history, memory or forensic studies in the same way as it does international humanitarian or human rights law and numerous different measures, as exemplified in Table 4.1. The term was only coined in the 1980s and 1990s when the first TRC were held in Latin America and South Africa, later, when vetting and reparation policies were put in place and trials were held in Eastern Europe, the Balkans and Sub-Saharan Africa, TJ became a discipline in the 1990s. Over the past two decades the concept of TJ has undergone dramatic changes in its definition and scope. Earlier on in the mid-1980s onwards, the term described a transition process at the time of the Latin American transitions, in particular in Argentina and Chile, and later during the war in Yugoslavia, after the collapse of the Soviet Union and its satellite states and after the end of the apartheid regime in South Africa and the genocide in Rwanda the concept was broadened. The international community, led by the UN, looked for different avenues to guarantee a peaceful transition from autocracy and violence to peace and democracy. International and hybrid tribunals were seen as one way to promote peace and democracy, while truth commissions and reparation were also used for the same purpose. It was at that moment that reference was made to the (perceived) successful post-war trials in Nuremberg and Tokyo between 1945 and 1949 and an attempt was made to create similar tribunals for other post-conflict societies, such as Yugoslavia and later Rwanda. These trials were attempts to shift violent conflicts towards peace by using international jurisdiction and human rights standards. Interestingly enough, the Tokyo Tribunals that prosecuted Japanese war crimes from 1946 to 1948 were mentioned far less frequently as a best practice of TJ, although these trials also had a significant effect on the

Japanese post-war democratisation process and on the development of the principle of universal jurisdiction. With the end of the apartheid regime in South Africa in the early 1990s and the massive transition processes in Eastern Europe since 1990, along with the Rwanda genocide in 1994, a huge demand for more TJ measures emerged. This was based on the assumption that trials would help to prevent perpetrators from committing mass atrocities in the future, or at least would contribute to punishing those who had committed them in the past. These developments dramatically influenced the scope of TJ as we know it today.

In addition to the tribunals and courts established in the 1990s, the UN passed its first general guidelines on TJ in 2006, and in 2009 the UN General Assembly called for an 'International Year of Reconciliation', calling upon all countries, both democratic and non-democratic, to contribute to peaceful and stable transitions and transformations.[1] The donor-funded International Centre for Transitional Justice (ICTJ) founded around 2001 started fostering public debates and TJ advocacy on the international level and curbed the professional field for TJ consultancy. The Centre defines its work and thus TJ as justice adapted to societies transforming after a period of pervasive human rights abuse, yet without placing any time limits on the length of the period of transition. The founders knew that in some cases these transformations happen suddenly; in others, they may take place over many decades, even after democracies have been more or less consolidated.[2] Many other NGOs, agencies and networks such as No Peace Without Justice, The IDEA, Human Rights Watch, Amnesty International, as well as national and local CSOs, joined the new trend in promoting TJ as a way to foster peaceful transition and satisfying the needs for truth and justice by millions of victims. For many years it was victim orientated but shifted to a more balanced concept in which both victims and victimisers are dealt with in their respective ways.

TJ is seen today as an ongoing process mainly driven by victims and survivors, but also alleged perpetrators and the successive generations who seek either justice or rehabilitation. The challenge for policy makers and civil society alike is to balance the demand for truth and the condemnation of perpetrators, on the one hand, with demands for impunity and

---

[1] UN General Assembly, International Year of Reconciliation, 2009, Addendum 61st session, UN Doc A/61/L.22/Add.1,20 November 2006.
[2] International Center for Transitional Justice, *Home Page.* ictj.org (last accessed December 2015).

amnesties on the other. Executive and legislative powers in many transition countries believe these claims and challenges to be directly relevant to democratic consolidation.[3]

Although the recent attempts at building a generalised explanatory theory of TJ are promising and will not be ignored, we must bear in mind that these attempts, such as the ones by Winter,[4] Dube,[5] Grodsky,[6] Hansen[7] and Caney,[8] to name but a few, are still in an early stage. More comparative and long-term evidence-based studies are needed to establish such a theory. The current attempts link TJ measures to Rawls' concept of justice,[9] as well as to other existing theories such as the theories of transition, transformation or reconciliation. They start with the normative assumption that TJ measures contribute to transforming society and to establishing a new normative benchmark of justice based on human rights, which generally speaking also serves as a ground for democracies. Caney, for example, explained why a theory of TJ – if ever established – must be normatively rooted in the concept of global justice, namely because global justice is based on universal human rights norms and standards, without which no democratic regime consolidation can take place. Winter argues that a theory of TJ can reply to those who claim that TJ consists of helpful tools for new and established democracies, because democracies attain continuous legitimacy through citizens, and TJ measures can facilitate seeking this legitimacy.[10] Thus it is not only the fact that TJ measures are anticipated, but rather by whom and how they are used that makes all the difference. In his recent book *Transitional Justice in Established Democracies*, Stephen Winter aimed to develop a political theory based on a theory of legitimacy and regime change and consolidation. He stated that TJ legitimises the new order by indicating that political institutions will henceforth

---

[3] J. McAdams (ed.), *Transitional Justice and the Rule of Law in New Democracies*, p. 15.

[4] S. Winter, 'Towards a Unified Theory of Transitional Justice', *International Journal of Transitional Justice*, 1, 1–21.

[5] S.I. Dube, 'Transitional Justice Beyond the Normative: Towards a Literary Theory of Political Transition', *International Journal of Transitional Justice*, 5 (2011), 177–197.

[6] B. Grodsky, 'Re-Ordering Justice: Towards a New Methodological Approach in Studying Transitional Justice', *Journal of Peace Research*, 46 (2009), 819–837.

[7] T.O. Hansen, 'Transitional Justice: Towards a Differentiated Theory', *Oregon Review of International Law*, 13(1) (2011), 1–46.

[8] S. Cany, *Justice Beyond Borders: A Global Political Theory* (Oxford: Oxford University Press, 2006).

[9] J. Rawls, *Theory of Justice* (Harvard University Press, 1971).

[10] S. Winter, 'Towards a Unified Theory of Transitional Justice', *International Journal of Transitional Justice*, 7(2) (2013), 224–244, 3.

bear a very different character, despite necessary continuities.[11] He high-lights that the role citizens and participation play is pivotal and focuses on actors when studying the role and possible impact of TJ measures in democracy. These actors are the ones who can legitimise institutions, and it is also these actors who can legitimise TJ measures.[12] State institutions learn to respond to citizens' claims for redress in ways that are respectful of newly implemented human rights. Nonetheless, Winter admits that his theoretical approach has some limits, because it focuses on interpersonal justice more than between citizens and political institutions – which is the focus of this book – but nevertheless assumed that this interpersonal justice positively affects democracy in the long run.

But none has thus far argued that TJ can also contribute to authoritar-ian regimes, which is mainly due to the fact that hardly anyone has looked at how dictators and authoritarian leaders 'successfully' use TJ measures to strengthen their governance model. Winter, for example, looked at situ-ations where the regime aimed to establish a well-functioning democracy. While he concluded that TJ might not be the only way to stop violence related to past injustice and to increase the legitimacy of (new) institu-tions in any given society, a correlating link to regime change or transition is missing.[13]

This is where the present systematic comparative case study can add to the theoretical debate in regime consolidation and transformation, as well as to autocracy and democracy studies focusing on TJ instead of other policies. I have started with the assumption that TJ measures can con-tribute to more than just interpersonal justice. They can also strengthen or weaken institutional performance, doing so in either an upward or downward spiral. But in order to prove this, I have to take other contex-tual variables into account. Such contextual variables could be whether the post-conflict country results from war or dictatorial regime change, the severity of crimes committed, the regional context and the level of involvement by international organisations. Although such variables deserve being mentioned and they do play a role for the process of con-solidation, they will not be systematically assessed, because they are part of the independent and contextual variables. This study also takes into account whether a regime's previous experiences with democracy existed,

[11] S. Winter, 'Transitional Justice in Established Democracies: A Political Theory', *International Political Theory* (2014), 17.
[12] Ibid., p. 22.
[13] Ibid., pp. 225–226.

but will not make systematic reference to it. Any type of past experience is of course important to take into account, since political and societal actors in regime transition carry the legacy and experiences of the past with them. The experience of Germans with the Weimar Republic (1918–1933), Spain's first democratic experiment during the Second Spanish Republic (1931–1936), and Turkey's short democratic interventions during Atatürk's successor regime in the 1950s, all determine the future of the new regime. However, it appears of little to no relevance when it comes to arguing in favour or against TJ measures whether a society had democratic experience in the past or not. I therefore use this analytical framework in a two-way flow of causality and spiral forms leading to a cumulative circular interaction between institutional consolidation and TJ measures, over a longer period of time. The aim is to compare, qualitatively assess and define possible patterns of interlinkage.

When Ruti Teitel[14] and Priscilla Hayner[15] analysed transitional periods in Africa and Latin America in the 1980s and 1990s, they came to the conclusion that TJ measures are somewhat crucial for social and political stability and thus form the foundation of a stable democracy. Both argued that none of the concepts of rule of law, constitution building and institution making can be understood without drawing at least some links to TJ. Hayner added that truth commissions during periods of transition and transformation are essential for justice and accountability in young democracies and are thus prerequisites for democratisation and consolidation processes. In the early 1990s, Martha Minow observed that after mass atrocities and human rights violations in the second half of the twentieth century, historical memory, narratives, memorials, recognition, truth commissions and forgiveness were somewhat interlinked when re-establishing societal trust, but that due to a lack of research there was little evidence that they contributed to democracy.[16] One of the most profound works on this case study is by James Gibson, in which he reviewed the TRC and TJ process in South Africa.[17] He emphasises that truth – or rather facts – about the past contribute to reconciliation, which in and of itself impacts democratic regime change and even consolidation. In

---

[14] R. Teitel, 'Transitional Justice Globalised', International Journal of Transitional Justice, 2 (2008), 1–4.
[15] P.B. Hayner, Unspeakable Truths, Facing the Challenges of Truth Commissions (New York/London: Routledge, 2002).
[16] M. Minow, Between Vengeance and Forgiveness.
[17] J.L. Gibson, Overcoming Apartheid: Can Truth Reconcile a Divided Nation? (New York: HSPC Press, 2004).

this process, he argues, it is important that blame and responsibilities for past atrocities are placed on all members in societies who violated the law of human rights, otherwise TJ has no positive impact and recurrence to injustice might occur.[18] This is where democratic institutions, in particular an independent judiciary, is crucial to change the haunting past of recurrence and repetition of a corrupt regime. Nevertheless, the direct impact of these measures remains difficult to prove. The idea that trials or truth commissions alone contribute to 'justice cascades', as Sikkink argued, is therefore much disputed.[19]

What the TJ community seems to agree on is that it takes more than punishment of perpetrators to transition from one regime to another. The current 'global justice' theory debate, initiated by Caney[20] and Winter, has triggered the urge for a more comprehensive theory of TJ, indicating that we are still at the beginning of seeing the short and long-term impact of TJ measures.[21] The simplest way to describe the current state of the art is that a theory of TJ combines theories of justice with those of transformation and new institutional legitimacy. Winter put it most boldly when stating that TJ can contribute to stopping cycles of violence by improving the legitimacy of (new) state institutions. In order to do so, people's claims for justice need to be addressed, either by domestic or international political elites and society.[22] One way of doing this is by using TJ instruments and mechanisms to turn a vicious cycle of repetition of violence and vengeance into a virtuous one through atonement. The division of TJ into punitive, historical, reparatory, administrative and constitutional measures, as Teitel does in her first attempt to define TJ, is a helpful guide in understanding the broader concept of justice to which TJ measures contribute.[23] This study aims to further explain and specify Teitel's work on this topic.

Finally, parallel to the development of the notion of TJ, the concepts of justice as democracy and global justice began to shift at the turn of the new millennium and have since reached new heights. Striving for TJ is often seen as equivalent to pursuing justice in general. Tom Campell turns to John Rawls and Jürgen Habermas to explain that justice requires

---

[18] J.L. Gibson, 'The Contribution of Truth to Reconciliation', 409–432.
[19] K. Sikkink, *The Justice Cascade. How Human Rights Prosecutions Are Changing World Politics* (New York: W.W. Norton & Company, 2011).
[20] S. Caney, *Justice Beyond Borders*.
[21] S. Winter, 'Towards a Unified Theory of Transitional Justice', 1–21.
[22] S. Winter, *Transitional Justice in Established Democracies*, p. 225.
[23] R. Teitel, *Transitional Justice*.

democracy in order to flourish. Justice thus requires a statehood and/ or comparable local, domestic or international (independent) governance institutions that adhere to a proper democratic process and rule of law.[24] TJ measures can contribute to this process in a mutually reinforcing and circular way. But Campell also highlights that settling political disagreements in court-centred settings weakens formal and administrative justice.[25]

Similar to Habermas' concept of social justice and the idea that critical theory and equality are an integral part of 'deliberative democracy', TJ aims to overcome inequality by means of human rights compliance and to attain a higher level of justice and inclusion of society through specific measures.[26] One of TJ's many goals is thus to diminish the social inequality that was the root cause of the conflict. Distributive justice by means of reparation and compensation are some of the ways to confront the inequalities of the past. Nevin Aiken described distributive justice as a way to move towards societal reconciliation in deeply divided societies. In order to have such an effect, TJ measures need to be associated with real and tangible change in the socio-economic conditions of former antagonists. Thus to include socioeconomic and legislative reforms that lead to compensation, reparation or other means of restorative justice is a way towards a more equal and democratic society.[27] Aiken used the example of South Africa where reparation and other socio-economic benefits related to compensation of past injustice were offered as one direct way for citizens to engage with (new) governmental institutions. Reparations were closely bound up with questions of justice and a way to counterbalance a potential 'justice deficit' for victims, caused by the granting of conditional amnesties to perpetrators.[28] These amnesties were the result of a negotiated deal between state institutions and victimisers in order to convince the victimisers to testify to at least 'something' in front of the TRC in the late 1990s.

Yet, employing too many TJ measures can spoil effective governance and regime consolidation, because they put too much pressure on both old and new elites, on victimisers and victims alike, to do 'something' about the past, even when parts of society are not yet ready. Actors and

---

[24] T. Campell, *Justice*, pp. 243–245.
[25] Ibid., p. 256.
[26] J. Habermas, 'Justice and Solidarity', *Philosophical Forum*, 21 (1989), 32–53.
[27] N.T. Aiken, *Identity, Reconciliation and Transitional Justice, Overcoming Intractability in Divided Societies*, A GlassHouse Book (London: Routledge, 2013), p. 162.
[28] Ibid., p. 185.

institutions have to balance and sometimes constrain public interests in order to reach an inclusive and pluralistic decision-making process for all members of society, victims and victimisers alike. TJ measures are tools to balance public interests after times of conflict and violence. Sometimes they aim to achieve retributive justice, sometimes they restore socio-economic equality and sometimes they seek truth. In one of the earlier books on vengeance and reconciliation in the 1990s, Martha Minow highlighted the importance of balancing TJ measures, stating that 'truth and justice are not the same'.[29] After hundreds of case studies and much evidence on how TJ measures work, the challenge of balancing TJ measures is still high on the agenda.[30]

Undoubtedly, the 1990s paved the way for the current interest in TJ research. The benchmarks have shifted and nowadays the (re-)implementation of human rights standards during regime change and during the path towards consolidation is more relevant than ever. The use of human rights benchmarks has turned many 'state heroes' into criminals responsible for thousands of innocent deaths, disappearances and displacements. Among them are, for example, Spain's first military dictator Primo de Rivera from 1923 until 1930 and Turkey's autocratic leader Kemal Atatürk from 1923 until 1938, who were seen as faultless heroes and founders of their states but are today viewed more as autocratic leaders who were responsible for more than one human rights violation. On the one hand, streets and public squares are named after them, thus sending a silent message to citizens that 'committing crimes against humanity is not so bad after all' or at least that you can get away with it. Yet, at the same time the number of citizen initiatives in these countries continues to grow, streets are renamed and statues of these leaders are removed from display. Those who committed mass atrocities do not seem to serve as role models for future generations. Is this a success of TJ and its many public debates and involvement in social media? TJ did indeed play a role in these developments over the past decades. Its measures and tools shifted the scope and perspective of how we assess good and bad leadership of the past and in the future. No longer is the number of deaths someone has caused the criterion for being a role model, but it is instead the number of lives saved.

[29] M. Minow, *Between Vengeance and Forgiveness*, p. 9.
[30] Interestingly enough the mission statements of the UN, EU, AU and the Organisation of American States have never glorified those who started or won wars (a practice that had been accepted before), but instead acknowledged the grief of those nations that had suffered and aimed to establish peace and welfare for all. This indicates that a first paradigm shift had already occurred in 1945 and then again in 1990 after the end of the Cold War.

At the same time, introducing TJ measures requires prudence and leadership. In most post-militant and dictatorial countries, spoilers of the democratisation process are waiting in the wings for the first mis-step that will allow them to rally their forces. That was the case in Spain and continues to be so in Turkey. James McAdams has long opted for prudent, and thus slow, TJ processes. According to McAdams, political calls for trials, truth commissions, reparations and even amnesties ought to be negotiated with elites of the previous regime and not imposed without warning.[31] Trials in particular can be a dangerous intervention during transition processes. Although they have a particular relevance to regime change because they aim to (re)establish the rule of law, they can be perceived as a tool in the hands of new political elites engaging in 'crusades to root out the dictator' and can become disputes that have little, if anything, to do with the realisation of justice let alone the delegitimisation of the past regime and the legitimation of the current one.[32]

One of the most well-known instruments of TJ is the Rome Statute for the ICC of 1998. Since its establishment we clearly see a normative shift towards victims receiving more attention than those who perpetrated the crimes. Teitel claimed it to account for the conscious construction of a distinctive term to address the justice associated with periods of radical political change following previous oppressive rule. She highlighted how criminal justice responded to the predecessor regime's repressive rule (referring later to the UN Security Council resolutions on the ICTY and ICTR).[33] She has also strongly linked the rise of TJ to the establishment of the ICC in The Hague in 1998, and to the earlier tribunals of the ICTY (1993) and ICTR (1994), as well as to the hybrid tribunals for Sierra Leone, Cambodia and Lebanon. The ECtHR in Strasbourg and the Inter-American Court (IAC)of Human Rights in Costa Rica have also addressed allegations of human rights violations in a TJ context during the past few decades, thus contributing greatly to the TJ debate, and to global criminal justice overall.[34] Thus, a mix of judicial and non-judicial, official and non-official mechanisms, instruments, strategies and approaches to acknowledge the wrongs of the past, either within a divided and conflict-torn society or between neighbouring countries, frame today's concept of

---

[31] J.A. McAdams (ed.), Preface, *Transitional Justice and the Rule of Law in New Democracies*, p. xii.
[32] Ibid., p. x.
[33] R. Teitel, 'Transitional Justice Globalised', 1–4, at 1.
[34] L. Viaene and E. Brems, 'Transitional Justice and Cultural Contexts: Learning from the Universality Debate', *Netherlands Quarterly of Human Rights*, 28 (2010), 199–224.

TJ. These measures seek for reconciliation and reintegration so as to bring former conflicting parties or divided societies together into functioning relationships through political partnerships by using political institutions to address the challenges of a once divided and conflict-torn society.

Although most of the measures used during the earlier European transitional processes of the 1950s and 1980s were not labelled as TJ, they can be considered as such. Amnesties, reparations, civil trials, memorials and pensions as forms of compensation for political prisoners and victims were among the first measures to be applied in the first five years of transition in many countries, including Germany, the Netherlands, France, Greece, Portugal and Spain. Although many of these measures were considered to have a meaningful contribution in some way to regime change and later to democratic consolidation, there was no clear claim that they were connected. But in response to the rise of TJ since 1990, the *Encyclopaedia of Transitional Justice* states that most modern states apply some measures that qualify as TJ.[35] Yet, the appropriateness of TJ measures and the progression of reconciliation processes very much depend on regional circumstances. Although these circumstances will only be dealt with marginally in the case studies, it can be said that the European normative legal and political framework with its three major international organisations impacted and framed the democratisation process in the countries I deal with in this book. That regional framework consists of the EU, the Council of Europe, and the OSCE. The latter has more influence on TJ in post-communist Eastern and Central European countries. These institutions provide normative and legal frameworks for the conduct of TJ, such as the EU External Action Service's (EEAS) Human Rights and Democratisation policies. The EEAS is today one of the strongest promoters of TJ measures around the world through its support of civil society initiatives, truth commissions, trials, memorials and other instruments of acknowledgement and criminal justice.

But however the larger concept of TJ is framed, the debate about its use or misuse, impact or contribution to societal and political processes continues to be widely debated. One aspect is that of historical truth, a common narrative and the 'right to truth', the latter of which has its roots in the human right to a fair trial (Article 9 of the UN International Covenant on Civil and Political Rights and Article 6 of the European Convention

---

[35] L. Stan and N. Nedelsky (eds.), *Encyclopaedia of Transtional Justice* (Oxford: Oxford University Press, 2013).

on Human Rights). Elazar Barkan stressed that the only way societies can overcome historical injustices that can negatively impact societies in transition is with a common narrative and historical truth. Overcoming this historical injustice is important because otherwise a strong sense of victimisation can affect the mutual understanding between different groups of society, perpetrators and victims alike. Consequently, this sense of victimisation can once again divide societies and thus deconsolidate regimes. A minimum agreement about what happened in the past and a common narrative shape new social identities that contribute to democracy.[36] According to Barkan, a narrow or biased understanding of historical facts has often led to enduring injustice, which we can see in Russia and many other former dictatorships today, which has a non-pluralistic society and authoritarian regime.

The so-called 'white spots of history' or denials of what really happened in the past always serve as feeding grounds for myths and speculations, as was the case for many years in post-Franco Spain and Turkey until TJ measures such as commissions of inquiry, memorials, and others were slowly implemented. Jeff Spinner-Halev argued that if these white spots remain untouched, culture of impunity and mistrust remains the norm not the exception. The white spots can then easily lead to the creation of new myths that again lead to acts of vengeance or arbitrary justice and thus new outbreaks of violence.[37] This also explains why contemporary fully fledged consolidated democracies such as Australia, Canada or Germany put significant resources and state capital into TJ measures. As Hazan accentuated, without a minimum agreement from all sides that 'something went wrong' in the past as well as agreement on some common denominators, a TJ process should not even be considered as it would be a waste of time and money.[38] As a consequence, those who are able to shape the historical narrative or determine the facts, often expressed in terms of the numbers of dead and wounded, can easily manipulate and use the narrative and facts for further acts of vengeance and crimes, as Minow has already noted in her earlier studies. The best prevention against vengeance is to allow for open discourse, international and interdisciplinary history and truth commissions, trials, wide-ranged media engagement, and discussions of public memory so as to avoid one-sided and individual 'fact-finding missions' and interpretations of the past. The case studies

---

[36] E. Barkan, *The Guilt of Nations*.
[37] J. Spinner-Halev, 'From Historical to Enduring Injustice', 574–597.
[38] P. Hazan, 'Measuring the Impact of Punishment and Forgiveness, 19–47.

in this book make it evident that private and public memory – and thus narratives that are constructed either in the family or in public media and political discourse – are fundamental to the way in which TJ measures are applied.

Powerful international allies support the concept of TJ. First among these was the UN, and later the EU and the African Union (AU). In 2011 the World Bank co-published the first World Development Report on Conflict, Security and Development, in which the authors emphasised the potential link between TJ and societal and democratic development – or at least peaceful stability.[39] International actors support many TJ projects and measures in emerging democracies in the hope they will contribute to increased stability. Apart from the EEAS, development agencies such as USAID and the Germany Development Cooperation GIZ also finance truth commissions, fund memorials and foster trials around the world. International NGOs often conduct work on the ground, and depend on the massive donations that are given for TJ measures.

In the end, the rapidly developing field of TJ research has put forward multiple case studies with examples of best practices and processes. Not surprisingly, some of the major recent publications in this area are on social transition and transformation;[40] the performance of tribunals and hybrid courts;[41] victimisation and reconstruction;[42] TRC;[43] the impact of

---

[39] P. de Greiff, 'Transitional Justice'.

[40] N.J. Kritz (ed.), *Transitional Justice*; J. A. McAdams (ed.), *Transitional Justice and the Rule of Law in New Democracies*; K. McEvoy and L. McGregor (eds.), *Transitional Justice from Below, Grassroots Activism and the Struggle for Change* (Oxford: Hart Publishing, 2008); J. Priban, P. Roberts and J. Young (eds.), *System of Justice in Transition, Central European Experience Since 1989* (Farnham, UK: Ashgate, 2003); L. Stan (ed.), *Transitional Justice in Eastern Europe and the Former Soviet Union, Reckoning with the Communist Past* (New York: Routledge, 2008).

[41] M. A. Drumbl, *Atrocity, Punishment, and International Law* (Cambridge: Cambridge University Press, 2007); M.J. Falcon y Tella and F. Falcon y Tella, *Punishment and Culture: A Right to Punish?* (Leiden/Boston: Martinus Nijhoff, 2006); A. O'Shea, *Amnesty for Crime in International Law and Practice* (London: Kluwer Law International, 2004).

[42] P. Rock, *Constructing Victims' Rights: The Home Office, New Labour and Victims* (Oxford: Oxford University Press, 2004); H. Strang, *Repair of Revenge: Victims and Restorative Justice, Clarendon Studies in Criminology* (Oxford: Oxford University Press, 2002).

[43] M. Freeman, *Truth Commissions and Procedural Fairness*; T. Godwin Phelps, *Shattered Voices, Language, Violence and the Work of Truth Commissions* (Philadelphia, PA: University of Pennsylvania Press, 2004); R.I. Rotberg and D. Thompson (eds.), *Truth Versus Justice: The Morality of Truth Commissions* (Princeton, NJ: Princeton University Press, 2000).

apologies,[44] amnesty laws,[45] impunity;[46] the importance of historical memory and justice;[47] reparations;[48] and on reconciliation processes in general.[49] It is impossible to name and revisit all these studies, although some of the most recent ones will be introduced later throughout this study. As will be shown, the many efforts to show any effect that TJ measures can have led to a number of revealing studies and research projects. A large N-study in an access to justice project at Tilburg University, aimed to determine whether TJ measures influence people's perceptions. The study divided TJ into different justice categories and discovered that procedural, interpersonal and informational justice measures impact the quality of distributive and restorative justice based on general concepts of justice.[50] This outcome indicates that interpersonal or societal justice is closely linked to distributive and restorative justice, a finding that plays a major role in TJ research and echoes Winter's theoretical concept of TJ as explained earlier. Furthermore, the aim of the multi-disciplinary research project, which is ideally linked to this study, is to investigate the impact of TJ on democratic institution building carried out in the United

[44] M. Gibney, R.E. Howard-Hassmann, J-M. Coicaud and N. Steiner (eds.), *The Age of Apology, Facing Up to the Past* (Philadelphia, PA: University of Pennsylvania Press, 2008).

[45] K. Brounéus, *Rethinking Reconciliation Concepts, Methods, and an Empirical Study of Truth Telling and Psychological Health in Rwanda* (Uppsala: Uppsala University, 2008); M. Abu-Nimer (ed.), *Reconciliation, Justice and Coexistence, Theory and Practice* (Lanham, MD: Lexington Books, 2001); D. Bar-Tal, and G.H. Bennink, 'The Nature of Reconciliation as an Outcome and as a Process', in Y. Bar-Siman Tov (ed.), *From Conflict Resolution to Reconciliation* (Oxford: Oxford University Press, 2004), pp. 11–38; A. Benson Brown and K.M. Poremski (eds.), *Roads to Reconciliation, Conflict and Dialogue in the Twenty-First Century* (New York: M.E. Sharpe, 2005); M.-H. Ross, 'Ritual and the Politics of Reconciliation', in Y. Bar-Siman-Tov (ed.), *From Conflict Resolution to Reconciliation* (Oxford: Oxford University Press, 2004), pp. 197–223; J. Spinner-Halev, 'Education, Reconciliation and Nested Identities', *Theory and Research in Education*, 1 (2003), 51–72.

[46] C. Villa-Vicencio and E. Doxtader (eds.), *The Provocations of Amnesty, Memory, Justice and Impunity* (Trenton, NJ: Africa World Press, 2003).

[47] A. Barahona de Brito, C. Gonzaléz-Enríquez and P. Aguilar, *The Politics of Memory*; E. Barkan, *The Guilt of Nations*, pp. 63–90.

[48] C.K.B. Barton, *Restorative Justice, The Empowerment Model* (Leichhardt: Hawkins Press, 2003); D. Roche, *Accountability in Restorative Justice, Clarendon Studies in Criminology* (Oxford: Oxford University Press, 2003).

[49] K. Brounéus, *Rethinking Reconciliation Concepts*; M. Abu-Nimer (ed.), *Reconciliation, Justice and Coexistence*; D. Bar-Tal, and G.H. Bennink, 'The Nature of Reconciliation as an Outcome and as a Process', pp. 11–38; A. Benson Brown and K.M. Poremski (eds.), *Roads to Reconciliation*; M.-H. Ross, 'Ritual and the Politics of Reconciliation', pp. 197–223; J. Spinner-Halev, 'Education, Reconciliation and Nested Identities', 51–72.

[50] Hague Institute for the Internationalisation of Law, *Measuring Access to Justice in a Globalising World* (Utrecht: HiiL/Tilburg University/Utrecht University, 2010).

Table 4.1 *Categories of Transitional Justice Measures (examples)*

Acknowledgement	Restoration	Criminal Justice	Silence
History commissions	Reparation	Application of	Blanket or
Truth commissions	Restitution	international	conditional
Apologies	Compensation for	human and	amnesties
Memorials	past injustice	humanitarian law	Silence pacts
Public Debates	Quota and	Criminal justice	
Film	affirmative	Tribunals and ad hoc	
Literature	action	tribunals	
Schoolbooks	Restoration of	Trials	
Scientific research	historical sites	Security system	
open archives	Exhumation of	reform	
Media involvement	mass graves	Condemnation or	
Symbolic naming		probation	
of victims and		Vetting and lustrations	
perpetrators			

Kingdom and the Netherlands, of which I had the pleasure to be one of two principle investigators. Until 2016 we went on to investigate whether there is a direct link between some TJ measures and democratic institution building.[51] Not surprisingly, there were no direct links but correlating ones between TJ and democratisation and the quality of democracy, as we found out by looking at cases such as Chile, South Korea, Japan, East Germany or Hungary and Uganda.

Based on the long list of literature, cases studies and practices noted above, I identify four key areas of TJ, consisting of mechanisms and tools of (1) acknowledgement, (2) restoration, (3) criminal justice and (4) silence (see Table 4.1).

Acknowledgement of past wrongdoings is the most pivotal measure in any TJ process because it is based on the willingness of various actors to acknowledge that 'something went wrong' in the past. Other measures such as reparations, trials or memorials can follow. But if political actors and the regime refuse to acknowledge the misdeeds of the past, TJ is very unlikely to happen at all. Without actors' willingness to employ these

---

[51] ORA-ESRC-NWO, Research Project: The Impact of Transitional Justice on Democratic Institution Building, 2013–2016, The University of Utrecht, Netherlands, and the University of East London in United Kingdom, www.tjdi.org.

tools to acknowledge that 'something went wrong', a successful TJ process is very unlikely. Acknowledgement as a catalyst, for example, includes commissions of inquiry, history, and truth telling; apologies by political or private stakeholders; and the establishment of memorials and memorial days. Additionally, acknowledgement can be carried out through initiating and responding to public debates, making films and documentaries, publishing literature about the past, introducing past wrongdoings and historical facts in school textbooks, conducting scientific research and opening archives, allowing media involvement, and naming victims and alleged perpetrators. These measures are mainly victim focused.

Second, TJ measures of restoration can be summarised as acts that involve reparation, restitution, rehabilitation or compensation for victims of expropriation, eviction, imprisonment or illegal killings. They can easily be assessed through qualitative data and have, therefore, been the subject of intensive investigation in numerous case studies. Alongside substantive and financial compensation or restitution, restoration includes measures for establishing working relationships between former combatants in public institutions through quota systems, reconciliation and reintegration programmes, restoration and maintenance of memorials, and/or the public exhumation of mass graves. Individual restorative measures such as compensations to individuals for their particular suffering have been proven to be very effective in terms of victim satisfaction, but it must be noted that this is only one type of restorative TJ measure. Such individual measures have to be seen in the larger context of TJ, which acknowledges and quantifies the loss of many lives and the years of living under oppression across time. Without this approach, TJ measures will lose their meaning for future generations. A good example of a restorative TJ measure is Rule 150 of the 1948 Hague Convention on Reparations, which has become customary international law and is applicable to all countries and societies. It holds that the responsible state is obliged to make full reparations for the injury caused by the internationally recognised wrongful act for which it is responsible. The restoration of Armenian churches in Turkey or synagogues in Germany has a direct link to these international customary rules. This type of measure is also victim focused.

The third and most prominent category is that of criminal justice, which is also often equalised with TJ as such. Courts apply international human rights law, international criminal law, humanitarian law or domestic criminal law to confront past injustice and perpetrators. Often this type of TJ also pushes for the reform of national criminal justice legislation. Criminal justice focuses predominantly on perpetrators, as do vetting measures and lustration policies. International (human rights) norms and instruments help to set out a legal framework for tribunals and the new national court system. In this process, it is crucial to ensure a judiciary that can adequately deal with cases from the past, in particular when dealing with the prohibition of retroactivity, which all post-authoritarian systems struggle with. Criminal justice measures also aim to combat impunity, establish and reform security services, and condemn perpetrators of the former regime. The ICC Statute of 1999 has been an important TJ criminal justice tool, with its emphasis on individual accountability being equal to state accountability with respect to past injustices.

Fourth, silencing the past through de facto amnesty laws or conditional amnesties is the most common TJ measure that governments in transition apply. It is also the most disputed one. Such an approach can include amnesty laws or informal 'silence pacts' (agreements between old and new political elites made shortly before or after transition takes place), as was the case in post-war Germany and post-Franco Spain. Most amnesty laws that are issued during regime change or in the first five to ten years thereafter include the release of political prisoners held by the previous regime, including all those who were against the previous regime or in some type of collaboration with it. In addition, the Spanish amnesty laws of 1976 and 1977 (which have been a blueprint for amnesty laws in other transition countries) exempt all those from prosecution who had been politically active before regime change, including Francoists. These measures can be issued through informal agreements or national laws and are therefore not immediately regarded as impunity measures. Amnesty laws can encourage perpetrators to surrender without (yet) having to face punishment. They also allow perpetrators to testify in front of truth commissions or other commissions of inquiry without fearing long-term prison sentences. Nevertheless, they also contribute to a culture of impunity and repetition of injustice.

Other ways of issuing de facto amnesties are 'reintegration' or 'rehabilitation' laws that reinstate functionaries from the previous regime, for example lawyers and technocrats, in new offices with new titles. These last-resort TJ measures often turn into habits, political traditions, and can finally lead to a culture of impunity. Therefore, amnesty laws should be conditional and agreed upon or changed by means of a referendum when the time is right, while always attempting to ensure that impunity is avoided.

As has been shown, the appropriate use and mix of TJ measures vary from country to country and from case to case. In some conflict-driven and post-dictatorial societies, governments may reluctantly and carefully only apply one or two TJ measures. This is often a spontaneous reaction to domestic or external pressure before elections take place; or TJ measures are applied to please the international donor community or seek membership in international organisations. Since TJ measures only have a spiral effect on regime consolidation if a set and/or mixture of such rules are applied over a longer period of time; spontaneous or single application of TJ, as a form of window-dressing, is unlikely to impact societal behaviour or regime consolidation. Moreover, even if a legislature decides to pass TJ measures, there is no guarantee that the executive or judicial branches will respond favourably, as seen in West and East Germany and Turkey.

In the future it will be more difficult for transition countries to deny claims for TJ, since international claims of justice are increasingly based on customary human rights law and international humanitarian law, which apply without strict time limits after crimes and injustice have happened. Statutes of limitations and the limits due to laws on retroactivity exist in every jurisdiction but can be overturned by international jurisdiction or through the application of customary law.[52] Even a century after atrocities took place, governments in established democracies such as in the United Kingdom, France or Canada, are called upon to respond appropriately to past injustices by setting up trials or commissions of inquiry. A good example of this is the international claim in 2015 calling on Turkey to finally recognise the Armenian genocide, which took place over 100 years ago.

The exertion of international pressure on political actors who employ TJ measures, along with incentives, must not be underestimated in any transition process, let alone during regime consolidation. Although Germany made significant efforts to join the UN in the 20 years after World War II, it only succeeded in 1973 after having made concessions to the international community and its own domestic politics. Some of these concessions included TJ measures; for example, the trials of guards in concentration camps. Even though West Germany had various statutes of limitations on mass murder, for political – if not democratic – reasons, it loosened and changed them in the 1970s. Serbia is a current example that has many parallels with post-war Germany when it comes to the denial of, concession to and finally compliance with international standards and TJ. In order to become a member of the EU, Serbia had to cooperate

---

[52] For a good overview of the role and development of international customary law in the context of TJ see: R. Zajac Sonnerholm, *Rule of Law after War and Crisis, Ideologies, Norms and Methods* (Antwerp: Intersentia, 2012), pp. 130–143.

with the ICTY and employ a number of TJ measures. Turkey had to make similar concessions to the Council of Europe and the EU in terms of TJ measures to foster EU accession talks around 2005. Similarly, Rwanda was required to cooperate closely with the ICTR in order to receive international financial support from the World Bank. These examples show that international incentives (or pressure) and the desire for integration into the international community must not be underestimated when studying TJ measures. It is of course another question whether the TJ measures that arise from these pressures and incentives actually contribute to democratic regime consolidation. In Rwanda, for example, TJ measures led to another authoritarian regime.

External pressure is only one side of the coin and should be seen as incentive policies for governments and means for civil society groups to exert pressure, rather than as an end in and of itself. In the case of Turkey, the ECtHR is the main international body that pushes for more TJ and emphasises the need to come to terms with the legacy of the past 100 years. This strongly impacts Turkey's domestic politics and international relations. Turkey's external relations are very much determined by its former violent relationships with its neighbouring countries and the same is true within the country in terms of its repressive politics towards minorities. The unresolved issue of the thousands of disappeared and murdered Kurds in eastern Anatolia since the 1980s and since 1974 in Northern Cyprus influences many parliamentary debates, the EU accession talks, the quality of NATO membership and other aspects of foreign policy up to the present day. Domestically, a large number of these minorities within the country will only see the government as trustworthy and legitimate if the government in Ankara acknowledges and comes to terms with this past.[53] External pressure and incentives, as well as the pressure from below, can thus no longer be ignored. Decisions by the ECtHR have had a great effect on investigation laws in the case of the disappeared Kurds and a commission to investigate lost property of Greeks in Northern Cyprus was set up prior to some major EU accession talks in 2004.

Hazan has stressed that unless there is public or citizen-driven transparency or monitoring procedures of the implementation of TJ measures, these measures may prove ineffective and instead become a convenient alibi for inertia.[54] Such transparency and monitoring procedures can only

---

[53]   E. Brems, 'Transitional Justice in the Case Law of the European Court of Human Rights', 282–303.
[54]   P. Hazan, 'Measuring the Impact of Punishment and Forgiveness', 19–47.

be guaranteed if democratic institutions work somewhat effectively, guarantee fundamental freedom rights and leave room for participation of societal and political actors from all sides. Thus, at least formally or constitutionally, democratic institutions must be in place in order to implement and establish any TJ instruments and mechanisms effectively, and this is when the mutually reinforcing and spiral interaction between TJ and regime consolidation begins.

There is by no means a homogeneous picture of TJ measures and tools. There is also no formula that specifies which TJ measures to use at what time and in which combination. Yet, by finding some cumulative causation with regime development over a longer period of time, we can study what kind of TJ measures were used by whom, for what purpose, and whether they had a positive or negative affect on regime consolidation.

5

The Case Studies: Germany, Spain and Turkey

The different regime types I look at in this book are post-authoritarian or post-dictatorial regimes that made a commitment to democracy. They all went through longer or shorter periods of regime change and later consolidation, but yet with very different outcomes and qualities. East and West Germany are cases of regime consolidation after 1949 and the case of Spain deals with transition and consolidation after 1975, and in Turkey we look at the period starting in 1987 and 1989 when the country made a strict political commitment to democratic reforms and accession to the EC. However, Turkey did not move towards a consolidated democracy in the sense of 'civil society consolidation'[1] over the past three decades despite many institutional reforms and international incentives. Instead the country has turned back towards an authoritarian regime after massive and systematic restriction of civil society and the exclusive use of TJ measures.

As mentioned earlier, I deliberately do not take socio-economic or historical-cultural characteristics into account much when comparing the impact the legacies of totalitarianism and authoritarianism had on these countries, because it goes without saying that historical and economic context, and even the fact that these countries are placed in Europe, affect the outcome of consolidation, so does the fact that their actors all use TJ measures. However, I focus on the actors and the institutions of regimes that are formally committed towards democracy and how they use or abuse TJ.

Spain's transition came as much as a surprise as the German one, although under very different conditions. After General Franco's death, Spain's transition government and the king used TJ measures sporadically and was influenced by political majorities within the country to

---

[1] W. Merkel, *Systemtransformation, Eine Einführung in die Theorie und Empirie der Transformationsforschung*, p. 124.

appease certain victim groups and to reconcile a number of – but not all – social groups. Although external pressure from the Council of Europe, the EU and the United Nations came much later, both civil society and government responded to this pressure. In both cases during the first 20–25 years since transition began, TJ measures were used in a politically tactical way to (1) prevent victim demands from becoming too loud; (2) in order to rehabilitate and reintegrate victimisers and former elites into the new regime; and (3) to foster integration into international or European organisations, such as the EC or the UN. Moral or ethical reasons for atonement, compensations or even trials did not play much of a role during regime change.

Turkey serves as a control, or rather 'test case' in this comparative study. Between 1989 and the present day, the Turkish government has made numerous efforts towards democratic reform, motivated by desires of joining the EU and reconciling its conflict-torn society. Due to pressure from within the country (in particular from the Kurdish minority population) as well as from the international level, the government has made dramatic efforts to reconcile with formerly oppressed groups within Turkey, but also with its neighbouring countries such as Cyprus, Armenia and Greece and to come to terms with its past. It made concessions to minorities within the country and also towards former elites. The Turkish government continues to face difficult diplomatic relations with many neighbours due to its wrongdoings, wars and crimes of the past under the Ottoman Empire. Turkey is seen as a long-term formal, but deficient, democracy with strong affiliations to Europe and at the same time a sad and long history of war, internal conflicts and authoritarian leadership. Turkey had passed the stage of constitutional and somewhat institutional consolidation but not attitudinal or behavioural.

According to most democracy rankings that rank countries by their level of freedom rights, corruption, equity and so forth, Germany is seen as the most solid democracy among the case studies. It is listed as the eighth strongest democracy worldwide. Spain is listed at 16th place and does not experience a dramatic increase or decrease in its performance over the past years. In contrast, Turkey is listed at 65th place on a scale of 110 countries and has seen a significant decrease in its performance since 2011.[2] According to the Quality of Democracy

---

[2] D.F. Campell, T.D. Barth, P. Plötzlbauer and G. Plötzlbauer, *The Quality of Democracy in the World*.

scheme, out of 113 countries worldwide, the country went down from 62nd to 69th by 2015 and its level and quality of democracy continues to fall downward.[3] In other rankings, such as the 2012 Worldwide Democracy Index, Germany ranks 14th, Spain 25th and Turkey ranks 88th. And by 2015, according to the Quality of Democracy Ranking scheme, Germany comes 7th out of 113 countries worldwide and Spain comes 19th. Germany has improved its record by one over the past years, but Spain went down by three points between 2012 and 2015.[4] What matters about these rankings is the tendency because their indicators on how to measure democracy often vary. But both rankings find similar results and are likely quite similar to what hypothetical rankings of TJ measures in each country would find, if there were such rankings. Finally, some indices list Germany and Spain as full democracies and Turkey as a hybrid regime. All rankings include civic and citizen trust and confidence in the regime as indicators and consider political culture and the level of participation beyond elections and voter turnouts crucial for the outcome of the ranking. Out of ten possible points for democratic performance, Germany and Spain score between 7.0 and 8.3 on political culture. This is a rather solid base for civic trust in political institutions. They score 6.0 out of 10 in terms of citizen participation, which is a rather average score. Turkey, however, scores around 5.0 on both scales, with increasing significant flaws in trust based on disenchantment with the regime and issues of legitimacy.[5] Although these rankings, benchmarks and indices can only give indications as to how these countries perform in general, it is interesting to note that all these indices come to more or less similar results when assessing democratic performance of institutions, participation and levels of accountability.

All of the case study countries addressed here qualify for a long-term qualitative and explorative comparison because they are different in their qualitative performance, but nevertheless have democratic institutions in place. Ultimately, this is a case-oriented qualitative comparative assessment with an explanatory approach towards regime consolidation or deconsolidation. Although all case study countries

[3] Democracy Ranking Association, 'Quality of Democracy Ranking 2015', see: democracy-ranking.org/wordpress/welcome/about-us/ (last accessed August 2016).
[4] Ibid.
[5] Democracy Index 2012, 'Democracy at a Standstill. A Report from The Economist Intelligence Unit'. www.eiu.com (last accessed November 2014), p. 20.

have incorporated formal democratic institutions with democratic constitutions and norms, they nevertheless remain different in terms of consolidation. The manner in which and intensity with which TJ measures have been used in these cases have contributed to these different pathways. The process of regime change, consolidation and deconsolidation in these countries can be divided into phases commencing with the initial regime transition and change (including the implementation of a new constitution, a multi-party system, elections), followed by regime consolidation, outcomes which can be determined based on levels of citizen participation, attitude and behaviour, the level of decentralisation, the growth of civil society and international engagement with the UN, Council of Europe or European Community/ Union.[6] East and West Germany, Spain and Turkey had similar commitments to international organisations such as the UN; and West Germany, Spain and Turkey were particularly committed to the EU, the Council of Europe, the ECtHR, the OSCE and NATO. This means that all four regimes were subject to similar external pressure, incentives and interferences. They all experienced governmental shifts and reforms after their experience with (military) dictatorships, one-party regimes, wars, genocides, oppression or grave human rights violations. Their political systems supported secular policies and did not – in principle – close themselves off to TJ measures.

In 1949 in both East and West Germany, the Allies and the international community were largely responsible for the imposition of TJ and implemented TJ measures hastily. This was not the case in Spain in 1975 and Turkey around 1989, where the TJ process was slowly developed over a longer period of time. Yet, in all four of these countries, the way TJ measures were implemented or rejected depended often on constitutional set-ups and political willingness of policy makers at that time. Nevertheless, in all countries TJ only took off when civil society and victim groups started engaging in it and used them as a tool to seek justice. Measures such as reparations, trials, compensations, amnesty laws and memorials were used by political actors for tactical and later, with the support of civil society, also for moral reasons which eventually led to regime consolidation in some cases.

---

[6] Tony Judt has argued that European countries democratise and unite after, and to distinguish themselves from, a violent and atrocious past, regardless of whether they have been victims or victimisers. T. Judt, *Postwar. A History of Europe Since 1945* (New York: Penguin Books, 2005).

5.1   Germany

Already in the last days of World War II in 1945, the Allies imposed democratic reform on post-war Germany under the Allied Control Council Laws
(*Kontrollratsgesetze*), which set the foundation for the TJ process in both
the Federal Republic of Germany (West) and in the GDR (East) shortly
after. Until 1948, the Allied forces, in particular the United States, United
Kingdom, the Soviet Union and France, passed a number of decrees ordering the newly established German political elite to take up cases of criminal justice and to deal with the issue of reparation and compensation of
wartime survivors and countries that had suffered under German occupation. Yet, shortly after, East and West German regime change and consolidation processes diverged in different directions.

West Germany's path to democracy and stability has often been
divided into several phases that historians and analysts such as Wolfum[7]
and Von Weizäcker[8] have marked by the simple dates of 1949, 1969
and 1989, which correlate with the timespan between 1945 and 1949
(the post-war phase), the mid-1950s to the 1960s (democratisation
phase), and the mid-1960s to 1989 (the consolidation phase) and later
the subsequent phase after 1990 to the present (the renewal phase).
A similar divide holds for the East German path towards authoritarian rule. These phases also coincide with the first, second, third and
now fourth post-war generations in Germany. In West Germany, the
first phase was initiated by the Allied powers under the slogan of the
'four Ds': demilitarisation, denazification, democratisation and decentralisation.[9] This led to a relatively intensive period of prosecution of
those responsible for war crimes, of which the most famous trials are
the Nuremberg trials between 1945 and 1948. All litigations were based
on the Allied Control Council Act No. 10 from 1945 that determined
that Allied and German courts were to prosecute all those who had
committed war crimes during World War II. At the time, the German
interim governments and administrations in the east and the west recognised the dire need to pass the law quickly after the war had officially ended in May 1945, in order to avoid arbitrary violence and
vengeance killings by victims or survivors against those whom they

---

[7] E. Wolfrum, *Die geglückte Demokratie, Geschichte der Bundesrepublik Deutschland von
ihren Anfängen bis zur Gegenwart* (Bonn: Klett Cotta, 2007).

[8] R. von Weizsäcker, *Drei Mal Stunde Null? 1949, 1969, 1989* (Berlin: Siedler Verlag, 2001).

[9] E. Wolfrum, *Die geglückte Demokratie*, p. 26.

believed were responsible. A greater number of acts of vengeance were recorded in East Germany than in West Germany. Regardless of where they occurred, the governments' intention was to reduce them as much as possible, as they were seen as a threat to the security and stability of the new regimes.[10] But with around eight million registered NSDAP members (a tenth of the whole population) and around five million to be potentially indicted, both east and west faced immense challenges of TJ. Although acts of revenge, such as pogroms, continued against Nazis and German citizens in and outside Germany for many years to come, the trials were an attempt to reduce the desire for vengeance. An estimated three million Germans died from injuries sustained from war after 1945. More than six or 12 – depending on the count – million refugees came not only from eastern Europe, but also from France, the Netherlands, Austria or Belgium where they had belonged to German minority or Nazi supporters and were now expelled as an act of vengeance.[11] It should be noted that at that time it was often considered 'appropriate' to use expulsion and revenge as a type of reparation for crimes committed during the war. International or universal jurisdiction did not exist at that time and human rights law was just beginning to develop. However, the need to confront this law-less situation led to the establishment of the UN High Commissioner for Refugees and other international efforts to deal with similar situations in the future.

In the American, British and French military zones most trials took place immediately after the war ended, between 1945 and 1946. Most of these trials were held in German courts and conducted by German judges under the Allies' supervision. The Allies soon took into account that more than 90 per cent of all German judges at that time had been judges, prosecutors or attorneys under the Nazi regime and were thus highly inflicted by Nazi ideology. The reason for this, apart from the fact that the Allies themselves lacked sufficient resources to conduct all trials, was the belief that Germans ought to take ownership of their 'own' crimes of the past. The Nuremberg trials were the exception not the rule because they did not involve German-trained judges. Between 1946 and 1948, trials in German courts of those who actively supported

---

[10] D. Cohen, 'Transitional Justice in Divided Germany after 1945', in J. Elster (ed.), *Retribution and Repatriation in the Transition to Democracy* (Cambridge: Cambridge University Press, 2006), pp. 59–88.

[11] E. Wolfrum, *Die geglückte Demokratie*, p. 29.

the Nazi regime, for example in the business and industry sectors, resulted in over 95,000 convictions for Nazi war crimes. Of those convicted, most were German and Austrian nationals and a large number of the convicted had been found guilty of war crimes committed in Eastern Europe and therefore fell within the jurisdiction of the Soviet-controlled zone, where – as we will see later – fair and open trials were far from guaranteed. Nevertheless, also in East Germany and the former occupied countries – now under Soviet control – thousands of alleged Nazi perpetrators had been tried and the majority of them executed. In comparison to these numbers, the conviction rate in West Germany was remarkably low and far below 10 per cent, also due to the fact that many of those who supported the Nazi regime remained in political, economic and judicial positions of power.

During the early stage under Soviet occupation, the new communist regime in the East engaged in its own acts of vengeance, which led to a high level of mistrust amongst Germans in Soviet-imposed institutions soon after the war had ended. It soon became evident that the many East German citizens who had never experienced justice under the Nazi regime, would also be denied justice under the communist regime and Soviet power. Many victims of both the Nazi regime and later the communist regime would have to wait until reunification in 1989 for their first chance at justice.

During the 1940s, roughly 50,000 people were convicted in Europe of Nazi crimes for their roles as collaborators or supporters of the regime, and about half of these convictions took place in East and West Germany. In West Germany alone around 5,000 persons were convicted of severe crimes against humanity before 1949, with over 800 sentenced to death. Many thousands more were convicted of lesser crimes to long-term sentences. Two-thirds of all Nazi defendants were tried in East Germany under Soviet occupation without any access to legal representation or justice. When these (often non-public) trials resulted in sentences of immediate execution without the possibility to appeal the sentence, it instilled fear and mistrust in citizens.

Both East and West Germany never launched any TRC or commission of inquiry that included open public hearings, civil engagement or involvement of citizen groups until 1949. Public accountability and transparency was not high at these times and specific TJ measures were hardly known at that time. Instead, the main TJ tools were trials and reparations, but often dealt with behind closed doors and with little publicity.

The conviction rate for the trials held throughout Europe was around 25 per cent.[12]

There is an abundance of literature describing and assessing the Nuremberg Trials and the hundreds of other local trials that took place in the different occupied sectors of Germany before 1949. I will not revisit it here in great detail because my case study only focuses on the period after 1949. I will only highlight some of the facts and figures from these earlier studies that are relevant to better illustrate the TJ process on both Germanys.[13] Altogether between 1945 and 1949, over 180,000 persons (mainly Germans) were tried for war crimes, but not necessarily convicted, based on over 12,000,000 documents that the Nazis left behind in 1945 in the US, French and Soviet sectors alone. This does not include the hundreds of thousands of Germans interned and later released due to the decision at the beginning of the transition process to only focus on punishing those who committed the more severe war crimes.[14] After the establishment of the two states in 1949, West Germany paid over 135 billion marks (approximately 77 billion euro today) in war reparations, paying most of these reparations between 1952 and the 1960s. It was during this later period that West Germany paid Israel 3.5 billion marks in 'global reparations'. These reparations were not compensation for any direct legal effect of the Nazi regime on Israel, since Israel did not exist as a country at the time of the Nazi regime. Rather, these reparations materialised out of international pressure to officially acknowledge the great injustice and deathly violence that millions of Jews had to suffer under the Nazi regime.

Germans in both parts of the country saw most of these TJ measures as imposed on them. They saw the reparations as punishment for having lost the war. Opinion surveys showed that in both West and East Germany, civil society and former Nazi supporters alike resisted regime change prior and after 1949. In particular, anti-democratic sentiments were publicly expressed in both East and West Germany. In West Germany many believed that the country was not ready to become a fully sovereign democracy because too many people still believed in the Nazi ideology.

[12] D.O. Pendas, 'Seeking Justice, Finding Law: Nazi Trials in Postwar Europe', *Journal of Modern History*, 81 (2008), 354–355.
[13] Many sources are available from this period of German history. For a good overview see: C. Vollnhals, *Entnazifierung. Politische Säuberung und Rehabilitierung in den vier Besatzungszonen 1945–1949* (Munich: dtv Verlag, 1991) and H. Glaser, *1945 Beginn einer Zukunft, Bericht und Dokumentation* (Frankfurt: Fischer Verlag, 2005).
[14] D. Cohen, 'Transitional Justice in Divided Germany After 1945', pp. 59–88.

There alone, the percentage of Germans that considered the Nuremberg trials 'fair' fell from 78 per cent to 38 per cent between 1946 and late 1950s, after they saw the results of the first trials.[15] Many Germans perceived these trials as 'victor's justice' because none of the Allied powers' war criminals, namely Soviet, French, British or US soldiers, were ever dealt with during these public trials. This scepticism was similar to what James Gibson observed during the TJ process in South Africa: if blame is not put on all sides, TJ measures will most likely not have any positive influence on democratic regime change or consolidation.

In 1949, when the Allied forces transferred the western and eastern German sectors back to the hands of semi-sovereign governments, the newly existing democratic institutions (in West Germany) faced a serious lack of legitimacy, and so did the socialist institutions in the East. The Allies urged both governments to continue with trials because, at that time, trials were seen as the only way to cleanse future governmental administrations of possible war criminals and anti-democratic powers. The desire to establish strong power structures was one of the reasons the Allied Control Commission asked the West German government and the prime ministers of the Federal States (*Länder*) in 1948 to meet and create a new constitution for West Germany. As a reaction to the developments in the western occupied zone, a parallel constitution building process took place in East Germany between 1948 and 1949 under the supervision of the Soviet Union. This step indicated that reunification of the two Germanys would no longer be an option at that time. Germans on both sides felt disappointed once again as their interests and needs were not taken into account. The West German constitution, the Basic Law (*Grundgesetz*), was established in May 1949. It was influenced by the 1948 Universal Declaration of Human Rights (UDHR) from December 1948 as well as the draft documents of the European Convention on Human Rights (ECHR) in 1949 and was thus one of the most modern constitutions at that time. Some of the creators of the UDHR and the ECHR had been sitting as judges or lawyers through the Nuremberg trials. Thus, the experience of the trials influenced the declaration and conventions that followed and subsequently the German Basic Law. Germany's laws were watched closely by western powers in order to ensure they complied with the new international norms being established. These laws were later often used in the political rhetoric of

---

[15] A.J. Merritt and R.L. Merritt, *Public Opinion in Semisovereign Germany: The HICOG Surveys, 1949–1955* (Urbana, IL: University of Illinois Press, 1980), p. 101.

the Cold War disputes. In East Germany the (communist) constitution was established in the same year, shortly after that of West Germany. The East German constitution contained no references to international human rights norms and instead based itself on the political power of the communist party.

The first elections were held in both Germanys in 1949. Already at that time it was clear that most Germans, in East and West, perceived the occupation and the fact that Germany lost much of its territory after the war as a general 'payment' or reparation for its war crimes. Germans felt that this was enough payment for the atrocities that were committed in their names. Fifty per cent of the German Reich's territory fell either to the Soviet Union and its satellite states or to France. Industry and cities were destroyed and large parts of the population had perished or kept the status of refugees. Therefore, long before the issue of the Holocaust was on the agenda, the first claims of restitution and TJ came not from victims of concentration camps or forced labour but from German citizens claiming restoration of property and social justice. Among all victims of the war, the Germans saw themselves as the first in line. The genocide under the Nazi regime and its consequences was not a primary concern in either East or West Germany until the early to mid-1950s, and even then it was only dealt with among some intellectuals, victim groups or among governments. Tactical concessions towards governments elsewhere in Europe, Israel and the international community were made, but without any understanding of the grave injustices committed by the Nazi regime. Delegitimisation of the Nazi regime took place very slowly in West Germany. Delegitimisation took place more quickly in East Germany, since the East German government did not see itself as the successor regime to Nazi Germany.

While at first, most Germans did not engage in a process of national catharsis, this changed dramatically over the following decades. Hundreds and thousands of acts of compensation and reparation were issued, trials held, memorials established and schoolbooks revised. Evidence of regime consolidation became only visible 20-plus years after the end of the war, once active citizen participation started taking place. In East Germany, authoritarian rule manifested itself and cumulated in building a wall and establishing an 'Iron Curtain' between the two countries. In the years since reunification in 1989, and despite the integration of the authoritarian East German regime, unified Germany has scored well under the top ten countries on quality of democracy and institutional performance. It ranks above most other democratic countries in the world. Recent democracy barometers indicate a high level of freedom, human rights control, equality and citizen participation.[16]

First Decade: 1949–1959

In 1949, Germans on both sides of the Iron Curtain desired to put the past behind them (*Fertigwerden mit der Vergangenheit*), as expressed by the first West German president, Theodor Heuss, after the first West German elections in the summer of that year.[17] From today's perspective, this might seem rather odd, but it illustrated that indeed, only four years after the atrocious regime had ended, Germans and their political elite hoped that the past would no longer interfere in their political affairs once trials had been completed and reparations were paid. It also shows that the years to come were an experiment in terms of linking TJ measures to the way Germans would understand and exercise their own responsibilities for war crimes and the atrocities as such, even if they had not committed them directly. In the first years of regime transition, the aim by the main opposition party, the Social Democrats (SPD) at that time, some intellectuals, writers and a few victim organisations, was to achieve a common narrative that it was not 'only' a few Nazis, but that the population as such had a shared responsibility. But they were yet in the minority. Their hope was that this would also allow the population to reflect upon the urgent need for a new, different (democratic) regime. A public opinion survey conducted prior to the first elections held in 1949 by the German Institute for Democracy (later the Allensbach Institute), revealed that the majority of Germans neither strongly supported nor opposed the Nazi regime. It showed further that 60 per cent of citizens with a higher level of education tended to dislike or oppose the Nazi regime and its atrocities more than those without that level of education. However, the academic and intellectual elite, let alone victim organisations, were rather small, as many had fled the country or been exiled. Interestingly enough, those asked in the surveys were fully aware of the Holocaust and persecution of minorities, but did not want to use the word 'killing' or 'murder' in that context, nor did they wish to accept a shared responsibility of all Germans for these atrocities. For the majority of Germans, the Jews were expelled, persecuted or disappeared during a period that ended in 1945. It

---

[16] Democracy Barometer, Center for Democracy Studies Aarau. 'Germany: Basic facts 2007'. www.democracybarometer.org (last accessed August 2013).
[17] Ibid., p. 50.

seemed as if the German psyche was not ready to openly face the painful truth, although everyone knew the real fate of those persecuted, expelled and tortured.[18] This denial showed that there was an understanding that it was a deeply rooted anti-democratic ideology and widespread belief that caused the atrocities of World War II and that therefore a change of attitude and behaviour towards democracy was important. The survey also indicated that West Germans were willing to obey the new rules of the democratic constitution, but that they were not familiar with these rules and did not fully understand what the separation of powers entailed – let alone accountability, transparency of free participation.[19] Although a process of national catharsis had started to begin, but only German nationals living in Germany at that time were able to take part in it. Those formerly enslaved, excluded or persecuted and thus no longer living or working in Germany, did obviously not take part in this catharsis.

Politicians reacted and responded to citizens' perceptions, highlighting the illegitimacy of the past regime bit with yet little reference to an alternative future. At the same time, anti-Semitism and prejudice against Jews was still widespread among Germans in both East and West Germany at that time, which indicates how the Nazi ideology prevailed for a very long time. Over 40 per cent felt reservations against Jews and many believed that more Jews had survived and remained in Germany than was actually the case. Prior to the war, there were over 500,000 Jews registered as citizens in Germany, and yet by 1949 only around 20,000 remained in the country. The majority of Germans believed that reconciliation and reparations with the Jews and Israel in particular was necessary (54–60 per cent). But unlike attitudes towards this 'payment justice', only 40 per cent believed that those responsible for the crimes should be prosecuted.[20] There was an evident discrepancy between attitudes towards reparations on the one hand, and towards prosecution on the other. Thus, it was not a lack of acknowledgement but a lack of knowledge on how to deal with the past in an adequate way. In summary, it was believed that the state, not the citizens, should take responsibility for the past. Twenty-eight per cent even thought that prosecution of perpetrators would be illegal because German law prohibited retroactive application of the law.[21]

[18] D. Cohen, 'Transitional Justice in Divided Germany after 1945', pp. 59–88.
[19] Institute für Demoskopie Allensbach: *Das Dritten Reich: eine Studie über Nachwirkungen des Nationalsozialismus, Gesellschaft zum Studium der öffentlichen Meinung* (Allensbach am Bodensee: Institute für Demoskopie Allensbach, 1949).
[20] Institute für Demoskopie Allensbach, *Deutsche und Juden*, pp. 12–16.
[21] Ibid., p. 14.

After holding elections and legislative meetings in September and October 1949, East and West Germany were officially established as semi-sovereign states under Allied forces. The East German government was under the complete control of the Soviet Union and, therefore, the powers that ruled in Moscow. It was led by a one-party government, namely the East German Socialist Unity Party of Germany (*Sozialistische Einheitspartei Deutschlands, SED*). The Soviet Control Council issued Order no. 201, which stated that the new East German authorities should continue to try Nazi perpetrators, but it would not further supervise this process unless it was opportune.[22] The West German government under the leadership of the conservative Christian Democrats (CDU), on the other hand, was under constant surveillance by the Allied High Commissioner of the western forces. The countries on either side of the Iron Curtain enjoyed neither full sovereignty nor independence in setting up their new regimes. Both regimes, the communist-socialist and the liberal-democratic one, were imposed upon the populations with very different constitutional provisions. Yet, the governments in each Germany formally committed to democracy during the constitution-building process. Regime change in East Germany took place quickly, as a consequence of the Stalin Note of 1952. This document demanded a neutralised Germany since the Soviets aimed to take over more of Germany in light of the still-present threat of the Cold War turning into a hot war. It took a further six years before the western Allies recognised West Germany as a quasi-sovereign state.

Meanwhile, due to the anti-democratic character of the East German constitution, in which the communist and socialist elite aimed to govern alone through a single-party system, pluralism was a farce and any efforts of democratic regime change or consolidation soon came to a standstill. Consequently, a workers' rebellion against the communist regime took place in 1953 and was suppressed violently by Soviet tanks with the killing and injuring of hundreds of protesters. The regime turned against its own citizens and in the subsequent years millions of East Germans fled to the west. Those citizens who suffered under the Nazi regime and realised that their claims for reparation would not be recognised under communist doctrine, soon expressed their unhappiness with the one-party government. In the same year one of the very few victim organisations in the

---

[22] H. Leide, *NS-Verbrecher und Staatssicherheit, Die geheime Vergangenheitspolitik der DDR* (Göttingen: Vandenhoek and Ruprecht, 2005), pp. 39–43.

east that existed since 1947, the association of those persecuted under the Nazi regime (*Verein Verfolgte des Naziregimes*) was dissolved by the Stasi because this CSO aimed to look for Nazi perpetrators to try them in their own capacity and thus undermined the government's efforts to dominate the TJ process. Many of their members fled to West Germany as a consequence. This uprising was an early warning of the dysfunctional character of the regime in the east. In the 1950s, the only way to openly show one's dissatisfaction with the communist regime was by fleeing the country across the open borders into West Germany, otherwise known as voting against the communist regime 'by foot'. An average of 350,000 citizens per year left the country, many of them highly qualified young people who would have otherwise have helped to build a new civil society. It led not only to a political brain drain but also to a dramatic economic breakdown in the east.

Ten years after the Nazi regime collapsed, massive protests in the east and the continuous large refugee flow from the east to the west marked the end of any serious democratisation process in East Germany. Although the East German government successfully used TJ measures such as memorials, trials and reparations to delegitimise the Nazi past, it could not use them to effectively legitimise itself.[23] It soon became clear that there would be no inclusive TJ process and it was later left entirely to the Stasi and thus the state secret service to decide who was a Nazi and was supposed to be show-trialled, imprisoned or executed, and who was not. The same was true for victims. It was the SED doctrine and thus the politburo that decided who was officially a victim of the Nazi regime and who was not. Open and fair trials or public dialogue were not an option. The measures were used in an entirely exclusionary way, commemorating predominantly communist victims and using TJ trials to purge the regime of political opponents, regardless of whether these were seriously suspected of Nazi crimes or not.[24]

East Germany was eventually included in the Warsaw Pact, whilst West Germany joined NATO and the EC. Nevertheless, during the first post-war decade, neither side was able to join the UN due to the Hallstein Doctrine. This doctrine was proclaimed by West Germany and denied the de facto political division of Germany. The division of East and West Germany also had consequences for restitution claims that were brought;

---

[23] Federal Archives Germany (Bundesarchiv, Berlin), *Marxism and Leninism*, BA-DY/30/IV2/13–431.
[24] Federal Archives Germany, GDR Department for Reparation DC 2, p. 650.

countries that held diplomatic relationships with West Germany filed their reparation claims in Bonn, whilst those who had ties with East Germany filed their TJ claims in East Berlin. The few countries that had ties to both Germanys filed their claims in both. The list of countries filing reparations included countries like Belgium, Denmark, France, Norway, Finland, Austria, Italy and the Netherlands. The SED leadership in the east was of the opinion that western countries that had not yet established diplomatic ties for ideological reasons with them were not countries the communist-socialist regime wanted to be allies with and therefore denied restitution claims from those countries. Any country that was perceived as anti-communist or hostile to the east was not eligible for reparations. Israel's request to receive reparations from East Berlin was ignored by the SED until reunification in 1990. This shows how highly politicised TJ measures were and it became evident that granting or denying repara-tions was less about the people who had suffered, or the recognition of the individual or collective responsibility needed to achieve a national cathar-sis, and more about political opportunities.

In January 1950, the Soviet administration in East Germany trans-ferred all restitution claims, political prisoners and alleged Nazi crimi-nals to the SED-controlled administration. In subsequent years, the SED bribed countries such as France to establish diplomatic ties with them instead of with West Germany. In France, for example, Nazis had sto-len many artefacts from private households and museums and brought them to museums in Germany or kept them privately. The West German government put reparation procedures in place to return these artefacts but also mainly for political purposes to regain trust among the govern-ments in Paris and Bonn and to facilitate external relations. At that time the government in Bonn aimed to be reintegrated into the western alli-ances. If these stolen artefacts happened to be stored in an East German museum, the SED government in Berlin did not feel bound to reparation agreements between Bonn and Paris and thus kept them until they were useful blackmail material for political negotiations with France.[25] In 1951, for example, East Germany denied restitution claims from French muse-ums or victims unless museum directors in France agreed to pressure the French government to establish diplomatic ties with East Berlin.[26] By means of the general restitution laws imposed upon them by the Allied

[25] H. Weber, *Die DDR 1945–1990: Oldenbourg-Grundriss der Geschichte*, No. 20 (Oldenburg: Oldenbourg Wissenschaftsverlag, 2011).
[26] Federal Archives Germany, GDR Department for Reparation DC 2, p. 650.

forces, both East and West Germany were under legal obligations to return goods that had been confiscated during Nazi occupation without conditions, but there was no domestic or external supervision of East and West German compliance with that law.

Prior to reunification in 1990, all measures that can be seen as TJ measures in East Germany had been in the hands of the Soviet post-war administration. This administration employed a top-down approach until the end of the communist-socialist era. Among the goods claimed for restitution were many artefacts that were privately owned. Hundreds of pages of lists with names, addresses and the artefacts lost can also be found in the German archives. This testifies to the immense efforts to count and list all stolen property, or at least that which was supposed to be returned. But the most important goods claimed in restitution proceedings were manufacturing machines, horses and agricultural machines that were then located in German industries and in high demand for rebuilding the devastated country. Therefore, many of the claims for the return of machines etc. were dealt with reluctantly because these were also needed to rebuild the country. People and private industries had to give notice if they had any stolen goods, but often ignored this rule. The German railway company, the Reichsbahn, for example, was under an obligation to return trains and wagons they had stolen from France and other countries. The East German Department for Reparation and Restitution Claims tried to settle arguments, paying compensation instead of granting restitution, because it feared that soon the SED regime would be without enough industrial machines to produce and transport goods for its own people. At the same time, the East German government also had to pay large restitution sums to the Soviet Union, payments that constantly weakened East Germany's economic power and eventually led to violent resistance in 1954. West Germany did not have to deal with such extreme pressure, but was nevertheless pressed by the Allies to respond to compensation claims of Holocaust survivors.[27]

To free themselves of the dilemma the restitution claims imposed on them, and to avoid a de-industrialisation of their emerging economies, East and West Germany soon lobbied for 'global restitution' and to close that chapter of the past once and forever. The governments of East and West Germany feared a second 'post-World War trauma', similar to what the Weimar Republic experienced after World War I. This referred to the

---

[27] D. Cohen, 'Transitional Justice in Divided Germany after 1945', pp. 59–88.

Weimar Republic's obligation to pay large sums of reparations to France and the United Kingdom, which eventually also fuelled the Nazi propaganda and led to resentments against the victors of that war, in particular France and the United Kingdom. Thus, bias and an opaque TJ policy contributed at that time to some extent the rise of Hitler's Nazi Party in Germany. Some of these reparation measures from World War I had only been completed in 2014.

In the 1950s, however, the main difference between East and West Germany in terms of restitution had to do with the political regime type and the willingness to truly democratise or not. Many former members of the Nazi Party were still in influential positions in West Germany and many of them remained fanatical about Hitler's Germany, whereas the communist elite in East Germany was mainly opportunistic towards Moscow. In West Germany, Chancellor Konrad Adenauer from the CDU, whose own past was impeccable, believed that the reconstruction of the country would be impossible without enlisting the competent bureaucrats of the Third Reich.[28]

The different political doctrines in East and West Germany also led to different ways of reacting to TJ claims. In 1952, and from one day to the next, the SED regime considered all restitution claims from Germany to be fulfilled and stopped responding to claims from other countries, except to those from the Soviet Union.[29] This was in order to avoid further external pressure and internal turmoil. Thus, for the sake of regime stability, TJ measures of restitution were eliminated and claims ignored. Such decisions cleared a path towards deconsolidation.

Apart from the different paths towards regime change and consolidation, governments on either side of the Iron Curtain shared the burden of the deep legacy of the atrocious and totalitarian regime that lasted until 1945 and the fear of its return. The haunting shadow of Nazi ideology and Nazi elites threatened both regimes, albeit in different ways. The Third Reich left the legacy of massive crimes against humanity based on an anti-democratic ideology, attitude, behaviour, as well as institutions that were never democratically legitimised. Free civil society and voluntary engagement had been absent, killed, exiled or imprisoned. On both sides, this legacy heavily influenced the country's process of regime consolidation, while both countries were forced by their allies to deal with their past for

---

[28] J. Elster, *Closing the Books, Transitional Justice in Historical Perspectives* (Cambridge: Cambridge University Press, 2004), pp. 252–254.

[29] Federal Archives Germany (Budesarchiv), GDR Department for Reparation DC 2, p. 652.

different reasons. In East Germany, the legacy of anti-democratic thinking made it easier for the new elite to establish a new dictatorial regime.
Public accountability of civic participation was restricted.

The Allies made sure that reparation and restitution claims were
also manifested through trials and legal reforms in both East and West
Germany. This served mainly a re-education effect and cleansed future
political institutions of Nazi perpetrators. Systematic vetting and lustration processes, like those used in unified Germany after 1990, were not in
place in the 1950s. Trials were seen as the best way to deal with personal
responsibility for the past.

Thus, it was private initiatives by survivors and intellectuals that
pushed for a TJ process. Survivors of the regime soon started writing and
publishing about their experiences in concentration camps and their suf-
ferings whilst under persecution. Already in 1946, Eugen Kogon, a survivor of a concentration camp, wrote one of the most renowned novels
about the Nazi regime (*Der SS-Staat*) with detailed evidence of how the
regime came into existence, as well as a description of its terror and torture policies. Although neither widely distributed nor popular, such early
testimonials of camp survivors were later used in trials and in school
curricula.[30] Personal narratives and evidence in book form or plays also
served as proxies for non-existing truth commissions. Hans Fallada's 1947
book and later film 'Everyone Dies Alone' (*Jeder Stirbt für sich allein*),
was an early effort to come to terms with the private past of ordinary
citizens, despite censorship from the American allies. The book aimed
to show the dilemma of ordinary citizens who started to followed Hitler
and the Nazi movement, but who later had doubts and showed signs of
disobedience that costs many of them their lives. On both sides of the
country, Germans saw themselves predominantly as victims of the Nazi
regime, instead of as perpetrators or bystanders. Consequently, the first
four to five years of West Germany's democratic experiment and regime
change was a period of economic, personal and political anxiety filled
with a large number of trials against perpetrators and Nazi collaborators
and massive reparation claims both from inside and outside the country. Since democratic transition started in 1949, West Germany's political administrations and institutions were filled with technocrats who had
no reliable experience with democracy and who needed to learn whether
judges would actually apply the rule of law and parliamentarians would

---

[30] H. Glaser, *1945 Beginn einer Zukunft*, pp. 197ff.

adhere to their own consciousness instead of loyalty to a political leader. Consequently, heated parliamentary debates on how to deal with the past commenced. These debates were mainly about whether war criminals should be judged under domestic criminal codes or international customary law (since international human rights law did not exist at that time) and whether there should be an expanded general amnesty for all former officials and military members. Opposition leaders from the Social Democratic Party (*Sozialdemokratische Partei Deutschlands*, SPD), including many of those who had survived concentration camps, raised their voices. SPD leader Kurt Schumacher was one of them. As soon as a parliament had been put into place in 1949, he triggered a debate stressing that 'Hitler's barbarianism' and the Holocaust that murdered over six million Jews dishonoured the whole German nation. He argued that Germans as a society would therefore need to come to terms with their past if they wanted to be seen as a trustworthy nation again.[31] This was an isolated political voice at that time, and led to Tony Judt's later assessment that Schumacher was among the only politicians at that time that could have provided a clear moral compass for Germans. Taking moral responsibility was not common at that time. TJ measures were introduced, if at all, only for tactical and strategic political reasons. The SPD could not compete with Adenauer's conservative CDU, which brought most of the Germans who had been bystanders and former Nazi collaborators under their umbrella. It was simply the majority of Germans at that time. And it was Adenauer himself who explicitly expressed the desire to leave the past behind and to grant clemency to Nazi perpetrators.[32] During parliamentary debates, only a few emphasised the long-term character of the TJ process that was to follow the first trials and reparations. Carlo Schmid, one of the creators of the German constitution, stated during a parliamentary debate that reconciliation with Israel and those 'Jews and other Germans who had been killed, but also those who resisted the regime and often paid for it with their lives, should be addressed in an honorary book of the German nation'.[33] This was an early TJ effort to make Germans understand that individuals made and supported or resisted the Nazi regime and thus taking or acknowledging individual responsibility for the past

[31] D. Dowe (ed.), *Kurt Schumacher und der 'Neubau' der deutschen Sozialdemokratie nach 1945*, No. 13 (Bonn: Friedrich Ebert Foundation, 1996).
[32] T. Judt, *Postwar. A History of Europe Since 1945*, p. 268.
[33] H. Dubiel, *Niemand ist frei von der Geschichte', Die nationalsozialistische Herrschaft in den Debatten des Deutschen Bundestages* (Munich/Vienna: Hanser Verlag, 1999), pp. 44–45.

was closely connected to how they would deal with each other in the present and the future, and consequently the way Germans would make use of democratic institutions. The imaginary honorary book that Schmid called 5 Vor 12 (Five Minutes to Midnight) never came about. There was not enough support either in parliament or in public. It was a metaphor for how Germans should view themselves: a nation that had been violently divided by Hitler and that desperately needed reconciliation. These moral aspects were raised in the early TJ and transition process, but mostly represented the views of elites, of which there were only a few left since most had been killed or had left in exile. Schmid's warning of the return of the Nazi doctrine had little effect and mistrust prevailed among citizens towards and within institutions. Because of this, many victims, such as Holocaust survivors living in the diaspora, had little confidence in their fellow citizens and institutions upon their return to Germany.[34]

Instead, one of the first TJ measures the West German parliament launched independently of Allied supervision was not a punitive one, but an amnesty one. This law granted indemnity from prosecutions (Straffreitheitsgesetz) was passed in December 1949, benefiting 800,000 people. These people would have otherwise been prosecuted under the Allied laws from 1945. This quasi-amnesty law was enacted as a result of pressure by interest groups that represented former Nazi elites, for example those that did not pass the 'denazification procedures' under the Allies (for example, Deutscher Beamtenbund and Vereinigung der Entnazifizierungsgeschädigten e.V.). These groups exerted pressure on the Adenauer government, expressing the belief that the denazification procedures, which were in fact quasi-vetting procedures, went too far by imprisoning those who had only loyally served the regime, without actively participating in war crimes or genocide. These people saw themselves as the 'real' victims of victor's justice and of the denazification process that had been in place since 1945. Generally and depending on how the numbers were counted, 3.5 million people, mostly members of the Nazi Party, benefited from the amnesty law.[35]

Interestingly enough, the West German government passed this quasi-amnesty law only three months after the state had been established, prior to granting any additional reparation, compensation or other legal TJ measures, and granted freedom for all those who had been charged with 'minor'

---

[34] M. Fulbrook, Dissonant Lives. Generations and Violence through the German Dictatorship (Oxford: Oxford University Press, 2011).

[35] D. Cohen, 'Transitional Justice in Divided Germany after 1945', pp. 59–88.

sentences.[36] The de facto amnesty law (*Entnazifizierungsschlussgesetz*), also called the Art. 131 law, allowed all former state officials (mostly technocrats such as lawyers and administrators) who were in office prior to 1945 to return to work in their previous political and state positions. Parliament also passed a guideline to accompany this law that regulated compensation of those state officials who had been expelled or disadvantaged by the Nazis while working for the former German Reich government, regardless of whether they were Jews or not. It was an amnesty law for both those who were expelled from their positions for political reasons and those who were accused of having collaborated with the Nazi regime prior to 1945. This type of clemency law, because it was illustrated as rehabilitation and not amnesty but which was de facto an amnesty law, was interestingly enough used in Spain 30 years later after that country turned to democracy in 1975.

A reason for this amnesty law was articulated already in 1946 by the American Military Commander in Germany, Lucius Clay, who expressed his concern regarding the lack of qualified men in the civil service. Many German civil servants had been called to the front lines of the war and had perished there. The ones who were not called and thus remained in Germany had often been devoted members of the Nazi Party. These civil servants had subsequently been purged from office, imprisoned or tried – but later amnestied under the 1950 laws.[37] Moreover, since there were few highly educated women, there were not enough female judges, lawyers or administrators to replace the previous male bureaucrats who had either died during the war or were removed due to Nazi sympathies. The government was in such great need of technocrats to build up its new democratic institutions that they called for any German citizen from within or outside state boundaries to return to the country to serve as lawyers, doctors and civil servants. Remigration, as it was called, was aimed at those who were formerly expelled from Nazi Germany and now came back mainly from the United States to West Germany. It was an official policy issued by the West Germany governments. Lawyers, political scientists and other skilled technocrats were expected to bring back new democratic ideas that would fuel and inspire the new institutions in the west. Many followed the call, but also some remained abroad. Only a few German Jews heeded the call and returned to Germany, including the lawyer Fritz Bauer, who later

---

[36] Straffreiheitsgesetz, 31 December 1949, BGBl, German Civic Penal Code, p. 37.
[37] T. Judt, *Postwar, A History of Europe Since 1945*, p. 56.

became attorney general of the Federal State of Hesse and conducted the first Auschwitz Trials in Frankfurt in 1963.

The West German government saw no other solution to the lack of trained civil servants than to pass an amnesty law that would allow removed civil servants to regain their positions so that the institutions could start running again. By 1951, after the enactment of the amnesty law, most civil servants were back in office. In Bavaria alone, 94 per cent of the judges and prosecutors were former members of the National Socialist Party as were 77 per cent of the finance ministry employees. The overall majority of Germans supported these measures. Furthermore, in the West German Foreign Ministry, 30 per cent of the officials had been members of the party and almost 60 per cent were former members of the SS, Gestapo or other radical Nazi agencies.[38] It is plausible that such high numbers of previous regime members in the civil service contributed to the widespread reluctance and even fear among citizens and victims to openly address the atrocities of the past. It is certain that the various de facto amnesty laws privileged Nazi Party elites because of the government's urgent need for highly skilled lawyers, business people, physicians and other skilled functionaries. In 1954 another law was passed that had consequences on trials. In the years that followed, fewer than 50 people were tried and brought to justice for mass murder and war crimes. The reluctance of the West German judiciary was so strong that the public hardly took notice of the government's continuing commitment to the Allies' laws to indict those responsible for war crimes.[39]

At the same time, and after some of the initial chapters of 'representative consolidation' by norms and standards were closed,[40] Adenauer's government feared that if West Germany failed to 'reintegrate' former bystanders and low-level perpetrators into the new democratic regime, large parts of the old Nazi elite would not adhere to the new democratic experiment and might even attempt to undermine it. The young regime also had to deal with claims by victims from all sides. Among them were international victims' organisations and foreign governments. The American Jewish Claim Commissions and the German Jewish Council both demanded to be more included in the restitution and compensation

---

[38] Ibid., pp. 57–58.
[39] G. Werle, 'Der Holocaust als Gegenstand der bundesdeutschen Strafjustiz', *Neue Juristische Wochenschrift*, 45(40), 2529–2532.
[40] W. Merkel, Systemtransformation, *Eine Einführung in die Theorie und Empirie der Transformationsforschung*, pp. 118–123.

decision-making processes on laws and practice. In 1955, the German Jewish Council wrote to Adenauer several times, urging him to hear and respond to their claims for compensation and acknowledgement.[41] The government did so reluctantly, while continuing to privilege war veterans and those German refugees who lost all their property in the former eastern territories of the Reich after the war. The political and organised voices of these veterans and refugees were simply louder than those of the Holocaust survivors, of which only a few remained in the country. Victims of the 1936 Nuremberg Racism Laws did not get on the political agenda until later and did not play a significant role as an electorate or political constituency. Moreover, Adenauer saw that social peace and reconciliation depended more on those living in the German territory, meaning war veterans, refugees and those who had the privilege of not having lost lives or property. Plus, victims and survivors who were now residents of other countries than West Germany did not belong to the constituency of the chanchellor and neither to his electorade.

The dilemma of the successful regime change towards democracy centred on how many of the old elites should remain in office or be excluded. Vetting procedures were not sufficiently designed and were applied arbitrarily, as well as being applied differently from one Federal State to another. Nevertheless, due to movies, novels and a growing free media scene in the mid-1950s, a public debate slowly began to arise on questions of individual and collective responsibility, which had some eye-opening effects on many citizens. Adenauer himself avoided direct criticism of the recent German past and of the present problems with democracy. Instead, he often blamed the ineffective pressure put upon Germany in the east by the Soviet Union and the western Allies for West Germany's continuing problems with democracy.[42]

In East Germany, the regime faced the same problems of transition and consolidation as West Germany. Although it did not match with the communist propaganda, former loyal Nazi technocrats and officers were also desperately needed to keep the country running.[43] Thus the SED regime aimed to 'convert' these former Nazis into Communist followers – even though it was only on paper. Around 12 per cent of the new technocratic SED elites were former NSDAP members. 'Reintegration' and de facto amnesty of old Nazi elites and skilled workers in both the communist and

[41] Federal Archives Germany (Bundesarchiv, Koblenz) B-136 Bundeskanzleramt – 1144, no. 183, Zentralrat der Juden, 4 November 1955.
[42] T. Judt, *Postwar, A History of Europe Since 1945*, p. 270.
[43] T. Judt, *Postwar, A History of Europe Since 1945* (New York: The Penguin Press, 2005) Ibid., p. 60.

the democratic West Germany regime were among the most common TJ measures applied in the post-war Germanys. In West Germany the old Nazi elite covered between 20 and 60 per cent of all governmental offices in the new ministries in Bonn. Among the one most influenced was the Foreign Ministry with around 66 per cent of officers with a NSDAP past.[44]

At the same time, citizens of East Germany experienced years of Soviet oppression and arbitrary trials of Nazi perpetrators. The arbitrariness reached a peak with the secretly held Waldheim[45] trials against alleged Nazi perpetrators in 1950. These trials supposedly intended to be the eastern counterpart to the Nuremberg trials in West Germany. By January 1950, over 15,038 remaining war criminals were transferred from Soviet custody to the East German authorities to be tried. Most of those indicted had been in prison since 1945. Some had already been tried under Allied forces and others had never seen an attorney. The list of those who were considered victims was long and often arbitrary. Rumours of victor's justice and arbitrary revenge were widespread. All members of society were affected by these trials: communists who had opposed the Nazis, those who escaped concentration camps, those who fought in the international brigades during the Spanish Civil War, Roma and other ethnic minorities, Jews who survived deportation and extermination and other atrocities. Since many of these people had no documentation that proved that they had been persecuted, enslaved, expelled or expropriated for political or ethnical reasons, proving victimhood was difficult. For those who could prove their status as victims, the state guaranteed compensation and certain privileges.[46] The main purpose of the 1950 Waldheim trials was political. The trials were used to create a myth that all Nazi perpetrators had been convicted and that the country had thus been cleansed of all political evil. That was not the case in reality, but was a myth the government proclaimed. The East German regime's attorneys filed over 100 cases a day and had to try people within a few minutes on evidence that was more than dubious. The result was that of around 3,400 accused perpetrators, approximately 40 per cent were convicted for up to 15 years, whilst the other 60 per cent was either sentenced to death (32 persons), sentenced

---

[44] Martin Sabrow and Christian Mentel (eds.), *Das Auswärtige Amt und seine umstrittene Vergangenheit. Eine deutsche Debatte* (Frankfurt am Main: Fischer, 2014).

[45] H. Wentker, *Justiz in der SBZ/DDR 1945–1953: Transformation und Rolle ihrer zentralen Institutionen*, Veröffentlichungen zur SBZ-/DDR-Forschung im Institut für Zeitgeschichte (Oldenburg: Oldenbourg Wissenschaftsverlag, 2001).

[46] Gesetzblatt der DDR, German Democratic Republic, 18 February 1950, Nr. 14, Opfer des Faschismus.

to life-long detention (146 persons) or up to 25 years imprisonment (2,000 persons).[47] Twenty-five were shot dead in the stand immediately after the 'trial' in which no lawyers were allowed to defend the accused. This is the official historical version of criminal justice in East Germany.[48] Among those put on trial were children who had been imprisoned in 1945 because they had been members of Hitler's youth groups at the age of 14, or civilians such as a young saleswoman who had used old German Nazi newspapers and anti-Soviet propaganda pamphlets in Russian – which she could not read – to wrap food in and was thus accused of anti-Soviet propaganda. She was considered a war criminal because she had insulted Russians when using the pamphlet to wrap meat and vegetables and received over five years in prison.[49] That sort of criminal justice took place in most East German courts, in particular during the Waldheim trials with the desire to demonstrate to the new hegemon in Moscow that East Germany was free of Nazis. These trials did not adhere to the rule of law or principles of justice, as they took place entirely behind closed doors and were reported to be exclusive by nature, only punishing those who could be potential political enemies to the new regime. The only cases dealt with in public were a few in June 1950 in Waldheim for propaganda purposes (although international observers were not allowed, let alone an independent press). The process served to support socialist ideology and to show the SED alliance with Moscow. Thus we see how in East Germany, TJ tools were used to cleanse the new regime of old elites, who were portrayed as a danger to the new regime. Furthermore, these tools were used to show East Germany's pure loyalty to the new occupying,

[47] Federal Archives Germany (Bundesarchiv, Berlin), *Marxism and Leninism*, BA- DY/ 30/ IV2/13–431 and 432. These practices lasted until well into the 1950s and also soon became public. East Germany accused a NSDAP Party member of collaboration even though he was a member of the Socialist Party prior to and after the war and had been detained in Nazi concentration camps until 1945. However, because he had been forced to work as a prison guard in these camps he was seen as guilty. While working in this capacity, he allegedly denounced Soviet prisoners of war who were then tortured and abused by Nazi prison guards. Because he denounced Soviet prisoners of war, he was charged as a war criminal and received a life sentence. Another prisoner received 20 years in prison because he had worked as a soldier in the German military helping to transport machines from the Soviet Union to the German territory; he was charged as a traitor to the Soviet allies. Although many of these charges involved war crimes of some sort, the charges themselves were purely political and arbitrary and meant to intimidate the general public, keeping in mind that most Germans had never experienced a fair trial during their lives.

[48] H. Leide, *NS-Verbrecher und Staatssicherheit*, pp. 39–43.

[49] Federal Archives Germany, *Marxism and Leninism*, BA-DY/30/IV2/13–431.

yet non-democratic powers, the Soviet Union. Many of these trials were against ordinary citizens and those who opposed the newly emerging SED regime. TJ was used to manifest a new regime, through use of terror, fear and suppression.[50] Many of those tried were even former communists or socialists and their only alleged 'war crime' had been that they were against Soviet-style communism. Other prominent war criminals had already been tried in Nuremberg, Poland and elsewhere. Those that were left by 1950 were former Nazi technocrats or prison guards at concentration camps. The higher political elite had been tried or were about to be tried. But what is remarkable for the observation of the spiral effect of TJ on regime consolidation is the fact that these trials were entirely exclusionary and biased.

The standards of evidence and proof relied on protocols and investigations the Soviets had conducted from 1945 to 1949 after occupying East Germany, rather than on original Nazi documents. The 'Waldheim judges' were loyal members of the party, not necessarily lawyers or judges and often without any legal training or experience at all. Many of them had been craftsmen, tailors, salesmen, electricians or mine workers before they were appointed legal officials. International and humanitarian law was unknown to them. The lack of qualified lawyers was due to the fact that trained lawyers at that time had been trained under the Nazis.[51] Lawyers who had been members of the Nazi Party most likely fled to West Germany. Moreover, some communist lawyers had often been persecuted or tortured under the Nazis or not sufficiently trained because communists were denied higher education during the Third Reich. This dilemma led to the fact that hundreds of unqualified lawyers determined the fate of thousands of citizens. This was not a good start for establishing trust in the judiciary and it was uncertain whether citizens would trust such an arbitrary and politically dominated judiciary in the future. While in East Germany many judges were unqualified but loyal to the new regime, those in West Germany were qualified but only loyal to the old regime.[52]

Eventually, in these early years of transition it became clear that due to its ideological authoritarian communist direction, all TJ measures by the East German government would not catalyse independent institutions,

[50]   H. Weber, *Die DDR 1945–1990*.
[51]   H. Wentker, *Justiz in der SBZ/DDR 1945–1953*.
[52]   M. Fulbrook and A. Port (eds.), 'Becoming East German, Socialist Structures and Sensibilities after Hitler', *Publications of the German Studies Association* (New York: Bergham Books, 2013).

let alone democratic ones, but instead serve solely political purposes. The institutions in East Germany were not accountable to citizens, let alone transparent or independent and they denied any citizen participation.

But due to the bad performance of the judiciary in both Germanys, mistrust and a lack of confidence in the new institutions developed quickly on both sides of the Iron Curtain. This was mostly based on the fact that the massive number of trials in East and West Germany were perceived as victor's justice, from which, for example, Soviet or American war criminals were excluded. Whilst there is an estimate that over one million women were raped by Allied military forces on all sides and thousands of alleged war criminals were victims of arbitrary vengeance and 'justice' by Soviet, American, French or British troops, these crimes were never prosecuted or, if so, they were never made public. This hampered the consolidation process because it fuelled the existing mistrust and conspiracy among the new institutions and citizens. Keith Lowe illustrated the massive crimes of vengeance and revenge committed by Allied forces as well as by Germans, Poles, Russians, Dutch, French, Italian, Ukrainians and Czechs after World War II in his bestselling book *Savage Continent*. In the aftermath of the war, the lack of a minimum sense of rule of law cost millions of civilians and prisoners of war their lives even after the end of war had been declared.[53] In fact, the comparison between Nazi cruelties and alleged Allied atrocities was a constant theme in the public debate at that time, as Jon Elster illustrated.[54] Both the Allied command and the German authorities had to react to these often false accusations as well as to downplay German atrocities in comparison to the Allied ones. Therefore, delegitimisation and demystification of the Nazi past and what really happened and who was responsible for it was urgently needed – on all sides. Instead, only a handful of those who took brutal revenge on civilians for the German occupation were ever convicted in public. Therefore, millions of Germans perceived the type of justice brought by the new regimes under the Allied Forces as biased and perpetuating injustice, a perception that Jeff Spinner-Halev and Gibson have also observed in many other twentieth-century TJ processes.[55] The Allied commanders saw it as an urgent matter to install tribunals for German war criminals as

---

[53] K. Lowe, *Savage Continent, Europe in the Aftermath of World War II* (London: Penguin Books, 2013), pp. 75–180.

[54] J. Elster, *Closing the Books*, p. 255.

[55] J. Spinner-Halev, 'From Historical to Enduring Injustice'; and J.L. Gibson, 'The Contribution of Truth to Reconciliation', 409–432.

early as possible to avoid further reduction in trust due to arbitrary acts of revenge against Germans. Otherwise this public perception would have a destabilising effect on the consolidation process.

Yet, the sources of the mistrust were not just the trials in Nuremberg and the lesser-known ones in Waldheim, but also the experience that many citizens had during the Weimar Republic from 1919 to 1933. At that time, democratic institutions had also been in place, but were badly executed, like the electoral system that brought Hitler into power in 1933. Those with the experience of both failed regimes prior to and after 1933 were sceptical towards the Nuremberg trials in the first place and were also hesitant to trust the new democratic regime, since the previous attempt at democracy failed to deliver peace and stability. At first, both sides were under pressure to do better than the previous democratic regime, but failed due to lack of mechanisms to bring civil society stronger into the democratic game, as before. Germans had learned after all that formal democratic institutions did not automatically equate to good democratic practices, the rule of law or justice. Additionally, many citizens were more concerned with safety issues and less with debates regarding democratic culture. They feared that the Soviet-imposed Berlin blockade of 1948 would divide the country even further, which later turned out to be the case. The Cold War showed its ideological face of ugly power games, played out beyond people's real interests and both the urge for regime change and TJ were often used as tools in a game that was merely about power.[56]

Throughout the first decade of regime change, the number of prosecutions of war criminals slowed down dramatically in West Germany, although they were still in the hundreds. First, a statute of limitations and quasi-amnesty laws were passed on lesser crimes in 1950, as mentioned above. But nevertheless around 5,200 persons were still convicted in the following years, the majority of them in local courts.[57] At the same time the West German legislature also wanted to respond to many citizens' demands to 'finally close the files' of the Nazi regime and leave the past behind.

Many parliamentarians in Bonn had already decided to put a full stop to prosecutions (*Schlußpunkt*) since according to them 'enough' Nazi perpetrators had already been convicted and imprisoned. In September 1951,

---

[56] A.J. Merritt and R.L. Merritt, *Public Opinion in Semisovereign Germany*, p. 100.
[57] C. Vollnhals, *Entnazifierung*, p. 62.

Chancellor Adenauer had given a keynote speech in the German parliament in which he recognised the suffering endured by the Jewish and other people and affirmed that Germany would make moral and material reparations.[58] Although the reference to morality was more a rhetorical one at that time, it was at that date that West Germany started to take responsibility for its past as the successor to the Third Reich and introduced an unprecedented TJ process. Reparations (compensation) for individuals who suffered in concentration camps were seen as a novelty at that time, although today they are an expected element of many TJ processes.

In the beginning Chancellor Adenauer was in a constant dilemma and thus issued two parallel policies; one that was inward looking and one that was outward looking. The first one was to satisfy public opinion at home and the other to reintegrate West Germany in the international arena. TJ processes were seen as a tool, or as Pierre Hazan described it, a 'great laboratory' in which actors could experiment with different measures to achieve the anticipated political goals.[59] At the same time as Adenauer's political statement towards the world and his attempts at integration with the western Allies, the West German parliament passed another de facto amnesty law (*Entnazifizierungsschlußgesetz*) permitting the reinstatement of another large group of alleged perpetrators, namely over 39,000 convicted or excluded persons who had been removed from office under denazification proceedings in the 1940s. This way, Adenauer kept the critical voices in the country satisfied while he continued with his two policies of TJ and regime consolidation. And yet the trials also continued, although at a much lower intensity. As indicated earlier, the federal courts tried thousands but only convicted over 600 people in the following years; a number that was much lower than the figures before 1951.[60] Despite the fact that there were fewer alleged perpetrators left, the figures also slowed down due to the lack of political will to prosecute.

The inward-looking TJ policy of the Adenauer administration allowed for the enactment of more quasi or de facto amnesty laws. This was the way parliament responded to public pressure. At that time, almost 25 per cent of the population – one out of four in each family – had either been affected by the denazification and vetting procedures of the Allied forces

---

[58] P. Hazan, *Judging War, Judging History. Behind Truth and Reconciliation* (Stanford, CA: Stanford University Press, 2007), p. 20.

[59] Ibid., p. 21.

[60] D. Cohen, 'Transitional Justice in Divided Germany after 1945', pp. 59–88.

or had suffered personal or professional consequences, such as no longer being allowed to exercise their professions. In particular, it was people with higher education, such as lawyers and elites, who were affected by these vetting and lustration procedures because they had made their career under the Nazi regime and thus many of them remained somewhat loyal or at least indoctrinated by it. At the same time these technocrats were also greatly needed in the newly established institutions and bureaucracy.

Up to 66 per cent of people became affected by these vetting procedures but were also viewed as extremely unfair and as a matter of victor's justice. Even among those who were not subject to these procedures, 33 per cent still perceived them as unfair.[61] The new government and political institutions in Bonn had a legitimacy deficit and felt the need to react. That is why they did so by issuing more amnesty laws. Moreover, the government needed a new strategy, it could no longer only use TJ to delegitimise the Nazi regime, but would have to start using TJ to legitimise the new regime. However, the amnesty law did not much contribute to it. Instead, they meant to silence and appease the society for the moment under the umbrella of 'reintegration' and 'rehabilitation' as the laws were officially titled.

Nevertheless, some cases against perpetrators continued; for example, against those physicians who murdered thousands of prisoners in concentration camps for medical experiments and who then went back to practising in German hospitals after 1945. Those cases often lasted years, starting in the 1950s and ending in the 1960s. This was partly due to a lack of political will, but also to lack of evidence. Many of the atrocities and war crimes had been committed by the Nazi troops in central and eastern Europe and the documents that could prove it were often in the hands of the Soviet government officials who refused to release them to western authorities, due to Cold War power games. Many of the defendants' cases ended in probation due to the fact that the country needed physicians and many judges were thus reluctant to sentence these doctors to prison. There was not only a lack of physicians, but also a permanent shortage of other skilled people, lawyers and technocrats and trying them would have affected the Republic administratively as well as economically; at least,

---

[61] Institute für Demoskopie Allensbach, *Die öffentliche Resonanz der Entnazifizierung. Ergebnisse von Bevölkerungsumfragen. September 1948 und November 1953*. Gesellschaft zum Studium der öffentlichen Meinung (Allensbach: Institute für Demoskopie Allensbach, 1954), pp. 2 and 3.

this was the fear. The result was a dilemma that neither the West German government, the public nor the judiciary could solve. The same was true for the East German administration at that time.

The easiest solution for the West German judiciary was to put these people on probation, in the hope that they would not embrace Nazi ideology and crimes again, but would instead just do their work. What seemed to be most important for the newly established judiciary was the fact that the few cases that did end in imprisonment were reported outside the country and helped external foreign policies, showing that the German government was serious about delegitimising the previous regime and was trying once again to be a reliable partner in the international political arena.[62]

Despite the rather low numbers of convictions and the reinstatement of most former elites and technocrats, the Allied forces supported the reluctant TJ process in the hope that not pushing too hard for trials and convictions would speed up the economic and political development in the country and the subsequent democratisation process. In 1952 an internal US report on the democratic developments inside West Germany stressed that denazification certificates or the 'washing powder certificates' (*Persilscheine*), as they were called, which benefited lower-ranked technocrats most of all, would avoid social instability. Those certificates were seen as a TJ measure to reintegrate or give amnesty to perpetrators, thereby allowing them to participate in the democratic consolidation from which they would otherwise have been excluded. The reinstatement of former Nazis into offices was thought to be less dangerous to stability than a technocratic vacuum or these people retreating underground.

Regime change and democratic transition in West Germany was, in the end, a 'democratic revolution by decree', or an imposed and monitored democratisation process. Germans were told that from 1949 onwards they were to adhere to democratic principles, or else they would never become a sovereign country again. The Allies hoped that with the trials of thousands and the convictions of hundreds, Germans would understand the illegitimate character of the previous regime and thus embrace the new democratic one. Accordingly, it was hoped that in the long term people would change their attitudes and behaviour and become democrats.[63] But without a forward-looking TJ policy that would become impossible.

---

[62] Federal Archives Germany (Bundesarchiv, Koblenz) B-136 Bundeskanzleramt – 1880, cases.
[63] D. Cohen, 'Transitional Justice in Divided Germany after 1945', p. 68.

Therefore, the western Allies, mostly the Americans and the British, pushed for both formal and informal re-education programmes, in which reflection on the past was seen as crucial for people's understanding of the value of democracy. Education camps for young Germans were soon established in the American Allied sector under the name 'German Youth Activities'. These education camps aimed to teach Germans democracy through games, films and comics.[64] The United States also rolled out the Marshall Plan for Europe, which provided Germany and other countries with financial support and created educational programmes for the general public. Some of the short films shown for free at the cinemas were aimed at fostering understanding for the injustice of Germany's anti-democratic past and stressed the importance of democracy in the future. Information on how decisions are made in a democracy, why economic growth is important for stability and how to solve problems in a peaceful manner were the core content of these programmes. It was soon agreed that in order to convince the German population of the benefits of the new political system, Germans must confront their gruesome and undemocratic past and prepare for an alternative democratic future.[65]

East Germany also launched re-educational programmes. Equally propaganda oriented in nature, these programmes aimed to convince the public that the socialist system was better than the 'capitalistic and imperialist' one of the west. It focused more on delegitimising the western concept of living than the Nazi past and was rather an effective tool used on the new generation and to legitimise the new regime as opposed to the west, but not towards the past. What both re-education programmes in West and East Germany in principle shared were the condemnation of Nazi atrocities. Second, they both were committed to a (formally) democratic system. Third, they tried to win legitimacy for the respective new governmental and administrative structures. In East Germany, a communist dictatorship in the name of democracy of the working class was manifested, while in West Germany a liberal but consensus-based democracy developed.

Finally, and after a lot of international pressure, the Luxembourg Accord was signed in 1952. The agreement obliged West Germany to issue official reparations[66] to Israel, where a great number of members of the Jewish

[64] K.H. Jarausch, *Die Umkehr. Die Deutsche Wandlungen 1945–1995* (Munich: DVA, 2004).
[65] T. Judt, *Postwar, A History of Europe Since 1945.*
[66] J. Thompson, *Taking Responsibility for the Past, Reparation and Historical Justice* (Cambridge: Cambridge University Press, 2002).

diaspora sought refuge, as well as to those countries that had suffered great losses under Nazi occupations. The West German government saw this agreement not only as a way to deal with past injustice with monetary or technological compensation measures to the state of Israel, but also as a way to increase the international recognition of West Germany. Adenauer soon understood that Germany's way forward was to seek integration in the west and not as a standalone state, especially after the threat of the Stalin Note in 1952.[67] Partially as a result of this, and partially due to American and Israeli pressure, the West German government labelled the Luxembourg Accord the first Compensation and Reparation Agreement (*Wiedergutmachungsabkommen*). The Luxembourg Accord contained reparation measures for Jewish victims and survivors of Nazi Germany who immigrated to Israel before the end of 1945. This was a novelty in international law, which, at the time, did not provide for such forms of reparations. Nevertheless, the reparations arranged in the Luxembourg Accord should not be seen as an acknowledgement of past injustice or as based on a feeling of moral duty. The agreement in 1952 was the first of many agreements made by the West German government as part of its policy to be accountable for its legal status as successor state to the Third Reich. The reparations were thus a matter of official and formal state accountability and not a move towards reconciliation or apology based on ideals of morality. Moreover, there were no signs at that time of any wider public debate that would have supported apologies or reconciliation based on moral obligations. A public opinion poll conducted in 1952 by the Allensbach Institute confirmed that 44 per cent of West Germans thought that reparations to Israel were redundant and only 11 per cent thought they were justified. Almost half of the West German citizens cared less about the Luxembourg Accord in particular when granting reparation to people who lived outside Germany, than they did about measures for those living in the country.[68] It mirrored the Adenauer administration's consensual efforts at that time in which it tried to balance the interests of the 'victims at home' against those of the Holocaust, who mostly lived outside Germany and had become citizens of other countries – and thus also were no longer an important potential electorate for political parties. Both groups claimed compensation from the government, and most of

---

[67] R. Ludi, *Reparations for Nazi Victims in Postwar Europe* (Cambridge: Cambridge University Press, 2012).

[68] A. Primor and C. von Korff, *An allen sind die Juden und die Radfahrer Schuld* (Munich: Piper Verlag, 2010), p. 109.

them received it. But the focus was internal, due in large part to the influence of former war veterans and refugees who had become members of federal or state parliaments or the judiciary and favoured domestic reparation programmes. Consequently, in the first open vote in parliament regarding the reparations to Israel, only 106 out of 215 members of parliament agreed to payments. They did not understand why West Germany would owe anything to Holocaust survivors, since Germany had already paid for its crimes by losing the war (being liberated was not an alternative slogan at that time), losing half of its territories of the Reich, living in destroyed and damaged cities and by enduring the monetary and judicial consequences that followed. The Luxembourg Accord did not receive a majority in votes and reparations were eventually decided upon by governmental decree because Chancellor Adenauer saw the long-term political benefit of the Accord.[69] For many years to come, the large majority of German citizens and parliamentarians continued to regard themselves first and foremost as misled 'victims' of the Nazi regime, having been seduced by Hitler and his regime. Holocaust and prison camp victims and survivors were seen as a sad and tragic consequence of Hitler and the Nazis' wrongdoings.

Thus, more so than the number of trials, convictions and reparations, the greatest achievement of these TJ activities was the very slow but steady contribution to promoting an understanding of the severity of the atrocities committed by the Nazi regime, and the criminality and thus responsibility this implied. Delegitimisation of the Nazi regime and constitutional consolidation of the new regime was the primary objective of any TJ initiative taken during the first decade. One must bear in mind that there was no blueprint of best or worst TJ cases available and it was not evident at that time how trials, vetting procedures, reparations and the constant reminding by opening old wounds would positively affect the consolidation process in the country. West German TJ policies were not comparable to post-war and regime-building policies anywhere else in the world at that time. This was the first time a successor state to an atrocious regime felt obliged to pay large sums as reparations (*Wiedergutmachung*) to a country that had not even existed at the time that the war crimes were committed. Not surprisingly, the West German government did not get much domestic support for these actions. Nevertheless, as Adenauer

---

[69] P. Steinbach, 'Vergangenheit als Last und Chance: Vergangenheitsbewaeltigung in den 50er Jahren' in J. Weber (ed.), *Die Bundesrepublik wird souveraen 1950–1955* (Munich: BLpB, 1998), p. 348.

had anticipated, West Germany's external relations benefited tremendously from such measures in the long term, which in turn led to more democratisation internally over time, too. Thus, in the first decade after regime change, tactical and strategic reasons for using TJ tools prevailed. And, according to Hazan's observations, even though moral motivations would come later, strategic ones remained present throughout the whole TJ process.[70]

Civil claims for restitution were seen internally as a potential threat to economic growth, the stability of institutions, and to Germany's reputation. There was hardly any citizen pressure for granting restitution until the first trials against individuals responsible for war crimes brought up by the public in Kiel against a former euthanasia doctor in Auschwitz, and in Ulm against ten Gestapo members in 1958. Yet, the new (reformist) German elite knew they had to respond to the international and the growing domestic pressure and the tensions of the Cold War coming from the east. The one was external and came from West European neighbour countries and the United States and the other pressure was domestic and came from the growing civil society and victim organisations. Even though many of the claimants were not a part of the electorate because they lived outside Germany, they played an important role in building democratic institutions.

The sheer number of civil society (victims) groups that lobbied governmental institutions in the 1950s illustrates how many victim organisations the West German government had to pay tribute to.[71] There were those who considered themselves victims of denazification, claiming that they were incorrectly considered Nazis by the Allied forces. Additionally, there were groups with political power, such as the *Bund der Vertriebenen*, an alliance of Germans who had been expelled from Eastern Europe. This

---

[70] P. Hazan, *Judging War, Judging History*, p. 24.
[71] In the 1950s, there was an endless list of self-proclaimed victims, which included 'prisoners of war' (Verband der Kriegsheimkehrer); the group of 'returned POWs' (Verband der Spätheimkehrer); the association of the 'victims of fascism' (Bund der Opfer des Faschismus); the group of those 'persecuted under the NS-Regime' (Verfolgte des NS Regimes); the Federation of Resistance Fighters (Förderation der Widerstandskämpfer); the agency for those 'affected by the 1935 Nuremberg Race Laws' (Zentralverband der durch die Nürnberger Gesetze Betroffenen e.V.); the 'politically persecuted Social Democrats' (Politisch Verfolge Sozialdemokraten); and the association of 'displaced people' with refugee status (Bund der Vertriebenen), to name but a few. The last of these organisations was among the largest and most militant pressure groups of the time and gained significant political influence in the following years.

alliance claimed *inter alia* the 'right to a homeland', and pressured the government to raise the issue of their lost homes with the Allies and the UN.[72] The 'right to a homeland or return' was never recognised as a human right and these individuals never obtained the right to return to their homes in Eastern Europe. Citizen participation in pressing for victim interests was high and democratic institutions had to respond frequently and in a non-biased manner.

As each interest group was recognised as victims, they grew in importance due to their entitlement to financial benefits and other forms of compensation. These benefits or compensations were not necessarily financial or material, because the petitioners claimed lost territory or houses that now were located in Poland, Czechoslovakia or the Soviet Union and could not be returned. Instead, the claimants gained political influence, professional promotions or benefited from other types of affirmative action. Most of the petitioners received refugee status (*Vertriebenenstatus*) and could consequently benefit from informal compensation by receiving state positions in governmental institutions.

Although the general public wanted to forget the past and focus on the future, a significant group of writers and artists, many of whom were either survivors of the oppression and concentration camps or emigrants who had returned to Germany, started to revisit the past in films, books, plays and slowly gained a public voice. Some have been mentioned earlier, but since 1949 widely screened films such as *The Call* (*Der Ruf*) were an example of a voice that indicated that racism and anti-Semitism remained strong in Germany. The film received international awards and was shown at the Cannes film festival. It reflected the hostile and anti-Semitic atmosphere after 1945 that would remain in German society for years to come.[73]

During this first decade of West German regime change and consolidation phase, anti-Semitic graffiti remerged again and was found on newly restored synagogues and memorials, consisting of slogans like 'Juden raus' and 'Heil Hitler'. It became obvious that Nazi ideology and anti-Semitism still existed in many levels of society and would require constant opposition, regardless of the recent establishment of democratic

---

[72] A. Demshuk, *The Lost German East. Forced Migration and the Politics of Memory: 1945–1970* (Cambridge: Cambridge University Press, 2012).

[73] The film is about an emigrated Jewish professor who returns to a German university after the war, willing to help to rebuild the terror-torn German nation but all he receives is resentment, harassment and hostility. He dies after his return due to mental anguish and disappointment at the lack Germans' willingness to change.

institutions and re-education programmes. Such artistic endeavours also showed that anti-Semitism and racism was a problem for society as such and a threat to democratic regime change in particular. Anti-Semitism and pro-Communist slogans were seen as threats from the right and left-wing opposition. The new and obviously still fragile regime in the west had to deal with right-wing and old Nazi elites on the one side, and at the same time with an ever-growing number of radical left-wing actors, many of whom were supported by the East Germany secret service in an attempt to weaken the West German consolidation process. Government records show that many of the members of these pro-Communist groups were young people who once were in Hitler's youth organisations and had now turned to a new anti-democratic ideology, that of communism.[74] Hence, the once radicalised youth continued to be a threat to the regime consolidation.

The establishment of the West German Constitutional Court (*Bundesverfassungsgericht*) in 1949 attested to a willingness to strengthen the rule of law and the Basic Law. Although a similar court had existed under the Weimar Republic, the West German court had a slightly different mandate and played a crucial role in upholding human rights norms and democratic values as guaranteed under the Basic Law. Ruling by constitutionality (*Verfassungsgerichtsbarkeit*) as it has later been described became one of the pillars of German democracy and marked the significant period of 'constitutional and representative consolidation' as phrased by Wolfgang Merkel, and yet slowly moved to one that would determine change in attitude, behaviour and eventually the solid engagement by civil society.[75] Nevertheless, in the beginning, neither the legislative powers, the Federal States, nor the judiciary had significant experience with this new constitutional setup and thus it remained to be seen how this new institution would gain the trust of citizens and aid democratic institution building. Over the years, the Constitutional Court has evolved into a special kind of review organ and is often the last resort in political disputes, including those dealing with the past, its perpetrators and victims. At the same time, legally and in terms of values, in 1950 the proclamation and ratification of the European Convention on Human Rights and Fundamental Freedoms (ECHR) was a milestone in the promotion of human rights

---

[74] Federal Archives Germany (Bundesarchiv, Koblenz), BA-136 Bundeskanzleramt – 1745, 95ff, p. 428.
[75] W. Merkel, Systemtransformation, *Eine Einführung in die Theorie und Empirie der Transformationsforschung*, pp. 110–154.

after World War II in Europe. It is the first legally binding human rights instrument monitored by the ECtHR, to which West Germany was a contracting party since 1959 and which slowly also became a benchmark for new values and norms in German constitutional law.

In order to understand why the majority of West Germans felt that the TJ measures were a form of victor's justice or even punishment, one must consider the context. The majority of West Germans saw the Nazi war crimes as crimes that were committed by individuals – not by the state or society as a whole. Indeed, this individual responsibility was what the Nuremberg trials had aimed to emphasise, for the first time in history. The average German thus did not see themselves responsible and therefore punishable under the law for these crimes. In their view, Nazi perpetrators had nothing to do with the German population as a whole.[76] On the other side, 'Germans in general' were of the opinion that they had already paid as a collective for all the crimes, aggression and atrocities during the war because they had lost territory, property and far too many lives. Thus, why issue any TJ measures in the first place?

This dilemma continues until the present day in the collective memory. On the one hand, the Nuremberg trials are a milestone in the history of international law, as individuals were held responsible for mass crimes for the first time in history.[77] Yet, on the other hand, these trials and the individualistic approach they took led to the impression that the millions of bystanders and silent supporters of Hitler had nothing to do with the Holocaust. The combination of recognising individual responsibility and acknowledging collective responsibility only took place two and three generations after regime change. Meanwhile, West Germans were busy struggling for survival and the unemployment rate was of greater political concern than reckoning with the past. In 1956, more than ten years after the end of World War II, the West German public once again sought a final debate (*Schlußstrichdebatte*), which was only the beginning of many more demands to finally 'forget'.[78]

By that time and due to the increasing hostility and change of political climate worldwide because of the Cold War and the Korean War, the western Allies (in particular the American administration) shifted its focus to the other side of the globe, to where the Cold War had turned fierce once again. Although West Germany was thought strong enough to

---

[76] T. Judt, *Postwar. A History of Europe Since 1945*, p. 54.
[77] R. Teitel, *Globalizing Transitional Justice*, p. 30.
[78] D. Cohen, 'Transitional Justice in Divided Germany after 1945', pp. 59–88.

stand on its own two feet, it was clear that both parties needed each other. The western Allies needed West Germany in order to establish a strong counter-balance in central Europe against the Soviet empire, and West Germany needed the Allies to withstand the threat from the east. The best way to achieve these goals was to create an economically strong and democratic state that was able to defend the western Allies against the Stalinist regime. TJ was seen as one of the many tools to help reach that goal.

At that time, as it would be expected, the communist regimes in Europe, under instructions from the Soviet Union, rejected the informal invitation to join the Council of Europe. Later this had consequences for the TJ process, since the fundamental rights enshrined in the ECHR would come to enter political and institutional practice during the decades to come. The West German Constitutional Court made reference to fundamental rights, albeit reluctantly at first due to inexperience with incorporating international standards into domestic law.

Meanwhile in East Germany, the SED leadership decided on the most appropriate manner to deal with the past without any public input. Citizen or victim participation was not appreciated unless it was organised by the party. Genuinely consulting citizens holding fair and open trials were unheard of. The most important post-war day of memorial in the east occurred on 8 May, commemorating the day the Soviet army liberated Nazi Germany. This TJ measure was organised in a top-down way and consisted of parades and events that reckoned with the past. The new SED regime imitated and perpetuated much of the propaganda that the Nazi regime had employed.[79] The socialist-communist party knew this propaganda had been successful, to some extent at least, under the old regime and used it for their own purposes under the new regime. The SED believed that the manipulation of data, exclusionary TJ processes and constant reminders of how bad the Nazi regime was would work to delegitimise the past regime and legitimise their own.[80]

Other TJ measures were implemented by SED politburo decree. Mass graves were exhumed, memorials at former concentration camps were established and victim groups were classified. Communists who had been prisoners of the Nazi regime were considered the most important

[79]   M. Fulbrook and A. Port (eds.), 'Becoming East German'.
[80]   A. von Saldern, 'Öffentlichkeit in Diktaturen, Zu den Herrschaftspraktiken in Deutschland des 20. Jahrhunderts' in G. Heydemann and H. Oberreuter (eds.), *Diktature in Deutschland – Vergleichsperspektive, Strukturen, Institutionen und Verhaltensweise* (Bonn: Bundeszentrale für Politische Bildung, 2003), pp. 442–475.

if not the only victims. Jews, Sinti and Roma, homosexuals and even social democrats or other ethnical, religious or political minorities that survived the horrors of the concentration camps were hardly mentioned at all. The SED had control over all publications and organised the publishing of communist stories of survival from concentration camps, like Bruno Baum's 'Resistance in Auschwitz' (*Widerstand in Auschwitz*) and Agnes Humbert's 'Soldiers Without Uniforms' (*Soldaten ohne Uniform*). These books were obligatory reading for schoolchildren as they portrayed a realistic but at the same time strictly communist view of Nazi terror. Non-communist friendly stories, for example from Germans who had suffered repression under the Soviet occupation, or faith-based groups that were suppressed by the Nazis, were not published. But stories of those who suffered from American on French acts of vengeance after the war in the west were also not allowed.[81]

Over time, the narratives told in West and East Germany developed in different directions. Within a few years after 1949, two different narratives about the Nazi past came into existence. In East Germany, the government hurried to implement as many top-down and exclusive TJ measures as possible to delegitimise the past and celebrate their victory. In West Germany, TJ measures were mostly implemented under pressure from external powers but a bit more inclusive by nature. West Germany struggled to find a common narrative for the Nazi regime, as is illustrated by the case of the attempted military coup by German officers against Hitler on 20 July 1944. This attempted coup was seen first as betrayal but, since the 1980s, has been viewed as one of the main acts of resistance against the Nazi regime and, much later, this day became a memorial day in West Germany. East German historians did not mention this event at all, because it would show that even members of the Nazi Party opposed Hitler which was not part of the official communist narrative.[82] Citizen participation was initially weak on both sides, but increased significantly in West Germany throughout the 1950s.

As East and West Germany were competing with each other on ideological grounds and had different experiences of the Cold War, each country dealt with the issue of restitution claims differently during the first decade after regime change. The formal and legal foundation of the West German

---

[81] M. Fulbrook and A. Port (eds.), 'Becoming East German'.

[82] German Federal Archive GDR. Executive Board of the Victims of National Socialism (Zentraler Parteivorstand VVD (Verein Verfolgter des Nationalsozialismus) DY 55/V 2 78/1/2).

government's approach was formed by the fundamental freedoms and human rights proclaimed by the international community, such as the UN and the Council of Europe. The east, however, adhered to the Soviet ideology that human rights, as declared in the UDHR, were incompatible with communism. Equality between people was not in the ideological doctrine of the communist states, as it would have meant that landowners had the same rights as workers. Fundamental rights and freedoms, on which the UDHR and the European Convention is based, contradicted communist ideology and, in particular, Soviet political practice.[83] As such, the Soviet Union abstained from voting for the UDHR in 1948 in Paris, as did all of its satellite states. Communist values and norms propagated disparity between the bourgeoisie and proletariat. In their ideological setup there was no norm system to overcome this inequality by peaceful means, only by force and strict laws.

The East German constitution was grounded on Soviet doctrines and proclaimed East Germany as a socialist democratic state in which citizens' rights were paramount. Yet, functional democratic structures that could serve people's post-war claims were not developed and claims could only be submitted directly to the party leadership, which was free to (arbitrarily) decide whether reparation was due. Administrative legislative structures and free elections would have contradicted the major doctrine of the communist regime, the dictatorship of the proletariat. Instead, the party complied with communist ideology, believing that East Germany would reject the anti-fascist and anti-Nazi position and embrace a 'new' dictatorship, now led by the 'working class'.[84]

While East Germany was strengthening its dictatorship, West Germany was struggling with its fragile democratic institutions and the lack of an independent judiciary. Although West German citizens were formally guaranteed the right to file their claims and lobby and participate in the legislative arena, this was far from the case in practice.[85] The majority of the West German electorate consisted of citizens who had not experienced the suffering of the concentration camps (those who had survived had mostly emigrated abroad) but instead represented

[83] A. Mihr, *Amnesty International in der DDR, Menschenrechte im Visier der Stasi* (Berlin: Links Verlag, 2002), pp. 146–160.
[84] M. Fulbrook and A. Port (eds.), 'Becoming East German'.
[85] A. Weinke, 'West Germany: A Case of Transitional Justice, Avant La Lettre?' in N. Wouters (ed.), *Transitional Justice and Memory in Europe (1945–2013)* (Antwerp et al: Intersentia, 2014), pp. 25–61.

refugees to Germany who had suffered severe losses in Eastern Europe. These refugees were the dominant victim groups throughout the 1950s on the political TJ agenda in Bonn and many of their pressure groups claimed the human right to self-determination mentioned in the 1948 UDHR. They interoperated this human right as their right to repatriation to Eastern Europe, in the occupied territories by Soviet powers (nowadays Poland, the Baltic states, the Czech Republic, Slovakia, Hungary, Romania, etc.) which was never granted or taken up at the UN level, because there was no such right for repatriation and thus no realistic chance that six or more million refugees would be able to return to their homes; this could be guaranteed neither by the West German government nor by the Soviets. But the West German government had to react to these claims and did so by establishing a commissioner for reparations (*Beauftragten der Bundesregierung für Wiedergutmachung*), who collected claims on behalf of the refugees. In a second stage, the commissioner collected claims by those who had suffered Nazi crimes and whose property was confiscated before 1945. The West German government also established a Ministry for Displaced Persons and Refugees (*Bundesvertriebenenminister für Flüchtlinge*).[86] It was supposed to be a TJ measure, even if it was strongly abused for political reasons. This was where most former Nazi elites played a role in the new regime and this particular TJ mechanism soon became a political tool in the consolidation process. The assigned Minister for Refugees, Oberländer, was a former high-ranked Nazi Party member and was highly controversial among the political elites. He had to resign from office in the 1960s, at the moment in which the first post-regime change generation came into power and would no longer tolerate high-ranked Nazi Party members in leadership positions.[87]

The government and the international community had to respond to claims from many citizens who perceived themselves as victims of the war. To deal with the millions of German refugees displaced throughout central Europe the UN created the UN High Commissioner of Refugees in 1950. Thus, as part of the TJ process, it was German refugees who were among the first to be acknowledged by Allied powers and the UN as victims of the war, particularly in West Germany. Chancellor Adenauer was under immense pressure to compensate these refugees. He did so by

[86] Federal Archives Germany (Bundesarchiv, Koblenz), B-136 Bundeskanzleramt-4689.
[87] Federal Archives Germany (Bundesarchiv, Koblenz), B-136 Bundeskanzleramt-4699.

positioning them in the abovementioned ministries, before granting any claims for reparations from any other groups or countries.[88]

Victims of the Nazi regime who filed claims from the Netherlands, France or Denmark were dealt with exclusively under the category of reparations, because these were money transfers to a foreign country. Neither Bonn nor East Berlin responded with apologies or acknowledgement based on any moral ground. Nonetheless, starting already in 1949, the World Jewish Congress kept requesting a public and moral apology from the West German government. West Germany denied and so did the East. In 1951, the Israeli government under David Ben-Gurion requested another formal apology, recognising the Holocaust and the reparations to the Israeli state. The latter was later agreed to in the already mentioned Luxembourg Accord, but an apology was not issued.[89] Adenauer feared that if he were to issue an official moral apology, it would lead to protests among his own constituency (and potential electorate), of which the majority were refugees from the former eastern German territories – known for their very conservative approach in dealing with the past. Thus any of these TJ measures was highly politicised from the beginning onwards. Moral aspects played little or no role at all.

The Allied High Commissioner in West Germany, John McCloy, commented several times on the resistance of the German government to apologise for the atrocities of the past, stating that the way the Germans dealt with their past and behaved towards Jewish victims would be a test for consolidation of their democracy. In his eyes, West Germany in the 1950s was far from passing this test.[90] Yet, through rising external pressure in 1952, the mutually reinforcing interaction between institutions and TJ had started to begin. West Germany had made use of a number of TJ measures, including trials, vetting, formal apologies for war crimes, amnesty laws, reparations, compensations, re-education programmes, public debates, culture and (some) memorials. Victim groups slowly started to emerge and faced no major restrictions or limits, although their success depended on how well they were connected to the political regime at that time.

[88] Federal Archives Germany (Bundesarchiv, Koblenz), B-136 Bundeskanzleramt-4698.
[89] P. Steinbach, 'Vergangenheit als Last und Chance: Vergangenheitsbewaeltigung in den 50er Jahren', p. 347.
[90] M.A. Weingardt, *Deutsche Israel- und Nahostpolitik. Die Geschickte einer Gratwanderung seit 1949* (Frankfurt/Munich: Campus Verlag, 2002), p. 74.

Adenauer made concessions and was tactically responsive but not truly apologetic. Safeguarding his government and fostering western integration were his foremost motives.[91] Germany's first formal and public apology to all Jews only took place in 2000 and ten years after reunification, when the federal president of reunified Germany, Johannes Rau, spoke in the Israeli parliament, the Knesset. It was more than an official duty; it also symbolised that a politically and territorially divided Germany had found a way to reconcile itself.

Meanwhile, vetting procedures continued and of the one in ten Germans who had been a member of the Nazi Party NSDAP (*Nationalsozialistische Deutsche Arbeiterpartei*) prior to 1945 (the NSDAP and its sub-organisations had a total of ten million members). As explained earlier, many of them returned to comfortable positions five years after the end of World War II.[92] Any further vetting measures were left in the hands of the Federal States. Each Federal State dealt differently with Nazi perpetrators; some excluded them from higher public office, while others 'reintegrated' them and even gave them political leadership positions. But vetting procedures and reintegration laws varied per Federal State, which often led to incoherent lustration procedures. The Allied High Commissioner, to whom the government and the Federal States were accountable, accepted this compromise and refrained from arguing that the Nuremberg trials had already indicted those who were most responsible for the war crimes of the past.

But the way the government dealt or did not deal with the Nazi past was also a 'thankful tool' for the opposing parties or governments. The instalment of Nazi elites in the West German administrative system was enough reason for the East German government to argue that 'all former Nazis have forever moved to West Germany where they enjoy successful careers and the continuation of their policy.'[93] The 'Bonner Republic', as it was called, named after the interim capital Bonn in West Germany, was seen by the communist regime as a prolongation of the former Nazi regime. The SED was de facto correct because, due to the amnesty laws in West Germany, a large number of members of the Nazi party remained in public positions. However, the SED regime never did allow for any open and self-critical dialogue about its own TJ measures and amnesty laws and instead criticised the west for not sufficiently delegitimising the Nazi

91 Federal Archives Germany (Bundesarchiv, Koblenz) Box number 136–4960.
92 Federal Archives Germany (Bundesarchiv, Koblenz) Box number 136–4960.
93 H. Weber. '*Die DDR 1945–1990*'.

regime. Compensations to war victims, restitution to citizens of former occupied territories in Europe or criminal prosecutions of perpetrators were only useful for strengthening ties to Moscow. In this sense, both East and West Germany used TJ for tactical and strategic reasons to achieve their different political goals, such as the general compensation laws (*Bundesentschädigungsgesetz*) issued since 1953 in the west, which was amended and adjusted several times throughout history.[94]

Reconciliation and TJ in East Germany meant paying large reparations in the form of money and industrial goods to Moscow or other 'communist brother countries'. Although the SED regime granted massive restitution claims of confiscated property in the first years from countries such as France, Belgium and the Netherlands, in their official political doctrines there was no room for TJ measures with Israel. Later they did not respond at all to any of these countries' claims and victims.[95] All efforts by the Jewish Claims Commission or the state of Israel to claim compensation or reparation of around 500 million US dollars failed. In 1952 Moscow issued a doctrine that stated that reunification with West Germany had to be accomplished (of course under sole communist governance) before any claims for restitution from Israel or other Holocaust survivors could be considered.[96] In order to be acknowledged as 'victims of fascism' in the east one had to either be communist or socialist and to have suffered or been tortured under the Nazi regime in concentration camps. Other victims of the Nazi regime, such as religious or ethnic groups that were now citizens of East Germany, were neither considered victims nor received compensation.[97]

In West Germany, compensation to those who survived the Nazi camps was a technocratic response, not a moral one. Moreover, the rehabilitation and compensation of refugees and the 'victims' of the denazification process (those who did not succeed in being cleared of Nazi connections) were clearly prioritised above the rehabilitation and compensation of those who had suffered severe physical and mental injuries, lost lives, family or homes. This unjust prioritisation slowly became unacceptable

---

[94] U. Guckes, 'Opferentschädigung nach zweierlei Mass? Eine vergeichende Untersuchung der gesetzlichen Grundlagen der Entschädigung für das Unrecht der NS-Dikatur und der SED-Dikatur', *Berliner Wissenschaftsverlag*, 33 (2008), 33.

[95] C. Kleßmann, *Die doppelte Staatsgründung, Deutsche Geschichte 1945–1955* (Göttingen: Vandenhoeck and Ruprecht, 1991).

[96] A. Timm, 'Alles umsonst? Verhandlungen zwischen der Claims Conference und der DDR über 'Wiedergutmachung' und Entschädigung', *Hefte zur DDR Geschichte*, 32 (1996).

[97] U. Guckes, 'Opferentschädigung nach zweierlei Mass?', 38–45.

for other victim groups.[98] These groups had grown in number and had become organised around the world. Claim letters arrived from Vienna, New York or Jerusalem.

Despite the many flaws, constitutional and representative democratic regime consolidation slowly came about as the spiral effect slowly showed signs of mutual reinforcement in the mid-1950s. People started trusting institutions once the institutions took their claims seriously, although the procedures were still far from perfect. Newspaper articles in the international press and protest letters from all corners of the world reached the government in Bonn to demand increased acknowledgement of past crimes and of reparations. However, the government denied these claims for the most part, arguing that due to pressure from the Allied forces, it had to make concessions to all sides, to both victims and victimisers alike, and therefore could not address all claims at once.

One of the most prominent and disputed cases of a former Nazi elite in a high governmental position was that of Hans Globke. His rehabilitation and instalment as Adenauer's Secretary of State led to enduring disputes in parliament, among victim groups and civil society, up until the end of the Adenauer era. Globke had never been a NSDAP member but a legal adviser who worked on the drafting of the 1934 Nuremberg Race Laws that led to the persecution and extermination of Jews and other ethnic minorities. This law has since been recognised as the point that marked the beginning of the organised genocide. Those opposing Globke, mainly the SED regime in East Germany, called him a Nazi perpetrator at Adenauer's side. The SED government used Globke's instalment as an example of West German moral corruption and had remarkable success in generating mistrust towards the government in Bonn. In a letter dated from 1949, Adenauer publicly announced that Globke had been officially 'denazified' by Allied US forces after 1945 because Globke had never been a member of the NSDAP – even if he had embraced Nazi ideology.[99] Instead, so Adenauer claimed, Globke had tried to ease the 1934 Race Laws. But that was a common excuse at that time for former Nazi collaborators to explain why they had not openly opposed the regime.[100] This explanation that Adenauer gave in the first generation of regime

[98] Federal Archives Germany (Bundesarchiv, Koblenz), B-136-Bundeskanzleramt-504.
[99] Federal Archives Germany (Bundesarchiv, Koblenz) B-136 Bundeskanzleramt, Adenauer correspondence 14 November 1949.
[100] Federal Archives Germany (Bundesarchiv, Koblenz) B-136 Bundeskanzleramt – 3801, fiche 1, letter 14 November 1949.

consolidation, set a precedent, which many of his successors and governmental officials followed when answering questions from journalists and international organisations about their political affiliations and private life before 1945. If they had been officially denazified by the Allies or had been beneficiaries of the quasi-amnesty laws of 1949 and 1951, they no longer took personal responsibility for the past.[101] In later years however, it became evident that many denazification and vetting certificates issued by the Allies had been granted rather hastily after superficial and subpar investigations. At the time, many of the files on the NSDAP members were held under Soviet surveillance in East Berlin and were therefore neither accessible to the West German government nor to the western Allies. Only decades later would these be made public. Nevertheless, Adenauer made it clear to everyone that integration of those who had gone astray was more important for building a functioning democracy than memory, an apology and justice.[102]

During the first decade of transition and regime change, it was crucial for the credibility of the new regime that all chancellors and government leaders had a visible record of their non-alliance with the Nazi regime. In this way, the past was omnipresent in politics, and so was, albeit indirectly, TJ as well. A chancellor such as Konrad Adenauer, or politicians such as Kurt Schumacher or Willy Brandt were seen as those with the most impeccable record, due to the time they spent in prison camps or in exile. Often, politicians were pressured to prove their resistance against the Nazi regime around times of election. Despite the fact that the majority of the members of government and in parliament could not prove this, the pressure existed, but it was left to the electorate whether they thought it to be a relevant matter for governing the country or not. Overall, this was part of the process of delegitimising the old regime and legitimising the new one.

In West Germany, the Hallstein Doctrine hampered Adenauer's and later chancellors' policies to come to terms with the past. This doctrine held that West Germany would not establish or maintain diplomatic relations with any state that recognised East Germany until Germany was reunified under its former borders. Named after Walter Hallstein, a West German politician and a refugee who escaped communism in East Germany, this doctrine was a strategic compromise with the millions of refugees from the east. But this policy prevented both German states from

---

[101]   Federal Archives Germany (Bundesarchiv, Koblenz) Injustice (B-136 Bundeskanzleramt – 3904, fiche, statement 12 September 1963.
[102]   J. Herf, *Divided Memory*, p. 267.

gaining membership in international organisations such as the UN and hindered any attempts at reconciliation between the two Germanys. It was imposed by the government in Bonn upon all countries that tried to establish diplomatic relations with East Germany and led to a friend-enemy politics that soon influenced all political and administrative policies in Europe. One was either with West or East Germany; diplomatic relations with both was nearly impossible, except for the Allied powers. On both sides of the Iron Curtain, the policy of 'if you're not with us, you're against us' remained in place throughout the majority of the Cold War period. The doctrine was finally abandoned in 1968, thus paving the way towards UN membership for both countries in 1973 for which the official acknowledgement of a two-state solution was a requirement.

In West Germany, it soon became evident that the legacy of the past heavily impacted on the newly formed democracy. The West German Criminal Code contained laws that restricted freedom rights with the excuse that the young democracy had to be 'protected' from its radical enemies, such as communists or Nazis. Citizens did not trust the institutions (enough), and the institutions did yet not trust the citizens to be 'ready for democracy' yet. After some initial euphoria, the consolidation process slowed down whenever these laws hampered a fully fledged TJ and democratisation process. Those who were indicted in Germany for mass murder or crimes against humanity during World War II were convicted under the provisions for murder and mass murder in the German Criminal Code, not according to international criminal law, which did not exist at that time. Thus, some of the sentences for those who had committed massacres during the war were very low. This was in part due to the weakness of the West German judiciary that remained, even though the law was amended several times in the following decade to meet international demands.

The obstacle posed by the many Nazi-trained judges and lawyers remained. These people had worked in high-ranking Nazi courts and were able to impose their own view of the Nazi past on these new laws by means of their judicial decisions. As a consequence, a deviation from the Nuremberg convictions took place in the 1950s. Many of those convicted at Nuremberg appealed to the newly established West German courts after 1949 and had their sentences revised.[103]

---

[103] Yet some only faced charges after 1949 and had not been tried in Nuremberg, either because they had been among the millions in prison camps in the Soviet Union and only

Nevertheless, citizen claims for more TJ measures slowly led to governmental and institutional responses. In 1958 one of the first criminal justice processes under the new criminal code took place in the court in Ulm, in the US occupied zone. The 1958 Ulm trials of former SS members were a milestone of regime consolidation and TJ and had direct spiral consequences on furthering institutional development, leading to the 1958 inauguration of a central office of investigation for Nazi crimes (*Zentrale Stelle der Landesjustizverwaltungen zur Aufklärung nationalsozialistischer Verbrechen*) in Ludwigsburg.[104] Convening these trials was an important TJ step that led to many more indictments, reparation payments, lustrations and other TJ measures. The judiciary realised that without solid facts, data and documentation, any trial or vetting procedure would again trigger emotions, conspiracy theories, acts of vengeance and forms of anti-democratic activities. The Ulm trials dealt with the prosecution of ten alleged members of Nazi Germany's Special Security forces (*Gestapo Einsatztruppe*) who were charged with killing more than 5,500 Jews on one specific occasion in the occupied Baltic territories during World War II. These members had already been indicted in 1953, but the case was suspended due to the lack of political will and the lack of public support at that time. Any conviction of 'good German citizens' – as many of these former high-ranked Nazis were seen – was considered to be counterproductive at that time and silence was preferred. In 1958, the state attorney tried to bring the case a second time, and not surprisingly faced opposition from the public again.[105] But this time the younger and new generation of state attorneys succeeded, due to the fact that the majority of the prosecutors in this case had opposed Hitler, which was unusual at the time. Some of the prosecutors were of Jewish descent and had practised law in Germany before being expelled and returning to Germany after the war and only now started to 'dare prosecution'. This was a window of opportunity that was used to create more trials in the future. However, since the judiciary and law profession was still so heavily populated by judges loyal to the former Nazi regime, by the end of the first decade during regime change only 6,000 of the 100,000 persons who had been indicted on charges of support and collaboration with the Nazi regime were ultimately convicted.[106]

released in the 1950s or because they had successfully hidden or fled prior to 1949 and only returned in the 1950s, if ever.

[104] A. Weinke, 'West Germany: A Case of Transitional Justice', pp. 25–61.
[105] G. Werle, 'Der Holocaust als Gegenstand der bundesdeutschen Strafjustiz', 2529–2530.
[106] N. Frei, *Hitlers Eliten nach 1945* (Munich: Deutscher Taschenbuchverlag, 2003).

The Ulm trials caused a shift not only in German courtrooms, but also in society in general. All those accused were sentenced to between five and 15 years imprisonment. The proceedings were surprisingly well received by many policy makers at that time and triggered an urgently needed debate concerning the German judiciary and its understanding of collective guilt and responsibility. It seemed that at this time, 15 years after the war had ended, there was a critical mass in society to accept a debate about responsibility. Until the trials in Ulm, most accused perpetrators saw themselves merely as bystanders or subordinates of the system, but not as individually responsible perpetrators. That blame was always placed on Hitler, Heydrich or Himmler and all the others 'heavy weights' that had already died or been sentenced in Nuremberg. However, the time was right for a debate about who among the so-called ordinary citizens, soldiers and officers of the armed forces had been a perpetrator, collaborator or otherwise responsible. Opening the scope for potential war criminals led to many more trials and convictions in subsequent years. This acceptance of individual responsibility for the atrocities of the Nazi regime also had to do to with the growing level of trust in the new judiciary.[107] Even with many Nazi judges still in office, the foundation of a new constitution and newly appointed impartial, 20+ generation judges meant that the judiciary was becoming trustworthy. In addition to this, people started to bring cases without fear, once they saw that neither the accuser nor the accused would suffer heavy reprisals. Still, many, if not millions of victims never did file suit because they could not emotionally bear confronting those who had persecuted them and who were now living better lives than the victims. The trials that did follow resulted in realising the original aim of TJ measures, the symbolic attribution of responsibility showing that the new democratic regime would deal with criminals in adherence with the rule of law and human rights. Consequently, public debate about these trials triggered many of the subsequent proceedings, including the Auschwitz prosecutions in Frankfurt in 1963, almost two decades after the Holocaust ended.

In the east, the SED government stopped any possibility of citizen-driven TJ by decree. The SED declared all restitution claims closed as of 1952 and refused to respond to any further claims, for example to those from Israel. There was no change in attitude or behaviour on the institutional side. Trials that did not serve the purpose of stabilising the

---

[107] D. Cohen, 'Transitional Justice in Divided Germany after 1945', pp. 59–88.

communist regime were non-existent. Instead, propaganda, official commemoration days and biased memorials replaced public debate. Mass ceremony and public parades to commemorate communist victims of the
Nazi regime were used by the leadership as the main TJ measure to deal
with past.

During this time, the economic development and growth in West
Germany allowed the government to respond more positively to claims
for financial compensation. Chancellor Adenauer knew that reparations
to those who suffered from Nazi occupation was the price Germany had
to pay for integrating into western alliances and pacts such as NATO, thus
guaranteeing West Germany's stability and security during the Cold War
period. Despite not always having public support on his side, Adenauer
saw this integration as guaranteeing the best possible protection for
Germany in the event of military action between the Soviet Union and
the United States. Since West Germany still did not have any manner of
defence, it was highly vulnerable to the Cold War powers and Adenauer
knew that if it came to war between the United States and the Soviet
Union, West Germany would be in a very insecure position. This choice
for integration was thus a strategic choice for security, and so it was for TJ.

Another factor that also impacted the slow take-off of the spiral effect
to democratic regime consolidation in West Germany during the first
decade of transition was the fact that many democratic-minded elites
were still in exile or had been killed during the war. Therefore, a new
democratic elite had to be constituted; a process that needed time. This
had a significant impact on the political culture of the country, which was
often dominated by those who had no or little experience with pluralistic
thinking and respect for others.

In a similar vein, the neo-Nazi graffiti (such as the Nazi Swastika) that
began to appear frequently at the time the Ulm trials took place also
expressed dissatisfaction with the new democratic system. Some citizens
continued to be true believers in the *Führer cult*, while others believed
that a 'tame dictatorship' (*gemäßigte Diktatur*) would be better for West
Germany than a fully consolidated liberal democracy. They feared that a
democracy based on pure human rights principles, such as freedom of
expression and participation, would only lead to chaos and disorder, and
that the country was not ready for fully fledged democracy.[108] This showed

---

[108] Federal Archives Germany (Bundesarchiv, Koblenz) BA-136 Bundeskanzleramt – 1745,
p. 161.

that those generations who had grown up knowing only the methods of a dictatorship lacked experience with democratic institutions and with the benefits a pluralistic and free society can offer everyone. Again, time was needed for citizens to become acquainted with chaotic parliamentary debates, differences of opinion and having multiple political parties to choose from.

Many believed that absolute freedom of expression was the main threat to the fragile West German democracy. This led later to the compromise position of 'militant democracy' (*wehrhafte Demokratie*), which entailed limiting basic freedoms, such as the right to expression, by forbidding Nazi or communist discourse and symbols in public and political parties that was sympathetic to the Nazi ideology in order to defend democracy.[109] Legislative powers passed laws that allowed charges to be brought against those who made anti-Semitic statements, with sentences of up to two years in prison.[110] Trials were held against those who violated victim memorials, Jewish cemeteries and synagogues.[111] This concept of militant democracy has since been adopted by other post-conflict, emergent democracies, such as Rwanda in 1994.

Attorney Fritz Bauer tried to counteract these fears of democracy, drawing a more realistic picture of what really happened in the past. Instead, he heavily criticised the West German government for the amnesty laws it passed in 1949 and the years following, because these laws were, in his eyes, the real threat to regime consolidation. Bauer often wrote about his concerns that the early release of Nazi criminals would endanger the fragile democratic institutions. Because of these statements, former Nazis and members of the SS often threatened his life. In an article published as early as 1952, he wrote that the German military officers, such as Graf Stauffenberg, who had been convicted by Nazi courts after an unsuccessful coup attempt against Hitler on 20 July 1944, were still considered traitors of the German Reich (*Landesverräter*). Although public opinion and the urge for commemoration of Hitler's opponents had risen by 1970, it was almost absent in the 1950s. In 1951, 30 per cent of the population thought that those who

---

[109] N. Frei (ed.), *Transnationale Vergangenheitspolitik. Der Umgang mit deutschen Kriegsverbrechern in Europa nach dem Zweiten Weltkrieg* (Göttingen: Wallstein Verlag, 2002).

[110] Federal Archives Germany (Bundesarchiv, Koblenz) BA-136 Bundeskanzleramt – 1745, pp. 172–186.

[111] Federal Archives Germany (Bundesarchiv, Koblenz) B-136 Bundeskanzleramt -4404.

attempted the coup of 20 July were rightfully executed, although the majority did not have a strong opinion about it. Only in 1970 did those who approved of the execution drop to 7 per cent, whereas the group of people who had always believed that it was unlawful rose to 40 per cent. This was due in part to the fact that fewer people remembered the controversies around these trials in 1944, and more wanted to forget all about it.[112] It was only towards the end of the first decade and when the regime slowly consolidated that a critical mass of younger citizens arose that wanted to put an end to the black-and-white picture of Germans being the bad perpetrators while everyone else in Europe identified him or herself with the idea of a liberator.

Despite these developments in later years people like Fritz Bauer were still considered a threat to the country's old and powerful political elites and he received many threats since he entered office in 1956. Then, in 1968, Bauer was found dead in his bathtub. Some conspiracy theorists claimed that the mysterious exiled organisation of SS officers executed him for his efforts to come to terms with Germany's Nazi and SS past. Many Jewish victims' organisations and survivors believed that former SS officers acting in secret killed him and many others during these times. Despite this unresolved case, similar acts of alleged revenge by former Nazi elites had happened throughout the first decades of transition and transformation and were a sign of mistrust and lack of confidence in political institutions.

Bauer was one of the very few promoters of legal reforms and restitution claims in the 1950s. Furthermore, intellectuals, academics and philosophers such as Theodor W. Adorno and Max Horckheimer who spoke and published to a rather small community, but eventually expanded their reach in the 1960s, also sided with Bauer. The majority of intellectuals who asked for more TJ were often of Jewish or socialist background and had suffered oppression under the Nazis and were thus deeply concerned about the continuation of anti-democratic thinking in the new republic. It was their own past experience that fuelled their plea for more restitution measures, trials and other TJ processes. The writer Bertold Brecht advised the same in East Germany prior to his death in 1956. Nevertheless, those who spoke out and asked for more trials and public acknowledgement did often suffer anonymous death threats and intimidation from private persons.

---

[112] Institute für Demoskopie Allensbach, *Der 20 Juli 1944. Ergebnisse einer Bevölkerungs-Umfrage über das Attentat auf Hitler* (Allensbach am Bodensee: Institute für Demoskopie Allensbach, 1970), p. 2.

Obviously, taking individual responsibility for the past was painful. Many preferred to see themselves as victims of the Nazi regime instead of taking collective or individual responsibility for the past and for their role as bystanders and victimisers. This was equally the case on both sides of the Iron Curtain. In East Germany, many remained ignorant of the atrocities and crimes committed by Germans against Jews and other minorities. Anti-Semitism continued to exist in Eastern Europe, too.[113] It became clear that there was very little reason to believe that the new political communist elite would do better at implementing the rule of law than the Nazi regime had. By the end of the decade, dictatorship had been reinstalled, albeit in red instead of brown. The political elite in East Germany was once again cleansed of its Jewish population, and old stereotypes and anti-Semitic tendencies were not dealt with in a self-reflective manner. Although the SED regime did not instrumentalise Jewish stereotypes for its own agenda, even Jewish communists did not stand a serious chance of having worthwhile careers under the regime.

After the dramatic reappearance of anti-Semitism in West Germany, the Allies and federal agencies continued their efforts to 're-educate' Germany. This method was called 'grassroots democracy' (*Basisdemokratie*) and included revision of textbooks, publishing of photographic records and tours of the infamous death camps in addition to the ongoing criminal prosecution of perpetrators.[114] At the same time, the media played an important role in civic participation by raising awareness and presenting a different perspective of the past. One of the major daily newspapers, the *Süddeutsche Zeitung*, placed a uniquely polemic article in 1958 entitled 'The Murderers Are Still Among Us' (*Noch sind Mörder unter uns*), noting the fact that the amnesty laws passed between 1949 and 1951 had allowed war criminals to continue to reside in German society and have a significant negative effect on the development of democracy in the country.[115] The SED regime in East Germany made a successful cinema movie with

---

[113] One example is the trial of the Jewish communist leader Slánský in Czechoslovakia in 1952. He was sentenced to death, together with other Jewish communist leaders, as a result of party rivalry. The motivations for this were purely anti-Semitic and affected East Germany as well, where Jewish and loyal communist party leaders who had already suffered in Nazi concentration camps were requested to suddenly leave office. O. Groehler, 'Der Holocaust in der Geschichtsschreibung der DDR', in B. Moltmann, Bernhard et al. (eds.), *Erinnerung, Zur Gegenwart des Holocaust in Deutschland West und Deutschland Ost* (Frankfurt am Main: Arnoldsheimer Texte, Haag und Herchen Verlag, 1993), pp. 47–63.

[114] A.J. Merritt and R.L. Merritt, *Public Opinion in Semisovereign Germany*, pp. 7–9.

[115] *Süddeutsche Zeitung*, 11 July 1958.

the same title for their anti-west propaganda, illustrating that the old elites were still in power in West Germany, in both business and in politics.

After a decade of experience with new regimes, victim groups of all backgrounds started to organise themselves more systematically and began to bring claims. In 1959, for example, victims of the racist Nuremburg laws (1936) formed a central agency for those affected by these laws (*Zentralverband der durch die Nürnberger Gesetze Betroffenen*). After being officially recognised as a victim group, they protested loudly in 1959 after a synagogue in Cologne was severely damaged by Nazi sympathisers. Their voices were heard and large public and political protests occurred.[116] By then it became clear that immediate negative repercussions against these victim groups was no longer opportune. This also marked a shift towards regime consolidation by using TJ measures to acknowledge these victims as rightful citizens of society and to delegitimise the Nazi regime. Although the public fear and mistrust slowly began to vanish, the presence of anti-Semitic discourse remained for a long time. In 1959, the American Jewish Committee, of which many members were former Holocaust survivors, wrote to Adenauer asking him to address their annual congress in Washington DC on the issue of whether anti-Semitic tendencies would endanger democratic development in Germany. Adenauer responded with a keynote address emphasising that there was no danger of massive anti-Semitism in Germany and that there was no threat to democracy. According to Adenauer, the majority of Germans would not and could not embrace anti-Semitism and the atrocious Nazi past had been overcome. He argued that the reported incidents of anti-Semitic slogans and violent acts were simply remnants of a number of individual opinions.[117] He was not naive when making these statements, but reflected on the majority of Germans who, despite the far too many incidents of anti-Semitism, did not want to return to the old Nazi regime.

But despite Adenauer's efforts to persuade the international community that there was no threat from West Germany towards the world, it was not long before international support and protests began to pressure the government and local authorities to do more about this remaining anti-Semitism. In response to it, the parliament in Bonn amended Section 130 of the West German Criminal Code on 'sedition' and hate speech

---

[116] B-136, Bundeskanzleramt – 1745, pp. 70ff.

[117] Federal Archives Germany (Bundesarchiv, Koblenz) B-136 Bundeskanzleramt – 5864, Grusswort des Herrn Bundeskanzler fier das American Jewish Committee 21 October 1959.

(*Volksverhetzung*). This was an attempt to suppress anti-constitutional parties and aimed to prohibit extreme right-wing neo-Nazi parties as well as left-wing communist parties.[118] Today, it is often referred to as the Law on Holocaust Denial and is found in the current German Criminal Code. This law places limits on the freedom of expression of those who deny that the Holocaust ever happened and on those who attempt to justify the Holocaust. This was a concrete way the West German government could mitigate the fear of those abroad that anti-Semitic sentiments were experiencing a revival in Germany. Decades later, international human rights organisations such as Human Rights Watch criticised the law for restricting the freedom of expression and thus weakening democracy. A prohibition on Holocaust denial entered into international law in the twenty-first century and was adopted by most European states in 2005, after a resolution by the European Parliament.

Section 130 underwent several revisions over the decades and today's provision on Holocaust denial allows for the prosecution of those who used hate speech to defame other groups. Some German analysts argued that the restriction of freedom of expression was a sign of weak and fearful or 'tamed' democracy at that time. The majority of Members of Parliament always justified the restriction of freedom of speech and assembly in relation to activities, publications or films that glorified the Holocaust and neo-Nazism. As early as 1952, the Socialist Reich Party (*Sozialistische Reichspartei*), a successor to the NSDAP, and the Communist Party of West Germany (*Kommunistische Partei Deutschlands, KPD*) were forbidden on the basis of similar restrictive laws and the threat they were seen to pose to democracy. This illustrates that the young democracy had to learn to handle radical views that were part of the legacy of dictatorship. Whether the means used by the legislative powers were always democratic is debatable. Thus, restrictive laws as well as amnesty laws were a steady companion of TJ measures and institution building at that time.

But debates in the West German parliament on how to deal with the political legacy of the Third Reich continued. On the radical right, the German Reich Party (*Deutsche Reichspartei*), established in 1950, was a fusion of a number of right-wing and nationalist parties that did not receive many votes in the first West German elections. The party leadership was composed of former high-ranking NSDAP officials who wanted

[118] J.S. Brady, B. Crawford and S.E. Wiliarty, *The Postwar Transformation of Germany, Democracy, Prosperity and Nationhood* (Ann Arbor, MI: University of Michigan Press, 2002), p. 42.

to reinstall the former German Reich and its nationalist policies and strictly opposed any TJ process in the country. Their supporters were former Nazis and many were refugees from former German territories in the east. There were several attempts to exclude the party from parliament through legal measures between 1953 and 1964, but they failed, because the party was not entirely unconstitutional. Instead the National German Party (*Deutsch Nationalistische Partei*) attracted more votes with a less radical party programme. Keeping this political party, with obvious Nazi sympathisers, in the minority position in parliament was a tactical decision. The party's small number of seats in parliament did not pose a threat to democratic decision making and yet made those 'old Nazis' visible and in this way publicly controllable. The worst that could have happened was to force them to go underground and continue to commit acts of revenge and other serious threats to society. There were never any attempts to include the party in governmental coalitions, but their radical views held power over a significant number of voters. Because even though many Germans did not agree with the way victor's justice was imposed, they did not support nationalist parties either. But this was not due to the instalment of TJ measures; it was due to the fact that the majority of Germans could not 'forgive' Hitler and his Nazis for seducing them into war. Hazan has argued that although many Germans did not become fully fledged democrats overnight, the national catharsis of the past had sufficient effect in the first decade after regime change to prevent a massive return to authoritarian rule.[119]

Slowly, the use of TJ measures, however reluctantly, led to dramatic increases in political engagement and demands for more human rights in West Germany.[120] Moreover, the fact that the two Germanys competed with each other during the post-war decades in terms of legitimacy unexpectedly fostered the development of democracy and human rights in West Germany. The West German government exerted tireless efforts to be the 'better democratic regime'; a regime that was more democratic, freer and more economically successful than its communist 'brother' in the east. This competition, as well as international pressure, forced both governments to undertake substantial efforts to limit the influence of previous political elites on regime development. At the same time, the political alliances and loyalties towards the occupying powers (the United

---

[119] P. Hazan, 'Measuring the Impact of Punishment and Forgiveness, 19–47.
[120] L. Wildenthal, *The Language of Human Rights in West Germany* (Philadelphia, PA: University of Pennsylvania Press, 2012).

States and the Soviet Union) dominated the TJ process. As a consequence there were 'formal democracies' based on democratic constitutions on either side of the Iron Curtain's 'cold front', but one turned to become more paternalistic and authoritarian in the east and the other one became slowly more liberal.[121]

In East Germany, the main narrative was told from the perspective of the communist resistance movement and its victims. In West Germany, most conservative political actors identified with those who had fled from former eastern territories that were now under Soviet occupation or part of the Soviet Union. These competing narratives also provided the soil for political activism to grow during the first 15 years after the war ended. During this first decade after regime change, historians from East and West Germany only agreed on one fact: the Nazis were the main perpetrators. The rest was still up for debate. It was not until the 1960s and 1970s that the narratives about the past on either side of the Iron Curtain began to change, when the first generation of citizens born 20-plus years after the war started to raise their voices.

Second Decade: 1960–1969

After a decade of dramatic political and legal reforms, change, heated debates and diametrical transitions, the Eichmann trial in Jerusalem in 1961 marked the beginning of a new era of consolidation. West Germany began to deal with its past differently and Chancellor Adenauer saw the need for wider public debate. The change in attitude and political agenda setting among political and civil society actors became evident during this decade. By its end of this decade, the West German constitutional and representative consolidation stage would shift dramatically to one that also complied more with democratic principles albeit with all actors and institutions in society still struggling to fully adhere to it.[122] But throughout the second decade anti-democratic sentiments and unconsolidated pockets of violence were still widespread.

Parallel to a major shift in TJ policies in West Germany and the trial in Jerusalem, the East German government decided to build a wall and fence between East and West, which divided both states and marked the dramatic cessation of any democratisation efforts in the east. Many of

---

[121] R. von Weizäcker, *Drei Mal Stunde Null?*
[122] W. Merkel, Systemtransformation, *Eine Einführung in die Theorie und Empirie der Transf ormationsforschung*, p. 124

those who struggled to cross the Iron Curtain to the west paid for it with their lives. Yet, as Mary Fulbrook has described in her analysis of the two Germanys at that time, it was this decade that was the beginning of the 'normalisation' of the political regimes in East and West Germany – the one becoming more dictatorial and the other one more democratic.[123]

The Auschwitz trials began in Frankfurt in 1963 and lasted, with some interludes, until 1968. Although the German High Court had already ruled in 1959 that individuals should be tried for the crimes of murder they had committed before 1945, the statute of limitations in the German Criminal Code continued to pose a difficult hurdle to further prosecution.[124] However, it had been 20+ years since the end of World War II and there was now a new politically mature generation and enough critical public mass that would be able to face more openly the darkest part of German history. This second post-war decade is the period that Gabriel Almond and Sidney Verba would have looked at to test whether a political and civic culture had developed. It did. Moreover, the number of public cultural events, novels, films and debates about the war grew exponentially in this period. At the same time, the question about civic trust in the institutions was raised.[125]

Investigations into Nazi perpetrators had been going on since the late 1950s, mainly on the initiative of Attorney General Fritz Bauer. He tried to indict many of the leading officers who had served in the concentration camps of Auschwitz and who had, under the new regime in West Germany, turned into 'ordinary' and well-respected businessmen, pharmacists or physicians. Many de facto amnesty laws also provided much protection. These men and some women never left Germany and feared no indictment; never thinking that they would be held to account for the crimes they committed or were responsible for. Most Germans at that time were still convinced that the Nuremberg trials had dealt with the past in legal terms once and for all.

Therefore, the series of Auschwitz trials that started in Frankfurt in December 1963 must be seen in the context of the constant (international) pressure from survivors and victims as well as the West German government's desire to become a fully fledged respected member of the international community and more so of the UN. Last but not least, the time was ripe for these trials because a new generation of post-war Germans,

---

[123] M. Fulbrook and A. Port (eds.), *Becoming East German.*
[124] A. Weinke, 'West Germany: A Case of Transitional Justice, pp. 25–61.
[125] G.A. Almond and S. Verba, *The Civic Culture.*

as well as the many victims who had been politically active such as Bauer, Eugon Kogon, Karl Jaspers, and Kurt Schumacher had tirelessly appealed to the German conscience to see the benefit in dealing with the past as a way to also legitimate the new regime. The trials ended with the symbolic convictions of over 20 persons, as a sign of the harm individuals can do, and the responsibility they have. This symbol was directed not only at victims but also at many perpetrators who at that time were still in hiding, had disappeared or had never been caught.[126] Second, the trials had an educational aspect. They showed that the West German rule of law regime was strong enough (or rather ready enough) to deal with the worst atrocities in a way that did not threaten democracy. Despite the many shortcomings of post-war judiciary and its failure to sufficiently indict Nazi perpetrators, what also become an issue in the Frankfurt Auschwitz trials was the question of why these atrocities had been committed and why previous generations had contributed to the Nazi regime, either actively or as bystanders.[127] This was the moment in which dealing with the past shifted from merely a tactical and strategic choice to a moral one.

The Eichmann trial in Jerusalem[128] and the subsequent trials in Frankfurt were broadcast on German television, radio and covered in other media. Although television was still rare in ordinary households, most people were aware of the trials. The trials and later judgments gradually counteracted the policy of clemency, not just in West Germany but also throughout Europe. The moral and legal failings, both of the accused and the judiciary, came to light. Social elites from the realms of business, politics and culture showed remorse, many for the first time. Until this time, the Adenauer administration had used reparations to deal with issues of TJ as part of its foreign relations and integration policy. The administration had not yet taken an inward-looking approach and only a few had made the connection between TJ and the quality of democracy. Opinion polls in 1960 indicated that more than 80 per cent of Germans did not think much about the wrongdoing during World War II or the Nazi regime in their daily lives. That changed a bit with the Auschwitz trials, but the other major concern among people was future orientated. They did care about issues such as that of reunification, economic development and the threat

[126] D.O. Pendas, *The Frankfurt Auschwitz Trial, 1963–1965.*
[127] N. Frei (ed.), *Transnationale Vergangenheitspolitik*, p. 22.
[128] I will not go into detail about its contentious jurisdictional aspects, as others have written about this extensively. See for example: H. Arendt, *Eichmann in Jerusalem: A Report on the Banality of Evil* (New York: Penguin Books, 2006).

the Cold War posed. Problems of anti-Semitism or prosecutions of Nazi perpetrators were not among the day-to-day concerns.[129] However, after 1963 a place like 'Auschwitz' was no longer taboo and the term 'concentration camp' became synonymous with all places of Nazi terror. Hence, here too we see how a TJ measure, namely trials, catalysed a debate about a past that had been almost forgotten. As Bauer would have argued, this debate was important for the strengthening of democracy because it delegitimised the past and legitimised the new regime and its consolidation efforts.[130]

At the time of the trials in Jerusalem and Frankfurt, East Berlin felt under pressure and thus decided it needed its own Auschwitz trial. In response to what happened in the court rooms in Frankfurt in 1966, the SED politburo held a public show trial in East Berlin against a former Auschwitz SS physician Horst Fischer and sentenced him to death. He had been untouched until then, because the SED regime needed his skills and he turned out to be loyal to the communist regime. The main purpose of this trial was to send a strong signal to the world (not to its own citizens) that the SED regime was also willing to deal with the past for the sake of international recognition. Equally to Adenauer, the SED politburo was hoping for international recognition and subsequent UN membership.

Following these trials, a number of memorials were put in place in both East and West Germany, such as at camps in Bergen-Belsen (West), Dachau (West) or Buchenwald (East). The former Dachau concentration camp in Bavaria, for example, was inaugurated as a memorial only in 1965, based on the initiative of survivors. Although the Federal States usually supported these initiatives, local citizens did not always welcome such a memorial in their neighbourhood. Now that the crimes in concentration camps were named and categorised, thanks to the trials, such memorials reached a different acceptance among the general public because they were evidence of the past and used by the government to delegitimise the Nazi regime. Research and investigation into the past started to emerge slowly, in academia, but also in families and neighbourhoods. Nevertheless, in the West most memorials were established only at the initiative of survivors and victims and not state institutions, only later receiving governmental support and funding for

---

[129] Institute für Demoskopie Allensbach, *Das Einstellung in aussenpolitischen Fragen. Ergebnisse repräsentativer Bevölkerungsumfragen des Instituts für Demoskopie, 1957–1960* (Allensbach am Bodensee: Institute für Demoskopie Allensbach, 1960).
[130] A. Weinke, 'West Germany: A Case of Transitional Justice, pp. 25–61.

maintenance. From the beginning on, the government did not own the TJ process; also, it was eager to control it both in the East and the West. Because unlike the case in dictatorial East Germany, memorials in West Germany were not created through a top-down approach, but almost exclusively bottom-up with later financial embracement by governments of the Federal States.

During the Frankfurt trials, citizen awareness and engagement became stronger and, not surprisingly, the government in Bonn reacted to it. The parliament passed a resolution urging all foreign countries that had evidence of Nazi atrocities to pass the documentation to the Ministry of Justice. The minister issued the office of the attorney general, Bauer, to facilitate bringing more charges against perpetrators in the future. The dam had broken and hundreds of claims swamped the offices of the attorney general and the government in the following years. As a consequence, in 1965 a range of documents, including witness reports and other evidence of war crimes, was sent to the Attorney General's office and West German authorities from around the world. Documents that proved Nazi crimes came from the former occupied territories and beyond such as France, Belgium, Denmark, Yugoslavia, Greece, Luxembourg, the Netherlands, Norway, Austria, Poland, Czechoslovakia, the Soviet Union, the United States and Israel. The data provided insight into places where Jews, members of other minorities and political dissidents had been tortured and exterminated.[131] Some countries such as Italy, Romania and Hungary did not respond to the official request from Bonn due to their own involvement in war crimes or because their governments held them back for political reasons. The SED regime sent hardly any documentation to West Germany. This was not because East Berlin had no proof of Nazi crimes; in fact all main former Nazi ministries had been located in the then-occupied Soviet Sector in Berlin and thus most evidence about the details of mass murder and genocide was bunkered in archives in East Berlin or Moscow.[132] Rather, it was because the East German authorities were waiting for the 'right' moment when they could use these documents to discredit West Germany. Any moral obligation to hand over evidence about the fate of millions of murdered people was absent. For the dictatorial regime in the East, TJ measures were thankful tools to play out any political game that was possible at that time.

---

[131] Federal Archives Germany (Bundesarchiv, Koblenz) B-136 Bundeskanzleramt-3173, note from 22 October 1965.
[132] D. Cohen, 'Transitional Justice in Divided Germany after 1945', pp. 59–88.

In 1966 and 1967 West Germany moved from the conservative Christian party to a coalition with the SPD. Interestingly enough, this was a coalition in which a former NSDAP member Kurt Kiesinger (as chancellor) and CDU and the former Nazi dissident and emigrant, Willy Brandt (as vice-chancellor), SPD, led the government from 1966 until 1969. In a way, this team was symbolic for the transition that had finally taken place. But for many, the transition was too slow and it was unbearable to see a former NSDAP member as chancellor. Student protests increased, and in 1968 Beate Klarsfeld, a French-German citizen who had dedicated her life to exposing Nazi perpetrators, slapped acting Chancellor Kiesinger in the face during a CDU party congress, screaming 'Nazi, get out of office!' (*Nazi, tritt zurück!*). Her action was highly controversial at the time, but made it into the international press and later in the history books because of its symbolic relevance for the changing attitudes among the new generation of post-war Germans.[133]

During these years of a political shift in government, the shift in TJ policies also took place. International cooperation in hunting Nazi criminals increased and the support from citizens in West Germany to deal with the past grew slowly. When the Nazi archives in East Berlin were finally opened in 1990 and more evidence came to light, many of the victimisers had already died and could no longer be tried. And it was not just East Germany that held back information for political reasons. West Germany also failed to hand over evidence to East Germany and Moscow, if trials against Nazi perpetrators were held in satellite states controlled by the Soviet Union. Only in the 1990s, after German reunification, did the United States and Soviet Union authorities also hand over some of the remaining documents and evidence to the German government.

Yet, in the mid and late 1960s the rise in free and voluntary citizen involvement in this period was fundamental for regime consolidation. One of the reasons for this rise was the insufficient way their governments had dealt with the past in previous years. Although it was still disputed whether West Germany should adopt laws to allow the prosecution of people for crimes against humanity (they never were), the Frankfurt Auschwitz trials showed the political and social necessity of holding perpetrators accountable. The attention given to the Auschwitz trials showed the willingness of citizens to learn more about what happened under Nazi rule. Additionally, these trials tested the independence of the judiciary.

---

[133]   A. Weinke, 'West Germany: A Case of Transitional Justice', p. 47.

The trials are seen as a turning point in the development of the German judiciary and democracy, because they triggered a number of debates in the parliament in Bonn between lawyers and the public. The wider public recalled earlier writings by the German philosopher Karl Jaspers from 1946 on what he had called the necessary debate on 'German collective guilt' and how this guilt impacted the legitimacy and behaviour of the post-war democratic institutions and the judiciary.[134] At the time Jaspers wrote about guilt and legitimacy, it did not receive much attention, but his work was republished in the 1960s, and received a large readership among the new generation.

The debate about responsibility, not only of the state towards victims, but also of citizens themselves, finally began in the 1960s and has continued ever since. This debate was reflected in the highly disputed book by Alexander and Margarethe Mitscherlich, *Impossibility to Mourn* (*Unfähigkeit zu Trauern*) in 1967, which illustrated the dilemma that many Germans still felt at that time over whether to reject personal ties to and responsibility for the atrocities altogether, or instead leave it to governmental institutions to deal with the claims. This difficulty in accepting collective responsibility was, in part, the result of trials, which by their very nature focus on individual and not collective responsibility. The new generation had to 'learn' and understand collective responsibility.

The Auschwitz trials of 1963 were only the first in a series of trials that prosecuted individuals who had been directly involved in the murders. One of the trials that followed the Frankfurt Auschwitz trials was the Treblinka trial, held at the District Court in Düsseldorf between 1964 and 1970. Eleven highly ranked SS officers were convicted and over 100 witnesses were heard. As a result, the general public came to realise the full extent of the crimes that had been perpetrated in occupied Poland. In the subsequent years, separate trials dealt with personnel from other concentration and extermination camps, including a trial between 1963 and 1965 on the camp in Bełżec, one in 1966 on the camp in Sobibor and later, from 1975 to 1981, a trial on the camp in Majdanek. These trials were more than just a means of convicting old and presumably no longer dangerous former prison guards; they were used by the wider public, the media and politicians to promote certain political agendas and standards for Germany's political doctrines on domestic and international politics.

---

[134] K. Jaspers, *Die Schuldfrage, Für Völkermord gibt es keine Verjährung* (Munich: Piper Verlag, 1979).

Their main purpose was to legitimise and consolidate the new regime and show that a new and matured judiciary in West Germany followed the rule of law, which was a constitutional one.

And by 1965, 20 years after the war had ended and the time that the first post-war generation came onto the stage. Some of them radicalised in a right or left-wing direction that was often connected to the way the West German authorities dealt with the past. The media covered all the trials connected to the Nazi past, and these measures also entered into the cultural spheres of theatre, novels and cinema.[135] Victim organisations and NGOs claimed their space. The Council of Protestant Churches in Germany, for example, one of the largest religious communities in the country, sent a letter to Adenauer in 1964, addressing both him and the German public with a statement on the importance of the Auschwitz trials for German democracy. According to the Council, the trials were the only way, besides other punitive measures, to get Germans to acknowledge, reconcile themselves with and recover from the past. After all, the Nazi terror had destroyed the solidarity and common ties among the people, which was only slowly restored.[136] As Almond and Verba have repetitively emphasised in their assessment about the importance of political culture, these trials would not only affect legal regime consolidation that made them a turning point in German history, but also demonstrate how political and civic actors dealt with individual responsibility and brought perpetrators to justice.

With these citizen-driven trials taking off, another landmark stage of consolidation had been passed, which was indicated by the fact that all 'sub regimes', such as civil society, judiciary or media, within the regime were interacting and confronting a painful past without major censorship – albeit it still existed due to the restrictive laws that the West German parliament had passed earlier. But more and more, political parties, civil society and interest groups, political and societal elites, and the judiciary were all engaged in dealing with the past and citizens' attitudes, opinions and behaviour were shaped by a respect for minorities that legitimised the new regime.[137] The important role of diverse, diffuse and independent citizen groups and cultural activities, as highlighted by Merkel and Hans-Jürgen Puhle, can be seen during this period. The spiral effect of

---

[135] A. Weinke, 'West Germany: A Case of Transitional Justice', pp. 25–61.
[136] Federal Archives Germany (Bundesarchiv, Koblenz) B-136 Bundeskanzleramt – 4917, Der Rat der Evangelishend Kirch in Deutschland, 15 March 1964.
[137] W. Merkel and H.-J. Puhle, *Von der Diktatur zur Demokratie*, p. 138.

mutually interacting institutions, measures and actors continued slowly in an upward direction.

Further delegitimisation through public media and cultural events of the Nazi regime was taking place at full speed. In October 1965, Peter Weiss' theatrical play *The Inquiry* (*Die Ermittlung*), which covered the controversies of the Auschwitz trials, became a success in East and West German theatres and somewhat surprisingly was performed widely on both sides of the Iron Curtain.[138] And towards the end of the first round of Auschwitz trials in 1965, the West German parliament launched a debate about amending the statute of limitations (*Verjährung*) for murder and the 1953 compensation laws.[139] These laws had already been amended in 1956 and 1960 in order to prosecute remaining perpetrators of war crimes and compensate victims of the Holocaust. The government had been responsive to requests in this regard, but no large-scale trials had been started, except in Ulm. Nevertheless, in 1965 the statute of limitations for murder was extended again after great public attention and pressure.[140] It was not the last extension. Because of this, a new dimension of this debate was addressed by delegates from a younger generation who argued that prosecuting war crimes and mass murder would strengthen the rule of law in Germany, and thus also citizens' trust in the judiciary. Furthermore, it would increase Germany's credibility elsewhere in the world, which was a strong argument even for conservative minds.

Interestingly enough, references to international human rights norms, such as the UDHR and the ECHR, were used in parliamentary debates and among legal circles. The ECHR was one of the few international human rights documents with legal character in Germany at that time, a fact that convinced many lawyers of its utility. It encouraged national courts to prosecute individuals regardless of statutes of limitations, including the atrocities of the Nazi regimes.[141] Thus, the legal practice needed to reflect these provisions and abolish sooner or later the limitation of the law that allowed prosecuting mass murder. But in order to do that, one had to publicly recognise that the massacres happened during World War II qualified as such crimes.

---

[138] Bundeszentrale für Politische Bildung (ed.), *Auschwitz auf der Bühne. Peter Weiss: Die Ermittlung, in Ost und West* (Bonn: Bundeszentrale für Politische Bildung, 2008).

[139] U. Guckes, 'Opferentschädigung nach zweierlei Maß?', 36–37.

[140] *Der Spiegel*, NS-Verbrechen, Verjährung, Gesundes Volksempfinden, No. 11, Hamburg 1965, pp. 30–44.

[141] H. Dubiel, *Niemand ist frei von der Geschichte*, pp. 109–110.

Dealing with right-wing radicals continued throughout the second post-war decade and beyond. This fight had kept the government busy during the first decade, and now since the mid-1960s on top of that, leftist radicalisation began to emerge among the younger generation. One thing both left and right-wing groups had in common was their belief that the Nazi past had been dealt with in an inappropriate way. The Socialist German Student Union (*Sozialistische Deutsche Studentenbund*), which existed as early as 1946, started to remobilise and became more radical in the 1960s, with some financial and logistic support from East Germany. One of the Socialist German Student Union's grounds for mobilisation and radicalisation was the presence of a number of former Nazi bureaucrats still holding power in high administrative positions in Bonn and in the judiciary despite the many trials. The group feared these and other former Nazis would lead to the 'renazification' of Germany, unless they were purged. After not getting sufficient response from government for their claims, they radicalised. It was this radicalisation that was a response to the many undealt pockets of Germany's Nazi past and the response to the de facto amnesty laws from 1950 onwards.[142] Once the left-wing groups radicalised against the Nazis, there was automatically a movement on the right-wing side, vigorously defending the myth that Germans were the first and real victims of Hitler Germany.

The SPD distanced itself from the left-wing radical students' movement, which went on to become even more radical and violent in its claims and later actions. The movement turned into a leading radical leftist opposition group, calling itself the Extra-Parliamentary Opposition (*Außerparlamentarische Opposition, APO*), because they felt that the presence of former Nazi members in parliament prevented the legislative branch from responding sufficiently to their claims. The democratic system in West Germany was, in their view, not democratic at all, but far too infiltrated with Nazis and their legacy. Some members of the radical movements later supported terror attacks against politicians and economic elites. In this way, an unconsolidated pocket of democracy emerged in West Germany: the left-wing terror groups, who with their terror acts submerged and weakened the consolidation process. They were formed by radical claims and fears of Nazi infiltration and re-emergence of a new totalitarian Nazi state. One branch emerged later into the terror

---

[142]   V. Knigge and N. Frei (eds.), *Verbrechen erinnern, Die Auseinandersetzung mit Holocaust und Völkermord* (Bonn: Bundeszentrale für Politische Bildung, 2005), pp. 362–370.

group called the Red Army Faction (RAF). Its members, among them not but a few intellectuals, were held responsible for various killings of the political and economic elite in Germany until the 1970s and became West Germany's major unconsolidated pocket since the war. The West German parliament responded by limiting certain human rights in order to combat these groups. Parliament restricted freedom of expression and association and labour rights for those who were allegedly members or supporters of mainly left-wing radical groups. These acts led to a parliamentarian justification for the restriction of fundamental rights and to the concept of 'militant democracy' (wehrhafte Demokratie). Freedom of expression, movements and work were limited and the government claimed that with this response it was 'militant' enough to combat terrorism. Interestingly enough, this concept had initially been created to defend the fragile German democracy against former Nazis and their resurgence in the 1950s, but was much more forcefully applied against the left-wing radical groups.

Meanwhile, West Germany strengthened its ties with the Allies. The Élysée Treaty between France and West Germany in 1963 institutionalised regular meetings between the Ministries of Foreign Affairs, Defence and Education, which led to a number of reconciliation programmes for both countries' future generations. This is an example of using TJ in the foreign policy arena. In the years that followed, many more activities in the area of TJ were initiated, mainly targeting the youth and young elite to rebuild mutual trust on all levels among Germany's neighbouring and once-occupied countries. Restoring trust between Paris and Bonn was the main motivation behind these measures. But remorse and a sense of moral duty grew slowly among the two countries. It was only in 1988 that a Franco-German Council took place that established regular meetings and consultations.

In addition to left-wing radicalisation, right-wing parties continued to pose a threat to democratic development as well. The West German parliament asked the Minister of the Interior to list all movements, groups or NGOs that could qualify as 'right wing' in order to have an overview of citizen movements that could threaten the stability of the still-fragile democracy. Such citizen movements had been a topic of parliamentary debate as early as 1961 and the lawmakers wished to know which NGOs could be a serious threat to democracy and how to pass new regulations condemning right-wing initiatives.[143]

---

[143] Federal Archives Germany, Koblenz, B-136 Bundeskanzleramt-4404, note 13 February 1964.

Despite these motivations, the fact that more sympathisers with the Nazi regime than with leftist movements were in positions of power, meant that restrictions were applied more often to left-wing movements than right-wing ones. Not surprisingly, by 1967 67 per cent of Germans again asked for a *Schlußtrich* and sought to leave the Nazi past behind and in 1968 the West German parliament passed emergency laws (*Notstandsgesetze*) that limited the fundamental freedoms of members of communist, socialist or other radical left-wing groups. Such laws were never passed for Nazi supporters. Instead these laws led to a number of imprisonments of left-wing public protesters.[144]

At the same time as these shifts and debates in West Germany society, Germans who lived abroad continued to face hostility in the host countries. These political and social hostilities were often based on the host countries such as the Netherlands, France or Belgium's inability to come to terms with its own past and involvement in war crimes or inhumane behaviour during World War II. Instead, whenever anti-Semitism arose in France, Belgium, the Netherlands or Switzerland, locals were convinced that it 'had to be the Germans' who had done it. There was a strong sense in these countries that only Germans could be anti-Semitic and violate human rights. This led to an atmosphere that even impacted business, foreign policy and political ties between Germany and its European partners. West German ambassadors abroad were alert to these anti-German sentiments and many of them reported back to the West German Foreign Ministry that many European countries saw Germans as easy scapegoats that impacted all aspects of transnational relationships. In their view, this was because the French, Dutch or Belgians themselves were even more reluctant than the Germans to come to terms with their Nazi past as collaborators, and as such with their own history of anti-Semitism.[145]

In response to this trend, the West German Foreign Ministry wrote a 20-page document explaining what German embassies and consulates should do to respond to anti-German propaganda. It mainly urged the embassies to better explain and illustrate how West Germany had developed itself since 1945 and the efforts that had been undertaken to deal with its past. At the same time, with the support of the Marshall Fund, the West German government tried to encourage more democratic awareness programmes within its own country. This constituted the West

---

[144] H. Dubiel, *Niemand ist frei von der Geschichte*, pp. 50–95.
[145] Federal Archives Germany, Koblenz, BA-136 Bundeskanzleramt – 1745.

German two-part regime consolidation strategy at that time; one part was directed at Germany's external relations and the other was inward looking. The main concern at that time was that the democratic achievements of post-war Germany were not sufficiently understood both outside and inside the country and hence some extra efforts needed to be undertaken.[146]

Meanwhile, in East Berlin the SED regime's democratic shortcomings in not allowing free elections, controlling business and preventing free public participation and civil society were directly linked to its one-party dictatorial structure. The second decade would show whether the seeds planted in 1949 would slowly grow to become effective. On both sides of the Iron Curtain consolidation continued in a different direction in East Berlin and the government tightened control over its citizens after the building of the Wall in 1961. The SED regime failed to acknowledge the shortcomings of a one-party 'democracy' in terms of pluralism, transparency or accountability but firmly believed it would succeed, even though many citizens had already fled to West Germany for economic and political reasons. By 1961 around three million East Germans, 15 per cent of the population, had already fled. The SED government reacted swiftly to this mass migration by building the Wall in East Berlin in August 1961, which marked the end of any democratic attempts in East Germany, because it de facto 'imprisoned' its own citizens. From then on, surveillance, suppression and restrictions were a daily practice. It was impossible for citizens to reflect self-critically on their past, which was particularly troubling since a new post-war generation had emerged in East Germany as well, asking their parents' generation 'what did you do during the war?' But no public debate was allowed that went beyond the official doctrine that Nazis were evil and communists good.

With the Wall in place, the SED regime dramatically lost legitimacy. In order to hold power, the SED regime had to 'imprison' its people behind a 1,400 km-long fence in order to stabilise the regime. The Iron Curtain was drawn immediately and the division between the two Germanys was complete, at least for the time being.[147]

Consequently TJ priorities shifted as the Cold War reached new heights and a new generation entered the political arena. The focus turned from representative and institutional consolidation to a more value-orientated and attitudinal one in which people needed to adhere to common

---

[146] Federal Archives Germany, Koblenz, BA-136 Bundeskanzleramt – 4369, fiche 5.
[147] M. Fulbrook and A. Port (eds.), 'Becoming East German'.

principles and believe in the democratic regime and not just to follow its new rules. In West Germany, this meant a shift from legal obligations to more rule-of-law practice by conviction, while in East Germany party doctrine played a larger role than ever and democratic principles became irrelevant. Although the pursuit for moral responsibility towards the past slowly arose because, for the post-war generation, an ethical and moral approach to the past was the only option, on both sides, the only place where people could express their moral concerns freely about the past was in West Germany. The 'social capital', the basis for civic trust based on reciprocity and civil engagement, as Robert Putnam phrased it, developed mainly in the west of Germany.[148]

It was still the case under the chancellorship of Adenauer, which lasted until 1963, during which he commissioned a study on whether European countries would once again be able to trust West German democracy. Moreover, this study investigated to what extent a shift had taken place in how history was taught in the German education system. The study focused on the extent to which former Nazi officials had been reintegrated into official positions without being vetted. The cases of former Nazi officers and bureaucrats such as Hans Globke, Theodor Oberländer and Gerhard Schröder were well known abroad and raised questions.[149] The trust, or lack therefore, that other countries had in West Germany was a serious matter that impacted Germany's aim to fully integrate into international organisations, such as the UN and Council of Europe. As mentioned above, because of this in 1960 the diplomatic service and the Ministry of Foreign Affairs urged its government to take the initiative, because the reputation of Germans and Germany continued to be very negative abroad. There was a lack of trust in German institutions due to the fact that people such as Globke and Oberländer were highly ranked officials in executive offices. And this distrust would not only affect politics but also business, so they feared. Adenauer kept responding by claiming that it was necessary to increase foreign awareness programmes highlighting the achievements of German democracy since 1949.[150]

Indeed and despite all efforts, it took decades before the rest of Europe started to come to terms with its own anti-Semitic and fascist past, and

---

[148] R.D. Putnam, *Making Democracy Work*, p. 167.
[149] Federal Archives Germany (Bundesarchiv, Koblenz) BA-136 Bundeskanzleramt – 1745, pp. 277–280.
[150] Federal Archives Germany (Bundesarchiv, Koblenz), BA-136 Bundeskanzeleramt – 4369, Auswärtiges Amt, pp. 4–5.

consequently made its peace with Germany. For the time being, it was convenient to place the blame on Germans for more than just a generation after the war. The constant blame also led to another negative effect, namely the cultivation of collective guilt among German citizens. Interestingly enough, this feeling of guilt was particularly strong among those who were born after the war. In particular the younger generation started to believe that they and their parents' generations were the only ones who were responsible for the persecutions and atrocities during World War II and that subsequently Germans and Germany would need to take all the blame for the war and the crimes committed. But this was not what the philosopher Karl Jaspers had meant with his definition of 'guilt' (Die Schuldfrage) in 1946. He even denied the possibility of collective German guilt, arguing that because there is no collective morality there cannot be collective guilt. Guilt can only be individual and depends on the intentions of the perpetrator and individual responsibility as defined by means of trials. Thus what he had asked for in 1946 was bottom-up initiated trials against perpetrators as they eventually took place in Ulm in 1958 and in Frankfurt in 1963, but not collective guilt. Jaspers had been one of the most enthusiastic and optimistic observers of the Nuremberg trials in 1945 and 1946 when he published his book. It was the first intellectual reflection on the Holocaust and Nazi terror. He emphasised that Germans had to become aware of the fact that they all shared and carried individual guilt, if they had not opposed the regime, albeit to very different extents: some had moral guilt, while others had criminal guilt.[151] However, despite the author's attempts not to be misinterpreted, the idea of collective German guilt had already taken hold in the collective consciousness and resulted soon in the concept of 'German guilt', which remained a solid paraphrase for decades.[152] This collective guilt positioned others as collective beneficiaries of this guilt. It also filtered through, for example, into the official German state doctrine to have specific state and thus collective responsibilities towards the state of Israel, for example.

More than 20 years after the transition, societal perceptions had changed and what Adenauer had officially called 'Allied loyalty' was seen now as treason to many Germans who suffered from the catharsis of the war. As Wolfgang Zapf and Dankwart Rustow have noted, it was at this

---

[151] K. Jaspers, Die Schuldfrage, Von der Politischen Hoffnung Deutschlands (Munich: Piper Verlag, 1946).

[152] D. Cohen, 'Transitional Justice in Divided Germany after 1945', pp. 59–88.

time, thanks to a new generation, that rules (such as the constitutions of 1949) and practices (such as trials and TJ measures in the 1950s) became habitualised in citizen and elite norms, indicating that the regime had been consolidated.[153] The trials, memorials and public dialogues in the 1960s was evidence of this development. Rustow has always argued that one generation is the minimum period necessary for transition to take place,[154] a position supported by observations made by Merkel, Puhle, Almond, Verba, Juan Linz and Alfred Stepan. But this generation needs to be educated in this post-authoritarian and pro-democratic spirit, otherwise it won't take ownership of democratic values. We can see an example of how the new post-war generation contributes to regime con-solidation in the public reaction to anti-Semitic acts in the 1960s. It was not only government authorities that reacted but also thousands of citi-zens who gathered on the streets of West Berlin, Bonn and Freiburg to protest against re-emerging anti-Semitism throughout the 1960s and this growing civil society marked a turning point in West German political culture. Political education started to receive more public funds and pub-lic exhibitions as part of TJ policies on 'coming to terms with the past' (*Vergangenheitsbewältigung*) were state-sponsored. Under the slogan 'unatoned Nazi justice' (*ungesühnte Nazijustiz*) many were finally able to debate who was held responsible for the atrocities. The media reported this widely.[155] This was the decade when the media became heavily involved in TJ. *Der Spiegel*, one of the main West German political maga-zines, came to see it as its responsibility to initiate debates about World War II every so often, and has done so until the present day.

Manfred Kirchheimer, a Jewish-German constitutional lawyer who had immigrated to the United States in 1937 and who retained great influence in the legal discourse in Germany, published in 1961 a major work (first in English and later in German) on political justice in Germany. He high-lighted that throughout history, victor's justice is often political justice. Kirchheimer argued that this was the case for the Nuremberg trials as well. He saw the trials as an effort by the Allied powers to legitimise their power and their occupation of defeated Germany, without paying much attention to the legitimisation of the new German institutions. Nevertheless, he also emphasised that the trials had a strong preventive character too as they aimed to avoid future atrocities and war crimes and made people aware

---

[153] W. Zapf, 'Mondernisierungstheorien in der Transformationsforschung', p. 177.
[154] D.A. Rustow, 'Transition to Democracy: Toward a Dynamic Model', p. 347.
[155] *Der Tagesspiegel*, 4 March 1960.

that whoever commits such crimes will not remain unpunished.[156] His works were heavily cited in the 1960s and are considered to be one of the first in-depth analyses of the impact that TJ measures can have in a postwar or conflict-ridden society in positive or negative ways. He was part of what was called the Frankfurter School, a group of left-wing intellectuals and professors, formerly based at the University of Frankfurt, a university that employed many intellectuals and professors that had emigrated to the United States after 1933 and later returned to Germany. After returning to the University of Frankfurt in 1950, members of the Frankfurter School such as Theodor Adorno, Max Horckheimer and their scholars such as Jürgen Habermas (a member of the new post-war generation) analysed the impact the Nazi legacy of terror and the Holocaust had on societal behaviour and democratisation in West Germany. Their interest was in how TJ legitimised the new regime. One of their main arguments was that the Nazi regime had eliminated the role of the individual subject in society. Both victims and perpetrators were turned into objects and willing bystanders that served a higher purpose, which eventually led to one of the worst mass killings and atrocities in human history. Individual trials and responsibility, and thus accountability, could nevertheless break that vicious circle of mistrust and vengeance. This anti-democratic mentality had to be overcome by the new democratic practice. With their publications and radio broadcasts, the members of the School greatly influenced the (left-wing) student movements and protests against the conservative politics of the 1960s.

But Karl Jaspers continued to express his great concern and disappointment about the slow democratic developments in post-war Germany when he republished his book in 1962. He confessed that he had hoped that the Nuremberg trials would educate the Germans and strengthen their trust in the rule of law and democracy, but this had not happened. In his view, this failure was due to the fact that the Allied judges, while following correct legal procedures, missed the opportunity to issue justice on all sides. As Gibson has explained, such failures to issue justice arise frequently in TJ processes around the world. In Jaspers' assessment, the Nuremburg trials were a window of opportunity for increasing trust in the rule of law and democracy, since it was the time when the national catharsis and anxiety among Germans was

---

[156] O. Kirchheimer, *Politische Justiz, Verwendung juristischer Verfahrensmöglichkeiten zu politischen Zwecken* (Frankfurt am Main: Europäische Verlagsgesellschaft, 1981), pp. 473ff.

higher than it had ever been before or would be thereafter. Unfortunately, Jaspers claimed, this window of opportunity had been squandered. He argued in line with what Keith Lowe has called 'missed opportunities'.[157] It was a mistake not to charge those in the Allied forces who committed acts of revenge against Germans. Even though the quantity and consequences of Allied crimes were not equal in the magnitude to those of the Nazis, they were war crimes that deserved punishment. If the Allies had tried all war criminals equally, regardless of their country or army of origin, it would have set a strong moral precedent and re-established Germans' trust in law and justice.[158] The failure of the Allies to do so meant that an opportunity was missed to use the trials to legitimise the new rule-of-law abiding regime.

Hence, 20 years after the trials, Jaspers believed that the biased character of the Nuremberg trials was one of the root causes of the lack of trust in the judiciary. The reality was that for reasons of 'peaceful reintegration' and due to the de facto amnesty laws from 1950 onwards, far too many Nazi sympathisers were still holding high positions in West Germany. An official open-ended vetting or lustration policy did not exist at this time and there was never a systematic screening of ministers or other public servants to see whether and to what extent they had been involved in war crimes or other atrocities of the past. Yet, an indirect vetting procedure was conducted through the propagandist politics of East Germany. One of the most prominent examples is the Minister for Refugees and Displaced People, Theodor Oberländer (mentioned earlier), who had taken his office as a form of 'compensation' and appeasement towards former powerful Nazi members. He was known to the Allies and was often controversial. Although Oberländer had been involved in mass executions of Jewish civilians during the war, he nevertheless remained a West German minister for over ten years. In 1960 the SED regime in East Berlin conducted a show trial against Oberländer (in his absence) and convicted him to death (in East Germany the death penalty was still used). Although the evidence against him was dubious, since the documents remained only in the hands of the SED politburo, the trial resulted in a push from the West German public for holding Oberländer to account. The public pressure was so strong that he resigned from office. Thus, even in the absence of an official West German vetting procedure, this East Berlin show trial led to Oberländer's resignation, which showed the power public pressure started

---

[157] K. Lowe, *Savage Continent*, pp. 75–180.
[158] K. Jasper, *Die Schuldfrage*, pp. 92–93.

to have on political change, at least to some extent, and only 20 years after the war. Once again, a TJ measure, although rather dubious in kind, was responsible for the removal of perpetrators from high-ranking political offices. Because the East German ruling had no authority in West Germany, the trial did not prevent Oberländer from being a parliamentary delegate from 1963 to 1965. This case illustrates on the one side the failure of the West German judiciary to prosecute war crimes, but it also marked the beginnings of citizen-driven claims for more TJ and more democracy.

In the years that followed, many debated whether regime change and democracy are affected by how political elites and society deal with the past. The issue of reparations was a recurrent issue on the political agenda. In 1968, serious, long-lasting debates on reforms to the 1946 Allied Laws took place in parliament, which resulted in granting more reparations and in the revision of the original law (*Lastenausgleichsgesetz*). This debate would have had different results in the 1950s and was a sign of consolidation.

By the time the decade came to an end in 1969, the parliamentary delegate Walter Scheel, who later became president of West Germany, noted how crucial it was for the government to respond in an adequate and non-violent way to the left-wing student protests. These protests raised – among others – questions about the past involvement of members of the government in the war, as the case of Oberländer had previously illustrated. It had to be taken seriously in order to increase trust in the new democracy, and Scheel criticised the parliament's restrictive and anti-democratic reaction to the student protests. Yet in response to him, many conservative parliamentarians (many of them former members of NSDAP) doubted that the students' concerns were authentic and suspected that they were supported and paid for by the SED regime and its secret service; a fear that was only partly proven true after the Stasi files were opened in 1990.[159] Both the shadows of anti-Semitism and communism were widely feared by the West German public.

The influence of Cold War propaganda was always considered when gauging the effect of TJ measures and democratic performance. Yet the propaganda was a double-edged sword. Permanent competition between the two regimes triggered West Germany to compete to be the 'better democracy' and seek international recognition and acceptance into

---

[159] H. Dubiel, *Niemand ist frei von der Geschichte*, p. 121.

major international organisations, especially the UN. However, at the same time, conservative parliamentarians' constant mistrust of left-wing movements and vice versa hampered an open dialogue with the left-wing youth organisations. The TJ process in West Germany at that time was thus trapped in a tangled web of domestic efforts to strengthen democratic institutions, to receive international recognition, and to deal with the 'internal rivalry' between the West and East German governments.

Moreover, within West Germany there was a continuous competition between different groups of victims that had started immediately after the end of the war. At the beginning, for Germans it had been evident that they themselves were the most important victims of all. First they were seduced and betrayed by Hitler and later they lost half of the Reich's territory, as well as property and lives in abundance. Thus, the idea that 'others' were also victims of the Nazi regimes was only shared by a small group of people and predominantly those who had survived concentration camps. Public memorials initiated by 'other' mainly Jewish victim groups, commemorating the millions exterminated by the Nazis, were seen as 'competing' with the commemoration of the millions of dead German citizens, as well as with the million refugees and displaced persons and with those whose family members had perished during combat. There was a clear 'hierarchy of victimhood' and German victims – not even German Jews – were placed at the top by the government. In response to this, the West German government officially avoided public apologies towards the other types of victims since acknowledging past injustice with an apology could have led to more claims from more victims organisations, such as Jewish NGOs, slave labour forces or Sinti and Roma or from family members of the victims of the Nazi euthanasia programme. All of them raised their claims later in time, but in the 1960s their voices only started to be heard. But the bottom-up approach to TJ had already started and needed to be either embraced by the government in order not to lose credibility and trust, or suppressed – as in the East.

In 1969 both the new chancellor, Willy Brandt, and his now vice-chancellor, Walter Scheel, emphasised in parliament that democracy needed to live up to its ideals and not only be acknowledged on paper. In dealing with questions about the past from the younger generation, Scheel and his government generated new debates about restitution, in order to strengthen West Germany's democratic culture. It was such a top-down approach to respond to victims' claims that triggered more civic and also legal and political engagement of various actors and thus fuelled the upward spiral of consolidation.

A mix of TJ measure such as trials, compensations and memorials created a 'historical and moral balance' at that time, which paved the way to more democratic behaviour by acknowledging victims on all sides and thus avoiding major citizen resistance towards the new regime.[160] While the issue of who should be considered a 'real' victim remained, the category of victimhood rapidly expanded during this second decade.

The hesitant and insecure attitude towards TJ changed when the country became economically stable and when compensation payments were no longer seen as a threat to the economic prosperity. Germans did not generally feel that the billions of marks paid in compensation prevented them from sending their children to school or led to low-quality public infrastructure. Thanks to the economic growth, many TJ measures could be issued and thus contribute somewhat to the upward spiral effect after 20 years and more.

Meanwhile, since the SED had erected the Wall in East Berlin in 1961, it was not only a manifestation of two separate Germanys and ideologies, but also an indication that the two Germanys would deal separately with their common Nazi past. In East Germany, the government continued to respond only to the Soviet Union's claims for reparation, based on the argument that Nazi Germany had killed more Soviets than any other civilians anywhere during the war. That was de facto true. TJ measures in East Germany were centrally organised by the state and/or central party for their own interest and use. If any other TJ measures arose, these were suppressed. When TJ claims were citizen-driven, they were considered hostile and they were believed to have been instigated by the 'Nazi regime' in West Germany.[161] In contrast, West Germany was pushed by international as well as growing bottom-up pressure to take full responsibility for all crimes committed during the Nazi regime and World War II. This meant that the West German government had to respond to a much wider spectrum of claims and victims than the SED leadership did. An exclusionary, top-down TJ approach, such as that seen by East Berlin's politburo was difficult in the west, due to growing civic engagement and claims. In contrast to the dictatorship in the east, Bonn had to deal with the concerns of all and could not just imprison or expel those considered undesirable – a policy frequently applied by East Germany. Yet, West Germany could not respond to all demands for TJ measures at the same time and was thus

---

160 Ibid., p. 83.
161 H. Weber, *Die DDR 1945–1990.*

forced to set priorities. Plus, democratic elections were often the only way of indirect TJ, because election campaigns brought up debates about the past of candidates. The very different ways the two German governments responded to citizen claims for TJ measures illustrated the type of political regime they aimed to be. The one only responded to claims from one particular group while the other to more diverse types of claims for reparations and justice.[162] Despite the fact that both sides used the narrative of past for power games whenever it suited them, the key difference is that Bonn did not entirely ignore victims' and citizens' claims, while the SED regime in East Germany did. This was one of many indications that the regime in East Germany was making an authoritarian turn. Hegemonic regimes such as the SED one, as Steven Levitzky and Lucan Way phrase it, use the status of democracy as a facade, while in practice concentrating power in the hands of the few and exerting control over all judicial or political processes and CSO movements in the country.[163]

But despite all these changes and shifts in TJ policies, two decades after the war there was still no shared narrative and no common sense of responsibility towards the past, let alone any common German identity between the east and the west.[164] This was in part due to, and maintained by, the fact that public debates and school curricula in East and West Germany contained different narratives of the past. Thus, even if West German politicians had wanted to put massacres against Soviet citizens during the war on the political agenda, this would have been played down in schoolbooks for reasons of Cold War politics. This was also true for East Germany, which rejected responsibility for the Holocaust because according to official SED doctrine, all surviving Nazi perpetrators were either located in the west or had been successfully tried in the political trials in Waldheim, Leipzig or Torgau, which implied that there was no need to deal with the Holocaust or claims from Israeli citizens. According to the official version of history, all crimes of the past had been atoned. The SED regime grounded its narrative of the past on the liberation of the country by the Soviets, and thus on the anti-fascism doctrine of which the Berlin Wall was more than a symbol. At the same time, the new regime needed to produce new enemies in order to ensure that their propaganda against West Germany remained alive and believable.[165] But even the

---

[162] J. Thompson, *Taking Responsibility for the Past*.
[163] A. Levitsky and L.A. Way, *Competetive Authoritarianism, Hybrid Regimes after the Cold War* (Cambridge: Cambridge University Press, 2010), pp. 6–7.
[164] M. Fulbrook and A. Port (eds.), 'Becoming East German'.
[165] H. Weber, *Die DDR 1945–1990*.

most authoritarian regime, as the SED regime was, sought legitimacy and needed its citizens for this. The only way the politburo could garnish legitimacy was through propaganda, including massive public events and ceremonies at memorials and memorial days. Without this propaganda that is intrinsic to any authoritarian regime, citizens would increasingly drift away from socialist doctrine.

Ironically enough, the SED's Cold War game of naming and shaming West German public figures for their Nazi past unintentionally promoted consolidation of West Germany. The fear that one's own past could be 'discovered' and revealed by files carefully guarded in the hands of the SED leadership, kept many old elites from returning back into power and corrupting governmental policy and weakening democratic institutions in the west. As the Oberländer case illustrates, these East German efforts to discredit West Germany could actually work in West Germany's favour.

Thanks to East Germany's sleepless propaganda machinery that put pressure on West Germany and the rise of a new (more liberal and fearless) generation in West Germany, regime consolidation and TJ claims mutually reinforced each other in spiral ways in West Germany. Throughout the 1960s, the West German parliament revisited the highly controversial 1953 compensation laws regarding Israel and broadened the spectrum of TJ measures. It also revised many laws, including those concerning mass murder, and purged more and more former NSDAP members from high-level political positions. It became more evident that there were cumulative causalities and correlations between the behaviour of parliament and the executive on the one hand, and TJ measures on the other. This is one of many examples that illustrate Gerardo Munck and Jay Verkuilen's theory of cumulative causalities during regime change.[166] Claims for restitution by victims, trials and the emergence of memorials triggered even more claims, and thus also responses from the executive, judicial and legislative powers. Yet there was the continuous fear that too many restitution claims or too many trials would weaken democratic institutions and increase unrest among citizens, thus having the negative spiral effect Rustow predicted.[167]

Setbacks were a common part of the consolidation process on both sides of the Iron Curtain and the spiral went up and down and was never linear as shown in Figure 2.1. For example, in 1966 the West

---

[166] G. Munck and J. Verkuilen, 'Conceptualizing and Measuring Democracy', 29.
[167] D.A. Rustow, 'Transition to Democracy: Toward a Dynamic Model', 344.

German Ministry of Finance refused further claims from Jewish victims organisations in the United States because the 1956 reparation law (*Bundesentschädigungsgesetz*) and the 1957 restitution law (*Bundesrückerstattungsgesetz*) had already cost the West German state five times as much as they had anticipated when the first agreement had been reached in 1952. But by then only 15 per cent of all victim claims had been dealt with and many remained open and thus new measures needed to be installed. Instead of the estimated three or four billion marks, the expenses rose to around 20 billion marks (approximately 10 billion euros) for retirement benefits of survivors of concentration camps, in only one decade. This sum did not include the over 450 million marks (approximately 220 million euros) that West Germany had paid to the Jewish Conference for Material Claims against Germany (*Härtefond für jüdische Verfolgte*). This money was tax money and it was only because of the country's economic growth that West German citizens were able to accept the fact that they had been paying for Nazi war crimes for so long. Many Germans felt they had already paid the price for the Nazi regime with their lives, bodies, homes and territory or by having survived the Soviet gulags. They were not convinced that they should have to keep paying compensation to others.[168] But the government continued paying reparations for tactical political reasons mostly. Officially, the reparation payments to Jewish victims were classified as development aid and, ironically enough, most of it was given to Israel in the form of arms and weapons. At the same time Adenauer feared that if victim organisations gained more compensation, the right-wing parties in Germany (including his own conservative party, of which many were former NSDAP members) would seize the moment to revitalise German nationalism on the back of anti-Semitism. Thus the balancing of TJ with regime consolidation was a daily challenge for him and his successor administration and is in general a common element in consolidation processes, as Philipp Schmitter has noted.[169] If the Right had opposed Adenauer's policy, it would have been the end of the German democratic experiment as the many claims and pressures from abroad would have increased the number of radical and anti-democratic supporters. Thus, the Minister of Internal Affairs asked once more for a '*Schlußstrich*', a final instalment of compensation. However, that final instalment never came. In a letter from 1966,

---

[168] K. Lowe, *Savage Continent*, pp. 75–180.
[169] P.C. Schmitter, 'The Quality of Democracy'.

the Minister's office referred to the fact that many right-wing parties had already benefited far too much from the public debate about restitution. In his opinion, right-wing parties had gained a disproportionate number of seats in the Federal States' parliaments due to the victim claims for more restitution, which was not shared among the public for the reasons given above. The Minister's office also mentioned that victim organisations, such as the German branch of the Central Jewish Council, ought to understand the sensitivity of this matter and should no longer expect an increase in money, because it would only play into the hands of those who oppose the new democratic regime. Still, regardless of the political situation in Germany, victim groups based abroad annually increased their demands, endangering West Germany's ability to pay any restitution at all in the future.[170] Interestingly enough, the representatives of the West German claims' commissions understood Adenauer's fears and refrained from bringing more claims until the elections had passed.

For survivors of the Nazi regime who lived in Soviet-controlled and occupied countries, compensations by the West German government were impossible to reach. If, for example, forced labour requested (rightful) compensation from West Germany, the Soviet governments would have considered them traitors and collaborators with the West German regime. It was better for these victims, of which there were thousands, to remain silent until 1990 because after the end of the war and upon their return to the Soviet Union, many of them had been branded as German collaborators for the simple fact that they were forced to work for Germans. Despite having survived Nazi terror, they were seen as Nazi collaborators because they survived. Sadly enough, because of this, the Soviet military deported many of these victims to Siberian gulags shortly after their return to the Soviet Union and thus victimised them again.[171]

For some time in West Germany, citizens were rather sceptical towards radical democratic shifts and coalitions between social democrats and conservatives. Eventually, Willy Brandt (SPD) became chancellor in 1969 and, along with him, the first post-war generation of political elites entered into administrative, judicial and political positions, changing institutional performance. Brandt aimed for a change in political behaviour and agenda setting concerning the past and thus TJ. The CDU's long, previous hold on power had become a reason for international and domestic advisers

---

[170] Federal Archives Germany, Koblenz, BA-136 Bundeskanzleramt 3314, 6 April 1966.
[171] Federal Archives Germany, Koblenz, B-136 Bundeskanzleramt 3314.

to doubt the development of Germany's political culture. To further the consolidation of democracy, it would have been better to have more frequent power shifts. Brandt's succession was seen as a test of democracy and many people wondered whether his government could calm the student demonstrations and the radical movements that had arisen on both the left and right side of the political spectrum. Yet consensual democracy had its advantages, too. After some years of an unsuccessful coalition, parliamentarian debates became more civilised and the two opposing parties started to listen to each other.

At first, the left-wing student protests continued, even becoming stronger towards the end of the 1960s. They reflected a varied set of interests, including anti-Vietnam War sentiments, pro-communist sympathies but also the fear that too many Nazis would regain power in Germany. Some thought that it would only be a matter of time until the last Nazi officers would retire or die, but others raised the concern that much of their ideology and anti-democratic thinking was already transferring to the next generation, becoming a serious threat to democratic consolidation. The most prominent of these sceptical minds in West Germany was Ralf Dahrendorf, a liberal intellectual and politician who later became a leading academic in Oxford. He publicly raised his serious concerns about the anti-democratic culture in Germany that was, in his view, due to the Nazis still being in powerful positions. He also expressed concerns that this anti-democratic culture would provoke radical left-wing responses including terror, death and murder.[172]

Because of these fears of Nazi ideology still influencing German culture, violent opposition groups gathered towards the end of the 1960s and a smaller group of journalists and intellectuals formed the radical terror group, RAF. For decades to come, the RAF became a serious unconsolidated pocket in German democracy and consolidation process because of its violence. The RAF believed that because the Nazi regime had not been fully delegitimised, there would be a revitalisation of the old Nazi elites and the creation of another authoritarian right-wing neo-Nazi state. Furthermore, they assumed that democratic means alone could not stop the revitalisation of the Nazi regime, as Kiesinger's chancellorship had proven. Therefore they saw no other way out than turning to violence and underground guerrilla actions. The authorities in West Germany reacted not only with massive policing, but also

---

[172] R. Dahrendorf, *Gesellschaft und Demokratie in Deutschland* (Munich: Piper Verlag, 1965).

in a rather radical and undemocratic way too. Overwhelmed by the threat from the left-wing movement, which the government believed was entirely controlled by East Germany and the Soviet powers, parliament passed the 1968 Emergency Act (*Notstandsgesetz*). According to this Act, the Federal States were permitted to capture and imprison left-wing suspects without fair trials. In theory this law also applied to right-wing activists, but in practice it proved only to be used to target leftist movements. This law was widely condemned as unconstitutional, anti-democratic and a traditionally autocratic way to respond to citizens' demands for more democracy. These measures were a logical consequence of the militant democracy Germany adhered to.[173] The Emergency Act marked the beginning of a 15-year period of an unconsolidated pocket in West German democracy, triggered by the failure to fully delegitimise the Nazi regime in the years before. In response to this, the RAF reacted with terror attacks on parliamentarians, judges, businesspeople and whoever was seen to represent in some way the old Nazi regime. The government used these threats to justify limiting the freedom of assembly and demonstration, as well as to intervene by force if they thought peace was threatened.

The western Allied forces, in particular the United States, did not intervene at that time, although this law reminded many observers of the former Enabling Act (*Ermächtigungsgesetz*) that Hitler had installed in 1933, which gave the NSDAP a free hand in prosecuting, imprisoning and charging whomever the Nazis felt opposed them. This comparison fuelled fear in those who saw old nationalist movements regaining power over the country. It was only after German reunification in the 1990s when the East German secret service files were made public that it was proven that the RAF had acted for the most part independently, apart from some financial and logistic support from East Berlin. Although the SED did not create the RAF, it saw the radical group as a welcome 'ally' in their fight against the Bonn regime.

After the Berlin Wall was erected, the East German government soon started to see a strategic advantage in becoming a member of international human rights treaties, such as the International Covenant on Civil and Political Rights (ICCPR) or the International Covenant on Economic, Social and Cultural Rights (ICESCR). However, East Germany never planned to implement these treaties in institutional policies or let them

---

[173] K. Hanshew, *Terror and Democracy in West Germany* (Cambridge: Cambridge University Press, 2012).

have any impact on criminal codes.[174] East Germany held the belief that TJ was only useful in so far as it furthered the 'socialist fight' against anyone who seemed to threaten the socialist project. This was exemplified by SED political and administrative elites' view that only communist victims of fascism should be recognised as victims of human rights abuses or as political prisoners. Only those communists who had fought against the Nazi regime were considered freedom fighters and everyone else was seen as an enemy of the regime.[175] In this way, the communist regime in the east ignored its own political human rights abuses and its thousands of political prisoners. This tactic did not work in the long run.

Nevertheless, in the mid-1960s the SED regime was already fearful of losing more ground to the west.[176] This fear was due to the large number of East German citizens that preferred the political system in West Germany to that in East Germany. Government-controlled opinion polls from 1965 and the following years showed citizens in East Germany complaining about the lack of freedom and democracy under SED rule. Over 22 per cent of all responses emphasised the fact that freedom of expression should be better respected. Those who dared to argue that true democracy could only be realised in West Germany suffered repercussions for saying so. Eventually, towards the end of the 1960s the SED could no longer hide its power deficit. Their citizens wished to have real choices between the candidates in elections. The fact that these elections were staged was not mentioned in the official interpretation of the survey.[177] At the same time, a growing number of citizens in West Germany supported the democratic regime and over 50 per cent agreed that the Nazi regime had been an illegitimate and unjust regime (*Verbrecherregime*).[178] These two different tendencies in the east and west illustrate the two diverging spirals towards democratic consolidation in West Germany and towards autocratic consolidation in East Germany, as well as showing the links between the selective and exclusive abuse of TJ measures and the

[174] A. Mihr, *Amnesty International in der DDR*.
[175] C. Hölscher, *NS-Verfolgte im 'antifaschistischen Staat', Vereinnahmung und Ausgrenzung in der ostdeutschen Wiedergutmachung (1945–1989)* (Berlin: Metropol Verlag, 2002), pp. 200ff.
[176] M. Fulbrook and A. Port (eds.), 'Becoming East German'.
[177] German Federal Archive GDR Institute for Marxism and Leninism DY/30/IV A 2/, pp. 13–30.
[178] Institute für Demoskopie Allensbach, *Demokratie-Verankerung in der Bundesrepublik Deutschland: Eine empirische Untersuchung zum 30 jährigen Bestehen der Bundesrepublik* (Allensbach am Bodensee: Institute für Demoskopie Allensbach, 1979), p. 99.

subsequent downward spiral making the regime more of a surveillance one, based on strong propaganda policies that instrumentalised the Nazi past for its own political ideology and power.

In 1968, around the time of West Germany's abolition of the Hallstein Doctrine, another Soviet satellite state, Poland, submitted a draft resolution to the UN Human Rights Commissions targeting West Germany's many half-hearted TJ efforts. But Poland wanted to make West Germany's UN membership conditional on West Germany's payment of more reparations to eastern European victims of war crimes and crimes against humanity.[179] Poland emphasised that the reparations must be paid to the communist states rather than to the individuals themselves. But West Germany had already decided in 1952 that compensation to individual victims instead of states was the preferred policy when it came to reparations. This was more then a propagandistic game, it was a policy statement on how to atone and reckon with the past. Collective payments would neither place the individual as victim nor as perpetrator in the centre of TJ.

But Poland also made this demand because it realised that it had to prevent Eastern bloc citizens from having direct contact with West German authorities and individuals. If their own citizens (among which there had been many victims of Nazi terror) were to have direct contact with the former 'enemy', so that West Germany could distribute benefits and financial compensation to the victims personally, the idea of the atrocious and hostile German Nazi would vanish and could undermine the totalitarian communist regimes. Although the West German government in 1968 was not the same from 1933 or 1945, even so that was the picture that Eastern European propaganda was drawing. Full reconciliation between Eastern bloc citizens and former perpetrators had to be avoided. Moreover, individual compensation entailed a risk that citizens would compare West German compensation to that of their own state. They would ask why the 'enemy state of West Germany' redresses its atrocious past through compensation funds, when 'my brother and friend, the Soviet Union', who also committed horrendous war crimes, never even mentions it? This would have eroded the strict narrative of the 'good communist state' versus the 'bad western imperialist'. In the 1990s, these fears came to the surface when citizens in Poland and elsewhere across Eastern Europe stated that

[179] German Federal Archive GDR Institute for Marxism and Leninism DY/30/IV A 2/, pp. 13–30.

they could forgive Germans, but could not forgive the Russians, since Russians had never come to terms with their own war crimes. West German diplomats at the UN feared that if they were to strongly oppose Poland's resolution, it would trigger anti-German sentiments among other UN Member States.[180] Instead, Bonn responded by showing all of the reparations they had paid since 1949, showing that West Germany had done their 'homework'. With this, the West German government turned against the east and started to demand that Eastern European states also take responsibility for their role in the atrocities of the past, specifically calling on Poland, Czechoslovakia and Hungary – of which large parts of the population and political leadership had been in close collaboration with the Nazis – to not only acknowledge their own collaboration but also compensate and return the property of over six million German refugees who had suffered major acts of post-war vengeance after 1945.

In the years to follow, TJ measures became more and more part of political games in the international arena. In the end, the West German foreign ministry simply declined Poland's request at the UN. Internally, the diplomats emphasised once again that West Germany had made large reparation payments around the world and had taken criminal justice and other TJ measures in a less biased way than in the east. Yet, West Germany was wisely advised to refrain from strong countermeasures against the Polish attempts so as not to spoil West Germany's application for full UN membership. The change of strategy at the UN was based on an internal memo from the West German Chancellery to refrain from taking an active position, so as to prevent Eastern European countries from recognising East Germany as the only legitimate German state.[181] In the end, as a compromise on the international level, TJ concerns were entrusted to the UN Human Rights Commission. In 1970 the Commission passed a modest resolution on restitution acts and responsibilities. This resolution generally encouraged but did not oblige all UN Member States to take responsibility for war crimes and their consequences, a message also

---

[180] UN Doc GA 1727 Plenary Meeting, 2391(XXIII) Convention on the Non-Applicability of Statutory Limitation to War Crimes and Crimes against Humanity, Twenty-third Session, New York, 26 November 1968.

[181] Federal Archives Germany (Bundesarchiv, Koblenz) B-136 Bundeskanzleramt - 3314, Prüfung der Krioteroen zur Bestimmung der Entschädigung für Opfer von Kriegsverbrechen und Verbrechen gegen die Menschlichkeit durch den Generalsekretär der Vereinten Nationen 26 March 1968, and -6381Aufhebung der Verjährung für Mord und Völkermord 22 April 1969.

meant for parties involved in the recent wars on the Korean peninsula, Algeria, Vietnam and Angola, such as the United States, the Soviet Union, France, China and Portugal. Since this was not a binding resolution it had little effect at the height of the Cold War.

Domestically, the struggle between old and new elites continued on all sides and would do so even in the following post-war decade. In West Germany, the weekly right-wing journals such as *New Politics* (*Neue Politik*) that emphasised the achievements of the Reich over the democratic tendencies in Germany lost ground. Another radical right-wing group, the German Reich Party, the successor to the NSDAP, was finally dissolved in 1964. Many more radical right-wing groups disappeared by the end of the decade due to public disapproval and lack of political support.[182] Nevertheless, some remained, but became inactive as their members became too old to harm the system. One such group was the former armed militant groups of the Nazi regime, the SS (*Schutzstaffel*) aid and support association, the Quiet Help (*Stille Hilfe*), a citizen-driven initiative that called itself 'quiet' because it did not want to get into public controversies. This group supported former SS officers' family members who were in social economic need, since many SS officers could never reintegrate into West Germany's new political and economic elite due to their failing the denazification process or because a family member remained in prison. The Quiet Help was officially registered and was active for many years, even after Germany's reunification in 1990. Multiple citizen-driven initiatives, even those that did not support the new democratic regime, were widely recognised and registered as associations or NGOs at that time in order to avoid them going underground or failing to submerge the still not fully consolidated democracy. On the other side it was a sign that the new democratic regime would accept diversity and pluralism of association – as long as they would not use violence and act unconstitutionally. Nevertheless, the controversial support of the new political regime still showed its fragile side from time to time. In 1968, Kurt Sontheimer's second edition of his book on anti-democratic thinking in the Weimar Republic (*Antidemokratisches Denken in der Weimarer Republik*) made the link to the lack of democratic political culture in West Germany, but this was widely and publicly contested.[183] The additional chapter on West

[182] Federal Archives Germany, Koblenz, BA-136 Bundeskanzleramt – 1745, p. 45.
[183] K. Sontheimer, *Antidemokratisches Denken in der Weimarer Republik, Studienausgabe mit einem Extrateil, Antidemokratisches Denken in der Bundesrepublik* (Munich: Nymphenburger Verlagshandlung, 1968).

Germany in the 1968 edition was later withdrawn from bookshops after completely selling out. No reprint was allowed. It was censored due to the fact that it hit the core weakness of the government in Bonn, namely the lack of systematic lustration procedures among the far too many former Nazi elites in office. The second edition of the book fuelled the left-wing resistance and was thus seen as a threat to stability by governmental officials. These officials even believed that this chapter of the book was organised by the East German secret service, the Stasi hence causing further mistrust to dominate public discourse about democracy. This suspicion was often legitimate, because the SED had installed an entire department in East Berlin, the Department Eleven within the central Stasi headquarters Department IX that was only responsible to look for Nazi perpetrators in the west to undermine the regime in Bonn. In the 1960s this Department IX started to launch annually the so-called 'brown book' with the names of former Nazi elites still in office in the West German administrative system, such as the Foreign Ministry, judges and other federal or state ministries throughout the country.

But alongside the battle between East and West over 'who had more Nazis remaining in office', civil and public engagement took place at full speed. Many NGOs for victims, human rights, peace and humanitarian aims started to grow in West Germany, most of them rooted in Christian or left-wing movements, such as Amnesty International in 1961. Action Reconciliation Service for Peace (*Aktion Sühnezeichen*), founded by the Evangelical Church in Germany, was the most prominent NGO in West Germany that reached out to former occupied countries that had suffered under Nazi terror, helping to rebuild or build memorials and working together with Holocaust survivors abroad. This NGO started to send volunteers to the Netherlands as early as 1958, and in 1961 to Israel and other countries. The Action grew rapidly towards the end of the 1960s and soon received public and state support and has since been one of the main actors in the reconciliation process between Germany and those countries that had suffered Nazi terror. In East Germany, however, the nature of the dictatorship prevented any such volunteer organisation or civil society movement from being established. The East German regime used its hardest weapon against any civil society rise, the Stasi, to suppress any TJ initiative that was not governmental owned. Any efforts to participate in the global peace movement were restricted and activists were often imprisoned. All reconciliation efforts, for example youth group exchanges with eastern European states, were organised by the central government.

Meanwhile, in the west, the radicalisation of both right and left-wing groups escalated in 1967. On 2 June 1967 a German police officer shot the left-wing student Beno Ohnesorg at an anti-government demonstration in West Berlin. The student was part of a left-wing movement that feared the return of Nazi politics. The police officer who killed him was never successfully tried and in 2009, and after consulting East German Stasi files, it became evident that the police officer had been a secret operative of the East German government, under orders to cause as much unrest and disorder as possible in the western Allied sector of Berlin. He succeeded in his mission as the left-wing movements, specifically the RAF, recruited heavily from groups that felt the government had responded insufficiently to Ohnesorg's violent death. The radical 'movement of 2 June' named after the day of Ohnesorg's death, also committed various terrorist acts against alleged right-wing Germans in the following years.[184]

The majority of these protesters were non-violent and many of those who organised the peace or civil rights movements at that time later became known as the generation of 1968 in Germany. It was the 20+ generation. The term '68er' was used to denote a group of people who were mainly left wing; Willy Brandt supporters who massively distanced themselves from their parents' (Nazi) generation. James McAdams cited this moment as a major turning point for TJ and regime consolidation in German history, arguing that the government's 'neglect of the obligation to seek retribution for past crimes promoted widespread cynicism among the German population about its government's commitment to make a full break with authoritarianism, and from the perspective of some observers, it ultimately contributed to the violent rejection of German democracy by many young people after 1968'.[185]

The government reacted to the spread of left-wing violence with violent measures, but also by claiming to take more cautious measures and not to ignore the claims of this generation in the years to come. Willy Brandt stated it would 'dare' to allow more democracy. This was an occasion that Oskar Thoms et al. have characterised as the state taking ownership of TJ again.[186] And thus, whilst the 20+ generation in West Germany raised its voice against the remaining former NSDAP members now back in office, the same generation in East

---

[184] E. Wolfrum, *Die geglückte Demokratie*.

[185] J.A. McAdams (ed.), *Transitional Justice and the Rule of Law in New Democracies*, p. x.

[186] O.N.T. Thoms, J. Ron and R. Paris, 'State-Level Effects of Transitional Justice', 329–354 at 329–342.

Germany was rather silent (and oppressed) and many more even content with the way the SED had strengthened or consolidated the dictatorial regime through its steady anti-fascist propaganda. Christian Olivo assessed the East German 20+ generation's silence and found two causes for it. First, the post-war period's anti-fascist ideology had created a far-reaching political consensus between state power and intelligentsia in the east. The historical guilt of Auschwitz disciplined both sides, because even those who rebelled against the SED regime did not necessarily want to abolish it because it was left-wing in itself (although suppressive, but to reform it. The socialist-communist ideology seemed reasonable, although the reality looked very different. Second, the lack of free press meant that the new generation was heavily influenced by the official propaganda that all Nazis had fled to the 'neo-fascist west', leaving none remaining in East Germany.[187] This belief prevailed even despite the case of Horst Fischer, the former Auschwitz SS physician, in 1965 which had proved that Nazi elites had remained and operated in East Germany well into the 1960s. The possibility of deporting, or rather 'selling', regime critics to West Germany continuously hindered consolidation of the opposition in East Germany. Thus, the student protests in Prague and other communist countries in 1969 hardly affected the regime in East Berlin.

Interestingly enough, in the west unconsolidated pockets such as RAF terrorism arose during this period due to the lack of delegitimisation of the Nazi regime. The West German government went so far as to fight these left-wing terror groups with anti-democratic and illegal means underground, in the name of state security. It was only in 2008 that the city of Berlin inaugurated a memorial in honour of Ohnesorg's death and the violent abatement of the demonstrations in the late 1960s. However, radicalisation in the West did not end there. In one of the defining moments for the 1968 generation, a right-wing student tried to assassinate the left-wing student leader Rudi Dutschke in West Berlin. This student believed that Dutschke, and the communist views that he and other 68ers believed in, would take over Germany. Dutschke, who was known for his loud criticism of the government because it employed former members of the NSDAP, barely survived the murder attempt. In 1979, more than ten years after the assassination attempt, Rudi Dutschke died of his injuries. Today streets, buildings and

---

[187] C. Olivo, *Creating a Democratic Civil Society in Eastern Germany: The Case of the Citizen Movements and Alliance 90* (New York: Palgrave, 2001), pp. 62–63.

organisations are named after him and he is seen as one of the icons of German left-wing political resistance and the 20+ generation against the remaining traces of the Nazi regime of that time.

All this illustrates that TJ in Germany cannot be separated from its democratisation process. It was at this moment when the analyst and writer Kurt Sontheimer accused German parliamentarians of tolerating nationalist parties to legitimise the use of force against student protesters and those who had formed the extra-parliamentary opposition and protest movements. In his eyes, the democratic experiment in West Germany had failed, and the current political elite ran the risk of paving the way for another non-democratic or rather non-fully consolidated system in the country. He saw this risk being caused in part by the lack of TJ measures and the fact that the population never learned to self-reflect and take moral responsibility. He argued that coming to terms with the past (*Vergangenheitsbewältigung*) was a way to learn from history and past injustices in order to establish a better, more humane, democratic order. Instead, Sontheimer feared citizens were not encouraged to sufficiently detach themselves from nationalist and anti-democratic thoughts. He believed that Germany only issued TJ measures because of international pressure and the fear that Germany would be excluded by international organisations, the Allies or other countries in the world. In his eyes, the shift of the 1960s was not sufficient to strengthen democracy.[188] He was not unheard but fully democratic consolidation would indeed take place much later.

During an internal rally in 1969 between Chancellor Brandt and leaders of labour unions in West Germany, Brandt clarified that he would not let any more laws, censorship or restriction of political freedoms pass while he was in power. He hoped for a democratic solution to the problem of those that threatened democracy.[189] This marked one of the most prominent moments of the West German history of regime consolidation and TJ. It was finally acknowledged that democracy could not flourish without a self-critical understanding of the past, for which TJ measures were necessary.

The following years, however, showed that Brandt could not ignore the fact that radical movements from the right and the left were continuing to attack each other and in the 1970s left-wing movements committed terrorist attacks. When Brandt became Chancellor of West Germany in 1969

---

[188] K. Sontheimer, *Antidemokratisches Denken in der Weimarer Republik*.
[189] Federal Archives Germany, Koblenz, BA-136 Bundeskanzleramt- 4406, note 6 March 1969.

he promptly reacted to the radicalisation. Brandt said he 'dared' to allow more democracy, meaning that West Germans would have to practise and experience more respect for each other, more pluralism and inclusion of left-wing thoughts, which had been labelled hostile by the conservative and nationalist majority in the country since 1949. Brandt also pushed his government and the parliament to accept his policy of rapprochement (*Annährung*) towards East Germany and to accept the deals he made with Poland and the Soviet Union in later years. His policy was highly controversial and was criticised by media and political opponents. He was ahead of majority opinion in the electorate and other interest groups at that time, even in his own party. Although Brandt paved Germany's way to UN membership, eased relationships with the Soviet Union that led to the establishment of the Commission on Security and Cooperation in Europe (CSCE) in 1974, his friendly policy towards East Germany – and the discovery that he had a Stasi spy operating in his office – eventually cost him his position. In 1974 he had to resign from office. Although his resignation had many reasons, one was that because of his liberal and reconciliatory attitude towards the east (as opposed to Adenauer's towards the west) and his demand for internal reconciliation in Germany, he was the political enemy of many old Nazi sympathisers and refugees. Yet, despite his three short years in office as chancellor, he managed to turn the West German political culture towards more civic consolidation, and thus beyond the existing constitutional, representative and institutional and even attitudinal consolidation, using Merkel's categories again to illustrate the stages.[190]

In summary, the first post-war generation had a remarkable impact on the quality of the functioning of democratic institutions in West Germany. As opinion polls at the time showed, the majority of people during the 1960s in West Germany adhered to democracy as a concept and there was no way to go back to autocracy,[191] despite the radicalisation of political groups. The question for the third post-war decade was whether West German democracy would leave its militant character behind and instead become a more consolidated democracy. And for East Germany the question was whether the regime would be able to preserve its stability, and that would mean more authoritarian control.

[190] W. Merkel, Systemtransformation, *Eine Einführung in die Theorie und Empirie der Transformationsforschung*, pp. 199–204.

[191] L. Diamond and L. Morlino, *Assessing the Quality of Democracy* (Baltimore, MD: Johns Hopkins University Press, 2005).

Third Decade: 1970–1979

The third post-war decade began with Brandt's 1969 challenge to 'dare' to have more democracy and to continue the democratic consolidation process when allowing for more civil society engagement and (painful) dialogue about the past. For the first time, he linked Germany's regime consolidation to the unatoned legacy of World War II. His kneeling in front of the ghetto memorial in Warsaw in 1970 became a symbol for how closely both aspects were linked. He saw reconciliation as a long-term process that would eventually benefit the society and the democracy in West Germany. At the same time, indictments against alleged Nazi perpetrators and in particular concentration camp guards continued. Between 1970 and 1989 over 6,000 people were indicted and around 200 sentenced to prison.[192]

In East Berlin, Erich Honecker became leader of the SED politburo, but hopes that he would grant the young and restless generation more liberties soon vanished. He increased and standardised political repression throughout the country and thus consolidated the dictatorship more and more.

At the same time in West Germany and after Brandt's inaugural speech, and his visit to the memorial of the Jewish Warsaw ghetto in Poland, he caused an affront to the millions of German refugees from the former territories in the east. In the eyes of many Germans, the Poles together with the Soviets were seen as the victimisers of millions of Germans by those refugee organisations in West Germany. Brandt kneeled before the memorial and made a formal apology to all victims in the name of the German nation. This official and moral acknowledgement by the head of the successor government of the Nazi regime triggered a new era of consolidation and TJ. His subsequent apology, which was the first of its kind in the twentieth century, was the illustrative symbol of the shift to moral responsibility. Decades later, when many heads of state apologised in 1995 for their inability to prevent the Rwandan genocide in 1994, they followed in Brandt's footsteps. Today, to apologise for mass atrocities has become a common practice among politicians using TJ measures. It has almost become inflationary. But why would such a gesture in 1970 in Warsaw change all political agendas in Europe and ease the tensions of the Cold War, whereas today it has become a political ritual in most TJ processes?

---

[192] N. Frei, *Hitlers Eliten nach 1945* (Munich: Deutscher Taschenbuchverlag, 2003).

It was a first step of acknowledgement that later also led to restorative justice.

After passing the first step towards consolidation in the early 1960s, it became imperative for Brandt to increase civic trust in institutions. His prostration and apology in Warsaw led to that trust, in particular in regaining trust among the neighbouring countries. The following year he received the Nobel Peace Prize for his efforts. This again encouraged citizens to engage in TJ and encouraged foreign governments to have diplomatic relations with West Germany. In this way, the mutually reinforcing effect continued.

The attempts to democratise more in the west also meant to indict more Nazi perpetrators in the subsequent years. This did not remain unnoticed in the east, but the SED regime only reacted in ritualising its annual commemorations of its glorious anti-fascist fight more and more. CSOs and victims organisations that were not governmental run or controlled could no longer operate in public.

The process in the west instead has been described by Michael Naef and Jürgen Schupp as an engagement between the individual and institutions in which the trusting citizen freely transfers assets to another person or institution, without controlling their actions or having the possibility to retaliate.[193] When citizens saw and experienced political actions based on a sense of morality, such as Brandt kneeling before the memorial – but also the many private initiatives, such as the Action Reconciliation Service for Peace – this contributed to citizen trust and thus the upward spiral of the mutually reinforcing trend between institutions and TJ continued.

Eventually, in the subsequent years West Germany signed diverse friendship and rapprochement treaties with Poland and the Soviet Union, thus marking the beginning of a new policy towards the east and the beginning of the end of the Cold War. Before and after his visit to Warsaw, Brandt triggered parliamentary debates on how German society was dealing with its past. He was the first post-war chancellor who called for a debate about whether 8 May 1945 should become a national holiday and commemoration day of German liberation, albeit without success. Many conservatives in parliament considered Brandt's proposal unacceptable; the old elite maintained that the German Reich was *defeated*, not liberated. Additionally, this proposal received very little support because 8 May

---

[193] M. Naef and J. Schupp, *Measuring Trust. Experiments and surveys in Contrast and Combination* (Bonn: IZA, 2009), p. 3.

was already the official East Germany commemoration day of liberation. Brandt and others emphasised that this debate revealed the direct relation between how Germans reflected upon the Nazi past and their present understanding of democracy. Germans, in Brandt's eyes, tended to radicalise political opinions and behaviour regardless of whether they were on the left or right of the political spectrum. Germans would need to learn tolerance and to respect diversity among each other if they were to experience democracy to a fuller extent.[194] According to the regime change theories of the present day, we would say that West Germany needed to progress towards being an inclusive society.[195] At the time, democracy was not necessarily perceived as an accomplishment that would liberate Germany from Nazi terror and oppression, but rather as something that had been imposed upon the country. Democracy was seen almost as a penalty for having terrorised Europe with the Nazi dictatorship for over a decade. Despite this, political analysts in the 1970s saw no serious threat to democracy anymore. It had become 'the only game in town' for the majority of Germans, according to these observations, albeit unconsolidated pockets continued to exist.

But the harm these unconsolidated pockets from the right and from the left could do is shown by correspondence between Brandt and Ephraim Kishon, an Israeli writer who published widely in Germany at that time. After the attacks on the Israeli Olympic team by a Palestine terrorist group during the summer Olympics in Munich in 1972, many Jews feared visiting West Germany. Thus, in October 1972 friends had advised Kishon not to enter Germany to advertise his latest book, since German authorities could not guarantee his safety and since attacks on Jews were still prevalent. Kishon contacted Brandt, urging him to guarantee his safety, arguing that West Germany needed people like him to show that there was a 'new' Germany that one could trust.[196] Brandt agreed and guaranteed Krishon's protection. Krishon's visit to Germany went by without any difficulties but his case illustrated how deep the mistrust towards Germans and Germany still was at that time, despite the fact that 25-plus years had passed since the war.

After West Germany's treaty with the Soviet Union, both East and West Germany finally became members of international organisations

[194] H. Dubiel, *Niemand ist frei von der Geschichte*, pp. 131–140.
[195] P.C. Schmädeke, *Politische Regimewechsel*, p. 33.
[196] Federal Archives Germany (Bundesarchiv, Koblenz), B-Bundeskanzleramt 136–4374, Ephraim Kishon letter to Willy Brandt, 2 October 1972.

such as the UN in 1973. Meanwhile, West Germany enhanced its role in the Council of Europe and the EC. This played an important role in West Germany understanding its responsibility for establishing peace and stability in Europe on the basis of joint human rights norms and standards.[197] For most of its existence, East Germany remained a party to the Warsaw Pact and did not question the Soviet hegemon. In East Germany, when the first post-war generation demanded more independence and rights after the CSCE Helsinki Act of 1975, the SED regime suppressed these movements and restricted fundamental freedoms.[198] Most of the individuals involved in such movements ended up as political prisoners which reached a peak number despite legal reforms in the 1970s. A free and open discourse concerning the responsibilities of the post-war generation, let alone the SED government, for the injustice and terror that occurred before 1945 on German territory was equally denied.[199] Instead, political persecution of those who even compared the totalitarian Nazi state with that of the communist SED regime increased.[200] Whereas in West Germany coming to terms with the past started to become part of the civic culture and thus TJ measures became a political decree and a prerequisite for any political and societal agenda towards the international community, East Germany maintained the official version that the SED regime was 'anti-fascist' by nature and thus did not need to respond to any citizen's or victim's claims for TJ.[201] At the same time, between 1975 and 1981, the West Germany District Court of Düsseldorf held the Majdanek Trials, named after the concentration camp in Poland where over 80,000 people were murdered. The West German trials were part of a long history of trials for the war crimes that were committed at this camp. The first trials were held by the Soviets in Poland in 1944 towards the end of the war and after the concentration camp had been freed by Soviet forces. It was West Germany's longest and most expensive trial, lasting 474 sessions and convicting 16 highly ranked Nazi officers and prison guards – of which many were women – of war crimes. They were sentenced to a minimum of three years imprisonment. It was a rather

---

[197] D. Senghaas, *Von Europa Lernen Entwicklungsgeschichtliche Betrachtungen* (Frankfurt am Main: Suhrkamp Verlag, 1982).

[198] E. Wolfrum, *Die geglückte Demokratie*, pp. 283–304.

[199] M. Fulbrook and A. Port (eds.), 'Becoming East German'.

[200] A. Mihr, *Amnesty International in der DDR*.

[201] H. Lichtenstein and O.R. Romberg (eds.), *Täter-Opfer-Folgen. Der Holocaust in Geschichte und Gegenwart* (Frankfurt am Main: TRIBÜNE Zeitschrift zum Verständnis des Judentums, 1995).

symbolic and insufficient trial because too many witnesses had passed away or were not allowed to testify or travel to West Germany since they lived under the communist regimes in Eastern Europe.[202]

Two of the most prominent groups that fuelled the unconsolidated pockets of democracy were the Bader-Meinhof Complex and the RAF, which enjoyed growing support in the early 1970s.[203] Members of these groups kidnapped, killed and robbed those who they believed represented the old and new elite establishment. The RAF described itself as a communist and anti-imperialist 'urban guerrilla' group engaged in armed resistance against what they deemed to be a fascist state – the Bonn Republic. Their founders were academics and journalists, who feared a return to Nazi dictatorship because of the many old elites still in high-level positions and political functions. In 1970 they started to go underground and commit terrorist acts, robberies and killings against politicians, bankers and industrial leaders. They bombed a US air force compound in Germany and committed over three dozen assaults, many of which resulted in deaths. The authorities and government retaliated, killing and imprisoning a number of these members, often without the necessary authority from democratic institutions.

The unconsolidated pocket of left-wing violence reached its peak in 1977, after 34 homicides and an RAF hijacking of a German Lufthansa plane in Mogadishu in Somalia, a failed attempt to blackmail the West German government to release imprisoned RAF members. After the hijacking failed, many of the RAF prisoners in Stammheim committed collective suicide. Shortly after, the abducted president Hans Martin Schleyer of the German Federation of Employers was murdered as an act of revenge. But they targeted Schleyer not only because of his outstanding elitist position in West Germany, but because he used to be a member of Hitler's SS troops during World War II. His homicide symbolised what the RAF violently claimed to aim at: to free Germany from a re-emerging old Nazi elite. It was the culmination of violence during a period that had been a clear failure for democracy and the rule of law in Germany under the new chancellorship of Helmut Schmidt. Due to massive counter-terrorism acts, but also thanks to more TJ and because the RAF lost ground in their anti-regime arguments, the RAF was disbanded in the 1980s – a fact that was only officially recognised in 1998.

---

[202]   P. Heberer and J. Matthäus (eds.), *Atrocities on Trial, Historical Perspectives on the Politics of Prosecuting War Crimes* (Washington, DC: US Holocaust Memorial Museum, 2008).

[203]   E. Wolfrum, *Die geglückte Demokratie*, pp. 261–271.

In hindsight, this period is often seen as a warning to legislative powers against enacting highly restrictive laws.[204] Stricter anti-terrorist laws (for example Art. 129a of the German Criminal Code) led to more resistance among civil movements. These laws were introduced after contentious parliamentary debates and a resolution that German democracy was militant enough to defend itself against terrorism, yet still able to leave many human rights and basic constitutional rights unaffected. This only led to further mistrust.[205] More legislation followed; for example, a law criminalising anyone aiming to create a group allegedly planning to use terror (*Bildung terroristischer Vereinigungen*). The question at that time was whether a consolidated democratic regime needed yet another law to combat terrorism or whether it was a lack of implementation and of letting those opposing the regime to participate more freely in public. Obviously, it felt it needed it.

The concern was whether the government would continue down the slippery slope of anti-democratic measures, as Sontheimer had feared. All these decrees and laws aimed at restricting basic human rights, such as the right to free assembly, the right to free speech or to exercise one's profession was to control the new emerging 20+ generation and their claims for more truth through accountability and transparency. The law was never abandoned, although it was revised after the German High Court in 1978 criticised it for allowing the prosecution of people just because there was an allegation that they might be creating a terrorist group. Nevertheless, the fact that courts in Germany dealt with this issue also indicated that there was an open discourse and that such anti-democratic laws could be changed.

This period was a test for attitudinal and behavioural consolidation and because it was a painful period paired with violence and counter-violence it was also called the 'German autumn', an apocalyptic expression used to express the fear of a return to a repressive regime. But it was also a period of political awareness and moral attribution to the past. In the same year of the High Court's decision, in 1978 Kurt Filbinger, prime minister of the federal state of Baden-Wuerttemberg, had to resign from office due to public pressure after his Nazi past was revealed.

The governments both on a federal level as well as in the states in general pointed mainly to the fact that the government had to respond

---

[204] H. Dubiel, *Niemand ist frei von der Geschichte*, pp. 145–151.
[205] K. Hanshew, *Terror and Democracy in West Germany* (Cambridge: Cambridge University Press, 2012).

to public needs and interest, both concerning the Nazi past as well as the threat that the RAF posed to democracy. Although Chancellor Brandt had promised more democracy and liberty, militant democracy still prevailed in the legislature and increased under the chancellorship of Schmidt. Despite Brandt's liberal views and his commitment to more democracy, he passed yet another decree on radicalisation (*Radikalenerlass*) in 1972. This measure allowed public and private employers to expel employees and public servants from office if the employees were suspected of sympathising with communist or left-wing movements.[206] Teachers, postal workers and other public servants were affected. Special police units were formed and laws to restrict freedom of manifestation and expression were passed. Although these units were later abolished, they left a mark: the legacy of repressing freedom of expression.

It must be acknowledged that a significant portion of the younger generation did silently sympathise with these radical left-wing movements. Many did not believe that it would be possible to solve the political conflicts and disputes that existed in West Germany in a peaceful or democratic manner.[207] Yet, these beliefs were only a sign of unsuccessful regime change, incomplete consolidation and a lack of trust in democratic institutions, for which the old elites were most responsible. And this triggered dissatisfaction among citizens with democracy. According to a Eurobarometer survey in 1973, approximately 55 per cent of West Germans were not very or at all satisfied with democracy, and only 39 per cent were fairly satisfied.[208] By the end of the 1970s and after substantial democratic reforms, 70 per cent of Germans reported being fairly satisfied and 10 per cent very satisfied. This indicates that West Germans had come to accept democracy as 'the only game in town' more than they had in the 1960s, but they also remained sceptical.[209] As much as the late 1960s convinced West Germans that returning to the past was not an option, it took another decade before the regime was truly consolidated.

Meanwhile, cultural events also fuelled the shift from a purely tactical and strategic use of TJ to the acknowledgement of German moral

---

[206] E. Wolfrum, *Die geglückte Demokratie*, pp. 330–334.

[207] K. Hanshew, *Terror and Democracy in West Germany.*

[208] European Union, Eurobarometer Surveys, Germany 1973.09, http://ec.europa.eu (last accessed August 2013).

[209] European Union, Eurobarometer Surveys, Germany 1979.04, http://ec.europa.eu (last accessed August 2013).

responsibility and consequently a morality based use of TJ measures. One example is the 1978 US TV film series *Holocaust* that portrayed a German Jewish family fleeing Nazi Germany in the 1930s. This film triggered a shift in public opinion. The number of those who considered Germany's past reprehensible increased. By 1978, around 71 per cent of Germans agreed that the Nazi regime was an atrocious and unjust regime, which also meant that radical neo-Nazi movements would receive increasingly less acceptance among the public.[210] Civil society increasingly compared the past to the present and tried to learn from the past. Eventually, the legislature had to respond to this change in society, and radical laws were abolished.

With the series about the Holocaust, the issue of Nazi terror came into both East and West German living rooms and was widely discussed on both sides of the Wall. Twenty years earlier it would not have received the same positive responses as it did in 1978. The TV series also influenced public life, school education and affected political thinking for months, if not years, thereafter. The difference between the TV series and previous writing, lectures and documentaries about the past was that it reached almost everybody in society, young and old, and especially schoolchildren. After this, the term Holocaust became part of the German discourse and dominated any debate, including in parliament, on the Nazi past.[211]

In addition to the endless efforts to enact and revise laws, deal with terror, prohibit civil organisations, organise cultural events, hold public debates and organise memorials, another factor was what to do with former technocrats of the Nazi elites. Retirement benefits and pensions soon became another issue in the wider field of TJ.

But by then it was evident that TJ brought more benefits to German society than restrictive policies, for German domestic and international politics, as well as business and investments abroad. It became official doctrine to commemorate the Holocaust and remember victims, in particular in West Germany's foreign relations with the United States and Israel. The correlation between TJ and responsiveness of institutions remained strong.

---

[210] Institute für Demoskopie Allensbach, *Demokratie-Verankerung in der Bundesrepublik Deutschland.*

[211] H. Welzer, 'Der Holocaust im deutschen Familiengedächtnis' in V. Knigge and N. Frei (eds.), *Verbrechen erinnern, Die Auseinandersetzung mit Holocaust und Völkermord* (Bonn: Bundeszentrale für Politische Bildung, 2005), pp. 362–378.

Yet, controversies about how to deal with the past continued. In the summer of 1979 parliament debated whether the statute of limitations on crimes connected with genocide and the Holocaust should be finally abolished. Germany was about to close the files on World War II perpetrators because the statute of limitations had once again expired while many of the alleged perpetrators were still free citizens. In the end and after heated debates in and outside parliament, the delegates abolished the law that restricted prosecution of mass murder or crimes against humanity, thus opening the door to prosecution of those alleged to have committed genocide without time limits. Although this ended the parliamentary debates, it did not end the debate regarding democratic legitimacy. In the years following, the majority of delegates across all political parties came to be more open for abolishing the statute of limitation for crimes committed under the Nazi regime and they strongly opposed amnesties and clemency which led to a change in politics.[212] The statute of limitations for mass murder was abolished and this led to both the abolition of the 1972 law on radicalisation (*Radikalenerlass*) and the statute of limitations (*Verjährungsfrist*) on crimes against humanity. From that point on, mass murders and thus crimes connected to the Holocaust could be tried at any time in Germany and this has since become a pillar of criminal justice measures under German law and thus contributed to strengthening the rule of law in the country.

In this same period the SED regime in the east constantly changed and revised its laws to make them more compatible with the needs of the people, trying to ease tensions and give more liberties. However, in fact, the regime only succeeded in tightening its dictatorial grip on society. But at the same time in the west, without the continuous pressure from the UN or the Council of Europe on West Germany, many basic freedom rights would have not been installed either.[213] And because the east was in constant competition with the west it also formally reformed the penal code, but because the Stasi made sure that the execution of such liberty rights was limited, they existed on paper only. Thus, both the integration in an international human rights regime and the growing bottom-up pressure triggered democratic reforms and leveraged the rule of law and compliance with human rights in West Germany. In the East, however, the spiral went further down.

---

[212] K. Hanshew, *Terror and Democracy in West Germany*, pp. 160–174.
[213] H. Weber, *Die DDR 1945–1990*.

Fourth Decade: 1980–1989

If it were not for the fall of the Berlin Wall in 1989, the fourth post-war decade would have been seen as the one of stability for the two regimes: the autocratic-totalitarian regime in the east, and the liberal consensus-orientated democratic regime in the West. Instead, it was a decade of erosion through civil rights movements, citizens' claims and increasing participation that had a significant impact on political culture. On both sides of the Iron Curtain, a new generation of politicians, tech-nocrats, judges, as well as civil activists in search of their identity, dared to look back to 1945 and allowed themselves to feel remorse and moral responsibility. They demanded more than just atonement, trials and con-victions, counting the dead, or granting reparations. The Holocaust and the issue of German guilt had entered the public domain and media long ago and, more than any previous generation, this one identified with all victims of Nazi terror: communists, Jews, Roma, homosexuals and other ethnic minorities. In West Germany not a single week passed without the German media addressing the Nazi past in films, reports, media columns or talk shows. Researchers and academics soon filled libraries with their studies, doctoral theses, documentaries and conference reports on what had happened, when, how and why. For this generation, it was normal to see and hear parliament debating the creation of memorial days, trials of former concentration camp guards, the inauguration of memorials and the establishment of compensation funds. There were no longer any his-tory books that denied the facts of the war crimes committed by the Nazis, although the precise interpretation of these historical facts remains con-tested even now. The massive, bottom-up demand for TJ had significant impact on German political perception and democratic behaviour, on both sides of the Wall even though in the east it could not be approached in the same way as in the west.[214]

TJ measures were no longer just the concern of an elite, exclusive circle of intellectuals and victims or only a response to Allied pressure and vigi-lance. Instead, they became part of both Germanys' civic cultures. This was a period characterised by naming perpetrators and victims of the Third Reich through criminal charges and memorials. Prior to this shift, perpe-trators and victims had simply been labelled as 'Nazis', 'Sinti' or 'Jews', but later turned into big memorials around the world. Now, people wanted to

---

[214] E. Wolfrum, *Die geglückte Demokratie*, pp. 391–430.

differentiate more. The desire to reckon with the past and the perceived moral obligation to redress past wrongs, spilled over to influence the political relationships between German and former occupied states and territories all over Europe, in particular France and Poland. Interestingly, when the Berlin Wall came down on 9 November 1989 the West German Chancellor Helmut Kohl was on a state visit to Poland.[215] Some linked this moment and Kohl's presence in Poland with another highly significant moment of post-war history 20 years earlier: Chancellor Brandt kneeling before the Warsaw memorial in Poland in 1970. Thus one can argue that the way TJ is linked to any consolidation process in Germany had also always been closely related to the relationship of reunified Germany with Poland. The fact that the Poles had suffered tremendously under the Nazi occupation and that Auschwitz is located in Poland, was one of the key issues in this relationship.

But let me start at the beginning of the decade. It started with the West German federal elections of 1982. Power changed hands from the social democrats back to the conservative CDU. Soon thereafter, Chancellor Helmut Kohl, himself a historian, gave a number of landmark speeches dealing with the past. In this third post-war decade, TJ slowly moved towards becoming state doctrine, a position that was solidified after reunification. Although Kohl was not always sensitive in character, dealing with the past (*Vergangenheitsbewältigung*) was a key issue for him, and he practised it widely in German external relations and in domestic politics.[216] He aimed to revitalise German self-esteem, moving away from a guilt-ridden post-war generation towards a generation that could take responsibility for what happened in the past. In his inauguration speech to the German Bundestag in 1982, he emphasised that he wanted to give Germans more confidence in their achievements since 1945 and to shift the focus from atonement to responsibility. In 1984, he addressed the Israeli Knesset in Jerusalem and spoke about Germany's special responsibility towards Israel, one that goes beyond normal foreign relations. He also spoke about the mercy he and his generation had been given by not having to carry any personal guilt for the Holocaust. The 'mercy of being born late' (*Gnade der späten Geburt*) – meaning born towards the end of or after World War II – became a metaphor that reflected the post-war generation's feelings at that time. Kohl also indirectly confirmed that

---

[215] M.E. Sarotte, *The Collapse. The Accidental Opening of the Berlin Wall* (New York: Basic Books, 2014).

[216] D. Cohen, 'Transitional Justice in Divided Germany after 1945', pp. 59–88.

the post-war generation that entered into politics in the 1960s, as he did, would make their decisions on a different basis than those who had experienced the war and who perhaps had something to hide. In 1984, West Germany officially recognised the assassination attempt against Hitler on 20 July 1944 and remembered the opposition leaders who once had been considered traitors executed by the Nazi regime, now as resistance fighters. The so-called 'men of 20 July' had been controversial for over 40 years. In the first decades after World War II, it had been impossible to raise the question about these resistance fighters openly because there were too many NSDAP elites in office who would never agree to commemorate the 'men of 20 July' as rightful objectors to the Hitler regime. Forty years later that perception has shifted dramatically, not only due to the 20+ and 68er generation, but also because novels, films, documentation and the media had revealed some of the facts around 20 July 1944. Now, 60 per cent of all West Germans thought it was a heroic act, whereas only 12 per cent thought it had been wrong.[217]

Kohl inaugurated a German history museum in Bonn. The Home of German History (*Haus der Geschichte*) was primarily focused on post-war democratic history and the development of West Germany after the war. Until then, German history had been largely dominated by everything that had happened up until 1945 and not beyond. This was due in part to the division of the country, the Hallstein Doctrine and the 'blind spots' of political leadership. As a result, a common narrative among historians still had to be created on how to interpret the early post-war era. This museum led to public debates on whether German citizens should be proud of their democratic achievements as much as they should have a sense of responsibility for what happened prior to 1945. The museum project was realised in 1986, but only opened in 1994 due to German reunification in 1990.

Meanwhile in the east the civil rights movement rose more and more against the regime, but so did the neo-Nazi movement, too. The SED regime did not know how to react as it had always ignored the fact that there could be any traces of Nazism left in the anti-fascist SED regime. In 1983, however, one of the last trials against a high-ranked Nazi perpetrator took place in East Berlin. Heinz Barth had been accused of massacres against civilians during the war and thus been sentenced to life

---

[217] Institute für Demoskopie Allensbach, *Wiederstand im Drittem Reich. Wissen und Urteil der Bevölkerung vor und nach dem 40. Jahrestag des 20 Juli 1944* (Allensbach am Bodensee: Institute für Demoskopie Allensbach, 1985), p. 5.

imprisonment. This was one of the last cases but a public one, in order to show to the world that attempts to indict Nazis also took place in the east.[218]

In 1985, a year after Kohl's response to the public domain on how to deal with the past, President Richard von Weizäcker (CDU) held a land-mark speech in the Federal German Bundestag declaring 8 May 1945 the liberation day from Nazi Germany.[219] This represented a significant shift in the interpretation of the German perspective on World War II – similar to the one on the 'men of 20 July'. Fifteen years earlier, Chancellor Brandt had failed to introduce this debate to the public. However, at this time, the common narrative switched from the idea that Germany had lost the war and sustained millions of German victims to the belief that Germany had been liberated from Nazi dictatorship. The current generation came to see the loss of the war as a chance to experiment with democracy. In a survey conducted in 1985, when West Germans were asked which event and date over the course of the past 40 years had been the most strik-ing and important in their collective memory, their answer was 8 May 1945, the date they saw marking the radical and imposed regime shift. Surprisingly enough, this date was seen as more important than for exam-ple the RAF violence, the establishment of the Republic in 1949 or the recent instalment of Pershing rockets in West Germany in 1983.[220] This illustrated how relevant the war and its consequences had been in col-lective memory, although the focus had shifted from Germans being the victims to having been the victimisers.

At this time, the upward spiral of regime consolidation slowed down and started to turn into regime manifestation. The debate concerning the historical interpretation of the Holocaust that started in 1986 in West German media and among historians and philosophers (*Historikerstreit*) marked that phase. This debate was also inspired by a Frankfurt play by Rainer Werner Fassbinder that made indirect reference to the remaining anti-Semitism and the legacy of the Holocaust in Germany while por-traying Jewish stereotypes. Shortly afterwards, a German parliamentar-ian and a city mayor made anti-Semitic comments on how 'powerful' Jewish business people were still in Frankfurt and elsewhere. Despite

---

[218] E. Wolfrum, *Die geglückte Demokratie*, pp. 261–271.
[219] H. Dubiel, *Niemand ist frei von der Geschichte*, pp. 198–200.
[220] Institute für Demoskopie Allensbach, *Der 8 Mai und die Deutschen. Ergebnisse einer Repräsentativumfrage im Auftrag des Bundespresseamts* (Allensbach am Bodensee: Institute für Demoskopie Allensbach, 1985), p. 3.

all the efforts to reveal and demystify the past, hidden anti-Semitism seemed to break out again – or in other words, denying anti-Semitism never worked to restrain it. A strong democracy ought to be able to tolerate these debates without fearing regime collapse. Yet, at first, the comments by the mayor became a public scandal, which also led to political and academic debates about individual responsibilities during the Holocaust. Due to these cultural activities referencing the need of more TJ in the years that followed, public debate focused almost exclusively on the Jewish victims of the Holocaust, and less on all the other millions of victims the war had claimed.[221] In comparison to earlier decades and to East Germany, these debates were held freely and without major repercussions for those who led them, although stereotypes about Jews were still widespread.[222]

Leading historians and intellectuals such as Habermas led the historical debates at the time, bringing to light controversial left and right-wing opinions on Hitler's motivation as to why he initiated the persecution and genocide of the Jews.[223] The main controversy was whether the Holocaust was a unique genocide of its kind and even specific to Germans, or a genocide that could be repeated anywhere at any time in the future. The question was never finally answered, even after the 1994 genocide in Rwanda and the parallels some drew between those atrocities and Nazi terror. These debates had an indirect impact on democratic culture and citizen trust in public institutions. Regardless of their outcome, the fact that these debates could be held peacefully without major insults or terror threats from either side of the political spectrum was a novelty in West Germany. An opinion poll from that year shows that the majority of citizens supported strict consequences for public figures and politicians who made anti-Semitic or stereotyped comments about Jews in public. Seventy-one per cent of Germans believed that those public officials should either resign from office or apologise for their expressions against Jews.[224] At the same time, 66 per cent of the population also wished that they could finally leave the past behind.[225]

Many West German politicians still showed great insensitivity towards the past. They did not so much deny the wrongdoings of the past, as they

---

[221] E. Wolfrum, *Die geglückte Demokratie*, pp. 391–392.

[222] Institute für Demoskopie Allensbach, *Deutsche und Juden*, p. 48.

[223] R.J. Evans, *Im Schatten Hitlers? Historikerstreit und Vergangenheitsbewältigung in der Bundesrepublik* (Frankfurt am Main: Suhrkamp, 1991).

[224] Institute für Demoskopie Allensbach, *Deutsche und Juden*, p. 59.

[225] Ibid., p. 76.

debated the consequences to draw from them. Above all, they asked the question whether German responsibility for the past should impact political doctrines (as it did in foreign policy) and whether an individual should take responsibility if one's parent had been actively involved in the atrocities of the past. An example of this can be seen in the political scandal around Philipp Jenninger who was chair of the West German parliament in Bonn in 1988. In a speech in November 1988 to remember the 1938 Jewish pogroms (*Reichskristallnacht*) he asked whether Jews themselves were somewhat responsible for, or at least provoked, the crimes committed by the Nazis because of their 'different Jewish' behaviour.[226] The speech was criticised internationally by the media and across the political spectrum in Germany. Shortly after his presentation, Jenninger had to resign from office, which was also a first in the history of parliament, bearing in mind that only 20 years earlier a former member of the NSDAP could become chancellor. It has never been clarified whether he made his comments unintentionally or with the intention to provoke. The reaction of parliamentarians and the public, however, showed that in this fourth decade since regime change, making such comments was inappropriate and could cost one one's office; as opposed to what had been the case in the 1950s and 1960s.[227]

At the same time in the east, Erich Honecker, still head of the SED regime, sought more international recognition and aimed to be invited to speak on behalf of the 'other' Germany in Washington DC. He knew that his best chance of fostering strong relations with the United States would be via recognising the victimhood of millions of Jews and thus to establish ties with Israel. In 1988 he allowed the renovation of the main synagogues in East Berlin (formerly the largest in Germany) and invited religious and civil leaders from Israel for its inauguration. It was an act of TJ and establishing ties with Israel, but despite his attempt to finally recognise his own regime's responsibility to reckon with the past, Honecker was never invited by western Allies and in the following year the Berlin Wall fell.

Meanwhile, throughout the 1980s trials against Nazi perpetrators continued, particularly focused on finding alleged perpetrators around the word. The Los Angeles-based Salomon Wiesenthal Centre reinvigorated its systematic search for hidden perpetrators in order to extradite them, if necessary, to West Germany where, thanks to the legal reforms of the

[226] H. Dubiel, *Niemand ist frei von der Geschichte*, pp. 217–218.
[227] D. Cohen, 'Transitional Justice in Divided Germany after 1945', pp. 59–88.

1970s, they could still be tried. Some were also tried in the countries where they were resident. Every time an extradition or bringing of charges was successful, it was taken up in the press. Nevertheless, it was at the same time more of a moral verdict than a legal one. Trials could take years, and often those convicted were too old to actually go to prison.

There was also another major political shift that drove regime consolidation. The generation of 1968 gained political power and moved from the streets into parliament. The Green Party appeared on the political scene for the first time, making a strong statement that TJ was fundamental to German democracy and consolidation and that they would push for it. In 1982 and 1983, the Green Party entered the West German parliament under its charismatic leader Joschka Fischer who, 20 years later, became foreign minister of reunified Germany. The Greens made sure that radical right-wing speeches and arguments were countered and made it clear that not only West Germany, but also both Germanys had a unique and specific responsibility towards Jews and for the Nazi past as a whole. Kohl pushed for a 'moral change' (*geistig moralische Wende*) in Germany and a normalisation of its foreign relationships with Israel, France, Poland and other countries, as well as with the victim groups and survivors, although he did not clarify what 'normalisation' meant.[228]

In the east, however, a generation similar to the 1968 one in West Germany never emerged, and the citizen movements that did emerge in the 1980s were rather late, even by Eastern European standards. Therefore, regime consolidation by civil society never occurred in the east and therefore the regime was never fully legitimised and had to rule by coercion only. This kind of failure in democratic consolidation was a frequent one in other countries, too, as described by Linz and Stepan.[229] Yet, in the 1980s, over 300 mainly peace and environmental movements (with around 15,000 people in a country that held around 18 million citizens) took off in East Germany. The majority of these movements acted locally, aiming to change or 'improve' the SED regime, but not necessarily to abolish socialism. Thus, while these groups did not engage in a major critique of the system, they did criticise the functioning of this particular socialist regime function. Under the umbrella of the Evangelical Churches, these groups protested against corruption, war, Stasi surveillance, environmental pollution and lack of freedom in the east. Yet, they did not necessarily connect the current authoritarianism of the regime

---

[228]   H. Kohl, *Erinnerungen 1982–1990* (Munich: Droemer Verlag, 2005), p. 51.
[229]   J.J. Linz and A. Stepan, *Problems of Democratic Transition and Consolidation*, pp. 56ff.

to the fact that the past regime had never been delegitimised. This was a lost generation in terms of TJ, partly because of successful SED propaganda against Nazism and partly because of the fact that those who truly opposed the SED regime had already fled to the west in the 1960s and subsequent decades.[230]

At the height of the Cold War there were more protests than ever against the US decision to base more nuclear bombs in West Germany. This increase in protest affected West Germany's civil society and peace movements, of which mainly the 1968 generation were members. West Germans feared nuclear war more than reunification with the communist east and strongly believed that reconciliation between the two countries was possible, although it would require making compromises. In opposition to the demands of the peace movement, the United States installed more nuclear weapons on West German soil, indicating an erosion of the 'stability pact' between the east and the west that had kept the world more or less free of war until that point. The United States placed nuclear weapons in West Germany and the Soviet Union did the same in East Germany in the name of self-defence and deterrence. This even triggered the East German peace movement, including many churches (*Schwerter zu Pflugscharen*), out of which grew a civil and human rights movement that launched the Monday demonstrations of 1988 and 1989 and which contributed to the fall of the Berlin Wall.[231] These were the only years in which there was effective citizen mobilisation in East Germany, according to Olivo.[232] At the centre of the movement was the fact that people on both sides of the Iron Curtain had become aware that if a war between the east and west were to break out, they would be the primary targets of complete destruction. In West Germany, the peace movement linked the current threat of war with the memory of the past. Intentionally or not, this resulted in citizens on both sides of the Wall using the slogan 'Never again war!', a variation on the earlier 'Never again Auschwitz' (a slogan that had only been used in West Germany).

While East Germany heavily suppressed peace protests and activists had to go underground to avoid prison, protesters in West Germany became more institutionalised and organised, often led by CSOs and the Green Party. As a consequence, in West Germany the anti-nuclear

---

[230] C. Olivo, *Creating a Democratic Civil Society in Eastern Germany*, pp. 62–64.
[231] E. Neubert, *Geschichte der Opposition in der DDR 1949-1989 (Forschungen zur DDR-Gesellschaft)* (Berlin: Christoph Links Verlag, 1998).
[232] C. Olivo, *Creating a Democratic Civil Society in Eastern Germany*, p. 62.

war, peace and human rights movement that marched every year at the East German border for peace and reconciliation was a strong and significant constituency. This movement combined demands for peace and reconciliation, based on an overall awareness of the atrocities that potential war could lead to, as learned from the joint narratives of World War II. The past was always present in these political debates, as was TJ.

At this time, however, political debates were less emotional and the accusations less personal that they had been in the past, perhaps due to the fact that many of the accused perpetrators, bystanders, survivors, and resistance fighters were either no longer alive or were retired from prominent positions. It is by no means a coincidence that it took until after Weizäcker's speech in 1985 that the thousands of death sentences rendered by the Nazi High Court were seen as unjust verdicts and invalid according to the norms of the 1980s. The West German parliament acquitted these victims *post mortem*, at a time in which hardly any of the old elites were still in office and thus no longer opposed this decision.

As illustrated by Jon Elster, it is a pattern that a society can only move on once its past has been demystified, the regime fully delegitimised and the files have been opened so that memorials are established and trials are being held without restrictions.[233] The public West German debates of the late 1980s were thus of a different quality than those in the 1950s or 1960s and far less polemic. Newspaper headlines by Springer Press, a conservative publishing house, for example, continuously led to public debates among left and right-wing movements, but in a less destructive way than in the 1960s. Springer Press was accused of being conservative and pro-right wing and of having rather strict anti-communist views and was held accountable for the impact it had on public opinion. Ever since the end of World War II, Springer had owned the largest media consortium in West Germany. The articles of its main daily publications such as *Bild* or *Die Welt* newspapers justified anti-communist laws and other restrictive measures against those who threatened German democracy, which of course, in their view, were the left-wing movements. Springer Press had been a big defender of militant democracy and had great influence on public opinion. This media outlet stood in contrast to the rather left-wing, often pro-socialist press that had gained ground in German public opinion, in particular among academics. These outlets, such as

---

[233] J. Elster, *Closing the Books.*

Der Spiegel, Süddeutsche Zeitung, Frankfurter Rundschau, all became very strong in the 1980s, again thanks to the 1968 generation which occupied many of the media sectors by then. This cannot be ignored when explaining the political shift towards TJ and how to deal with the past. One of the spiral effects was that victims and interest groups other than Jewish claims groups became actively involved in society and politics in the 1980s. They not only 'dared' to be more democratic, they also dared to use more TJ. Public awareness changed as well. German victims of deportation and refugees from the east were no longer seen as victims on the same level as Holocaust victims. The notion of collective memory, moral responsibility and a shared (unfalsified) narrative, which had been anticipated by Kohl and von Weizäcker, slowly replaced the term collective guilt in the public arena.

Yet, it became apparent that progressive TJ movements and politics do not necessarily work together in harmony. Not surprisingly, the 1980s were also the decade of a thriving neo-Nazi movement in both Germanys. Above all, this indicated that many of the past myths about the 'heroic German race' had not been sufficiently demystified or delegitimised. Although the neo-Nazi movement never reached a critical mass, let alone serious political influence, it threatened people with hate speech, thus threatening social peace on both sides of the Iron Curtain. Anti-Semitic movements and attacks against Jewish cemeteries led to new forms of thinking about the Holocaust and more policies and how to educate and provide information about the past. In East Germany, the SED regime applied its usual state-centred top-down approach, imprisoning people who took part in anti-Semitic action without allowing any public debate. The main newspaper in the east, *Neues Deutschland*, was a party propaganda outlet and thus state-controlled. An open, let alone controversial public debate about anti-Semitic tendencies, Neo-Nazi movements or TJ in general was not possible. Instead, and all of a sudden, the SED discovered TJ again as a useful tool for political concessions in reaching diplomatic ties with Israel and thus inaugurated memorials and celebrated prominent German-Jewish artists and communists, many of whom had been Holocaust victims and therefore had remained in the east.[234] This was a new era in East Germany's top-down TJ approach and in its foreign policy. In the 1980s, the SED politburo aimed to protect the country from international criticism that it had not sufficiently fought Nazism and thus had to show how to combat anti-Semitism. Another example of the

---

[234] O. Groehler, 'Der Holocaust in der Geschichtsschreibung der DDR', pp. 47–63.

East German regime's top-down approach to TJ is the restoration of the largest German synagogue in East Berlin that had been destroyed during the *Reichskristallnacht* in 1938 and remained untouched for over 40 years. As indicated earlier, in 1988 the SED ordered it restored to satisfy international pressure and to strive for recognition. This was not for moral reasons, but because the regime aimed for diplomatic ties with Israel and wanted to avoid neo-Nazi groups undermining the power of the one-party regime and its reputation abroad. It was the time of appeasement politics, the de-escalation of the Cold War and the opening up of the east. It was now, finally, that the SED did for tactical reasons what the Adenauer government had done 30 years earlier.

At the same time, suppression by the Stasi grew even stronger as the civil rights movement and the neo-Nazi movement became stronger, both posing a serious threat to communist doctrine and one-party rule. The right-wing movement often used violent means to express its disagreement with the political regime, such as the desecration of Jewish cemeteries. Although such violent neo-Nazi acts also happened frequently in West Germany, the manner in which they were dealt with by the regime was different by that time.

In West Germany, neo-Nazi attacks at the Oktoberfest in Munich and the killing of a Jewish publisher in 1980, garnished public attention for the movement, but more protest against the neo-Nazi movement. This neo-Nazi movement rose up at the same time as – and was soon outnumbered by – the peace movement. Nevertheless, the neo-Nazi movement remained a serious concern for all political leaders. Many of the members were prosecuted and indicted under Section 130 of the West German Criminal Code, a provision that was part of the German move towards militant democracy. One could be indicted under Section 130 for singing the Nazi Horst Wessel anthem in public, promoting anti-Semitic protest, denying or attempting to justify the Holocaust, displaying the Nazi Swastika or associated symbols, or celebrating Hitler's birthday in public. Charges ranged from financial penalties to up to five years in prison, although defendants were most often released on bail and only received minor penalties of several hundred marks. Although Hitler nostalgia and Holocaust denial were illegal, it became clear that punitive measures alone could not halt the tide of neo-Nazism. Education and awareness programmes were installed again and 're-integration' and 'exit' programmes were launched for Nazis who wanted to leave the right-wing movement, although it was not always clear whether this led to success. The difference between the neo-Nazi movement in the 1980s and that of previous decades was that the movement of the 1980s was almost exclusively composed of second post-war generation members who had never been through a war or seen a concentration camp. In the previous decades, the neo-Nazi sympathisers had been war veterans or former NSDAP and SS members who aimed to preserve the 'nationalist glory of the past'. They saw themselves as elites and celebrated their nostalgia in closed circles. Such groups had little in common with the new nationalists who fuelled the racist and xenophobic movement in the 1980s. Public institutions reacted with increased surveillance of right-wing and neo-Nazi groups.[235]

In the 'new dictatorship' in the east, another radicalisation of the young generation started taking place 20–25 years after the Berlin Wall was built and the Iron Curtain was closed. Similar to the first post-war generation and its radicalisation in the 1960s, it was now predictable that not only a left-wing movement would start questioning the governance practice of the SED regime, but that also a neo-Nazi movement would become active. These groups posed a real dilemma for the communist regime, since, according to its official propaganda, East Germany had successfully eliminated all Nazis in the country. But the new right-wing groups violated Jewish cemeteries and proclaimed the Third Reich as a successful era in German history. In 1987, the East German neo-Nazi movement had approximately 1,000 members in a country with around 18 million inhabitants. Some of these members raided a church concert of a rather left-wing activist group in East Berlin. Their actions undermined the official propaganda of the SED, illustrating that the SED's suppression of open dialogue about the past had not created a socialist culture, as the communist leaders had hoped it would.

At the same time, human rights and civil society movements in East Germany grew out of the peace movement. These movements focused on two points: first, protesting the threat of a nuclear war; and second, joining a civil rights movement such as *Solidarność* in Poland or *Charta 77* in Czechoslovakia. This movement had no direct connection to Germany's past, but was a result of the government's failure to openly deal with World War II and to become more democratic. Accordingly, this movement directly targeted the suppressive SED regime.[236]

During this decade, citizen engagement and civic trust reached a peak on both sides of the Iron Curtain. Citizens used formal and public

[235] E. Wolfrum, *Die geglückte Demokratie*, pp. 391–430.
[236] E. Neubert, *Geschichte der Opposition in der DDR 1949–1989*.

channels to make their demands with legal means, petitions and peaceful protest. It weakened the regime in the east but strengthened the one in the west. In the west, civil protest and growing citizen engagement in politics led to large political shifts and changes and thus to more accountability and responsiveness from the executive and legislature. Open and public debates were held and the questioning of the historical narrative of the past took place. The peace movement rose and executive and legislative powers had to respond in a more sensitive fashion to their claims. The 'paternalistic' or 'militant' democracy of the early post-war years had disappeared and been replaced by 'citizen democracy'. But by 1989, civic turmoil and unrest in East Germany rose and in the west the large majority of Germans were either fairly satisfied or very satisfied with democracy (78 per cent had a high level of civic trust in institutions).[237]

In November 1989, public pressure and civic engagement led to the fall of the Berlin Wall and eventually to the reunification of East and West Germany. From then on, TJ and democratic institutions were closely linked in the new transitional process in East Germany with a short period of regime change that quickly turned into consolidation.

This rupture and regime shift in 1989/90 took place under completely different conditions than the regime change of 1945. One of the reasons was the change in morality and the awareness about human rights norms and standards among the wider public. As Kathryn Sikkink and Beth Simmons have noted, human rights norm diffusion starting already at that time was part of the larger process of delegitimisation of autocratic regimes around the globe.[238] These certainly did have an effect on East Germany and, due to the pressures from below, the SED regime passed rehabilitation (de facto amnesty) laws for all political indictments and sentences (*SED-Unrechtsbereinigungsgesetze*) one week prior to the fall of the Wall in November 1989. These laws were aimed at easing tensions in society.[239] These quasi-amnesty laws were not only aimed at the massive number of political prisons in East Germany, but also intended to account for all 'political crimes' by the SED leadership. This was similar to what

---

[237] European Union, Eurobarometer Surveys, Germany 1989.11, http://ec.europa.eu (last accessed August 2013).
[238] K. Sikkink, *The Justice Cascade*; and B.A. Simmons, *Mobilizing for Human Rights*.
[239] J. Arnold, 'Zweiter Teil. Ergebnisse im Einzelnen. 3.Bundesrepublik Deutschland/DDR' in A. Esser, U. Sieber and J. Arnold (eds.), *Strafrecht in Reaktion auf Systemunrecht. Vergeichend Einblicke in Transtiosprozesse, Transitionsstrafrecht und Vergagenheitspolitik* (Berlin: Max Planck Institute für ausländiches und inteternationales Straftrecht, 2012), pp. 314–315.

many regimes in transition did, such as the Adenauer government in 1949 and King Juan of Spain after Franco's death in 1975. Seeing the end of the regime coming, the political elites took any measure they could to preserve as much status as possible and avoid future prosecution. It is more the rule than the exception that this will lead to a culture of impunity that can hamper democratic development as was the case in the early years of West Germany.[240]

However, once the regime made these and other concessions to quell the growing unrest in the country and to appease the 'Monday protesters' throughout the cities in East Germany, more exposure for the regime followed. The rather peaceful 'revolution' of the autumn of 1989 made it clear that time for change was long overdue and that citizens would determine how the second German dictatorship in the course of a century would be dealt with. It was citizens who had dissolved the 'shield and sword' of communist power, the Stasi headquarters in East Berlin, in November 1989 and who had turned it into a centre of commemoration and education. There was no military intervention this time, a fact that certainly determined the role TJ would play in dealing with the communist past.

Between November 1989 and the spring of 1990, members of the political SED elite and the Stasi were highly intent on destroying, burning and shredding tonnes of files and documents that could prove the use of suppression, human rights violations and corruption to keep the 'socialist revolution' going. This showed that the SED and Stasi feared TJ measures and citizen acts of vengeance.[241] The remaining political SED elite that was officially still in power after November 1989 immediately planned to establish their own commissions of enquiry as early as December 1989 and planned to include civil rights movements in dealing with the past. The SED reacted fast, using the promise of TJ measures and the justice and truth they could bring, to ease citizens' demands and the violence on the street. The measures promised by the SED included amnesty laws and reforms of the secret service and other institutions.[242] Political elites knew, either consciously or unconsciously, that democracy – whatever that might entail – could only be attained with TJ measures. Later

[240] J.E. Mendez, 'In Defence of Transitional Justice', pp. 1–26, at p. 1.

[241] A. Sa'adah, Germany's Second Chance. Trust, Justice, and Democratisation (Cambridge, MA: Harvard University Press, 1998), p. 217.

[242] P. Bock, Vergangenheitspolitik im Systemwechesel. Die Politik der Aufklärung. Strafverfolgung, Disqualifizierung und Wiedergutmachung im letzten Jahren der DDR (Berlin: Logos Verlag, 2000), p. 143.

in March 1990 the civil rights movement in East Germany demanded its own independent commissions of inquiry and further TJ measures. Thus, during the year prior to and the year after reunification with West Germany, the East German interim parliament (composed mainly of old SED elites), passed a number of rehabilitation and amnesty laws as a TJ package to deal with the dictatorial past. This package included restitution for property (which was later paid by West Germany) and rehabilitation measures. Yet, it also included a number of measures meant to allow communist party members to keep their positions in the government and bureaucracy of the state.[243] This plan did not work, as after reunification the joint German parliament introduced long-lasting lustration and reparation policies that counteracted the earlier political initiatives. The year 1989 was a milestone for both regime change and regime consolidation, because it was clear to all from the beginning that the unified country could not transition from one regime to another without the application of at least some TJ measures. This was a phenomenon that had been accepted across the globe, and one that would be put into place in many countries in the decades that followed.

Fifth Decade: 1990–1999

In 'Germany's Second Chance', Anne Saʼadah illustrated the challenges and missed opportunities that Germany experienced after reunification in 1990. She wrote about the disappointments, compromises and identity crisis that the unified country faced during this decade.[244] Saʼadah particularly focused on the intertwining and spiral relationship of various actors and institutions that struggled between trust, legitimacy and the adequate use of TJ measures. As Hazan, O'Donnell and Schmitter have emphasised, it is this first decade during which the roadmap between the will to consolidate with the support of TJ is drafted and result will be seen much later.[245]

By the end of the 1990s, all possible TJ measures had been introduced and applied, either in dealing with the legacy of World War II or with the legacy of the communist past in East Germany. Moreover, the 1990s saw the coming together of two different approaches to TJ – that of West Germany and that of East Germany – in the one country united. Because

[243] Ibid., pp. 412–417.
[244] A. Saʼadah, *Germany's Second Chance*.
[245] P. Hazan, *Judging War, Judging History*, p. 31.

of that, this decade marked the most intense era in terms of TJ and regime consolidation, because it had to deal with two TJ processes at the same time – the ongoing post-World War II one and the new post-SED regime one. Although the unification in October 1990 came a bit by surprise, the reunified government had learned from the risks that too many or too few TJ measures at the same time can impose on consolidation. Even after the first fair and free elections on East German soil in March 1990, the new mixed political elites and actors in East Berlin who had already started to set up their own truth commission and mapped out possible trials, and so forth, were in a weak position to negotiate their own transition process with their western counterparts.[246] Only half a year later, the reunification of October 1990 made the outcome of the elections obsolete.

Without doubt, too many trials at once, biased lustration processes and exclusionary reparations to a few but not all victim groups can weaken this process if those responsible for past crimes are not *all* targeted on an equal basis. The benchmark for successful TJ was whether old East German elites would seek a recurrence of the former Stasi-based regime and receive a lot of support of citizens or if they would become an integrated part of all Germany without causing any unconsolidated pocket of democracy by the end of the decade.

Unique to any post-communist country in Eastern Europe, Germany saw the expulsion of all communist elites, all at once, from office through massive vetting procedures, thousands of trials in extraordinary chambers dealing with political and property claims, opening of the notorious Stasi records and establishing a truth and history commission in the German parliament. Within seven years after reunification the parliament had passed three laws to eradicate SED injustice, issued trials and massive vetting procedures, charged and compensated thousands of citizens who had been deprived of their property, been abducted or put into prison for political reasons.[247] TJ measures applied on East Germany meant overall acknowledgement and criminal justice through vetting and lustration procedures and reparations by dealing with property issues of the past. Most of these measures were symbolic, since East Germany no longer legally or politically existed after 1990. Jon Elster has stated that

---

[246] Interview with Martin Gutzeit, Federal Commissioner for the Stasi Files in the State of Berlin (Berlin, June 2015).

[247] For an overview of the German measures and laws after 1945 and 1990, respectively, see: S.F. Kellerhoff, *Learning from History – A Handbook for Examining Dictatorships*, *Gedenkstaette Hohenschoenhausen* (Beier, Wellach, Berlin, 2013).

the post-communist elite was surprisingly passive and opportunistic in Eastern Europe and the TJ process was rather technical and bureaucratic.[248] The installation of TJ measures was confronted with less resistance than it was in the period between 1945 and the fall of the Wall.

Juan Espindola has assessed the TJ process in unified Germany concerning the east and has concluded that its main achievement has been the public exposure of former perpetrators, leading to delegitimisation of the communist regime and those responsible for it.[249] He described a truly anti-communist TJ process, with the sole purpose of delegitimising the SED regime, without seeing much need to legitimise the new democratic regime, since the institutions were mostly copied from West Germany and thus already in place. But this was also a missed opportunity, as it 'imposed democratic institutions' instead of allowing people to build them up, and has haunted East German political and civic culture since the 1990s, i.e. in how to treat and deal with minorities, a high level of xenophobia and neo-Nazi movements and other radical, nationalistic views which are much more frequent in the east than in the west.

This decade could also have been a moment for dealing with the West German past between 1949 and 1989, including the wrongdoings and human rights abuses of West German authorities against the RAF and other left-wing opposition groups during the Cold War. However, Germany neglected to deal with this past at all, thus making the TJ approach biased against East Germany. Blame was not put on all sides, but only on those who collaborated with the SED regime (and only if they were not prominent West German politicians). West German collaborators with the SED regime were hardly brought to justice. Many East Germans, even those who had risked their lives protesting on the streets of Leipzig and Berlin prior to 9 November 1989 (the day the Wall felt), perceived this way of dealing with the past, the total defeat of alternative elites from the former GDR and the swift imposition of democratic and liberal values as victor's justice, similar to how Germans perceived the trials of their former political and military elites after 1945.

Nevertheless, regime change and consolidation in the east through accession continued swiftly and in a much more diverse and self-critical – albeit not ideal – way than ever before. The situation was such that McAdams referred to East Germany as a completely defeated regime that

---

[248] J. Elster, *Closing the Books*, p. 252.
[249] J. Espindola, *Transitional Justice after German Reunification, Exposing Unofficial Collaborators* (Cambridge: Cambridge University Press, 2015), p. 239.

the West German authorities in Bonn 'inherited' in 1990. According to McAdams, 'they did not have to worry about the kinds of concerns that have made the pursuit of transitional justice in other settings so precarious and complicated . . . there were no contending military elites in the wings waiting to reassert themselves should their country's democratically elected leaders appear to go too far in their reckoning with past crimes.'[250] German authorities almost immediately introduced a functioning bureaucracy and there was never any serious social instability in the newly united regime. However, there was the risk of dividing the young reunified country into a 'winner' and 'loser' side, which indeed happened in the following decades.

It was almost a simple technocratic transition, but the hearts and minds of 18 million people still had to be won.[251] A survey from October 1990 showed that a large majority of Germans had great confidence in the (new) democratic regime. Seventy-five per cent of all respondents expressed their overall satisfaction and trust in the regime – a regime that many East Germans had previously only known from television. Only 22 per cent expressed no satisfaction with these institutions.[252] Public opinion was influenced by the fact that it was the financially well-equipped western institutions that were imposed on the smaller-sized eastern part of the country. Thus institutions and actors in the east could not grow out of themselves, make their mistakes, renegotiate laws and policies with groups, and thus often led to marginalisation of political opinion and thus their radicalisation in the east which remained way beyond another post-communist generation in 2015. Nevertheless, the idea that it 'would take at least a generation' to overcome the cultural and political cleavages and to fully adhere to democratic rules soon became common in German public life and the majority of people adapted. This TJ process would be less punitive or restorative and instead more about establishing a common narrative and culture among all Germans.

Nevertheless, this TJ was issued in a rapid and massive way. The Unity Treaty provided the provisions for TJ of the coming years, defining in particular individual responsibility for injustice and crimes, especially political crimes in the east, and the possible consequences in terms of vetting and lustration procedures. The Unity Treaty also dealt with property

---

[250] J.A. McAdams, 'Communism on Trial', p. 239.
[251] A. Sa'adah, Germany's Second Chance, p. 59.
[252] European Union, Eurobarometer Surveys, Germany 1990.11, http://ec.europa.eu (last accessed August 2013).

issues arising from both the Nazi and the communist dictatorships, such as the expropriation of Jewish property under the Nazis and subsequently also under the communist regime. After 1990, the unified government had to deal with the past of two dictatorships at the same time. But overall the dictatorship of the SED regime with all its shortcomings and crimes always stood in the shadow of the crimes and atrocities of the Nazi regime. To put equal attention, let alone mobilise large parts of civil society in all of Germany to support both TJ processes equally, was almost impossible and was soon given up on. TJ of the SED regime remains mainly a matter of courts, administration, foundations and private initiatives in federal states of East Germany.

The Stasi files were made public in 1990, and in 1992 parliament decided to set up a commission of formal inquiry into the causes and consequences of the SED dictatorship. The commission (*Enquette Kommission des Deutschen Bundestages*) met over a 25-month period from 1992 to 1994 with 16 members of parliament from all political parties, 11 academic advisers, and others. Forty-four public hearings and 150 subcommittee hearings led to several volumes of testimony and stories about the past. The commission was deemed a success and parliament decided on a second round of investigation in 1995.[253] Joachim Gauck, the first director of the Stasi Record Office, expressed his view that if 'after more than 55 years of Nazi and communist dictatorship in East Germany, citizens were going to trust elected officials under the new democratic system, it was important that those officials be trustworthy.'[254] In Gauck's view, public exposure and opening the Stasi files was a response to the East German citizens' demand that persons who had conspired with the regime should be deemed unsuitable for public position. Nevertheless, only a handful of high-ranked officials have ever been put on trial, and thousands SED technocrats, although indicted, remained untouched. Espindola has interpreted this fact that so few collaborators have been tried and imprisoned as the result of an attempt to 'reincorporate' them into the system, even as opening the files and public exposure meant a rather unambiguous reprobation of those people's missteps in the past.[255] With this policy the judiciary aimed to avoid parallel societies and new division among Germans.

---

[253] J.A. McAdams, 'Reappraising the Conditions of Transitional Justice in Unified Germany', *East European Consititutional Review*, 10(1) (2001), 53–59.
[254] J. Espindola, *Transitional Justice after German Reunification*, p. 214.
[255] Ibid., p. 215.

According to Gauck and Hermann Weber (one of the most distin-
guished scholars of German totalitarianism at that time), the two German
dictatorships from 1933–1945 and 1949–1989 displayed similarities
in their mechanisms of oppression and totalitarianism.[256] For the new
'Berliner Republic', as the unified Germany was called, it was officially
equally important to deal with both of these past regimes. Nevertheless, in
reality, TJ measures were unfortunately split: the Nazi past and the communist past were two different avenues on the road to consolidation. The
TJ process of the communist past was left to and kept by East Germans,
while dealing with the Nazi Germany past remained in the hands of West
German intellectuals, academics, media and CSOs. West Germans did
not care much about East Germans' difficulties in adjusting to the new
democratic regime, let alone the new culture, narrative and behaviour.
On the other side, East Germans often shook their heads when listen-
ing to the controversies surrounding West Germany's 'collective guilt and
responsibility' sentiments. Easterners did not share the collective guilt
of the 1968 generation, let alone their sense of responsibility. To East
Germans, Jews were not seen as having been more victimised in the concentration camps and atrocities of the war than communists, prisoners of
war and dissidents of the Hitler regime or all the other millions of victims.
The point that the racism laws were an inherent part of the Nazi policy
and supported by a large part of Germany and which had led to the killing
of millions of people based on the nature of their birth, and which made
that dictatorship so unique in history, was not captured by many East
Germans at that time.

Reunification also brought with it a chance to face democratic flaws and
obstacles. Because the expectations of reunification and regime change
had been so overwhelmingly high among East Germans, dissatisfaction
soon arose. Dissatisfaction with the democracy had more than doubled
in the three years after reunification and, surprisingly enough, on both
sides. By 1993, almost half of all Germans (47 per cent) were not very
satisfied or not at all satisfied with democracy, and most of them were
East Germans who had expected other ways of dealing with their past.
East Germans were particularly disappointed with a perceived lack of
justice that the few trials and vetting procedures had apparently brought
about. In their eyes they had been conducted in an unfair way.[257] After

[256] H. Weber, *Die DDR 1945–1990*.
[257] European Union, Eurobarometer Surveys, Germany 1993.11, http://ec.europa.eu (last
accessed August 2013).

East Germans experienced and came to understand that democracy is a day-to-day process of compromise and that nothing can be taken for granted, they started to doubt whether democracy was really the best way to go. Thousands of political victims of the SED regime started to demand more justice and compensation by means of restitution of lost property. A federal foundation for political prisoners of the SED regime, already established in West Germany in 1969, became one of the key players pressuring government and parliament to find solutions to these demands. Another one was the NGO for victims of Stalinism (*Opfer des Stalinismus*), the largest membership organisation of victims that suffered SED and Soviet suppression since 1945 and from 1949 onwards. Although the government responded with a number of 'victim' laws including compensation, rehabilitation and restitution measures, the government also started a general debate about whether these people should be considered victims at all. Why not call them heroes who dared to oppose and fight against an unjust regime? Instead of political recognition, they received financial compensation. While this compensation in and of itself was not disputed, the method and means were.[258] Although the other half of the country remained rather satisfied with regime consolidation, the shift to more negative views indicated increased scepticism and disillusionment after the initial euphoria about democracy in 1990. Nonetheless most levels of regime consolidation as described earlier by Merkel, such as the constitutional consolidation, the representative or by attitude and behaviour were rather quickly achieved. The final level of democratic consolidation, however – namely to include civil society as a permanent motor of democracy – needed time and was far from being completed in the 1990s.[259] It would need a generation at least. Since West Germans were in the majority, they dominated the TJ discourse, much to the dissatisfaction of victims of the SED regime. In the West German TJ discourse the Holocaust was the main focus, not the SED regime's massive human rights violations.[260]

The Unity Treaty (*Einigungsvertrag*) in 1990 between the two Germanys and the four former Allied powers – France, Russia (Soviet

---

[258] S. Plogsted, *Knasmauke: Das Schicksal von politischen Häftlingen der DDR nach der deutschen Wiedervereinigung* (Giessen: Psychosizial – Verlag, 2010).

[259] W. Merkel, Systemtransformation, *Eine Einführung in die Theorie und Empirie der Transformationsforschung*, pp. 110–154.

[260] J. Danyel (ed.), *Die geteilte Vergangenheit, Zum Umgang mit Nationalsozialismus und Widerstand in beiden deutschen Staaten* (Berlin: Akademie Verlag, 1995).

Union), the United Kingdom and the US, ensured that war memorials, particularly in former East Germany, would be maintained on the territory of Germany. Although the Soviets emphasised their own version of World War II history in these memorials, the Treaty was clear on this issue. The former Allied victors' commemorations of World War II had to be respected – even though, for many Germans, these memorials were symbols of massive violence, arbitrary killings of civilians, the systematic rape of women, show trials and 40 years of oppression.[261] This posed a paradox: the victimisers were commemorated as heroes whereas the victims were not even mentioned – a situation that reminded many of the dilemmas Chancellor Adenauer faced in the early 1950s with regard to the German refugees. The government responded with memorials for victims of the communist regime. The Soviet memorials of honour that are close to the Brandenburg Gate and in the Teptow district of Berlin are some of the most prominent results of the Treaty, although they are ironically often mistaken for German war memorials. In addition to this, the Treaty provided for the withdrawal of Soviet troops from East Germany. The reunified German government paid for the removal, reintegration and housing of Soviet soldiers returning to the Soviet Union, not only as an act of reconciliation, but also as an indication that the Soviet government was in financial trouble and more than fragile. In the end, and in hindsight, many have wondered who this agreement humiliated more, the Soviets or the Germans? Most importantly, the Treaty revised and updated the German laws of restitution from the 1950s. Between the fall of the SED regime in November 1989 and the reunification of Germany in October 1990, the East German interim government made it clear that past injustice and, in particular, the political imprisonment of 150,000 East German citizens under conditions of ill-treatment or torture, had to be acknowledged. In September 1990 the East German parliament passed a rehabilitation (de facto amnesty) law for those who had been prosecuted for exercising their freedom rights, regardless of whether they were communist or in opposition.

One of the first public and parliamentary debates that linked TJ with consolidation was in 1991 when it was discussed whether Berlin should be reinstated as the capital of Germany. This debate indirectly reflected the question of how reunified Germany would deal with its past. According to the 1949 German Basic Law, to which East Germany had acceded, the

[261] K. Lowe, *Savage Continent*, pp. 75–180.

capital of Germany would be Berlin after reunification. Yet, the parliamentarians from the younger, post-war generations wanted a more open debate on whether this was actually necessary. Bonn had since become the symbol of a successful, peaceful, and moreover consolidated democratic regime in the west. Berlin, on the other hand, had been the capital city of two German dictatorships, a Nazi and a communist one, in one century alone. Despite doubts and concerns, the parliamentarians voted in favour of Berlin. The parliamentary debate as such was interesting, as it indicated the role the past and TJ played in Germany's regime change. During the days and weeks of the debate, parliamentarians from all factions discussed questions of the past, not only concerning World War II, the legacy of both the Nazi regime and the SED regime, recent history, historic symbols and their meanings, as well as what Jan Assmann later called the German 'cultural memory'.[262] Moving the capital back to Berlin was all about how the country would deal with its past in the future and about consolidation, too. Many parliamentarians feared that Berlin's negative legacy of Nazi and Communist dictatorships was too loaded with unsuccessful attempts at consolidation. They feared Berlin as a capital to be a bad omen, because once again it would mean that Germany had to rebuild democracy in parts of its own country where democratic culture had been absent for over six decades, if it had ever been present at all. Now that Germany was a fully sovereign state, it could no longer rely on the Allied forces to check whether democratic consolidation was actually succeeding. It was up to the Germans themselves, and to their neighbouring states, in particular Poland and France, to watch its further development. Nevertheless, the government could count on international support especially after Germany was further embedded in the EU in 1992 and later took a significant lead as a country symbolising Europe's unity after the German reunification process went on fairly smoothly. But first of all domestic fears were also fuelled by international politics. More than a few governments in Europe and beyond feared that a reunified strong Germany would return to autocratic forms of governance once it regained its sovereignty and that nationalist feelings would once again gain ground. These fears were not without reason, although democracy was on firm ground at this time. Those who won the first debate in parliament argued that it would be good to show that Berlin could finally be a place where

---

[262] J. Assmann and J. Czaplicka, 'Collective Memory and Cultural Identity', New German Critique, Cultural History and Studies, 65 (1995), 125–133.

a strong democracy could flourish and be 'the only game in town'. At the same time, it still had to be proven that the citizens were ready for a fully fledged democratic state with a fully sovereign government.[263] It took until the end of the 1990s before the capital finally moved to Berlin, which was a striking symbol of an effective and legitimised regime, alongside a record number of TJ measures being put in place.

Initially, the moral aspect of TJ measures was not addressed, neither by former SED leaders nor by members of the East German notorious secret service and the Stasi never apologised. And as Wolf-Dieter Meyer, Chair of the NGO Victims of Stalinism has phrased it, as long as former Stasi officers were not publicly tried and sentenced, any moral sentiment to come to terms with the past would be absent in the wider public in the eastern part of Germany. Too many victims of the SED regime feel that they have not received the justice they aimed for.[264] In the parliamentary truth and history commission (*Enquete Commission of the German Bundestag*), the legislature made clear that any facts or evidence of past oppression could lead to criminal prosecution and personal consequences.[265] It was clear that the number of amnesties granted in 1950s must be avoided, but at the same time the new laws were viewed in combination with rehabilitation laws. This meant that, in the end, SED perpetrators benefited from de facto amnesties. While an official amnesty law was never on the table, the sentences given to perpetrators were so minor that they could almost qualify as acts of clemency. At the same time, there were enough West German administrators, technocrats, lawyers and otherwise skilled persons available to replace the East German communist elites all at once. Thousands of East Germans lost their jobs in public service shortly after reunification or were downgraded in their positions due to lustration processes.

As a consequence of the federal commission of inquiry, until 1998 the parliament passed a law that dealt with the files the Stasi had kept on individuals, as well as with the archives held by state-run research institutes in the former GDR.[266] The law laid down the foundation for one of the longest ongoing vetting and lustration episodes in history, allowing for

---

[263]   H. Dubiel, *Niemand ist frei von der Geschichte*, pp. 249–256.
[264]   Interview with Wolf-Dieter Meyer, Chair, Organization of Victims of Stalinism (Vereinigung Opfer des Stalinismus, VOS), Erfurt, 22 January 2016.
[265]   J.A. McAdams, *Judging the Past in Unified Germany* (Cambridge: Cambridge University Press, 2001), p. 101.
[266]   Ibid., pp. 23–87.

systematic scans of millions of German citizens, in the east and the west, in public office. Today the Stasi files are open to researchers and investigators and have provided material to hundreds of academics, journalists and novelists writing about the 40-year-long dictatorship.

But 'competing memories' or the prioritisation of one set of victims of Nazi terror over victims of SED terror prevailed. As a response to this, the parliament issued more commemorations and other TJ measures than any other country in the world. Yet, the sheer number of TJ measures does not necessarily say anything about how consolidated the regime is, let alone how democratic. The point raised is who initiates and who embraces these measures?

This decade also brought up the debate about the public holiday and commemoration day of the end of World War II. Many proclaimed 8 May to be an official holiday for all Germans, to commemorate liberation from Nazi terror. A majority of East Germany favoured this day but it failed due to the dominance of West German conservative policy makers who did not share the common narrative of the east. Thus a common narrative about World War II, as Elazar Barkan had proclaimed it, was once again to be established in unified Germany. Although for some Federal States in former East Germany, for example in Mecklenburg-Vorpommern, the day remains an official commemoration day.

On the sixtieth anniversary of the end of World War II, the German parliament commemorated the day of German liberation, but without declaring it a national holiday. How to deal with this important day in German history became an example of and intriguing aspect of Germany's TJ policies, considering that most European countries that were affected by German occupation, for example France, Russia and the Netherlands, celebrate the day of liberation from Nazi occupation in May as a national holiday.

In 1995 Chancellor Kohl invited the heads of states of the former Allied powers and turned the day into a state act confirming Germany's unity and new role in Europe. For the first time since 1945, foreign representatives were invited to address the German Bundestag and the Bundesrat.[267] In summary, 50 years after World War II, the first official reconciliation ceremony took place between Germany and its former 'enemies' in the occupied territories from World War II. With this type of commemoration, Kohl made it clear that a unified Germany had been defeated in order to be liberalised and had only now become a fully recognised and

[267] H. Dubiel, *Niemand ist frei von der Geschichte*, pp. 262–274.

sovereign member of the international community. It was also a symbolic act towards the new and old elite in East Germany. This day was a day of liberation for all Germans, not only for some. Regime consolidation was no longer questioned during this decade; but it was mistakenly taken for granted.

If unconsolidated pockets of democracy are marked by the level of violence and sabotage by groups who oppose democratic agenda setting and decision making, then some minor branches of these pockets also arose in Eastern Germany, often labelled as right-wing and neo-Nazi nationalistic movements which had problems accepting a diverse, pluralistic society. Nevertheless, some international observers stated that all major state obligations for reconciliation were technically fulfilled after 1949 and after 1989, respectively.[268] However, what was missing was the moral duty to reconcile the divided East German society, i.e. Stasi officers with their victims. This moral obligation to learn from history, to atone and reconcile, was impossible to pass by laws or to impose on people. It needed to grow in the years to come. But civil society grew and so did voluntary engagement, often with heavy financial support by the governments. This is the reason why, today, Germany has a number of federal foundations for remembrance that respond and tackle TJ demands from the past. They are semi-governmental entities that deal with these issues and aim to increase civic culture and trust through education and memory.

German authorities' responsiveness to victims and perpetrators claims was high, although sometimes rather hasty. They faced strong opposition and engaged in debates on the extent to which TJ, and in particular restitution policies, could heal the wounds of the past, whilst at the same time strengthen democracy. 'White spots' in Germany's two dictatorships' past still needed to be found and dealt with. Often, these were discussed openly, although there were also parts of the past that were not openly talked about, such as massacres or individuals collaborating with the Stasi or Nazis.[269]

At one point, the country was divided by the question of whether the former head of the communist party and leader of the SED regime,

---

[268] J.E. Mendez, 'In Defence of Transitional Justice', pp. 1–26.
[269] I. Drechsler (ed.), *Getrennte Vergangenheit, gemeinsame Zukunft* (Munich: DTV, 1997); N. J. Kritz (ed.), *Transitional Justice*; P. Reichel, *Vergangenheitsbewältigung in Deutschland. Die Auseinandersetzung mit der NS-Diktatur von 1945 bis heute* (Munich: C.H. Beck Verlag, 2001).

Erich Honecker, should be prosecuted for his individual and political responsibility for the killings at the Berlin Wall, the massive number of political prisoners and general oppression. Honecker fled Germany in 1991, sought refuge in the Chilean Embassy in Moscow and was later extradited to Berlin to be tried. He was released for health reasons and exiled to Chile in 1992, where he died in 1994. This case, more than any other, indicated the difficulties faced by the German judiciary in trying to reconcile the West German criminal code with the former East German criminal code. McAdams has argued that according to the German constitutions, the Basic Law, the value of human life outweighs the public clamour for retribution, thus entailing that Honecker's poor health was a valid reason not to try him.[270] This example of a rather weak post-communist German judiciary led to the fact that most trials that followed had more of a symbolic and restorative purpose to 'teach the rule of law' than a punitive one. This led to resentment among victim groups. Only a handful of the SED elites were tried, most of them on the basis of complicity, with only minor charges or suspended sentences being handed down.[271]

Another striking parliamentary and public debate about regime consolidation and TJ took place on the issue of the federal commemoration day of reunification, 9 November. According to some observers, 9 November 1989 was the 'happiest day in Germany's history', the day the Berlin Wall fell by peaceful means and by virtue of the will of the citizens. For many it was thus evident that this day must become the most important national holiday. However, 9 November is a heavily burdened date in Germany's history. This day in November was the night of pogroms, the *Reichskristallnacht* in 1938, when Nazis looted Jewish synagogues and killed Jewish citizens, a day that is often seen as the beginning of the Holocaust. The compromise was to declare 9 November a national commemoration day, primarily of the events in 1989, while not converting it into a national holiday to avoid any possible insult to Holocaust victims. Today, most celebrations of 9 November take place around the remains of the Berlin Wall and no public representative or governmental official has failed to mention the events of 1938 when observing this day. But the official holiday for German reunification is now 3 October, the date on which the German Unity Treaty was signed in 1990.

---

[270] J.A. McAdams, 'Communism on Trial', p. 258.
[271] A. Weinke, 'West Germany: A Case of Transitional Justice', pp. 25–61.

Another cultural event that contributed to the common narrative of Germans, was the 1993 Hollywood release *Schindler's List*. This film was watched widely throughout the country in the following years. It brought back aspects of the Nazi past into citizens' living rooms and shaped their understanding of it, but this time in a unified country and supported by a majority of Germans, unlike the film *Holocaust* 25 years earlier. Throughout the decade, it became clear that dealing with the legacy of World War II remained mainly in the hands of West Germans. In the east those who cared about TJ were either too busy with the SED dictatorship or simply cared less about the Nazi past because it was still widely perceived as the responsibility of the west to deal with it. Films and textbooks about the East Germans' unjust past surfaced only much later for the wider public but were not prohibited. As in any TJ process a common narrative and the catharsis had to be there, in order to trigger public debates; however, since the East German regime was toppled by its own people and not through a defeat, this soon came about. And thus in the first decade after reunification the Nazi legacy was much more present in the popular narrative than the SED dictatorship in overall Germany, but that soon changed.

Meanwhile public and private foundations aimed to support citizen-driven initiatives to commemorate or compensate the victims of past injustice – on all sides. The Holocaust Memorial in Berlin for all murdered Jews in Europe, for example, was a citizen initiative that started in 2003, after a decade of heated public debate starting in the mid-1990s. Although today it is part of a federal foundation, it started as a public-private initiative driven by German-Jewish citizens, many belonging to the 1968 generation. The projects were realised mainly through private donations from Germany and around the world. These were citizen-driven initiatives later embraced and supported by parliament and turned into federal agencies or supported by them. The same was true for the foundation dealing with the SED Dictatorship (*Stiftung Aufarbeitung SED Diktatur*). After the end of the commissions of inquiry, in 1998, the German parliament debated and enacted a law to establish a federal and state-owned foundation with the aim to commemorate, educate and investigate the dictatorial past of East Germany. But it also supported private institutions with tax money. Many more initiatives pushed by civil rights movements, victims and other private initiatives rose in the subsequent years with a clear mandate to delegitimise the past and to improve the democratic culture in the east.

Many countries have since copied the TJ model that German authorities and civil society had constructed since 1949, although their effect is not necessarily the same in other countries due to very different causes and consequences of past conflicts, dictatorships and how political actors and CSOs use them.[272]

A much more controversial issue of restitutional justice in 1990 was property issues. In 1992 a law passed by the new parliament regulated compensation for those expropriated under communism. Trials were reluctantly or carefully initiated and the legal advisers to the Ministry of Justice identified around 11 types of crimes relating to the SED dictatorship. Among those were crimes of espionage, killings at the border of West and East Germany (136 people were killed during their attempts to cross the Berlin Wall between 1961 and 1989), corruption, perversion of justice and ill-treatment of prisoners. Over 700 cases had been dealt with in federal courts, although not all those involved were East Germans. During these proceedings, no charges for crimes against humanity were ever brought, much to the discontent of many former East German citizens and victims of decades as political suppression. Approximately 5,600 investigations of espionage took place up until 1997, with a few more taking place after that date. Approximately one-third of the people investigated were former West German citizens who had collaborated with the SED regime, in which case the investigation became a joint TJ issue for East and West Germany. Yet, most of those tried had been in leadership positions in East Germany and were soon replaced or officially 'retired from office' after reunification in October 1990. The highest number of investigations took place before 1993; after that the number of denouncements and prosecutions decreased. This was also due to the fact that a functioning judiciary was soon put in place after 1990 (with lawyers and attorneys from the west) and neither laws, nor the application of laws nor the practice of how to run a court independently needed to be explored or learned – as would be common in times of regime change. Thus, the (few) cases that were brought up for trial were dealt with in a rather rapid but efficient way because there was no need to retrain lawyers or judges, as most of them were West Germans and their independence was almost guaranteed by the simple fact that they had never lived or worked under the SED regime.[273] By 1997, 98 per cent of all cases had been closed, but only 2 per cent had resulted in successful prosecution

---

[272] T.D. Olson, L.A. Payne and A.G Reiter, *Transitional Justice in Balance.*
[273] J. Espindola, *Transitional Justice after German Reunification.*

and sentences of up to two years in prison. Most of those indicted received a suspended sentence or probation. The main reason for the low number of charges and the high number of suspended sentences was the fact that after 1990 the country of East Germany no longer existed, and the Stasi was entirely dissolved, and thus those who had committed crimes no longer posed any risk for the democratic society of the (new) reunified Germany. There was no significant threat of recurrence, and therefore almost all those sentenced for crimes such as ill-treatment and espionage received parole.[274] This also indicates that trials functioned as a way to introduce East German (and West German) citizens to a functioning judiciary, whose aim was to reintegrate perpetrators into society whenever possible. A major goal often claimed by TJ was to increase the level of rule of law. The president of the German Constitutional Court, Ernst Benda, emphasised this when he mentioned, during the proceedings against Honecker in 1991, that the trial had the potential of becoming a 'learning process' for the new citizens of the east.[275] Egon Krenz, a former member of the SED politburo and the last head of government before the Wall fell in November 1989, was one of the few high-ranked politicians who were eventually prosecuted. He was charged with homicide for the order to shoot to kill (Schießbefehl) at the border of West and East Germany in the period before 1989. Dozens of citizens had lost their lives at the border crossing as they tried to flee the dictatorial regime. The attorney general started prosecution in 1993 and Krenz was sentenced to six and a half years imprisonment for giving and maintaining these orders, which violated international customary human rights law at that time. After various revisions and declines of his appeals in 1996, 1997 and 2000, the German Constitutional Court upheld his conviction, as did the ECtHR in 2001.[276] He was imprisoned in Berlin and released in 2003, serving the rest of his sentence on parole. Krenz's case was part of the effort to respond to the victims' claims and to show that what had happened under the regime was unjust and violated human rights. Moreover, the trial showed that the German Rechtsstaat was capable of delivering justice for the past and future. The fact that Krenz

---

[274] K. Marxen, G. Werle and P. Shäfter, Die Strafverfolgung von DDR Unrecht. Fakten und Zahlen (Berlin: Humboldt University Berlin and Stifung Aufarbeitung DDR Diktatur, 2007).

[275] J.A. McAdams, 'Communism on Trial', p. 259.

[276] ECtHR, Case of Streletz, Kessler and Krenz versus Germany, Appl. Nos 34044/96, 35532/97 and 4480/98, Judgment, Strasbourg, 22 March 2001.

was prosecuted and sentenced to substantial jail time was, however, the exception and not the rule.

These mainly symbolic efforts to establish justice caused much discontent among former East German opposition leaders and members of the civil rights movements. Many East Germans expected nothing less than a miracle from the West German political regime and were without further surprise disappointed. They expected revenge and not a rule of law. Bärbel Bohley, a prominent civil rights activist from East Germany (who had been imprisoned several times by the SED regime) expressed the frustration many felt with the symbolic convictions that were often nothing more than symbolic acknowledgement of past wrongdoings forcing many Stasi officers to early retirement but more or less doing nothing. She therefore paraphrased an oft-quoted sentence, 'We wanted justice and got the rule of law instead' (*Wir wollten Gerechtigkeit und stattdessen bekamen den Rechtsstaat*).[277]

In another case, an East German soldier who killed a person attempting to flee at the East and West German border in 1972 was given a suspended prison sentence of 22 months. When he appealed to the ECtHR, the Court ruled that even under East German law the right to life, and thus basic human rights principles, had to be respected. The Court held that the soldier had made a conscious decision to kill the person who wanted to flee.[278] Yet again, this case was more of a symbolic act than anything else. The sentence could by no means capture the violent and dehumanising acts or the criminal intentions of the SED regime to suppress and terrorise the people of East Germany. But the courts in Germany held the view that since the country of East Germany and the SED regime no longer existed there was no threat of recurrence. That was one of the reasons why the sentences were often so low. Moreover it was a matter of principle to uphold the rule of law and if one wanted 'to educate' the East German public that democracy was about rule of law and not about revenge, that meant that regardless of how unjust and inhumane the communist regime was personally perceived by many, the laws had to be respected.

Implementing TJ measures such as public trials, commissions of inquiry, memorials and foundations was one thing. Changing people's minds and winning their trust for democratic institutions, however, was

---

[277] W. Hassemer, *Strafrechtliche Aufarbeitung von Diktaturvergangenheit Aus Politik und Zeitgeschichte* (Bonn: Aus Politik und Zeitgeschichte, APuZ 35–36, 2011), pp. 48–54, at 49.

[278] E. Brems, 'Transitional Justice in the Case Law of the European Court of Human Rights', 299.

a much longer and enduring challenge. One of the highly contested matters was whether basing lustration judgments on files and records from a dictatorial regime and its corrupt Stasi was fair and just. The Stasi had violated many human rights in collecting the information by spying on their own citizens, and much of the information came from fraudulent or false statements.[279] It had terrorised the majority of citizens but it was a philological and much more subversive terror than a physical one and therefore justice was difficult to get in court.

The fact that little about the past was included in schoolbooks and curricula, and that, until very late in regime consolidation, very few movies or cultural events took place in reunified Germany, shows that Germany did not prioritise dealing with the SED period. Most TJ efforts aimed at re-establishing a legitimate regime and strengthening the existing democracy, not at working through the SED history. TJ was used to promote state-supportive values and habits, mostly among East Germans, as Stephen Winter has observed.[280] Nevertheless, approximately 18 million citizens, or one-quarter of the total population of reunified Germany, had no experience with democracy.[281] And yet, they were thrown into a consolidated regime expected to behave like any citizen in a long-term mature democracy.

Therefore it was not too much of a surprise that disorientation and radicalisation among the wider public in the east was common in the 1990s and beyond. Racist, anti-Semitic and xenophobic attacks increased dramatically in the first years and even led to murderous attempts against asylum seekers, indicating that an anti-democratic culture was still alive in this part of the country. These attacks never posed a real threat to further consolidation, but nevertheless left traces of unconsolidated pockets. As a result of intensive democracy and civil education programmes, these attacks decreased from over 1,000 to 500 per year by the late 1990s, but did not disappear completely. In 1992 alone the German Federal Office of Protection of the Constitution noted 1,163 crimes and attacks with a xenophobic, racist or anti-Semitic motive, the large majority of which took place in the eastern part of Germany, in Hoyerswerda, Rostock, Magdeburg and smaller towns. Some of these attacks resulted in the death of foreigners, many of whom had been brought to East Germany during

---

[279] S. Glatte, 'Judging the (East) German Past. A Critical Review of Transitional Justice in Post Communist Germany', *Oxford Transitional Justice Research*, 5 (2011), 18.
[280] S. Winter, *Transitional Justice in Establisched Democracies*, p. 32.
[281] E. Wolfrum, *Die geglückte Demokratie*, pp. 431–485.

communist times as contract workers from Vietnam or Mozambique. At the same time, East and West German civil protest movements against racism and xenophobia united, starting in Munich in southern Germany. Within weeks after the killings of Vietnamese contract workers in East Germany in 1992, three million Germans around the country set up 'candle chains' by which they posted candles as a sign of peaceful disagreement and protest against those crimes. This civil engagement was a mix of the fully formed West German civic culture and the very weak but emerging one in the east. But neo-Nazi attacks that also resulted in murder crimes often remained untouched. This was a political and administrative disaster for the German National Security Agency, the Federal Investigation Bureau (*Bundesnachrichtendienst*, BND), which had long underestimated the harm that these neo-Nazis in the east – and also the west – could cause. Since the anti-communist hype of the 1960s, the German Secret Service had continued to focus on left-wing movements instead of right-wing ones.

Alongside this the TJ activities continued and were costly, in particular the vetting and lustration procedures. It was a unique experiment in opening up archives far before the usual waiting period of between 30 and 70 years. These specific German lustration laws opened the East German files held by political institutions and the secret service, despite international rules on closure for privacy protection. Other Eastern European regimes which found themselves in a similar situation, such as Hungary, Romania or Poland, watched German TJ efforts carefully but failed to install many of them in their own country due to lack of money, rule of law or support from civil society.

Nevertheless, vetting procedures had initially led to a certain uneasiness on the side of perpetrators and victims alike in East Germany; in the end, it resulted in a successful practice that other transitional countries have attempted to copy. It is possible that this was such a successful measure, and that the files were not misused for major acts of revenge, because stable institutions, such as the judiciary and legislature and a free media were already in place by the time reunification took place. Rules and regulations that reflected the basic principles of human rights and equality, as well as a strong judiciary, were already in place to consider claims. Thus, rather than using TJ measures to establish a rule of law, these measures were used to conduct a 'fact-based and values-oriented reappraisal' (*Aufarbeitung*), as Joachim Gauck has called it.[282] As a consequence, civic trust in the German Constitutional Court has been exceptionally high for

[282] J. Espindola, *Transitional Justice after German Reunification*, p. 1.

THE CASE STUDIES: GERMANY, SPAIN AND TURKEY

decades. Citizens affected by potential misuse knew they could demand their rights in court. Some citizens went to claim them before the ECtHR and Germany's Federal Court had to implement the ECtHR's decisions.[283] Throughout this decade, it became evident that serious efforts to leverage democratic culture in former East Germany was not moving past the elite circles of those who once were in opposition to the SED regime, members of the church and civil rights movements who had been engaged with the 'peaceful revolution' in 1989. Attitudinal and behavioural regime consolidation was slow, although on its way. It was difficult for the 18 million East Germans who had never experienced public, open and pluralistic debates about the Nazi past, let alone their own communist past, to practise this dialogue and reflections. Public events about the SED regime often ended in heated discussions. There were hostility, polemics and mistrust between those who had been victims of the SED regime and those who had not. The debate about the East German past was somewhat different than the debate about the Nazi past since it was much longer ago.[284] Even with a non-corrupt police and independent judiciary in place, some incidents of revenge and intimidation by former Stasi agents against former dissidents were reported and had to be prosecuted. But many of the former SED victims did not dare to confront and face those responsible for the SED state terror and human rights abuses because they feared the hidden strong arm of former Stasi agents. Those who had spied on each other were neighbours, friends, colleagues or family members, which made it very difficult to reconcile and apply TJ measures.

The strong push to remove agents and politicians who had been involved in the SED regime from office as soon as possible, along with many laws and regulations – including international human rights law, reduced sentences, parole and large pensions after 1990 – was not necessarily perceived as justice. Although this may have been a political necessity, the public did not perceive it as fair.[285] East Germans' in-depth experience with democracy gave them the perception that the rule of law was merely a technocratic tool that did not necessarily correlate with individuals' sense of justice. These feelings were also reflected in a 2000 general evaluation of the post-1990 TJ process. Citizens' and victims' perceptions were not affected by the fact that there was wide-scale compensation and rehabilitation and that thousands of perpetrators and

---

[283] A. Weinke, 'West Germany: A Case of Transitional Justice', pp. 25–61.
[284] E. Wolfrum, *Die geglückte Demokratie*, pp. 431–485.
[285] A. Sa'adah, *Germany's Second Chance*, p. 145.

elites were tried and either sentenced or deprived of their position due to lustration laws. Martin Gutzeit, a former dissident and later the commissioner for the Stasi files in the Federal State of Berlin, explained 'that all these TJ measures did not necessarily lead to more citizen engagement; they served a mere technical purpose and helped us to know what had happened'. However, he also added, 'the opening of the files did increase the trust in the public sector and institutions, and that was its main achievement'.[286] However, in general the process during the first decade was widely perceived as independent, transparent and accountable and not corrupted, although for many it was seen as incomplete.[287]

Bohley and many other former dissidents from the civil rights movement in East Germany (many of whom had spent several years as political prisoners until 1989) were now members of new civil rights movements and political parties in reunified Germany. The New Forum (*Neues Forum*) and later the Green Party (*Bündnis 90 die Grünen*) are evidence of this shift. Today's Green Party carries the title 'Alliance 90, the Greens' and is the only political party whose name makes a direct link to the democratic shift and reunification of 1990. The subsequent Socialist and Communist Party, the PDS (*Partei des demokratischen Sozialismus*) was the only party with a direct link to the SED. The PDS existed from 1989 until 2007. Although controversial, the existence of this party was important to filter and absorb the millions who supported the previous dictatorial regime, people who otherwise might have turned to undemocratic means.[288] The existence of the PDS gave them a way to have their voices heard. These people had needs and demands like everyone else and wanted fair treatment and not winners' justice, as the accession of East Germany to the west was perceived by most former members of the SED regime and the Stasi. Although they were ignoring the fact that it was the first freely elected East German parliament in 1990 which voted for the accession and unification with West Germany, the fact that hundreds of thousands of East German citizens opposed reunification and the decline of the communist regime was not to be ignored for the sake of peace and stability. This is why TJ measures had to be carefully applied. With the legalisation of the successor party of the SED, the PDS, the aim was to reintegrate them while at the same time not repeating the mistake

---

[286] Interview with Martin Gutzeit, commissioner for the Stasi files in Berlin (Landesbeauftragter für die Stasiunterlagen, Berlin) in his office in Berlin, 6 July 2015.
[287] J. Arnold, 'Zweiter Teil', pp. 364–367.
[288] A. Sa'adah, *Germany's Second Chance*, pp. 271–276.

of giving them highly ranked positions in politics, as Adenauer had done with Oberländer and Globke in the 1950s. It was an attempt towards an inclusive TJ process. Supporters of the former regime were therefore allowed to create political parties and other pressure groups, but they had to pass a vetting procedure if they wished to hold political office. As a result of this, many were excluded from higher public offices.[289] A decade later, the PDS moved away from its strict socialist or communist outreach with a 'left-wing' focus, and in 2007 it renamed itself the New Left (*Die Linke*), distancing itself from Marxism and communism and declaring itself a left-wing party focusing on solidarity.

The 1990s saw parties and movements that included both those from the elite of the former regime and those who had been victimised. Elites from the former regime were allowed to participate in the new regime, under the same conditions as everyone else. Yet, this was not always perceived as fair, since those who had been imprisoned for years, if not decades, had lost their youth and health because of the oppressive regime and received compensation worth less than the pensions the former Stasi offices received due to their early 'retirement' after failing the vetting procedure. Although victims, and in particular former political prisoners, were all officially recognised as victims and had been granted access to their files, they never received an apology from former SED party leaders, such as Egon Krenz, let alone Erich Honecker. Nevertheless, the intense vetting and lustration procedures of the 1990s excluded almost all former GDR political elites from re-entering parliament or the administration. By October 2000, all SED cases were statute-barred, making it impossible to continue to try former regime members.

Thus, the country continued to struggle with the intertwining benefit of TJ and democratic institutions in particular when the competing memories of World War II and the SED regime had to be taken into account, although the first dictatorship was the one that all Germans shared in memory. When a private research institute, the Reemtsma Institute for Social Research in Hamburg, held in 1997 a large exhibition about the war crimes committed by the German soldiers during the war (*Deutsche Wehrmacht's Ausstellung*), it caused unexpected tensions amongst the public, even though the war had already ended 50 years previously. The exhibition contested most Germans' interpretation that it had been a small military elite that had committed the atrocities of the Holocaust.

---

[289] J. Espindola, *Transitional Justice after German Reunification*.

This was the common narrative about this part of the past. However, this exhibition showed ordinary soldiers (fathers and grandfathers) as among those who committed the atrocities. The exhibition reignited the debate about German bystanders and the responsibility for crimes against humanity held by more than just a small SS elite, more so in the west than in the east.

The German sample only illustrated the similar challenges that all former post-communist countries in the east faced in terms of TJ and memory. In 1996, the Parliamentary Assembly of the Council of Europe (PACE) issued a milestone resolution, Resolution No. 1096, on 'measures to dismantle the heritage of former communist totalitarian systems'. This resolution was meant as a political statement to all of the Council of Europe Member States that transition carries the risk of failure if not conducted properly. Many national institutions, lawyers and NGOs used this resolution as a benchmark to refer to when facing difficulties with democratic institutions and their reluctance to come to terms with the past.[290] Internationally, due to the amount of transition and post-conflict society during that period, much attention was placed on individual victims; the importance of individual claims, instead of only state responsibility, grew, and the way the German justice system dealt with its own past was often observed with great interest. How to deal with the past in legal terms also impacted the reforms in penal and criminal codes.

By the end of this decade in 1999, in East Germany satisfaction with the new regime slowly increased again, but the trust in the political institutions still remained much lower than that of all Germans (38 per cent to 59 per cent). At the same time, a Eurobarometer survey showed that opinions remained stable at the extreme ends of the spectrum. Nine per cent of the population was either 'very satisfied' or 'not at all satisfied' with the way democracy worked, which indicated that the overwhelming majority was satisfied with the regime.[291] It was only towards the end of the decade that it became evident that TJ measures would pay off and people slowly saw the advantage of rule of law over revenge. Confronting the unjust past and arguing about whether, and to what extent trials should be issued, challenged the public to think about democratic values and human rights.

---

[290] J.A. Sweeney, *The European Court of Human Rights in the Post Cold War Era. Universality in Transition* (London/New York: Routlege Research in Human Rights Law, 2013), pp. 18–19, 75.

[291] European Union, Eurobarometer Surveys, Germany 1999.11, http://ec.europa.eu (last accessed August 2013).

The fifth post-war decade, and the first post-communist one, was without a doubt the most important one for citizen-driven consolidation in Germany since World War II. In this vein, Anne Sa'adah concluded her essay on Germany's second chance with the statement that 'without trust, there is no democracy'.[292] This echoed Martin Gutzeit's experience that all the TJ measures primarily served to enhance civic trust. By this time, TJ was an integral part of political doctrine, civil society and civic culture, although the extent to which this was the case differed per region. TJ measures were used whenever opportune to trigger or test institutional performance and were a catalyst for civil engagement.

Sixth Decade: 2000 to 2010 and Following Years

McAdams concluded on the tenth anniversary of the fall of the Berlin Wall, that 'a decade's worth of wrestling with the wrongs and injustices of the GDR era seemed to be given definitive legitimation when the Bundestag chose Stasi files commissioner Joachim Gauck to represent the interest of eastern Germany's civil rights activists at the anniversary celebrations over the Wall's fall'.[293] Joachim Gauck, who later became president of Germany from 2013 to 2017, used his speech in 1999 to address all the shortcomings and disappointments of the civil rights movement and of the victims of the SED regime. Yet, he also emphasised that the revolution of 1989 and its aftermath was a gift to German democracy. Regime change was the result of a citizen-driven movement, instead of the result of violent defeat. This fact certainly determined the progress of the transition. By the end of the sixth post-war decade and second post-communist decade, there had been more than 40,000 cases of lustrations and thousands of trials. These were all individual cases; lump sum payments to groups, general reparations and general accusations did not occur. Yet, many victims still felt that justice had not sufficiently been done. Despite this, civic trust in democratic institutions had increased which also indicated the surveys. The mutually reinforcing spiral seemed to have progressed upwards in terms of trust and responsiveness and, consequently, also in terms of regime consolidation. If, arguing alongside Larry Diamond and Leonardo Morlino, the existing German democracy had its own role in this, since the high-quality democratic performance of institutions was

---

[292] A. Sa'adah, *Germany's Second Chance*, p. 277.
[293] J.A. McAdams, *Judging the Past in Unified Germany*, p. 157.

already in place, consolidation was therefore never truly threatened after reunification in the east.[294]

Thus many TJ measures continued to focused on individual needs, not collective ones. They largely aimed to achieve moral justice and did not prioritise punitive measures.[295] Victims needed to be convinced that legal measures benefited all Germans and that they delivered no more justice than absolutely required by the nature of the offences. But this process was not only an 'educational exercise' for East Germans. Consolidation is part of a long-term transformation process and thus never really ends. The light-handed approach taken in regard to former members of the SED regime, especially in contrast to the fact that TJ continued without restriction in regard to the Nazi past, might partly account for the increasing electoral success of The Left (*Die Linke*, the successor party to the SED) in eastern Germany. Claus Offe and Ulrike Poppe, the latter a former dissident, have argued that The Left and its constituents were perversely able to profit from the lack of criminal justice measures applied against members of the SED, of which many were now party members of The Left. The failure to use punitive measures might have failed to demystify the SED regime and made them continue their politics, just under a different label.[296] A critical reflection of what was just and unjust never really took place among SED members. And external pressure, such as from cases pending at the ECtHR, decreased. After a decade, all cases at the ECtHR had been resolved, or were regarded as too minor to peruse, due to international law and the fact that there was no fear of the previous regime regaining power.[297]

Around the year 2000 scholars continued to disagree on whether it was proper to compare the post-war TJ process with the process of the post-communist period. Although political institutions emphasise that both processes occurred according to international standards and that there can be no competition between those that suffered in the war and those that suffered in East Germany, various observers disagree. Ulrike Guckes, for example, conducted a comparative investigation of both German regime consolidation processes – the first one from 1949 until

---

[294] L. Diamond and L. Morlino, *Assessing the Quality of Democracy*.
[295] J.A. McAdams, *Judging the Past in Unified Germany*, p. 88.
[296] C. Offe and U. Poppe, 'Transitional Justice in the German Democratic Republic and in Unified Germany' in J. Elster (ed.), *Retribution and Reparation in the Transition to Democracy* (Cambridge: Cambridge University Press, 2006), p. 267.
[297] J.A. Sweeney, *The European Court of Human Rights in the Post Cold War Era*, pp. 45ff.

1989 and the second one from 1990 onwards – from which she concluded that the victims of the Holocaust were better compensated and received more justice than those of communist terror, even taking in consideration that the crimes and level of injustice have been different. According to Guckes, this is due to the fact that post-war West Germany was under immense international pressure to redress its crimes and that such external pressure often pushes a government to respond more than pressure from domestic actors and victims does.[298] Whether this is in fact the case is disputed, but it does show the dangers of allowing the desire for successful democratic regime change to override the implementation of a non-biased TJ process.[299]

The East German TJ process, however, was often perceived as an internal affair. Significant external pressures, such as from the Council of Europe, the OSCE or the EU let alone the UN are not reported. This resulted in a TJ process that was very different from the West German post-war one, and had the consequence that victims of the SED regime felt like second-class victims. In reunified Germany, the bargaining power of the East German victim groups, which were already marginalised groups in East Germany, was relatively limited. Justice against former elites played a less significant role than these groups hoped in 1990.[300] If these groups were organised, it was because West German civil society leaders had taken over, including many who had fled East Germany decades before the regime ended – and now had returned in different official functions. There were very few genuine civil society groups that had emerged from those who risked their lives on the streets of Leipzig and Erfurt in 1988 and 1989.

Despite some dissatisfaction among victims of the SED regime, the overall satisfaction with the democratic regime rose steadily from 2000 to 2010, increasing from 47 per cent among East Germans in 2003 to 55 per cent in 2010, and in West Germany from 72 per cent to 79 per cent, and has continued to rise since.[301]

In 2000, after a decade of parliamentary initiatives, the compensation fund for forced labourers during World War II (*Stiftung Erinnerung,*

[298] U. Guckes, 'Opferentschädigung nach zweierlei Mass?', 68–69.
[299] J. Espindola, *Transitional Justice after German Reunification.*
[300] S. Glatte, 'Judging the (East) German Past', 14.
[301] T. Petersen, D. Hierlemann, R.E. Vehrkamp and C. Wratli, *Gespalten Demokratie. Politische Partizipation und Demokratiezufriedenheit vor der Bundestagswahl* (Gütersloh: Bertelsmann Stiftung, 2013), p. 17.

Vernantwortung Zukunft, EVZ) was finally established. This is a joint governmental and civil institution, similar to the many others Germany has established to deal with its past. Established 60 years after the first deportations of people from Eastern Europe to do forced labour in the agricultural sector or war industry, this compensation fund was the last parliamentary measure for groups that had suffered great injustices during World War II. It was a legislative and private response to responsibility and remorse. It had been difficult to establish anything of that sort during the Cold War when more of the forced labourers were still alive. The reason was simply that the large majority of these victims came from Eastern Europe, Russia and the Ukraine, which had been in the grip of the Soviet Union. To acknowledge these individuals as forced labourers would have put them in danger. Stalin would have accused them of being traitors and collaborators with the Nazis and they would risk deportation to the Gulags. The ability to recognise the injustice this group experienced only came about in the 1990s. The narrative of the forced labourers is not a black-and-white story and can be difficult to grasp with linear causalities, just as so many other stories of the war are. When, ten years after reunification, German parliament and the companies that benefited most from the forced labour finally addressed the issue, it revealed a new dimension of TJ. The initiative was entirely driven by civil society, including citizens, victims and industry. The government only supported the initiative much later, finally establishing a foundation under public control. These are examples that illustrate the spiral interlinkage of TJ and regime consolidation and the fact that when civil initiatives – for whatever reason – are taken up by government, the level of trust among institutions and citizens increases.

This was a milestone, and in the years to come more companies and other entities started to take responsibility for the past – although legal measures had not yet been taken. The lack of legal measures was mainly due to the fact that most of the German companies directly involved in the Holocaust (for example, IG Farben and Krupp) had already been tried during the Nuremberg Tribunal under pressure from the Allies. This was the first time that compensation funds had been established under federal law (*Bundesstiftung*), filled with money from German industry and private corporations that had benefited from forced labour until 1945, such as BASF, Volkswagen, Beyer and Mercedes Benz and that had not been found guilty at all or partially guilty at the Nuremberg Tribunal. This type of compensation fund was a new TJ tool, showing that Germany was continuing as a laboratory for TJ, as Hazan had once described it.[302] After compensating the forced labourers, the remainder of the fund was used to benefit a federal foundation dedicated to educational and awareness-raising activities in the field of TJ throughout Europe, with a particular focus on those countries from which forced labourers were taken to Germany. In this way, this foundation combines reparation, restitution, compensation and education.

And yet the past continued to impact democratic consolidation; for example, by the notorious Section 130 of the West German Criminal Code (*Para. 130 Volksverhetzung*). Since 1949 this paragraph haunted Germany's way to deal with the past and it was revised several times. This provision, which prohibited denial of the Holocaust and denial of other mass killings and atrocities, underwent further transition. In the twenty-first century, parliamentarians and politicians debated whether this provision should finally be repealed, since it restricted the freedom of expression and could be considered anti-democratic and a violation of human rights. This provision had been a symbol of militant democracy, and this type of democratic practice – namely to limit freedom of expression – was only meant to be a temporary stage in the development of German democracy. This provision's repeal would have been another milestone in the improvement of German consolidation. For many, it would have meant that the legacy of the Third Reich had finally been left behind and that democracy could be fully embraced. However, the law was not abolished. It was extended in 2011 and it later became mandatory that all EU Member States implement a similar law into their national legal framework. The question remains whether such a law strengthens or weakens democracy.

While the EVZ compensation fund provided monetary compensation, the claims for commemoration and symbolic reparations continued. This was driven in part by the fact that there were now multiple generations of people who had not directly experienced World War II or the communist regime. In Eastern Europe, the focus was on coming to terms with the communist past, more than on the Nazi past. Thus, government initiatives, international NGOs and international organisations, undertook significant efforts to commemorate the past by declaring years of commemoration or launching TJ tools such as the UN Office of the High Commissioner for Human Rights (OHCHR) in Geneva. In

[302] P. Hazan, *Judging War, Judging History*, p. 21.

2005, the UN General Assembly declared 27 January as the International Holocaust Remembrance Day. This was the day that Soviet troops entered the concentration camps in Auschwitz and allegedly freed the prisoners (it is not clear whether the prisoners were freed by the Soviet troops or in fact freed themselves). Germany adopted this day as an official day of commemoration, as did many other countries. The 'globalisation of the Holocaust', as some call it, took place on 13 October 2005 when the EU parliament passed a resolution on the remembrance of the Holocaust, as well as of anti-Semitism and racism, encouraging the observance of the International Holocaust Remembrance Day in all the EU Member States. The International Holocaust Remembrance Day has entered into the collective memory and has become part of the way Europe deals with its past.[303] Ruti Teitel has described this process as 'globalising transitional justice'.[304] This globalisation of the Holocaust and of TJ marks a shift in how political and civil actors deal with the legacy of totalitarianism and violence.

As global commemoration has become more common, the responsibility for commemoration as a tool for dealing with the past is no longer only Germany's, but is shared by the EU and many more countries. Holocaust remembrance is today seen as a way to encourage critical reflection among younger generations.[305]

In the same year that the EU passed the law, in 2005, the Holocaust Memorial for murdered European Jews in Berlin was inaugurated, underlining that this was part of Europe's collective memory. As mentioned above, the Memorial was the result of civil pressure, although eventually the German parliament also supported the initiative and established a federal foundation to raise money to build the memorial. The important aspect here is that survivors and CSOs initiated these TJ measures. These examples illustrate how the TJ process has quickly changed from a top-down one (either initiated by governments or international pressure) to a bottom-up and civil-driven one. During this decade, almost all TJ activities were the result of civil or private initiatives, to which state authorities eventually responded.[306]

---

[303] U. Jureit and C. Schneider, *Gefuehlte Opfer, Illusionen der Vergangenheitsbewaeltigung* (Stuttgart: Klett Cotta, 2010), p. 91.

[304] R. Teitel, *Globalizing Transitional Justice*.

[305] A. Mihr, 'Why Holocaust Education Is Not Always Human Rights Education', *Journal of Human Rights*, 16(4) (2015), 525–544.

[306] M.H. Ross, 'Ritual and the Politics of Reconciliation', pp. 197–223.

It took a decade before East German intellectuals, writers and film-makers dealt with the notorious SED in ways that were accessible to all Germans. The real shift took place around 2002 when East German film-makers and authors shaped the common narrative with their popular films and literature. Monika Maron's novel *Endmoräne* in 2002, Christa Wolf's *Ein Tag im Jahr* in 2003, and in particular the 2006 internationally broadcast film *The Life of Others* (*Das Leben der Anderen*) brought the SED reality to the living rooms of all in Germany and beyond.[307] Similar to the film *Holocaust* and later *Schindler's List*, these films created a common shared memory and narrative and triggered civil engagement. In her assessment of the different German generations, Fulbrook argued that the shift in values only came with a common generational memory and understanding of the past. She referred to this as 'history from within', in which cultural activities play a pivotal role.[308] Fifteen years after the end of the SED dictatorship, members from the younger generation, a generation that never consciously participated in or experienced the communist regime, demanded – as a group – answers to their questions about the past.

A culture of apology and commemoration has long replaced the technocratic reparations and restitution in German consolidated democracy. The recent decades have shown governments, but also CSOs, private initiatives, and individual politicians across the political spectrum apologising on behalf of former governments or on behalf of previous generations. TJ has become a matter of individuals dealing with their countries' past and thus also a matter of dealing with questions of both national and individual identity. However, surveys from 2006 and 2008 showed that public support for vetting was divided. Around 50 per cent was in favour and 50 per cent against the continuation of the vetting procedures, although all groups attested to the importance these procedures had in the first years after reunification.[309]

It would take pages to document all civil society initiatives that were active in Germany during these first two decades of reunification. For 20 years an abundance of educational, cultural programmes dealing with past was initiated (although the past was often dealt with in a way that

[307] N. Hodgin and C. Pearce (eds.), *The GDR Remembered, Representation of the East German State Since 1989. Studies in German Literature, Linguistics and Culture Studies* (New York: Rochester, 2011).
[308] M. Fulbrook, *Dissonant Lives.*
[309] J. Espindola, *Transitional Justice after German Reunification*, pp. 4–5.

was biased against East German history). Money was not as much an issue for TJ in unified Germany as was the willingness of civil society to engage with it. Today, no governmental official would dare imply that the SED regime or the Nazi regime was just or that victims need not be acknowledged. Rather, current disputes revolve around what is the best way to acknowledge victims, reintegrate perpetrators and compensate victims. Trials, commissions of inquiry, compensation, textbook reforms, media coverage and public debates, both in and outside of parliament, have become a daily factor in Germany's political and social life. Yet, a 2012 compelling TJ survey among high school students and the wider public revealed that there is little understanding of the difference between the two German dictatorships of the twentieth century, or of democracy. Fifty per cent of students with and without an immigrant background thought that neither the Nazi state nor the SED regime were dictatorships. They thought that there was little difference between then and now because the one is remembered only by its war and the other by the Wall without reflecting on the political ideologies that caused the war and the Wall. Only one-third of all students could clearly identify East Germany as a dictatorship, most of whom were students from East Germany. The majority of students did not consider the SED regime as an unjust regime that violated human rights – a finding that alerted many NGOs, media and foundations that dealt with these issues. Parliamentary outrage surged and fault was found with the way the past had been dealt with, namely with facts and figures but without any contextualisation of the present. This aligned with Martin Gutzeit's assessment that the TJ process in Germany is more knowledge-driven than value-driven.[310] Because dealing with the past in a purely historical way fails to create an understanding of what distinguishes a free from a non-free society.[311] Since this moment, people have acknowledged the failure of German history books, countless memorial sites, Holocaust education programmes, trials and lustration processes to make a clear connection with democratic values over dictatorial ones. The result is a relatively limited understanding of democracy. This of course does not mean that more initiatives for recognition or memorials should not be started, but that focusing on democratic values and empathy with victims of past

---

[310] Interview with Martin Gutzeit, Commissioner for the Stasi files in the state of Berlin, 6 July 2015.
[311] Forschungsverbund SED Staat, Schüler halten Demokratien und Didkaturen für gleichwertig No.181/2012 (Berlin: Free University Berlin Press Release, 2012).

injustice must be a fundamental part of these initiatives which continued to exist way beyond 2010.

Today, the world is shifting towards individual claims and individual responsibilities. International human rights law is driving the change of this perception, as is the ICC and other tribunals that have set new norms and standards of international and universal jurisdiction, which dramatically impact every situation of regime change, consolidation and TJ.[312] This was also illustrated by the ICJ's 2012 ruling in *Germany v. Italy* on massacres during World War II is a prominent and symbolic instance of democratic states' accountabilities shifting.[313] It also illustrates that the catharsis of Nazi Germany's crimes is still ongoing in Europe and is thus something that German politics cannot ignore. For the time being, the ICJ (an institution of the state-centric UN) confirmed international legal doctrine that only states – and not individuals – could demand lump-sum reparations from foreign states. The case dealt with claims brought by former forced labourers from Italy in Germany for compensation in Italy in 2007, and later before the ICJ in The Hague. This lead to discussions on how governments should deal with individual claims. Whereas Italian courts had held that Germany must also compensate individuals for war crimes, in addition to the lump sum they had paid to Italy earlier, the ICJ decided that the current standard of state sovereignty and immunity against individual claims could not allow individuals to bring claims against a foreign state. This shows that international law has not yet fully developed beyond a state-centric perspective, although the individual criminal responsibility enforced by the ICC shows a shift in this regard. Somewhat linked to these developments on international jurisdiction and criminal justice one has to consider two of the recent German criminal justice cases against notable Nazi perpetrators in 2015 and 2016. In 2015 a former prison guard of Auschwitz was convicted and jailed to four years after being found personally guilty for being an accessory of the murder of over 300,000 people while serving at Auschwitz concentration camp. A case, therefore, of individual responsibility that would never expire. And in 2016 a 94 year-old former prison guard of Auschwitz was convicted in a court in the German city of Detmold for being an accessory to the murder of

---

[312] K. Sikkink, *The Justice Cascade.*

[313] Ruling of the International Court of Justice, The Hague on Italy versus Germany, 3 February 2012. ICJ decision: icj-cij.org/docket/files/143/16897.pdf and commentary: www.internationaljusticeathunter.wordpress.com/2012/02/27/icjs-ruling-on-germany-v-italy/ (last accessed November 2015).

at least 170,000 people at the death camp. More than anything, these trials had not only the purpose for the very few living survivors of Auschwitz to testify, delegitimise the previous regime and face their perpetrators, but also to prove how resilient the German judiciary had become over these years, and how it would deal with crimes against humanity not only of the past but also in the future and thus legitimise the democratic regime one more time.

These trials reflect international developments in these matters and thus impact consolidation processes around the world. If international law was to develop past this state-centric position, any individual who was a victim of a crime against humanity could sue the responsible government or intergovernmental organisation. But it is also feared that such a possibility would lead to courts ruling individual compensation from states, which would be seen to undermine state sovereignty. This is a dilemma that will have to be solved in the future, but the examples from Germany have shown that trials generally strengthen the regime and do not undermine it.

Brief Summary of Germany

During the first two decades after 1949, a synchronic development between regime change, consolidation and TJ measures took place in East and West Germany. Whereas constitutional and representative consolidation was quickly achieved on both sides, the attitudinal and behavioural one was very different and the final democratic one, namely by civil society, only took place in the west. In the east the top-down dictatorial approach on how to deal with the past remained repressed from the 1970s onwards whereas at the same time West Germany consolidated its democracy.[314] TJ measures played an important role in strengthening and mobilising civil society in West Germany. TJ was used for tactical and strategic reasons and to make political concessions on both sides of the Iron Curtain. But in East Germany TJ remained a top-down approach to exercise control over the historical narrative and through this strengthen the dictatorship, while in West Germany TJ became a tool for citizen engagement in a way that somewhat reflected and supported democratic values and norms. Starting in the third post-war decade, a vital and critical 20+ generation started participating in consolidation and TJ

---

[314] W. Merkel, Systemtransformation, *Eine Einführung in die Theorie und Empirie der Transformationsforschung*, pp. 139ff.

processes. In East Germany, however, all activist members of this generation were exiled, suppressed or imprisoned. Thus, in East Germany there was no critical mass of people using TJ measures to delegitimise the past, let alone to reform the existing regime as a dependent variable towards democratic consolidation.

Until 1989 one of the major differences between East and West Germany was that in the east the SED government used TJ measures for ideological and tactical reasons for their alliance with the new hegemon, the Soviet Union; whereas in West Germany this approach also existed in the beginning towards the Allied Forces, but was slowly complemented and sometimes even replaced by a citizen-driven, bottom-up approach after the student movement and the change of government in the late 1960s. The 'Bonner republic' slowly learned to accept TJ as more than just a tool to gain external legitimacy and international recognition. TJ became a catalyst for more civil engagement and thus trust in West German institutions. In East Germany, TJ remained centrally organised by the SED regime, while citizen ownership of dealing with the legacy of World War II was either fully controlled or forbidden. This led to consolidation of dictatorial regime based on exclusive TJ measures.

Consequently, in the Federal Republic as well as in the GDR, TJ delegitimised the previous Nazi regime, while at the same time legitimising the new regimes, even though in different ways. This parallel narrative worked for the first post-war generation because all narratives aimed to delegitimise the same past. However, in order for the TJ measures to keep contributing towards democratic consolidation for the next generations, the way they were applied had to change. Instead of the government applying the measures top-down, it was now citizens themselves who had to drive the movement, based on a feeling of moral duty and empathy. This was the critical moment at which political actors had to transfer TJ to the citizens. This transfer meant that TJ measures were no longer only the tactical and strategic tools of governments.

When the second post-war generation emerged in the 1960s and 1970s, the circular cumulative causation between institutions, TJ and actors became clear. Merkel has explained this as the moment when the civil society finally engaged with the state as a type of sub regime that legitimated and consolidated state institutions.[315] East Germany's SED leadership never intended to democratise the country and used, for example, memorials and trials as tools for authoritarian regime consolidation,

[315] W. Merkel, *Systemtransformation* (1999), pp. 145–146.

leaving no room for a critical approach. In West Germany, however, Chancellor Brandt and his successors used these measures to respond to citizen pressure, which legitimised the governments and state institutions slowly, in a cumulative way. It was only in this period that citizens started feeling a moral responsibility, which was crucial for the spiral effect between TJ and the legitimation and strengthening of (democratic) institutions. After reunification in 1990, TJ measures continued. During this first decade after reunification, TJ's tactical purposed merged with moral and civil motivations, but it was clear that it would still take a generation before citizens fully embraced the understanding and behaviour of a democratic society.

But since the rupture of the SED regime was triggered by their own citizens and not by defeat, the TJ process in unified Germany was also from the beginning onwards greatly citizen-driven in the east, although predominantly by Stasi victims and CSOs that had been in opposition to the SED regime, not by the general public. It was the former suppressed and persecuted opposition that after the fall of the Berlin Wall issued the commission of inquiry, the trials, the memorials, and so on. However, because there were quickly strong democratic state institutions transferred from the west to the east after the reunification in October 1990, they soon took over and formalised the TJ process.

This case study of 'three' Germanys in 70 years shows that in order for TJ to contribute to democratic regime consolidation, five conditions must be met. First, democratic institutions must be in place and governmental authorities have to comply with basic fundamental human rights principles (even though this will be improved by consolidation over time). Second, a minimum set of TJ measures must be applied and, thirdly, these must be applied during the course of at least a decade in order to achieve results in terms of civic trust. Fourth, social and citizen-driven demands (national catharsis and narrative) need to exist or be constructed to redress grievances and to turn the process into a moral one. The fifth and final condition is that a country in transition needs to have some sort of external and international engagement with international organisations such as the Council of Europe, the EU or the Allied Forces and the UN that can monitor, incentivise or pressure the transition and transformation process.

Whereas for West Germany and unified Germany these conditions were mostly met, even if in a non-linear process, citizen-driven TJ and thus civil society and citizen-driven consolidation never occurred in East Germany. Instead, in East Germany TJ was only applied in a top-down exclusive manner. The dependent variables thus showed different results even though the same or similar TJ measures such as trials, compensation, memorials and reparations in both regimes applied throughout the decades. Where the two countries differed was on the variable of civil engagement with TJ. While in West Germany institutions, civil society, victim groups and TJ mutually reinforced each other; this was not the case in East Germany. On the contrary, the top-down use of TJ undermined civic trust in institutions, leading to dictatorship.

5.2 Spain

When the Spanish dictator General Francisco Franco died on 20 November 1975 a new head of state, King Juan Carlos, was already in place. Spain had not seen a massive civil protest movement or a peaceful revolution to topple the dictator, thus placing Spain in a special transition process. Nevertheless, in this raptured transition a young and internationally trained King Juan Carlos took over as the constitutional monarch with support from the successor government of Francoists and slowly introduced democratic reforms. Because of this constellation and the 'pact' formed between the opposition and remnants of the former regime, Spanish consensus-based democracy is often called a 'pacted' or negotiated democracy in transition. In this pact, the king and the new and predominantly socialist and communist political forces agreed in the first two years after the regime change on serious constitutional compromises in order to avoid civil protests or even a civil war. It was of primary importance to pacify the country and pull it out of its economic and political standstill. Since the 1930s, Spain had been heavily political divided into a left-wing and right-wing faction, which meant that this type of pacted transition would only allow very few TJ measures due to the lack of political willingness to compromise.

Spain's transition and democratisation was part of the widely assessed 'third wave' of democratisation and is viewed in the context of the other southern European countries that successfully transitioned to democracy in the 1970s.[316] Spain is an example of how a country can have a successful democratic regime change and consolidation, even after a history of almost four decades of fascist dictatorship, and despite pockets of violence, separatism and terrorism during the consolidation process and without much of a TJ process. Constitutional, institutional and

---

[316] J. J. Linz and A. Stepan (eds.), *Problems of Democratic Transition and Consolidation.*

thus representative consolidation was soon accomplished, but change in behaviour and active engagement by civil society took a long time in Spain. Merkel phrased the Spanish democratic consolidation process as being faster than the West German one after World War II. It was completed by around 1985, because of the large support by civil society, around 78 per cent, to the democratic regime.[317] However, this support for the new democratic regime can also be disputed. The regime was by far not fully consolidated in 1985 because terror attacks prevailed, separatist movements continued and civil society activities were still overshadowed by intimidations and thus unconsolidated pockets remained a steady annoyance towards full consolidation. It was a rather general support of the new regime set up by the king and reformist by intimidation and a lack of alternative because the large majority of citizens feared a return to the period of civil war and dictatorship. Civil actors were largely intimidated by the silence that was driven by the fear of Spaniards to turn the wheel back towards civil unrest and even war due to the undealt past of the Franco regime that was not delegitimised at this stage.

Nevertheless, as Merkel, Morlino, Linz and Stepan repeatedly observe, Spain's transition was different from that of the other southern European countries. Since Spain's regime change did not happen in the context of civil upheaval or revolution, there was no critical mass of people to instantly call for restorative or retroactive TJ measures to deal with the 'perpetrators of the past'. This was different in Greece and Portugal, where regime change did not happen so peacefully, and where a civil movement existed and caused the regime change to happen. In Spain, most of the old fascist elites remained in power and continued to successfully disseminate a 'fear of chaos', with which they had successfully governed the country for over four decades.[318] There was not much resistance from below. This led to an almost obsessive search for political consensus among all parties involved in the transition process. Thus, even though some victim groups raised their voices and demanded a search for their loved ones' remains, they soon quieted down.[319] Today we know that the number of victims of the Franco regime ran into

---

[317] W. Merkel, Systemtransformation, *Eine Einführung in die Theorie und Empirie der Transformationsforschung*, pp. 199–204.

[318] C. Humlebaek, 'Party Attitudes Towards the Authoritarian Past in Spanish Democracy' in A. Costa Pinto and L. Morlino (eds.), *Dealing with the Legacy of the Authoritarianism: The 'Politics of the Past' in Southern European Democracies* (New York: Routledge, 2011), p. 74.

[319] Liberation policies were introduced in the 1960s for economic reasons and due to pressure from the United States, which saw Spain as a country in which it could set up US

the hundreds of thousands, a magnitude that was largely unknown at that time. From 1975 onwards, the old elite ensured that the dark side of Franco's law and order regime remained hidden. Measures such as trials, vetting procedures, and history or truth commissions were not among the primary choices to delegitimise the past regime, if there even was a will to delegitimise the past at all. Moreover, even though some TJ measures were applied, this only happened on the local, municipal or private levels and pension funds – although these measures were never officially declared as a part of any TJ process. As a result, the wider public was largely unaware of the measures or their delegitimising effect in the first years. It was only at the beginning of the twenty-first century, a generation after Franco's death, that a 20+ generation of young Spaniards took to the streets to demand more TJ. Some regional and state governments supported these initiatives, but only very slowly. The government only ever implemented TJ measures for tactical or strategic reasons, such as to benefit coalition negotiations or negotiations with the regional governments. The central government did not primarily intend these measures to build trust in the new regime's institutions, although it was a welcome side effect. The first two post-Franco governments decided not to apply TJ measures such as trials or vetting procedures for strategic reasons, to avoid reinforcing cleavages in society. It was feared that any implication that former victims were the 'winners' under the new regime and that the former perpetrators were the 'losers', would destabilise the country and deepen the cleavage between 'right' and 'left' that existed for over half a century. One must bear in mind

military bases along the Mediterranean Sea during the Cold War. It needed these bases to prevent the Soviet Navy from passing through the Strait of Gibraltar. Spain opened itself up to tourism and the industrial modernisation of the country. Thousands of Spaniards left to work in France, Switzerland or England, and at the same time hundreds of thousands of foreigners entered the country, and brought with them ideas of different political regimes. The Franco regime was a non-totalitarian but nevertheless dictatorial and fascist regime. The authoritarian elite consisted of landowners, members of the church, members of the military and last but not least members of the judiciary (who later played a significant role in TJ). The economic and social reforms were deemed necessary to keep up with Western development. These reforms prevented Spain from turning into a 'Third World' country, defenceless and dependent on foreign economic help. Most beneficiaries of the loyal Franco elites owned large amounts of property and territory in the country, and therefore determined the country's economic and political future. This is even more evident when one takes into account the fact that the country depended on the agricultural sector for its economic success. Roughly 80 per cent of Spain's gross national income came from that sector, which meant that only a few educated and trained people were needed to manage the country's economic development.

that a majority of those who held state positions, on both the regional as well as on the central level, followed Franco's doctrine firmly. And almost 100 per cent of those who worked in the security sector were Francoists at the time of transition.

Spanish society had been divided since the beginning of the Civil War in 1936 until long after its end in 1939. Generally speaking, one half was socialist or republican and the other half fascist Franco supporters, mostly Catholic conservatives. When the regime change began, there was a serious risk that the sides would turn against each other, leading to turmoil and vengeance instead of reconciliation.

The new interim government responded to some demands for TJ, although they did so mostly locally and quietly. On private and interpersonal levels, the government ensured pension funds for former political prisoners and organised local memorials and commemorations of the Civil War victims. This was never done in a transparent way or on the national level, but rather as a result of local or individual negotiations often depending on the will of local leaders. Hence, unsurprisingly, it was not until the first post-Franco generation some 25 years later that people were able to move past their fear and on to the streets in Madrid, Bilbao, Barcelona and elsewhere asking for TJ – beyond the claim for peace and the end of ETA terror which had a long tradition already.

The four decades of Spanish regime consolidation and TJ can be characterised in two ways: (1) the interlinkage between institutional reforms, constitution building, amnesty laws and reform of the military and security sector; and (2) the interlinkage between reparations, acknowledgement, national memory laws and individual compensations for victims by the states. Only during the representative and behavioural stage of consolidation did the spiral effect materialise and gain speed and visibility. Yet, during the first decade, the lack of an active opposition and civil society movement meant that the TJ process did not really take off until the beginning of the twenty-first century. The whole process of regime consolidation, both with and without TJ measures, is thus often labelled an 'amnesic reconciliation' process, a process in which justice and truth were meant or imposed to be silenced for the majority of citizens in the country.[320]

---

[320] J.M. Tamarit Sumalla, 'Transition, Historical Memory and Criminal Justice in Spain', *Journal of International Criminal Justice*, 9 (2001), 731.

Three main societal factors thwarted TJ measures' contribution towards upward spiral consolidation during the first two decades. The first factor was the presence of Franco elites in key political institutions, the judiciary, church and economy. Even today, many former supporters of the France regime still hold these key positions. The second factor was that the domestic state security institution (such as the Guardia Civil) was still loyal to the old regime. The third and final factor was the influence of the Catholic Church, which strongly opposed the socialist and communist elites' involvement in the (new) game of democratic power sharing. Nevertheless, the Church was to some extent interested in revealing its own wrongdoings during Franco's dictatorship, although it took the Church until the 1960s to finally admit its misdeeds. But the Catholic Church was one of the first groups in the country to call for reconciliation long before Franco died and some, albeit limited, TJ measures. However, as long as the new king did not insist on revisiting the past and as long as citizens were too intimidated to insist on this, there was no need for public or governmental apologies, acknowledgement, restitution or trials.

There are similarities between Spain and post-war Germany in how they dealt with the past during their first two decades of transition. Both did so only hesitantly and reluctantly, and only as a tactical or strategic move to satisfy international or domestic (and in the case of Spain, regional and local) pressure. Both feared the collapse of the fragile democratic system – through acts of violence and revenge – if the past returned to haunt the new regime. Silence and amnesty were seen as the easiest of all solutions to maintain stability. The governments employed TJ measures in a very limited way so as to avoid high political costs, whether violent, economic or international in nature. Even then, the governments of Germany and Spain only ever used these measures as a result of tactical concerns and with the intention to appease society and compensate those who were seen as posing a threat to stability. Pensions for former political prisoners were seen as the only state tool of recognition at that time for Spain. TJ measures such as dismantling Franco statues and issuing memorials for the dead and oppressed could only be used by local governments, and always depended on the political leadership in the specific village or town. If the leadership was communist or socialist, there was a higher likelihood that TJ measures would be used to delegitimise the Franco regime, but not automatically. Because of the long period of 'silence', 'oblivion' and fear, TJ measures such as trials, commissions of inquiry and public apologies were less likely to be used than measures such as amnesties and memorials.

The Spanish transition to democracy prompts the question of whether TJ methods are needed to strengthen and consolidate institutions.[321] Yet, the answer is given by the prevailing existence of unconsolidated pockets of Spanish democracy and why they exist. For example, the Guardia Civil's attempted coup d'état in 1981, the ongoing ETA terror in the Basque Country and the separatist movements in Catalonia, all show the defects in Spanish institutional and democratic performance. These 'violent pockets' show that democracy is negatively affected by the lack of recognition of past injustices, specifically the lack of naming victims and perpetrators and the lack of criminal justice.[322] The failure of democratic institutions to systematically issue TJ measures to delegitimise the Franco regime triggered radical movements and terror groups, which led to more undemocratic behaviour from institutions. For example, interrogators used systematic torture long into the 1990s to extract evidence from prisoners because the interrogators 'had never learned better'. Trust in new institutions could only grow very slowly and was often hampered. In a turbulent and uncertain transition period between 1975 and 1981, King Juan Carlos saw himself as the reconciler of a divided society. He used the powers Franco transferred to him to reform the armed forces, introduce the first amnesties of political prisoners in 1975 and 1976, and install a parliamentary monarchy. All these top-down policies led to peaceful institutional reforms, but not yet to democratic culture or behaviour. By 1978, all of the democratic institutions were in place but far from being consolidated. Observers have thus often called 1979 and the following years the era of shift from regime change to (the very slow and slippery road of) consolidation.[323]

Prior to and during the Spanish regime change, it was mostly the communist and socialist left that had not emigrated to Latin America or Europe that provided political opposition. These former exiles formed the intellectual and leftist opposition that arose following a difficult liberalisation policy that had been introduced by Franco in the 1960s. This policy tried to ease political tensions in society but also triggered more civil engagement and underground activities against the regime.[324] In

---

[321] One of the most comprehensive compilations summarising this process is edited by G. Alonso and D. Muro (eds.), *The Politics of Memory of Democratic Transition*.
[322] J.M. Tamarit Sumalla, 'Historical Memory and Criminal Justice in Spain'.
[323] M. Kneuer, *Demokratisierung durch die EU*, p. 218.
[324] P.B. Radcliff, *Making Democratic Citizens in Spain. Civil Society and the Popular Origins of the Transition, 1960-1978* (London: Palgrave Macmillan, 2011).

the early years of transition, members of the new left-wing political parties, such as the PSOE in Madrid or Barcelona, spoke various languages and easily held high-level talks with foreign diplomats in French, English or German for the simple reason that they had spent most of their lives abroad in exile. Because of their international connections and ties, they received financial and logistic support from abroad, mainly titled as support funds, mainly from Germany, England and France to build their political (leftist) constituency in Spain.

King Juan Carlos introduced the first major political reforms only months after he succeeded Franco. These reforms led to the first free elections. At that time, Spain was hit by a severe economic crisis and half a million citizens went on strike. These strikes were organised by the long-forbidden communist and socialist labour unions, which sought greater participation in the political process. Their strikes led to political reforms and amnesties for political prisoners.[325] The interim government faced pressure from two sides: from citizens on the one side, who sought rapid (economic and political) reforms in favour of those who had been oppressed for far too long; and, on the other side, from the old Francoist elites, the Falange, who feared losing power. During this time citizens' calls for reparation, compensation and acknowledgement of the previous regime's crimes increased, but still remained rather small. The TJ tools that were generously applied were amnesty laws at that time. To secure a peaceful transition, Juan Carlos not only granted amnesty to Franco's political prisoners but also to all Francoists in the judiciary, in high-ranked political positions and beyond, as well as to the members of Franco's political police and security forces.

Almost half of the Spanish population was directly or indirectly victimised, either during the Civil War or under the Franco regime. Individuals had been killed, tortured, disappeared or kept in Franco's prison cells. They had been put into forced labour camps and children had been abducted, but all these crimes were well silenced. To demystify them would have needed an open and public debate, truth commissions or other forms of TJ, which did not happen until around the year 2000.

Instead each household had a 'family narrative' of victimisers and victims, often under false allegations. On the other side of the spectrum, as Pablo Sánchez León has noted, were people with an understanding of

---

[325] B.N. Field, 'Interparty Consensus and Intraparty Discipline in Spain's Transition to Democracy' in G. Alonso and D. Muro (eds.), *The Politics of Memory of Democratic Transition. The Spanish Model* (New York: Routledge, 2011), pp. 71–93.

citizenship that did not distinguish between radical and violent politics and other aspects of cultural life, such as the Guardia Civil, the police and the Franco supporters that were still in the majority of those who held public office.[326]

Consequently, the violent past was very much alive and present during the first post-regime change decades – and there was no public debate to deal with it. Those who sought political responsibility in the newly formed democratic institutions faced the dilemma of whether to bring past perpetrators to justice. The new political elite, most of which came out of exile and/or were left wing, knew that victims and victimisers would have to continue to live side by side and that many victimisers would have to remain in office because the new regime needed their skills. In this respect, Spain faced a situation that combined the worst elements of both post-1945 and post-1989 Germany: old technocratic and political elites needed to stay in power because there were not enough skilled and trained individuals to replace them (like post-war Germany), and at the same time victims and victimisers had to live alongside each other in the same streets and houses (like post-1989 Germany) and often greatly mistrusted or hated each other. Because of this, it often seemed best to only grant symbolic monetary compensation or amnesty laws, instead of launching a moral debate about the values of the past. Those who dared to do otherwise often had to suffer social and even violent repercussions.

The government thus decided to leave the past alone, to 'forget' it or at least to silence it in order not to jeopardise the transition process. The public, without much opportunity to take an alternative path, generally supported this approach. It entailed an unwritten pact of silence, or a 'Pacto de Olvido'.[327] In 1977, the king, interim government and representatives of almost all opposition movements, signed the Moncloa Pact. This pact silenced the past and closed the doors to a substantive TJ process for the first 20 years of transition.[328] Analysts such as Linz and Stepan emphasise that Spain had learned the lessons of the Civil War, and knew how hurtful it was to divide the country into republicans, socialists and communists

---

[326] P. Sánchez León, 'Radicalization Without Representation. On the Character of Social Movements in the Spanish Transition to Democracy' in G. Alonso and D. Muro (eds.), *The Politics of Memory of Democratic Transition. The Spanish Model* (New York/London: Routledge, 2011), pp. 95–111, at p. 108.

[327] C. Humlebaek, 'The "Pacto de Olvido"' in G. Alonso and D. Muro (eds.), *The Politics of Memory of Democratic Transition. The Spanish Model* (New York: Routledge, 2011), pp. 183–198.

[328] J.J. Linz and A. Stepan, *Problems of Democratic Transition and Consolidation*, pp. 92–93.

THE CASE STUDIES: GERMANY, SPAIN AND TURKEY 273

on the one side and royalists and Francoists on the other side, and had transformed this into a positive factor that aided the transition.[329] The consequences and lessons learned from the past only came to light much later and entered politics after one generation had passed. Around the year 2000, and after many hopeless efforts by small victim groups, citizens started to demand more TJ, and not only in court.

The legacy of the past was omnipresent in 1975, in particular among the opposition parties whose predecessors had been heavily suppressed and killed under Franco. Thus, not surprisingly, underground movements emerged shortly after Franco's death. The Basque Homeland and Freedom Movement (*Euskadi Ta Askatasuna*, ETA) emerged as early as 1959 and frequently challenged and threatened the Franco regime in the following years by means of deadly terror acts. It continued after Franco's death, because ETA believed the regime in Madrid had only changed its colour, not its content. The Catholic Church, although a strong supporter of Franco's regime, slowly became more sensitive to the changes in the country after it launched a review on its 'non-Catholic' role in the Civil War in the late 1960s. In this report, the Church indicated its co-responsibility for the massacres that occurred. In the 1990s, the Church finally dared to publicly criticise some of its own past wrongdoings and distanced itself from the violence of the past. The fact that the Church took the first step also indicated that citizens had changed. The heads of the Spanish Catholic community realised that by being more self-reflective and self-critical, they could win citizens' trust, in particular from those who had supported the communist and socialist movements.

War crimes, crimes against humanity, arbitrary killings, torture, disappearances committed during the Spanish Civil War between 1936 and 1939, and the continuing White Terror (carried out by Franco) and Red Terror (carried out by the communists), resulted in between 300,000 and 400,000 victims in total. These numbers did not even include the allegations of approximately 300,000 child abductions during that time. Newborn babies from leftist Republican, socialist or communist women, mostly in custody, were abducted (after being declared dead) and trafficked as orphans to loyal Christian or Franco supporters. Including these babies, the number of victims to be dealt with might be more than one million between 1936 and 1975. These victims were not officially acknowledged during the early period of regime change, and were only

[329] Ibid., p. 88.

sporadically and often privately recognised during the first two decades following the end of Franco's regime. It soon became clear that if the country was to undergo an open TJ process, the atrocities on both sides would come to light. It was doubtful whether the judiciary, which was dominated by Francoists, would have been able to handle this. And around 2000 it also became clear that in order to reconcile this troubled and divided society, one had to deal with the horror of the past, acknowledge it, atone for it and name those who were responsible, in order to finally unite and reconcile the society, otherwise democracy would always face flaws and unconsolidated pockets.

While Spain's regime change was pacted, its lack of accountability for past atrocities undermined the consolidation process. On the one hand, the Francoists enabled a peaceful transition on their terms, including the installation of a king. This did not prevent the country from becoming somewhat democratic, but it did prevent it from becoming a resilient and high-quality inclusive democracy. Those favouring Franco saw the human rights violations committed in the past as a necessary means to fight unrest, Bolshevism, communism and other threats to the Spanish nation. Thus, according to the Francoists, the measures were justified and there was no need for criminal or restorative justice. One of the reasons why fascist movements could survive in Europe long after the defeat of Nazi Germany in 1945 was that those movements in Portugal, Spain and Greece were seen as strongholds against the emerging communist power from Moscow. The autocratic governments and juntas stayed in power in southern Europe because they served the western powers by providing a fortification against communism.[330]

Another TJ measure, reform of the paramilitary police (the Guardia Civil), took over ten years. The Guardia Civil alone was responsible for the killing of an estimated 100,000 people. Many of their victims died of torture or ill treatment. The majority of the murders were acts of revenge aimed at intimidating and terrorising the Spanish population, an aim the Guardia Civil succeeded in achieving. State terror governed the country until 1975, but also continued later into the 1980s, undermining regime consolidation. Thereafter, Franco's legacy remained visible in the lives of Spaniards with his numerous statues

---

[330] A. Quiroga, 'Salvation by Betrayal: The Left and the Spanish Nation' in G. Alonso and D. Muro (eds.), *The Politics of Memory of Democratic Transition. The Spanish Model* (New York: Routledge, 2011), pp. 135–158.

in public places and mandatory school trips to his burial place at the Valle de los Caidos (Valley of the Fallen) near Madrid. This burial place turned into a memorial for all those who fought during the Civil War on Franco's side and positioned him as the main hero of the battle against the republicans. Although this memorial had once been a forced labour camp for prisoners, and these forced labourers built his mausoleum, this aspect was never commemorated. The Valle de los Caidos is probably the most controversial symbol of Spain's struggle with TJ. It remains one of the largest memorials to a fascist state leader in the world. Only recently has it been suggested that it should be converted into a memorial for all victims of the Franco reign of terror between 1936 and 1975.

Shortly after Franco's death, the Spanish education sector was barely reformed. The Spanish Catholic Church kept its privileges and overall influence on the Spanish education system, thus preventing any open debate about past atrocities, let alone about reconciliation.

The European Community (and later the EU) and the United States exerted pressure on Spain to introduce democratic reforms. Europe wanted Spain to become a member of the EC as soon as possible, in order to reintegrate the country into the democratic fold and to have influence over its future development. Regime consolidation went alongside these efforts. The EC triggered massive economic, infrastructural and societal reforms, along with political ones, like the installation of a multi-party system. The United States wanted Spain to become a member of NATO, which would secure the military bases in Spain against the Soviet Union while also influencing military reform in the country. The Spanish government chose to join NATO for various reasons – bearing in mind that this was still the time of the Cold War. One of the side effects of joining NATO was the need to reform the Spanish military. According to Merkel's assessment of the Spanish transition and consolidation process, the military's rehabilitation was a crucial part of regime consolidation. It was in the king's and the government's interest to avoid any litigation against the military leaders in order to safeguard peaceful transition and transformation.[331] Thus, joining NATO allowed the government to alter the military's role in a peaceful manner; in particular, the roles of old generals who were loyal to Franco long after his death. The military was seen as one of the root causes of 'Spanish fear' during the period of transition.[332] European

---

[331] W. Merkel, *Systemtransformation* (1999), p. 293.
[332] L.M. McLaren, *Constructing Democracy in Southern Europe*, p. 267.

and US external pressure had significant influence on regime consolidation because it purged those who could potentially hinder democracy.

The main threat to regime change, however, was the lack of delegitimisation of the past and thus also the flaws and subsequent violent paths to legitimise the new regime. Anti-democratic and separatist movements in Spain claimed legitimacy based on the fact that Franco's nationalist view of Spain was still alive and would never allow any true autonomy or human rights. These movements had millions of supporters. Needless to say, citizens, in particular in the Basque Country and in Catalonia, engaged little with the new democratic institutions they thought still represented the Franco regime. Citizens often regarded these institutions as illegitimate, which stalled Spain's path towards democratic consolidation, thus creating the first unconsolidated pocket. Why should trust be placed in the newly reformed judiciary if those once in power and responsible for committing crimes never faced prosecution under the democratic regime? Judges and attorneys, most of them educated under the Franco regime, would never speak in favour of those who once opposed the Franco regime, despite a new constitution.[333]

The government's lack of responsiveness in the first three post-Franco decades permanently weakened the consolidation process and prevented it from being resilient to crises. According to the Democracy Barometer, Spain's democratic quality scores are today slightly above average. Between 2000 and 2015, however, the political regime faced some dramatic crises and changes to which it has not proven that resilient, due to a lack of tradition in accountable and transparent measures. Consequently, according to rankings by the Quality of Democracy Rankings, in 2015 it lost ground by three points and scores number 19 on a scale out of 113 countries.[334] Although its institutions are stable, the country had suffered flaws due to the fact that the executive and legislature have continuously restricted rights and undermined the rule of law. The government and the judiciary permitted the use of undemocratic means, such as torture and violations of the right to a fair trial, to combat ETA terrorism in the 1980s and 1990s. A better balance between executive and legislative powers was only established after 1994, when the government lost its majority in parliament.[335]

---

[333] P. Aguilar, *Memory and Amnesia. The Role of the Spanish Civil War in the Transition to Democracy* (New York/Oxford: Berghahn Books, 2002).

[334] The Democracy Ranking Association, Quality of Democracy Ranking 2015, see: democracyranking.org/wordpress/welcome/about-us/ (last accessed July 2016).

[335] Spain, Basic Facts 2007, Democracy Barometer, Center for Democracy Studies, Aarau, www.democracybarometer.org (last accessed August 2013).

The unconsolidated pockets of ETA terrorism and its consequences and causes were always linked with the failure of government efforts to introduce TJ measures to delegitimise the Franco regime.[336] Ending ETA terrorism has become a measure of how successful, strong and resilient Spain's democratic institutions have been. Interestingly, in parallel with ETA's decline between 2011 and 2015, Spain's efforts in terms of TJ measures have increased dramatically.

First Decade 1975–1984

In November 1975 King Juan Carlos cooperated or rather 'pacted' with the Francoist Falange to ensure a peaceful regime transition to democracy. It was a tense time, as many Spaniards feared the power gap between those who had been oppressed and those who feared losing power would drive the country back into a civil war. Many of the state elites, technocrats and politicians were loyal to the ideas and concepts of a centralistic, non-democratic fascist regime. To these people, pluralism meant 'chaos' and democracy meant 'uncertainty of leadership'. The reforms installed included dramatic changes from how the country had been governed thus far. In addition, generations of citizens who had never experienced pluralism in parliament, participation in elections or the rule of law were confronted with rapid democratic reforms. Therefore, a pacted or negotiated transition based on a consensual democratic regime was seen as the best of all bad options.

The first years of regime change were crucial for setting the legal and political framework for future elections and legal reforms, including pathways for consolidation. TJ measures were not foreseen as a means for delegitimising the Franco regime, because the king, most of the political elites, the judiciary and the military remained in power. It was not a complete shift, but rather opening up of the regime, namely to allow political parties to establish, to allow CSOs to form, reintroducing labour unions and overall allow for fair and free elections and reform of the constitution. Silence on the one side and incorporation of those once opposed to each other on the other side, was the dominant two doctrines at that time.

Whether TJ measures would be introduced to delegitimise and demystify the previous regime was debated mostly at a regional level, in the

---

[336] O.G. Encarnacion, *Democracy Without Justice in Spain. The Politics of Forgetting* (Philadelphia, PA: University of Pennsylvania Press, 2014), p. 29.

so-called *autonomias,* or locally. Many soon rejected a systematic TJ process, due to the fact that too many old Francoists remained in important
positions in government and administration and to challenge them with
TJ measures would have hampered this transition. TJ measures were left
to a few isolated local initiatives that 'dared' to employ such measures.
Thus, one could have soon come to the assumption that TJ measures are
best made use of only in societies that had suffered atrocious war, genocide and suppression with a subsequent complete shift of political and
institutional elites, but not in pacted transitions like in Spain and later in
Latin America and Eastern Europe – which was partly the case.

The dismantling of statues or memorials to Franco by left-wing movements and victims of the regime stopped in the late 1970s. Private initiatives to build memorials remained the exception. One such private
initiative was the 1979 inauguration of the memorial in Pozos de Caudé
in Aragon for communists murdered during and after the Spanish Civil
War. This location had served as the execution place of Franco's opponents during and after the Civil War. Many of these local and private
failed initiatives marked a retreat into the private sphere, which provided a basis for myth formation on both sides since the doors to his-
torically grounded arguments about the past remained locked for the
time being. Most often, those who tried to commemorate their murdered
loved ones were intimidated by their Falange neighbours and were thus
silenced again.[337] Public debates, media coverage and academic research
on Spain's past were unseen in the country at that time, although not
only because of intimidation by those who were slowly losing power in
society but also because no independent commission of inquiry existed
and no public acknowledgement had been expressed. In retrospect, these
fears may seem unreasonable, but to those at the time they were justified
by the events of 1981. Interestingly enough, it is widely understood that
both sides had something to hide, making it easy for the pact of silence
to remain in place.

Now, in 1975 and the following years, amnesty laws and pension funds
were the more obvious but also most silent measures often used in pacted
transitions. In December 1975, the interim government led by Adolfo
Suarez, the first appointed prime minister after Franco's death, leader of
the Union of Democratic Centre (Union Centro Democratico, UCD) and
former leading figure of Franco's National Movement, passed a decree

---

[337]   W.L. Bernecker and S. Brinkmann, *Kampf der Erinnerungen, Der Spanische Bürgerkrieg in
Politik und Gesellschaft, 1936–2008* (Nettersheim: Verlag Graswurzelrevolution, 2008).

on the revisions and nullification of administrative sanctions for communists, which were issued in 1939 straight after the Spanish Civil War. In the following years, the government passed decrees on extra pensions for seriously injured war victims, which everybody, communists and fascists alike, could benefit from.[338] The problem, however, was that there was no independent commission that would be able to determine who qualified as a victim. Since there was no governmental engagement and public debate about the past, no history or truth commissions, no tribunal installed, no vetting process, no opening of the Franco archives or anything of that kind, it was entirely up to the administrative powers to decide on the local level and from case to case whom to grant compensations or some form of acknowledgement of victimhood. Those decisions were mainly in the hands of old Francoist elites, who insisted on clear evidence and documentation of victim status.[339]

Although democratic institutions and procedures were put in place, it was evident from the beginning that consolidation would never be straightforward. In 1976, vice prime minister and a minister of the interim parliament, the Cortes, and a former minister under Franco, Manuel Fraga Iribrane, introduced a programme for democratic reforms that would legalise political parties and pave the way for pluralism and elections. The government and the quasi-parliament adopted this 'Law for Political Reform' (*Ley para la Reforma Política*) and the law came into force despite mass protests. As a result of the law, Franco's fascist nationalist movement, the National Movement (*Movimiento Nacional*), which had operated in a semi-single party system, transformed itself into various different parties. The main dispute among the political elite was whether to allow the Spanish communist party to take part in the political process. This party represented those the Franco regime had fought for over 40 years. Their leaders lived in exile, mainly in France and some in the Soviet Union. The main veto powers, as Merkel has called them, or the former political elites under Suarez and Fraga, eventually agreed to allow the party's participation, thus paving the way for regime consolidation.[340] Shortly thereafter, in 1977 thousands called for retribution for the murder of opposition leaders in police custody prior to Franco's death.[341] The veto

---

[338] J.M. Tamarit Sumalla, *Historical Memory and Criminal Justice in Spain. A Case of Late Transitional Justice*, Series on Transitional Justice, 14 (Antwerp et al.: Intersentia, 2013), p. 61.
[339] O.G. Encarnacion, *Democray Without Justice in Spain*, chapter 1.
[340] W. Merkel, *Systemtransformation* (1999), p. 293.
[341] W.L. Bernecker and S. Brinkmann, *Kampf der Erinnerungen*.

powers rejected this call, believing that they had compromised enough and any public trial or commission of inquiry on past injustice would have increased the unrest in the country – thus the fear of the leading policy-makers at that time.

Thus the new regime was under constant violent threat from either radical separatists or socialists on the one side and the loyal Francoists on the other side, all defending their cause and legacy by means of violence. The 1977 Massacre of Atocha, in which members of the Guardia Civil allegedly killed eight labour lawyers, is an example of the political agreement not to punish those associated with the Franco regime. Linz and Stepan have stated that due to the lack of a strong civil society (except, perhaps, in the Basque Country and Catalonia) there was no outcry to expect when these killings happened. But interim president Alfonso Suarez realised how precarious the situation was and initiated political reforms in the same year that would allow for indictments of those who did such murderous attempts and reforms that would later also allow for some modest TJ measures. That is why Linz and Stepan often called this transition a 'reforma pactada-ruptura pactada', a pacted reform agenda that determined future regime change, a very top-down approach by the government in response to the growing pressure from below.[342]

The majority of the communist or socialist party leaders, both those returning from exile and new leaders, pleaded for a negotiated but radical shift (ruptura pactata) based on a 'rupture by death', meaning that there was no break with the past as such, let alone a strong opposition or civil rights movement demanding such a break, but rather a Franco-approved transition into leadership. The fact that an old man had died of sickness and had already prepared for a pacted transition, made the case for citizen-driven TJ rather weak. Neither Franco nor his political advisors had intended the regime to remain unchanged, so the break was not a real rupture with the past, but a negotiated 'rupture'. In January 1975, ten months before Franco died, a master plan for transition to democracy was already in place for a pacted and thus negotiated peaceful transition for all groups in society after Franco's death. The plan included parliamentary elections, adherence to the rule of law by an independent judiciary, adherence to international human rights and the young king becoming head of state. Yet, there is no doubt that Franco meant this all to take place

---

[342] J.J. Linz and A. Stepan (eds.), *Problems of Democratic Transition and Consolidation*, p. 111.

under the strict surveillance of the National Movement, the Falange.[343] This pacted transition, or the 'Rise of Forgetting' as Omar Encarnacion called it, later became a case study for many political scientists interested in whether or not such a 'planned and negotiated' transition had led to real consolidation of Spanish democracy.[344]

At the end the pacted break-up of the Franco regime was possible due to the king's role as negotiator and mediator. He went much further than Franco had anticipated. Juan Carlos installed people of confidence as his assistant 'negotiators'. Many of these people of confidence were members of the Franco movement but educated abroad and who nevertheless seemed dedicated to putting in place democratic reforms. They enjoyed trust from those on both sides; from those who remained loyal to Franco and those who wanted steady democratic reforms. The main obstacles lay in the strength of the armed forces, the military, the Guardia Civil and police forces, to which democracy meant nothing but chaos and the end of the many political privileges they had enjoyed.

Meanwhile millions participated in strikes and protests in 1976 and the following years, manifesting their discontent with the democratic reforms and the government had to respond to the pressure from the streets. 'Liberty, amnesty and autonomy' (*libertad, amnestia y autonomia*) was one of the slogans heard on the streets of Spain's main cities.[345] Hundreds of thousands of people demonstrated and dozens of demonstrators were killed arbitrarily by the Guardia Civil during the first peaceful protests in 1976. The protesters wanted freedom for all political prisoners, respect for rights, and autonomy for the different states and regions in Spain. Protestors in Barcelona and Bilbao fought for more decentralisation and autonomy against a centralised government (as centralisation was a symbol of Franco's power). This fight was a sign of liberation from the age-old propaganda of one nation and Franco's rhetoric of a glorious Spanish heritage and tradition. In fact, like an earlier generation of post-authoritarian Germans, the Spaniards were decidedly inhibited about nationalism, and preferred being Catalan, Basque or Andalusian rather than 'Spanish'.[346] The democratisation and denationalisation in southern Europe also led to

---

[343] Fundación Francisco Franco, Archive. *Documento de trabajo para la preparación de una asociación política*. 3rd version. January 1975. Fiche 10109, Madrid, pp. 2–14.
[344] For a good summary of this process, see: O.G. Encarnacion, *Democracy Without Justice in Spain*, chapter 2.
[345] L.M. McLaren, *Constructing Democracy in Southern Europe*, p. 155.
[346] T. Judt, *Postwar: A History of Europe Since 1945*, p. 702.

a new approach to Europe: the 'Europe of the Regions'. Under this principle, Europe was governed through regional administrations and governments. For some Spaniards, it meant in essence being Andalusian, Basque
or Catalan in Europe. Nevertheless, it was this urge for independence and
connecting to pre-Franco identity paths in the Spanish periphery, such as
in Catalonia and the Basque Country, that was among the major driving
forces for both regime consolidation and TJ, as illustrated by many examples in Ricard Vinye's compilation on *The State and the Memory*.[347] If TJ
and regime consolidation correlated during the first post-Franco decade
at all, it was in these autonomous regions. It is here where TJ measures
soon became tools in the hands of civil society, overall victim groups and
regional governments. But they hardly made their way through to the
central government in Madrid.

Interestingly enough, those who claimed amnesty for political prisoners on the streets of Bilbao, Seville or Barcelona were not necessarily
united. Some wanted amnesty for communists in prisons, while others
wanted amnesty for Basque nationalists, separatists or other intellectuals
who were being incarcerated. The range of those imprisoned was wide
and so were those protesting for their freedom. There was no clear divide
between victims and victimisers and that did not make the negotiations
easier for the king. He had to decide to whom to grant amnesty.[348]

Terror and violence continued underground. The ETA representatives
targeted the headquarters of the Guardia Civil, which they saw as a continuous symbol of oppression of the Basque people. Another anti-Franco
terror group, the GRAPO (*Grupo de Resistencia Anti-Fascista Primero de
Octubre*), targeted the Guardia Civil because it saw its chance to install
a communist regime in Spain now that Franco was dead. The GRAPO
was a communist armed force against fascism and the Falange that was
founded in 1975, months before Franco's death. The organisation grew
in the following years and committed terror acts. The Guardia Civil and
the Spanish Secret Service fought both groups with equally brutal and
illegal means. The new regime, however, responded with secret deten-
tions, ill-treatment and unfair trials of those captured and interrogated
under anti-terror laws. Yet the GRAPO continued its plan to install a

---

[347] R. Vinyes (ed.), *El Estado y la Memoria, Gobiernos y Ciudadanos Frente a los Traumas de
la Historia* (Barcelona: Memorial Democratica, 2009).

[348] M. Perez Ledesma, '"Nuevos" y "Viejos" movimientos sociales en la transicion' in
C. Molinero (ed.), *La transición: treinta años después de la dictadura a la instauración y
consolidación de la democracia* (Barcelona: Ediciones Península, 2006), pp. 117–126.

Marxist-Leninist state. Since it saw the United States as the main loyal partner to the Franco regime – and its successor government under the king – the GRAPO sabotaged US military facilities. Opposing Spain's fragile path to regime consolidation in the first two decades after regime change, GRAPO carried out a number of terror acts against police officers, members of the Guardia Civil and civilians. It was only in 2007 that the radical arm of GRAPO dissolved itself, by then having lost most of its supporters (similar to the fate of the RAF in West Germany around the same stage in the consolidation process). This was interestingly enough at the same time that the Historical Memory Law was finally passed and consolidation was no longer disputed.[349]

By the late 1970s there was little hope for a mutually reinforcing take-off between TJ mechanisms and democracy, due to the lack of both. In the Basque Country, Basque nationalists and the violent terrorist organisation ETA pleaded for a total amnesty for (their) political prisoners and those who had been convicted of murdering Franco supporters. The interim president of the government, Adolfo Suarez, and King Juan Carlos denied their request in 1976. This resulted in many more acts of violence by ETA against both security forces and civilians. At the same time, approximately 75 per cent of citizens were in favour of amnesty laws for political prisoners without any limits on who could qualify. This indicated that citizens overall wanted stability by any means, knowing that victims and victimisers would have to continue to live side by side without any atonement. Yet, by supporting these measures, they sacrificed justice and the spiral went downwards.

Increasing demand from the public forced the president and the king to react and pass amnesty laws. Juan Carlos also wanted to include members of the military and the Catholic Church in the amnesty, although strikes and protests against this inclusion continued during the first decade. The economic crisis contributed to the unrest and the abundant number of strikes. This 'worker's rebellion' also symbolised the divide in society in general: on the one side, the working class mostly supported the socialist or communist party and thus opposed Franco; while on the other side the privileged elite, business people and landowners had supported Franco. By the end of the 1970s, workers had been on strike for a total of 150 million hours. In comparison, workers in 1975 had only been on strike for 14.5 million hours. These strikes severely threatened Spain's

---

[349] J.M. Tamarit Sumalla, *Historical Memory and Criminal Justice in Spain*.

season-dependent, agricultural and tourist economy, thus also threatening the regime change's success. Fear that the country would return to
Francoism kept citizens silent for the sake of quasi-tranquillity.[350] 'Fear'
became thus the most persisting perception by which the government
justified its top-down approach of reforms and the rejection of any TJ
measures at that time.

Parliament passed the first amnesty law in 1976, covering a wide range
of political prisoners. But because of it, acts of vengeance continued,
including the 1977 Massacre of Atocha. It was such incidents, of which
there were many, that caused citizens to fear the beginning of another violent outbreak and even a civil war between the 'two Spains': the left (red
shirts) and the right (white shirts). This alarmed all those who wished to
hold human rights abusers to account. Demands for TJ measures were
made, but either ignored or half-heartedly followed up on. There was also
no significant external pressure by the EC or other international bodies
and CSOs to foster their instalment. Dealing with the past and bringing Francoists to justice would risk triggering a new civil war. Society
still appeared too divided and the democratic institutions too fragile to
protect against this threat. In the eyes of the political leadership at that
time, TJ measures would have carried the risk of aggravating the division, potentially leading to the re-emergence of violent acts of vengeance.
Instead this fear and tension resulted in a second amnesty law in October
1977, which again equalised all 'political acts' and put in place amnesty for
those responsible for them.[351]

Instead of a democratically negotiated regime change, Spain's transition became an 'amnestied' one, which sacrificed justice and the rule of
law. Eventually, the king concluded an agreement between the former
elites and those in opposition. Most of the latter were socialists, communists or regional-nationalists who led separatist movements in Catalonia
or the Basque Country. The agreement of silence or forgetting (*pacto de
silencio* or *pacto de olvido*), as it was often called, was seen as the only
way to proceed with democratic reforms without risking any further outbreaks of violence. Fear, mistrust and lack of experience with democratic
institutions were already deeply rooted in society and dominated the first
decade of democracy. With the recent violent experience and the political
killings on all sides of the political spectrum in mind, old and new elites,

[350] P. Schmidt (ed.), *Kleine Geschichte Spaniens*, pp. 479ff.
[351] Spain Law 46/1977, Ley de amnistia, 15 October 1977, Gazette n°248, 17 October 1977,
pp. 22765–22766, Reference BOE-A-1977–24937.

intellectuals and opposition leaders chose not to threaten their future by bringing up the past. Little was published, either academically or in terms of novels or films, that indicated that the people could deal with the past in a public space. Publishing about the past could only be done from abroad and preferably not in Spanish. As a result, the Franco past remained something that was only discussed in the family. Even today, every Spanish family knows who in the family fought on the white side and who on the red side.[352]

No one expected an official apology from Adolfo Suarez, the first appointed prime minister who was later elected president of democratic Spain, although his party, the UCD (*Unión de Centro Democrático*), was mostly composed of former Francoists. Reparation payments, the installation of historical commissions, public debates and condemnations were not the first issues openly discussed.[353] But the more silent or 'oblivious' the society was about the previous regime, the more obvious it became that atrocities must have happened in the past. It became clear that something was being masked, something that could interfere greatly with the democratisation process. It reflected how deeply the injustice and fear had gone through all social layers. Those who could legally claim a fair trial or compensation feared that their claims would trigger unrest and disrupt societal peace; as a result, a culture of impunity for past injustices arose and compromised the country's judiciary.[354] The failure to delegitimise the past also led partly towards a downward spiral effect in democratic development. Civic trust was difficult to develop and instead violence and revenge grew stronger.

The so-called rupture with the political past was finalised when the Communist Party was legalised in 1977 and democratic elections could finally take place. As mentioned before, that was not to delegitimise the previous regime, but rather to add more pluralism to the existing one. Parties such as the PSOE (*Partido Socialista Obrero Español*), the Communist Party (*Partido Communista Español*), the conservative right-wing *Allianzia Popular* (later turning into *Partido Popular* or PP) and the UCD representing those Francoists who 'converted to

[352] J.C. Monedero, *La transición contada a nuestros padres. Nocturno de la democracia española* (Madrid: Catrata, 2011).
[353] A. Mihr, 'From Reconciliation to the Rule of Law and Democratisation', *Web Journal of Current Legal Issues*, 1 (2009) online at: http://webjcli.ncl.ac.uk/2009/issue1/mihr1.html, 1 (last accessed December 2010).
[354] W.L. Bernecker and S. Brinkmann, *Kampf der Erinnerungen*, pp. 243–244.

democracy overnight' were registered for the first elections in 1977. The UCD won the first democratic elections with almost 35 per cent of the votes and Suarez became president as expected. The PSOE only managed to get 29 per cent of the votes and could not form a significant coalition with the other left-wing parties, although it did move from 0 per cent to almost 30 per cent of the vote. The close election results reflected the divide between left and right in society. The fact that the successors to the previous regime won is not unusual in post-autocratic regimes, as citizens have the most confidence in someone they already 'know' from the previous regime – even if s/he had been part of it. Communist or socialist candidates could not yet demonstrate any track record of democratic performance and hence many citizens were rather sceptical of them. Mistrust of unknown new political actors was still high among the public. In that context, electing Suarez, who was at the same time a leading member of the Falange, was seen as the best compromise. The major opposition party PSOE, which represented hundreds of thousands of victims and oppressed people, became the second-biggest party, leaving all other parties far behind and achieving a remarkable and surprising result. The left-wing parties felt pressured by their more radical members to promote a less consensus-based and less silent approach to the past. Consequently, the communist and socialist parties made much greater reference to the persecution suffered in Spain during the Franco era than others.[355] The 'new' parties in the new democratic 'game in town' still had to gain the confidence of citizens so that they could also govern. Because neither the PSOE nor the Communist Party were seen as facilitators of peace and security, let alone economic growth, they could not gain a majority. Conveniently, Spain had a head of state already in place who did not require any political legitimation. The king became something of a guarantor for what citizens wanted most: peace, security and unity. He subsequently became a proxy for all the TJ measures that were never installed or openly addressed. As such, Juan Carols acted as a personalised TJ mechanism, probably the only ever in European history. He pushed for more democratic reforms on the one side and for some modest memorisation and acknowledgement of victims, pension funds or other activities that would qualify as TJ – whenever needed – hoping to restore unity in the country. Most of all, he stood for reconciliation.

---

[355] P. Aguilar, *Memory and Amnesia*, p. 239.

But even after the first elections, the society was still unable to replace all the pre-existing bureaucrats with new technocratic elites due to the fact that those who opposed the regime had been in exile or in prison, or had been denied access to universities and other administrative education. This left many of them with a low level of education and training and no bureaucratic skills, preventing socialists or communists from taking up higher-level positions in the new democratic regime. Instead, public administration, ministries, universities and the education sector were filled with members of the Falange or the neo-Francoist nationalist movement. Regime consolidation was still a long way away. It was evident from the beginning that it would take a generation or two for the Francoist public servants to be replaced. Installing any TJ measure remained therefore a sensitive matter and could only be done if it served tactical political purposes, such as tactical reparations. After the amnesty law of 1977 'imposed' a level of silence on the past, the government slowly and carefully issued reparation to specific and selective groups of victims, usually in the form of pensions.[356] Nevertheless, citizens were far from having a common narrative of the past and the only reconciling factor in society was the king, which was not a strong enough base for an intertwining regime change and TJ process. Not surprisingly, at the same time, insurgencies by the military and the Guardia Civil continued, because people did not use the judiciary or the parliament to solve their political disputes, but instead violence and terror. Their opposition to the democratic changes increased after the rehabilitation of incarcerated members of the Communist Party (under the amnesty laws) and after the Communist Party was given the ability to participate in elections. Some of the perpetrators of these insurgencies were indicted and sentenced, but it took a long time before the violence abated. Meanwhile, the police continued to carry out torture.

Efforts to apply restitutional justice faced a wall of silence and intimidation until the mid-1980s, while executive powers struggled to create harmony between new and old political elites in government institutions.[357] At the same time, the ETA and other groups continued committing attacks. This showed the discontent many citizens felt with the reforms and their mistrust in the shift of government in Madrid. It was a clear sign of the weakness and fragility of the regime, thus increasing

---

[356] C. Humlebaek, 'Party Attitudes Towards the Authoritarian Past in Spanish Democracy', p. 76.
[357] J.M. Tamarit Sumalla, *Historical Memory and Criminal Justice in Spain*, pp. 68–75.

the unconsolidated pockets of Spanish democracy. The terror groups did not see holding elections as a sufficient break with the past. Laws such as the Statute of Autonomy were passed to counteract separatist movements already in 1978. The laws affirmed that more political autonomy should be given to the Autonomous Communities and increased their political participation in the central parliament.[358] The hope was that this law would undermine political violence. Throughout the change and consolidation process these terror groups posed a serious threat to democratisation and they were the main weakening factor for the regime.[359]

Nevertheless, the Moncloa Pact as the 'pact of silence or 'pact of forgetting' as it was also called, indirectly acknowledged and confirmed that great injustices had been committed in the past.[360] But the downside of this was that a culture of impunity was soon established that would haunt the necessary democratic regime consolidation. Without an independent judiciary with independent, not loyal, Franco judges, neither the rule of law nor civic trust could barely take place. The improper functioning of the judiciary, which was filled with judges, attorneys and lawyers from the previous regime, actually increased over time. Trials against perpetrators let alone against members of the Falange were hardly ever initiated and, when they were, they were never held in public.[361]

But a spiral is never linear, and thus change continued, albeit often in a hazardous way. The amnesty laws paved the way for a constitutional referendum in 1978. Without the amnesty laws, the old elites would have never agreed to this referendum. In the Basque Country, a left-wing citizen movement called 'Amnesty and Liberty' (only for their own people of course) was launched, while a right-wing movement called for the boycott of the constitutional referendum.[362] The constitution was in the end a compromise for both. This marked a major shift towards party pluralism and civil society engagement, which is a prerequisite for democratic regime consolidation.

Thus, many of those who had suffered political oppression even made their approval of the constitutional referendum conditional on these laws.

---

[358] J.J. Linz and A. Stepan, *Problems of Democratic Transition and Consolidation*, p. 103.
[359] W. Merkel, *Systemtransformation* (1999), p. 296.
[360] J.E. Mendez, 'In Defence of Transitional Justice', pp. 1–26.
[361] J.M. Tamarit Sumalla, *Historical Memory and Criminal Justice in Spain*, pp. 63–66.
[362] Archive Historical Memory, Salamanca, Campaign materials, Archive of Historical Memory, Salamanca, INCORPORADOS, Camaign Material Basque Country 'Sin amnstia ni liebertades politicas no afirmes con tu vota la monarquia contunardora del franqueismo' and 'Por la Amnestia y la Libertad – Abstencion!' Caja (box) 1598.

These groups did not anticipate the fact that Francoists would also benefit from these amnesty laws, but eventually they were part of the compromise as well. On the other hand, if Franco's followers had not benefited from this amnesty, they would never have supported any constitutional referendum. It was a trade-off, but nevertheless opposition from right-wing movements to the draft constitution was significant, with many fearing that they would lose their privileged status. At the same time, as the left-wing parties called for the amnesty, the right-wing parties and Francoists campaigned against the constitutional draft in 1978 with slogans such as 'Yes to Spain – No to the constitution' ('*Si a España – no a la constitución!*') on the basis that the conditions set out in the constitution were not right for them.[363] The fear in the 'generation of victimisers' was that this constitution would eventually serve to hold them accountable for their wrongdoings.

The historical and collective (unspoken) narrative continuously and indirectly intervened in regime change policies. If, for example, history or truth commissions were used to deal with the past, many of the myths that led to flaws and vicious circles of violence and amnesty could have been broken. For example, shortly before the referendum on the constitution in 1978, public debates arose in relation to dealing with the past. The conservative-run media, such as the *ABC* daily newspaper (previously a Franco-supporting paper) did not mention the term 'civil war' once, let alone write about any responsibility the Falange had in it, whereas the newly established left-wing newspaper *El País* mentioned civil war in almost 40 per cent of its editorials. This type of rhetoric also showed how divided the country remained and that there was no common narrative during the first post-Franco decade; a situation that would persist for another two decades.[364] In the end, the referendum took place and clearly confirmed a desire for democracy over dictatorship and for the slow but steady dismantling of the old Franco institutions. With a 77 per cent election turnout, of which 95 per cent voted 'yes', the referendum was a major success, although the conservative powers maintained a grip on the country and TJ remained taboo. Discussions around decentralisation and the adoption of the Statute of Autonomy followed.

[363] Archive Historical Memory, Salamanca, Campaign materials, Archive of Historical Memory, Salamanca, INCORPORADOS, Caja (box) 1598.
[364] J. Rodrigo, *Cautivos, Campos de Concentración en ll España Franquista, 1936–1947* (Barcelona: Critica, S.L., 2005), p. 321.

Soon afterwards, Spain received official support, or rather pressure, from other EC Member States in its economic and political and institutional transformation. Thus representative consolidation was anticipated, but a behavioural or attitudinal one was yet to come about. A mix of old and new elites in power, especially at the level of the federal or autonomous states, designed a decentralised autonomous federal state composed of the Autonomous Communities. As a result, the Communities' new statutes received immense support from the EC, which invested in the underdeveloped regions and Autonomous Communities in the country and thus supported decentralisation and consequently moved power from Madrid to the peripheries. The EC believed that economic growth through better infrastructure and industrialisation would also strengthen democratic forces and lead to democratically minded citizens. This 'Marshall Plan' for the southern European countries in transition at that time (Greece, Spain and Portugal) was called the EC Structural Fund, and had the same intention as the Marshall Plan did 40 years earlier for northern Europe and Germany: improve public infrastructure and skills and the economy so that the path towards democracy will be easier. The plan worked, but would have been more effective if TJ measures had been included in the plan, a sentiment similar to one the former Allied Commander for West Germany in the 1950s, Commander Clay, had once noted about the consolidation process in West Germany: the consolidation process in West Germany worked better with TJ than without it.

In the EC, in particular in Germany and France, governments understood that only a quick integration into the EC and active membership in international organisations would enable foreign powers to influence democratic institution building in Spain.[365] Spain's willingness to democratise and participate economically in the European Common Market was a formal requirement of becoming a member of the EC. Yet, it was exactly the fact that its institutions were far from stable and solid that triggered EC Member States to embrace Spain even more strongly. The EC hoped that once Spain was a member, it could influence and facilitate the development of Spain's institutions, even if at the beginning Spain did not completely fulfil all the criteria of a democracy since, for example, it lacked an independent judiciary and the Guardia Civil often operated outside its legal authority. But in all that, the systematic application of TJ

---

[365] U. Liebert, *Neue Autonomiebewegung und Dezentralisierung in Spanien. Der Fall Andalusien* (Frankfurt am Main: Campus Verlag, 1986).

measures was not a requirement for any international membership during the first post-Franco decade (which was very different from Germany after 1949). For those in Spain who wished to democratise faster, such as King Juan Carlos and the opposition parties like PSOE, the EC's interference was welcome. They could use the EC as an excuse when arguing with former Francoist supporters – it was the EC that demanded all of these democratic reforms, not only the PSOE or Juan Carlos. It is a common tactic for young democracies and their supporters to engage with international organisations in order to gain support in their 'fight against conservative anti-democratic' forces within their own country.[366] This was also true for Spain's early commitments in the UN, the Council of Europe and NATO.

As indicated earlier, the main significant political shift took place with the referendum on the constitution in 1978. Yet it did, however, indirectly pave the way for much later TJ measures and somewhat for the reconciliation of the 'two Spains', although it would take another generation. Instead, during the first transition years, Guardia Civil, who had lost their scope of action as a result of the democratic reforms, fought all democratic efforts after 1978. They argued that the transition from dictatorship to democracy had resulted in more chaos than order. In other words: 'Under Franco there was peace and security, now under democracy that respects communists and socialists, there is only chaos and insecurity.' In fact, protests and strikes continued to be a daily annoyance and threatened the economic upswing. In the early years of transition, people generally did not trust the new regime, instead favouring peace over freedom and even over justice, as opinion polls from 1976 show.[367] In one year, the protests and strikes resulted in over 460 injuries and even some deaths in the streets of Madrid, Barcelona and Bilbao. The past continued to haunt the transition period and people feared another civil war. The outbreaks of violence and the acts of terror seemed so similar to those of the 1930s that even those who most strongly opposed Franco and had suffered imprisonment under him did not dare to break the pact of silence and deal with the past.[368]

---

[366] M. Kneuer, *Demokratisierung durch die EU*, pp. 140–244; and J.M. Magone, 'The Role of the EEC in the Spanish, Portugese and Greek Transition' in G. Alonso and D. Muro (eds.), *The Politics of Memory of Democratic Transition. The Spanish Model* (New York: Routledge, 2011), pp. 215–236.
[367] P. Aguilar, *Memory and Amnesia*, pp. 260–261.
[368] Ibid.

But after constitutional consolidation in 1978, the government could slowly allow for reacting to TJ claims, and did so albeit reluctantly and hesitantly. On 18 September 1979, the government adopted an Act ensuring pensions, medical assistance and social support to the widows and other family members of individuals who were injured or died in the Civil War as an act of TJ. Five years later, in 1984, the socialist government increased the pension funds for those who had served in the Republican Army.[369] The problem with acknowledgement and TJ measures was being able to find adequate evidence to justify their use. Without open public discourse, history commissions or forensic analysis of the hundreds of unrevealed mass graves from the Spanish Civil War, it was difficult to prove who were victims and who were victimisers because trials were off-limits. Instead, amnesties and pension funds for victims were put in place in the first five years of transition and were an indirect form of acknowledgement of past injustices.[370]

Democratic efforts were weakened by the many cases before the administrative courts resulting from family feuds. They were often proxies for the lack of TJ trials and resembled old enmities from the Franco past and often resurfaced as administrative cases. The real cause for these claims was the desire to settle old scores between different factions and families that dated back to the Spanish Civil War. Thus, in some way, these cases can be seen as 'hidden TJ claims'. In the absence of official trials people looked for proxies. Land or property disputes often served as a proxy for the quest for justice. Many of the minor cases that came before the Spanish administrative courts were in fact a result of never openly discussing disputes or vengeance of the past. Although it was evident that political change would only take place if people in the villages dared to talk, organise themselves in interest groups and face the past, this did not take place until the 1990s.[371]

In January 1981, President Adolfo Suarez resigned from office. Days later an ETA member died in prison from torture. This unfortunate combination of events caused serious tensions in Spanish society and was proof of the weak basis for representative consolidation. It led to further provocations from ETA, a strong governmental response and yet another major general strike in the Basque Country, which spread a sense of chaos

---

[369] J.M. Tamarit Sumalla, 'Transition, Historical Memory and Criminal Justice in Spain', 740.
[370] P. Aguilar, *Memory and Amnesia*, p. 191.
[371] B. Schlee, *Die Macht der Vergangenheit. Demokratisierung und politischer Wandel in einer spanischen Kleinstadt* (Baden Baden: Nomos, 2008).

throughout the country. Weeks later, due to uncertainty about the country's political future, the power gap and the absence (or rather silence) of decision-making powers to openly confront the democracy gaps in the country, the Guardia Civil, under General Antonio Tejero Molina, wanted to restore law and order. Arguing that the democratic institutions had failed to keep order in the country, Tejero Molina launched a coup on 23 February 1981, during a meeting of Spain's lower house, the Congress of Deputies. No one was seriously injured, but it was the biggest threat to regime consolidation in the first decade, causing people to fear a return to dictatorship. Many Spaniards, most of them communist supporters, had already packed their belongings, ready to cross the border to France (again) as their parents and grandparents had done in 1936 when Franco seized control in Spain. The coup was closely related to the failure to delegitimise the previous regime and the UCD could no longer contain the tensions caused by the economic crisis (with almost 20 per cent unemployment), the regionalisation in state autonomies and federalisation, the violent acts by the separatist group ETA, and the reluctance from a significant part of the Spanish Armed Forces, including the Guardia Civil. All actors needed to accept the constitution and the democratic regime and in order to do that the political elite had to distance itself from the past. Unconsolidated pockets were at their height in 1981. Nevertheless, due to the public intervention of the king, the coup failed. After holding the parliament and cabinet hostage for 18 hours, the Guardia Civil surrendered. In a nationally broadcast television speech on the day of the coup, Juan Carlos – wearing his Captain General of the Armed Forces uniform – denounced the coup and urged the continuance of the democratically elected government. He asked the guards to return to their barracks. The incident showed that the young democracy was unstable and (still) depended on the willingness and conviction of a single leader, especially the king. At that time, the majority of the population by no means saw democracy as 'the only game in town', but the subsequent imprisonment of the military personnel involved in the coup, and the trials completed in 1982, made this a crucial year for regime consolidation. As Linz and Stepan have stated, '[t]he trials helped to consolidate democracy because they showed how divided and without an agenda the military "alternative" really was'.[372] The Guardia Civil officers who had launched the coup were sentenced to 30 years in prison that same year and more were convicted with lower sentences. This

---

[372] J.J. Linz and A. Stepan (eds.), *Problems of Democratic Transition and Consolidation*, p. 110.

was the first time citizens had ever seen state institutions ensure justice be served against the Guardia Civil.[373]

In April 1981, parliament passed a law to install an ombudsman (*defensor del pueblo*) to take up citizens' claims and concerns in respect to the continued corruption and human rights violations by state forces after 1975. This office had been long anticipated, as it was intended to safeguard those human rights set out in the 1978 constitution, but it now finally became a matter of urgency. The government started to appreciate citizen participation and saw it as a vehicle to aid democracy, rather than impede it. The ombudsman had no power to take claims from the past, but was meant to signal that under the new regime, human rights violations should no longer occur and would be taken up by the judiciary. Although the first ombudsman was only appointed in 1982 with rather limited powers, the development indicated responsiveness to citizens' needs. According to Merkel, consolidation only really began to take place when the PSOE won a majority in the 1982 elections.[374] Five years after regime change took off, trials, pension funds, and public acknowledgements of wrongdoings of the Franco elites started to (slowly) delegitimise the Franco regime.

Suarez's government had already initiated some cultural and memorial TJ activities that indirectly acknowledged past wrongdoings, although it was – if at all – for tactical political reasons and not for moral ones. One such informal activity was ensuring the return of Picasso's most well-known painting, the 1937 *La Guernica*, from 'exile' in New York to Madrid in 1981.[375] This was a memorial act of reconciliation between the central government and the Basque country and peoples who asked for more recognition of the suffering they had to endure under Franco. The government had started negotiations in 1977 with the aim of satisfying Basque claims for recognition of victimhood in the Spanish Civil War and the Franco regime's responsibility for killing thousands of Basque people. The government responded to the Basque claims, but the return of the painting offended many of the Falange members who had supported the massacres against the 'disobedient' Basque people. For the Falange, the painting was an affront. Picasso's painting depicts the atrocities during the Spanish Civil War and the destruction of the holy place in the Basque region

---

[373] J.M. Tamarit Sumalla, *Historical Memory and Criminal Justice in Spain*, chapter 5.
[374] W. Merkel, *Systemtransformation* (1999), p. 296.
[375] P. Aguilar, *Memory and Amnesia*, pp. 200–201.

by – at that time – allied German, Italian and Spanish forces. After its return, it was displayed in the Reina Sofía Museum of Modern Art in Madrid. In terms of TJ this was one of the government's few early symbolic acts that acknowledged past injustices.

Based on the events of the previous year, in 1982 a shift in government took place and the PSOE gained an absolute majority and fostered economic reforms benefiting labourers. But the trauma of 1981 remained and the PSOE took actions to avoid a second attempted coup although most of their political leaders had suffered repression or exile under Franco, remained silent and did not openly deal with the past. Fears that Franco's shadow would return, for example in the form of judges and technocrats, were omnipresent in all families and all institutions.

But inward-looking TJ policies such as amnesties, memorials or symbolic acts and pension funds can only trigger more TJ if there are external incentives that continue to exert pressure on the process. In the case of Spain, the EC was the only source of such pressure and, since Spanish civil society was so weak, it took a long time before more TJ was triggered and the spiral effect could take off. The PSOE government adopted policies to achieve a more rapid integration into the EC and NATO, hoping that international integration would trigger more necessary changes in political institutions, the military and the security forces. The PSOE hoped that international pressure would lead to the dismantling of the Guardia Civil and the Falange, since the constitution restricted internal forces from achieving this goal. The fact that even the Socialist governments continued complying with the 1978 pacts agreed among the various political parties and labour unions at the president's seat in the Palace of Moncloa (a place in the University District of Madrid), the so-called 'Moncloa Pacts' showed the willingness to adhere to agreements and constitutional law. According to Guillermo O'Donnell and others, the importance of this willingness for a democratic culture must not be underestimated, even though it meant that Francoists remained largely unpunished.[376]

In the subsequent years, pressure from the EC increased, as it aimed to prevent yet another fascist coup. This process led to Spain joining NATO in 1982 and the EC in 1986. Political power shifted between conservative and social democratic governments in 1982, 1996 and 2004. After the first legislative term of the PSOE government ended in 1986 at the end of the first post-Franco decade, Spanish democracy was internationally recognised as consolidated, after its first round of constitutional

---

[376] G. O'Donnell, J. Vargas Cullell and O. M. Iazzetta, *The Quality of Democracy*, pp. 56–69.

consolidation in 1978 and 1979. Interestingly enough, it was also during this period, around 1986, that parliament passed a law rehabilitating military personnel oppressed by Franco.[377] Researchers and politicians have long disputed whether it was the EC membership that marked the major democratic shift of regime change and consolidation. It is evident that Spain joined the EC not because of its excellent economic performance (the official criteria to seek membership at that time), but because European states wanted the EC to have a grip on the country's fragile democracy. 'Holding a firm grip' was not an official criterion, for obvious reasons.

It soon became evident that the PSOE government would risk sabotage within democratic institutions, such as the courts or ministries, if they did not serve the interests of the former victimisers of the Franco regime to the same extent as they did those of their own supporters. Thus, in adherence to the 1978 agreements and constitution, the left-wing government left those from the 'white' side in peace and slowly introduced some TJ measures for their own supporters. Jose Tamarit summarised these and other silent measures of reparations as tools for TJ issued since King Juan Carlos' Royal Decrees (*Real Decreto-Ley*) in 1978. To this, the PSOE government added formal acknowledgement in the form of contributions to social security in 1984. In 1986 they issued an 'incorporation act' for members of the army who had pushed for democratic reforms within the former regime (before Franco's death), and were thus expelled from the army. Under the PSOE, they were rehabilitated and received full pensions. Nevertheless, during all this time the Amnesty Act of 1977 remained untouched while any TJ measures thus had to work around this Act, but abolishing it was unthinkable. Instead, the PSOE government slowly started issuing reparations and letters of acknowledgement and started to support cultural and popular events that acknowledged the past. Seeing that the government was willing to acknowledge past injustice triggered the civic engagement of those millions of victims who were predominantly supporters of the PSOE government. Yet, Tamarit also concluded that the government 'failed to consider the period of almost forty years of dictatorship, thus revealing that the young democracy did not find a way to express its attitude towards the previous regime.'[378]

---

[377] Later in 2001, under the conservative governments, the guerrillas were rehabilitated. C. Closa Montero (ed.), *Study on How the Memory of Crimes Committed by Totalitarian Regimes in Europe Is Dealt with in the Member States* (Madrid: CSIC, 2010), pp. 94–95.

[378] J.M. Tamarit Sumalla, *Historical Memory and Criminal Justice in Spain*, p. 69.

A majority of the new communist or socialist political elites kept ties with their former exile residences, such as Germany, France and Latin America. Political foundations such as the German-based Friedrich Ebert Foundation and others financially and politically supported the new and often politically inexperienced PSOE leaders – not always by legal means and often with non-declared money transfers. At that time, external support was an important factor in regime consolidation. It steered political parties and civil engagement, and due to the fact that many citizens were too intimidated to discuss the past, civic trust had to be slowly re-established. A large left-wing citizen movement started to grow, comprised of members who had suffered in Franco's prisons, campaigned for women's and human rights and against nuclear power, as well as against membership of NATO.[379] The PSOE government soon became in favour of NATO membership in 1982, after deciding that it would help to reform the security and military sectors with new methods of security defence based on civil codes, too.[380] Apart from seeking membership of the EC and enhancing its role in the UN, membership of NATO was seen as a key way to integrate Spain's main veto powers, the military and security sector, into the international community and, moreover, it led to the dismantling of old generals who were firmly loyal to the former regime.[381] Another important by-product of NATO membership and the fact that the Spanish army would be integrated into NATO forces was that all high-ranked military leaders would need to communicate in English, the official NATO language. The old military generals of Franco's time had to be replaced by new, young military leaders who were trained in the United States and Canada, like King Juan Carlos himself. This turned out to be an indirect way of 'purging' or vetting former elites. By replacing the old generals with new internationally trained ones, Spain removed its old military elites from important positions, thus also getting rid of the threat they had always continued to pose to the government. The military forces were cleansed of Francoist, anti-democratic members and westward-looking individuals were sworn in.

---

[379] A. Quiroga, 'Salvation by Betrayal', pp. 135–158.
[380] Campaign materials, Archive of Historical Memory, Salamanca, INCORPORADOS, Caja 1601.
[381] Starting in the 1950s, and thus with Franco's consent, NATO forces were based in Spain, giving these forces control over a large part of the access point to the Mediterranean Sea and the Atlantic.

International integration and monitoring by the United States and Europe was the first step in delegitimising previous dictatorial habits. At the same time a bottom-up and citizen-driven approach to reckon with the past slowly started to grow. Local TJ initiatives in villages throughout the country hesitantly sought to exhume mass graves from the Civil War in order to demystify and thus delegitimise the domestic and local Francoist elites. They faced major resistance, however, since many members of the Falange continued as mayors and local administrators. Thus the main consolidating intertwining affect between TJ measures and institutions took place, mostly, if at all on local levels throughout the country, but not necessarily supported by the government through public statements or financial support. And time was running out, because each year there were fewer people alive who remembered the war, the arbitrary killings and mass executions of the Franco regime of the 1930s and 1940s. Although legacies and stories were passed on from eyewitnesses to their children, it would be a challenge to find mass graves somewhere under the huge wheat fields of Galicia, in Catalonia or Castilla y Leon. On the other hand, exhumations in the 1980s would have directly confronted still-living perpetrators and their influential families with the fact that men, women and children had in fact been buried at night in mass graves outside the villages. Yet, failing to address these crimes would make it very difficult to demystify the legend of Franco being a liberator and guardian of the Spanish nation.[382]

The establishment of new universities and a broader non-Christian and non-Falange education system in the 1980s, fostered by left-wing political voices, led to a new desperate need for trained academic staff that was more critical to Christian or Francoist education type and which later became key to the TJ process that started around 2000. Large civil educational programmes were launched. The Catholic Church, which had dominated the education system in Spain for centuries and strongly supported Franco and the king, made sure that its Catholic values and the former Franco regime were not among the disputed issues in the educational programmes' curricula.[383]

Meanwhile, King Juan Carlos and the PSOE government tried to appease and hold together the 'two Spains' after the turbulence in 1981. But at the same time and because of the coup, unconsolidated pockets of democracy began to remerge again. Shortly after the coup, the ETA

---

[382] J.M. Tamarit Sumalla, *Historical Memory and Criminal Justice in Spain*, p. 99.
[383] O.G. Encarnacion, *Democracy Without Justice in Spain*, chapter 3.

was thought to have found a new cause, thus raising its violent voice again and kidnapping and murdering a prominent politician of the PP in the Basque Country. As a result, the political arm of ETA, the *Heri Batasuna* party, reacted more strongly than ever against 'the centralism of Madrid' and demanded the establishment of an independent Basque Country, including the Basque region of France. Hence, the conflict between the Guardia Civil and ETA started again, although this time not under a dictatorship, but under fragile democratic institutions. In a way ETA's terror has always been an indicator of the progress and pace of Spain's democratic consolidation. The more ETA violently responded to governmental policies, the less likely these were to dismantle ETA's base, whose members and supporters justified their killings and attacks by pointing to the lack of delegitimisation of the Franco regime. ETA's violence even led to the socialist government condoning illegal action against them, for example the disappearances and torture of ETA members.[384] The way ETA moved in their violent cause has since been a benchmark for observers of Spanish democracy and whether or not it succeeded in overcoming its last unconsolidated pocket, that of separatist terror.

Spain's centralist government had been the Basque nationalists' bane for decades and continued to be so after the reforms in 1977, the Statute of Autonomy in 1979 and after the PSOE won the elections, even though it had guaranteed the Basque Country and Catalonia the greatest level of autonomy seen up to that point. This was not enough for those who sought complete independence from the Spanish state. The concept of statehood and/or nationhood was always a core issue in political fights between the periphery and the central government. In the Basque Country, the Statute of Autonomy was sufficient neither for *Heri Batasuna* nor the Basque nationalist governing party (*Partido Nacionalista Vasco*, PNV), which was the more moderate branch of Basque nationalism that formed the regional government from 1980 to 2009.[385] By claiming a right to self-determination, the PNV sought to detach itself from Spain despite its already existing financial privileges, such as tax autonomy. Those striving for independence employed the old image of the oppressive centralist powers in Madrid, arguing that Franco's legacy remained in all central governments, regardless of whether they were led by the UCD or the

---

[384] J.J. Linz and A. Stepan (eds.), *Problems of Democratic Transition and Consolidation*, p. 107.
[385] D. Nohlen and A. Hildebrand, *Spanien, Wirtschaft – Gesellschaft, Politik, Ein Studienbuch* (Wiesbaden: VS Verlag 2005), pp. 310–311.

PSOE. It was easy for ETA and the PNV to argue in such a manner, since Franco had never been officially demystified or delegitimised. The state responded by violently disrupting ETA's manoeuvres. As stated earlier, the PSOE government even used anti-democratic and illegal means to combat the terror attacks. It launched anti-terror liberation units (*Grupos Antiterroristas de Liberatión*, GAL), which acted outside the legal and judicial rule of the constitution and contributed to the anti-democratic tradition of solving security problems with violent means, including illegal killings and abductions. In this way, both the GAL and ETA fuelled the unconsolidated pockets. Trials and the dismantling of Franco's legacy would have been more effective, perhaps.[386]

Although the PSOE government declared several ceasefires between itself and ETA, the group has continued to terrorise the country until the present day. ETA remains the prime example of radical nationalism and separatism in Spain and Europe, claiming to be a 'non-state actor' with many Basque followers. It has succeeded in intimidating the Basque and Spanish populations alike, as the Guardia Civil also did, although with different political motivations. Basque people have always been intimidated both by the Guardia Civil on the one side and by the ETA on the other side, a fact which has greatly impacted their voting behaviour and attitude towards democratic culture.[387]

For a long time into the period of democracy and free elections in the 1980s, many Basques did not dare to vote for anything other than the nationalistic PNV party because they did not trust that ballots were truly secret. They worried that somehow 'ETA's silent eyes and ears' would know who voted for which party and that those who did not vote for the PNV or *Heri Batasuna* would face repercussions or intimidation from ETA. Until recently, nationalist parties in many of the villages and rural regions of the Basque Country received a large proportion of votes during the elections. Nationalism, even if regional in nature, does not leave much room for pluralism.

There have been more than 860 ETA terror victims since 1970. On average, this means ETA was responsible for two victims a month for roughly 40 years, many of them civilians. All attempts to turn the organisation

---

[386]   U. Liebert, *Modelle demokratischer Konsolidierung* (Opladen: Leske und Budrich, 1998), p. 194.

[387]   D. Muro, 'The Basque Experience of Transition to Democracy' in G. Alonso and D. Muro (eds.), *The Politics and Memory of Democratic Transition. The Spanish Model* (New York/ London: Routledge, 2011), pp. 159–181.

into a civil organisation with a strong political branch adhering to democratic principles have failed. Although ETA lost significant support over time, it was difficult to convince ETA members to deradicalise if, in their eyes, those who were responsible for Basque oppression were still in high-ranking offices in Madrid and elsewhere – and, of course, either members of the Falange or collaborating with them. As long as the myth of the past worked in ETA's favour so that it could portray the current regime as having links to Franco, ETA could successfully continue its terrorist activities. Separatist propaganda with violent consequences and parts of the population's voting behaviour has meant that the democratic order in the Basque Country was not consolidated. Even if these factors have not permanently obstructed Spain's consolidation process, they have certainly impaired it. This impairment of democratic consolidation has actually benefited ETA because it allows ETA to keep Franco 'alive' as an enemy. Without this, the group would have lost ground and many supporters. I argue that if TJ measures such as history commissions, memorials and even trials had been put in place to deal with the past and shed some light on the terror from all sides until 1975, most of ETA's victims would still be alive today.

Despite its difficult start and the drawbacks, violence, reluctance and shortcomings of democratic regime change, the period after 1982 is considered the second transition phase or consolidation phase, or the phase of representative and behavioural consolidation. The first attempts to establish an official memory culture can be found in this period.[388] Linz and Stepan, again, have pointed to the 80 per cent popular support for democracy by 1982, the necessary economic and social reforms and the success of the PSOE under Felipe Gonzales as having enabled the new system to consolidate only seven years after Franco's death.[389] Nevertheless, the low election turnout illustrated many voters' great dissatisfaction with the political transition. Therefore, some observers find that consolidation only took place in the mid-1980s, after comprehensive reforms of the legal and military apparatus and the removal of the Francoists from power.[390] Marianne Kneuer, for example, has argued that consolidation did not occur until 1986, after decentralisation was further advanced and membership of NATO and the EC were achieved.[391] The general consent

---

[388] C. Molinero (ed.), *La Transición, Treinta Años Despues de la Dictatura a la Instauracion y Consolidacion de la Democracia* (Barcelona: Atalaya, 2006).

[389] J.J. Linz and A. Stepan (eds.), *Problems of Democratic Transition and Consolidation.*

[390] W. Merkel and H.-J. Puhle, *Von der Diktatur zur Demokratie*, p. 297.

[391] M. Kneuer, *Demokratisierung durch die EU*, p. 219.

lies in the fact that the shift of government and the membership in the EC marked the stage of democratic consolidation.

Generally speaking, by the end of the first post-Franco decade in and around 1985, the country was still politically divided. According to Eurostat, 51 per cent of the population was rather satisfied and trusted the institutions, leaving around 40–50 per cent rather unsatisfied or expressing no opinion.[392] The 'satisfaction' indicator was not surprising, as it reflected how divided the country still was between those who had supported the previous Franco regime and those who had suffered under the previous regime and supported the new one.

Second Decade 1985–1994

Ten years after Franco's death, 76 per cent of the population was proud of the transition Spain had made. This sense of pride was particularly strong on the left, after the PSOE won the election in 1982 and the violence on both radical ends, left and right wing, decreased.[393] The second post-Franco decade included institutional reforms and executive and legislative responses to citizens' demands for more TJ. For Merkel and others, the democratic regime was consolidated by that time.[394] Towards the end of this decade, the first post-Franco generation emerged. Yet, this decade is one in which also many democratic flaws and unconsolidated pockets of democracy remained or re-emerged.[395]

Hundreds of thousands of Falangistas still annually celebrated Franco's birthday (4 December) and the date of his death (20 November). He enjoyed great support among citizens and civil society hardly protested against the glorification of Franco, also due to the fear that to challenge his followers would end in many more acts of violence. Masses of people made annual pilgrimages to his grave at the Valle de los Caidos, the official war memorial and a TJ tool that Franco had used to manifest his own autocratic power. This annual pilgrimage did not remain unnoticed and even received media coverage. The only compromise made with Franco's successors in terms of memorials was that the anniversary of the start of

---

[392] European Union, Eurobarometer Surveys, Spain 1985.11, http://ec.europa.eu (last accessed August 2013).

[393] J.J. Linz and A. Stepan (eds.), *Problems of Democratic Transition and Consolidation*, p. 109.

[394] W. Merkel, Systemtransformation, *Eine Einführung in die Theorie und Empirie der Transformationsforschung*, pp. 196ff.

[395] J.J. Linz and A. Stepan (eds.), *Problems of Democratic Transition and Consolidation*. And Polity IV Project www.systemicpeace.org/polity (last accessed December 2014).

the Spanish Civil War was neither commemorated in public nor in parliament. The government tried to limit the provocation this had caused each year to the millions of victims of the war and the regime due to the still unresolved disappearances and abductions during and after the war since 1939. Here, too, King Juan Carlos played the main reconciling role in this strongly divided society. In 1985, on the tenth anniversary of his coronation, he inaugurated a monument in Madrid to all who gave their life for Spain, not distinguishing between communists, republicans or Falange. This was the first public inclusive TJ measure of its kind in Spain and acknowledged all victims. The wider public and Spaniards who felt their sacrifices had never been acknowledged received this gesture very positively.[396]

But most of the time, the government acknowledged the past only very minimally through indirect TJ measures such as pension funds for former political prisoners of the Franco regime or private memorial activities that at least the government did not officially forbid. Citizens were only able to fully legitimise the democratic regime when it guaranteed the 'order' of the Franco era (in other words the absence of war) while providing them with more freedom and development than they had before. This was a difficult balancing act for the transitional government to maintain.[397] Because of the culture of impunity, silence and forgetting, even the PSOE government combatted violent threats to the stability of the country with equally silent and anti-democratic means. Its main tool was the GAL (*Grupo Antiterrorista de Liberacion*), an anti-terror death squad established illegally by officials of the government that continued the dirty war against ETA and other groups that formed a threat to the government. In the 1980s, the GAL and its activities remained largely unnoticed by the wider public, but eventually came to light as a result of media investigations. By the early 1990s reporters did not have to fear repercussions themselves and openly published their findings. This was followed by a multitude of political scandals with legal consequences, which in 1996 cost the PSOE leader and President Felipe Gonzalez his position. Eventually, about 20 years after regime change, the first post-authoritarian generation of political decision makers slowly started to dare to speak up.

Individual compensation and the public acknowledgement in the form of pensions and small memorials remained two of the most successful TJ

---

[396] P. Aguilar, *Memory and Amnesia*, p. 208.
[397] Ibid., pp. 261–264.

304 REGIME CONSOLIDATION AND TRANSITIONAL JUSTICE

measures throughout all Spanish legislative periods, including between 1985 and 1994. The payments for past injustices and suffering by way of pensions acknowledged that 'something went wrong', that the recipients had unjustly suffered and were entitled to compensation. Plus, each government extended these measures' scope and the number of beneficiaries for decades to come. In June 1990, the PSOE government again issued monetary reparations and expanded the scope of people who were entitled to it. It aimed to reach those who suffered imprisonment for political reasons at any time – on both sides of the political spectrum. However, any other type of restitution, for example measures to aid in the return of lost or appropriated property were not considered, although claims slowly started to appear.[398]

It was not until 1993, towards the end of the second post-war Franco decade and during the last PSOE legislature, that the party included the importance of (finally) coming to terms with Spain's violent past in its political manifesto. Until then it had adhered to the pact of silence. It only dared to address the past when immediate threats from the previous political and military elite seemed to have vanished and when the new generation arrived on the political scene. In addition, PSOE was motivated by the need to respond to the growing national catharsis. And by that time in the early 1990s, surveys showed that 40 per cent of the population regarded the unaddressed past of the Spanish Civil War as a major issue and to which the government had to respond in one way or the other. A few years later in 2000, over 50 per cent thought it was an important issue to deal with. This group included many members of the younger generation.[399]

As civil society movements emerged, NGOs such as Amnesty International put TJ on the agenda under the label of 'fighting impunity' and by drawing comparisons to other countries in the world, in particular in Latin America and the Balkans, which had already started using TJ measures. If less democratised countries used TJ measures to speed up their democratisation and peace process, it was not left unnoticed in Spain, too, despite all prior pacts and agreements. Some 20 years post-regime change, the government had to start responding to the internal and external pressure for TJ. A large part of the population on both sides seemed ready for it. Despite public concern for other current issues, such

---

[398] For examples, see: J.M. Tamarit Sumalla, 'Transition, Historical Memory and Criminal Justice in Spain', 729–752.

[399] P. Sánchez León, 'Radicalization Without Representation', pp. 95–111.

as economic growth or unemployment, dealing with the Franco past became an increasingly significant issue in electoral campaigns.

Meanwhile, the unconsolidated pockets hampered the upward trajectory of the TJ and consolidating spiral. The ETA terrorist activity in the Basque Country and the separatist movements in Catalonia and Galicia increased in parallel to the democratic reforms and dramatically illustrated that full reconciliation had not yet been achieved within Spain. The left and right, centre and periphery, those who enjoyed privileges and those who had been marginalised were still harshly divided. Political disputes and terror attacks in both peripheral locations like Catalonia and the Basque Country and in the centre of Madrid demonstrated this struggle. ETA sympathisers protested, for example, against the way 'its' prisoners were held and cases of torture and ill-treatment were reported. Over 500 prisoners, distributed over the entire country, were frequently exposed to torture, abuse, unfair court proceedings, as well as the violent work of the GAL anti-terror unit.[400] Nevertheless, the regime status quo remained stable and the danger of regressing back to an authoritarian regime change receded, even though civil engagement was still low and much of the population was still too intimidated to raise its voice.[401] But social transformation and the first attempts at establishing one official and nationally shared memory also grew hesitantly. Almost a generation had passed and talking about the past was still largely limited to the private sphere. Only slowly did literature, film and theatre start addressing the issues of the past and of the dictatorship.[402] But generally speaking in the 1980s and 1990s, schoolchildren learned more about the Nazi dictatorship in Germany and the military juntas in Latin America than they did about their own dictatorial past.

Because of Spain's democratic development and social reforms, satisfaction numbers started to change. By the end of the second post-Franco decade, Eurobarometer confirmed that citizens' opinions about state institutions had converged towards the middle. Seventy-five per cent of the population was fairly or not very satisfied and only 5 per cent very satisfied and 17 per cent not at all satisfied.[403] These figures also correlate

---

[400] J.J. Linz and A. Stepan (eds.), *Problems of Democratic Transition and Consolidation*, p. 115.

[401] R. Gunther, P. Nikiforos Diamandouros and H.-J. Puhle (eds.), *The Politics of Democratic Consolidation*, p. 151.

[402] P.J. Smith, 'Cinema and Television in the Transition' in G. Alonso and D. Muro (eds.), *The Politics and Memory of Democratic Transition. The Spanish Model* (New York/London: Routledge, 2011), pp. 199–211.

[403] European Union, Eurobarometer Surveys, Spain 1995.06, http://ec.europa.eu (last accessed August 2013).

with the wish for a general motion in Spain to finally put the past on the agenda.

It was thus the civil society and private research institutes that started to unravel the past. Historians, journalists, private initiatives, survivors and family members started gathering the first facts about the past, regarding cases of disappearances, illegal killings, 'accidents', torture and even rumours about abductions and concentration camps, which were slowly being made public. Academic papers and media reports mainly in *El Pais* and the Catalan paper *La Vanguardia* published articles about the Civil War and the Franco era and triggered public debates.[404] The TJ processes in Latin America (for example Argentina and Chile), as well as in post-communist Eastern Europe and the Balkans, continued to influence the development of TJ in Spain. While Spain was still struggling with its history because of the heavyweight amnesty laws from 1977, the post-communist and authoritarian regimes elsewhere in Europe, Africa or Latin America had already accepted the utility of TJ measures for building democracy – a development that neither the Spanish government, nor civil society or academia could ignore for much longer. Demands for trials, the abolishment of amnesty laws and exhumations also came up in Spain. Another fact that could not be ignored was the establishment of the ICTY in 1993 and the ICTR in 1994. Journalists or political analysts compared the atrocities of the present with the ones of their own past and questioned whether it was now perhaps time for trials. The only case brought between 1994 and 1996 was that of the student Enrique Ruano, who had allegedly been killed in police custody in Madrid in 1969. Although the Supreme Court valued the efforts to deal with this case, it came to the conclusion that due to statutes of limitation the case could not be dealt with. According to Julia Arnold, Spain generally dealt with its past with biased rehabilitation efforts, through amnesty laws and pension (compensation) until far into the new millennium.[405]

One can see that external incentives, in this case examples of TJ from elsewhere in the world, had a causal effect on citizen demands, the growth of civil society and waiting for the government's response. Thus, by 1995 it was not only the growth of civil society, the general satisfaction with the regime, the absence of violence and threat in the country that caused the rising claims for TJ but also the worldwide development in the TJ arena

---

[404] P. Aguilar, *Memory and Amnesia*, pp. 260–261.
[405] J. Arnold, 'Zweiter Teil', pp. 216, 330.

as such, putting TJ on the agenda of the UN and later also on the agenda of European institutions.[406]

Third Decade 1995–2004

After some initial (and often externally driven) attempts for TJ during the second decade, the third was the one during which civil society and TJ finally took off. Civil society movements demanding commemoration of and truth about the past dominated the third post-Franco decade. It was also the decade in which questioning the past became a moral imperative and civil society reached its peak. Even those who had no personal memories of Franco's regime felt the urge to explore their past. However, the third decade did not begin very promisingly. After the defeat of the PSOE in 1996, the conservative People's Party (PP) came to power and started idealising and mythologising the Franco era again as a period of stability and peace. All thoughts of implementing TJ measures, such as history commissions or commissions of inquiry, and the taking up of citizen claims for individual trials were put on ice. The new government might not have openly made pro-Franco propaganda, but it did try to prevent any official process that would have delegitimised him. One cannot forget that the strongest and most loyal supporters of the PP were former Falangistas and that the country was politically still greatly divided between pro- and contra-Franco followers. Since there was never an uprising against Franco and he was the only dictator in modern times who died in bed, the existence of national catharsis had to grow much slower and later than in other transition and transformation processes. Nevertheless, it did and the government had to respond to it. However, the PP continued to resist acknowledging and accepting responsibility for its own Franco-related legacy and foundation, such as for example the fact that the founder of the PP, Manuel Fraga, had been one of Franco's ministers, and remained an influential leader in the party.

Now in opposition, the PSOE no longer stuck to its self-imposed rule of silence as it did in 1982 when it first won the elections. In 1999, pressured by its large membership and together with the Catalan and Basque nationalists, it submitted a bill in which it suggested that Spanish Civil War exiles should be honoured with public compensation as an act of

---

[406] J.-C. Manier, 'La cultura de la transición o la transición como cultura' in C. Molinero (ed.), *La transición: treinta años después de la dictadura a la instauración y consolidación de la democracia* (Barcelona: Ediciones Península, 2006), pp. 153–171.

public acknowledgement. Following the examples of post-regime change, criminal justice processes elsewhere in the world and inspired by the birth of the Rome Statute for the first ICC in 1998, the draft bill focused on responsibility and the question of guilt for atrocities and war crimes committed between 1936 and 1939. The bill was rejected due to the low number of seats held by the left-wing parties in the parliament.[407] The governing PP, which held a majority in parliament, voted against the bill and angered those who were seeking more examination of the Franco regime. Instead, in 1999, almost as an act of provocation for those who sought TJ for the Franco area, the conservative government passed the Solidarity with the Victims of Terrorism Act, an act that embodied TJ in its most biased and exclusionary form. This Act was aimed at the victims of ETA and GRAPO terror and provided subsidies to all victims of terror acts since 1968. Most of these victims had been supporters of the Franco regime. Those who also benefited from these TJ measures were citizens who happened to be collaterally affected by these terrorist acts, although they were not the primary targets of the terrorist acts. The Act did not distinguish whether the violent acts and killings had been committed by ETA, the GRAPO, separatist movements or other left-wing terror groups, which was a step ahead in acknowledgement policies. However, given the timeframe to which it applied, this law clearly benefited one group of victims over others and raised many concerns in society. Enacting this law was another political move by the former elite to please its supporters.

The state terror carried out in the years prior to 1975 by the Guardia Civil and the secret police remained unatoned for. It was therefore rather dubious whether such governmental acts would lead to reconciliation in society. Curiously enough, the Act was later enhanced with the Historical Memory Law in 2007, which provided monetary compensation of 135,000 euros to the beneficiaries of the persons who died between January 1968 and October 1977, exactly the same period in which ETA had committed most of its terrorist attacks.[408] This law was seen as a compromise to obtain concessions from the PP to start dealing with victims during the Franco era – regardless of which side of the political spectrum they stood. By doing this, the law did not make any commitment at acknowledging the terror coming from the Franco regime. Most beneficiaries of the law were instead Franco supporters who had been injured or killed by ETA.

[407] O.G. Encarnacion. *Democracy Without Justice in Spain*, chapter 5.
[408] J.M. Tamarit Sumalla, 'Transition, Historical Memory and Criminal Justice in Spain', p. 742.

The victims of the GAL, however, were hardly ever compensated, which could be interpreted as confirming that the anti-democratic and illegal practices committed by the GAL were a legitimate way of conducting governmental business against GRAPO and ETA.

Throughout the third decade, the government could no longer resist external pressure and the spill over from other TJ developments. Two Spanish lawyers, Balthasar Garzón and Manuel Garcia-Castellon (both known for their liberal legal philosophy and with a family history as victims of the Franco regime) set proceedings into motion that eventually resulted in the arrest of the former Chilean dictator, General Augusto Pinochet, in 1998. Due to the 1977 Amnesty laws, these Spanish judges could not indict any Francoists, but they did the Chilean one. But that was part of their plan and first step towards TJ in Spain. They had planned a long-term TJ coup that they hoped would have a boomerang effect. Garzón had agreed to hear claims of human rights abuses against Spanish citizens by Latin American dictatorships under the 'popular action' (*accion popular*), which permits any Spanish citizen to pursue a case in the public interest.[409] Garzón and Garcia-Castellon hoped that if these cases were heard at the Spanish National High Court, the *Audiencia Nacional*, sooner or later cases would come up also concerning Spanish citizens who suffered under the Franco dictatorship. They succeeded only in part, but eventually did break the silence about the past, thus paving the way for many more TJ efforts in the next decade and a half. Interestingly enough, the lawyers' first attempts to try crimes under Franco came around the same time, namely 20-plus years after the regime change, as in West Germany, when Bauer had successfully tried the concentration camp guards.

The year 2000 (not surprisingly a generation after Franco's death) finally marked a major shift for the multiple causalities of regime consolidation. The fear of the past had given way to the generally positive experience citizens had with the new regime, which had been able to prevent the country dissolving into another civil war. Merkel's notion of 'consolidation by civil society'[410] had finally occurred. Values such as justice, freedom and democracy even began to outweigh the desire for order, which in any society is a sign of stability and consolidation. Last but not least, a new generation of educated and far more cosmopolitan young politicians and intellectuals entered the political arena and took the claims to

---

[409] O.G. Encarnacion, *Democracy Without Justice in Spain*, p. 134.
[410] W. Merkel, Systemtransformation, *Eine Einführung in die Theorie und Empirie der Transf ormationsforschung*, p. 124

the streets of Barcelona, Vitoria and Madrid.[411] Films, plays and novels that dealt with the Franco period increased dramatically. One of the most famous films was by Pedro Almodovar, *Live Flesh* (1998), which portrayed the painful and often uncertain transition period in Spain in the 1970s and triggered many overdue public debates. In 2001 the long-running TV show about the transition, 'Tell Me How it Happened?' (*Cuéntame cómo pasó?*), went on the air and became a milestone for initiating public debates and media coverage about the times around the year 1975. The show depicted numerous family stories from 1968 throughout the transition period until the 1980s. The show was watched by 40 per cent of the TV audience and was therefore one of the most popular TV shows ever in Spain, indicating citizens' need and desire to deal with their political past. The importance of this New Spanish Cinema (*neuvo cine espanol*), which had been initiated by the former PSOE government and slowly started showing results of triggering debates and societal engagement with the past, cannot be underestimated. It greatly affected the mutually reinforcing effect between the claim for more TJ and trust in the institutions.[412] Many Spaniards later referred to it as finally opening the door to investigating their own or their family's role under the Franco regime. In 2000, the journalist Emilio Silva Barrera, a leading figure in the civil society movement for TJ, searched for the remains of his grandfather who had 'disappeared' during the Civil War.[413] He dared to publish an article about his project in a local newspaper in the conservative PP-run city of Valladolid and asked for assistance from witnesses of the events at that time. Unintentionally, his request ended up launching a campaign to search for the bodily remains of an entire war generation. The public response was overwhelmingly positive, as almost every family in Spain had a story to tell. Witnesses, archaeologists and forensic pathologists volunteered assistance in the search for mass graves and with their exhumation. At this time, opinion polls showed that 51 per cent of Spaniards still remembered the Spanish Civil War and the dictatorship afterwards and regarded it as an important issue that needed to be dealt with. More and more people considered the past a 'negative period' and joined Silva's cause.[414] In the same year Silva created an NGO, the Association for Dealing with Memory and History (*Asociación para la Recuperación*

[411] P. Aguilar, *Memory and Amnesia*, p. 264.
[412] P.J. Smith, 'Cinema and Television in the Transition', pp. 199–213.
[413] E. Silva, *Las fosas de Franco. Crónica de un desagravio. Temas de hoy* (Madrid: Historia Selección, 2005).
[414] C. Humlebaek, 'Party Attitudes Towards the Authoritarian Past in Spanish Democracy', p. 84.

de la Memoria Histórica, ARMH), whose mission was to search for and exhume the mass graves of the Franco era. Initially a voluntary organisation, the Association acted via an Internet forum. It was not awarded any national allowances until the Historical Memory Law entered into force in 2007 under a new PSOE government. ARMH's initiatives spread rapidly around the country in its hundreds run by citizen-driven and voluntary branches across the country in almost all Autonomous Communities and some smaller towns, leading to the identification of over 1,300 individuals in more than 70 mass graves that had been sealed for over 70 years. Most of the graves were in the rural parts of Castile and in the north of Spain, where Franco encountered the most resistance to his fascist regime. Despite the intimidation and personal threats aimed at those involved in the ARMH's work, it was seen as a milestone in the TJ process of Spain.[415] ARMH made Franco-era memories more public and led to a discussion about a common narrative of the past, a discussion that is still in progress. Yet, according to Emilo Silva, historical memory largely remains a private and family matter although ARMH brought it onto the political agenda.[416] But knowing about the past and speaking about it in public without fear are two different things. Processing the past and processes of reconciliation accelerate the growth of trust in political institutions, especially when citizens who have experienced injustice see the public punishment of those responsible for the injustice.[417] But that was a long way ahead, although for the upward spiral to gain speed the developments and initiatives around 2000 were essential.[418]

Due to the fact that the conservative PP government contained many members from the previous Franco regime, it avoided official recognition of and governmental debates about the Spanish Civil War and the 40 years of Franco's reign. It was not until 20 November 2002, upon an initiative from the left-wing opposition and under great public and civil society pressure, that the Spanish parliament acknowledged for the very first time all victims of violence and injustice from the Spanish Civil War and the Franco era. Thus, 27 years after Franco's death and a 20+ generation later for the first time in its history, the government and parliament jointly responded to public demands to officially acknowledge the atrocities of the past. This condemnation was an act of responsiveness, although

---

[415] E. Silva, *Las fosas de Franco*.
[416] Interview with Emilio Silva Barrera Madrid, 8 May 2011.
[417] M. Minow, *Between Vengeance and Forgiveness*.
[418] H.-J. Lauth, 'Die Qualität der Demokratie im interregionalen Vergleich', pp. 89–110.

it was not intended to hold anyone individually accountable for his or her wrongdoings. It had no legal consequences for those responsible for the killings, abductions and disappearances of millions. And yet the government also knew that in the 27 years that had passed, a new generation had grown into potential voters. It would be worthwhile to compete for their votes and address these issues.[419] However, one year later, when the national parliament called for a commemoration session to remember the unjust past, the PP abstained from participating in the event, although it did not prevent it either.[420]

The founding of NGOs like the ARMH and other Memory Associations and the condemnation in parliament triggered many local and civil initiatives, led by second- or third-generation survivors and victims' grandchildren. The mutual reinforcing spiral effect went off again. In turn, these local and civil initiatives triggered further events and parliamentary debates. This was not only caused by this generation's desire to search for their identity, but also by the lack of fear of repercussions for doing so. The plethora of civil and public initiative and debates was a fundamental indicator of the strengthening of civic trust and thus also of the strengthening of institutions. Even though the PP government initially refused to financially support such initiatives, there was a clear break with the silence and fear of the past.

In December 2000, the Catalonian regional parliament unanimously condemned the crimes of the past. Interestingly, the regional branch of the PP also voted in favour of this condemnation, as they knew that many of their supporters felt more Catalan than Spanish and were critical of the central government in Madrid. But this was more than a joint legislative response; it had dramatic consequences on the level of citizen participation and legal claims. The resolution called the past a 'barbarous act' against citizens, and condemned this act both in moral and political terms.[421] It was a milestone in terms of parliamentary responses.

Despite such measures at the regional level, all central governments at that time did not yet see TJ measures as a systematic tool or as a means to leverage and consolidate democracy. If TJ measures were used, it was

---

[419] La Vanguardia, 'El Parlamento condena el franquismo', 21 November 2001, p. 15.
[420] El Mundo, 'Congreso de los Diputados: Todos los grupos parlametarios, excepto el PP, homenajean a lo represaliados del franquismo', 1 December 2003, www.elmundo.es (last accessed August 2014).
[421] La Vanguardia, 'EL PP se suma "sin reservas" a la condena del Parlament al franquismo', 14 December 2000, p. 26.

only ever for political strategic reasons, for example because TJ measures served parties' political agendas before an election or to respond to citizen needs. Hence, the PP's political agenda on the national and regional level struggled with TJ. The party had the most to lose if its clean image as the guarantors of law and justice in the country was challenged. When in government, the PP even commissioned a 'counter-attack' against TJ measures by generously subsidising the National Foundation in Memory of General Francisco Franco, which had been founded in 1976. Rather than subsidising NGOs such as the ARMH that aimed to dismantle and demystify Franco, the PP supported initiatives that commemorated his heroism. The privately held Franco Foundation holds Franco's private records and only selectively opens them to like-minded researchers. There is no independent research or public state archive that supervises the General's records and allows access to independent research, as is the case for all records concerning World War II and the communist past in East Germany, for example. Instead, the many dark sides of the Franco narrative must be extracted from information that is made available by testimonies, stories, pictures, oral history, literature and other sources of evidence, and this is what the many citizen initiatives such as the ARMH aimed to do. My visit to the Franco Foundation was an ambiguous one; they only allowed me access to documents that were cleared of any controversial political data beforehand and showed periodical time gaps.

In general the third post-Franco decade was an era of competing memories. One narrative was a result of the Falange's efforts to glorify Franco, while the other resulted from the millions of families and victims that demanded recognition of their losses, pain and injuries. The number of popular films, TV and radio shows, exhibits and publications by academics, filmmakers, writers and hobby historians increased in the following years. Most importantly, Franco's loyalists had no written record or evidence that they could use against these accusations. If they had, they would have brought this to the public attention. In many Autonomous Communities such as the Basque Country and Catalonia, hundreds of private initiatives to commemorate the atrocities and victims of Franco's regime brought more and more facts and evidence of the atrocious past to light and soon received governmental support.[422] Eventually, Franco's

<hr/>

[422] G. Herrmann, 'Documentary's Labours of Law: the Television Journalism of Montse Armengou and Ricard Belis', *Journal of Spanish Cultural Studies*, Special Issue (New York: New York University Press, 2008), pp. 193–212.

victims' narrative won out, finally succeeding to demystify and delegitimise Franco's image.

Meanwhile, Catholic bishops, as loyal supporters of the PP and the Falange, found themselves under public pressure to come to terms with their part in the atrocious past. They only slowly revisited their members' and supporters' role during the Franco period, although they had already made confessions in regard to the role of the Church during and after the war. Moreover, the Vatican had repeatedly blessed priests and nuns who were killed by republicans and communists during the Spanish Civil War, but had never acknowledged those who had been deliberately killed by Franco's soldiers with the consensus of the priests while seeking refuge in churches during the war. As a result, the debates about the superiority of victims and who had suffered continued among the Spanish public. Eventually, around 2006, the Vatican carefully revised its account of the war, acknowledging shared responsibility and the Church's wrongful support of the massacres carried out by Franco. Shortly before the Historical Memory Law came into force in Spain in 2007, representatives of the church acknowledged that some of their priests had committed injustices towards civilians. They furthermore expressed that the Catholic Church had also been involved in other acts of severe injustice in the past beyond the war, including the forced abductions of children.[423] The Vatican recognised at least 1,000 victims of the Spanish Civil War, mostly communists and thus members of the republican forces against Franco, whose suffering could be linked to the involvement of the Catholic Church. The Church feared that if it did not atone and become more critical of its own involvement in the Franco dictatorship, it would lose younger members in the years to come. Considering the strong role that the Catholic Church plays in the public and educational lives of Spaniards, this way of responding to claims and needs was an act of accountability and atonement.

However, where the desire for change prevails, so does resistance, which grew even stronger in the third decade, both among the neo-Falange (some would call it neo-Nazi) movement and the radical left-wing and communist movements. This was similar to the situation in post-war Germany. A generation after Franco's death, his statues could still be found in every major Spanish city. Different citizen initiatives attempted

---

[423] G. Alonso, 'Children of a Lesser God: The Political and the Pastoral Action of the Spanish Catholic Church' in G. Alonso and D. Muro (eds.), *The Politics of Memory of Democratic Transition. The Spanish Model* (New York: Routledge, 2011), pp. 113–134.

to ensure that Franco statues in heroic military poses were taken down. Cities that were governed by left-wing councils were often persuaded to take down the statues. Some statues, mainly those that portrayed Franco in a heroic position on horseback, were illegally taken down during the night by youngsters. Those who removed statues without city council consent risked being charged with disturbing public order. In 2002, citizen groups proposed that the government officially remove all monuments to the Franco era throughout the country, but the PP government at the central level and in many communities rejected this proposal. As a reaction, citizen protests and demonstrations by many organisations that had established their own historical memory groups, pressured for state and official support and acknowledgement of their actions. But whereas some aimed for official support, others could not wait any longer. They demolished statues of Franco, initiated private memorials for victims of the regime, exhumed mass graves and gave victims of the Civil War a proper burial.[424] The government's unwillingness to respond to the citizen demands for more TJ in this regard often led to violent and illegal actions. During public riots, angry citizens destroyed many Franco statues and street signs with names of Falange leaders or war heroes of the past. Such riots often took place in Zaragoza in Aragon, a region that had once been a Franco stronghold, reflecting the political divide and now the radical shift that was taking place in the country.

Parallel to these developments and due to fear that the PP government would retaliate, ETA terror became prominent once again and the group demanded immediate separation from Spain. The upward spiral of TJ stagnated and even reversed, due to the PP government's lack of response. And almost every time the PP held a majority in parliament, ETA terror re-emerged alongside. This development resembled the way the German government dealt with neo-Nazi movements and the RAF in the 1970s.

State institutions remained thus as repressive under PP leadership, which indicated that the unconsolidated pockets continued. In 2003 the *Heri Batasuna* party was outlawed after a court ruling declared that the party financed and supported ETA with public money. International human rights organisations such as Amnesty International were indignant and appealed to the public administration and the police to refrain from unnecessarily restricting freedom of expression. Such restrictive measures were not only anti-democratic but also ran the risk of

[424] W.L. Bernecker and S. Brinkmann, *Kampf der Erinnerungen*.

being wrongful acts under international human rights law.[425] Amnesty International and other NGOs also demanded an end to the period of impunity for the Franco era and demanded immediate condemnation of those responsible for human rights violations. They realised that as long as the perpetrators had impunity and remained hidden, terror groups like ETA or GRAPO would not refrain from using violence to combat the Francoists they believed still controlled Spanish democratic institutions. The lack of an independent judiciary, the Franco-friendly voices in parliament and a conservative president who celebrated Franco's legacy did not help to increase civic trust in order to strengthen democratic institutions.

Yet, the government did respond somewhat to these public claims. It did so not by prohibiting or prosecuting citizen initiatives, but by allowing private (local) history commissions to operate uninhibited. Textbook reforms, public protests for liberty and societal dialogues took place freely.[426] This post-Franco generation was also a significant group of potential voters for the PSOE and other leftist parties. The PSOE thus intensified its efforts to come to terms with the past to please these young voters. In December 2003, all parliamentary groups rendered institutional homage to the victims of Francoist repression and their families, which led to widespread support.[427]

Nevertheless, not disconnected from TJ movements elsewhere in the world, the Spanish TJ process took off towards the end of the third decade and it became politically fashionable to examine and atone and apologise for one's own past. Spain's political and civil actors could not resist this global development. The main goal was the same as everywhere – namely to reconcile divided societies. The permanent exchange between Latin America and Spain on private, business and political levels meant that the developments across the Atlantic did not remain unnoticed in Spain. In fact, the ideas for protests, memorials, exhumations of mass graves and installing local history commissions were mostly copied from

---

[425] Sección Espanola de Amnestia Internacional, Victimas de la Guerra civil y el régimen franquista: El desastre de los archivos, para privatización de la verdad, Madrid, 30 March, 2006, pp. 16–17.

[426] A. Barahona de Brito, C. Gonzaléz-Enríquez and P. Aguilar, *The Politics of Memory*; P. Aguilar, *Memory and Amnesia*; G. Gamio Gehri, 'Reflexiones sobre el Tiempo y los Espacios de la Reconciliación', *Cuadernos Idehpup*, *Instituto de Democracia y Derechos Humanos* (Lima: Pontificia Universidad Católica del Perú, 2004), pp. 52–66; C. Molinero (ed.), *La Transición*.

[427] C. Closa Montero (ed.), *Study on How the Memory of Crimes Committed by Totalitarian Regimes in Europe Is Dealt with in the Member States*, p. 147.

the TJ movements in Chile, Argentina and Guatemala at that time. The EU, the Council of Europe and the UN called not only on Spain but on all Member States to deal with their past, which intensified TJ claims in Spain, too. This international TJ trend was one to which the Spanish government had to respond, despite its notorious amnesty laws. Eventually Spanish society started showing less divisive opinions. Around 2004 surveys showed that slightly more than half of the population (52 per cent) was fairly satisfied with governmental institutions and their responsiveness to citizen needs, which included needs for TJ. At the same time, satisfaction with democracy in general nevertheless rose only slowly. Thirteen per cent of the population was very satisfied, whereas 32 per cent were not very or not at all satisfied, while the large majority was satisfied with this 'game in town'.[428] At this time, political institutions enjoyed the highest level of trust seen since the transition and also openly expressed their own satisfaction with the way democracy was working. The regime was consolidated, but it still suffered major flaws and moreover unconsolidated pockets of terror and separatism which were clearly linked to an unatoned and silenced past.

Fourth Decade 2005–2014

In 2011, Juan Carlos Monedero wrote a chapter in his book about the transition in Spain with the following title, 'If the transition was so wonderful, why then is Spanish democracy so weak?' (*Si la transicion fue tan maravillosa, per que la democracia espanola es tan debil?*).[429] This title best resembles the state of the democratic consolidation at that time. Democratic flaws caused by the continuous ETA terror, the lack of resilience in dealing with critical questions and the refusal of the courts to challenge the amnesty laws of 1977 and the high level of corruption on all sides were just some of the troubles that Spanish society was struggling with.

In 2004 the PSOE regained a majority in government. A large part of the PSOE's constituency was the younger generation and openly asserted that dealing with the past would impact the assessment of democratic performance. Thirty years after Franco's death, a more comprehensive and thorough TJ approach seemed possible, as did the continuation of regime consolidation.

---

[428] European Union, Eurobarometer Surveys, Spain 2004.04, http://ec.europa.eu (last accessed August 2013).
[429] J.C. Monedero, *La transición contada a nuestros padres*, p. 197.

The shift in government to the PSOE occurred because conservative President José Maria Aznar had made a serious mistake in his treatment of the victims of terror, only weeks before the elections. He had failed to realise that citizens would no longer buy into the black-and-white portrayal of 'good government' versus 'bad ETA separatism'. This strategy had worked for over 50 years, but now it seemed to have come to an end. Aznar's mistake started in March 2004, after Islamic extremists attacked a local train in Madrid on 11 March 2004, killing 191 people on the same day. Aznar falsely accused ETA of perpetrating the crime. NGOs and victims' organisations jointly commemorated the tragic date as '11-M' which today is part of Spanish collective memory. Victims' families pushed for clarification, investigations and compensation. Instead, Aznar wanted to use this case to accuse his strongest opponents, ETA, in an attempt to justify stricter and more violent measures against the separatist movements in the Basque Country. However, Aznar did not succeed in turning those with traditional Falange affinities against their lifelong left-wing opponents, because the victims of this attack came from all areas of society and the threat was part of a global terror movement. After the truth was revealed, the public punished Aznar for his false and unjustified accusations against ETA. The PP lost the respect and support of voters who voted instead for the PSOE, a party that promised to use strict and unbiased measures for dealing with terrorist acts and their victims. The victims and survivors of ETA as well as of the Islamic extremist terror attack, although different in kind, were united in their demands for clarification and demystification. The fact was that the Spanish government and judiciary had difficulties embracing the rule of law and indicting perpetrators regardless of their political persuasion, in particular when it came to the past. In order to increase trust in the judiciary, it was imperative that the government and judiciary learned to do so in the future.

The lack of rule of law and, in its place, the anti-democratic tradition of using the law and judiciary to further one's own political ends, was no longer feasible. If institutions such as the judiciary or the government had used the Franco era as an educational opportunity to learn to apply the rule of law and indict perpetrators of the past (even if only symbolically, as was the case in post-communist unified Germany and many other transition countries of that time) it might have contributed to more respect for the rule of law at a later stage. Aznar's failure in the 2004 elections also indicated that Spain's democratic culture had become stronger than he had expected, but that political institutions had not yet necessarily done the same. Aznar's false claims against ETA also triggered general debates about coming to terms with many other events of past injustice, including those of the Franco era. It was the box of Pandora that triggered the request for more TJ. The PP's misinformation with regard to the terrorist attacks made people wonder if the PP had also lied regarding the Franco past. The public sought the truth about the past and wanted to name those individuals who should be held accountable for their actions, regardless of whether they were dead or alive. This was a novelty in Spain. Since the time of representative consolidation in the 1980s, the election turnouts had more or less resembled the traditional political divide in Spain: the PSOE (for the former republicans and socialist) and the PP (for the royalists and Francoists). The parties usually won and lost seats by small percentages, each sharing around a minimum of 40 per cent of the seats in Parliament.[430] Spain was far from being a consensus-based democracy, a model that Lijphart would have recommended in order to successfully overcome cleavages. However, the generational shift pressured parties and governments to change their rhetoric and agenda to become more consensual in the political culture, marking a new era of attitudinal and behavioural consolidation.

The PSOE government kept its promise to atone for the past by appointing Maria Teresa Fernandez de la Vega shortly after the election in 2004 as head of a governmental commission to create a historical memory law. In the following years, she chaired the Commission to Repair the Dignity and Restore the Memory of the Victims of Francoism (*La Comisión para Reparar la Dignidad y Restituir la Memoria de las Víctimas del Franquismo*) and proposed the Historical Memory Law (*Ley de Memoria Histórica de España*), which was passed after months of heavy parliamentary debates in 2006. The law entered into force in 2007 and the commission was the first of its kind to inquire about the past, 30 years after the general amnesty laws and 70 years after the Spanish Civil War. Omar Encarnacion has called this period of regime consolidation a 'cultural revolution' in terms of civic culture, a 'revolution' that was much needed to complete Spain's democratic consolidation.[431] His assessment goes in line with Merkel's last two stages of democratic consolidation, namely behavioural through civic engagement.

Despite the fact that President Zapatero did not hold a majority in parliament, with the support of other parties, and with this law he turned the

---

[430] L.M. McLaren, *Constructing Democracy in Southern Europe*, p. 127.
[431] O.G. Encarnacion, *Democracy Without Justice in Spain*, pp. 160–161.

everlasting 'Pact of Oblivion' into a law of 'Remembrance'. In the following years, this law not only delegitimised Franco's 'heroic' past, but also
one of its most powerful supporters, the Catholic Church. This heralded
a new role for the Church, as religious symbols disappeared from public places (such as prisons, courts and military buildings), and abortion
and same-sex marriage were legalised. These reforms also reflected the
reluctance of the Church to deal with its own past. The leftist government
aimed to push the Church to finally accept its dubious role during the war.
Because until today, many churches in Spain post only the names on their
walls of those who fought and lost their lives on Franco's side. The many
thousands of civilians, republicans and socialists who were executed,
killed, imprisoned or raped are not mentioned, even though most of them
were Catholic believers and members of the community. Nevertheless, in
recent years, some churches have slowly updated their memorial walls
and thus committed to the new TJ policies.

During the PSOE's first year in power after the 2004 elections, the government enjoyed one of its highest levels of trust ever in Spanish history.
Fifty-one per cent of citizens reported having trust in the government.[432]
This figure slightly decreased and increased again over the years, but fell
dramatically towards the end of the decade, when the PP re-entered government in 2013. At that time only 8 per cent of citizens reported trust
in government while 91 per cent tended not to trust the government. The
spiral went downward, although not in challenging consolidation, but in
terms of democratic quality also linked to the lack of transparency and
accountability of governmental agencies, to which TJ is connected.

The reason for PP's re-election was not the lack of TJ under the PSOE,
but citizens' dissatisfaction with the PSOE's inability to effectively deal
with the financial crisis. Due to a lack of alternatives this meant that the
PP was bound to win the elections, despite the fact that it also had no solution to end the crisis. Corruption and high unemployment remain major
problems in Spain.[433] This shows that TJ alone is never enough to keep a
government in power or cause a government to lose power, although TJ
can facilitate and catalyse political elections and turnouts.

There is also a correlation between the failure of democratic institutions to deal with general crises (of any kind) and the way they learn to be

[432] European Union, Eurobarometer Surveys, Spain 2004.10, http://ec.europa.eu (last
accessed August 2013).
[433] European Union, Eurobarometer Surveys, Spain 2013.05, http://ec.europa.eu (last
accessed August 2013).

self-reflective and critical towards their own wrongdoings in the present and the past. I draw a link here to the fact that the Spanish legislative and judicial powers, let alone the government, never learned to deal with the unpleasant legacy of the past because they silenced or deliberately 'forgot' it. It was in this decade that the lack of institutional knowledge of how to deal with a crisis other than with undemocratic and violent means, or by simply silencing the crisis, showed its dark side. Dealing with the Franco past more transparently might have strengthened the institutions in a way that would have made them more able to cope with other major challenges such as the financial crisis since 2008 in a more effective way.[434]

Nevertheless, since 2000 the number of civil groups increased and their engagement and participation rose as thousands started to pose questions about the past. One of the strongest NGOs in dealing with the past was the Spanish division of Amnesty International, which distributed several expert papers and lobbied the government to finally stop impunity and silence and to apply TJ measures.[435] Around 2005 they started lobbying the government to make a law to deal with reparations for the family members of the thousands of disappeared and that would allow for exhumations and collaboration with the UN working group for disappearances, since the UN started to become involved in Spain's reluctant TJ process around that time. Furthermore, Amnesty International asked the government to establish more independent archives and release relevant documents, for example those that have been held in the Ministry of Defence since 1939 and that might lead to legal procedures.[436] But it has not only been NGOs and political parties that have mobilised in this way. Individual family members and descendants of victims chose the legal proceedings as a way to claim justice. Encouraged by the civil movements and the laws for remembrance, the first claims were filed at the Supreme Court (which was also responsible for military issues of the past)

---

[434] Conversely, in Germany at the time of this crisis the level of citizen trust in democratic institutions almost doubled from 24 per cent in 2003 to 44 per cent in 2013. This was because people trusted that the institutions had learned to deal with unpleasant legacies and shortcomings in other areas. See: European Union, Eurobarometer Surveys, Germany 2003.11 and 2013.05, http://ec.europa.eu (last accessed August 2013).

[435] Amnistía Internacional España, *España: poner fin al silencio y a la injusticia. La deuda pendiente con las víctimas de la Guerra civil española y del régimen franquista* (Madrid: Amnistía Internacional España, 2005).

[436] Amnistía Internacional España, *Víctimas de la Guerra civil y el régimen franquista: El desastre de los archivos, para privatización de la verdad* (Madrid: Amnistía Internacional España, 2006), pp. 16–17.

to revoke sentences and rehabilitate victims of Franco's arbitrary and illegal executions. Some of the cases went all the way to the ECtHR, but none ever succeeded. Family members were fully aware of their low chance of success, due to the non-revised amnesty laws of 1976 and 1977.

Despite all the failures to ever bring a superior under the Franco regime to justice, in 2007 and thanks to the History Law, the Supreme Court revoked the Military Tribunal's 1937 death sentence of Ricardo Puente, due to the formal unlawfulness of the tribunal at that time. This case aimed to illustrate the political motivation behind many of the thousands of arbitrary tribunal sentences during the war. In this case, as in many others, Puente was a republican and thus an enemy of Franco's troops and thus was going to be eliminated regardless of whether this was legal or illegal. Therefore, the Supreme Court's decision in 2007 was also a plea for the rule of law and thus for the strengthening of democratic institutions in modern Spain even 70 years later. Yet, according to some observers, the fact that this past political sentence was not questioned or publicly discussed during the sessions out of fear that it would trigger public protests was again a reason to doubt the progress of the rule of law.[437] But further appeals for the revision of death sentences for mostly republican, anarchist and communist victims of the Franco era, such as Julian Grimau in 1963 and Puig Antich in 1973, were almost all declined, even after CSOs and political institutions were in place. According to the lawyers who took up these cases, it was never a matter of winning or losing the case, but of showing the flaws of the judiciary. Bringing these cases before democratically installed courts was meant to show public and political actors that the past regime had been unjust and illegal, and that justice should be based on fundamental rights in the past and the present. According to Luis Fernando Para Galindo, a lawyer who argued the case of José Pellicer Gandía, who was executed in 1942, the main goal of these cases was to change people's awareness.[438]

After almost all cases were rejected by the Supreme Court, international pressure on Spain increased. In 2008, the ICTJ in New York launched a call to the wider public and government urging them to consider alternative measures in Spain. These NGOs, lawyers and victims were not necessarily aiming to have perpetrators imprisoned, but rather hoped for a symbolic act from governments and courts to revise the amnesty laws

---

[437] Tribunal Supremo España. Sala de lo Militar. Sentencia, Recurso, Revisión Penal. No 106/2004. Sentencia: 19 February 2007.
[438] Interview with Luis Fernando Parra Galindo in Madrid, 11 May 2011.

and end impunity. Instead, the Spanish government has indicated, on more than one occasion, that the amnesty laws and the agreements on the unwritten 'Pact of Oblivion' from the 1978 meetings at the Palace of Moncloa, mean that justice does not apply to all.

In its study, the ICTJ suggested that while the 1976 and 1977 amnesty laws hamper in-depth investigations and revocations, the judiciary could revise sentences according to their legal complaint mechanisms. In addition, the parliament could encourage courts to consider whether all defendants had enjoyed equality before the law. Last but not least, the ECtHR could give advice on how to revoke sentences despite amnesty laws. The Center's researchers argued that there are always ways for political and educational bodies to implement TJ measures, even if laws do pose some restrictions.[439] Moreover, victims' family members and leftist parties in parliament attempted to amend the law so that the judiciary would have broader powers of revision and be able to revoke sentences to rehabilitate victims of the regime. These attempts started in 1978 and were continuously taken up by groups of lawyers and CSOs in the 1990s without ever receiving the necessary majority of votes. Nonetheless, the legislature reacted and passed a number of smaller laws and decrees in the following years that had subsequent consequences for dealing with such claims. The majority of them dealt with issuing documents and subsidies from the central state to the Autonomous Communities, in particular Catalonia, which would make it possible to acknowledge and investigate the wrongdoings of the past.[440] But unsurprisingly, because of the strong resistance of the conservative branches in Spain, it took international state and NGO actors, as well as citizen-driven action in Spain's periphery, to finally trigger the Historical Memory Law and the first commission of inquiry in 2007. It was a response to the private efforts to investigate, commemorate and file cases on behalf of victims over the first two decades and with support from the Communities' government such as the one of Catalonia.[441]

Around the same time, in 2006, Pedro Almodovar's popular film 'Return' (*Volver*) was one more push for the national catharsis to take off. The film dealt with the unresolved questions of the 'frozen past' of

---

[439] J. Errandonea, *Estudio comparado de la anulación de sentencias injustas en España* (New York: International Center for Transitional Justice, 2008), pp. 29–33.
[440] P. Aguilar, 'Transitional or Post-Transitional Justice? Recent Developments in the Spanish Case', *South European Society for Politics*, 13 (2008), 417–433.
[441] R. Vinyes (ed.), *El Estado y la Memoria*.

the Franco era, drawing parallels between the characters in the film and people in contemporary Spain with an overwhelming success.[442] The film, and many subsequent novels and documentaries that told stories of this period, triggered public debates at a time in which public opinion and governmental responsiveness had changed dramatically. International incentives and pressure played their part in stimulating parliament to hold debates. Again, this bottom-up movement, a free media, novels, films and a free CSO movement paired with external interference was also a response to the PP government's silence.

The year 2006 was also an anniversary year for Spain, namely 70 years after the start of the Civil War, and the government in Madrid had to react somehow, although it did not know how and what to do about it. In March 2006, the Council of Europe issued a report condemning Francoism and the serious breaches of human rights committed after the war between 1939 and 1975. Importantly, the report did not only refer to the Spanish Civil War, which had already been condemned by all democratic parties in Spain, but also to the crimes that happened afterwards.[443] This gave the TJ process a new direction. With this report, the Council had followed a recommendation made by the Parliamentarian Assembly of the Council of Europe in November 2005, which urged the Spanish government not only to investigate crimes linked to the war, but also to officially condemn the Franco regime, install critical (as opposed to heroic) exhibits in the Valle de los Caidos, open archives to researchers and install a national committee to inquire into violations of human rights and so on.[444] This international pressure and the public pressure from below caused a 'sandwich situation' for the government in which it felt trapped between the claims for more TJ from two sides. It was stuck between international pressure and citizen demands and thus needed to respond if it wanted to remain credible. And it did so almost immediately and issued parliamentarian debates about the amnesty laws from 1976 and 1977, which eventually did not succeed in abolishing the laws but in creating a new one, the Historical Memory Law in 2007.

---

[442] S.R. Golob, 'Volver: The Return of/to Transitional Justice Politics in Spain', *Journal of Spanish Cultural Studies*, Special Issue (New York: New York University, 2008), 127–141.

[443] P. Burbidge, 'Walking the Dead of the Spanish Civil War. Judge Baltasar Garzón and the Spanish Law of Historical Memory', *Journal of International Criminal Justice*, 9 (2011), 753–781.

[444] Council of Europe, *Brincat Report – Need for International Condemnation of the Franco Regime, for Debate in the Standing Committee*. Doc. 10737, 4 November 2005.

It is not without the involvement of influential political actors that the EU watched Spain's TJ debates carefully in 2006 and 2007. Following the example of the Council of Europe, the European Parliament also condemned Spain for its slow process in coming to terms with its past. The condemnation was an initiative of the president of the European Parliament, Josep Borrell, between 2004 and 2007. Himself a Catalan and member of the PSOE and the European socialists, Borrell aimed to 'support' his party members in the Spanish government and parliament who wanted a revision of the amnesty laws or at least the implementation of the Historical Memory Law. He used the European Parliament as a 'boomerang' to exert external pressure to trigger a change in the political debate in Spain.

But the PSOE government under Zapatero did not hold an absolute majority of seats in parliament at that time and thus needed external push factors for which Borrell's initiative was the catalyst. His party had urged Borrell to issue the report in 2006 and to assure legitimate support from the EU. Borrell saw that one window of opportunity and on the seventieth anniversary of Franco's coup d'état and of the beginning of the war in 1936, he successfully launched the debate in the European Parliament. A group of 200 parliamentarians, among them representatives of the conservative Spanish parties, signed a request to the Spanish government to finally issue a Memory Law. They also pushed for an oral hearing by the EU Commission and the European Council explicitly calling for a debate on condemning the Franco regime and his coming to power on 18 July 1936. Borrell argued that Spanish democratic transition had been based on selective forgetfulness and suspension of memory and that now more TJ was needed to overcome the flaws that this caused in Spanish democratic consolidation. This did not remain unnoticed by the larger public in Spain. And along the shifts and developments of memory, the bookshops started to fill up with biographies, novels and documentary literature about the past and the Civil War and the sales went well. Although there was still a long way to go,[445] this year marked a final turning point in the twist between TJ and regime consolidation in Spain.

Observers such as Tamarit Sumalla have therefore argued that Spain's TJ process only started in 2006. According to Sumalla this was the year when specific requirements in the field of criminal justice, including the

---

[445] European Parliament, Debate, No. 4, 70 years after General Franco's coup d'état in Spain (Statements by the President and the political groups, Strasbourg, 4 July 2006.

duty to prosecute crimes of the past, became also part of Spain's internal criminal justice policy.[446] These years also illustrate how much Spanish political and democratic culture relied on the behaviour of contemporary social and political elites, rather than institutions, according to Merkel and Puhle's approach to regime consolidation.[447] As Richard Gunther, Jose Ramón Montero and Joan Botella have argued, the new elites (including King Juan Carlos) and the sides they took played a larger role in transition than the constitutional setup and the rupture and break with the past regime – in both restrictive and progressive ways. And one could add that the way that the king has been in many ways a personification of the Spanish reconciliation process and has never openly banned any TJ efforts, he has indirectly been a supporter of it. Spanish political culture had long been characterised by authoritarian and corporatist tendencies that had long undermined consolidation.[448]

Furthermore, the 2007 law gives guidelines and recommendations, for example recommending the removal of Franco statues in municipalities. If some are to remain part of Spanish cultural heritage, such as the Valle de los Caidos, they must be accompanied by critical voices, such as museums that explain the period.[449] This law responds to many demands from victim groups, such as the ARMH and the Spanish branch of Amnesty International. But another problem with Spanish consolidation remains – the amnesty laws from 1976 and 1977. The Historical Memory Law has been amended and extended several times in the past years. Later, the governmental commissioner for the law not only addresses memory processing in general but also looks into the possibility of compensation, reimbursement of private property, pension requirements and the overdue arrangement of dismantling public places featuring the names of 'heroes' from the Spanish Civil War.[450] It also supports initiatives to exhume mass graves to identify victims. Furthermore, it has started debates on the revision of the amnesty laws in 1977. But it also points out that the identification of victims and establishing the truth is not intended to be a public matter and only aims to reconcile the family members of those killed. But the law does not allow for judicial procedures or indictments. But

---

[446] J.M. Tamarit Sumalla, 'Transition, Historical Memory and Criminal Justice in Spain'.

[447] W. Merkel and H.-J. Puhle, *Von der Diktatur zu Demokratie*, p. 174.

[448] R. Gunther, J. Ramón Montero and J. Botella, *Democracy in Modern Spain* (New Haven, CT: Yale University Press, 2004), pp. 135–158.

[449] La Vanguardia, 'El Valle de los Caídos dejará de ser un templo de exaltación del franquismo', 18 October 2007, p. 17.

[450] W.L. Bernecker and S. Brinkmann, *Kampf der Erinnerungen*, p. 339ff.

regardless how modest this law may be, it did succeed in triggering further parliamentary debates, civil society initiatives, dismantling Franco statues, inauguration of memorials, exhumation of mass graves and public burials, TV debates, and overall media coverage about parts of the Franco past. All these TJ efforts triggered a change in attitudes, in behaviour and civic engagement that fuelled the upward spiral.

Yet, TJ policies were not necessarily supported by the overall majority and President Zapatero himself suffered personal insults from conservatives and other victims of ETA, which preferred a hard hand against ETA and which were mainly families with a PP background. Because ETA had always seen its terrorist acts as revenge for all that happened under Franco's rule, the victims of ETA terror had little sympathy with the fact that Franco's wrongdoings were made public, because it would have demystified it. During a public event in February 2006, unsatisfied ETA terror victim groups shouted 'Zapatero, go with your grandfather!' (*Zapatero, vete con tu abuelo!*), meaning that he should be executed just as his grandfather had been under Franco. This spontaneous insult became a political metaphor against the Memory Law in the following years and was cited widely in media and blogs to illustrate the still-existing irreconcilable divide and hatred between Francoists and socialists. Although the majority of Spanish society no longer felt this divide on a day-to-day basis, the smaller group of citizens that did expressed their discontent with parliament and the law in a way that exemplified the low level of democratic culture in Spain.

TJ continued due to the Historical Memory Law, for example, when in 2008 the Youth Branch of the Falange was prohibited from commemorating the anniversary of Franco's death at his grave at the Valle de los Caidos. This commemoration had been held without interruption since 1975, and thus the supporters and members of the neo-Falange were outraged. But the most prominent of all TJ measures that increased after the instalment of the law was the exhumation of the hundreds of mass graves and the DNA identification of thousands of victims. The office of the president (*Ministro de la Presidencia*) provided direct financial support to NGO initiatives in their search for mass graves for which the minister of finance (*Ministerio de Hacienda*) is responsible. In addition, the legislature opened the Civil War archive (*Centro Documental de la Memoria Historica*) in Salamanca to the public. This archive not only named the crimes of the Franco regime, but launched exhibitions, publications and investigations into them as well. It has no educational mandate, but its website is highly accessible and contains information and documents which tell many of the stories that Francoists had tried to keep secret for decades.[451] The archive was founded in 1938 and was used by the Franco regime to safeguard all documents from the Spanish Republic and Civil War.[452] It is hard to know how many of the files could have facilitated the TJ process in Spain because, between 1975 and 2008, most of the archive was cleansed and documents were destroyed or removed. Thus, many claim that such archives are useless for prosecution or litigation. According to Spanish laws, trials would need to be based on other sources of evidence and testimonies that have become scarce in modern Spain. If this was not enough, it has been agreed that these files cannot be used for legal or political purposes. Key terms such as 'use of force' or 'suppression' are not found in the files. Nevertheless, opening the archive is seen as one of the first attempts to publicly shine a light on 40 years of Spanish dictatorship, some 30 years after it ended. Not surprisingly and because of years of silence, the amnesty laws and the cleansed or closed archives, many victims' organisations found the Historical Memory Law insufficient and asked instead for legal investigation and prosecution of perpetrators. In 2008, Amnesty International again requested the government to start the first trials despite the laws and in respond to citizens' human rights to truth by making reference to existing international human rights and criminal law (such as crimes against humanity) as a door opener to finally trigger trials in Spain.[453]

Although this did not materialise, the claim arose again when one of the initiators of the earlier TJ process, the judge Baltasar Garzón was prosecuted for his attempt to investigate past crimes a few years later.

---

[451] Portal de Victimas de la Guerra Civil y Prepresaliados del Franquismo, http://pares.mcu.es/victimasGCFPortal (last accessed May 2011).

[452] Portada de Pares, Spanish Archives, http://pares.mcu.es (last accessed August 2014). After Madrid was conquered in 1938, all documents from the democratically elected government of the Second Republic (until 1936) were transferred to Salamanca. With the documents in a safe place, the Franco regime was then able to persecute and eliminate those who were registered in these archives without being interrupted by the opposition (mostly communists, republicans and socialists). Consequently, the archive was used as a main source of espionage against all opposition. The archives contain select information on mainly private donations from people of various backgrounds. Remarkably, most of the private documents were transferred to the archive after Franco's death – so as to make sure that the donors would not be pulled into any confrontation with protagonists of the old or new regimes. Nevertheless, its files have been largely cleansed by Francoists, who had more than 30 years to destroy and cleanse all materials they found disfavourable.

[453] Amnistía Internacional España, España: la obligación de investigar los crímenes del pasado y garantizar los derechos de las víctimas de desaparición forzada durante la Guerra Civil y el franquismo (Madrid: Amnistía Internacional España, 2008).

For Spain he played a similar role as did attorney Fritz Bauer in West Germany in the 1950s and 1960s, but his success and fate were different. At his first intervention to challenge the amnesty laws from 1976 and 1977, public opinion was on his side. Surveys conducted in 2008 showed that the Spanish Civil War remained in the daily memory of over 50 per cent of the population. Even more striking is that one in three individuals (30.5 per cent) was still fearful of speaking publicly about the past, although this number was significantly lower than it had been in previous years.[454] Less surprisingly, it appeared that the older generation disliked discussing their memories of the past in public because they feared repercussions and confrontations from their peers. But the general opinion meant that the majority was no longer afraid and dared to start asking questions and, moreover, dared to take the initiative in finding the truth. Yet, among the older population, the fear of direct consequences remained at the local level, where most of the forensic exhumations take place, since mass graves are generally found in remote, rural areas and not in major cities. According to Paco Etxeberria, a forensic analyst from the University of San Sebastian and one of the first volunteers to start exhumations in 2000, the fear continues because many of these forensic initiatives are still private and not public. Since the private initiatives are not always supported by the government, people fear their involvement with these initiatives might have negative repercussions.[455]

But according to the surveys by Paloma Aguilar, Laia Balcells and Héctor Cebolla-Boado the public attitudes towards the Franco era had shifted in favour of TJ. They found that over 50 per cent of Spaniards favour TJ measures, across the political spectrum, although those who have a 'republican past', or dead family members whose allegiance never became clear, favour TJ measures more than conservatives and they favoured prosecution of the authorities that violated human rights under Franco. The PP, other conservative forces and the Supreme Court have blocked such prosecutions, insisting that the amnesty laws cannot be changed and thus posted limits for judge Garzón's efforts to investigate.[456]

[454] C. Closa Montero (ed.), *Study on How the Memory of Crimes Committed by Totalitarian Regimes in Europe Is Dealt with in the Member States*, p. 368.
[455] Interview with Paco Etxeberria, Forensic Institute University of San Sebastian, during excavations of mass grave from Civil War, Puerto de la Mazorra close to Burgos, 7 May 2011.
[456] P. Aguilar, L. Balcells and H. Cebolla-Boado, 'Determinant of Attitudes Toward Transitional Justice: An Empirical Analysis of the Spanish Case', *Comparative Political Studies*, 44 (2011), 1397–1430.

Just a few years earlier in the debates around the Historical Memory Law, the leader of the PP, Mariano Rajoy (who later became the president of Spain), falsely claimed that the 'vast majority of Spaniards does not want to talk about the past, let alone about Franco'.[457] It should be borne in mind that today's families are largely 'mixed families', composed of some family members with a pro-Franco past and some with a republican orientation. In these cases, families share a common interest in discovering what happened to their family members on both sides, which creates political space for more TJ measures. Due to the massive public controversies around the law and the way on how to implement it, in November 2008, and with great public and parliamentarian support, the parliament passed two amendments to the Historical Memory Law. One of these amendments facilitated reparation and personal acknowledgement for those persecuted or repressed during the war and the dictatorship. The other granted Spanish nationality to the international brigade volunteers and those who were descendants of Spanish refugees, in the Law of the Grandchildren (*Ley de los Nietos*). By 2012, over 240,000 'grandchildren' (descendants of Spanish refugees) were granted Spanish citizenship, most of them from Latin America as an act of TJ.[458]

The law resembled a similar restitution law in Germany that granted descendants of Holocaust survivors German citizenship. But here again, the Spanish government followed the international TJ trend of acknowledgement and individual compensation or restitution in other countries. The Law of the Grandchildren, as these amendments were called, meant that descendants of refugees would benefit from some government compensation. Many of these third-generation descendants now live outside Spain in Latin America, France, Germany or Great Britain, but could potentially become an important constituency in the future. With the passing of this law, it became a wishful thinking to all parties and interest groups involved in TJ that this was only the beginning and that additional laws and punitive measures would soon be adopted. In 2009 an organisation called Psychologist Without Frontiers began providing support and advice to victims and relatives on how and where to search for the remains of their relatives with help from the government.

---

[457] The Guardian, 'Spain finally attempts to lay ghosts of the Franco era', 20 July 2006. www.guardian.co.uk (last accessed August 2013).

[458] El Pais, 'España suma casi 250,000 nuevos nacionales gracias a la "ley de nietos"', 30 March 2012. http://politica.elpais.com (last accessed August 2013).

Today hundreds of these CSO initiatives exist, but the law has not been extended, but rather due to the financial crisis and shift in government they have even been suspended.

This did not stop the judge Baltasar Garzón further investigating and calling for criminal justice in Spain. After his first unsuccessful efforts in the area of universal jurisdiction in 1998, he began to pursue the investigation and prosecution of Franco-era crimes. In 2005 he requested the investigation in the Autonomous Communities' provincial courts of an estimated 110,000 political killings under Franco. As one of the highest judges in the country, he openly criticised the amnesty laws of 1977. His position in this matter met with resistance from influential conservatives and Francoists, including many judges (and colleagues) in Spain's higher courts. The public debates about the amnesty laws had fuelled Baltasar Garzón efforts to continue his criminal investigation into the Franco regime's crimes. He argued that they had been crimes against humanity, in particular the thousands of illegal killings and disappearances during and shortly after the Spanish Civil War, and thus not covered by the Amnesty Laws of 1977, but well under international criminal law.

In May 2009 Garzón was indicted because he was allegedly 'violating the laws of 1976 and 1977' and his case was brought before the National Court (*Audiencia Nacional*), Spain's highest criminal court. The claim against him was that his efforts to bring Franco perpetrators to justice would go beyond the scope of the Memory Law from 2007. Although Garzón received strong support from victims' organisations, the influential ARMH, regional memory organisations, Amnesty International and even the ICC, as well as from many deputes and media, he failed to uphold his cause in front of the court. On the other side, he also received death threats, hate speech and other acts of sabotage that formed a daily annoyance. This procedure showed that the conservative forces were concerned about the pending questions about guilt and legal responsibility and wanted to suppress them, testing the rule of law once again. Until the court's final decision, Garzón was suspended from office in May 2010. But parallel to his defeat, different victims associations increased their protests. Every Thursday in the heart of Madrid at the Puerta del Sol in front of the town hall, protesters called for an end to impunity and the amnesty laws in Spain, thus showing solidarity with Garzón. The Mayor of Madrid, a member of the PP, later suspended these marches for justice. The Thursday protestors followed the examples of a prominent TJ initiative, namely the 'crying and protesting mothers' elsewhere in the world, in Turkey and Argentina and in other post-dictatorial countries, by which they publicise stories of the Franco-era victims.[459] With the PP in power, TJ seemed to have been restricted as much as possible. At the same time, the UN Human Rights Committee expressed its concern about Spain's constant refusal to reconsider its amnesty laws and the Committee asked the government to 'consider repealing the 1977 amnesty law and take necessary legislative measures to guarantee recognition by the domestic courts of the non-applicability of the statute of limitation to crimes against humanity'.[460] Although the UN Human Rights Committee's recommendation did not mention Garzón by name, it was evident the committee members were aware of his actions. The UN recommendations provided indirect support for his efforts to challenge the amnesty laws. In the following months, Amnesty International in London launched an international report addressed to the UN Committee against Torture stating that the Spanish government had failed to exercise its obligation under international human rights law to investigate cases of crimes against humanity and could not 'hide' behind the amnesty laws.[461] By classifying the Franco crimes as crimes against humanity, Garzón and his supporters had opened Pandora's box, because according to customary international law amnesty laws can never apply to crimes against humanity. The UN report supported his interpretation of the crimes under Franco and thus increasing the pressure on the government and parliament in Spain. Eventually, the UN Committee urged the government to revise the law, but without success.[462] Garzón himself saw these disputes also as a test case for whether the Spanish judiciary had indeed learned from the past and had become part of a modern legal regime based on international law and the rule of law, a test which Spain has not passed.

The issue was not so much about the content of the investigations that Garzón had started, since enough evidence of the 110,000-plus disappearances was already available and anybody could have brought it to court (and many other lawyers did so as well). Instead, it was about

[459] Manifestación de las víctimas del franquismo en la Puerta del Sol (Madrid) todos los jueves en la Puerta del Sol, Madrid de 20 a 21 horas. tercerainformaciñon.es (last accessed August 2013).
[460] UN Human Rights Committee. *ICCPR, Consideration of Report Submitted by State Parties under Article 40 of the Convenant*, Concluding observations of the Human Rights Committee, Spain, 94th session, Geneva 13–31. October 2008. Doc. CCPR/C/ESP/CO/5, Geneva, 5 January 2009, p. 2.
[461] Amnistía Internacional España, *Briefing to Committee Against Torture* (Madrid: Amnistía Internacional España, 2009), pp. 48–51.
[462] UN Doc. CAT/C/ESP/Q/5/Add.1., UN Committee Against Torture (CAT), New York, 22 September 2009.

him as a test case for how resilient the Spanish judiciary was to political influence and the legacy of the past. Apparently, it was not very resilient. After Garzón's suspension and during an open talk in 2011, he emphasised that the investigations he started, as well as 'his personal case', had the overall effect of shedding light on the level of (legal) corruption in Spain; a light that was necessary for the functioning of democracy (*para que la democracia funciona*).[463] This sentence was reminiscent of the one uttered by attorney Fritz Bauer the day before the Auschwitz trials in 1963. The Spanish Supreme Court, the majority of whose judges supported the PP (some with strong family ties to the Falange), had its chance to prove its independence by taking up the criminal charges brought by Garzón, but failed to do so. It argued instead that the amnesty laws prohibited retroactive investigations of whatever kind, according to Article 9 of the Spanish Constitution – regardless what international customary criminal law says. Although it is true that Article 9 contains such a prohibition, Garzón claimed that according to international human rights standards such a provision could not apply to crimes against humanity.[464] With the final judgment of the Supreme Court in February 2012, Garzón was suspended for life from practising law in Spain. This had the appearance of an act of cleansing even in a consolidated democratic regime. He was legally convicted for violating Spanish law and the constitution. The judgment also entailed that he could no longer practise as a lawyer and he later started working as a consultant in the TJ and peace process in Colombia, where his initiatives have brought many cases of crimes committed under dictatorships to light. While the court's decision was not an imminent threat to democracy in Spain, it showed how difficult it has been to attribute responsibility for past crimes and, at the same time, build a Spanish rule of law and democratic culture.[465]

In 2009 and parallel to these developments, a dramatic change in government took place in the Basque Country, almost bringing an end to ETA. The first PSOE-led government in the Basque Country

---

[463] Talk with Baltasar Garzón, Madrid, 6 May 2011.

[464] P. Burbidge, 'Walking the Dead of the Spanish Civil War'.

[465] In Latin American countries, it has proven possible to revise amnesty laws and to change statutes of limitation. This shows that the Spanish Supreme Court's reference to the prohibition of retroactivity in the Spanish constitution could not alone justify the expulsion of Garzón from office. Yet, interestingly enough, these developments have encouraged even more lawyers and victims organisations to continue with their efforts to challenge antiquated laws and elitist thinking in society.

reversed nearly 30 years of PNV nationalist and anti-TJ memory poli-cies. Textbook reforms, historical awareness raising and new language regulations changed the Basque social consciousness. In the same year the citizen-driven NGO, called the Basque Memory (*Euskal Memoria*) was founded by people who used to be active supporters of ETA and separatist claims, but later withdrew from these positions. They chose other means to deal with the past and looked to common Spanish and Basque history. They collected data and testimonials from vic-tims of terror, those who had been affected by ETA terror and by the violence, torture and disappearances caused by the Guardia Civil in police custody.[466] When one of the many ETA ceasefires was declared in 2011, it was seen as a sign that the time was ripe to reconcile under terms acceptable to both the central government and the Autonomous Communities. Since then, ETA has not re-emerged significantly and because the ceasefire remains active one can presume that ETA is about to dissolve itself.

In 2012, the PNV returned to power in the Basque Country, but the new government was more moderate than the previous one. In 2013, the Basque prime minister, a member of the PNV but in a coalition with the PSOE, announced a new plan on peace and human rights. This was a novelty in the Basque country, because it aimed to also look at crimes after 1975, such as the killings by ETA. Citizen demands and massive pro-tests calling for an end to ETA terror and radical separatism put pressure on the prime minister to respond. Many citizens called for normalising the situation and demanded that ETA prisoners be treated according to international standards. As a result of these pressures, the prime minis-ter developed a new policy, together with the Institute of Memory and Coexistence, and many prisoners were moved to prisons closer to home where they could receive family visits.

Around this time, a public debate broke out about the destiny of the Valle de los Caidos and how to finally turn it into a memorial and museum for all victims of the Civil War. Santiago Carrillo, a major leader of the com-munist and later leftist movement prior to and during transition, argued that this discussion only became possible because people were no longer afraid to ask questions and confront the past, but unfortunately this took

---

[466] J. Agirre, 'EUSKAL MEMORIA: Recovering the Memories of the Rejected People', *Politorbis, Zeitschrift für Aussenpolitik*, Tenth Anniversary of the International Criminal Court: The Challenges of Complementarity (Bern: Federal Department of Foreign Affairs Switzerland, 2012), pp. 123–125.

a generation and a few political shifts in government.[467] In the following years, political tensions relating to the past became less extreme, because they became also more public and thus the past had been publicly demystified. Thus, calls for the TJ reforms from civil society continued heavily and led to a significant but late delegitimisation of the Franco regime.[468]

Meanwhile publications about the Civil War continued to pile up on bookshelves and more films were launched. War veterans, victims of the war, observers and analysts on all sides shared their long-concealed experiences and beliefs. Many of these were very controversial, but had long been needed. Films, publications, novels and media coverage unblocking memories skyrocketed.[469] Authors like Pio Moa justified Franco's brutal war against his own compatriots, while others, like Paul Preston, called the massacres on civilians the 'Spanish Holocaust'. Regardless of whether these opinions were based on evidence, the fact that extreme views on all sides were possible without resulting in major repercussions was a sign of the growing confidence in the regime – or rather the varied character of democratic civil society, as Merkel and Puhle stated in their observations on regime consolidation.[470]

Preston's use of the term the 'Spanish Holocaust' serves as a superlative to demand the missing justice and atonement and to overcome the amnesty laws from 1977. Similarly, Ulrike Jureit and Christian Schneider claim that the term 'Holocaust' is today used as a 'universal container' for societies and countries to describe atrocities and events that have not been acknowledged or brought to justice. When this term is used, people expect some institutional response and acknowledgement that is in accordance with international human rights law.[471] Hence, in the following years, TJ measures were no longer disputed, although the government carefully controlled any TJ manoeuvre mainly by issuing only limited financial support for it, if any at all.[472] Nevertheless, the demand to finally bring Spanish perpetrators to justice, even if only symbolically, continues.[473] And so does international pressure.

---

[467] El Pais, 'En Busca de un Valle para todos los Caídos', 8 June 2011, www.memoriahistorica. org.es (last accessed August 2015).

[468] F. Gómez Isa, 'Retos de la justicia transicional en contextos no transicionales: El caso español', Interamerican and European Human Rights Journal, 3 (2010), 81.

[469] W.L. Bernecker, and S. Brinkmann, Kampf der Erinnerungen, p. 246.

[470] W. Merkel and H.-J. Puhle, Von der Diktatur zur Demokratie, p. 138.

[471] U. Jureit and C. Schneider, Gefuehlte Opfer, p. 100.

[472] R. Gunther, J. Ramón Montero and J. Botella, Democracy in Modern Spain (New Haven, CT: Yale University Press, 2004).

[473] J. Arnold, 'Zweiter Teil', p. 372.

In September 2013, the UN Working Group on Enforced or Involuntary Disappearance (established in 1980) visited Spain for the first time. It was unusual for a UN working group to visit a consolidated democratic country in Europe that claimed to have all legal, forensic and political means to deal with mass graves and the legal implications exhumations might have. The UN working group's visit was a reaction to serious claims by victims and CSOs concerning the failure of the Spanish government to investigate the hundreds of thousands still-disappeared victims of the Civil War and beyond in an open, transparent and overall unbiased way. For the Spanish opposition, international institutions (in particular those in Europe) had always been a welcome supporter of TJ in Spain, and the fact that this UN visit took place revealed the magnitude of the Spanish authorities' inability to deal with these issues, despite massive domestic pressure. The UN experts eventually questioned government officials on the government's willingness to ensure truth, justice, reparation and commemoration for the victims of enforced disappearances. The Working Group came to the conclusion that the government had not taken sufficient measures to deal with the estimated 100,000 disappeared and 30,000 abducted children during the dictatorship despite the law of 2007. They recommended more training of forensic personnel, authorities and judges on how to deal with these crimes of the past. Among other recommendations, they requested the government not to leave TJ in the hands of private initiatives, lawyers and NGOs alone. These initiatives need government support, for example to establish systematic databases that are protected and to arrange criminal prosecution. They concluded that the state must finally take the lead in the TJ process, otherwise the process would have no (positive) effect.[474]

The answers to questions of responsibility and the level of democratic institutions' accountability are undoubtedly the most difficult and consequential parts of regime consolidation. A careful historical and legal preparation is necessary before accusations are made. Its effects on social reconciliation, the democratic culture and social peace cannot be underestimated.[475] The financial crisis and the high unemployment rate in Spain

---

[474] Office of the High Commissioner for Human Rights (OHCHR), Spain: The State must assume a leadership role and engage more actively to respond to the demands of the relatives of the disappeared, Press Release, Madrid, 30 September 2013 ohchr.org/ (last accessed January 2014)

[475] D. Bloomfield, M. Fischer and B. Schmelzle (eds.), *Social Change and Conflict Transformation* (Berlin: Berghof Research Center for Constructive Conflict Management, 2010), p. 14.

dominated public debates towards the end of this decade and was the main reason for the significant decrease in the level of trust in government and public institutions. The way in which public institutions deal with and respond to any type of national crisis indicates levels of institutional quality. But the TJ laws, the European and UN pressure, also challenged the lack of transparency and accountability in Spanish democracy and showed its flaws that are usually visible in times of national crisis. But at the same time, the fact that civil society tirelessly pressured policy makers to respond to their needs for TJ measures – paired with pressure from the UN, the EU and the CoE – fuelled and catalysed the consolidation process furthermore. These initiatives fuelled the consolidation process even more and closed some of the unconsolidated pockets, such as in Catalonia and in the Basque Country, where it became more difficult for nationalist and radical groups to mobilise people with the simple fact that all governments avoid dealing with the past and therefore separation and independence is necessary from Spain. Although that alone has not ended the separatist movement in Catalonia claiming independence from Spain, it has changed the rhetoric and framework of arguments for independence. And as a result of this, by 2013 the fear of terrorism – which was once high in the opinion polls – has declined over the years, to zero per cent. This is the lowest rate ever in Spanish history and is also thanks to massive reconciliation projects and TJ measures towards the end of the fourth decade.[476]

Brief Summary of Spain

The case of TJ in Spain illustrates that the mutually reinforcing effect between sub regimes such as an active civil society and political institutions can lead to more democratic consolidation by lowering the level of radical movements and even terrorism.[477] The main challenge to regime consolidation in Spain was the irreversible amnesty laws of 1976 and 1977 that hampered any delegitimisation process of the dictatorial regime and which eventually cost many people's lives, because ETA and GRAPO justified their killings with the statement that 'Franco is still running the country' through his successors and there was no justice for those who suffered his suppressive regime. The notorious lack of open dialogue

[476] European Union, Eurobarometer Surveys, Spain 2013.05, http://ec.europa.eu (last accessed August 2013).
[477] W. Merkel and H.-J. Puhle, *Von der Diktatur zur Demokratie*, p. 175.

about the past and the subsequent terror led to a rather weak and fearful civil society that only dared to demand TJ 25 years after Franco's death with a new regime in charge.

Regime change and consolidation in Spain was slow and always showed major flaws and unconsolidated pockets. TJ measures were firstly only slowly implemented and were mainly used to garnish electoral support or when following international pressure. Due to the specific situation of the Spanish transition in 1975 and the strong divide into 'red' and 'white', 'left' and 'right' caused by the Spanish Civil War, political actors could only grant very modest and almost 'silent' TJ measures, such as amnesties and pensions in the first two decades. These were granted as a tactical concession to win over Franco supporters to prevent them from revolting against democratic reforms (which they eventually did anyhow). Fear and mistrust dominated the first two decades of transition, preventing the hundreds of thousands of victimised citizens from demanding reparations, let alone trials or vetting. In the same way, after 1982 and throughout the second decade of transition until the 1990s, TJ measures were used in a haphazard and sporadic way, in a way that resembled the haphazard and sporadic regime consolidation. ETA terror, the GAL's illegal activities and the attempted coup of 1981 were signs of the regime's upward and downward spiral switchbacks throughout the first two decades of regime development (see Figure 2.1). This was all related to the fact that TJ measures were never used as systematic catalytic tools to delegitimise the Franco past and legitimise the new regime – as would be the case with other policies of, for example, economics, education or infrastructure to consolidate a country's regime.

Nevertheless, the cumulative causations between the independent TJ and dependent variable of the consolidation process started in 1977 with the amnesty laws and massive political reforms after the 1978 constitutional referendum. Around the year 2000, large protests were held in Madrid and elsewhere, civil organisations mushroomed and urged the government to fulfil its moral obligation as a democratic government to acknowledge the past. Responding to these demands with TJ was not only strategic, it also contributed to a deeper pluralistic civic culture, which caused the previously slow upward spiral effect between the two variables to increase its speed.

TJ measures and 'dealing with the past' now took place to enhance citizen participation, democratic culture, governmental response, public dialogue and last but not least to slowly reconcile the country and set new political spectra which elections in 2015 have shown. The societal and political divide of the country into left and right is no longer obvious and a much more diverse set of CSOs and political parties contribute to the political agenda.

Without doubt, radical movements and terror on all sides has always slowed down the true behavioural and citizen-driven consolidation process, but once the causes of the Falange and ETA terror were demystified – thanks to public dialogue, forensics, films, novels, media and memorials – the country as a whole became more reconciled with its past and present. Separatism is still high on the political agenda in Spain, and has succeeded in referenda in 2015 in Catalonia to opt for separation, without being executed.

Spain is a case that shows that consolidation can occur even without large-scale vetting or lustration, without trials or commissions of inquiry, and with the lowest level of atonement thinkable, namely by way of amnesty laws, reparations and memorials. However, this low level of TJ often coincides with low-level regime performance and led to many haunting unconsolidated pockets in Spain which have cost many people's lives and hampered vivid participation by society in building a stronger trust in institutions. The fact that up to present times the political parties have difficulties dealing with crises, building coalitions and governing by consent, has its roots in the radical divide of the country and the lack of TJ. In 2016 the country was without an effective government for almost a year because of the incapability to build coalitions after the elections, which in return shed light on an insufficient mature political culture in times of crisis.

5.3   Turkey

In 1989, after decades of authoritarian military rule and pseudo-democracy, Turkey launched major democratic reforms that included TJ measures. High on the agenda was reconciling the very divided and conflict-torn society, although always under the banner of national unity and 'Turkishness'. Turkey applied for full membership to the European Community (later the EU) in 1987, indicating major political and cultural shifts in the country and society. The democratic reforms and the application for EC membership marked a turn away from the repetitive downward spiral of quasi-military, quasi-democratic shadow governments that had ruled the country since the 1950s, after initial attempts to democratise. Regime change and a long-lasting consolidation process could only begin towards the end of the 1980s.[478] Nevertheless, although no successful coup took place after 1989, representative consolidation only took off in and around 2001 and 2002 when the Party for Justice and Progress (*Adalet ve Kalkınma Partisi*, AKP) and its leader Recep Tayyip Erdogan gained a majority in parliament and issued democratic reforms – although he later withdrew or violated many of them. Until then democratisation had been overshadowed by a high level of state violence and a continuous low-intensity war in eastern Anatolia, in particular in the Kurdish territories. Turkey has a long record of human rights violations, abductions, arbitrary killings, disappearances or torture and a high level of corruption and employs highly restrictive measures against civilians, measures that continue today. The three major military coups of 1960, 1971 and 1980, and the attempt in 1997 that led to the government's resignation one last time and the other attempt in 2016 which finally marked the end of any democratic consolidation process and strengthened the power of the newly anticipated presidential autocratic system, increased citizens' reluctance to bring any issue of the past to light and consequently led to a culture of impunity.

Turkey's serious moves towards more democracy in 1989 and in 2002 were only modest and often externally driven shifts. Merkel's terms and level of consolidation best apply in the case of Turkey, highlighting that constitutional, representative, and even to some extent behavioural consolidation, in terms of norms and values, had occurred in the first two decades after reforms started around 1990. However, the massive suppression of civil society started again after 2005 and reached its peak ten years later. After the coup attempt in 2016 and the subsequent state terror and suppression, there was little hope that 'consolidation by civil society' would ever occur.[479] Instead, this time marked the return of the regime into authoritarianism.

But first, Turkey had made significant efforts to democratise since the 1990s. This was first done through its heavy security sector reform, a major TJ tool. It has made a difference in the consolidation process, but was never followed by civil reforms and implementation. Instead, the culture of impunity and violence has dominated Turkish society over decades and was easy to abolish. It constantly re-emerged, despite democratic

---

[478]   K. Öktem, *Angry Nation. Turkey since 1989* (London: Zen Books, 2011).
[479]   W. Merkel, Systemtransformation, *Eine Einführung in die Theorie und Empirie der Transformationsforschung*, p. 111.

reforms. Since the first transition in 1950, no military officials were ever convicted for crimes against civilians.

Turkey's first association agreement with the EC in 1959 and its first bid to join the community in 1963 has underpinned its political will for regime change, but it never materialised until its application for full membership in 1987 and subsequent reforms since 1989. Turkey's membership of the UN in 1945, the Council of Europe in 1949, NATO in 1952 and becoming a signatory to the UN Genocide Convention in 1950, has exposed the country's desire to be part of international alliances and a credible partner for negotiations, even in terms of human rights. Turkey has thus often shown its will for political reforms and has effectuated these reforms, however reluctantly, due to internal and external pressure, but it often failed to maintain and enhance new and fragile democratic institutions.

The country became party to the ECHR in 1954 and accepted the jurisdiction of the ECtHR in 1987 – not coincidentally the same year as its application to the EC/EU – and the possibility of individual claims in 1990. This led many individuals to bring claims and cases for TJ before the ECtHR with subsequent judgments and decisions that Turkey had to obey, leading to more democratic reforms in the years to come. This had an immense impact on the rule of law, and consequently encouraged citizens from other contracting countries, such as Greece and Cyprus, to file claims before the ECtHR for reparations against Turkey. The reforms that took place in Turkey after 1989 have been closely linked to the many ways in which TJ measures have been used to come to terms with the past, and today the country is a parliamentarian democracy with a multi-party system.

Mustafa Kemal Atatürk founded the Turkish Republic in 1923. Reforms in 1946 and 1950 allowed parties other than Atatürk's Republican People's Party (*Cumhuriyet Halk Partisi,* CHP) to participate in elections. Since then, the Turkish democratic process has undergone upward and downward spiral developments in terms of democratic consolidation, if any at all. After periods of liberalisation, periods of restrictions and constraints on freedom, rights followed and vice versa. Only until the time of serious EU accession talks around 2004 did the reforms continue. But despite these reforms the armed forces had always seen themselves as a stronghold of secularism against fundamental Islamic tendencies, and they view secularism as one of the pillars of a guided democracy – a viewpoint which led to another coup attempt in 2016 by these forces.

The specific constitutional privileges for the Turkish military have contributed to what is known as the 'deep state' in Turkey, a state that functions beyond the rule of law and instead depends on the will of one party or one leader. As of today, there is a great interlinking between military, elected government, the legislative branch and the judiciary, all of which ignore laws whenever it suits their interests, in particular when they act against separatist movements, such as those of the Kurdish minority or anti-nationalist groups. For a long time, the goal of all Turkish governments has been to keep the Turkish Republic and what remains of the Ottoman Empire unified at all costs. All governments have used the idea of a great Turkish nation and 'Turkishness' as a proxy ideology to keep the multi-ethnic and politically diverse state together. Keeping the nation unified is the benchmark against which all regime change, let alone consolidation, efforts have to be measured, even though this goal has also been used to justify violent and suppressive measures against citizens. Whenever left-wing, civil or separatist movements have challenged 'Turkishness', thereby also challenging the 'deep state' institutions, their members have suffered repercussions, prosecution, imprisonment and disappearances. That is why victims of the deep state are found all across the political spectrum. A culture of impunity is therefore deeply ingrained in Turkish politics and the level of trust in institutions is far below the international average. When TJ measures slowly started to be implemented, triggered by the government and the international community, these measures were taken up by civil society actors and led to slow increases in civic trust.

Neighbouring countries' demands for reparations or reconciliation date back to World War I and bilateral disputes between Turkey and Greece, Bulgaria, Greek Cyprus and Armenia have endured ever since. These demands are also seen as a threat to authoritarian regime stability (but not consolidation) because they challenge the 'myth of the greatness' of the Turkish nation and therefore also challenge the imposed unity of the multi-ethnic and very diverse and fragile society. But the biggest threat to the governmental grip on people comes from within the country, namely from its large and diverse minority groups and opposition movements, in particular the Kurdish and to some extent other religious minorities. Despite secularism, ethnicity and religion always played a major role in Turkish politics. For centuries minorities questioned the Turkishness and unity of the country, thus posing a major threat to the government's hold on power. As in the Spanish case, the Turkish government fought these movements with anti-democratic and violent means for a long time, without success. Throughout the decades, state institutions have been responsible for a number of gross human rights violations, torture and ill-treatment, illegal killings, disappearances, restrictions of fundamental freedom and using military forces against civilians.

When in the late 1990s TJ measures were finally and formally issued to deal with some aspects of the atrocious past, it was only because they served the tactical interests of the deep state in dealing with the enemies of 'Turkishness'. The rule of law, free and fair elections, a pluralist party system and broad civil participation (beyond state control) were always seen as threats to the unity of the country.

Today Turkey's anti-democratic tradition and disrespect for minority rights date back to the early 1920s in the 1923 Treaty of Lausanne. This treaty was negotiated after decades of internal and external wars that unsuccessfully tried to prevent the decay of the Ottoman Empire; its unity was seen as more important than active participation of minorities or citizens. Turkey (then the Ottoman Empire) was allied with Germany and Austria-Hungary in World War I, but stayed mostly neutral in World War II. The collapse of the Ottoman Empire and the following periods of war, gave rise to Turkish nationalism. This movement's main motivation was to preserve what was left of the country's territory and integrity. The Ottoman Empire had diminished to less than one-third of its former size. This dramatic reduction in size helps explain why the idea of 'Turkishness' and unity is so important in Turkish politics today. Turkey lost 85 per cent of its territory and approximately 75 per cent of its population after World War I. The Turkish military leadership used these facts to attempt to justify any means necessary to preserve Turkey's unity as much as possible, even though ethnic cleansing and other forms of atrocities, state terror and crimes were eventually used with this aim. Since the first shift in political power in 1950 to a government that committed itself to democracy but which was overthrown in 1961, the atrocious past of the Ottoman Empire has haunted Turkish politics. Elections were held prior to 1950, but with Mustafa Kemal Atatürk's CHP party being the only party until 1946, a serious shift towards democracy was impossible. It was only in 1950 that a power shift took place. In this year, the newly introduced multi-party system allowed the new Democratic Party (*Demokrat Parti*, DP) to take office. This party had been founded in 1946 as a 'democratic response' to the CHP. The party leadership aimed for democratic transition but did not succeed. Cold War politics were already on the horizon and Turkey provided a geopolitical security guarantee against the communist Eastern Europe.[480] This caused the window of opportunity for democratisation to soon close.

Nevertheless, in 1950 the legislature launched democratic reforms and made a clear commitment to democracy. The DP received over 50 per cent of the votes cast in the election. It stayed in power for a considerable time and led the political and modest democratic reforms until 1961, when the CHP regained power. During this first decade, several massacres and atrocities against Kurdish or Greek orthodox groups were committed by the military in the name of 'Turkishness'. Violence has a long tradition in Turkey and the genocide against the Christian Armenian minority during World War I; the looting of Kurdish villages in the 1930s; the pogroms and expulsion of Greeks in the 1930s; and the September 1955 pogroms in Izmir (Smyrna) and Istanbul against the Greek community, haunted every successor government and caused further state-driven crimes and massacres throughout the upcoming decades. This vicious cycle and dark past certainly determined the way regime change progressed (or not) and more so consolidation. TJ measures were seen as one possibility to break the vicious cycle of violence, suppression and vengeance. This is why TJ measures more than ever were seen by each government as tools and threats at the same time by the government during the brief period of representative and behavioural consolidation around 2005.

Today, democratic flaws and unconsolidated pockets are somewhat related to the fact that the country never really came to terms with the past of the Ottoman Empire and first Turkish Republic. The war crime most well known outside Turkey is without doubt the Armenian Genocide; an atrocity that remains largely unatoned for. During World War I, the Ottoman Empire under Sultan Mehmed V passed the deportation law of 1915 (*Tehcir* law). This law ordered the 'evacuation' of minorities such as the Armenians from the territory because they were suspected of collaborating with the Russian enemy and were hostile to the internal stability of the Ottoman Empire. The 'evacuation' eventually led to large-scale and uncontrolled killings and persecution of minorities of all kinds and finally to genocide. Kurds, Assyrians, Armenians, Christians and Azeris became victims of executions, deportations and

---

[480] I. Turan, *Turkey's Difficult Journey to Democracy: Two Steps Forward, One Step Back* (Oxford: Oxford University Press, 2015).

starvation on a massive scale under the law. The governments at that time aimed to regulate with it the so-called 'settlements' of Armenians and other minorities by relocating them to other places in the Ottoman Empire, which in effect meant the Syrian desert (which was then part of the Empire), where hundreds of thousands of Armenians died. The law emphasised that those deported should not be harmed and their property should be returned after the war. Many years later, the deportations, starvations, massacres and systematic killings of 1915 and subsequent years were classified as genocide, in accordance with the 1948 UN Convention on Genocide. The Ottoman Empire abolished the deportation law in 1916 because the many arbitrary, 'non-regulated' killings and acts of revenge that it caused had destabilised the region and the empire. However, the military and civilians continued to perpetrate massacres and violent deportations. The genocide only ended around 1918, after Turkey surrendered to Allied forces. After World War I, and under the new Sultan Mehmed VI, what was left of the Ottoman Empire affirmed its obligation to come to terms with war criminals in the Sultan's army who had already been denounced for arbitrary killings against civilians, mainly Armenians and Assyrians. In Istanbul, the Allied coalition pushed for trials. The court martials of generals and representatives of Sultan Mehmed who had been allegedly involved in the massacres and deportations of hundreds of thousands of Armenians, Kurds, Assyrians and Greeks were later transferred to Malta. The tribunals were promised by the Allied powers with the consent of the new government in Istanbul (capital of the Ottoman Empire at that time) to be held at the Paris Peace Conference between 1918 and 1920, but this never happened. Later, Article 226 to 230 of the 1920 Treaty of Sèvres between the Sultan and the Entente (Russia, France and Great Britain), confirmed that those responsible for war crimes should be put on trial – but these trials were largely suspended.

   The two Armenian and Turkish historians Vahakn Dadrian and Tanar Akcam described in detail how the opponents of the Sultanate regime launched these political but punitive tribunals to dismantle the Sultan's regime. However, there was not enough external pressure to lead to the success of these trials and no CSO or organised victim groups that could pressure from below. At times, the western entente was more interested in delegitimising the Sultan and carving up the Ottoman Empire than in punishing war criminals. These trials, if they accomplished anything, only provided victor's justice. They did not achieve reconciliation between

346 REGIME CONSOLIDATION AND TRANSITIONAL JUSTICE

the divided factions in Turkish society, let alone between Turkey and its former enemies.[481]

At most, the successor interim government run by the liberal Freedom and Coalition Party revised the Sultan's policies of the war. It encouraged deported Armenians who had survived to return to the Turkish mainland. Further, the interim government offered TJ measures in the form of relief to orphans and destitute villages, at least acknowledging the wrongdoings of World War I. Evidence given at trial in eyewitness reports from soldiers, politicians and Islamic clerics identified some of the past atrocities in detail. This led to the condemnation of the previous government's systematic annihilation (*imha*) of the Ottoman Armenians. Those responsible for this were sentenced to death in absentia. Although the sentences were never carried out because the perpetrators escaped (many of them to Germany, Turkey's ally in World War I) and little effort was made to bring them back to Turkey, some of them later became victims of individual vengeance and killings. Without international law being in place, judgments with effective consequences for perpetrators were not to be expected at that time.[482] The fact that the later Turkish government denied that a genocide had ever occurred in Turkey had to do with the political situation at that time, in which the matters of the past were not the most urgent problems to solve and were seen as a serious threat to unity.

Due to the chaos of the post-war struggles in the region and the ongoing massacres against the Armenian, Assyrian and Kurdish minorities, there was no serious chance for trials and prosecution. Non-ratified treaties and non-completed trials left it unclear whether the military or the successor government of the Empire would accept any responsibility for the war crimes committed by the predecessor state. When Kemal Atatürk came into power in 1923, he condemned the deportation of minorities but at the same time continued to discriminate against and expel members of the Greek, Armenian or Assyrian communities, but did not accept that the new Turkish Republic held any responsibility for war crimes committed under the Ottoman Empire. Needless to say, at

---

[481] For a good overview of the political developments in Turkey since 1923, see: S. Kredourie, *Turkey: Identity, Democracy, Politics* (Routledge, 2014); and I. Turan, *Turkey's Difficult Journey to Democracy*; and A.R. Usul, *Democracy in Turkey: The Impact of EU Political Conditionality* (London: Routledge, 2010).

[482] V.N. Dadrian and T. Akçam, *Judgement at Istanbul. The Armenian Genocide Trials* (New York: Berghahn Books, 2011).

that time there were no international institutions or legal mechanisms to execute international jurisdiction and no monitoring mechanisms such as the UN or EU that could have put pressure on the country in order to implement the court decisions. In this way, the Turkish situation differed from that of post-war Germany, in which the Nuremberg trials were held and the sentences enforced under Allied pressure. It was entirely up to the goodwill of the Turkish government to implement domestic and internal TJ procedures, or to grant reparations, restitution or other forms of acknowledgement of past crimes.[483] The new government used the TJ tribunal to delegitimise the previous government, but never intended the tribunal to bring about reconciliation with the victims.[484]

The 1923 Treaty of Lausanne, as well as various other treaties, caused the Ottoman Empire to lose most of its territory, leading to a fate similar to Germany's Weimar Republic. In order to overcome the harsh conditions and the humiliation of the treaties, Atatürk founded the first Turkish Republic. His aim was to recover as much territory and Turkish unity as possible. Any separatist intentions, for example from the Kurdish or Yezidi minorities, threatened this unity. The Treaty of Lausanne also gave rights to non-Muslims, mainly Christian and Armenian minorities in Turkey, hoping that this would safeguard them. After Atatürk's death in 1938, a new power structure came into place that made democratic reforms more possible. In 1946 a pluralistic party regime was introduced and in 1950 a non-CHP party was elected for the first time. Due to restrictive national legislation, it has been impossible to bring them to trial or to have a public debate. The lawyers of victims or human rights activists who attempted to bring those responsible to trial often faced severe repercussions, were sentenced to prison or fled into exile.[485]

But why do I mention the events of World War I and Atatürk's rise in detail? Because for the assessment of whether TJ measures have any

---

[483]   I. Turan, *Turkey's Difficult Journey to Democracy*, pp. 33–60.
[484]   As a consequence of continuing hostilities between Turkey and the Armenians, the Armenian Republic was established in 1920 to host those who had survived the genocide and to separate them from the Ottoman Empire. This was a result of the Treaty of Sèvres, which was never ratified by the Ottoman parliament or by the Turkish Republic, but with which the victorious states sought to resettle the citizens of the Ottoman Empire. Armenia was soon annexed by the Soviet Union and this association hampered Armenia from holding any legal or political claims against Turkey.
[485]   S. Kredourie, *Turkey: Identity, Democracy, Politics*.

influence on consolidation, even decades after massacres and injustice happened, one has to know why these measures failed in the first place and became a haunting shadow for the consolidation process in Turkey a century later. In the tradition of Atatürk's policies, the Turkish democratic institutions continued their aim to establish a secular state-based Turkishness, which aimed to lead to more democracy. Although nationalism turning into fascism was common at that time in many European countries, this nationalism remained a feature of Turkey's politics even after other European countries had distanced themselves from it, for example during the third wave of democratisation in the 1970s.[486] As one of the last authoritarian governed countries in Europe, Turkey has justified many of its cruel and anti-democratic activities as being in the best interests of the Turkish nation, regardless of how much suffering they might cause. Nationalists have since used Atatürk as a figure of integration and have given him an almost divine status. Up to the present day, Atatürk's portrait hangs in every office, school and cafeteria in the country, showing that the owner of that office or cafeteria is not against Turkishness and to ward off interference from the Turkish secret police. The day that these portraits are restricted to museums, where they belong in a fully fledged democracy, will be the day on which Turkey finally embraces the rule of law and makes its way to democratic consolidation. But with such extreme nationalism there is no room for pluralistic or multi-ethnic and religious ideas and thus no way for democratic practice. As Kemal Cengiz, president of the Turkish Human Rights Agenda Association (HRAA), points out, 'Turkish identity is based on its atrocities in injustice against minorities and others' and thus it is upheld only by suppression of others.[487] This is one of the many reasons why both democratic and pluralistic practises, as well as TJ measures, are seen as a threat to unity. TJ measures were only used if they served the one goal of all governments and political parties: a unified Turkish nation. Anything that could shatter the nationalistic unity is viewed with great scepticism. Around the year 2000 it became clear that this Turkish unity could not be maintained with nationalistic views only, let alone by force and fear, and this was the time when TJ measures also took off – bearing in mind the upcoming accession talks with the EU in and around 2005 and worldwide rise of TJ measures as a means of transition and transformation at that time.

---

[486] P. Ther, *Die dunkle Seite der Nationalstaaten. Ethnishe säuberungen im modern Europa* (Göttingen: Vandenhoek and Ruprecht, 2011).
[487] Interview with Orhan Kemal Cengiz, Ankara, 20 April 2011.

The Haunting Coup D'états

To better understand Turkey's non-consolidation process, the successful and unsuccessful coups are landmarks in this process. They are irreversible landmarks for TJ efforts, too. The military coup d'état in May 1960 led not only to the regaining of secular powers, but also to a change in the constitution. The military opposed the re-election of the DP and imposed new elections, which Atatürk's Republican People's Party won, signifying a shift in politics. The Turkish Armed Forces (TAF) often imposed death sentences after military coup d'états. One example is Adnan Menderes, who had served as prime minister and was later hanged on 17 September 1961 for treason following the coup d'état, along with two other cabinet members, Fatin Rüştü Zorlu and Hasan Polatkan.

A second coup d'état occurred a decade later, on 12 March 1971. The government under president Demirel was forced to resign after the commanders of the TAF issued an ultimatum to the president. Turkey's military leaders asserted the urgent need for a 'strong and capable government' that could redress the 'anarchical situation' in the country and demanded a new government. Refusing to accept this demand, they warned, would result in the armed forces taking over the administration of the country. The decision by the military high command to impose its will on the government followed three years of political violence and growing economic problems.

The years that followed were seen as a period of 'guided democracy', meaning that democratic powers could only move within the boundaries set by the TAF and the military aristocratic elites of the country. It turned into what was known as the 'deep state'. In the year after the coup, many alleged leftists, in particular students and intellectuals, such as the student leaders Deniz Gezmiş, Hüseyin İnan and Yusuf Aslan, were indicted, sentenced to death and hanged.[488]

Another aspect of Turkey's past that it has not adequately dealt with is its relationship with Greece and the possible reunification of Greek and Turkish Cyprus. The Turkish military invaded Cyprus in 1974 (upon provocation by the Cypriot Patriarch and the Greek government against the ethnic Turkish minority in Cyprus), forcefully dividing the island into its current split state. Forced evictions, the slaughter of men and many other severe crimes and atrocities were conducted by both parties during

---

[488] I. Turan, *Turkey's Difficult Journey to Democracy*, pp. 98–113.

the war. For mainland Turkey it meant that the years that followed were dominated by state terror and violence and there is little clarity about the crimes committed by the TAF or police inside Turkish territory, such as the massacre of labour unionists in Istanbul on 1 May 1977; the imprisonment and killing of young leftist students in 1978; the massacres of the Alevi towns Maras, Corum and Sivas; and many other unresolved state murders during the 1970s. Those who rebelled and demanded more liberty and democracy were seen as a threat to the Turkish nation state and were accused of being socialist radicals. As a result, TAF martial law took over almost every ten years.[489]

The third major coup d'état took place on 12 September 1980, with amnesty laws following for those generals and military officials who committed it. This was without doubt another victory for impunity. Between 1980 and 1984, a total of 50 people including 27 political prisoners were executed in Turkey, all of them alleged leftist and socialists. The date of 12 September 1980 has become one of the most traumatic in the common Turkish narrative.[490] Similarly to the attempted coup in Spain in 1981, this coup d'état showed the Turkish people the fragility of the regime and the strength of the military. Citizens had hoped for more democratic reforms in the 1980s, triggered by the changes and democratisation processes in their neighbouring countries in southern Europe and other parts of the world. They soon realised that this hope was in vain as many democratic reforms came to a standstill until Turkey's official application to the EC in 1987. The year of 1987 and subsequently 1989, when the application was accepted, are recognised as milestone years for regime consolidation.[491]

The country had to do more than just show willingness to reform its government; it also had to implement reforms and seek international acknowledgement. Turkey's unatoned for past haunted all regime change and consolidation efforts and often led to the return to an even more authoritarian regime, and maintained this character for most of its existence, as has been described by O'Donnell and Schmitter.[492]

Nevertheless, in the late 1980s, parallel to the emerging regime changes in Eastern Europe and South America, the Turkish government showed

---

[489]   F. Ahmad, 'Military and Politics in Turkey' in C. Kerslake, K. Öktem and P. Robins (eds.), *Turkey's Engagement with Modernity. Conflict and Change in the Twentieth Century* (London: Palgrave Macmillan, 2010), pp. 92–116.

[490]   I. Turan, *Turkey's Difficult Journey to Democracy*, pp. 113–115.

[491]   A.R. Usul, *Democracy in Turkey: The Impact of EU Political Conditionality*.

[492]   G. O'Donnell, P. Schmitter and L. Whitehead, *Transition from Authori-tarian Rule. Southern Europe*.

some indications of major reforms. Internal and external pressure from the Council of Europe has made Turkey refrain from executing any prisoners since October 1984. But only in 2004 did Turkey reluctantly abolish the death penalty to fulfil the EU Copenhagen criteria prior to EU accession talks.[493]

Nevertheless, and parallel to these signs of goodwill, in the years since 1984 the Turkish army has increased its presence in eastern Anatolia and has intensified its suppression of the Kurds, thus showing strong authoritarian tendencies. Allegations of disappearances, ill-treatment, torture, and arbitrary imprisonment, killings, bombing of Kurdish villages, and severe suppression and even deprivation of citizenship rights in the Kurdish enclave, still remain unaddressed. Hundreds of thousands of Kurds have been displaced or have fled the country, forming a strong Kurdish diaspora coalition in western Europe, particularly in Germany and Sweden. Eventually, this coalition came to exert significant pressure on the Turkish government. It soon became evident that 'guided democracy' would only fuel the vicious circle of violence, suppression and a low-intensity war against the Kurdish population. This approach was far from even triggering a serious transition to democracy. Since then, over 45,000 deaths on all sides have been reported and the government has had to change its approach.

But interestingly enough, the internal and external claims that pressured the governments into responding to Kurdish interests and demands have opened the door to regime consolidation. As Lauren McLaren has argued, in the case of Turkey, like in Spain, there is a low level of civil engagement in politics. While this might speed up consolidation because consensus has to be achieved among fewer groups,[494] the question is how solid the consensual grounds can be if they fail to include all citizens and, in particular, the new young intellectual elite such as students.

In Turkey, as in the other case studies, politicians primarily use TJ measures for strategic and tactical purposes. In 1986, a Greek-Turkish initiative for reconciliation was founded, and later in 1999 Greece sent humanitarian aid for the earthquake victims in Turkey as a sign of its willingness to reconcile.[495] It was positively received throughout the country

---

[493] M. Emerson, *Has Turkey Fulfilled the Copenhagen Political Criteria?* Center for European Policy Studies (CEPS Policy Brief No. 48, April 2004).

[494] L.M. McLaren, *Constructing Democracy in Southern Europe. A Comparative Analysis of Italy, Spain and Turkey* (New York/London: Routledge, 2010), p. 137.

[495] U. Üngör, *The Making of Modern Turkey* (Oxford: Oxford University Press, 2011).

and was a welcome first step towards reconciliation after decades of hostility and mistrust. Prior to the founding of the Turkish Republic, both countries had been at war with each other since Greece started its battle for independence from the Ottoman Empire in 1830. The culminating point was the Greco-Turkish War from 1919 to 1922. Both sides committed a large number of atrocities, ethnic cleansings and war crimes. By 1923, more than 1.5 million Greeks left Turkish territory in exchange for over half a million ethnic Turks leaving Greece. This was confirmed in an official agreement on resettlement between the two countries and was meant to be a legal solution. Ever since, ongoing disputes regarding this territory and the Aegean Sea have affected diplomatic ties and relationships. Nevertheless, it has been a priority for both governments to normalise their relations. In 1941, Turkey sent humanitarian aid to relieve the great famine in Athens, but pogroms against the Greek minority in Turkey continued until the 1960s. The most severe one took place in 1955 in Istanbul, when houses belonging to non-Muslims were destroyed. It was organised by a semi-legal and ultra-nationalist Special Warfare Command, which had earlier spread the incorrect message that Atatürk's native house in Thessaloniki in Greece had been attacked. With the semi-divine status that he enjoys in Turkey, it was easy to mobilise hundreds of volunteers who looted and killed non-Muslims, mainly Greeks as an act of revenge.[496] But as an act of TJ on both sides, today Atatürk's birthplace is a museum that attracts thousands of Turkish tourists every year and is supported by Greek authorities as an act of reconciliation between the two countries.

In recent years, Turkey's democratic experiment faced many challenges, and by 2015 the country is only ranked 69th out of 113 countries in terms of quality of democracy, accountability, transparency and participation of its citizens, fair and free elections, freedom of the press and NGOs.[497] And in July 2016, after decades of political improvements, there was another alleged coup attempt by the Turkish military – once more presuming to be the guardian of secularism and security in the country. President Erdogan responded to the coup with massive restrictions of freedom rights, mass imprisonment of political opponents and accusations of a conspiracy by the Fethullah Gülen movement and in particular the Kurdish parties. The

[496] Young Civilians and Human Rights Agenda Association (HRAA) (ed.), *Ergenekon Is Our Reality* (Ankara: HRAA, 2010), p. 6.
[497] The Democracy Ranking Association, Quality of Democracy Ranking 2015, see: www.democracyranking.org/wordpress/welcome/about-us/ (last accessed July 2016).

rule of law, free election and freedom of media and press, plus the war in Syria on the Turkish border, make it almost impossible for TJ activists, let alone Kurdish victim groups, to act freely and in cooperation with political institutions to strengthen the consolidation process.[498]

The Long Way to Democracy

Since 1989, Turkey has undertaken constitutional and legislative reforms and after the political shift to the AKP in 2001 and further elections in 2002, 2008 and 2010, many of these democratic reforms were partly or fully restricted again. They have introduced recognition of minority rights and religious freedom, and later paved the way for fairer trials and the ability to bring claims against perpetrators without suffering immediate repercussions by state forces. In the 2010 referendum on the constitution, the protection and quasi-amnesty for coup leaders was abolished, which opened up the way to trials against the military. The first round of trials, also known as the Ergenekon trials, ended in 2013 and there was another round in 2014 under dubious circumstances.[499] More trials against political enemies of Erdogan's AKP continued in 2016.

The mysterious Ergenekon group allegedly consists of over 100 generals, lawyers, National Security Council (MGK) members, party members and members of the gendarmerie's secret anti-terrorist organisation (*Jandarma İstihbarat ve Terörle Mücadele*, JITEM). The AKP government has driven these trials, while intellectuals and journalists who have tried to investigate the Ergenekon group and its trials were put in custody and convicted to long sentences in 2013. The group was accused of planning a coup d'état in 2007, also known as the sledgehammer (*Balyoz*) plan, which according to the allegations had been carefully planned since the AKP and Prime Minister Erdogan took office in 2002. The members of this group allegedly resumed the activities of the 'deep state'. Some of its members have been held responsible for killings of non-Muslim groups, such as Christian missionaries in Malatya, Turkey, in 2007 or the Armenian journalist Hrant Dink in 2007. Others, such as members of the secret service JITEM, have been indicted for operating as counter-guerrilla forces against the state whenever nationalist interests are at stake, such as cooperating with the Turkish Resistance Organisation in Northern Cyprus or

[498] Turkey's coup attempt, *The Guardian*, theguardian.com/world/turkey-coup-attempt (last accessed August 2016)
[499] U. Ungör, *The Making of Modern Turkey*.

acting against Alevi Kurds and Muslim Kurds in eastern Anatolia. Close ties to the Sursuluk case in 1996 and earlier coup d'états in 1971, 1980 and 1997 were investigated but with few sentences. The trials against the Ergenekon group have been called 'century trials', and in a way it was an exclusive TJ effort to deal with the past – followed by political repressions and persecutions. The trials were not based on the rule of law, let alone on international human rights standards. Instead, they were entirely politically motivated and thus a sign of autocratic consolidation in recent years.[500] Many observers classified them as political trials during which Erdogan 'cleansed himself' of military, secular and political opponents, instead of the other way round. This has led to heavy public protest of the use of this particular judicial TJ tool which was misused to purge Erdogan's political opponents and thus undermine democracy[501], and thus lead to the claim that as long as the rule of law cannot be halfway guaranteed, trials might not be the best of all TJ measures to install.

The constitutional referendum in 2010 was only the beginning of more constitutional and penal reforms but not democratic consolidation. On the one hand, the government argued that it had to make reforms to comply with EU norms, while on the other hand it faced pressure from domestic political opposition and pressure groups to undertake the necessary reforms.

Turkey's long process to regime consolidation is not exceptional, and therefore serves as an ideal test case in comparison to Germany and Spain. In Turkey, the executive, legislature and judiciary only respond to civil society's expectations of TJ if doing so serves a strategic political objective just as it did in Germany and Spain in the earlier years of transition. The governing AKP, which has been in power for over a decade since 2002, knows that EU integration can strengthen the country's geopolitical leadership role in the region and can make Turkey a legitimate and stronger partner for other allies such as NATO, IMF or the EU, but at the same time active and full membership in these organisations and overall in the EU are reciprocal. Later it would mean that Erdogan could not go on with his autocratic governance style, turning the country back into a dictatorship.

But first, for reasons of domestic stability and EU membership talks, the AKP government was always ready to respond to TJ claims to show

[500] Young Civilians and Human Rights Agenda Association (HRAA) (ed.), *Ergenekon is our Reality*, p. 24.
[501] I. Turan, *Turkey's Difficult Journey to Democracy*, pp. 175–195.

its commitment to the ongoing reforms – however half-hearted or strategic they may have been. This reform increased the number of private enterprises and thus provided access to political resources by citizens who had been excluded from the political process for generations, such as the Kurdish minority. It created new social elites that later exerted pressure in favour of maintaining ties with the EU and speeding up democratic reforms. However, despite these legal, political and economic reforms, the government knew that it had to settle the disputes with its neighbouring countries as well as within and among its own citizens. In fact, bearing in mind that some forms of protest and demands were only possible after 1989, the citizen-driven and externally pushed TJ process has gone rather rapidly.

Yet attempts to reckon with the past and with disappearances can be penalised under obscure and politically motivated articles in the penal code, particularly if the attempts can be framed as threatening Turkish unity. Access to justice, fair and independent trials and judges are not guaranteed in Turkey. Under the notorious Article 301 of the Turkish Criminal Code (effective since 2005), anyone who questions the Turkish nation and Turkishness can be punished. Merely calling the atrocities against the Armenian population 'genocide' is a crime under this article. A number of other provisions in the Criminal Code restrict freedom of expression, particularly in respect of offences against dignity (for example Articles 125–131). There was also a self-imposed prohibition by authorities on questioning the role of the military or pressuring them to take any responsibility for the country's past. These articles have intimidated many citizens over the decades, preventing them from questioning past or present wrongdoings. International organisations and observers have long demanded the abolishment of these articles.[502]

Democracy has thus always been weak if not absent in Turkey. Reauthorisation of the regime has taken place since around 2010 and the following years, culminating in the 2015 and 2016 presidential reforms, elections and alleged coup. According to the Bertelsmann Transformation Index (BTI), the country has since its first initial efforts around 2002 again declined over subsequent years. Out of all the 128 transition countries ranked in the BTI (not including any consolidated democracies), Turkey is number 20, with fairly solid democratic

---

[502] Parliamentary Assembly of the Council of Europe, *In the Aftermath of Hrant Dink's Murder*, Doc. 11187, 20 February 2007.

institutions scoring 8.0 out of 10.0 in 2012 but declining dramatically thereafter. Milestones in transition are the political reforms of 1999, the elections in 2002, the EU accession talks in 2005 and the subsequent democratic reforms that first increased the civil liberties and the number of CSOs – which then were massively restricted around 2015 due to anti-terror laws and the war in Syria. Thus, 20 years after its commitment to democracy, there is some evidence of an emerging democratic culture, similar to what the situation was in Germany and Spain 20 years after regime change. Yet Turkey's unconsolidated pockets of terrorist, separatist or other excluded groups are larger and more severe than the ones either Germany or Spain had to deal with. They mainly lie in eastern Anatolia and have to do with the unatoned past atrocities against the Kurdish minority. Therefore, Islamists, liberalists and ultra-nationalists oppose each other, sometimes with illegal means.[503] Nevertheless, citizens' movements and CSOs enjoy high levels of support and have succeeded in bringing about legislative changes, such as reforms concerning the Kurdish minorities, but there is still considerable resistance.[504] Similar to the BTI, the Polity IV Project Index ranks Turkey as a stable but not consolidated democratic regime because of its major democratic flaws, corruption, violence and re-emergence of a low-intensity war in the eastern part of the country since 2015. This index also confirms that the years since 1989 have been a major turning point in democratisation and regime change, but not for democratic consolidation. This provides justification for starting this assessment around 1989.[505] Because the regime is in its third decade of transformation and thus passed the 20+ generation – and not surprisingly faced major challenges between new and old elites – it lacks legitimacy and scores rather low in terms of effectiveness and responsiveness.[506]

First Decade 1990–1999

Turkey's first official accession application to the EC in 1985 was followed by an initial deferral, but the EC Member States continued to encourage

[503] S. Kredourie, *Turkey: Identity, Democracy, Politics.*
[504] Bertlesmann Transformation Index 2012, Turkey Country Report, BTI, Gütersloh 2012 www.bti-project.org (last accessed September 2014), p. 27.
[505] Polity IV Project, Turkey Authority Trends 1946–2010, Center for Systematic Peace, systemicpeace.org/polity (last accessed August 2013).
[506] M.G. Marshall and B.R. Cole, Global Report 2011, State Fragility Index and Matrix 2010. Center for Systematic Peace. www.systemicpeace.org/polity (last accessed August 2013), p. 3.

Turkey with its efforts to meet European standards and – interestingly enough – to settle matters with Armenia, Greece and Cyprus.[507] In 1989, the EC accepted Turkey's revised application from 1987 under the condition of re-establishing diplomatic ties with its neighbouring countries and slowly introducing TJ measures. The year 1989 was not only a turning point for central European history and regime change in the east, but also for Turkey. Turkey's path to regime consolidation cannot be seen independently from the developments in the rest of Europe or the Middle East. In the same year, the first private TV channel was allowed to broadcast in Turkey and Turgut Özal became the first non-military president of the republic. As Krem Öktem has noted, a period of proactive foreign policies finally began, which was fundamentally important for the process of regime consolidation.[508] These new policies would soon encourage various stakeholders and civil society actors to pressure for more TJ. The reasons for this pressure were multiple: first, the EC did not want to accept a country that was still in a 'war-like' situation with other member countries, such as Greece and later Greek Cyprus (which joined the EU in 2004), or with a country that had closed its borders and kept no diplomatic ties with a neighbouring country, such as Armenia. Second, Turkey's tense relationship with Armenia was due to unsettled accounts from the so-called 'events of 1915' (*1915 olaylari*), the Turkish government's official name for the Armenian Genocide. Turkey's official position was that these 'events' arose from inter-communal strife during World War I and it was not a genocide and therefore was not to be atoned for. Whereas Turkey counted an approximate 300,000 deaths, disappeared, exiled or wounded Armenians, the Armenian version is that 1.5 million people were killed in a planned genocide. Since the 1980s, the Turkish government has been searching for a way to defend and explain the atrocities of World War I to internal and external audiences, and in particular to the United States, the country that has exerted the most pressure on Turkey. The right hand of the TAF-led government, the military National Security Council (MGK), designed the official 'no-genocide' doctrine and governmental position on 'the events of 1915'. The MGK held that Armenians had always been treated well in the Ottoman Empire and in Turkey, but because some of them had collaborated with the Russian enemy during World War I, they were expelled and evacuated from their homes and lands to the Syrian

---

[507] K. Öktem, *Angry Nation*.
[508] Ibid., pp. 82 and 219.

dessert, where around 300,000 of them 'unfortunately' perished.[509] This has become the official doctrine and the answer to all TJ demands by Armenia and has caused ongoing tension between the two governments and citizens.

But eventually, the correlating and cumulative causal effect between TJ and regime consolidations took off in the 1990s.[510] In debates in the European Parliament, delegates recommended that Turkey acknowledge the Armenian Genocide and suggested making it a formal criterion for Turkey's EC candidacy, thus bringing TJ and democratic reforms on the agenda.[511] Although initially an official governmental commitment to democracy and human rights norms was enough to pursue the accession talks in the years to come.[512] But despite the official doctrine and politics, soft internal and external pressure showed consequences. Even though the Turkish government denied any involvement in genocide it did make concessions. In the following years it ratified more human rights treaties, which in turn led to more activism by human rights and NGOs, particularly Kurdish ones, demanding not only better treatment and justice but also TJ measures in general.[513]

In 1992, shortly after the government's official commitment to carefully reconsider its doctrine on past atrocities, the first government-certified book on the 'Armenian issue' was published in Turkish. This book addressed a wide public and attempted to justify the official governmental position on the events of 1915 – largely denying, of course, that the evacuation of Armenians between 1915 and 1918 came anything close to a systematic organised genocide.[514] It pre-emptively addressed the expected demands from Armenians and others to deal with the 'G' word (genocide). At that time, it was forbidden to refer to the Armenian issue

---

[509]   J.M. Dixon, 'Defending the Nation? Maintaining Turkey's Narrative of the Armenian Genocide' in A. Costa Pino and L. Morlino (eds.), *Dealing with the Legacy of Authoritarianism: The 'Politics of the Past' in Southern European Democracies* (New York/London: Routledge, 2010), pp. 125–143.

[510]   K. Öktem, *Angry Nation.*

[511]   B. Seyhan, *Politik und Erinnerung. Der Völkermord an den Armenien* (Bielefeld: Transcript Verlag, 2010).

[512]   Parliamentary Assembly of the Council of Europe, Written Declaration No. 147, on Democracy and Human Rights in Turkey, Doc. 5690, Strasbourg, 28 January 1987.

[513]   F. Türkmen, 'Turkey's Participation in Global and Regional Human Rights Regime' in Z.F. Kabasakal Arat (ed.), *Human Rights in Turkey* (Philadelphia, PA: University of Pennsylvania, 2007), p. 252.

[514]   T. Akcam, *Turkish National Identity and the Armenian Question* (Istanbul: Iletisim Yayinlari, 1992).

using that word. The government realised that if it was to use violence as a means to silence issues of the past, it had to act proactively against the idea that the atrocities of the past qualified as genocide.

In the early period of regime change, Ankara only reacted to these demands by denying them. And despite the political reforms violence and suppression against opposition continued and so did the war against the Kurds. Because the peace attempts by the government to come to an accord with the PKK did not succeed at that time, an alleged coup attempt – along with mysterious killings and massacres – took place in 1993, launched by the military with the aim of pressuring the government to find solutions to the problem. But instead of using TJ measures to partly respond to the claims by the Kurdish community and CSOs, denial about past and present atrocities and war crimes was the official doctrine at the time. As a consequence, another issue from the past made it onto the political agenda that served to pressure the government to reconsider its harsh position: the Cyprus issue. In 1995, the ECtHR ruled against Turkey for the first time on cases of ill-treatment and property issues in Cyprus. In the subsequent years, a total of several thousand cases were lodged against Turkey. Since then, the ECtHR has ruled on between 100 and 300 cases per year relating to Turkey's human rights policy. The government responded to this by highlighting the importance of human rights, such as the right to freedom of assembly or freedom of expression. At the same time the government used TJ measures to respond when the ECtHR ordered compensation for torture victims or when dealing with property rights in Cyprus and of other minorities in Turkey. Turkey saw itself as a rising geopolitical player in the region, taking on responsibility in NATO and other international organisations such as the OSCE. Turkey reacted to external pressure when the country achieved a tactical or strategic advantage in its geopolitical activities. At the same time, internal pressure grew slowly but steadily.[515]

Also in 1995, the ECtHR ruled against Turkey in matters of property rights and compensations, and the European Parliament awarded the EU's human rights Sakharov Prize to Leyla Zana, a Kurdish human rights activist and politician who has continuously suffered imprisonment and intimidation from the government. In choosing this recipient for the prize, the European Parliament sent a clear message to Turkey to address its past. In response, the Turkish parliament launched a study on

---

[515] K. Öktem, *Angry Nation*, p. 76.

the disappearances and victims of the war in eastern Anatolia – although rather than going public, it was instead intended to please the EU delegations at that time. Due to fear that it would lead to more claims for redress, this did not result in further consequences or public debate.[516] The Turkish parliament's response served the sole purpose of placating the international community.

During the further pre-accession talks with the EC in the mid-1990s, the number of domestic trials on torture and state violence increased, although the trials regularly failed to result in convictions.[517] The EC/EU and the Council of Europe supported media reforms in Turkey, which led to an increase in publications by governmental think tanks, parliamentary commissions and other official sources on unsettled past issues such as the Armenian Genocide, although these publications were controlled by the state. The government had one objective: disseminating its own version of what happened in the past which left little room for different opinions or independent research. Independent academic or historical research was not welcome and archives and records were only opened to a selective number of researchers loyal to the government.[518] The government realised that in this period debates on the past were mainly held at an intellectual and elite level, often only outside the country in international forums. Therefore, the Turkish government counteracted any allegations of past injustices with state-friendly publications that were often intentionally translated into English in order to target the international critical audience. Not surprisingly, the government could not stop independent research and dialogue, but the government was hoping to at least delay the process of free and open debates. It was, however, unsuccessful and the evidence of massacres, deportations, torture and killings inside the country was so prevalent that the government's efforts in this respect stopped at some stage. Millions of victims wanted to talk.

On 3 November 1996, government officials and members of the JITEM were involved in an arranged car accident in Susurluk – killing government officials and an ultra-right-wing businessman, most of whom were involved in the drugs trade. The subsequent trial against government

---

[516] D. Kurban, *Reparation and Displacement in Turkey, Lessons Learned from the Compensation Law, Case Studies on Transitional Justice and Displacement*, Brookings-LSE Project on Internal Displacement (New York: International Center for Transitional Justice, 2012).

[517] For an example of a trial failing to result in conviction, see the 1996 Manisa trials against policemen who were accused of torturing university students after a rally. See further: K. Öktem, *Angry Nation*, p. 256.

[518] J.M. Dixon, 'Defending the Nation?', p. 130.

and military officials supposedly responsible for the crash brought to light how closely the military, business and political elite were linked, and confirmed the idea of the 'deep state'.[519] For many Turks, the town of Susurluk thus stands for the 'deep state'. The subsequent first free and open trials in Turkish political history also revealed that JITEM – similar to GAL in Spain – used illegal and violent measures to kill members of the Kurdish liberation movements, communists, and other opposition members. Many of the victims of the illegal killings were members of the PKK. JITEM acted under the direct order of the TAF, which itself could not be held accountable by any democratic institution, including the judiciary, due to the impunity that the military enjoyed in Turkey. Yet, the founder of JITEM was involved in the car accident and had to testify in court on charges of membership in the Ergenekon, a mythical group that appeared to control the entire political fate of Turkey and received international attention during the trials until 2013.[520]

It is no surprise that the military planned another coup after the Sursuluk case in 1996 because it lost power. Yet, this time, the military was confronted by the fact that Turkey was in the process of EU accession and that the wider public was closely watching every step the country took. Turkey's strongest international ally, NATO, had clearly indicated that it would no longer tolerate TAF's interventions within the country against its own citizens. Regardless, the military planned a coup in 1997, but because of the warnings from abroad and the fear of a major uprising within the country, it shifted to 'only' issuing a threatening memorandum to the government, expressing the military's concerns about Prime Minister's Erbakan's inability to govern the country. To avoid violence, the prime minister resigned and therefore the 1997 coup attempt was the first in Turkey's history to be carried out without major bloodshed. It was nevertheless a victory for the nationalists against the Muslim-orientated government and another victory for the 'deep state'.

---

[519] U. Ungör, *The Making of Modern Turkey*.

[520] The so-called Ergenekon gang, named after a mysterious place in the Turkish mountains (and nobody knows whether it ever existed), was initially a group of national security officials who bypassed state legislation to use all means, including violence, to safeguard national unity in their favour. Later, also lawyers, writers, journalists and even university professors were thought to be part of this gang. Simply spoken, anybody who wanted to dismantle state authorities and was at the same time part of the security sector or political elite in the country, could be claimed to be member of the Ergenekon gang. Young Civilians and Human Rights Agenda Association (HRAA) (ed.), *Ergenekon Is Our Reality*, p. 8.

Meanwhile, under the watchful eye of the EU and the Council of Europe, the government continued its modest civil and security sector reforms, even though with heavy concessions to the armed forces. At the same time, a human rights movement continued to rise from the Kurdish community. Groups of lawyers, victims and family members of the disappeared started to organise themselves politically. They started bringing court cases against governmental authorities and the military, while also bringing attention to the fact that the Kurds, as the largest minority group in Turkey, were not adequately represented in Turkish politics.

In the years that followed, the government made concessions and sought reconciliation in an attempt to preserve national unity. However, the government also had to accommodate the military. In 1999, the legislature decided that those charged with ill-treatment and even torture would benefit from automatic suspension of trial proceedings. This illustrated that the government, while committed to democratic regime consolidation, always had to 'negotiate' and balance the interests of the 'shadow-government': the military and paramilitary forces. Although the government did respond to the victims of human rights violations by means of individual compensation, thereby acknowledging the ECtHR judgments, this alone was not enough to appease the country. Thus, towards the end of the decade, the government slowly started to use TJ measures such as the ECtHR decisions on compensation, measures of acknowledgement, public debates and exhumations to safeguard peace in the country, except for establishing a vivid, non-violent and free plural society.

Once the government made concessions to the Kurdish demands, the cry for more TJ became louder – and the mutual reinforcing spiral effect took off. Since the Kurds comprised 10 per cent of the Turkish population, they were an important constituency not only in elections but also for general peace and stability in the country. These demands were fuelled by the growing revelations about the past massacres against them. In 1990, Ismail Besikci published a book in Turkish on the massacres in the Kurdish Alevi town of Dersim (today Tunceli) between 1937 and 1938, which remained unknown until 1990. The government and the secret police were outraged about this 'discovery'. Besikci discovered that the Turkish military had killed most of the town's inhabitants – men, women and children alike – because the inhabitants had demanded language and religious rights, and Kurdish claims for TJ arose again. The book was denounced for its anti-Turkishness and was banned. In addition the author was convicted and spent more than ten years in prison, which was not an unusual political response at that time to anyone who revealed past atrocities. This was only one of many bans on Turkish writers, historians or journalists who aimed to shed light on past wrongdoings. And governmental responses aimed to intimidate the rest of the population.[521] The fact that the Turkish authorities feared a book that did not even mention present human rights abuses, but atrocities from more than 50 years earlier, showed how sensitive the issues of the past were and also how threatening public debate on the past and TJ measures were in the eyes of the public authorities.

The external pressure from European institutions soon had its own spillover effect and transformed into internal citizen-driven pressure, especially among the Kurds. Minorities and opposition groups soon took ownership of the possibilities that NGOs, the ECtHR and other external forces had provided them with, including TJ measures. The Turkish diaspora, which counted several million individuals around the world who had close ties to their families back in Turkey, started to influence political thinking in the country. These people also influenced the intellectual circles within the country and the new, internationally trained 20+ generation soon founded pressure groups and CSOs that acted internally and externally. More freedom rights allowed for more citizen participation and even though this window of freedom was soon to be closed again, it gave many CSOs a chance to form themselves and raise their demands for TJ. One of the strongest actors in the field was the independent Turkish Human Rights Association (*İnsan HaklariDerneği*, IHD), which has existed (mainly underground) since 1986. Even though its members have been in and out of prison and exile ever since, the IHD has remained a steady voice pushing for human rights, democracy, and later TJ in Turkey. Other victim groups soon arose, encouraged by the pressure from the EU, the ECtHR and the Sursuluk trials in 1996. Examples of such organisations are the Association for Solidarity and Support of Relatives of Disappeared People (*Yakınlarını Kaybeden Ailelerle Yardımlaşma ve Dayanışma Derneği*, Yakay-Der) and the Kurdish Mothers of Peace, also called the Crying Saturday Mothers because they protest every Saturday in main cities in Turkey to represent those who disappeared in the 1980s and 1990s. The Crying Saturday Mothers started to protest in 1995 and were at first largely rejected by

---

[521] M. Von Bruinessen, 'Genocide in Kurdistan? The Suppression of the Dersim Rebellion in Turkey (1937–1938) and the Chemical War Against the Iraqi Kurds (1988)' in G.J. Andreopoulos (ed.), *Conceptual and Historical Dimensions of Genocide* (Philadelphia, PA: University of Pennsylvania Press, 1994), pp. 141–170.

364   REGIME CONSOLIDATION AND TRANSITIONAL JUSTICE

the public in Istanbul and elsewhere outside the Kurdish territory.[522] However, unlike in earlier decades, the police did not interfere with these protests. Between ten and 30 mothers and relatives of those who have disappeared demonstrate every Saturday near Taksim Square in Istanbul. Until recently, the Yakay-Der and the Crying Saturday Mothers have met regularly, launched petitions, initiated trials and protested peacefully. Since the mid-1990s, it had been Yakay-Der, together with IHD and the International Committee Against Disappearances (ICAD), that have organised a series of special events to reckon with the past, drawing inspiration from other countries on means and substance.[523] They protested and lobbied for their cause during the international UN Week of Disappeared People (every last week of May of each year) and have become the loudest voice demanding TJ measures in Turkey ever since. Towards the end of the first decade in 1999, the scattered groups and events soon became more coherent and public and also became an issue in the Turkish parliament. The parliament responded by changing the law to give these civil rights movements more space and freedom, but later restricted them again. But at that time, the fact that members of CSOs or NGOs were less frequently imprisoned, for shorter periods, was also an indication that the government and the judiciary aimed to appease them, if not to reconcile with them.

Another consequence of the political reform was that NGOs soon started to spring up and thus pressure the government from below. Diversification within and among NGOs was inevitable and hundreds were soon established. The government in return responded to these new citizen-driven demands by installing formal governmental advisory committees on human rights in the following years.[524] Although imprisonments, disappearances, torture and intimidation of citizens and their initiatives was still a daily reality, improvements and changes soon became evident. The state responded to demands with promises of formal commissions of inquiry and by launching investigations of allegations of killings and disappearances. These actions were never meant to be a public statement; they were only the government's first attempts to respond to citizens' demands for TJ. It was clear the government would continue

[522] Amnesty International Turkey, 'Listen to the Saturday Mothers' (London: AI Index, EUR: 44/17/98, 1998).
[523] K. Öktem, *Angry Nation*, p. 167.
[524] B. Cali, 'Human Rights Discourse and Domestic Human Rights NGOs' in Z.F. Kabasakal Arat (ed.), *Human Rights in Turkey* (Philadelphia, PA: University of Pennsylvania Press, 2007), p. 230.

operating in a traditional authoritarian way and would want to be in control of 'citizen initiatives' and TJ processes. However, it soon became evident that it would be impossible for the government to keep up with all the new citizen-driven initiatives since the regime change started. CSOs from below relied on the external demands from Europe, whilst pressuring the government in Ankara to make more concessions towards TJ and a stronger constitutional, representative and institutional consolidation in the years to come.

The decade ended with the Turkish National Intelligence Agency's capture of the number one enemy of the state, Abdullah Öcalan. Öcalan was one of the founders of the Kurdish PKK who had been living in exile in Kenya at the time of his capture. His capture in February 1999 and his subsequent imprisonment and trial became a test for whether Turkey would move from an authoritarian to a democratic regime, and for whether the rule of law or the 'deep state' would prevail in the coming years. The fact that Öcalan was not sentenced to death but life imprisonment instead and the subsequent abolishment of the death penalty, was a sign of concession towards the Kurdish community and a way to start a TJ process.

Second Decade 2000–2009

In the year of Öcalan's capture and trial, the EU finally recognised Turkey's candidacy for membership. This decade marked the period of constitutional consolidation and started with good signs to move towards representative and behavioural consolidation[525], because decisions were taken mostly in a transparent and accountable way, trials were public, parliamentarian debates increased and Kurdish political parties became more visible on the political agenda, gaining more and more seats in parliament. This triggered more victim groups, and Kurdish demands for truth, justice and political acknowledgement. Domestic civil actors and elites and external stakeholders used the Kurdish and Cypriot demands and the anniversary of the Armenian Genocide to push for domestic reforms. The EU Copenhagen accession criteria explicitly demanded the implementation of human rights norms and minority rights into domestic law – and one way of complying with these norms was with investigations of past crimes, acknowledgement and compensation. The Kurdish population

---

[525] W. Merkel, Systemtransformation, *Eine Einführung in die Theorie und Empirie der Transformationsforschung*, p. 111ff.

benefited from these developments. The state of emergency in southeast Anatolia was lifted and the MGK was transformed into a purely advisory body. It became evident that the external pressure from the ECtHR and the EU accession criteria provided a major incentive to domestic pressure groups to seek further TJ measures and reforms, but it was just one element of many.[526]

Nevertheless, the Council of Europe only saw an indirect link between the decisions of the ECtHR and TJ in Member States. It was only in 2008 that the Council of Europe's High Commissioner for Human Rights, Thomas Hammerberg, stated that, without coming to terms with the past, a culture of impunity would prevail and impair regime consolidation anywhere, and particularly in Turkey.[527] In the first five years before and after the EU accession talks in 2005, official publications on the Armenian Genocide doubled, indicating the mental shift, and the regime shift, in Ankara and throughout the country.

Between 2000 and 2005 alone, close to the 90th anniversary and worldwide commemoration of the Armenian Genocide, hundreds of writers, journalists, artists and academics competed with government think tanks, state and military archives and ministries, in publishing about issues of the past. Government-supported agencies published around 45 official documents, studies and books to support the official governmental version of the events of 1915 in Armenia. This shows the immense pressure the government was under to counteract the international and domestic pressure and internal publications and broadcasting on the past.[528] In the year of the EU accession talks, which coincided with the 90th anniversary of the Armenian Genocide, the US Congress and later the French National Congress passed a resolution to condemn the Armenian Genocide and to urge the Turkish government to investigate these allegations and come to terms with their past by employing TJ measures.

In 2000 the prize-winning novelist and poet Kemal Yalcin aimed to publish a popular book titled *You Rejoice My Heart*, telling the hidden journey of Armenians in Turkey. Although his Turkish publisher had already printed the book, the publisher was ordered to destroy all samples prior to distribution in 2001, due to the heavy contestation of the

---

[526] F. Türkmen, 'Turkey's Participation in Global and Regional Human Rights Regime', pp. 249–261.

[527] J.A. Sweeney, *The European Court of Human Rights in the Post Cold War Era. Universality in Transition* (London/New York: Routledge Research in Human Rights Law, 2013), pp. 24–25.

[528] J.M. Dixon, 'Defending the Nation?', p. 130.

'historical narrative' and truth about the past. The book aimed to be one of the first published in Turkey that dealt with the question of the genocide, calling it the 'Turkish shame'. The book was later translated into German, English and Armenian, and received international recognition, going into several editions. But like Ylacin, who later moved to Germany in exile, dozens of authors and novelists have been convicted under Article 301 for writing about the Armenian Genocide in Turkish. As Ilter Turan has emphasised, Turkey's democratisation process has often taken one step backward for every two steps forward as seen during the first decade of regime change.[529] But due to immense pressure, the government had to deal with its past and thus launched a number of 'EU Harmonisation Packages', which distanced the government from the past, thus also delegitimising the past. Starting in 2000, these packages gradually introduced more liberties into national legislation.[530] The decade did not only start with a government response contributing a bit to the upward spiral, it also responded to the civil pressure from below that increased dramatically. Domestic victim groups like the Kurdish Crying Saturday Mothers, the Turkish BAR association, and intellectual elites like writers, journalists (many of whom had to pay with their lives or imprisonment), artists and academics claimed more freedom and now directly demanded an acknowledgement of past wrongdoings. Some of them referred directly to the ECtHR's decisions or the European Parliament's resolutions urging the Turkish government to change legislation and start investigating the past. Meanwhile, popular cultural life moved on and some academics and intellectuals thought that the time had come to openly debate the past.

Within Turkey, incrementally the internal and external pressure continuously pressured for a governmental response for TJ and political reforms, which indicates the cumulative causalities between TJ and consolidation in the long run. In 2001, the parliament introduced further political reforms granting more domestic, cultural and linguistic rights to the Kurds and giving room for political representation. In the same year, future prime minister Erdogan founded the AKP, which had a distinct open policy towards the Kurds and which would take major steps towards recognition of the past. In the 2002 elections the AKP received a

[529] I. Turan, *Turkey's Difficult Journey to Democracy*.
[530] B. Oran, 'The Minority Concept and Rights in Turkey: The Lausane Peace Treaty and Current Issues' in Z.F. Kabasakal Arat (ed.), *Human Rights in Turkey* (Philadelphia, PA: University of Pennsylvania Press, 2007), pp. 35–56.

large number of seats in parliament, partially due to Kurdish voters, and Erdogan became prime minister.[531] The party's policy would determine the pace of democratic progress and TJ measures over the next ten years, eventually ending around 2015. But at first, Erdogan made a clear commitment to democracy, although not one necessarily based on consensual democracy but rather on majoritarian democracy, which was established in the constitutional changes of 1982. At first, the AKP clearly favoured EU accession but also the unification of the country around Islamic values. With the AKP in government, an Ottoman revival took place in Turkey, highlighting the achievements of past sultans and the greatness of Muslim culture – all of which had been banned under Atatürk's secular policies and by the military.[532] Reconciliation efforts with Armenia or the Kurdish minority did not serve this ideological trend of Erdogan's AKP. But since suppression, intimidation, expulsion and violence no longer worked to guarantee state unity, Erdogan had to use other tools, such as the Ottoman revival and later, as we will see, even some TJ tools – also only in a strategic and tactical manner, if they served the purpose of national unity.

Much has been written about the rise and change of the AKP over the past decade, and thus will not be revisited here.[533] I will briefly summarise the main conclusions concerning the party's impact on regime consolidation swinging between democracy and authoritarianism. Since the AKP obtained executive and legislative power, TJ measures were widely used as strategic tools to purge the AKP of political opponents such as the military. AKP leaders held some military responsible for thousands of crimes and atrocities in eastern Anatolia. These were show trials for the wider public; TJ measures such as trials and commissions were misused to purge political opponents by Erdogan's power politics throughout his governance either as prime minister or later as president. On the other hand, Erdogan used TJ tools in a smart tactical and strategic way, for electoral purposes and to win Kurdish votes and the backing of intellectuals who sought an alternative to the existing parties. The AKP was not an Islamic party that embraced Sharia law or any other radical Islamic laws; rather, it saw itself in the tradition of many other European conservative parties that base their party programme on

---

[531]   K. Öktem, Angry Nation, p. 165.
[532]   I. Turan, Turkey's Difficult Journey to Democracy, p. 175ff.
[533]   For a good overview, see: W. Hale and E. Özbudun, Islamism, Democracy and Liberalism in Turkey: The Case of the AKP (New York: Routledge, 2011).

Christian values, such as the CDU in Germany or the PP in Spain. But, regardless of its self-definition, the reach of the AKP and its grip on the country has led to many more restrictive laws concerning freedom of information, expression and assembly. What is striking is that Erdogan has clearly identified the unconsolidated pockets in the country, namely the Kurds, and used all possible means and measures to win them for his party at that time.

Due to an electoral rule that mandated that parties could only enter parliament if they won more than 10 per cent of the vote, religious and minority parties were not able to enter parliament, although some splinter groups have received up to 25 per cent of the seats in total, but did not build a coalition. Yet in 2002, with the AKP in power, many of these parties were allowed to take their seats, which appeased these groups for a time.[534] The exclusion of minority or religious parties from the decision-making process had paralysed Turkish economic and political progress. Erdogan was determined to end this and in doing so also aimed to dismantle the TAF and the JITMR, the most powerful opponents to his government. He started this process by openly stating that arbitrary killings and disappearances as well as terrorist acts on both sides (by the Turkish military and the PKK) had been going on for far too long. Erdogan justified trials against his opponents by referring to unsettled accounts of the past and thus claimed the trials to be part of an overall TJ process of the country, albeit often exclusive and biased.

In the following years, TJ measures for Turkey's ethnic and religious minorities were based on two national interests: first, preserving the country's integrity and unity and, second, fighting a number of rebel Kurdish groups, in particular the continuously active PKK, which largely followed its leader, Abdullah Öcalan. Erdogan made more concessions and even allowed radical members of the PKK to become involved in parliament, so long as they refrained from violence. After its victory in 2002, the AKP also abolished the martial law and state of emergency that had governed the Kurdish region in Turkey since 1978. Due to the fact that Öcalan had been openly tried and his death penalty had been commuted to life in prison, the violence and protests in the territory calmed down and political participation increased, allowing more Kurdish parties to participate in elections. Turkey had passed its first test for upward spiral democratic regime consolidation. After legal reforms, more Kurdish interest and victim groups, intellectuals and journalists emerged. This also had to do

534 L.M. McLaren, *Constructing Democracy in Southern Europe*, p. 139.

with the fact that many of the TJ measures, such as the exhumation and memorialisation of victims, delegitimised the military arm of the government, which was also in the interest of the AKP. The government made concessions to Kurdish terrorist and separatist fighters and their political branches. The Kurdish language was allowed and the Kurds were also allowed to have their own television station in their language.[535]

Even more concessions were made on the eve of the EU accession talks in 2004, a period that is considered the all-time peak of the TJ process in Turkey. In 2002, the UN Special Rapporteur for Disappearances, Francis Deng, was finally allowed to enter the country after a number of rejections by the government, which denied that there had been any cases of disappearances in eastern Anatolia. Deng's report about the hundreds of thousands of cases of disappearances fuelled the pressure exerted by the EU, provoked strong reactions in Ankara, and eventually caused a shift in Turkish policies towards more democratic reforms and overall to TJ. Interestingly enough, at that same time, opinion polls conducted by Eurobarometer showed that civic trust in the Turkish government increased dramatically. Eighty per cent of those polled reported trust in the government and only 17 per cent tended not to trust it.[536] Yet, these figures shifted dramatically later in the decade. In the following years, when it became apparent that many of the promised reforms never took place and the regime would move back into more authoritarian practice, trust in government dropped to only 4 per cent.

One of the main reasons why the quality of Turkey's democracy had not improved for so long was the past governments' and legislatures' unwillingness or incapacity to control extremists with consensus-based rules and coalitions.[537] The main reason for the AKP's popularity in 2004 was exactly because it was able to make concessions. It introduced liberal reforms and was in favour of the EU. Some of the concessions made by the AKP qualify as TJ measures, such as the various compensation laws for the Kurdish victims. In the same year as the EU talks, the Turkish parliament issued a compensation law for victims of disappearances, which included the establishment of a commission to implement and monitor the law. The law compensated bodily harm, loss of property and loss of

[535] Amnesty International, *Amnesty International Report 2007 – Turkey* (2007).
[536] European Union, Eurobarometer Surveys, Turkey 2008.10, http://ec.europa.eu (last accessed August 2013).
[537] L.M. McLaren, *Constructing Democracy in Southern Europe. A Comparative Analysis of Italy, Spain and Turkey* (New York/London: Routledge, 2010), p. 170.

earnings and agriculture. Although this compensation commission was not independent from government influence, the law as such was remarkable. It aimed to compensate mostly Kurdish victims and descendants of those who had disappeared and been forcefully evicted since the 1980s, which totalled approximately one million people. No official figures exist, and while the government claims that the figure should be 950,000 people, Kurdish CSOs estimate around three million people have been killed, tortured and disappeared or have fled into exile.[538] With the compensation law, the AKP tried to respond to the pressure exerted by the EU – and to some extent to the UN – and by the many pending cases (around 1,500 at that time) filed by Kurdish victim groups and diaspora NGOs to the ECtHR to uncover the truth about the remains of their relatives. Notwithstanding, this was also the era in which worldwide TJ measures flourished.

The new law also responded to the growing civil society community inside the country and civil pressure by adhering to international norms and standards. This illustrates how external pressure or 'carrot and stick' incentives can be effective if combined with domestic politics and interests. In this case, the EU played a significant role in unifying divided elites, such as nationalists, Muslims, Kurds and human rights organisations, all of which were in favour of EU membership. This odd coalition helped to push through reforms, which again correlated with the effective and thus high-quality performance of democratic institutions.[539] The law accommodated many stakeholders and after it was issued the ECtHR stopped all further investigations and seemed satisfied. Yet, the law did not include a truth or justice perspective, nor did it arrange for those responsible for crimes to be held accountable under the criminal law. However, overall, it triggered a bottom-up and citizen-driven approach to regime consolidation that often used TJ tools to demand shifts and changes beyond mere compensation and acknowledgement.

Although the Kurdish branch of the IDH and the Istanbul BAR Association encouraged file claims and pressured the government, the changed laws did not always find favour among Kurdish victims. This was because the law also compensated members of the TAF who had been injured or killed while combating members of the PKK. The law recognised all victims of the conflict and, in this way, the law was similar to

538 Ibid.
539 Ibid., p. 240.

the amnesty or 'rehabilitation' laws in other countries, such as Spain. It was the government's compromise to acknowledge victims of the past era, regardless of whether they were Kurds or member of the TAF. Yet, the law was not completely neutral, let alone inclusive, in its approach if a victim – or their family members – could provide documentation proving the violation. Of course, many Kurdish villagers from eastern Anatolia did not possess such documents, whereas military officials tended to have ready documentation about their own people being killed or injured by the PKK because they had issued it themselves. This ad hoc and rather sporadic TJ measure created a new constituency of those who criticised the law. Like we saw in Spain, both amnesty and memorial laws often have a biased character and lack transparency. To be open to all sides, as Gibson had often claimed, was far from being the reality in Turkey.

In 2005, Erdogan almost apologised when addressing Kurds in Diyabakir, admitting that the 'state has done wrong in the past'. Additionally, he backed the state prosecutor to start a trial against a colonel responsible for arbitrary killings in the region who, again, was one of his opponents. Erdogan used this trial – which could be claimed to be a TJ measure – to cleanse himself of those who opposed him. On the other hand, the compensation law was a concession on which NGOs, parliamentarians and the EU could build upon. It not only eased the way for further talks with the EU, it also finally gave the UN bodies and others a chance to investigate cases of severe human rights abuses and disappearances in the country. By the end of 2010, the government had settled more than 133,000 applications for compensation, worth one billion euros and dealt with over 300,000 claims nationwide. However, no trials or truth commissions on the role of the security services or military were implemented, nor were plans made to do so.[540]

Meanwhile, dealing with the Armenian Genocide was not the Turkish government's primary concern at any time of its regime consolidation efforts. Erdogan's cost-benefit analysis did not weigh in favour of dealing with it. The Turkish government also wanted to avoid the billions of euros in compensation that post-war Germany had to pay for its genocide, in addition to trials, reparations and other TJ measures. These financial concerns also informed the government's decision not to recognise the events of 1915 as genocide. In addition, Armenia was not a major trade partner and the Azerbaijan-Armenia dispute about Nagorno-Karabakh, in which

---

[540]   D. Kurban, *Reparation and Displacement in Turkey*.

Turkey clearly sided with Azerbaijan, gave Turkey an additional reason to deny the genocide.

Despite the Turkish government's interests in denying the Armenian Genocide, the debate about these events, instigated by external stakeholders, has nevertheless been an important stimulus for talks about TJ and about democracy in Turkey in general. As indicated earlier, a more intense attempt to open the debate about the 'events of 1915' took place around 2005, the year of the 90th anniversary of the Armenian Genocide and also the year of Turkey's accession talks with the EU. This year was commemorated by Armenia and the Armenian Diaspora around the world and was internationally recognised. Pressure on Ankara increased and the government responded to both the international community (especially the EU) and to internal pressure. In light of the anniversary events coming up around the world (where Armenian diaspora lives) the AKP supported an NGO-driven attempt to establish a Turkish-Armenian Reconciliation Commission (TARC) between 2001 and 2004 with meetings in Geneva and Moscow, although it produced no results with consequences for the bilateral relationship. The TARC was mainly financed by US governmental and Armenian non-governmental agencies and discontinued its work with no further cooperation on either side. It was not an independent commission. Its main role was to bring Turkish and Armenian historians and experts to the table and facilitate discussions as a type of history commission, but it produced no lasting results. In 2002, the TARC asked the ICTJ in New York to facilitate a memorandum on the applicability of the UN Convention on the Prevention and Punishment of the Crime of Genocide of 1948 to the Armenian Genocide. The Turkish government, however, held its traditional position. At the same time, the Armenian Institute in Washington DC conducted another analysis, which concluded that the primary focus in dealing with the past should be establishing individual responsibility, and not the collective punishment of Turks. Although this analysis was published and triggered debate, it received no further governmental follow-up in Ankara.[541] But all this did not remain completely unnoticed by Turkish society and the condemnations of the genocide by the EU Parliament and the US Senate also led to some political reactions in Ankara.

---

[541] The Armenian National Institute, *The Applicability of the UN Convention on the Prevention and Punishment of the Crimes of Genocide to Events which Occurred During the Early Twentieth Century*, Legal Analysis Prepared for the ICTJ, 2003. umd.umich.edu/dept/armenian/news/ictj.pdf (last accessed September 2013).

The 'open door' atmosphere eventually triggered more citizen-driven approaches. In 2005, professors at the private Bilgi University in Istanbul launched the first ever public conference on the Armenian Genocide, entitled 'Ottoman Armenians During the Decline of the Empire: Issues of Scientific Responsibility and Democracy'. The conference was covered internationally, but far less so domestically. Neither the content of the debate nor the conclusion about the 'events of 1915' was new, but they stated that the Armenian Genocide was not only a matter of victims but also of victimisers and the successor state to the Ottoman Empire. On that occasion, Kurdish NGOs and civil society activists also raised their voices, making it clear that the deportations and exterminations of 1915 were not only targeted against Armenians, but against all minorities, including Assyrians, Kurds and Greeks. As such, the Armenian Genocide might be more appropriately called the Turkish Genocide, because the Armenians killed at that time were of Turkish citizenship and since hundreds of thousands of Turkish nationals with different ethnic and religious backgrounds (although at that time subjects of the Ottoman Empire) became victims of this genocide.[542]

Parallel to these events, between 2005 and 2007, a debate was waged about the restoration and inauguration of the Armenian Church. In response to the Council of Europe's recognition of the Armenian Genocide already in 2001 and the French parliament's recognition in 2006, the government in Ankara promised to restore and reopen Armenian memorials. Needless to say, the AKP wanted to keep ownership over the narrative and thus actively engaged in the debate, assured that it had justice on its side. In 2006 the Parliamentary Assembly of the European Parliament called on Ankara to finally recognise the events of 1915 as genocide.[543] This call followed an earlier attempt in 2001, by the European Parliamentarian Assembly of the Council of Europe, which was mainly ignored by the Turkish government.

But prior to, during and shortly after the accession talks, Turkey received positive international acknowledgement for the modest restoration efforts of Christian and Armenian churches in Turkey in the second post-transition period. One such example of Turkey's efforts to restore these churches was the Ministry of Culture's restoration of the Armenian Church on Akhtamar as a museum, which was inaugurated

---

[542] K. Öktem, *Angry Nation. Turkey since 1989* (London: Zen Books, 2011), p. 147ff.
[543] Parliamentary Assembly of the Council of Europe, Need for recognition of the Armenian genocide by Turkey, Doc. 11104, Strasbourg, 27 November 2006.

as an act to underline 'Turkish tolerance' towards its minorities in 2007. However, this whole project backfired on the government because of its biased and exclusive character and can be interpreted as a failure – or rather an abuse – of top-down TJ measures. The government had thus far only allowed for a top-down, strategically and tactically measured TJ process, controlling the narrative, the memorials, trials and reparations for the sole purpose of maintaining domestic stability under control of the AKP. CSO activities were low and strictly controlled in the case of the Armenian Genocide. The Turkish Nobel Prize Laureate for Literature, Orhan Pamuk, openly addressed this story and the half-hearted efforts at reconciliation and the shame the 'events of 1915' placed on all Turks because of the still non-existent acknowledgement of the Armenian Genocide. Following Pamuk's campaign against governmental abuse of TJ tools, he was convicted under Article 301 and received death threats. International protests followed and the accusations against him came to a halt, but he later went into exile in New York. He has been a symbolic figure for many activists and citizen-driven initiatives, signalling that it is time for the country to take moral responsibility for its past, a responsibility that goes beyond measures of restorative justice.[544]

In 2007, Prime Minister Erdogan called the whole restoration of the Armenian Church a 'retaliation against the Genocide claims' in an attempt to counteract the 'aggressive attacks against Turkishness' from the Armenian and European governments and diaspora, and to show instead how tolerant and modern Turkey was.[545] Erdogan did not see the restoration as an act of reconciliation for Armenia and Turkey, or for the divided Turkish society, but rather as a useful political instrument to silence Turkey's critics abroad. Erdogan emphasised that 'the history of the country is clean and no massacres and genocides have ever occurred'.[546] He saw no political, economic or diplomatic benefit from any reconciliation between Armenia and Turkey.

This case and the verbal battles between Erdogan and the international community also triggered long-awaited internal debates and discussions about whether regime change, let alone democratic consolidation

---

[544] Young Civilians and Human Rights Agenda Association (HRAA) (ed.), *Ergenekon Is Our Reality* (Ankara: HRAA, 2010), p. 13.
[545] B. Ayata, 'Tolerance as a European Norm or an Ottoman Practice? An Analysis of Turkish Public Debates in the (Re)Opening of an Armenian Church in the Context of Turkey's EU Candidacy and Neo-Ottoman Revival', Working Papers – KFG, Transformation Power of Europe, 41 (2012), p. 13.
[546] Turkisch Press.com, 16 April 2010.

in Turkey, had ever taken place. Pandora's box had been opened, and all efforts to close it through restrictive politics have failed or led to some sort of violent response on all sides. It was at this point that many other gruesome issues of the past started being openly debated, for example the massacres of Kurds in the 1920s. According to Ishak Alaton, a Turkish-Jewish businessman, people's engagement with the state had become stronger.[547] Among other things, this led to public debates, despite the existence of Article 301, but also to the imprisonment of many writers, journalists and academics.

One of the many outspoken intellectuals and civil actors at that time was the Turkish-Armenian journalist Hrant Dink. In January 2007, shortly before the inauguration of the restored Armenian Church, Dink – like Pamuk – commented on the different shades of the debate and on the political intentions behind it.[548] But unlike Pamuk, Dink paid for this with his life. He had noted that this TJ measure was only being used for tactical purposes and did not allow for public participation, and that therefore a moral feeling of responsibility for the past was still missing. Shortly after his comments, a fanatic nationalist murdered him in broad daylight, in front of his office in Istanbul. His murder became an international affair and a dramatic sign that despite all efforts to atone for the past in 2005 and 2006, Turkish society was not yet ready for general acceptance of, let alone moral responsibility for, the past. The nationalist-motivated homicide of a journalist was a signal to those who aimed to change this. It led to large protests and alignment between victims and many non-Armenians in Turkey. These protests went beyond the usual narrow elite group who had always criticised Turkish nationalism – mainly from exile abroad. In response to this murder, 100,000 people demonstrated on the streets in Istanbul in the largest protest in Turkish history. The protesters demanded transparency and accountability of those who were responsible for the killing.[549]

Almost immediately after the murder, the PACE pushed the government in Ankara – to no avail – to abolish Article 301 of the penal code in order to deal with the consequences of the murder and to eventually try

---

[547] Young Civilians and Human Rights Agenda Association (HRAA) (ed.), *Ergenekon is our Reality*, p. 43.

[548] B. Ayata, 'Tolerance as a European Norm or an Ottoman Practice?'.

[549] M. Sancar, 'Coming to Terms with the Past in Turkey: Being Realistic, Asking for the Impossible' in Heinrich Böll Foundation (ed.), *From the Burden of the Past to Societal Peace and Democracy* (Istanbul: Heinrich Böll Foundation, 2007), pp. 33–35.

the person who had committed it.[550] Hundreds of people attended Dink's funeral, using the slogan 'We are all Armenians', and meaning that they were all victims of Turkish nationalism.

Moreover, the protests in 2007 signalled that the new 20+ generation after 1989 was about to politically mature and demand what had not been possible for the past seven decades, namely a civic culture. Dealing or rather not dealing with the Armenian genocide exemplified how authoritarian the government still was – and would remain. Twenty years after the first serious democratic reforms, TJ measures became seen as a tool to improve the rule of law in the country and to ease tensions. In addition to the efforts to atone for and commemorate the Armenian massacres in 2005 and 2007, the slow TJ efforts on the Kurdish issue were also sped up. The influence of the Armenian, Kurdish and Cypriot issues on each other is undeniable. Encouraged by the conference at Bilgi University in 2005, an academic-driven initiative organised the fifth International Conference against massive Kurdish Disappearances in May 2006 in Diyarbakir. Kurdish NGOs, politicians, mothers of the disappeared and the political branch of the PKK initiated sit-down strikes, a photo exhibition and panel discussions with the relatives of missing persons. They also filed a complaint with the public prosecutor and demanded the punishment of the officials responsible for the disappearance of the missing persons.[551]

The Turkish middle class was concerned that any radical nationalist could kill someone who they deemed not Turkish enough and that Article 301 would prevent the killer's prosecution. They feared that any murderer who killed in the name of Turkishness would suffer no legal consequences, because he could claim to have acted in defence of Turkishness. This would of course mean a significant deterioration of the rule of law and undermine any democratic value, let alone the cry for justice, at the very least contributing to deep unconsolidated pockets in the system. The lawyers and judges at the responsible court in Istanbul had to react, for which many suffered repercussions. To some extent, Dink's murder trial was one of the few exceptions in the context of TJ, simply because it happened and because it was a benchmark judgment condemning the murderer.[552] Significant parts of society indicated that they would no longer

---

[550] Parliamentary Assembly of the Council of Europe, *In the Aftermath of Hrant Dink's Murder*, Doc. 11187, 20 February 2007.
[551] K. Öktem, *Angry Nation*, p. 168.
[552] Interview with Murat Belge, Istanbul, 13 April 2011.

accept censorship and prosecution when talking about the massacres of World War I or the persecution of Greeks, Kurds and other minorities. Another, wider public consequence of the dramatic shifts during this decade, and in particular between 2005 and 2007, was the fact that the government had to make concessions towards the new intellectual elite, middle class, NGOs and new generation.

These changes in policy and polity led to a number of official and unofficial meetings that contributed to TJ, such as the visit of the Turkish President Gül to an Armenian-Turkish football game in Yerevan in 2008. Surprisingly, two-thirds of the Turkish population supported this visit to Yerevan. In Armenia his visit was seen as a sign that Turkey was ready to finally discuss the genocide and deal with its past – which did not happen. According to Hasan Kanbolat, director of the Center for Middle Eastern Strategic Studies, it was all a matter of 'timing', not of preparation.[553] Until that time, the history taught in schools excluded many events of the past that remained strongly in the collective memory of the people. Therefore, there was a gap between individuals' experience at home and within communities, and at school or through the media, which has always been strongly controlled by the state.[554]

In May 2008 the government once again reformed the notorious Article 301, which led to a significant decrease of cases brought based on this article. As a result, in November of that year, 300 intellectuals sent President Abdullah Gül an open letter asserting that Turkey inherited the responsibility of the events of 1915 and that denying the Armenian Genocide unnecessarily prevented reconciliation with Armenia.[555] Following this letter, Gül issued an official statement in December 2008 saying that such a civil Armenian apology campaign is a sign of democracy because it exercises freedom of expression – which of course by no means would include a signature by a public official.[556] Although Erdogan later contradicted Gül's statement, it encouraged more civil engagement. Subsequently, and in solidarity with the initiators due to the public debate, some 30,000 Turks signed an online letter addressed to Armenians across the world

---

[553] International Crisis Group, 'Turkey and Armenia: Opening Minds, Opening Borders', *Europe Report*, 199 (2009), 22.
[554] L. Neyi, 'Oral History and Memory Studies in Turkey' in C. Kerslake, K. Öktem and P. Robins (eds.), *Turkey's Engagment with Modernity, Conflict and Change in the Twentieth Century* (London: Palgrave Macmillan, 2010), p. 445.
[555] International Crisis Group, 'Turkey and Armenia', 12.
[556] The Epoch Times, 'Turkey's President Defends Aermnai Apoligy Campagin', www.theepochetimes.com (last accessed December 2008).

apologising for the massacres and genocide in 1915. Nevertheless, the fear of suffering repercussions never completely vanished. Ankara has retained its position towards Armenia, despite its slight change in the notorious legal instrument of Article 301.

Towards the end of this second post-authoritarian decade, everyone had easy access to information about the past, thanks to the Internet. However, most of the literature, essays and displays about the Armenian Genocide or Kurdish massacres have been in foreign languages and are still thus only accessible to a small minority in the country. Publishing in English also offers protection, because the Turkish Intelligence Authorities will less likely censor the work. In 2008, the Kurdish Democratic Society Party (DTP) launched a wide public debate to call on the Turkish parliament to officially apologise to the Armenians for the events of 1915 and, in doing so, used the Kurdish word for genocide during the parliamentary debate. The party also called for the official governmental version of World War I to be changed and for the government to change its policies on minorities in Turkey. This indicated how quickly post-nationalism movements were progressing and how different political and civil groups were joining forces and using TJ measures to trigger more democratic reforms.[557] With the amendment of Article 301, NGOs such as the IHD, the Crying Saturday Mothers and Yakay-Der became bolder and made open calls for official apologies for enforced disappearances.[558]

In continuation to this, in 2009 the Turkish parliament commissioned (again) a memorial or statue for Turkish-Armenian reconciliation in Kars, a former Armenian town close to the Armenian border with Turkey, as a way to start talks between the two countries. The city of Kars has always been seen as symbol of commemoration and its development as an indicator for the level of Turkish-Armenian reconciliation and TJ.

But after the AKP's second term in government had started, reforms began to stagnate and citizens' claims were largely ignored, much to the disappointment of the Kurdish population. This was largely due to the missing 'carrot' and 'stick' of EU pressure. As a consequence, only 58 per cent trusted the government and 47 per cent tended not to trust the AKP anymore and remained divided in the following years.[559]

---

[557] J.M Dixon, 'Defending the Nation?', p. 133.
[558] E. Ustundag, *Government Should Apologize for Enforced Disappearances* (Istanbul: Bianet, 2009).
[559] K. Öktem, *Angry Nation*, p. 164.

Although at first the government remained rather quiet in response to the 20+ generation's calls for more consolidation and more TJ, Erdogan was afraid that sooner or later these debates would lead to indictments and questions about his leadership. Thus again, he used TJ for his own political purpose; welcoming the claims for more accountability towards the TAF as he himself aimed to indict high-ranking members of the military to rid his government of its strongest opponents. He soon discovered that dealing with the past through trials and recognition of past crimes, such as those committed against the Kurdish community, could help him to free himself from his own opponents. Thus the Ergenekon trials were initiated, including anyone who somehow and somewhat opposed AKP politics. Although legally speaking, the TAF cannot be held directly responsible for the crimes and atrocities committed prior to 1923 under the Sultanate or any government prior to 1982, military officials were highly sensitive to accusations concerning the massacres, pogroms and persecution of Kurds and Greeks. The TAF's fear was not so much personal indictments – many of them were already too old to go to jail – but the fear that the military would be disfranchised and demystified, and therefore no longer able to protect the unity of the country. The TAF's concern was that the country would fall into the hands of Islam. This is why the AKP, from the beginning of the reforms onwards, aimed to embrace Islamic groups as much as possible without losing sight of the secular forces.

By the same time, the issue of the Armenian Genocide had entered the wider Turkish consciousness, although opinion polls from 2008 showed that the vast majority of Turks (over 60 per cent) did not believe that the events of 1915 had resulted in genocide. However, 70 per cent expressed openly that it was genocide – a novelty in opinion polls – and 13 per cent believed that Armenians had been severely mistreated in the past.[560] It was positive that people felt more comfortable expressing opinions about the Armenian Genocide, something that would have been impossible only a few years before due to Article 301.

Under international vigilance and pressure, citizens continued their efforts for TJ. They held meetings; street demonstrations and conferences, like the one on TJ and Enforced Disappearances together with the New York and Brussels-based ICTJ in 2009 in Istanbul. In the same year, Turkish CSOs began a campaign to urge the government to ratify the UN Convention for the Protection of All Persons from Enforced

560 L. Morlino, 'Authoritarian Legacies', p. 180.

Disappearances. As a response to Kurdish pressure, the government allowed state television and more radio channels to be broadcast in Kurdish. Erdogan once again pulled out his strongest political tool, winning Kurdish votes and support through TJ measures. He responded to the increasing pressure from below when he announced his intention to launch a new initiative for a political solution to the conflict, before an audience of 400,000 Kurds in their regional capital of Diyarbakir. In 2010, the PKK announced a ceasefire, allowing a significant shift from a militant movement to political participation.

Third Decade 2010 and the Following Years

In 2010, the Turkish MetroPoll conducted a survey on whether or not citizens were aware that the US Congress and the Swedish Parliament had adopted a resolution on the Armenian Genocide to pressure the Turkish government to come to terms with it. Around 40 per cent of the population was aware of the fact that these foreign legislatures had done so, although it disapproved of these resolutions and instead agreed with the government's official version of what had happened.[561] Yet, this awareness indicated that people did follow international and national coverage of the Turkish past.

The issue reparations and restitution concerning the Kurdish and the Armenian issue was still high on the public agenda, and in 2011 Turkish writers and academics again sent an open letter on the Armenian Genocide and started a public campaign, which was followed by 11,000 signatures demanding an official apology for the genocide. The president and prime minister refused. However, this time Erdogan did respond directly to the demands, saying that there was no need for an apology because no genocide had taken place. The Turkish Republic, in his words, had no such problem.[562]

Looking to the next elections that were to be held in February 2011, Prime Minister Erdogan met (for the first time) with the Kurdish Crying Saturday Mothers in Istanbul to show that he took their concerns seriously, although this meeting did not have any further consequences.[563] At that time, Kurdish lawyers, human rights organisations and interest

---

[561] MetroPoll, 'Awareness of Oscar's and the Armenian Issue', March 2010, www.metropoll. com.tr (last accessed August 2013).
[562] Hürriyet Daily News, 'Armenian apology denounced by gov't', 6 June 2011.
[563] D. Kurban, 'Reparation and Displacement in Turkey', p. 10.

groups had filed over 1,500 court cases, although most were rejected due to lack of jurisdiction or otherwise dismissed. CSOs and lawyers argued that the government's first steps should be to stop harassing human rights defenders, start the exhumation and identification of the bodies in mass graves (especially in Kurdish provinces), establish a centralised database concerning forensic information of disappeared individuals and start prosecutions against those who handled the procedures regarding the enforced disappearances – namely the military, the secret police and the civilian police.[564] Over 80 mass graves, each containing between ten and 170 victims, had been found so far under the watchful eye of international organisations, lawyers, local initiatives and local municipalities.

Although the level of democracy and regime consolidation in Turkey was still many steps away from Linz and Stepan's assessment of 'the only game in town', the 20+ generation initiatives indicated that this is where the new young political and civic elite was ready to go.[565] Thus, the government and military response was harsh and violent in the following years, because civil society was not strong enough to hold out against it. But it was exactly this rising civil society, and their claims – among others – for more TJ, that were soon suppressed and around 2015 civil society was so intimidated and under surveillance, that consolidation by behaviour and conviction through civil society engagement was no longer possible.

But the more time that passed following the accession talks, the more evident it became that the EU could not have Turkey and Greek Cyprus both as Member States until they settled their territorial conflict with peaceful agreements and payment of reparations for those expelled during the war in 1974. TJ thus was no longer an optional tool, but a prerequisite to enter the EU. Since the Turkish invasion of northern Cyprus in 1974 and the division of the island, diplomatic relationships have been tense. They were eased somewhat when Greece actively supported Turkey's membership in the EU and when Greece and Turkey made an (unsuccessful) bid in 2002 to jointly host the 2008 UEFA Football Championship. These gestures did more for the reconciliation process than earlier diplomatic and economic ties had done altogether. Nevertheless, the EU-Turkey-Cyprus triangle remains a chief source of tension and conflict in the region. Greek and Turkish Cypriots have

---

[564] Turkish news agency Bianet.
[565] J.J. Linz and A. Stepan (eds.), *Problems of Democratic Transition and Consolidation*, p. 5.

both used violence in their attempts to expel and expropriate each other. Addressing issues of reparation and restitution as well as the acknowledgement of atrocities, pogroms and other forms of discrimination are slowly taking place during the process of Turkey seeking membership in the EU. Greek Cypriots rejected the 'Annan Plan' (named after the former UN Secretary General Kofi Annan) for a unified membership in the EU in a 2004 referendum, and as a consequence Greek Cyprus joined the EU.[566] As a means of compensation for this political disaster, the EU promised Turkey full membership soon. But for the time being, the Turkish northern part of the island had to return to its isolation and dependence on the Turkish mainland and Ankara's policies. Debates continue as to whether the northern part of Cyprus can join federally governed Cyprus on the basis of a single sovereignty and citizenship, meaning that Cyprus would have two federal states, one Greek and one Turkish. Today, an estimated 200,000 people are still displaced and thousands have disappeared since 1974. Many of the displaced people lost their property and houses during the intervention, a fact upon which most of the restitution claims against the other side are based. The need to reckon with these past crimes was slowly acknowledged when Greece, Cyprus and Turkey sought EU membership.[567] In this dispute and as an act of TJ, the ECtHR has ruled several times against both Cypriot sides (the Greek and the Turkish), ordering both sides to settle disputes over land and property.[568] In response to these judgments, the Turkish government established the Turkish Cypriot Immovable Property Commission (TRNC) in 2006 for compensation for occupied property, which was largely rejected by the Greek community.[569] Since then, the Commission has examined claims for restitution, compensation and exchange. By 2011, 974 applications had been lodged with the TRNC, with 151 of them concluded through friendly settlements and seven of them through formal hearings. Since then, many more restitution cases have been brought to the ECtHR and the court has repeatedly ruled against both Cypriot sides since the compensation measures for occupied property were largely rejected by the Greek community. Efforts to deal with this issue of the Turkish past continued into the third decade, and as of 2012 the ECtHR has rendered

---

[566] K. Öktem, *Angry Nation*, p. 140.
[567] International Crisis Group, 'Turkey and Armenia', 12.
[568] See judgments at www.echr.coe.int (last accessed August 2016).
[569] European Court for Human Rights (ECtHR), Court Chamber, Case of Loizidou versus Turkey, Application no. 15318/89, Judgment, Strasbourg, 18 December 1996.

around 207 Cypriot judgments on cases originating from Turkey, with many more still pending.[570] Meanwhile, the UN, the Council of Europe, the European Commission and the European Parliament have emphasised the importance of settling these disputes and to acknowledge, name and prosecute those who have been responsible for grave injustices and expropriation throughout the past decades. Until 2009, Turkey had more trials brought before the ECtHR on protection of property than any other Council of Europe Member State. With 544 judgments concerning, in particular, property claims in Cyprus and eastern Anatolia between 1959 and 2009, Turkey's record in this regard was way ahead of Russia's, another notorious Member State of the Council of Europe that struggles with its past and that has had around 380 cases adjudicated by the ECtHR.

These 'open wounds' of the past have constantly haunted each election campaign and each outbreak of violence in the country. The government constantly made concessions to ease the tensions, but often took one step back for every two forward.[571] For example, in 2006 in response to Turkish integration of minorities, the government abolished the mandate that ID cards were to state the holder's religion, a move that benefited Greek Orthodox, Armenians and Sunni Muslims and thus the Kurdish population to some extent. However, many of these measures were purely tactical. Their effects were only seen in the third decade. One can argue that these concessions – made for whatever reasons – also opened the door to more TJ measures and to the possibility that the judiciary and the legislature would respond to claims in accordance with human rights. The spiral between institutional reforms, TJ measures and civic trust slowly moved upwards.

Another strategic move was made between 2008 and 2013 with the initiation of the Ergenekon trials on past violence and with the trial of those allegedly responsible for the coup d'état in 1980 and other nationalist crimes. The way these trials were conducted over the course of five years has shed light on how regime consolidation had (not) progressed and thus the regime at its political and civil elites had not passed the test after 20-plus years to clear the next hurdle of democratic consolidation. When the trials finally came to an end in 2013 and 2014 it led to widespread political protest and outrage in the streets of Istanbul. At the same

---

[570]   E. Özbudun and F. Türkmen, 'Impact of the ECtHR Rulings in Turkey. Democratisation: An Evaluation', *Human Rights Quarterly*, 35(4) (2013), 988.
[571]   I. Turan, *Turkey's Difficult Journey to Democracy*.

time, trust in political institutions, the prime minister, the government and parliament was decreasing dramatically. Before the trials started, governmental institutions enjoyed a confidence rating of 7.9 points out of 10.0. This rate dropped to 6.5 in 2009 and went even lower in 2013 when it became evident that the trials were conducted in a biased way and that the AKP only wanted to purge itself of its political opponents. Erdogan reacted with populist and nationalist speeches and tried to gain support from religious leaders.[572] Islamisation of the party and Erdogan's policies followed and led to increasing authorisation of the regime, by later installing a presidential leadership with strong powers for Erdogan.

Erdogan pursued his 'zero problem policy of peace and cooperation' with all of Turkey's neighbours. Around EU accession talks in 2004 he launched his 'step ahead' policy for solving the Cyprus issue and also proposed normalising relations with the Kurdish minority. But by doing so, in 2010 he also indicated that the Cyprus issue would be resolved with the government in Athens, rather than the government in Nicosia (the capital of Cyprus), thus indicating that he would never accept Greek Cyprus as an independent federal state. As a result, he also stated that Northern Cyprus fell under Turkey's hegemony and was not an independent state, as it claims itself to be.[573] Around 2010 and later Erdogan responded in his own peculiar way to an earlier call from the Council of Europe, which urged Ankara to reach a settlement on the Cyprus issue by increasing trade between the two parts of the island and by respecting the cultural heritage of the Greeks in the Turkish part.[574] Although at first this gave incentives to acknowledge the atrocities, to come to terms with the past, to rehabilitate, to provide restitution, to bring perpetrators to justice and to establish a history and reconciliation commission, the purpose was clear: Cyprus had to return to its homeland, Turkey.

At the same time in eastern Anatolia the successful claims of Kurdish and other groups in front of the Court depended largely on the political moves of the AKP, which the majority seemed to support in 2007 according to MetroPoll. Before Erdogan (evidently) turned into an autocratic leader around 2014, his support was quite high, despite the rapidly

---

[572] MetroPoll, 'Social and Political Situation in Turkey-II, Image of Political Leaders and Confidence in Institutions', Strategical and Social Research Center Ankara, January 2009, www.metropoll.com.tr (last accessed August 2013).

[573] S. Tiryaki and M. Akgün (eds.), *The Heybeliada Talks: Two Years of Public Diplomacy on Cyprus*, Global Political Trends Center (Istanbul: Instabul Kültür University, 2011), p. 77.

[574] Parliamentary Assembly Council of Europe, Situation in Cyprus, Doc. 11727, Strasbourg, 30 September 2008.

decreasing level of civic trust. In 2007, for example, 58 per cent of citizens living in the Kurdish territory approved of the AKP government's policies, while only 30 per cent did not approve. The government's policy and level of responsiveness seemed to be successful.[575]

Baskin Oran, a writer and former professor of political science at Ankara University who has often been incarcerated, investigated and charged with high penalties for his critical expressions against the government, has pointed out that many of the violations of citizen rights and EU norms would have been prevented if TJ measures had been introduced at an earlier stage. He argued that the government would have initially lost trust if the 'heroic' past of the autocratic regime had been dismantled and demystified through acknowledgement of the Armenian Genocide or the pogroms against the Greeks in the 1950s and other religious minorities. However, if at least some TJ measures such as acknowledgement, debates, apologies or even trials had been implemented, Turkish society would have developed empathy with those suppressed and killed, which would have triggered reconciliation. In his view, this could have led to a much greater acceptance of current minorities and other ethnic groups. As a consequence, it could have (partly) prevented the mass killings and disappearances in eastern Anatolia in the 1980s and 1990s.[576]

But one of the main indicators to see whether TJ and consolidation were somewhat interlinked was the level of participation of the 20+ generation. It was high, but strongly controlled and suppressed by the political elite at that time. They questioned and challenged the Erdogan regime using the claims to deal with the past and thus not only delegitimising and demystifying the Ottoman and military past but also Erdogan's policies. Such is Leyla Neyzi's project on oral history. Neyzi is a university professor from the private Sabanci University in Istanbul who resembles what the 20+ generation political aims are. She has no personal ties to Armenians, but as an academic researcher she wanted to investigate her own Turkish identity and history. When I interviewed her in 2009, she said that the time of fear and secrecy was over at that time. But the fear to speak openly about the violent past returned around 2012 and 2013 when Erdogan made a bid for more power. But during less fearful times in 2009 and together with her team of students, she started studying former

---

[575] MetroPoll, 'Social and Political Situation in Turkey, A Study on Terrorism and Kurdish Issues in Southeast Region of Anatolia, Strategical and Social Research Center Ankara', November 2007, www.metropoll.com.tr (last accessed August 2013).

[576] Interview with Baskin Oran in Ankara in 2011.

Armenian villages in eastern Anatolia. Along with Armenian scholars and with support from German foundations and the German Ministry of Foreign Affairs, she interviewed descendants of survivors in Armenia as well as non-Armenians in the formerly inhabited Armenian villages in Turkey. She argued that even 100 years after the genocide, the history and story of the Armenian massacres are an open secret at the local level.[577] People remember, but have not dared to talk about these memories until now. Since the protests against Hrant Dink's murder in 2007, a more open atmosphere has developed and people feel less afraid to talk. Slowly, a consensus has emerged that it is time to tackle this period of history. In 2012 she released her results in the form of an exhibit, but had to be selective with the chosen location. Through this exhibit, villagers tell their stories which were documented in Turkish, Armenian and English. The exhibit travelled through Turkey, Armenia and beyond, and was only accessible 'upon demand' and mostly virtually, but it clearly illustrated the atrocities and injustice inflicted upon the Turkish-Armenian population at that time. Nevertheless, it must be mentioned that many books about the Armenian Genocide, including Neyzi's, were never available for purchase in Turkey and that exhibits like hers are shown in selective and non-public locations such as private foundations. These are private or academic initiatives, and by no means embraced by any government agencies or the Ministry of Education and, in the case of Turkey, they could hardly flourish. However, the little success and impact they have, these projects owe to the possibilities offered by the Internet, such as virtual memorials. Other such initiatives were those of the writer Murat Bardakci. He wrote one of the first books in Turkish with original documents from the time of the Armenian Genocide. It triggered wide debates and many questions. The author claimed that it would have been impossible to publish such a book ten years before. After the penal code reforms, the public protests and signed letters to the government, the publication of the book resulted in no serious repercussions, but was not widely read and was later censored.[578]

The United States launched (unsuccessful) 'normalisation protocols' between Turkey and Armenia after Erdogan's 'opening policies' in 2009 and 2010; his instalment of memorials and use of other TJ measures were part of a tactical concession the government in Ankara made to the

---

[577] Interview with Leyla Neyzi, Istanbul, 11 April 2011
[578] International Herald Tribune, 'Nearly a million Armenians, veiled by amnesia', 10 March 2009, p. 3.

international community and the United States in particular. This was the result of immense pressure exerted by members of the Armenian diaspora residing in the United States and France. In the protocols, both countries agreed to open crossing points between Armenia and Turkey on a border that had been closed since 1993.[579] Turkey had shown once again in only ten years its willingness to establish closer diplomatic ties with Armenia for tactical reasons. But the conditions were unacceptable to the Armenian government because it makes the acknowledgement of the genocide a precondition for serious talks and thus refrained from signing the protocols. The AKP argued that it was up to the Armenians to reach out to Turkey again to normalise the relationship between the two countries. This notwithstanding, the protocols were seen as a step towards EU accession for Turkey and have been confirmed by the Armenian Constitutional Court. But because of internal politics, a desire to please nationalist and Muslim forces and pressure from Azerbaijan, Erdogan pressured the Turkish parliament and his AKP to reject the protocols in 2010.

In 2009, the first Armenian-Turkish reconciliation memorial was erected in the already mentioned highly symbolic city of Kars. The Turkish artist Mehmet Aksoy called the 30 metre-high memorial the 'Statue of Humanity' (it depicted two persons reaching out to each other). However, it was taken down in 2011 after the protocols with Armenia failed and Erdogan called the statue ugly and a 'freak'. Erdogan directly asked for it to be demolished and it was taken down in the following months. Mehmet Aksoy reacted, saying he was 'really sorry, sorry on behalf of Turkey' about this act of demolition and assured both Armenian and Turkish citizens that he regarded it as his obligation to restore it one day and asked for moral forgiveness.[580] The memorial and its destruction stand like no other TJ measure as a sample for the tactical approach of the Turkish government to all TJ measures and its failure to catalyse any democratic consolidation process. Even more so, since after its demolition the writer, artist and blogger Bedri Baykam, who had staunchly supported the memorial, became the victim of an assassination attempt. He survived, left the country and the attempted assassin was at least prosecuted.[581]

---

[579]   D.L. Philipps, *Diplomatic History. The Turkey-Armenia Protocols* (New York: Columbia University Institute for the Study of Human Rights, 2012).

[580]   Frankfurter Allgemeine Zeitung, online version: 'Denkmal in der Türkei Mit der Abrissbirne gegen Versöhnung' (20 April 2011).

[581]   Exibart online journal, 'Erdogan tears down Kurdish-Armenian friendship monument', www.italy.exibart.com/_pdf/news.php?id_news=573 (last accessed April 2011).

Although the memorial was a minor act for reconciliation and minimal TJ tool, Erdogan's reactions and involvement illustrate the sensitive role that the past plays in politics and also the current state of democratic culture at that time, pushing away any further consolidation. Overall such TJ measures would question Turkish nationalism, which Erdogan needed to reinstall his autocratic regime. Thus over and over again, he expressed his discontent that the Armenian government would not accept his conditions for 'normalisation' between the two countries. This showed that the common narrative of the past remained in the hands of the government, rather than of society at large.

Nevertheless, the statue in Kars and the few exhibits about World War I in Turkish museums all show signs of how the government responded but also misused TJ to ease the pressure from the international community, CSOs and victims. In the Military Museum in Istanbul – the primary purpose of which is to glorify the Turkish army, wars and the military past – the first ever exhibit was opened in 2008 to address the Armenian Issue (with English subtitles), to satisfy visitors and pressure groups, both from outside and inside Turkey, by explaining the 'true' story of the Armenians and the threat they posed to the Ottoman Empire and now also to the Turkish Republic. Interestingly enough, the exhibit shows the same pictures of massacres and persecution, torture and deportation during the Armenian Genocide as the Armenian Genocide Museum in Yerevan, Armenia, yet with completely different titles and interpretation. In this memorial, the visitor learns that it is mainly Turks who were the victims of an Armenian (and Russian) violent and conspiratorial anti-Turkish movement, the sole objective of which was to harm Ottoman national unity.

It took Turkey more than two decades to establish a short window of opportunity of a fearless environment in which one could openly talk about the past prior and after 2005. But due to dramatic deconsolidation of the regime since Erdogan's run for the presidency in 2014, this fear to tackle past injustices has returned among much of the elite. Unconsolidated pockets had reached a threshold that could not compensate the democratic movement and by 2016 the government had restricted so many freedom rights, trialled and imprisoned dissidents of the regime and caused many more the leave the country, that it had entered yet another phase of authoritarian governance. The majoritarian 'winner takes it all' mentality of Turkish politics is still dominant in decision making. The public interpretation and perception of democratic institutions have seriously jeopardised the consolidation process.[582]

According to the polls, civic trust had risen to 43 per cent before Erdogan's presidency, and declined heavily afterward. The AKP government has lost almost half of the trust that it once enjoyed when it gained power in 2001.[583] Since 2010, this has divided the country roughly down the middle again. Since Erdogan knew that in 2011 the majority of his constituency would be in eastern Anatolia, he openly addressed the Kurdish massacres of the 1930s, particularly focusing once again on those that occurred in Dersim.[584]

Moreover, Erdogan promised to deal with these issues in what he called the 'New Resolution Process'. This is one of many examples of the rise of a new (electorally relevant) young generation and the emergence of public debates, films and publications to seek acknowledgement and even trials up to 25 years after serious transition started. Of course, at the same time, the revised but still in force Article 301 can be applied at any time. In addition, Oran Pamuk's exile is yet another indicator of the regime's instability, which is not willing or able to ensure his safety. A survey conducted in 2013 indicated that a small majority of Turks (51 per cent) disapproved of 'amnestied transitions', like those that occurred in Spain and Germany; thus a large part of the population would have supported trials and other TJ measures at that time aiming not only to delegitimise the previous governments but more so to legitimise the new one, if they would have allowed for it.

Nevertheless, one of the reasons why half of all Turks disapprove of this process for their own country is because it would include talks with the imprisoned PKK leader Abdullah Öcalan and thus would mean for some elites facing parts of their own unpleasant past. Seventy-five per cent of the respondents indicated that members of the PKK should not receive any amnesty. Not surprisingly, supporters of the Kurdish Party show strong support for amnestied transitions (77 per cent).[585] A generation into the process of transition, it became clear that the Kurdish issue

[582] L.M. McLaren, *Constructing Democracy in Southern Europe*, p. 171.

[583] European Union, Eurobarometer Surveys, Turkey 2010.06, http://ec.europa.eu (last accessed August 2013).

[584] O. Bakiner, 'Is Turkey Coming to Terms with Its Past? Politics of Memory and Majoritarian Conservatism', *Nationalities Papers: Journal of Nationalism and Ethnicity*, 41 (2013), 1–18.

[585] MetroPoll, Turkey's Pulse 'The New Resolution Process', Strategical and Social Research Center Ankara, April 2013, slide no. 18, www.metropoll.com.tr (last accessed August 2013).

was key to dealing with past injustices. This was the connecting issue in the spiral effect towards regime consolidation. Thus any democratic consolidation process in the future would largely depend on how future governments deal with the Kurdish issue.

But one more attempt for an open and fair way of dealing with the past should be mentioned here. In 2011, Turkey's largest television station began broadcasting a family soap in prime time that portrayed the Kurds in a positive light (*Ayrılık Olmasaydı: ben-u sen*). However, after seven weeks of broadcasting the show was stopped due to governmental interventions, and was only relaunched much later in 2012 and later cancelled. Intimidations and suppressions continued around that time and by 2015 President Erdogan had reissued military attacks against the alleged activities by the PKK in eastern Turkey with large destruction of Kurdish villages responding to violent provocations – a signal that any TJ process of any sort would be put on ice for the foreseeable future.

This was a time when many academics, lawyers, judges and prosecutors – the last strongholds of democratic reforms – continued to suffer repercussions. In a way, this time might remind one of what happened with Fritz Bauer and Baltasar Garzón in their respective countries. These men were also perceived as a threat to the silence that covered the past. In Turkey, the former chief prosecutor, Cihan Kansız, suffered a similar fate. In April 2011 he was appointed head of the judiciary's Ergenekon investigation. His appointment was sensational because he was best known for his work as a lawyer on the murder case of Hrant Dink.[586] In addition, he was a member of the Judges and Prosecutors' Association, YARSAV, an organisation that had criticised the Ergenekon investigation on a number of occasions. At first, Erdogan thought Kansız's nomination would ease the tension in society, but it had the opposite effect. Kansız wanted to shed more light on the cases and criticised the rule of law practice in Turkey. Unsurprisingly, he was removed from this position in 2012, only one year after his appointment, because his views were not in line with those of the AKP.

Olli Rehn, EU Commissioner for Enlargement, believed that the Ergenekon cases would be the key to Turkey's democratisation, but these hopes turned out to be in vain.[587] In 2011, Erdogan visited the European

---

[586] Hurriyet Daily Newspaper, English version http://web.hurriyetdailynews.com/ (last accessed April 2011).
[587] Young Civilians and Human Rights Agenda Association (HRAA) (ed.), *Ergenekon Is Our Reality*, p. 34.

Parliament and was again confronted with concerns about indictments of journalists and constraints on the freedom of the press. Erdogan defended the trials as a major achievement of rule of law and democracy but after the trials ended around 2013 it was evident that Erdogan had used this TJ tool to purge his political opponents.

But whilst the trials were ongoing, the constitutional referendum of 2010 took place which allowed the direct appointment of judges by the government (de facto by Erdogan himself) and thus weakened the independence of the Turkish judiciary. Ironically, two Turkish journalists, Mavioğlu and Ahmet Şık, who published a highly contested book about the Ergenekon case already in 2010,[588] were charged themselves in the Ergenekon trials. Even before these charges, no one had seriously thought that the trials would help Turkey face its past. Yet, due to greater participatory rights and citizen engagement (under international scrutiny), the path to democratic consolidation was not completely closed. International protesters together with Turkish academics, writers, journalists and human rights activists form a steadily growing voice in the country's TJ and democratisation process. Several civil society groups and NGOs (in particular IHD, Amnesty International and the Collective Memory Platform, which is comprised of family members of Kurdish, Alevi and Armenian victims) have repeatedly requested the Turkish government acknowledge the atrocities, come to terms with the past, prosecute perpetrators, and rehabilitate victims and those discriminated against. One of them is Hafıza Markezi, an NGO based in Istanbul which aims to collect data on past atrocities over the past century in Turkey. It aims to collect victims' personal narratives and to let the wider public know what has happened in eastern Anatolia throughout the century.[589] It also aims to bring perpetrators to justice and to establish history, truth or reconciliation commissions, although it operates mainly online and via Twitter. Its survival, however, depends largely on support and donations from abroad.

Meanwhile, Erdogan has tried to disrupt the old alliances of the deep state, in which nationalists, the military and organised crime together fought against separatists, Islamists and minorities. Yet, with the Ergenekon trials in his pockets, Erdogan went far beyond what is

---

[588]   The book is entitled *Between a Rock and a Hard Place* (Kırk Katır Kırk Satır): The Guide to Understanding Ergenekon and the Counter-Guerrillas, see: Hürryet Daily News, Özgür Ögret, New Books urge dropping blinders on Turkey's Ergenekon case (16 June 2010).

[589]   Hafıza Merkezi, www.hafıza-merkezi.org (last accessed February 2014).

acceptable in a democracy. *The Economist* titled its report of the trials 'Justice or Revenge?' in 2013 because of the unusually high conviction rate. Of the more than 270 people indicted, around 250 were convicted and 19 received life sentences. Erdogan's primary objective with these trials was to dismantle the TAF, intimidate its members and to remove them from leading administrative positions wherever possible.[590] The fact that Erdogan called himself 'the chief prosecutor of Ergenekon' indicated the lack of judicial independence and at the same time Erdogan's use of the trials for his own political gain. The initial hope for some TJ soon declined.

Shortly before the trial ended, parliament amended the armed forces charter. Generals had often cited this charter in the past to justify coups. The TAF's duty in the charter to 'protect and watch over the republic' was replaced with a more limited obligation to defend 'the Turkish homeland against foreign threats'. This amendment dismantled the military's power over internal affairs, which was now solely in the hands of the executive, the legislature and the judiciary. Such slow transformation of the military into an external defence-oriented organ was a successful way to reduce the risk of another coup.[591]

In the aftermath, the Ergenekon trials have become known as the country's longest-lasting political trials against the military (and many others who opposed Erdogan). What began with indictments against former and retired generals of the TAF for a plot from 1980 turned into a marathon of prosecutions against any individual, organisation or journalist who questions the policies of the AKP. The number of people prosecuted and investigated has reached over 500. Those indicted and convicted include members of the army, journalists, academics, bloggers, lawyers and even prosecutors, teachers, members of NGOs and politicians. There was widespread protest against the trials, both within the country and throughout the world, from all sectors and societal groups. These protests ironically aligned those who radically opposed each other: defendants of democracy, victim groups and the military.

Some observers also blame the EU for the decline of democracy in Turkey. Özbudun and Türkmen state in their evaluation of Turkey's democratic regime consolidation that the objections expressed by the EU Member States towards Turkey's full membership, even in the long term,

---

[590] The Economist, 'Turkish Politics, Justice or Revenge?' (last accessed 10 August 2013).
[591] N.S. Satana, 'Transformation of the Turkish Military and the Path to Democracy', *Armed Forces and Society*, 34 (2008), 359.

created a sense of hopelessness among the Turkish public.[592] Similar opinion is expressed by Ilter Turan, who had earlier warned that if the EU withdraws its support for Turkey, this could bring about anti-democratic developments and a slide back to authoritarianism, which it eventually did in 2016.[593]

At the same time, civil unrest, protests and international alliances against this downward spiral could not be held back – despite a strong 20+ generation and growing international support for TJ and democratic development. However, the spiral correlation between consolidation and TJ may pause for some time, as Rustow's model illustrated in phase two and three, but can still arise again.[594]

Some of the last freely organised CSOs protests and sit-ins in Gezi Park at Taksim Square started in 2013 and were sparked by the police's violent reactions to demonstrators. These demonstrators were protesting against a plan to build a shopping mall in the park and marked not only the generational shift but also the time when the regime turned autocratic again with its massive repressions against the protesters. In 2013 MetroPoll confirmed a fast-growing dissatisfaction and distrust in democratic institutions among citizens. Trust decreased from 65 per cent in 2010 to 48 per cent in 2012 and finally to 38 per cent in 2013. This downward trend continued after Erdogan became president of the country in 2014, with the aim of concentrating even more power in his hands. Subsequently strikes and more protests broke out and today these regular (and violent) protests rally against restrictions of freedom of the press, assembly and the government's encroachment on secularism. One of the major concerns for reformists is Islamisation of Turkey's internal policy. These reformists have been imprisoned, tortured and prosecuted and the downward direction of the spiral continues.

Around the same time in 2014, 60 per cent of the population believed that the government suppressed open and fair investigations and trials. Trust was already at one of the lowest levels ever.[595] The lower the trust, the higher the radicalisation among Kurdish and other civil society groups in 2014 and 2015 when Erdogan launched military strikes on eastern Anatolia. Civil movements, such as Taksim Solidarity – formed mainly

---

[592] E. Özbudun and F. Türkmen, 'Impact of the ECtHR Rulings in Turkey', 1008.
[593] I. Turan, *Turkey's Difficult Journey to Democracy*, p. 223ff.
[594] D.A. Rustow, 'Transition to Democracy: Toward a Dynamic Model', 337–363.
[595] MetroPoll, Turkey Pulse, 'Corruption and Government', www.metropoll.com.tr/research/political-research-9/1743 (last accessed August 2014).

with members of the 20+ generation and other NGOs, with more than 400,000 supporters around the country – demanded massive democratic reforms and an end to Erdogan's rule. Violence from left-wing opposition groups against the AKP, their offices and politicians increased and so did radical Islamist terrorist acts. In 2015, left-wing groups attacked AKP offices and held protests in all major Turkish cities on a weekly basis, while the police attacked Kurdish party offices and Islamists attacked Turkish facilities. The vicious cycle continued.

Those who believe that democracy is 'the only game in town' remain between 30 and 40 per cent and this crowd has not really increased significantly over the past few decades.[596] These are worrying indicators and Turkey is far from being a qualitatively high and thus stable and effective democracy, let alone a consolidated regime. The country remains divided. Despite March 2013 the leader of the PKK, Abdullah Öcalan, declared a ceasefire with his TAF opponents and asked the PKK followers to fight for their interests using political (that is democratic) means in parliament. The Kurdish party followed these instructions and was successful in the 2015 elections. However, at the same time, the events of 2015 and 2016 also led to the recurrence of violence between the TAF and PKK insurgents.

And in February 2014, after a controversial and violent 20-hour parliamentary debate, delegates of the AKP eventually passed a new law that gave Erdogan and his government sole authority over the judiciary. There was not enough civil society pressure to prevent it. After 'successfully' controlling the Ergenekon trails now, with this law Erdogan aimed to control the judiciary so that it would be possible to cover up his own cases of corruption and illegal activities among party members. Both the law and the judiciary were not in his hands and consequently any attempt to strive for more TJ. The AKP policy and the violent incidents after the earlier period of reform illustrate the low level of transparency and accountability.

Whilst radical movements and groups are prospering, another actor has come into the downward spiral game: the Fethullah Gülen movement. This is a Muslim movement that runs schools and higher education and keeps close ties with the business and science community.[597] But it is the movement's head, Gülen, whom Erdogan made personally responsible

[596] MetroPoll, Strategical and Social Research Center, Leaders and Public Trust in Institutions, Ankara, January 2013, www.metropoll.com.tr (last accessed August 2013).
[597] For an overview of the Gülen movement, see: K. Öktem, *Angry Nation*, p. 119; and I. Turan, *Turkey's Difficult Journey to Democracy*, p. 194ff.

for the failed coup attempt in 2016 and whom the president persistently persecutes and aims to put on trial in Turkey, if he can be extradited from his exile in the United States. What followed in the months after the coup attempt were arbitrary arrests, travel bans and persecutions of members of civil society, academics, writers, human rights activists, speakers of victim groups, journalists and members of opposition parties, which as we have seen in other TJ and democratisation processes is the core of any successful regime consolidation process.

Brief Summary of Turkey

Turkey surely proves to be a test case for regime consolidation in relation to TJ measures and the spiral model. A first upward and later downward spiral of democratic performance has been closely linked to the way TJ measures were used or abused by government for tactical reasons and by civil society.

Since 1989 the country has officially complied and adhered to all international duties, has issued major reforms, allowed civil society to grow and used TJ as tools for both. The EU accession talks in 2004 and 2005, the 90th anniversary of the Armenian Genocide in 2005, the rise of the AKP in 2002 and the emerging civil society powers in the Kurdish territories, first indicated a democratic regime consolidation between 2000 and 2005. Unfortunately, consolidation abruptly failed thereafter when international pressure decreased, civil society was intimidated, political trials emerged and emerging wars in the region could no longer restrain Erdogan's power grab, which cumulated in 2016 following the major decline of level of democracy since 2005 and thus a generation after the initial reforms and the commitments to democracy and TJ in 1989.

Apart from this TJ measures were used mostly in an exclusionary and biased way during these periods and the different elites were not able to establish the legitimacy they needed to push the spiral upwards. As Merkel and Puhle have phrased it for similar country cases, there is a major gap between the rights and democracy guaranteed in the constitution and how these are adhered to in practice.[598] It is not surprising that radicalisation on all political sides re-emerged, to which the government responded with arbitrary vengeance already in 2009 (reintroducing autocratic governance), massive suppression of protests in 2013 and a launch of internal air strikes in 2015.

---

[598] W. Merkel and H.-J. Puhle, *Von der Diktatur zur Demokratie*, p. 140.

Thus, the re-radicalisation of left wing and right-wing religious/nation-alist groups after 2013 is a consequence of the regime's return to authori-tarian tactics.[599] Yet, since the country's turn to democracy in the 1990s, TJ measures have been able to effect some cumulative causation, for example contributing to the rise of civil society engagement and ownership, an effect that has been noted in EU accession talks. Even in the early stage of regime change, Turkey fulfilled most of its commitments to TJ and when it did so this contributed to an upward spiral effect and mutually cumu-lative causalities between the independent and dependent variable, for example in the government's response to the Kurdish Crying Saturday Mothers, the establishment of Armenian memorials and in dealing with the Cypriot reconciliation process.

In 1989 democratic institutions and a willingness to comply with European norms were in place and governmental authorities responded to this with massive reforms over the course of the first decade. TJ measures such as commissions of inquiry, exhumations, trials and pub-lic debates were used (albeit in a very tactical and election-orientated manner) throughout the decades, although they remained almost exclu-sively under government control. Setbacks and restrictions in the first two to three decades are normal, since the feeling of moral responsibil-ity to atone for past injustices only comes about with the 20+ genera-tion, the generation that determines whether democratic consolidation succeeds or not. It takes at least one generation before civic trust can grow. In Turkey, this generation started to take the public stage between 2005 and 2015, with an increase in victim and citizen-driven organisa-tions, but which were massively and censored to act freely. Last but not least the impact of the international community – mainly the Council of Europe, the EU, UN, the Armenian diaspora, and the Cypriot govern-ment – was a major driving force for regime change through TJ. Thus, we see that the patterns of regime change and TJ in Turkey are very similar to those of Germany and Spain during the first two decades, but very different after 20-plus years when a new generation appeared on the political and civil stage.

However, the firm grip that Turkey's ruling AKP party and President Erdogan holds on the country, and Erdogan's use of Islam to give him moral authority, challenges this transition and has widened the coun-try's unconsolidated pockets, posing a major threat to democratic

---

[599] W. Merkel and H.-J. Wagener, 'Akteure', pp. 67–68.

consolidation.[600] TJ and democracy in Turkey are competing with many different narratives and belief systems and thus will always face challenges of re-authorisation of the regime. Yet, as Teitel has argued, the effect TJ has had globally cannot be ignored, even by the most authoritarian regimes, and thus it will most likely strike Turkish society sooner or later again as one of many tools to trigger regime change. In Teitel's view this is because TJ measures are 'changing [the] nature of rights protection, especially group conceptions of rights that may guide a way to deal meaningfully with the root cause of conflict and provide new parameters by which to identify and respond to political violence'.[601] Thus, even if Erdogan seeks more power whilst dividing the society again, sooner or later claims for reconciliation and democracy will re-emerge, despite or because of autocratic regime consolidation.

---

[600] Religious authorities do not play as important a role in Germany or even Spain as they do in Turkey. Such a faith-based transition process can put secularism at risk, which would damage the development of moral engagement and civic trust.

[601] R. Teitel, 'Globalizing Transitional Justice', p. 182.

6

Regime Consolidation through Transitional Justice

As shown in the cases of East and West Germany, Spain and Turkey TJ measures and consolidation of political institutions somewhat interact in an upward and downward spiral over a longer period of time. TJ measures can guide consolidation process, but the quality of democracy or level of consolidation depends on whether these TJ measures are applied in an inclusive or exclusive manner, whether they are implemented top-down only, or also citizen-driven and bottom-up. The more inclusive, the more democratic the regime as seen in West and later reunified Germany and Spain (once it is taking off); the more exclusive, the more regime consolidation tends towards authoritarianism as seen in East Germany and Turkey. The extent to which they do that depends on the interaction among political, civic and international actors and their respective institutions, i.e. parliaments, CSOs or international organisations such as the EU and the Council of Europe. TJ measures contribute to democratic consolidation in a way when there is a bottom-up and top-down international and governmental approach aiming towards the same consolidation target, as seen in the cases of West Germany and Spain. TJ measures contribute to authoritarian regime consolidation if they are exclusively used by governments in a top-down approach and, for example, to only please the international community and organisations or to appease opposition and minorities in one's own country for strategic reasons. For these reasons they are rather misused to manifest a certain political or ideological power and status; and when civil society is excluded from interacting to create their own narrative of justice of the past, as seen in the cases of East Germany and Turkey.

Nevertheless, East and West and reunified Germany, Spain and Turkey show a number of similarities in terms of regime change and consolidation, parallel to the rise or decline in use or abuse of TJ measures. Although during the first years of regime change, the governments in all the country case studies firmly expressed their commitment to democracy and thus also to political reforms and TJ measures. But at the same time they used TJ measures almost exclusively for tactical and strategic reasons, to manifest their external relations as well as to ease domestic demands or unrest during the first decade. Moral, ethical or citizen-driven concerns did not play a major role during the early transition process, that is to say in the first five to ten years of regime change. TJ measures are merely political tools during this period. More importantly, in the first years of regime change political elites tended to use TJ in a more exclusionary way, to strengthen their new regime type. Soon after the first years of transition, the regimes headed towards democratic (West and reunified Germany, Spain, partly Turkey) or authoritarian consolidation (East Germany, recently Turkey) after a decade. Specifically during the first and second post-regime change decade, all countries had to deal with unconsolidated pockets, such as terror or violent separatism, often related to the lack of TJ measures. Merkel's divisions in constitutional, representative, attitudinal and behavioural or civic consolidation phases after transition[1] are best illustrated by these case studies when we look at the mutual reinforcing use or abuse of TJ measures in relations to regime consolidation.

All countries or states passed the first two consolidation phases with democratic deficits and political shortcomings but no major damages or failures; but during the phases of behavioural and civic consolidation, TJ measures had to be pushed by victim groups and civil society in West Germany (and unified Germany) as well as Spain.[2] In East Germany and Turkey exclusive and selective sets of TJ measures were used by autocratic governments, i.e. celebrating in their TJ policies the communist victory or Turkish nationalism. They legitimised the new regime type in a one-sided narrative of the past to uphold the ideal of 'communism' or 'Turkishness' as a binding factor for state building.

The fact that unconsolidated pockets such as ETA terror in Spain, the RAF terror in West Germany or TAF terror in Turkey were strongly linked to the lack of or the refusal to delegitimise the past and demystify past dictatorships, underlines either the wrongful or the exclusive or unsystematic use of TJ measures during the first decade or two. But the systematic, inclusive and citizen-driven open use and change of TJ measures, for example the public lustration and expulsion of Nazi members from office in West Germany or members of the Stasi in reunified

---

[1] W. Merkel, Systemtransformation, *Eine Einführung in die Theorie und Empirie der Transformationsforschung*, p. 112f.

[2] P.C. Schmitter, 'The Quality of Democracy', *Journal of Democracy*.

Germany and the demystification of Franco's past by renaming streets and taking down statues and instead installing memorials for victims, had later helped to end or further prevent these unconsolidated pockets of terror and counter-terror to violently dismantle the shadow of the previous regime.

While in East Germany it soon became evident that the SED government was a dictatorial regime that used TJ in an exclusionary way, Turkey seemed to be a country that had taken two democratic steps forward and one authoritarian step backward. After the end of the first round of EU accession talks in 2005, international pressure on Turkey declined, leading to a slide towards authoritarianism in the following ten years. In West Germany (later unified Germany) and Spain, TJ's effects increased rapidly after two to three decades, when citizen and victim groups took more ownership of the TJ process. This increased civil participation and eventually led to the development of a civic culture.

Governments' responsiveness to citizen demands for TJ or reconciliation has always indicated the institutions' level of accountability and transparency. This in return indicated the level of civic trust and eventually consolidation. Thus, the mutually reinforcing interaction between state affairs, civil actors, elites and non-violent citizen engagement paired with international incentives, financial support or pressure for legal reforms, trials, inquiries, compensations or memorials, has contributed to strengthening institutions and actors and consolidating the democratic regime.[3] To ignore or suppress civic engagement and ignore international pressure will most likely lead to an autocratic consolidation, because it indicates or symbolises that the government has no interest in being held accountable, responding to citizen's claims or adhering to international human rights or other standards.

I used the image of spiral effect to describe and explain the confrontational relationship between external or interfering measures and domestic citizen-driven ones. In this study, I applied it to the mutually reinforcing effect that trials, commissions of inquiry, lustrations, vetting procedures, reparations, amnesties, memorials, films, public debates or media coverage, novels and literature can have on delegitimising and demystifying the past and stabilising a new political regime.[4] These measures are often financed or incentivised by international organisations, such as the EU or the Council of Europe or by NGOs and foundations or foreign and

---

[3] W. Merkel and H.-J. Puhle, *Von der Diktatur zur Demokratie*, p. 140.
[4] N. Deitelhoff and K.D. Wolff, 'Business and Human Rights', pp. 225–227.

international aid projects, such as EU structural funds or the Marshall Plan. In the cases of East, West and reunified Germanys, of Spain and Turkey, these spiral and cumulative causality effects started slowly in the first decade during constitutional and representative or institutional consolidation, to use these categories again. But the process sped up over the next decades in both directions toward democracy in West (and reunified) Germany and autocracy in East Germany. In East Germany it cumulated in the building of the Berlin Wall in 1961 which marked the end of any 'democratic experiment' in the east and at the same time it marked the year of the first Holocaust trials in Israel and later in West Germany, after which representative and attitudinal consolidation of democratic institutions took off once more.

The main difference is that TJ measures in authoritarian regimes are used by political elites only to stabilise their power, while in democratic regimes, over the course of about 20 years, TJ policies change from being top-town measures to bottom-up ones, thus reaching civil society and giving them additional tools to participate and thus legitimising the regime. To refer again to Rustow, O'Donnell or Linz and Stepan concepts of regime consolidation, it was intriguing to see how and when TJ measures contributed to consolidation efforts. The 'magic' turning point seems to be when the 20+ generation has politically matured and enters the political arena. This is when behavioural and attitudinal as well as civic consolidation finally takes off and democracy has a chance to become 'the only game in town' – or otherwise, as seen in Turkey (from approximately 2005 onwards) and East Germany (from approximately 1961 onwards), it is the point in time for the autocratic regime to radically suppress civic and democratic engagement. It's the time when the (new) regime has to face its toughest challenge, whether their leadership is capable or willing to share power and respond to civic engagement, or if they close the doors to new ideas and bottom-up civic movements.

West Germany (and reunified Germany) and Spain slowly moved to behavioural or civic consolidation[5] and after two decades using TJ measures in a more systematic and inclusive manner as a catalyst to change behaviour and the rhetoric of political and civic elites, of policy makers, journalists, judges or academics and triggered more participation among the 20+ generation. Despite the heavy drawbacks, such as the

---

[5] W. Merkel and H.-J. Puhle, *Von der Diktatur zur Demokratie*, p. 140ff. and W. Merkel, Systemtransformation, *Eine Einführung in die Theorie und Empirie der Transformationsforschung*, pp. 122–127.

radicalisation laws in West Germany in the 1960s and the indictment of Judge Garzón in Spain after 2000, generally the spiral motion developed over time, and the concession towards and the use of more TJ measures benefited from more stable democratic institutions and thus we can speak of a mutually reinforcing spiral effect.

6.1   TJ Measures as Catalysts for Change and Consolidation

Applying TJ measures (Table 4.1) gives political and civil actors an opportunity to break the vicious circle of vengeance, suppression of minorities and political violence that often lasted for centuries in the respective country. As outlined earlier by Rustow, Jeremy Sarkin and others, this process is generally understood as one that continues for several generations, an understanding that the present study confirms.[6] Nevertheless, even if a responsive government aims to break the vicious circle, it remains challenging for political actors to use TJ measures in a forward-looking way, to avoid the downward spiral of violence or the unquenchable desire that traps people in cycles of revenge, recrimination and escalation, to use Martha Minow's terms.[7] In other words, the pure fact that a regime uses TJ measures does not say anything about what the regime will become. Therefore, TJ measures are truly 'independent' (variables) in character and only become 'dependent' in the hands and minds of actors who can use them to further whatever purpose they wish.

One can see the similarities in all case studies during the first two decades after the regime's commitment to democracy. The interaction between institutional actors, their political and civic actors and TJ tools, exhibits the same patterns in all countries studied. But the spiral effect is usually only visible during the second decade and it depends on how TJ measures are intertwined with institution building and civic performance over a period of time. Although a democratic constitution and elected parliament seem to be a crucial rejoinder to mass violence and an unjust past, they alone are not enough. Democratic consolidation can only be fuelled if an active and diverse public and institutional response to the past is guaranteed by TJ measures, if the new regime is to be legitimated and stable.[8]

---

[6] J. Sarkin and E. Daly, 'Too Many Questions, Too Few Answers', 101–168; and D.A. Rustow, 'Transition to Democracy: Toward a Dynamic Model', 337–363.

[7] M. Minow, *Between Vengeance and Forgiveness*, p. 10.

[8] Ibid., pp. 22–23.

These catalysts flourish best in a human rights abating, inclusive, reinte-grated society that embraces pluralism and citizen participation. Because this is when justice can better be done for all groups of victims and vic-timisers regardless of their political or religious loyalties. In general, gov-ernments and citizens can use TJ measures immediately after the conflict has ended and as soon as there is at least some constitutional setup that allows for democratic participation, as was shown. Civil participation, the independence of institutions and forming NGOs must be guaranteed in the constitutional setup to give TJ measures a chance to later interact with civic and political institutions. In other words, TJ measures as catalysts or tools can be implemented when the formal margins of the (new) regime are in place, its institutions established and the political will to recon-cile dominates public discourse. That was not the case in East Germany because the constitutions privileged one victim group, the communist victims, over others. It was also not the case in Turkey when the AKP-led government refused the claims by Kurdish or Armenian victim groups and their representatives.

Therefore, this comparative study aimed to provide narrative proof for the theoretical assumptions made among TJ scholars as well as regime change and consolidation study scholars (named in the methodology chapter), who argue that TJ contributes 'somewhat' to democracy but without yet much proof or evidence. Scholars, such as Bloomfield and colleagues, have long emphasised the importance of civil actors as key to TJ measures. Without them, they are not effective. It is civil society that ought to contribute to reconciliation for it to work. This is fundamental for 'a democratic culture and thus create relationships between coun-tries, communities, neighbours, constituencies and individuals which will lead to trust in democratic structures'.[9] But thus far, there was lit-tle evidence that a free civil society correlates whether TJ measures are applied in an inclusive or exclusive manner and thus contribute to con-solidation. Similar to what Stephen Winter could only theorise but not prove, namely that TJ aims to establish or re-establish trust amongst divided societies and reintegrate them, because an integrated society is pivotal for any consolidation in a democratic regime. Hence, the coun-try cases presented here aim to illustrate that this is only the case if TJ is accompanied by citizen participation, which in turn can be triggered by the use of TJ measures. And in line with the UN guidelines for the

[9] D. Bloomfield, T. Barnes and L. Huyse (eds.), *Reconciliation after Violent Conflict* (Stockholm: IDEA Handbook, 2005), p. 14.

2009 UN International Year of Reconciliation when the UN highlighted that there is no successful democracy without rule of law and reconciliation of a divided society, to which TJ can contribute eventually, this study aimed to trace some of these TJ measures in relation to regime consolidation.[10]

And yet, the notion of TJ, its measures and methods have transformed dramatically over the past decades. TJ has moved from being an exceptional response to war crimes in the first place, then to dictatorships and military regime, to becoming a method and even strategy used to further a far broader array of interests held by non-state actors associated with the global tendency to democracy. Even though in very different time periods, political eras of Cold and post-Cold war, my findings show that neither Turkey, Spain nor reunified Germany could ignore the dramatic emergence of TJ in the 1990s. Today, almost all states in transition apply some if not an extensive number of TJ measures in order to be a reliable and legitimate partner for any negotiation process. This led to an expansion as well as to criticism of the role international human rights and international criminal law played in advancing democratisation and state building.[11]

Because of the rising urge for more TJ across the world, it has also become an inflationary tool or method for any political and civic actor in any regime constellation – even the most autocratic ones. It has been therefore necessary to show that TJ measures do not automatically lead to democracy, but can also have the opposite effect. Thus careful and inclusive application and consideration of who uses these tools, at what stage and with what aim, is helpful to assess their possible impact and effect.[12] The timing and sequencing in applying these mechanisms is fundamental to whether they result in democratic or authoritarian regime consolidation. For example, as seen in the cases of Germany and Spain, amnesty laws, memorials and reparations were the first measures implemented; truth commissions were never used, although trials were held in Germany and Turkey (albeit for very different purposes). There was no case in which all TJ measures, as outlined in the introductory chapters, were used at the same time and in specific sequence. Apologies, vettings, compensations

---

[10] A. Mihr, 'Das Internationale Jahr zur Aussöhnung 2009', *Zeitschrift für die Vereinten Nationen*, 1 (2010), 21–26.

[11] R. Teitel, 'Transitional Justice Globalised', p. 2.

[12] A.R. Champman, V. Baxter and H. Van der Merwe (eds.), *Assessing the Impact of Transitional Justice: Challenges for Empirical Research* (Washington, DC: USIP Press, 2009); O.N.T. Thoms, J. Ron and R. Paris, 'State-Level Effects of Transitional Justice', 329–354.

and other TJ measures might better be applied at different times in the transformation process, depending on how victims and victimisers have been or can be integrated into the new political system, for example during the constitutional and representative consolidation phase.

To see whether there is any catalyst effect in the short (transition) or medium (consolidating) term, it is helpful to look at the first ten years of transition. This is the time during which some of the TJ measures – albeit not all – are issued at least on paper. During this period of regime change, the road towards democratic or authoritarian consolidation is paved. The window of opportunity that opens when a majority of the population aims to address the past and seeks justice is short, as Hazan has pointed out, but can be used to install major political shifts, for example in the new constitutions, the penal code or civil law.

Citizens who just survived war, conflict and dictatorship have high expectations for a better life and usually opt for democracy as an alternative model to the previous regime. But they are often soon disappointed by the new regime due to their lack of experience and understanding of what democracy means – namely to take an active part and responsibility in the regime and not expect others to do it. Thus, governments need to react immediately to promote national unity, as was seen in Germany and Spain, and for all these purposes TJ measures are useful tools.[13] Thus, agreements to use TJ are often made during the first decade, but are only sufficiently executed if civil society and victim groups are ready to face the (sometimes painful) TJ process and if external pressure is strong enough and if it allows for free and equal civic participation, although government responsiveness to citizen demands is often limited in this first decade of transition, due to tendencies of radicalisation of new political and private actors in times of transition.[14]

As illustrated above, the TJ process must be launched in the most inclusive way possible in the first decade during the constitutional consolidation process in order to have any later effect at all (often by pilot projects), to address needs and desires of all those who were involved in or affected by the conflict. Once amnesty laws are passed, as was the case of Spain and West Germany before or right after the new regime has been set up, it is difficult to launch an open TJ process. To change or amend amnesty laws take a lot of political will, power and resources in the upcoming decades

---

[13] N.T. Aiken, *Identity, Reconciliation and Transitional Justice*, p. 184.
[14] W. Merkel, Systemtransformation, *Eine Einführung in die Theorie und Empirie der Transformationsforschung*, p. 112ff.

and can also often lead to public turmoil and violence, as seen in Spain, Turkey and West Germany.

Unconsolidated pockets and radicalisation of groups such as the PKK, the RAF or ETA are not unknown responses to impunity or amnesty laws. Victimisers' rights to a fair trial or fair vetting procedure is as important as victims' rights to reparation and acknowledgement of wrongdoings through compensations or memorials. However, as my case studies also show, it seems the new and often-fragile governments are never able to satisfy all victims' desires and expectations. Launching a completely inclusive TJ process is almost impossible in the early years of transition. Governments set priorities, which often benefit those who cry the loudest: external stakeholders, or victims and victimisers who are part of the new constituency and electorate – as was the case of West Germany after 1949 and Spain after 1975. Not surprisingly, victimisers are often able to 'cry louder' for their rights, as they form part of the former elites such as the German refugees and displaced persons after 1945, while victims still suffer from intimidation and discrimination as many Holocaust survivors did. Therefore, extra advocacy is needed on behalf of victims, a task that is often taken up by external or international stakeholders such as the Council of Europe, the UN or the EU, let alone international donors or NGOs. NGOs, think tanks or foundations and international organisations become proxy voices of those being victimised. In reality, these processes are far from ideal and are often exclusionary and biased. The goal is thus to achieve as much inclusiveness as possible with TJ measures in the first decade and to have institutions that operate with as much independence and transparency as possible.[15]

If this early window is used prudently to install TJ measures, then these tools have a chance of later being used in a non-biased way by civil society actors, which again can have a legitimising effect on the consolidation of the regime. If a defeated, tired, devastated, traumatised or poor population has a shared desire to use TJ tools in this way, it poses a chance for newly elected political elites and the democratic institutions to delegitimise traditional authoritarian rules and old elites. However, that is not necessarily the case in all traumatised societies. The new political and civic elites have to choose carefully which TJ measures to apply and when. Sequencing and timing play an important part in this circular cumulative

---

[15] E. Kristjansdottir, A. Nollkaemper and C. Ryngaert, 'Introduction', in ibid. (eds.), *International Law in Domestic Courts: Rule of Law Reform in Post-Conflict States* (Antwerp: Intersentia, 2012), vol. IX, pp. 1–15.

causal process, as shown in the case of Spain and West Germany in the first decade or two. In this respect, some TJ measures will only work after institutions have consolidated, to which TJ measures themselves contribute in a spiral manner.[16]

Overall, TJ measures are also key to the integration of victims and victimisers, and this integration is a prerequisite for a democratic consolidated regime. International donors, NGOs and charity organisations all aim to foster TJ with the aim of bringing peace, stability and democracy. Governments and security forces in the countries where TJ is needed have to guarantee the personal safety and security of both victims and perpetrators before they can proceed with implementation of TJ measures. In many post-conflict societies, such victims' safety and security cannot be guaranteed due to bigotry, stereotypes, old military elites still in positions of power, or ongoing acts of vengeance.[17]

As has been shown in the case of West Germany and later also Spain, the first step is to address and include victims, victimisers and bystanders of past injustice in the process. The extent to which TJ measures address all those who are reluctant, afraid or simply opposed to coming to terms with the past is also a 'stress test' for young regimes and their commitment to democracy. Sometimes this pathway is paved with failures and resistance among victims and victimisers on all sides, as was the case in all countries discussed here. This happens mostly during times of representative and behavioural consolidation phases, as illustrated by Merkel earlier, and thus in the first decade of transition.

In addition, any TJ initiative must take into account the different circumstances and types of conflict, as well as the country's early experience with democracy, its economic developments, and traditional governance structures. In a purely ideological conflict scenario, such as was the case in East Germany and partly in Turkey's struggle for Turkishness, members of national groups that were previously at war with each other can attribute the previous abuses to the former regime. But this can only work if there is true commitment to pluralism and diversity best represented by the political and civic spectrum of society.

TJ measures serve to unite divided countries and reconcile societies after periods of war, injustice and violence, as we saw in the cases of East and West Germany and Turkey. Bringing the young elite from the former conflict parties together can facilitate the mutually reinforcing process

---

[16] T.D. Olson, L.A. Payne and A.G. Reiter, *Transitional Justice in Balance*, p. 107.
[17] J.A. McAdams (ed.), *Transitional Justice and the Rule of Law in New Democracies*, p. xv.

between TJ and regime consolidation. Turkey is far from achieving this as of the near future. Instead Turkey's political elites have chosen backslides to autocracy.

In contrast, in a situation of domestic ethnic, political and linguistic or religious conflict – as was the case for Spain and Turkey – mistrust and hatred prevails and former combatants (victims and victimisers) continue to live side by side while maintaining their distinct identities, extremist views and religious animosities. This poses a tremendous risk to democratic regime consolidation and leads to very hazardous TJ measures, which is one of the reasons why TJ processes were so different in Spain and Turkey from the one in Germany.[18]

6.2 The Spiral Effect

As shown with the cases of East Germany and Turkey and partly Spain during the first two decades, the downward spiral can begin if the political leadership denies inclusiveness, free and open civic engagement and dialogue, either formally or informally. If TJ measures fail to place blame on all sides or are used exclusively for political purposes, this will lead to unconsolidated pockets and a downward spiral of regime development. It seems to be in the nature of the early transition process that TJ measures, if applied at all, are predominantly used in an exclusionary and tactical way due to bigotry, bias, legacies or old political ties and friendships among the political elites that do not allow for a fully fledged, transparent and accountable TJ process. In all case studies, governments have exempted former political elites from vetting procedures and instead issued amnesty laws, because of their strong alliances with them or because new governments fear acts of vengeance or violent resistance. Interestingly, the level and intensity by which this has been done differs per country and leads to different results. Impunity was hardly combatted at all in Turkey and Spain. But West Germany and Spain turned into democracies, despite unconsolidated pockets and aspects of exclusiveness, while Turkey has failed to overcome these pockets and East Germany never aimed to be truly democratic.

The spiral or cumulative causal path between civic and institutional consolidation and TJ measures has never been linear as illustrated in Figure 2.1. West Germany's path towards democratic consolidation had

---

[18] N. Kritz, 'Policy Implications of Empirical Research on Transitional Justice', pp. 13–22, at p. 19.

some slides back to non-democratic measures, and so did the Spanish consolidation process. Under West Germany's militant democracy occupational bans for radical right or left-wing sympathisers were imposed and the legislature passed a number of laws that resulted in a limitation of fundamental freedoms, such as expression, media, participation and work, among others, for the benefit of peaceful transition in the 1960s and 1970s. This is where the spiral went down for some years, although it later went upwards again. Similar it was the case when Spain aimed to fight separatist terror with their own anti-terror group, the GRAPO, and thus undermined the new democratic regime in the 1980s. Yet, Turkey's spiral went up and down over the decades but failed to fully recover from the downward trend starting slowly in 2005, intensifying around 2010 and cumulating in 2016.

Political actors, external and internal institutions, time, sequencing and generations matter in this spiral concept of mutual reinforcement. Most prominent in the spiral effect is the TJ category of criminal and restorative justice measures. This study found that punitive justice was not applied to punish all perpetrators immediately after transition, and that compensation with all available means was not offered comprehensively to all victims. This is because consensual executive and legislative powers had to balance the interests of all sides: perpetrators, bystanders and victims. Therefore, only small-scale TJ measures were issued for victims (such as memorials, reparations or pensions) and victimisers (amnesties). According to McAdams, there are times when the most responsible way of dealing with a legacy of human rights abuse is, in fact, to be silent about the former dictators' crimes and thus pass amnesty laws, as was the case in Spain. The aim is then to forget and if possible, forgive past offences in the interests of national security.[19] Although one does not have to agree with McAdams's assessment, it is a fact that all of the countries in this study opted for amnesty laws and forgiveness instead of atonement as with the 'reintegration' laws in West Germany or the agreements made in the Palace of Moncloa in Madrid, while at the same time continuing a process of democratic consolidation. This again raises the question whether and to what extent amnesty laws actually are part of the mutual reinforcing consolidation process after all?[20] Of course the short answer is that it depends on whether amnesty laws are blanked or conditioned.

[19] J.A. McAdams, 'Preface' in J.A. McAdams (ed.), *Transitional Justice and the Rule of Law in New Democracies*, p. xiv.
[20] The fact that TJ can contribute to either an upward or downward spiral during regime change has often been noticed but not systematically proven. The 2006 United Nations Resolution 60/147 on the 'Basic Principles and Guidelines on the Right to a Remedy

At the same time, too many TJ measures too soon can lead to inertia and will consequently hamper the positive spiral effect. We can conclude that the sequencing of TJ measures matters in this process.[21] However, there is no simple majoritarian rule or formula that determines the 'right' time or best measure. There is no formula but there are indications for when and how TJ mutually enforces (democratic) institution building. That is why it is a long-term spiral effect and not a mono-causal and linear one. Hence, one of the most striking comparative results in this study is the similarity of timing and sequencing between TJ measures and institutional response and vice versa in all countries in the first five to ten years and then later after the second decade. These similarities clearly indicated that once a tactical concession to use TJ measures was made, the spiral effect started and almost compelled society to take moral responsibility after some years.

In West Germany, for example, the spiral effect was triggered by the desire to join the western alliance and later the UN, which then paved the road for an open dialogue between the different actors within and outside Germany. In Spain it was the EU, the Council of Europe, NATO, and then later the UN and the media that criticised the lack of TJ. This pushed the country to introduce massive reforms in the 1980s and later after 2004. This was also the case for Turkey around 2004 and 2005, when serious accession talks with the EU took place and the ECtHR took some landmark decisions in terms of compensations. In all cases, civil society became active about 20 years after regime change during the civic consolidation period:[22] in 1968 in West and East Germany (although with little success); in 2000 in Spain; and somewhat around 2009 in Turkey, but followed by suppression. This 20+ years may be the point at which the spiral effect shows at its best. These 'turmoils' were brought about by a new post-conflict generation coming onto the public stage that was free

---

and Reparation for Victims of Gross Violations of International Human Rights Law and Serious Violations of International Humanitarian Law' indicate that TJ measures are one but not the only factor that contribute to regime change and democracy under *certain* conditions, namely when human rights principles are respected. This includes fair trials for victimisers and no differentiation between victims of human rights abuses. All countries in my study have partly failed in respecting human rights, which has led to different results. The difference in these results is due to the fact that in an autocratic government, there is very little to no citizen participation and thus TJ measures cannot fully affect democratic institution building in this type of regime.

[21] T.D. Olson, L.A. Payne and A.G Reiter, *Transitional Justice in Balance*, p. 105.

[22] W. Merkel, Systemtransformation, *Eine Einführung in die Theorie und Empirie der Transformationsforschung*, p. 124.

from responsibility for the past and free enough from fear to demand their country deal with past wrongdoings. This generation was also less indoctrinated by propaganda or ideology of the past. Yet, as we saw in Turkey, the violent and unjust backlash to this generational shift has been dramatic in 2011, 2013, 2015 and 2016 and started again a downward spiral in which TJ is used in an exclusive way to remanifest an authoritarian regime.

6.3   Regime Change and Consolidation

Now, enough has been said about the independent TJ variable and the spiral effect. The aim of this book is to illustrate regime change and consolidation as dependent variables influenced by TJ in a multi-casual way as shown in Table 1.1. Hence, the devil is in the detail. Hundreds of studies, political advisories and academic publications, international guidelines and recommendations have more than once highlighted this complexity. Yet, as I aimed to show the use and abuse of TJ measures to catalyse claims, petitions, concerns and grievances and, at the same time, prevent acts of vengeance or arbitrary violence, is probably the strongest contribution to regime consolidation, particularly during the representative, behavioural and civic phase.[23] If there is a mix of governmental, civic and international engagement, the mutual reinforcing effect between TJ and democratic consolidation is highest.

UN or EU and ECtHR norms, laws and decisions provide necessary incentives to speed up the consolidation process, as shown in the example of Turkey prior to EU accession talks. In response, civil actors and victim groups gain access to justice and political actors win legitimacy, which is pivotal for all stages of consolidation, as illustrated in Figure 3.1 – as is delegitimising the previous regime. If citizens see that their claims about past injustice somewhat materialise – for example because a court decides in their favour for acknowledgement or compensation, or because parliament issues a law that deals with past crimes instead of silencing them – then victims, bystanders and citizens alike will abstain from taking justice into their own hands by means of violence.

---

[23] Ibid., pp. 122–127.

To see whether there is any circular cumulative causation between effective democratic performance and TJ, I refer again to Juan Riado, an observer of the Spanish consolidation and TJ process. After having looked back on over 30 years of the democratic process in Spain, he stressed that citizen-driven associations and organisations (civic consolidation) rose after so many years because they had to defend 'the recovery of historical memory, if democratic institutions did not accept their demands it was not because they had adopted other political priorities or were following a different agenda but simply because they were not authentically democratic.'[24] His observations emphasised that the lack of systematically applied TJ measures after 1975 led to major flaws in the Spanish democratic consolidation process and to unconsolidated democratic pockets in the 1980s and 1990s. TJ measures can be a way to express values that are important to both authoritarian and democratic consolidation. But when these values are expressed freely and without coercion by citizens they are conducive to elite integrity, which is a factor in closing the gap between formal and effective democracy, as was determined by Ronald Ingelhart and Christian Welzel.[25] When this happens, the stage of using TJ measures for moral atonement or behavioural consolidation[26] has been reached; and as Riado has illustrated, this usually happens after a generation has passed and when victims and victimizers can start compromising and collaborating again. However, albeit the first two decades are the most difficult ones, blanket amnesty laws, as in the cases of Turkey and Spain, have never been shown to have any strengthening medium or long-term effect on democratic consolidation. The culture or impunity that they manifest hampers the rise of the rule of law in such a way that it is difficult to overcome or compensate it with other democratic tools and measures.

International pressure, incentives and TJ policies in Europe and elsewhere have bolstered state obligations to bring perpetrators of human rights violations to justice and to provide victims with reparations, regardless of the time that has passed since the commission of the crimes.[27] And these obligations played their part in consolidation

---

[24] J.M. Ridao, 'Democracy and the Past', p. 132.

[25] R. Ingelhart and C. Welzel, *Modernization, Cultural Change, and Democracy*, pp. 173–209.

[26] W. Merkel, Systemtransformation, *Eine Einführung in die Theorie und Empirie der Transformationsforschung*, pp. 112ff.

[27] UN Human Rights Committee, General Comment No. 31, 'The Nature of the General Legal Obligation Imposed on State Parties to the Covenant', UN Doc CCPR/C/21/Rev.1/Add.13, 26 May 2004, paras. 16–18.

in Spain, unified Germany and even in Turkey. They have incorporated TJ measures as a means to respond to pressure and of ensuring accountability and responsiveness to the international community and international organisations.[28] Ultimately, the rapidly developing international human rights and criminal law also catalyse consolidation,[29] in particular constitutional and representative consolidation of political elites and institutions.[30] In response to this, after the Cold War, think tanks, NGOs and international organisations have issued an endless number of toolkits and guidelines on how to incorporate TJ measures in national legislation. Today, these agents, actors or bodies are part of a complex external and international intervention mechanism, also considered as contextual variables, that affect almost all regime change and consolidation processes, including those that are already democracies, such as Spain and Germany. For the existing democracies, to leverage their 'consolidated quality' is the main incentive to continue with TJ polices.

Thus, even established democracies such as today's Germany and Spain are continuously confronted with claims from their citizens, diaspora communities of second- and third-generation victims, or the international community to come to terms with their past or at least to openly address it, as the 2011 attempts to try Franco's crimes during the civil war in Spain; or some of the last 'Auschwitz trials' in Germany in 2015 and 2016 have illustrated. Accordingly, it is almost impossible to determine when a TJ process starts or ends. Therefore I conclude that TJ is a constant helpful companion of regime development from change to consolidation.

Although, as has been shown, it seems that consensus-based democratic models are more likely to respond – although slowly – to TJ because there are more political parties involved and many of them represent victim groups, than liberal-majoritarian democracies from TJ. In majoritarian-led democratic systems, TJ measures can often be implemented more easily top-down and quickly than in consensus-based democracies. However, this is only the case if a majority in

---

[28] UN General Assembly, International Year of Reconciliation, 2009, 61st session, UN Doc A/61/L.22, 13 November 2006.
[29] M. Parlevliet, 'Rethinking Conflict Transformation from a Human Rights Perspective' in V. Dudouet and B. Schmelzle (eds.), *Human Rights and Conflict Transformation: The Challenges of Just Peace* (Berlin: Berghof Handbook Dialogue, 2010), pp. 15–46.
[30] W. Merkel, Systemtransformation, *Eine Einführung in die Theorie und Empirie der Transformationsforschung*, pp. 112f.

parliament supports criminal justice measures and is able to get their way.[31] Moreover, TJ in liberal-majoritarian democracies has a higher risk of being exclusionary than it does in a consensus-driven democracy, as most Western European political regimes are. While consensus-based democracies are slower in reaching agreement among all relevant actors, and often result in dramatic compromises, this type of democracy is more likely to attain a consensus-driven, albeit slower, TJ process, as was the case in West Germany and to some extent in Spain, after the first two decades. In Turkey, the consensual aspects of the regime have long been neglected and the AKP under President Erdogan has successfully established an authoritarian presidential regime. In East Germany neither model ever applied.

Even though most European democracies draw no clear distinction between liberal-majoritarian and liberal-consensual democracies, and instead have developed a mixed regime that is both liberal and consensual, the fact that transition countries in Europe opt for one particular system determines their political decision-making and later shows the slight nuances that also help to understand why TJ measures are more likely to be applied in one country than another. This is due in part to the fact that party coalitions, citizen participation and compromise are much more common in consensus-based democracies. This governance model is more inclined to take the different interests of very diverse groups into account that are pivotal for consolidation. Victim groups that aim for some representation in local or national parliaments have a higher chance of getting their voices heard in a consensual multi-party system.[32] Due to the multitude of parties, legislative setup is less polarised and also more balanced when addressing the interests of bystanders and victimisers versus victims. Almost needless to say, this regime type also barriers disadvantages in terms of decision making. Nevertheless, consensus-based democracies, such as West Germany and unified Germany, have also used radical – and even non-democratic – measures to restrict the actions of unconsolidated pockets, for example the laws on Holocaust denial or the 'radicalisation' decree in the 1960s. These counter-measures were far from establishing a diverse and pluralistic society.

---

[31] E. del Pino and C. Colino, 'National and Subnational Democracy in Spain: History, Models and Challenges', Working Paper No. 7, Instituto de Políticas y Bienes Públicos IPP, Madrid 2010.

[32] A. Lijphart, *Democracies, Patterns of Majoritarian and Consensus Government in Twenty-one Countries* (New Haven, CT: Yale University Press, 1984), pp. 30–33.

At the end what counts is whether and how the political system and regime allows for free citizen participation and civic engagement. Demands from victims and perpetrators groups (often former elites, such as the military and party members) induce the government to develop and implement policies. This triggers democratic processes and strengthens institutions, because the basic principles of responsiveness and participation have been fulfilled.[33] Therefore, when a regime consistently encourages and responds to citizens' demands, state institutions are of a higher quality than when citizens' claims are ignored.[34] If these claims are ignored, as was the case in East and West Germany and even Spain (during Franco) in the 1960s and post-Franco around 2000, and Turkey around 2010, violence and even terror re-emerges dramatically and weakens or ends the consolidation process.

Generally speaking, whatever democratic model one chooses, consolidation depends on how quickly and adequately political powers can or are willing to react, respond and adapt to citizens' demands, may they be from victims or victimisers, as illustrated with these case studies. This in return leverages and enhances accountability, transparency and civic participation. Yet it is true that some are able to do so faster than others due to their commitment to consensus or, alternatively, majoritarianism. If the constitution is set out in the wrong way, amnesty laws are blank, impunity, silence and mistrust prevails, then it will hamper civic consolidation.[35] But TJ measures can influence and shift circumstances and even influence whether a consensus or majoritarian-based approach works better, although there is some evidence that consensus-based democracy tends to enhance better democratic consolidation.[36]

The permanent exclusion or denial of victims' and thus often citizens' claims – even though there is dubious evidence for their victimhood – can still lead to unrest or violence in a deconsolidated or dictatorial regime, if the minority's interests are not taken into account, such as the Basques, Kurds or Jews. While unconsolidated pockets, such as RAF, ETA or PKK

---

[33] For more on the degree of fulfilment of the principles as a function of the quality of democracy, see: M. Bühlmann, W. Merkel, L. Müller and B. Wessels, 'The Democracy Barometer: A New Instrument to Measure the Quality of Democracy and Its Potential for Comparative Research', advanced online publication European Political Science (European Consortium for Political Research, Palgrave Journals, 2011), pp. 1–18.

[34] G.B. Powell, 'The Chain of Responsiveness', 91–105.

[35] W. Merkel, Systemtransformation, *Eine Einführung in die Theorie und Empirie der Transformationsforschung*, pp. 112ff.

[36] A. Lijphart, *Patterns of Democracy: Government Forms and Performance in Thirty-Six Countries* (New Haven, CT: Yale University Press, 1999), pp. 275–305.

terror, do not necessarily pose an eternal threat to regime consolidation, they will significantly hamper consolidation if they last much longer than a generation, as was the case in Spain and Turkey. Consensual regime setup allows the regime to function by incorporating minority rights in a sequenced and circular cumulative causal way. Governments are thus forced to represent and compromise on a broad swathe of interests, including those of victimisers or bystanders and must emphasise social justice, peace and the common wellbeing of societies.[37] On the other hand, one-sided punishment or victor's justice leads to a downward spiral of consolidation, as was the case in East Germany and is periodically still the case in Turkey by, for example, the government's denial and political instrumentalisation of the Armenian Genocide.

The level of participation and public involvement through organised civil movements, for example victim groups, survivors or descendants of the Armenian Genocide or the Holocaust, determines the strength or weakness of these institutions more than the creation of new ministries, the replacement of technocrats, or the appointment of delegates to parliament does. The extent to which a political regime is resilient to future crises and conflicts depends on its citizens' trust in these institutions and on how institutions respond to citizens' needs and demands to reckon with the past. In this context, the former UN Special Rapporteur on TJ, Pablo de Greiff, has phrased this effect in reference to regime consolidation as such that '[t]rusting an institution . . . amounts to assuming that its constitutive rules, values, and norms are shared by its members or participants and are regarded by them as binding'.[38] Thus, the way institutions deal with the past indicates their level of consolidated and consequently their resilience to other potential conflicts and crises based on injustice and inequalities in the present and the future. The extent to which a regime is open to learn from its errors and wrongdoings of the past – for which dealing with the past is a good exercise because it determines how leaders will deal with flaws and crises in the future. This leads to a spiral and mutual reinforcing effect to delegitimise and legitimise institutions and actors, because political institutions, political actors, victims and citizens learn to trust each other again. They do so with small steps and thus TJ and regime consolidation slowly mutually reinforce each other. The more citizens and policy-makers have experience in dealing with past injustices

[37] A. Lijphart, *Democracies, Patterns of Majoritarian and Consensus Government in Twenty-one Countries*, pp. 30–33.
[38] P. de Greiff, 'Transitional Justice', p. 11.

by bringing perpetrators to justice or issuing reparations, the more likely these societies will combat corruption and other forms of political fraud, injustice or crisis with democratic means. Hence, TJ mechanisms are able to assist in developing a culture of resilience.

The direct linear impact of TJ on democratic or authoritarian regime consolidation is probably difficult to ever prove, but we do know that TJ can trigger attitudinal or behavioural change and can eventually affect the development of civic culture.[39] The first task of democratic institutions, however, is to develop a rule-based, consensual and participatory political system in order for behavioural adherence and civic engagement to flourish in the first place.[40]

Tricia Olson, Leigh Payne and Andrew Reiter argue that applying only one or selective TJ measures while omitting others (for example, introducing commissions of inquiry and compensation funds but omitting trials) will have little or no effect on the sustainable democratic development in a country.[41] And Baxter adds that 'each TJ measure can have a different impact on different sectors of society', for example on elites or victims.[42] A holistic set of TJ measures might best serve regime change and consolidation in the best of all matters, as has been the case in West Germany when a 20+ generation and victims/survivors entered the political stage.

In line with many authors, Paul Gready, in his case of South Africa, denied any linear connection or direct causality between TJ and democratic consolidation at all. He argued that the strengthening of, for example, the independence of the criminal justice system, through both state and non-state involvement, is the only way to secure greater access to justice for all. In this way, such a reform *can* legitimise democracy, but does not automatically have to. It can therefore not *guarantee* legitimacy, but might contribute to it.[43] And Sikkink's approach in *The Justice Cascade* illustrated that prosecutions and trials have impacted human rights compliance by and through the appointment of a new judiciary, for example, and thus, to speak in Merkel's terms, strengthened representative consolidation.[44]

---

[39] T.D. Olson, L.A. Payne and A.G. Reiter, *Transitional Justice in Balance*, p. 105.
[40] L. Whitehead (ed.), *The International Dimensions of Democratisation, Europe and the Americas* (Oxford: Oxford University Press, 2006), p. 27.
[41] T.D. Olson, L.A. Payne and A.G. Reiter, *Transitional Justice in Balance*, pp. 141–145.
[42] N.J. Kritz, 'Policy Implications of Empirical Research on Transitional Justice'.
[43] P. Gready, *The Era of Transitional Justice: The Aftermath of the Truth and Reconciliation Commission in South Africa and Beyond* (New York: Routledge, 2011), p. 151.
[44] W. Merkel, Systemtransformation, *Eine Einführung in die Theorie und Empirie der Transformationsforschung*, pp. 112ff.

But all these case studies, samples and process tracing efforts are only half of the story of consolidation and do not say much about whether the country actually turns into a democratic or authoritarian regime. Sikkink reached a similar conclusion, namely that without a minimum set of democratic institutions and human rights and fundamental freedoms in place, it is impossible to prosecute perpetrators in the first place and thus democratic consolidation is almost impossible if one starts with a bias or exclusive legal system or constitution, such as was the case in East Germany. This would strengthen the argument that constitutional consolidation is somewhat necessary to start with the fully fledged TJ process. Hence, Sikkink implicitly stated that cumulative causality exists over a longer period of time, a period that she calls a 'cascade'. She alternately treated TJ and democratic institutions as dependent and independent variables, highlighting the fact that without a serious commitment to democracy, TJ measures are pointless.[45]

It is here that this book has aimed to build upon previous findings and existing literature and research. The assessment of whether, and if so how, TJ measures relate to regime consolidation as the dependent variable is therefore a step towards showing the cumulative causal correlation and spiral effect between the two, and that in fact there is a correlation. The effect can only be seen after at least one post-regime change generation and with the support of free and proactive citizen engagement and international involvement.[46]

[45] K. Sikkink, *The Justice Cascade*.
[46] W. Merkel, Systemtransformation, *Eine Einführung in die Theorie und Empirie der Transformationsforschung*, p. 124.

BIBLIOGRAPHY

J.M. Abad Liceras, *Ley de Memoria Histórica. La Problemática Jurídica de la Retirada o Mantenimiento de Símbolos y Monumentos Públicos* (Madrid: Dykinson, 2009).

H. Abromeit and M. Stoiber, *Demokratien im Vergleich, Einführung in die vergleichende Analyse politischer Systeme* (Wiesbaden: VS Verlag, 2006).

M. Abu-Nimer (ed.), *Reconciliation, Justice and Coexistence, Theory and Practice* (Lanham, MD: Lexington Books, 2001).

J. Agirre, 'EUSKAL MEMORIA: Recovering the Memories of the Rejected People', *Politorbis, Zeitschrift für Aussenpolitik*, Tenth Anniversary of the International Criminal Court: The Challenges of Complementarity (Bern: Federal Department of Foreign Affairs Switzerland, 2012).

P. Aguilar, 'Transitional or Post-Transitional Justice? Recent Developments in the Spanish Case', *South European Society for Politics*, 13 (2008), 417–433.

P. Aguilar, *Memory and Amnesia. The Role of the Spanish Civil War in the Transition to Democracy* (New York/Oxford: Berghahn Books, 2002).

P. Aguilar, L. Balcells and H. Cebolla-Boado, 'Determinant of Attitudes Toward Transitional Justice: An Empirical Analysis of the Spanish Case', *Comparative Political Studies*, 44 (2011), 1397–1430.

F. Ahmad, 'Military and Politics in Turkey' in C. Kerslake, K. Öktem and P. Robins (eds.), *Turkey's Engagement with Modernity. Conflict and Change in the Twentieth Century* (London: Palgrave Macmillan, 2010), pp. 92–116.

N.T. Aiken, *Identity, Reconciliation and Transitional Justice, Overcoming Intractability in Divided Societies, GlassHouse Book* (London: Routledge, 2013).

T. Akcam, *Turkish National Identity and the Armenian Question* (Istanbul: Iletisim Yayinlari, 1992).

T. Allen, 'Restitution and Transitional Justice in the European Court of Human Rights', *Columbia Journal of European Law*, 13 (2006), 1–46.

G.A. Almond and S. Verba, *The Civic Culture, Political Attitudes and Democracies in Five Nations* (London/Thousand Oaks, CA: Sage, 1989).

G. Alonso, 'Children of a Lesser God: The Political and the Pastoral Action of the Spanish Catholic Church' in G. Alonso and D. Muro (eds.), *The Politics of Memory of Democratic Transition. The Spanish Model* (New York: Routledge, 2011), pp. 113–134.

G. Alonso and D. Muro, *The Politics and Memory of Democratic Transition. The Spanish Model* (New York: Routledge, 2011).

Amnesty International Spain, *Briefing to Committee Against Torture* (Madrid: Amnesty International Spain, 2009).

Amnesty International Spain, *España: la obligación de investigar los crímenes del pasado y garantizar los derechos de las víctimas de desaparición forzada durante la Guerra Civil y el franquismo* (Madrid: Amnesty International Spain, 2008).

Amnesty International Spain, *España: poner fin al silencio y a la injusticia. La deuda pendiente con las victimas de la Guerra civil española y del régimen Francoista* (Madrid: Amnesty International Spain, 2005).

Amnesty International Turkey, *Listen to the Saturday Mothers* (London: AI Index, EUR: 44/17/98, 1998).

Amnesty International Spain, *Víctimas de la Guerra civil y el régimen Francoista: El desastre de los archivos, para privatización de la verdad* (Madrid: Amnesty International Spain, 2006).

M. Andrews, 'Grand National Narratives and the Project of Truth Commissions: A Comparative Analysis', *Media Culture & Society*, 25 (2003), 45–65.

Z. Arat (ed.), *Human Rights in Turkey* (Philadelphia, PA: University of Pennsylvania Press, 2007).

H. Arendt, *Eichmann in Jerusalem: A Report on the Banality of Evil* (London: Penguin Books, 2006).

Armenian National Institute, *The Applicability of the UN Convention on the Prevention and Punishment of the Crimes of Genocide to Events which Occurred During the Early Twentieth Century* (New York: International Center for Transitional Justice, 2003).

J. Arnold, 'Zweiter Teil. Ergebnisse im Einzelnen. 3.Bundesrepublik Deutschland/ DDR' in A. Esser, U. Sieber and J. Arnold, Jörg (eds.), *Strafrecht in Reaktion auf Systemunrecht. Vergleichend Einblicke in Transitionsprozesse, Transitionsstrafrecht und Vergangenheitspolitik* (Berlin: Max Planck Institute für ausländiches und internationales Straftrecht, 2012).

J. Assmann and J. Czaplicka, 'Collective Memory and Cultural Identity', *New German Critique, Cultural History and Studies*, 65 (1995), 125–133.

M. Avello, 'European Efforts in Transitional Justice', Working Paper No. 58, FRIDE, Madrid, June (2008), pp. 1–18.

B. Ayata, 'Tolerance as a European Norm or an Ottoman Practice? An Analysis of Turkish Public Debates in the (Re) Opening of an Armenian Church in the Context of Turkey's EU Candidacy and Neo-Ottoman Revival', Working Papers – KFG, Transformation Power of Europe, 41 (2012).

D. Backer, 'Civil Society and Transitional Justice: Possibilities, Patterns and Prospects', *Journal of Human Rights*, 3 (2003), 297–313.

O. Bakiner, 'Is Turkey Coming to Terms with Its Past? Politics of Memory and Majoritarian Conservatism', *Nationalities Papers: Journal of Nationalism and Ethnicity* (2013), 1–18.

A. Barahona De Brito, C. Gonzaléz Enríquez and P. Aguilar, *The Politics of Memory: Transitional Justice in Democratizing Societies* (Oxford: Oxford University Press, 2001).

Y. Bar-Siman-Tov (ed.), *From Conflict Resolution to Reconciliation* (Oxford: Oxford University Press, 2004).

D. Bar-Tal and G.H. Bennink, 'The Nature of Reconciliation as an Outcome and as a Process' in Y. Bar-Siman Tov (ed.), *From Conflict Resolution to Reconciliation* (Oxford: Oxford University Press, 2004), pp. 11–38.

E. Barkan, *The Guilt of Nations, Restitution and Negotiating Historical Injustice* (Baltimore, MD: Johns Hopkins University Press, 2000).

M. Barrington, Jr, *Social Origins of Dictatorship and Democracy: Lord and Peasant in the Making of the Modern World* (London: Beacon, 1993).

C.K.B. Barton, *Restorative Justice, the Empowerment Model* (Leichhardt: Hawkins Press, 2003).

F. Bauer, 'Eine Grenze hat Tyrannenmacht', *Geist und Tat*, 7 (1952), 194–200.

D. Beetham, *Democracy and Human Rights* (Oxford: Polity Press, 1999).

D. Beetham, E. Carvalho, T. Landman and S. Weir, *Assessing the Quality of Democracy: A Practical Guide* (Stockholm: International IDEA, 2008).

A. Benson Brown and K.M. Poremski (eds.), *Roads to Reconciliation, Conflict and Dia-logue in the Twenty-First Century* (New York: M.E. Sharpe, 2005).

W.L. Bernecker, *Anarchismus und Bürgerkrieg, Zur Geschichte der Sozialen Revolution in Spanien, 1936–39* (Nettersheim: Verlag Graswurzelrevolution, 2006).

W.L. Bernecker and S. Brinkmann, *Kampf der Erinnerungen, Der Spanische Bürgerkrieg in Politik und Gesellschaft, 1936–2008* (Nettersheim: Verlag Graswurzelrevolution, 2008).

D. Bloomfield, T. Barnes and L. Huyse (eds.), *Reconciliation after Violent Conflict* (Stockholm: IDEA Handbook, 2005).

D. Bloomfield, M. Fischer and B. Schmelzle (eds.), *Social Change and Conflict Transformation* (Berlin: Berghof Research Center for Constructive Conflict Management, 2010).

P. Bock, *Vergangenheitspolitik im Systemwechesel. Die Politik der Aufklärung. Strafverfolgung, Disqualifizierung und Wiedergutmachung im letzten Jahren der DDR* (Berlin: Logos Verlag, 2000).

H.E. Brady and D. Collier (eds.), *Rethinking Social Inquiry, Diverse Tools, Shared Standards* (Lanham, MD: Rowmann and Littlefield, 2004).

J.S. Brady, B. Crawford and S.E. Wiliarty (eds.), *The Postwar Transformation of Germany, Democracy, Prosperity and Nationhood* (Ann Arbor, MI: University of Michigan Press, 2002).

E. Brems, 'Transitional Justice in the Case Law of the European Court of Human Rights', *International Journal of Transitional Justice, Oxford Journals*, 5(2) (2011), 282–303.

H. Brighouse and I. Robeyns, *Measuring Justice, Primary Goods and Capabilities* (Cambridge: Cambridge University Press, 2010).

K. Brounéus, *Rethinking Reconciliation Concepts, Methods, and an Empirical Study of Truth Telling and Psychological Health in Rwanda* (Uppsala: Uppsala University, 2008).

J. Brueckner, 'Transitionasansaetze' in R. Kollmorgen, W. Merkel and H.-J. Wagner (eds.), *Handbuch Transformationsforschung* (Wiesbaden: Springer VS, 2014), pp. 89–97.

M. Bühlmann, W. Merkel and B. Wessels, 'The Quality of Democracy, Democratic Barometer for Established Democracies', *National Centre of Competence in Research (NCCR) Challenges to Democracy in the 21st Century*, Working Paper No. 10 (2008).

Bundeszentrale für Politische Bildung (ed.), *Auschwitz auf der Bühne. Peter Weiss: Die Ermittlung, in Ost und West* (Bonn: Bundeszentrale für Politische Bildung, 2008).

P. Burbidge, 'Walking the Dead of the Spanish Civil War. Judge Baltasar Garzón and the Spanish Law of Historical Memory', *Journal of International Criminal Justice*, 9 (2011), 753–781.

A. Cairns, 'Coming to Terms with the Past' in J. Torpey (ed.), *Politics and the Past, On Repairing Historical Injustice* (Lanham, MD: Rowman and Littlefield, 2003), pp. 63–90.

B. Cali, 'Human Rights Discourse and Domestic Human Rights NGOs' in Z. F. Kabasakal Arat (ed.), *Human Rights in Turkey* (Philadelphia, PA: University of Pennsylvania Press, 2007), chapter 14.

D.F. Campell, T.D. Barth, P. Plötzlbauer and G. Plötzlbauer, *The Quality of Democracy in the World* (Vienna: Democracy Ranking; Books on Demand, 2012).

T. Campell, *Justice* (London: Palgrave Macmillan, 2010).

S. Caney, *Justice Beyond Borders: A Global Political Theory* (Oxford: Oxford University Press, 2006).

A. Carkoglu and E. Kalaycioglu, *Turkish Democracy Today: Elections, Protest and Stability in an Islamic Society* (New York: International Library of Political Studies, 2007).

J. Clare, 'Democratisation and International Conflict: The Impact of Institutional Legacies', *Journal of Peace Research*, 44 (2007), 259–276.

P. Clark and Z. Kaufman (eds.), *After Genocide: Transitional Justice, Post-conflict Reconstruction and Reconciliation in Rwanda and Beyond* (London: Hurst & Co Publisher, 2008).

C. Closa Montero (ed.), *Study on How the Memory of Crimes Committed by Totalitarian Regimes in Europe Is Dealt with in the Member States* (Madrid: CSIC, 2010).

D. Cohen, 'Transitional Justice in Divided Germany after 1945' in J. Elster (ed.), *Retribution and Reparation in the Transition to Democracy* (Cambridge: Cambridge University Press, 2006), pp. 59–88.

D. Collier, 'Understanding Process Tracing', *Political Science and Politics* 44, 4 (2011), 823–830.

K.S. Cook, R. Hardin and M. Levi, *Cooperation Without Trust?* (New York: Russell Sage Foundation Series on Trust, 2005).

J.W. Creswell and V.L. Plano Clark, *Designing and Conducting Mixed Methods Research* (London: Sage, 2011).

A. Croissant and W. Merkel (eds.), 'Consolidated or Defective Democracy? Problems of Regime Change', *Democratisations, A Frank Cass Journal Special Issue*, 11 (2004).

V.N. Dadrian and T. Akçam, *Judgement at Istanbul. The Armenian Genocide Trials* (New York: Berghahn Books, 2011).

R.A. Dahl, *On Democracy* (New Haven, CT: Yale University Press, 1998).

R.A. Dahl, *Democracy and Its Critics* (New Haven, CT: Yale University Press, 1989).

R.A. Dahl, *Polyarchy, Participation and Opposition* (New Haven, CT: Yale University Press, 1971).

R.A. Dahl, *Who Governs? Democracy and Power in an American City* (New Haven, CT: Yale University Press, 1989).

R. Dahrendorf, *Gesellschaft und Demokratie in Deutschland* (Munich: Piper Verlag, 1965).

J. Danyel (ed.), *Die geteilte Vergangenheit, Zum Umgang mit Nationalsozialismus und Widerstand in beiden deutschen Staaten* (Berlin: Akademie Verlag, 1995).

M. Dauer and S. Voigt, 'Institutionen' in R. Kollmorgen, W. Merkel and H.-J. Wagner (eds.), *Handbuch Transformationsforschung* (Wiesbaden: Springer VS, 2014), pp. 47–62.

N. Deitelhoff and K.D. Wolff, 'Business and Human Rights: How Corporate Norm Violators Become Norm Entreperneurs' in T. Risse, S. C. Ropp and K. Sikkink (eds.), *The Persisting Power of Human Rights. From Commitment to Compliance* (Cambridge: Cambridge University Press, 2013), pp. 222–238.

A. Demshuk, *The Lost German East. Forced Migration and the Politics of Memory: 1945–1970* (Cambridge: Cambridge University Press, 2012).

Department of Peace and Conflict Research, Uppsala University: www.pcr.uu.se/research/research.htm

L. Diamond, *Developing Democracy: Toward Consolidation* (Baltimore, MD: Johns Hopkins University Press, 1999).

L. Diamond and L. Morlino, *Assessing the Quality of Democracy* (Baltimore, MD: Johns Hopkins University Press, 2005).

A. Dimitrova and G. Pridham, 'International Actors and Democracy Promotion in Central and Eastern Europe: The Integration Model and its Limits' in A. Croissant and W. Merkel (eds.), *Democratisations, A Frank Cass Journal, Consolidated or Defective Democracy? Problems of Regime Change*, Special Issue (New York: Routledge, 2004), pp. 91–132.

J.M. Dixon, 'Defending the Nation? Maintaining Turkey's Narrative of the Armenian Genocide' in A. Costa Pino and L. Morlino (eds.), *Dealing with the Legacy of Authoritarianism. The 'Politics of the Past' in Southern European Democracies* (New York/London: Routledge, 2010), pp. 125–143.

D. Dowe (ed.), *Kurt Schumacher und der 'Neubau' der deutschen Sozialdemokratie nach 1945*, No. 13 (Bonn: Friedrich Ebert Foundation, 1996).

I. Drechsler (ed.), *Getrennte Vergangenheit, gemeinsame Zukunft* (Munich: DTV, 1997).

M.A. Drumbl, *Atrocity, Punishment, and International Law* (Cambridge: Cambridge University Press, 2007).

S.I. Dube, 'Transitional Justice Beyond the Normative: Towards a Literary Theory of Political Transition', *International Journal of Transitional Justice*, 5 (2011), 177–197.

H. Dubiel, *Niemand ist frei von der Geschichte. Die nationalsozialistische Herrschaft in den Debatten des Deutschen Bundestages* (Munich/Vienna: Hanser Verlag, 1999).

Z. Dubinsky, 'The Lesson of Genocide', *Essex Human Rights Review*, 2 (2005), 112–117.

V. Dudouet and B. Schmelzle (eds.), *Human Rights and Conflict Transformation: The Challenges of Just Peace*, No. 9 (Berlin: Berghof Handbook Dialogue Series, 2010).

J. Dülffer, 'Zeitgeschichte in Europa – oder europäische Zeitgeschichte', *APUZ*, 1(2) (2005), 18–26.

D. Easton, *A Systems Analysis of Political Life* (New York: John Wiley & Sons, 1965).

J. Elster, *Closing the Books: Transitional Justice in Historical Perspective* (Cambridge: Cambridge University Press, 2004).

J. Elster, C. Offe and U.K. Preuss (eds.), *Institutional Design in Post-Communist Societies, Rebuilding the Ship at Sea* (Cambridge: Cambridge University Press, 1998).

M. Emerson, 'Has Turkey Fulfilled the Copenhagen Political Criteria?' in Center for European Policy Studies (ed.), *CEPS Policy Brief*, No. 48 (2004).

O.G. Encarnacion, *Democracy Without Justice in Spain. The Politics of Forgetting* (Philadelphia, PA: University of Pennsylvania Press, 2014).

J. Errandonea, *Estudio comparado de la anulación de sentencias injustas en España* (New York: International Center for Transitional Justice, 2008).

R. Escudero Alday, 'El Desarrollo de la Ley de Memoria Histórica por Parte de los Poderes Públicos' in *CIRZA, Guerra Civil y Represión: Historia y Memoria* (Zamora: Circulo Republicano Zamorano, 2010), pp. 105–128.

J. Espindola, *Transitional Justice after German Reunification, Exposing Unofficial Collaborators* (Cambridge: Cambridge University Press, 2015).

R.J. Evans, *Im Schatten Hitlers? Historikerstreit und Vergangenheitsbewältigung in der Bundesrepublik* (Frankfurt am Main: Suhrkamp, 1991).

M.J. Falcon y Tella and F. Falcon y Tella, *Punishment and Culture, a Right to Punish?* (Leiden/Boston: Martinus Nijhoff, 2006).

M. Feher, 'Terms of Reconciliation' in C. Hesse and R. Post (eds.), *Human Rights in Political Transitions: Gettysburg to Bosnia* (New York: Zone Books, 1999), pp. 325–338.

B.N. Field, 'Interparty Consensus and Intraparty Discipline in Spain's Transition to Democracy', in G. Alonso and D. Muro (eds.), *The Politics of Memory of Democratic Transition. The Spanish Model* (New York: Routledge, 2011), pp. 71–93.

L.E. Fletcher and H.M. Weinstein, 'Violence and Social Repair: Rethinking the Contribution of Justice to Reconciliation', *Human Rights Quarterly*, 24 (2002), 573–639.

K.J. Ford, N. Schmitt, S.L. Schechtmann, B.M. Hults and M.L. Dohrety, 'Process Tracing Methods: Contributions, Problems and Neglected Research Questions', *Organizational Behaviour and Human Decision Process*, 43 (1989), 75–117.

Forschungsverbund SED Staat, *'Schüler halten Demokratien und Diktaturen für gleichwertig' No.181/2012* (Berlin: Free University Berlin Press Realease, 2012).

D.P. Forsythe, *Human Rights in International Relations* (Cambridge: Cambridge University Press, 2000).

M. Freeman, *Truth Commissions and Procedural Fairness* (Cambridge: Cambridge University Press, 2006).

N. Frei, *Hitlers Eliten nach 1945* (Munich: Deutscher Taschenbuchverlag, 2003).

N. Frei (ed.), 'Transnationale Vergangenheitspolitik. Der Umgang mit deutschen Kriegsverbrechern' in *Europa nach dem Zweiten Weltkrieg* (Göttingen: Wallstein Verlag, 2002).

N. Frei, J. Brunner and C. Goschler (eds.), *Die Praxis der Wiedergutmachung, Geschichte, Erfahrung und Wirkung in Deutschland und Israel* (Göttingen: Wallenstein Verlag, 2009).

R. Fuchs and D. Nolte, 'Politikfeld Vergangenheitspolitik: Zur Analyse der Aufarbeitung von Menschenrechtsverletzungen in Lateinamerika', *Lateinamerika Analyse*, 9 (2004), 59–92.

M. Fulbrook, *Dissonant Lives. Generations and Violence through the German Dictatorship* (Oxford: Oxford University Press, 2011).

M. Fulbrook and A. Port (eds.), *Becoming East German, Socialist Structures and Sensibilities after Hitler*, vol. 6 (Publications of the German Studies Association, 2013).

W. Gagel, *Geschichte der politischen Bildung in der Bundesrepublik Deutschland 1945–1989* (Wiesbaden: VS Verlag für Sozialwiessenschaften, 1995).

G. Gamio Gehri, 'Reflexiones sobre el Tiempo y los Espacios de la Reconciliación', *Cua-dernos Idehpup*, Instituto de Democracia y Derechos Humanos (Lima: Pontificia Universidad Católica del Perú, 2004), pp. 52–66.

M. Gibney, R.E. Howard-Hassmann, J-M. Coicaud and N. Steiner (eds.), *The Age of Apology, Facing Up to the Past* (Philadelphia, PA: University of Pennsylvania Press, 2008).

J.L. Gibson, *Overcoming Apartheid: Can Truth Reconcile a Divided Nation?* (New York: HSPC Press, 2004).

J.L. Gibson, 'The Contribution of Truth to Reconciliation, Lessons from South Africa', *Journal of Conflict Resolution*, 50 (2006), 409–432.

A. Gil Gil, *La Justicia de Transición en España. De la Amnistía a la Memoria Histórica* (Barcelona: Atelier, 2009).

D. Gilmour, *The Transformation of Spain: From Franco to the Constitutional Monarchy* (London: Quartet Books, 1985).

H. Glaser, *1945 Beginn einer Zukunft, Bericht und Dokumentation* (Frankfurt: Fischer Verlag, 2005).

S. Glatte, 'Judging the (East) German Past. A Critical Review of Transitional Justice in Post Communist Germany', *Oxford Transitional Justice Research*, 5 (2011), 18.

C. Göbel, 'Authoritarian Consolidation', *European Political Science*, 10 (2011), 176–190.

T. Godwin Phelps, *Shattered Voices, Language, Violence and the Work of Truth Commissions* (Philadelphia, PA: University of Pennsylvania Press, 2004).

S.R. Golob, 'Volver: The Return of/to Transitional Justice Politics in Spain', *Journal of Spanish Cultural Studies*, Special Issue (New York: New York University, 2008).

F. Gómez Isa, 'Retos de la justicia transicional en contextos no transicionales: El caso español', *Interamerican and European Human Rights Journal*, 3 (2010), 81.

C. Goschler, *Schuld und Schulden, Die Politik der Wiedergutmachung für NS-Verfolgte seit 1945* (Göttingen: Wallstein Verlag, 2005).

T. Govier and W. Verwoerd, 'Trust and the Problem of National Reconciliation', *Philosophy and Social Sciences*, 32 (2002), 178–205.

P. Gready, *The Era of Transitional Justice: The Aftermath of the Truth and Reconciliation Commission in South Africa and Beyond* (New York: Routledge, 2011).

P. de Greiff, 'Transitional Justice, Security, and Development, Security and Justice Thematic Paper', World Development Report 2011, Background Paper, 2010.

B. Grodsky, 'Re-Ordering Justice: Towards a New Methodological Approach in Studying Transitional Justice', *Journal of peace research*, 46 (2009), 819–837.

O. Groehler, 'Der Holocaust in der Geschichtsschreibung der DDR' in B. Moltmann et al. (eds.), *Erinnerung, Zur Gegenwart des Holocaust in Deutschland West und Deutschland Ost* (Frankfurt am Main: Arnoldsheimer Texte, Haag und Herchen Verlag, 1993), pp. 47–63.

U. Guckes, 'Opferentschädigung nach zweierlei Mass? Eine vergleichende Untersuchung der gesetzlichen Grundlagen der Entschädigung für das Unrecht der NS-Diktatur und der SED-Diktatur', *Berliner Wissenschaftsverlag*, 33 (2008), 33.

R. Gunther, P.N. Diamandouros and H.-J. Puhle (eds.), *The Politics of Democratic Consolidation. Southern Europe in Comparative Perspective* (London: Johns Hopkins University Press, 1995).

R. Gunther, J. Ramón Montero and J. Botella, *Democracy in Modern Spain* (New Haven, CT: Yale University Press, 2004).

T.R. Gurr, K. Jagger and W. Moore, 'The Transformation of the Western State: The Growth of Democracy, Autocracy, and State Power since 1800', *Studies in Comparative International Development*, 25(1) (1990), 73–108.

J. Habermas, 'Justice and Solidarity', *Philosophical Forum*, 21 (1989), 32–53.

Hague Institute for International Law, *Measuring Access to Justice in a Globalising world* (Utrecht: HiiL/Tilburg University/Utrecht University, 2010).

W. Hale and E. Özbudun, *Islamism, Democracy and Liberalism in Turkey: The Case of the AKP* (New York: Routledge, 2011).

P. Hall, 'Political Science and the Three New Institutionalism', *Political Studies*, 4(55) (1996), 936–957.

T.O. Hansen, 'Transitional Justice: Towards a Differentiated Theory', *Oregon Review of International Law*, 13 (2011), 1–48.

K. Hanshew, *Terror and Democracy in West Germany* (Cambridge: Cambridge University Press, 2012).

P. Harris and B. Reilly (eds.), *Democracy and Deep-Rooted Conflict: Option for Negotiators* (Stockholm: Handbook Series IDEA, 1998).

W. Hassemer, *Strafrechtliche Aufarbeitung von Diktaturvergangenheit Aus Politik und Zeitgeschichte* (Bonn: Aus Politik und Zeitgeschichte, APuZ 35–36, 2011), pp. 48–54.

P.B. Hayner, *Unspeakable Truths, Facing the Challenges of Truth Commissions* (New York/London: Routledge, 2002).

P. Hazan, *Judging War, Judging History. Behind Truth and Reconciliation* (Stanford, CA: Stanford University Press, 2007).

P. Hazan, Measuring the Impact of Punishment and Forgiveness: A Framework for Evaluating Transitional Justice', *International Review of the Red Cross*, 88 (2006), 19–47.

P. Heberer and J. Matthäus (eds.), *Atrocities on Trial, Historical Perspectives on the Politics of Prosecuting War Crimes* (Washington, DC: US Holocaust Memorial Museum, 2008).

J. Henderson and P. Wakeham (eds.), 'Colonial Reckoning, National Reconciliation?: Aboriginal Peoples and the Culture of Redress in Canada', *ESC: English Studies in Canada*, 35(1) (2009), 1–26.

M. Heper and A. Güney, 'The Military and the Consolidation of Democracy: The Recent Turkish Experience', *Armed Forces and Security*, 26 (2000), 635–657.

J. Herf, *Divided Memory: The Nazi Past in the Two Germanys* (Cambridge, MA: Harvard University Press, 1997).

G. Herrmann, 'Documentary's Labours of Law: The Television Journalism of Montse Armengou and Ricard Belis', *Journal of Spanish Cultural Studies. Special Issue* (New York: New York University Press, 2008), 193–212.

N. Hodgin and C. Pearce (eds.), 'The GDR Remembered, Representation of the East German State since 1989' in *Studies in German Literature, Linguistic and Culture Studies* (New York: Peter Lang, 2011).

L. Holmes, *Post Communism: An Introduction* (Durham, NC: Duke University Press, 1997).

C. Hölscher, *NS-Verfolgte im 'antifaschistischen Staat', Vereinnahmung und Ausgrenzung in der ostdeutschen Wiedergutmachung (1945–1989)* (Berlin: Metropol Verlag, 2002).

C.M. Horne, 'Assessing the Impact of Lustration on Trust in Public Institutions and National Government in Central and Eastern Europe', *Comparative Political Studies*, 45(4) (2001), 439–440.

S. Horowitz and A. Schnabel, 'Human Rights and Societies in Transition: International Context and Sources of Variation' in S. Horowitz, and A. Schnabel (eds.), *Human Rights and Societies in Transition* (New York: United Nations University Press, 2004), pp. 3–25.

C. Humlebaek, 'The "Pacto de Olvido"' in G. Alonso and D. Muro (eds.), *The Politics of Memory of Democratic Transition. The Spanish Model* (New York: Routledge, 2011), pp. 183–198.

C. Humlebaek, 'Party Attitudes Towards the Authoritarian Past in Spanish Democracy' in A. Costa Pinto and L. Morlino (eds.), *Dealing with the Legacy of the Authoritarianism. The Politics of the Past in Southern European Democracies* (New York: Routledge, 2011).

C. Humrich, 'Critical Theory' in S. Schneider and M. Spindler (eds.), *Theories of International Relations* (London: Routledge, 2014), pp. 260–271.

S.P. Huntington, *The Clash of Civilization and the Remaking of World Order* (New York: Simon & Schuster, 1996).

S.P. Huntington, *The Third Wave. Democratisation in the Late Twentieth Century* (Oklahoma, OK: Oklahoma University Press, 1991).

S.P. Huntington, 'How Countries Democratise', *Political Science Quarterly*, 106 (1992), 579–616.

R. Ingelhart and C. Welzel, *Modernization, Cultural Change and Democracy: The Human Development Sequence* (Cambridge: Cambridge University Press, 2005).

Institute für Demoskopie Allensbach, *Das Dritten Reich: eine Studie über Nachwirkungen des Nationalsozialismus, Gesellschaft zum Studium der öffentlichen Meinung* (Allensbach am Bodensee: Institute für Demoskopie Allensbach, 1949).

Institute für Demoskopie Allensbach, *Das Einstellung in aussenpolitischen Fragen. Ergebnisse repräsentativer Bevölkerungsumfragen des Instituts für Demoskopie, 1957–1960* (Allensbach am Bodensee: Institute für Demoskopie Allensbach, 1960).

Institute für Demoskopie Allensbach, *Demokratie-Verankerung in der Bundesrepublik Deutschland: Eine empirische Untersuchung zum 30 jährigen Bestehen der Bundesrepublik* (Allensbach am Bodensee: Institute für Demoskopie Allensbach, 1979).

Institute für Demoskopie Allensbach, *Der 8. Mai und die Deutschen. Ergebnisse einer Repräsentativumfrage im Auftrag des Bundespresseamts* (Allensbach am Bodensee: Institute für Demoskopie Allensbach, 1985).

Institute für Demoskopie Allensbach, *Der 20. Juli 1944. Ergebnisse einer Bevölkerungs-Umfrage über das Attentat auf Hitler* (Allensbach am Bodensee: Institute für Demoskopie Allensbach, 1970).

Institute für Demoskopie Allensbach, *Deutsche und Juden, vier Jahrzehnt danach. Eine Repräsentativbefragung im Auftrag des STERN* (Allensbach am Bodensee: Institute für Demoskopie Allensbach, 1986).

Institute für Demoskopie Allensbach, *Die öffentliche Resonanz der Entnazifizierung. Ergebnisse von Bevölkerungsumfragen. September 1948 und November 1953. Gesellschaft zum Studium der öffentlichen Meinung* (Allensbach: Institute für Demoskopie Allensbach, 1954).

Institute für Demoskopie Allensbach, *Wiederstand im Drittem Reich. Wissen und Urteil der Bevölkerung vor und nach dem 40. Jahrestag des 20. Juli 1944* (Allensbach am Bodensee: Institute für Demoskopie Allensbach, 1985).

International Crisis Group, 'Turkey and Armenia: Opening Minds, Opening Borders', *Europe Report*, 199 (2009), 12.

K.H. Jarausch, *Die Umkehr. Die Deutsche Wandlungen 1945-1995* (Munich: DVA, 2004).

K. Jaspers, *Die Schuldfrage, Für Völkermord gibt es keine Verjährung* (Munich: Piper Verlag, 1979).

G. Jenkins, *Context and Circumstance: The Turkish Military and Politics* (New York: Routledge, 2005).

T. Judt, *Postwar. A History of Europe Since 1945* (London: Penguin Books, 2005).

U. Jureit and C. Schneider, *Gefuehlte Opfer, Illusionen der Vergangenheitsbewaeltigung* (Stuttgart: Klett Cotta, 2010).

M. Kaase and K. Newton, *Beliefs in Government*, Vol. V (Oxford: Oxford University Press, 1995).

M.M. Kaminski and M. Nalepa, 'Judging Transitional Justice: A New Criterion for Evaluating Truth Revelation Procedures', *Journal of Conflict Resolution*, 50 (2006), 383-407.

A. Kästner, 'Autokratieförderung' in R. Kollmorgen, W. Merkel and H.-J. Wagner (eds.), *Handbuch Transformationsforschung* (Wiesbaden: Springer VS, 2014), pp. 493-498.

T. Ka-ying Wong, W. Po-san and M. Hsiao Hsin-Huang, 'The Bases of Political Trust in Six Asian Societies: Institutional and Cultural Explanations Compared', *International Political Science Review*, 32 (2011), 263-281.

J. Keane, *Life and Death of Democracy* (London: Simon & Schuster, 2009)

S.F. Kellerhoff, *Learning from History - A Handbook for Examining Dictatorships* (Berlin: Gedenkstaette Hohenschoenhausen, Beier + Wellach, 2013)

C. Kerslake, K. Oktem and P. Robins (eds.), *Turkey's Engagement with Modernity; Conflict and Change in the Twentieth Century* (Basingstoke: Palgrave Macmillan, 2010).

G. King, R.O. Keohane and S. Verba, *Designing Social Inquiry, Scientific Interference in Qualitative Research* (Princeton, NJ: Princeton University Press, 1994).

O. Kirchheimer, *Politische Justiz, Verwendung juristischer Verfahrensmöglichkeiten zu politischen Zwecken* (Frankfurt am Main: Europäische Verlagsgesellschaft, 1981).

C. Kleßmann, *Die doppelte Staatsgründung, Deutsche Geschichte 1945–1955* (Göttingen: Vandenhoeck and Ruprecht, 1991).

M. Kneuer, *Demokratisierung durch die EU, Süd- und Ostmitteleuropa im Vergleich* (Wiesbaden: VS Verlag, 2007).

V. Knigge and N. Frei (eds.), *Verbrechen erinnern, Die Auseinandersetzung mit Holocaust und Völkermord* (Bonn: Bundeszentrale für Politische Bildung, 2005), pp. 362–378.

C.H. Knutsen, 'Measuring Effective Democracy', *International Political Science Review*, 31 (2010), 109–128.

H. Kohl, *Erinnerungen 1982–1990* (Munich: Droemer Verlag, 2005).

B. Kohler-Koch, T. Conzelmann and M. Knodt, *Europäische Integration – Europäisches Regieren* (Wiesbaden: VS Verlag, 2004).

R. Kollmorgen, 'Mondernisierungstheoretische Ansaetze' in R. Kollmorgen, W. Merkel and H.-J. Wagner (eds.), *Handbuch Transformationsforschung* (Wiesbaden: Springer VS, 2014), pp. 77–88.

S. Kredourie, *Turkey: Identity, Democracy, Politics* (London: Routledge, 2014).

K. Kreiser and C.K. Neimann, *Kleine Geschichte der Türkei* (Stuttgart: Reclam, 2003).

L. Kriesberg, *Constructive Conflicts: From Escalation to Settlement* (New York: Rowman and Littlefield, 1998), pp. 329–331.

E. Kristjansdottir, A. Nollkaemper and C. Ryngaert, 'Introduction' in ibid. (eds.), *International Law in Domestic Courts: Rule of Law Reform in Post-Conflict States*, Vol. IX (Antwerp: Intersentia, 2012), pp. 1–15.

N. J. Kritz (ed.), *Transitional Justice, How Emerging Democracies Reckon with Former Regimes*, Volume I General Considerations; Volume II Country Studies; Vol. III Laws, Rulings and Reports (Washington, DC: United States Institute for Peace, 2004).

N.J. Kritz, 'Policy Implications of Empirical Research on Transitional Justice' in H. Van der Merwe, V. Baxter and A. R. Chapman (eds.), *Assessing the Impact of Transitional Justice: Challenges for Empirical Research* (Washington, DC: USIP Press, 2009), pp. 13–22.

D. Kurban, *Reparation and Displacement in Turkey, Lessons Learned from the Compensation Law, Case Studies on Transitional Justice and Displacement*, Brookings-LSE Project on Internal Displacement (New York: International Center for Transitional Justice, 2012).

W. Kymlicka, *Contemporary Political Philosophy: An Introduction* (Oxford: Oxford University Press, 2002).

D. Lambach, 'Legitimitaet' in R. Kollmorgen, W. Merkel and H.-J. Wagener (eds.), *Handbuch Transformationsforschung* (Wiesbaden: Springer VS, 2014), pp. 599–604.

C.K. Lamont, *International Criminal Justice and the Politics of Compliance* (Burlington, VT: Ashgate, 2010).

H.-J. Lauth, 'Die Qualität der Demokratie im interregionalen Vergleich – Probleme und Entwicklungsperspektiven' in G. Pickel and S. Pickel (eds.), *Demokratisierung im internationalem Vergleich, Neue Erkenntnisse und Perspektiven* (Wiesbaden: VS Verlag, 2006), pp. 89–110.

H.-J. Lauth and U. Liebert, *Im Schatten demokratischer Legitimität* (Opladen/ Wiesbaden: Sozialwissenschaftlicher Verlag, 1999).

J.P. Lederach, *Building Peace: Sustainable Reconciliation in Divided Societies* (Washington, DC: United States Institute for Peace Press, 1998).

B.A. Leebaw, 'The Irreconcilable Goals of Transitional Justice', *Human Rights Quarterly*, 30(1) (2008), 95–118.

H. Leide, *NS-Verbrecher und Staatssicherheit, Die geheime Vergangenheitspolitik der DDR* (Göttingen: Vandenhoek and Ruprecht, 2005).

S. Levitsky and L.A. Way, *Competitive Authoritarianism, Hybrid Regimes after the Cold War* (Cambridge: Cambridge University Press, 2010).

H. Lichtenstein and O.R. Romberg (eds.), *Täter-Opfer-Folgen. Der Holocaust in Geschichte und Gegenwart* (Frankfurt am Main: TRIBÜNE Zeitschrift zum Verständnis des Judentums, 1995).

U. Liebert, *Modelle demokratischer Konsolidierung* (Opladen: Leske und Budrich, 1998).

U. Liebert, *Neue Autonomiebewegung und Dezentralisierung in Spanien. Der Fall Andalusien* (Frankfurt am Main: Campus Verlag, 1986).

A. Lijphart, *Democracies, Patterns of Majoritarian and Consensus Government in Twenty-one Countries* (New Haven, CT: Yale University Press, 1984).

A. Lijphart, *Patterns of Democracy: Government Forms and Performance in Thirty-Six Countries* (New Haven, CT: Yale University Press, 1999), pp. 275–305.

J.J. Linz, 'Crisis, Breakdown, and Reequilibration', in: J.J. Linz and A. Stepan (eds.), *The Breakdown of Democratic Regimes* (Baltimore, MD: Johns Hopkins University Press, 1978).

J.J. Linz and A. Stepan, *Problems of Democratic Transition and Consolidation. Southern Europe, South America, and Post-Communist Europe* (Baltimore, MD/London: Johns Hopkins University Press, 1996).

J.J. Linz and A. Stepan, *Toward Consolidated Democracies'*, in Diamond, Larry and Plattner, Marc F., *Consolidating the Third Wave Democracies, Themes and Perspectives* (Baltimore, MD/London: Johns Hopkins University Press, 1996), pp. 14–33.

S.M. Lipset, *Political Man* (Baltimore, MD: Johns Hopkins University Press, 1980).

S.M. Lipset, 'Some Social Requisites of Democracy: Economic Development and Political Legitimacy', *American Political Science Review*, 53(1959), 69–105.

K. Lowe, *Savage Continent, Europe in the Aftermath of World War II* (London: Penguin Books, 2013).

R. Ludi, *Reparations for Nazi Victims in Post-war Europe* (Cambridge: Cambridge University Press, 2012).

J.A. McAdams, *Judging the Past in Unified Germany* (Cambridge: Cambridge University Press, 2001).

J.A. McAdams, 'Communism on Trial: The East German Past and the German Future', in J.A. McAdams (ed.), *Transitional Justice and the Rule of Law in New Democracies* (Notre Dame, IN: University of Notre Dame Press, 1997), pp. 239–267.

J.A. McAdams, 'Reappraising the Conditions of Transitional Justice in Unified Germany', *East European Consititutional Review*, 54 (2001), 53–59.

J.A. McAdams (ed.), *Transitional Justice and the Rule of Law in New Democracies* (Notre Dame, IN: University of Notre Dame Press, 1997).

K. McEvoy and L. McGregor (eds.), *Transitional Justice from Below, Grassroots Activism and the Struggle for Change* (Oxford: Hart Publishing, 2008).

L.M. McLaren, *Constructing Democracy in Southern Europe. A Comparative Analysis of Italy, Spain and Turkey* (London/New York: Routledge, 2008).

P.C. McMahon and D.P. Forsythe, 'The ICTY's Impact on Serbia: Judicial Romanticism Meets Network Politics', *Human Rights Quarterly*, 30 (2008), 412–435.

J.M. Magone, 'The Role of the EEC in the Spanish, Portuguese and Greek Transition' in G. Alonso and D. Muro (eds.), *The Politics of Memory of Democratic Transition. The Spanish Model* (New York: Routledge, 2011), pp. 215–236.

J.C. Manier, 'La cultura de la transición o la transición como cultura' in C. Molinero (ed.), *La transición: treinta años después de la dictadura a la instauración y consolidación de la democracia* (Barcelona: Ediciones Península, 2006), pp. 153–171.

K. Marxen, G. Werle and P. Shäfter, *Die Strafverfolgung von DDR Unrecht. Fakten und Zahlen* (Berlin: Humboldt University Berlin and Stiftung Aufarbeitung DDR Diktatur, 2007).

S.L. Mazzuca, 'Access to Power Versus Exercise of Power, Reconceptualizing the Quality of Democracy in Latin America', *Studies in Comparative International Development*, 45 (2010), 334–357.

J.E. Mendez, 'In Defence of Transitional Justice' in J.A. McAdams (ed.), *Transitional Justice and the Rule of Law in New Democracies* (Notre Dame, IN: University of Notre Dame Press, 2001), pp. 1–26.

W. Merkel, *Systemtransformation* (Oplanden: Leske & Budrich UTB, 1999).

W. Merkel, *Systemtransformation* (Wiesbaden: VS Verlag, 2008).

W. Merkel, Systemtransformation, *Eine Einführung in die Theorie und Empirie der Transformationsforschung*, 2nd edition (Wiesbaden: VS Verlag, 2010).

W. Merkel and H.-J. Puhle, *Von der Diktatur zur Demokratie, Transformationen, Erfolgsbedingungen, Entwicklungspfade* (Opladen: Westdeutscher Verlag, 1999).

W. Merkel and H.-J. Wagener, 'Akteure' in R. Kollmorgen, W. Merkel and H.-J. Wagner (eds.), *Handbuch Transformationsforschung* (Wiesbaden: Springer VS, 2014), pp. 63–74.

W. Merkel, H.-J. Puhle, A. Croissant, C. Eicher and P. Thiery, *Defekte Demokratie* (Opladen: Leske und Budrich Publisher, 2003).

W. Merkel, E. Sandschneider and D. Sengert (eds.), *Systemwechsel 2, Die Institutionalisierung der Demokratie* (Opladen: Leske und Budrich, 1996).

A.J. Merritt and R.L. Merritt, *Public Opinion in Semisovereign Germany: The HICOG Surveys, 1949–1955* (Urbana, IL: University of Illinois Press, 1980).

A. Mihr, *Amnesty International in der DDR. Menschenrechte im Visier der Stasi* (Berlin: Links Verlag, 2002).

A. Mihr, 'Human Rights in Europe: Origins, Institutions, Policies and Perspectives' in R. Seidelmann and A. Vasilache (eds.), *European Union and Asia, A Dialogue on Regionalism and Interregional Cooperation, Transformation, Development, and Regionalisation in Greater Asia* (Baden-Baden: Nomos, 2008), pp. 197–220.

A. Mihr, 'Transitional Justice and the Quality of Democracy: From Democratic Institution Building to Reconciliation' in A. Mihr (ed.), *Transitional Justice: Between Criminal Justice, Atonement and Democracy* (Utrecht: SIM – Netherlands Institute of Human Rights-Utrecht University, 2012), pp. 11–52.

A. Mihr, 'Turkey, Transitional Justice and Reconciliation' in S. Lavinia and N. Nedelsky (eds.), *Encyclopedia of Transitional Justice*, Vol. 1 (Cambridge: Cambridge University Press, 2012).

A. Mihr, 'Das Internationale Jahr zur Aussöhnung 2009', *Zeitschrift für die Vereinten Nationen*, 1 (2010), 21–26.

A. Mihr, 'From Reconciliation to the Rule of Law and Democratisation', *Web Journal of Current Legal Issues*, 1 (2009). Online at: http://webjcli.ncl.ac.uk/2009/issue1/mihr1.html (last accessed December 2010).

A. Mihr, 'Transitional Justice and the Quality of Democracy', *International Journal of Conflict and Violence*, 7(2) (2013), 298–313.

A. Mihr, 'Why Holocaust Education Is Not Always Human Rights Education', *Journal of Human Rights*, 16(4) (2015), 525–544.

M. Minow, *Between Vengeance and Forgiveness, Facing History after Genocide and Mass Violence* (Boston, MA: Beacon Press, 1998).

C.R. Mitchell, 'Conflict, Social Change and Conflict Resolution. An Enquiry', in D. Bloomfield, M. Fischer and B. Schmelzle (eds.), *Social Change and Conflict Transformation* (Berlin: Berghof Handbook Dialogue Series, 2010), pp. 13–36.

C. Molinero (ed.), *La Transición, Treinta Años Despues de la Dictatura a la Instauracion y Consolidacion de la Democracia* (Barcelona: Atalaya, 2006).

J.C. Monedero, *La transición contada a nuestros padres. Nocturno de la democracia española* (Madrid: Catrata, 2011).

L. Morlino, 'Authoritarian Legacies, Politics of the Past and the Quality of Democracy in Southern Europe: Open Conclusions' in A. Costa Pinto and L. Morlino (eds.), *Dealing with the Legacy of Authoritarianism: The 'Politics of the Past' in Southern European Democracies* (New York: Routledge, 2011), 507–529.

L. Morlino, *Democracy between Consolidation and Crisis; Parties, Groups and Citizens in Southern Europe* (Oxford: Oxford University Press, 1998).

L. Morlino, 'What Is a "Good" Democracy?' in A. Croissant and W. Merkel (eds.), *Democratisations, A Frank Cass Journal; Consolidated or Defective Democracy? Problems of Regime Change, Special Issue* (New York: Routledge, 2004), pp. 10–32.

M.E. Morell, 'Survey and Experimental Evidence for a Reliable and Valid Measure of Internal Political Efficacy', *Public Opinion Quarterly*, 67 (2003).

G. Munck, 'Ten Fallacies About Qualitative Research', *Qualitative Methods, Newsletter of the American Political Science Association*, 3(1) (2005), 2–5.

G. Munck and J. Verkuilen, 'Conceptualizing and Measuring Democracy', *Comparative Political Studies*, 35(1) (2002), 5–34.

D. Muro, 'The Basque Experience of Transition to Democracy' in G. Alonso and D. Muro (eds.), *The Politics and Memory of Democratic Transition. The Spanish Model* (New York/London: Routledge, 2011), pp. 159–181.

C. Murphy, *A Moral Theory of Political Reconciliation* (Cambridge: Cambridge University Press, 2010).

G. Myrdal, *Rich Lands and Poor: The Road to World Prosperity*, World Perspectives Edition, Vol. XVI (New York: Harper and Brothers, 1957).

M. Naef and J. Schupp, *Measuring Trust. Experiments and Surveys in Contrast and Combination* (Bonn: IZA, 2009).

M. Nalepa, *Skeletons in the Closet: Transitional Justice in Post-Communist Europe* (Cambridge: Cambridge University Press, 2010).

V. Navarro, *Bienestar Insuficiente, Democracia Incompleta* (Barcelona: Anagrama, 2009).

E. Neubert, *Geschichte der Opposition in der DDR 1949–1989 (Forschungen zur DDR-Gesellschaft)* (Berlin: Christoph Links Verlag, 1998).

K. Newton and P. Norris, 'Confidence in Public Institutions: Faith, Culture, or Performance?' in S. J. Pharr and R. D. Putnam (eds.), *Disaffected Democracies, What's Troubling the Trilateral Countries?* (Princeton, NJ: Princeton University Press, 2000).

L. Neyi, 'Oral History and Memory Studies in Turkey' in C. Kerslake, K. Öktem and P. Robins (eds.), *Turkey's Engagment with Modernity, Conflict and Change in the Twentieth Century* (London: Palgrave Macmillan, 2010).

D. Nohlen and A. Hildebrand, *Spanien, Wirtschaft - Gesellschaft, Politik, Ein Studienbuch* (Wiesbaden: VS Verlag 2005).

G. O'Donnell, 'Delegative Democracy', *Journal of Democracy*, 5 (1994), 55–69.

G. O'Donnell and P. Schmitter, *Transition from Authoritarian Rule. Prospects for Democracy*, Parts I–IV (Baltimore, MD: Johns Hopkins University Press, 1986).

G. O'Donnell, P. Schmitter and L. Whitehead, *Transition from Authoritarian Rule, Southern Europe* (Baltimore, MD/London: Johns Hopkins University Press, 1986).

G. O' Donnell, J. Vargas Cullell and O.M. Iazeetta, *The Quality of Democracy, Theory and Applications* (Notre Dame, IN: University of Notre Dame Press, 2004).

D. O'Pendas, *The Frankfurt Auschwitz Trial, 1963–1965: Genocide, History, and the Limits of the Law* (Cambridge: Cambridge University Press, 2006).

A. O'Shea, *Amnesty for Crime in International Law and Practice* (London: Kluwer Law International, 2004).

C. Offe, *Herausforderungen der Demokratie, Zur Integrations- und Leistungsfähigkeit politischer Institutionen* (Frankfurt/New York: Campus Verlag, 2003).

C. Offe, *Varieties of Transition: The East European and East German Experience* (Cambridge, MA: MIT Press, 1997).

C. Offe (ed.), *Demokratisierung der Demokratie, Diagnosen und Reformvorschläge* (Frankfurt, New York: 2003).

C. Offe and U. Poppe, 'Transitional Justice in the German Democratic Republic and in Unified Germany' in J. Elster (ed.), *Retribution and Reparation in the Transition to Democracy* (Cambridge: Cambridge University Press, 2006), 239–269.

K. Öktem, *Angry Nation. Turkey Since 1989* (London: Zen Books, 2011).

C. Olivo, *Creating a Democratic Civil Society in Eastern Germany: The Case of the Citizen Movements and Alliance 90* (New York: Palgrave, 2001).

T.D. Olson, L.A. Payne and A.G. Reiter, *Transitional Justice in Balance, Comparing Processes, Weighing Efficacy* (Washington, DC: US Institute of Peace, 2010).

B. Oran, 'The Minority Concept and Rights in Turkey: The Laussane Peace Treaty and Current Issues' in F.Z. Kabasakal Arat (ed.), *Human Rights in Turkey* (Philadelphia, PA: University of Pennsylvania Press, 2007), pp. 35–36.

E. Özbudun and F. Türkmen, 'Impact of the ECtHR Rulings in Turkey's Democratisation: An Evaluation', *Human Rights Quarterly*, 35(4) (2013), 985–1008.

M. Parker, *From the Burden of the Past to Societal Peace and Democracy. Coming to Terms with the Past: Why?, When?, How?* (Istanbul: Heinrich Böll Foundation, 2007).

M. Parlevliet, 'Rethinking Conflict Transformation from a Human Rights Perspective' in V. Dudouet and B. Schmelzle (eds.), *Human Rights and Conflict Transformation: The Challenges of Just Peace* (Berlin: Berghof Handbook Dialogue, 2010), pp. 15–46.

T. Parsons, *Social System* (New York: Routledge, 1951).

D.O. Pendas, *The Frankfurt Auschwitz Trial, 1963–1965: Genocide, History and the Limits of the Law* (Cambridge: Cambridge University Press, 2010).

D.O. Pendas, 'Seeking Justice, Finding Law: Nazi Trials in Postwar Europe', *Journal of Modern History*, 81 (2008), 347–368.

M. Perez Ledesma, '"Nuevos" y "Viejos" movimientos sociales en la transicion' in C. Molinero (ed.), *La transición: treinta años después de la dictadura a la instauración y consolidación de la democracia* (Barcelona: Ediciones Península, 2006), pp. 117–126.

T. Petersen, *Freiheit und bürgerschaftliches Engagement. Ergebnisse einer Repräsentativumfrage im Auftrag der Herbert Quandt-Stiftung* (Bad Homburg: Herbert Quandt-Stiftung, 2012).

T. Petersen, D. Hierlemann, R.E. Vehrkamp and C. Wratli, *Gespalten Demokratie. Politische Partizipation und Demokratiezufriedenheit vor der Bundestagswahl* (Gütersloh: Bertelsmann Stiftung, 2013).

P. Pham and P. Vinck, 'Empirical Research and the Development and Assessment of Transitional Justice Mechanisms', *International Journal of Transitional Justice*, 1 (2007), 231–248.

D.L. Philipps, *Diplomatic History. The Turkey-Armenia Protocols* (New York: Columbia University Institute for the Study of Human Rights, 2012).

D.L. Phillips, *Unsilencing the Past: Track Two Diplomacy and Turkish-Armenian Reconciliation* (Oxford: Berhang Books, 2005).

E. del Pino and C. Colino, 'National and Subnational Democracy in Spain: History, Models and Challenges', Working Paper No. 7, Instituto de Políticas y Bienes Públicos, IPP, Madrid (2010).

S. Plogsted, *Knasmauke: Das Schicksal von politischen Häftlingen der DDR nach der deutschen Wiedervereinigung* (Giessen: Psychosizial – Verlag, 2010).

G.B. Powell, 'The Chain of Responsiveness', *Journal of Democracy*, 5(4) (2004), 91–105.

S. Power, *A Problem from Hell; America and the Age of Genocide* (New York: Harper Collins Publisher, 2002).

J. Priban, P. Roberts and J. Young (eds.), *System of Justice in Transition, Central European Experience Since 1989* (Farnham, UK: Ashgate, 2003).

G. Pridham, *Designing Democracy, EU Enlargement and Regime* (New York: Palgrave Macmillan, 2005).

G. Pridham, *The Dynamics of Democratisation: A Comparative Approach* (London/ New York: Continuum, 2000).

A. Primor and C. von Korff, *An Allen sind die Juden und die Radfahrer Schuld* (Munich: Piper Verlag, 2010).

R.D. Putnam, *Making Democracy Work, Civic Traditions in Modern Italy* (Princeton, NJ: Princeton University Press, 1993).

R.D. Putnam, S.J. Pharr and R.J. Dalton, 'Introduction: What's Troubling the Trilateral Democracies?' in S.J. Pharr and R.D. Putnam (eds.), *Disaffected*

Democracies, What's Troubling the Trilateral Countries? (Princeton, NJ: Princeton University Press, 2000), pp. 3–27.

A. Quiroga, 'Salvation by Betrayal: The Left and the Spanish Nation' in G. Alonso and Diego Muro (eds.), *The Politics of Memory of Democratic Transition. The Spanish Model* (New York: Routledge, 2011), pp. 135–158.

T.K. Rabb and E.N. Suleiman (eds.), *The Making and Unmaking of Democracy; Lessons From History and World Politics* (New York/London: Routledge, 2003).

P.B. Radcliff, *Making Democratic Citizens in Spain. Civil Society and the Popular Origins of the Transition, 1960–1978* (London: Palgrave Macmillan, 2011).

M. Rafti, 'A Perilous Path to Democracy, Political Transition and Authoritarian Consolidation in Rwanda, Discussion Paper', Institute of Development Policy and Management, IOB, University of Antwerp, Discussion Paper (2008).

C.C. Ragin, *The Comparative Method; Moving Beyond Qualitative Strategies* (Berkeley, CA: University of California Press, 1987).

J. Rau von Koester, *The Nagorno-Karabakh Conflict between Armenia and Azerbaidsan: A Brief Historical Outline* (Berlin: Verlag, 2008).

J. Rawls, *Theory of Justice* (Boston, MA: Harvard University Press, 1971).

P. Reichel, *Vergangenheitsbewältigung in Deutschland. Die Auseinandersetzung mit der NS-Diktatur von 1945 bis heute* (Munich: C.H. Beck Verlag, 2001).

J.M. Ridao, 'Democracy and the Past' in *Politorbis, Zeitschrift für Aussenpolitik*, Tenth Anniversary of the International Criminal Court: The Challenges of Complementary (Bern: Federal Department of Foreign Affairs, 2012).

D. Roche, *Accountability in Restorative Justice, Clarendon Studies in Criminology* (Oxford: Oxford University Press, 2003).

P. Rock, *Constructing Victims' Rights: The Home Office, New Labour and Victims* (Oxford: Oxford University Press, 2004).

J. Rodrigo, *Cautivos, Campos de Concentración en la España Franquista, 1936–1947* (Barcelona: Critica, S.L., 2005).

R. Rohrschneider, 'Institutional Quality and Perceptions of Representation in Advanced Industrial Democracies', *Comparative Political Studies*, 38 (2005), 850–874.

R. Rose, *Understanding Post-Communist Transformation: A Bottom Up Approach* (London: Routledge, 2009).

V. Rosoux, 'Human Rights and the Work of Memory in International Relations', *Journal of Human Rights*, 3 (2004), 159–170.

M.H. Ross, 'Ritual and the Politics of Reconciliation' in Y. Bar-Siman-Tov (ed.), *From Conflict Resolution to Reconciliation* (Oxford: Oxford University Press, 2004), pp. 197–223.

R.I. Rotberg and D. Thompson (eds.), *Truth Versus Justice: The Morality of Truth Commissions* (Princeton, NJ: Princeton University Press, 2000).

D.A. Rustow, 'Transition to Democracy: Toward a Dynamic Model', *Comparative Politics*, 2(3) (1970), 337–363.

M. Sabrow and C. Mentel (eds.), *Das Auswärtige Amt und seine umstrittene Vergangenheit. Eine deutsche Debatte* (Frankfurt am Main: Fischer, 2014).

A. Sa'adah, *Germany's Second Chance. Trust, Justice, and Democratisation* (Cambridge, MA: Harvard University Press, 1998).

M. Sancar, 'Coming to Terms with the Past in Turkey: Being Realistic, Asking for the Impossible' in Heinrich Böll Foundation (ed.), *From the Burden of the Past to Societal Peace and Democracy* (Istanbul: Heinrich Böll Foundation, 2007), pp. 29–36.

P. Sánchez León, 'Radicalism Without Representation, on the Character of Social Movements in the Spanish Transition to Democracy' in G. Alonso and D. Muro (eds.), *The Politics and Memory of Democratic Transition. The Spanish Model* (New York/London: Routledge, 2011), pp. 95–111.

J. Sarkin and E. Daly, 'Too Many Questions, Too Few Answers: Reconciliation in Transitional Societies', *Columbia Human Rights Law Review*, 35 (2004), 101–168.

M.E. Sarotte, *The Collapse. The Accidental Opening of the Berlin Wall* (New York: Basic Books, 2014).

N.S. Satana, 'Transformation of the Turkish Military and the Path to Democracy', *Armed Forces and Society*, 34 (2008), 357–388.

A. Schaap, *Political Reconciliation* (New York: Routledge, 2005).

W. Schabas, *An Introduction to the International Criminal Court* (Cambridge: Cambridge University Press, 2011).

W. Schabas and S. Darcy, *Truth Commissions and Courts: The Tension Between Criminal Justice and the Search for the Truth* (Dordrecht: Kluwer Academic Publishers, 2001).

B. Schlee, *Die Macht der Vergangenheit. Demokratisierung und politischer Wandel in einer spanischen Stadt* (Baden Baden: Nomos, 2008).

P.C. Schmädeke, *Politische Regimewechsel, Grundlagen der Transitionsforschung* (Tübingen/Basel: A. Francke Verlag, UTB, 2012).

M.G. Schmidt, *Demokratietheorien, Eine Einführung* (Wiesbaden: VS Verlag, 2006).

P. Schmidt (ed.), *Kleine Geschichte Spaniens* (Stuttgart: Reclam, 2004).

P.C. Schmitter, 'An Introduction to Southern European Transition' in G. O'Donnell, P.C. Schmitter and L. Whitehead (eds.), *Transition from Authoritarian Rule. Southern Europe* (Baltimore, MD/London: Johns Hopkins University Press, 1991).

P.C. Schmitter, *The Quality of Democracy: The Ambiguous Virtues of Accountability* (Florence: European University Institute, 2003).

P.C. Schmitter, 'The Quality of Democracy: The Ambiguous Virtues of Accountability', *Journal of Democracy*, 15(4) (2004), 47–90.

P.C. Schmitter and N. Guilhot, 'From Transition to Consolidation, Extending the Concept of Democratisation and Practice of Democracy', *Geojournal Library: Democratic and Capitalist Transition in Eastern Europe*, 55 (2000), 131–146.

U. Schneckener, 'Models of Ethnic Conflict Regulations: The Politics of Recognition' in U. Schneckener and S. Wolff (eds.), *Managing and Settling Ethnic Conflicts* (New York: Palgrave Macmillan, 2004), pp. 18–39.

C. Schneider and P. Schmitter, 'Liberalisation, Transition and Consolidation: Measuring the Components of Democratisation' in A. Croissant and W. Merkel (eds.), *Democratisations, A Frank Cass Journal; Consolidated or Defective Democracy? Problems of Regime Change*, Special Issue (New York: Routledge, 2004), pp. 59–90.

E. Schniter, R.M. Sheremeta and D. Sznycer, 'Restoring Damaged Trust with Promises, Atonement and Apology', Capman University, University of California, 22 December 2011. ssm.com/abstract=1975976 (last accessed February 2014).

M. Schulte-Mecklenbeck, A. Kühberger and R. Ranyard, 'The Role of Process Data in the Development and Testing of Process Models of Judgement and Decision Making', *Judgement and Decision Making*, 6(8) (2011), 733–739.

G. Schweizer, *Die Türkei – Zerreißprobe zwischen Islam und Nationalismus* (Stuttgart: Klett Cotta, 2008).

D. Senghaas, *Von Europa Lernen Entwicklungsgeschichtliche Betrachtungen* (Frankfurt am Main: Suhrkamp Verlag, 1982).

D. Senghaas, *Zum irdischen Frieden* (Frankfurt am Main: Suhrkamp Verlag, 2004).

G. Seufert and C. Kubaseck, *Die Türkei, Politik, Geschichte, Kultur* (Munich: Beck Verlag, 2004).

B. Seyhan, *Politik und Erinnerung. Der Völkermord an den Armenien* (Bielefeld: Transcript Verlag, 2010).

K. Sikkink, and C. Booth Walling, 'The Impact of Human Rights Trials in Latin America', *Journal of Peace Research*, 44 (2007), 427–445.

K. Sikkink, *The Justice Cascade. How Human Rights Prosecutions Are Changing World Politics* (New York: W.W. Norton & Company, 2011).

E. Silva, *Las fosas de Franco: Crónica de un desagravio*, Temas de hoy (Madrid: Historia Selección, 2005).

B.A. Simmons, *Mobilizing for Human Rights, International Law in Domestic Politics* (Cambridge: Cambridge University Press, 2009).

E. Skaar and A.J.R. Dahl, *Dealing with Violent Past. The Impact of Transitional Justice* (Bergen: CMI, CHR, Michael Institute, 2012).

G. Skapska, 'Moral Definitions of Constitutionalism in East Central Europe, Facing Past Human Rights Violations', *International Sociology*, 18 (2003), 199–218.

P.J. Smith, 'Cinema and Television in the Transition' in G. Alonso and D. Muro (eds.), *The Politics and Memory of Democratic Transition. The Spanish Model* (New York/London: Routledge, 2011).

K. Sontheimer, *Antidemokratisches Denken in der Weimarer Republik, Studienausgabe mit einem Extrateil, Antidemokratisches Denken in der Bundesrepublik* (Munich: Nymphenburger Verlagshandlung, 1968).

J. Spinner-Halev, 'Education, Reconciliation and Nested Identities', *Theory and Research in Education*, 1 (2003), 51–72.

J. Spinner-Halev, 'From Historical to Enduring Injustice', *Political Theory*, 35 (2007), 574–597.

C.L. Sriram, *Confronting Past Human Rights Violations: Justice vs. Peace in Times of Transition* (New York: Frank Cass, 2004).

L. Stan (ed.), *Transitional Justice in Eastern Europe and the Former Soviet Union, Reckoning with the Communist Past* (New York: Routledge, 2008).

L. Stan and N. Nedelsky, *Encyclopaedia of Transitional Justice* (Oxford: Oxford University Press, 2013).

E. Stanley, 'Evaluating the Truth and Reconciliation Commission', *Journal of Modern African Studies*, 39 (2011), 505–546.

P. Steinbach, 'Vergangenheit als Last und Chance: Vergangenheitsbewaeltigung in den 50er Jahren' in J. Weber (ed.), *Die Bundesrepublik wird souveraen 1950–1955* (Munich: BLpB, 1998), pp. 333–373.

H. Strang, *Repair of Revenge: Victims and Restorative Justice, Clarendon Studies in Criminology* (Oxford: Oxford University Press, 2002).

J.A. Sweeney, *The European Court of Human Rights in the Post Cold War Era. Universality in Transition* (London/New York: Routledge Research in Human Rights Law, 2013).

J.M. Tamarit Sumalla, 'Historical Memory and Criminal Justice in Spain', *Series on Transitional Justice*, 14 (2013), 371–374.

J.M. Tamarit Sumalla, 'Transition, Historical Memory and Criminal Justice in Spain' *Journal of International Criminal Justice*, 9 (2001), 731.

J. Tanaka, *Japan's Comfort Women: Sexual Slavery and Prostitution During World War II and the US Occupation* (London: Routledge, 2002)

C. Taylor, *Multiculturalism, Examining the Politics of Recognition* (Princeton, NJ: Princeton University Press, 1994).

R. Teitel, *Globalizing Transitional Justice* (Oxford: Oxford University Press, 2014).

R. Teitel, 'How Are the New Democracies of the Southern Cone Dealing with the Legacy of Past Human Rights Abuses?' in N. Kritz (ed.), *Transitional Justice: How Emerging Democracies Reckon with Former Regimes*, Vol. 1 (Washington, DC: US Institute of Peace, 2004), pp. 146–153.

R. Teitel, *Transitional Justice* (Oxford: Oxford University Press, 2000).

R. Teitel, 'Transitional Justice Globalised', *International Journal of Transitional Justice*, 2 (2008), 1–4.

P. Ther, *Die dunkle Seite der Nationalstaaten. Ethnische Säuberungen im modern Europa* (Göttingen: Vandenhoek and Ruprecht, 2011).

J. Thompson, *Taking Responsibility for the Past, Reparation and Historical Justice* (Cambridge: Cambridge University Press, 2002).

O.N.T. Thoms, J. Ron and R. Paris, *The Effects of Transitional Justice: A Summary of Empirical Research Findings and Implications for Analysts and Practitioners* (Ottawa: CIPS Working Paper, 2008).

O.N.T. Thoms, J. Ron and R. Paris, 'State-Level Effects of Transitional Justice: What Do We Know?', *International Journal of Transitional Justice, Special Issue: Transitional Justice on Trial – Evaluating Its Impact*, 4 (2010), 329–354.

Tilburg Institute for Interdisciplinary Studies of Civil Law and Conflict Resolutions Systems (TISCO) (ed.), *A Handbook for Measuring the Costs and Quality of Access to Justice* (Appeldorn/Antwerpen/Portland: Tilburg Institute for Interdisciplinary Studies of Civil Law and Conflict Resolution Systems, 2009).

C. Tilly, *Democracy* (Cambridge: Cambridge University Press, 2008).

A. Timm, 'Alles umsonst? Verhandlungen zwischen der Claims Conference und der DDR über "Wiedergutmachung" und Entschädigung', *Hefte zur DDR Geschicht*, 32 (1996).

S. Tiryaki and M. Akgün (eds.), *The Heybeliada Talks: Two Years of Public Diplomacy on Cyprus, Global Political Trends Center* (Istanbul: Istanbul Kültür University, 2011).

B. Torgler, 'Trust in International Organizations: An Empirical Investigation Focusing on the United Nations', *Review of International Organizations*, 3 (2008), 65–93.

J. Torpey (ed.), *Politics and the Past, On Repairing Historical Injustice* (Oxford: Rowman & Littlefield Publishers, 2003).

I. Turan, *Turkey's Difficult Journey to Democracy: Two Steps Forward, One Step Back* (Oxford: Oxford University Press, 2015).

F. Türkmen, 'Turkey's Participation in Global and Regional Human Rights Regime' in Z. F. Kabasakal Arat (ed.), *Human Rights in Turkey* (Philadelphia, PA: University of Pennsylvania Press, 2007), pp. 249–261.

U. Ungör, *The Making of Modern Turkey* (Oxford: Oxford University Press, 2011).

M. Ure, 'Post-Traumatic Societies: On Reconciliation, Justice and the Emotion', *European Journal of Social Theory*, 11 (2008), 283–297.

E. Ustundag, *Government Should Apologize for Enforced Disappearances* (Istanbul, 2009). www.bianet.org/english/human-rights/118902-governments-should-apologize-for-enforced-disappearances

A.R. Usul, *Democracy in Turkey: The Impact of EU Political Conditionality* (London: Routledge, 2010).

H. Van der Merwe, V. Baxter and A.R. Chapman (eds.), *Assessing the Impact of Transitional Justice: Challenges for Empirical Research* (Washington, DC: USIP Press, 2009).

T. Vanhanen, *Democratisation. A Comparative Analysis of 170 Countries* (London: Routledge, 2003).

R. Vetik, 'Multiculturalism as a Model for Democratic Consolidation' in D-B. Schlosser and R. Veik (eds.), *Perspectives on Democratic Consolidation in Central and Eastern Europe* (East European Monographs, 2001), pp. 22–30.

L. Viaene and E. Brems, 'Transitional Justice and Cultural Contexts: Learning from the Universality Debate', *Netherlands Quarterly of Human Rights*, 28 (2010), 199–224.

C. Villa-Vicencio and E. Doxtader (eds.), *The Provocations of Amnesty, Memory, Justice and Impunity* (Trenton, NJ: Africa World Press, 2003).

R. Vinyes (ed.), *El Estado y la Memoria, Gobiernos y Ciudadanos Frente a los Traumas de la Historia, Direcció General de la Memoria Democratica de la Generalitat de Catalunya* (Barcelona: Groupo RBA, 2009).

S. Voigt, 'Values, Norms, Institutions and Prospects for Economic Growth in Central and Eastern Europe' in S. Pejovich (ed.), *The Economics of Property Rights II* (Cheltenham: Edward Elgar, 1996), pp. 303–337.

C. Vollnhals, *Entnazifierung. Politische Säuberung und Rehabilitierung in den vier Besatzungszonen 1945–1949* (Munich: dtv Verlag, 1991).

K. von Beyme, *Systemwechsel Osteuropa* (Frankfurt: Suhrkamp, 1994).

M. Von Bruinessen, 'Genocide in Kurdistan? The Suppression of the Dersim Rebellion in Turkey (1937–1938) and the Chemical War Against the Iraqi Kurds (1988)' in G.J. Andrepoulos (ed.), *Conceptual and Historical Dimensions of Genocide* (Philadelphia, PA: University of Pennsylvania Press, 1994), pp. 141–170.

A. von Saldern, 'Öffentlichkeit in Diktaturen, Zu den Herrschaftspraktiken in Deutschland des 20. Jahrhunderts' in G. Heydemann and H. Oberreuter (eds.), *Diktature in Deutschland – Vergleichsperspektive, Strukturen, Institutionen und Verhaltensweise* (Bonn: Bundeszentrale für Politische Bildung, 2003), pp. 442–475.

R. Von Weizsäcker, *Drei Mal Stunde Null? 1949, 1969, 1989. Deutschland europäische Zukunft* (Berlin: Siedler Verlag, 2001).

H. Weber, *Die DDR 1945–1990: Oldenbourg-Grundriss der Geschichte*, No. 20 (Oldenburg: Oldenbourg Wissenschaftsverlag, 2011)

B. Weiffen, 'Der vergessene Faktor – Zum Einfluss von Transitional Justice auf die Entwicklung von Rechtsstaatlichkeit in Demokratisierungsprozessen', *Zeitschrift für Vergleichende Politikwissenschaft* (Comparative Governance and Politics), 5 (2011), 51–74.

M.A. Weingardt, *Deutsche Israel- und Nahostpolitik. Die Geschickte einer Gratwanderung seit 1949* (Frankfurt am Main/Munich: Campus Verlag, 2002).

A. Weinke, 'West Germany: A Case of Transitional Justice, Avant La Lettre?' in N. Wouters (ed.), *Transitional Justice and Memory in Europe (1945–2013)* (Antwerp: Intersentia, 2014), pp. 25–61.

C. Welzel, 'Effective Democracy, Mass Culture, and the Quality of Elites: The Human Development Perspective', *International Journal of Cultural Studies*, 43 (2002), 317–349.

H. Welzer, 'Der Holocaust im deutschen Familiengedächtnis' in V. Knigge and N. Frei (eds.), *Verbrechen erinnern, Die Auseinandersetzung mit Holocaust und Völkermord* (Bonn: Bundeszentrale für Politische Bildung, 2005), pp. 362–378.

H. Wentker, *Justiz in der SBZ/DDR 1945-1953: Transformation und Rolle ihrer zen-tralen Institutionen*, Veröffentlichungen zur SBZ-/DDR-Forschung im Institut für Zeitgeschichte (Oldenburg: Oldenbourg Wissenschaftsverlag, 2001).

G. Werle, 'Der Holocaust als Gegenstand der bundesdeutschen Strafjustiz', *Neue Juristische Wochenschrift*, 45(40) (1992), 2529-2535.

L. Whitehead, *Democratisation, Theory and Experience* (Oxford: Oxford University Press, 2002).

L. Whitehead (ed.), *The International Dimensions of Democratisation, Europe and the Americas* (Oxford: Oxford University Press, 1996).

E. Wiebelhaus-Brahm, *Truth Commissions and Transitional Justice: The Impact on Human Rights and Democracy* (New York/London: Routledge, 2010).

E. Wiesel, 'Preface', in D.L. Phillips, *Unsilencing the Past: Track Two Diplomacy and Turkish-Armenian Reconciliation* (Oxford: Berghahn Books, 2005).

L. Wildenthal, *The Language of Human Rights in West Germany* (Philadelphia, PA: University of Pennsylvania Press, 2012).

R.A. Wilson, *The Politics of Truth and Reconciliation in South Africa: Legitimising the Post Apartheid State* (Cambridge: Cambridge University Press, 2001).

R.A. Wilson, 'Anthropological Studies of National Reconciliation Processes', *Anthropological Theory*, 3 (2003), 367-387.

S. Winter, *Transitional Justice in Established Democracies, A Political Theory*, International Political Theory (London: Palgrave Macmillan, 2014).

S. Winter, 'Towards a Unified Theory of Transitional Justice', *Journal of Transitional Justice*, 1 (2013), 1-21.

D. Wippman, 'Atrocities, Deterrence, and the Limits of International Justice', *Fordham International Law Journal*, 23 (2000), 473-488.

E. Wolfrum, *Die geglückte Demokratie, Geschichte der Bundesrepublik Deutschland von ihren Anfängen bis zur Gegenwart* (Bonn: Klett Cotta, 2007).

S. Woolpert, C.D. Slation and E.W. Schwerin (eds.), *Transformational Politics, Theory, Study and Practice* (New York: State University of New York Press, 1998).

H.M. Yavuz (ed.), *The Emergence of a New Turkey, Democracy and the AK Parti* (Salt Lake City, UT: University of Utah Press, 2006).

Young Civilians and Human Rights Agenda Association (HRAA) (ed.), *Ergenekon Is Our Reality* (Ankara: HRAA, 2010).

R. Zajac Sonnerholm, *Rule of Law after War and Crisis, Ideologies, Norms and Methods* (Antwerp: Intersentia, 2012).

W. Zapf, 'Mondernisierungstheorien in der Transformationsforschung' in K. von Beyme and C. Offe (eds.), *Politische Theorien in der Ära der Transformation*, PVS Sonderheft, No. 26 (Opladen, Wiesbaden: Springer VS, 1996), pp. 169-181.

J. Zielonka, 'The Quality of Democracy after Joining the European Union', *East European Politics and Societies*, 21 (2007), 162-180.

Archives

Archive Historical Memory, Salamanca. Campaign materials. Archive of Historical
Memory, Salamanca. Caja: 1598, 1601.

BA-136 Bundeskanzleramt – 175

BA-136 Bundeskanzleramt – 504

BA-136 Bundeskanzleramt – 1745

B-136 Bundeskanzleramt – 1880

B-136 Bundeskanzleramt – 3173

B-136 Bundeskanzleramt – 3314

BA-136 Bundeskanzleramt – 3801

BA-136 Bundeskanzleramt – 3904

B-136 Bundeskanzleramt – 4369

BA-136 Bundeskanzleramt – 4404

BA-136 Bundeskanzleramt – 4406

BA-136 Bundeskanzleramt – 4689

BA-136 Bundeskanzleramt – 4698

BA-136 Bundeskanzleramt – 4699

Bundesarchiv B 136–4960

Federal Archives Germany (Bundesarchiv, Koblenz).

Federal Archives Germany. GDR Department for Reparation DC 2.

Federal Archives Germany (Bundesarchiv, Berlin).

Federal Archives Salamanca.

Federal Republic of Germany, Federal Law (Bürgerliches Gesetzblatt, BGBl.) 1950.

Fundación Francisco Franco, Archive. Documento de trabajo para la preparación
de una asociación política. 3Rd version. January 1975. Fiche 10109, Madrid.

German Democratic Republic Department for Reparation (Amt für Reparation)
BA-DC 2 652.

German Democratic Republic Executive Board of the Victims of National Socialism
(Zentraler Parteivorstand VVD (Verein Verfolgter des Nationalsozialismus)
DY 55/ V 2 78/ ½.

German Democratic Republic Institute for Marxism and Leninism, SED
Government, Dept. of Law (Institut für Marxismus Leninismus beim ZK der
SED, Bestand Staat und Recht) BA-DY/ 30/ IV 2/ 13–431; -432 and DY/30/
IV A 2/ 13–30.

German Federal Archive GDR. Executive Board of the Victims of National Socialism
(Zentraler Parteivorstand VVD) (Verein Verfolgter des Nationalsozialismus)
DY 55/V278/1/2.

Interviews

Baltasar Garzón. 6 May 2011, Madrid.

Emilio Silva Barrera. 8 May 2011, Madrid.

Luis Fernando Parra Galindo. 11 May 2011, Madrid.
Martin Gutzeit, Federal Commissioner for the Stasi Files in the State of Berlin. Berlin, June 2015.
Orhan Kemal Cengiz. 20 April 2011, Ankara.
Paco Etxeberría: Forensic Institute University of San Sebastian during excavations of mass graves from Civil War. Puerto de la Mazorra close to Burgos. 7 May 2011.

Media and Internet Sources

Beethman, David, IDEA, Democracy Assessment: www.idea.int
Bertelsmann Transformation Index 2012, Turkey Country Report BTI, Gütersloh 2012 bti-project.org and bertelsmann-transformation-index.de
Center for the Study of Global Governance, Global Civil Society Reports; www.lse.ac.uk/Depts/global/index.htm
Council of Europe, Brincat Report – Need for International Condemnation of the Franco Regime, for Debate in the Standing Committee. Doc. 10737, 4 November 2005.
Democracy Barometer, 'Germany: Basic Facts 2007'. Center for Democracy Studies Aarau. www.democracybarometer.org (August 2013).
Democracy Barometer,. 'Spain: Basic Facts 2007'. Center for Democracy Studies Aarau. www.democracybarometer.org (August 2013).
Democracy index 2012, 'Democracy at a standstill'. A Report from The Economist Intelligence Unit: www.eiu.com (last accessed November 2014).
Democracy Ranking Association, Quality of Democracy Ranking 2015, http://democracyranking.org/wordpress/
The EpochTimes, 'Turkey's President Defends Armenian Apology Campaign', www.theepochetimes.com, 18 December 2008.
Eurobarometer, http://ec.europa.eu/public_opinion/index_en.htm
European Parliament, Debate No. 4: 70 years after General Franco's coup d'etat in Spain (Statements by the President and the political groups, Strasbourg, 4 July 2006).
European Union, Eurobarometer Surveys. Germany 1990. http://ec.europa.eu (August 2013).
European Union, Eurobarometer Surveys. Spain 2013. http://ec.europa.eu (August 2013).
Freedom House, www.freedomhouse.org (last accessed July 2016).
The Guardian, 'Spain finally attempts to lay ghosts of the Franco era', 20 July 2006. www.guardian.co.uk (August 2013).
The Guardian, 'Turkey's coup attempt', www.theguardian.com/world/turkey-coup-attempt (August 2016).
Hurriyete Daily Newspaper, English version: http://web.hurriyetdailynews.com/. 6 April 2011.

Hürriyet Daily News, 'Armenian apology denounced by gov't', 6 June 2011.

International Center for Transitional Justice, www.ictj.org/en/tj/.

International Center for Transitional Justice, What is Transitional Justice, 2009. Online paper: http://ictj.org/sites/default/files/ICTJ-Global-Transitional-Justice-2009-English.pdf (October, 2013).

International Herald Tribune, 'Nearly a million Armenians, veiled by amnesia', 10 March 2009, p. 3.

Manifestación de las víctimas del franquismo en la Puerta del Sol (Madrid) todos los jueves en la Puerta del Sol, Madrid de 20 a 21 horas. www.tercerainfor-maciñon.es (August 2013).

MetroPoll, Awareness of Oscar's and the Armenian Issue, March 2010, www.metro-poll.com.tr (August 2013).

MetroPoll, Turkey's Pulse 'The New Resolution Process', Strategical and Social Research.

Center Ankara, April 2013, slide no. 18, www.metropoll.com.tr (August 2013).

MetroPoll, Strategical and Social Research Center, Leaders and Public Trust in Institutions, Ankara, Januar 2013, www.metropoll.com.tr (August 2013).

M.G. Marschall and B.R. Cole. Global Report 2011. State Fragility Index and Ma-trix 2010. Center for Systematic Peace. www.systemicpeace.org/polity (August 2013).

El Mundo, 'Congreso de los Diputados: Todos los grupos parlamentarios, excepto el PP home-najean a los represaliados del franquismo'. 1 December 2003. www.elmundo.es

NCCR Democracy Barometer for Established Democracies, National Center of Competences in Research, Challenges to Democracy in the 21st Century, Zürich; www.nccr-democracy.uzh.ch/nccr/knowledge_transfer/ip14

El País, 'España suma casi 250.000 nuevos nacionales gracias a la "ley de nietos"', 30 March 2012. http://politica.elpais.com

El País, 'En busca de un Valle de los Caídos', 8 June 2011. www.memoriahistorica. org.es

Parliamentary Assembly of the Council of Europe, 'In the aftermath of Hrant Dink's Murder'. Doc.11187, 20 February 2007.

Parliamentary Assembly of the Council of Europe, Written Declaration No. 147 Democracy and Human Rights in Turkey. Doc. 5690, 28 January 1987.

Polity Index IV, www.systemicpeace.org/polity/polity4.htm

Polity IV Project, Turkey Authority Trends 1946–2010. Center for Systematic Peace www.systemicpeace.org/polity (August 2013).

Portada de Pares, Spanish Archives: http://pares.mcu.es

Portal de Víctimas de la Guerra Civil y Represaliados del Franquismo: http://pares. mcu.es/víctimasGCFPortal (May 2011).

Süddeutsche Zeitung, 'Noch sind Mörder unter uns', 11 July 1958.

Der Tagesspiegel, 4 March 1960.

La Vanguardia, 'El Parlamento condena el franquismo'. 21 November 2001.

La Vanguardia, 'El PP se suma "sin reservas" a la condena del Parlamento al franquismo'. 14 December 2000.

La Vanguardia, 'El Valle de los Caídos dejará de ser un templo de exaltación del franquismo'. 18 October 2007.

Vanhanen   Democracy   Index,   www.prio.no/CSCW/Datasets/Governance/ Vanhanens-index-of-democracy/

Legal documents

Convention (I) for the Amelioration of the Condition of the Wounded and Sick in Armed Forces in the Field. Geneva, 12 August 1949.

Straffreiheitsgesetz, 31 December 1949, BGB1, German Civic Penal Code.

Gesetzblatt der DDR, German Democratic Republic, 18 February 1950, Nr. 14.

Spain Law 46/1977, Ley de amnistia, 15 October 1977, Gazette n°248, 17 October 1977, pp. 22765–22766, Reference BOE-A-1977–24937.

Second Protocol of the Hague Convention of 1954 for the Protection of Cultural Property in the Event of Armed Conflict, 26 March 1999. (Art. 38.)

European Court for Human Rights (ECtHR), Court Chamber, Case of Loizidou versus Turkey, Application no. 15318/89, Judgment, Strasbourg, 18 December 1996.

ECtHR, Case of Streletz, Kessler and Krenz versus Germany, Appl. Nos 34044/96, 35532/97 and 4480/98, Judgment, Strasbourg, 22 March 2001.

UN Human Rights Committee, General Comment No.31 The nature of the general obligation imposed on State Parties to the Convenant. Doc.CCPR/C/21/ Rev.1/Add.13, 26 May 2004.

Council of Europe, Parliamentary Assembly. Need for international condemnation of the Franco regime. Report, Political Affairs Committee. Doc. 10737, 4 November 2005.

UN-General Assembly, Resolution adopted by the General Assembly on the report of the Third Committee (A/60/509/Add.1) 60/147. Basic Principles and Guidelines on the Right to a Remedy and Reparation for Victims of Gross Violations of International Human Rights Law and Serious Violations of International Humanitarian Law, UN Doc A/Res/60/147, March 2006.

UN General Assembly, International Year of Reconciliation, 2009, 61st session, UN Doc A/61/L.22, 13 November 2006.

UN-General Assembly, International Year of Reconciliation, 2009, Addendum, 61st session, UN Doc A/61/L.22/Add.1, 20 November 2006.

UN Doc A/HRC/24/42 Human Rights Council, Report of the Special Rapporteur on the promotion of truth, justice, reparation and guarantees of non-recurrences, Pablo de Greiff, Geneva and New York, Twenty-fourth session, 28 August 2013.

UN Human Rights Council, Special Rapporteur on the promotion of truth, justice, reparation and guarantees of non-recurrence, Pablo de Greiff, Doc. A/HRC/ 21/46, 9 August 2012.

Office of the High Commissioner for Human Rights (OHCHR), 2006. *Rule-of-Law Tools for Post-Conflict States: Mapping the Justice Sector, HR/PUB/06/2*, New York and Geneva: United Nations.

Office of the High Commissioner for Human Rights (OHCHR), 2006. *Rule-of-Law Tools for Post-Conflict States: Prosecution Initiatives, HR/PUB/06/4*, New York and Geneva: United Nations.

Office of the High Commissioner for Human Rights (OHCHR), 2006. *Rule-of-Law Tools for Post-Conflict States: Truth Commissions, HR/PUB/06/1*, New York and Geneva: United Nations.

Office of the High Commissioner for Human Rights (OHCHR), 2006. *Rule-of-Law Tools for Post-Conflict States: Vetting, an Operational Framework, HR/PUB/06/5*, New York and Geneva: United Nations.

Tribunal Supremo España. Sala de lo Militar. Sentencia, Recurso, Revisión Penal. No 106/2004. Sentencia: 19 February 2007.

Spain Law 52/2007, Ley de la Memoria, concerning those who suffered persecution or violence during the Civil War and the Dictatorship, 26 December 2007, Gazette n° 310, 27 December 2007, pp. 53410–53416, Reference BOE-A-2007–22296.

Office of the High Commissioner for Human Rights (OHCHR), 2008. *Rule-of-Law Tools for Post-Conflict States: Reparations Programmes, HR/PUB/08/1*, New York and Geneva: United Nations.

UN Human Rights Committee, ICCPR, Consideration of Report Submitted by State Parties un-der Article 40 of the Convenant, Concluding observations of the Human Rights Committee, Spain, 94th session, Geneva 13–31 October 2008. Doc. CCPR/C/ESP/CO/5, Geneva, 5 January 2009.

UN Committee Against Torture (CAT), UN Doc. CAT/C/ESP/Q/5/Add.1 New York, 22 September 2009.

Office of the High Commissioner for Human Rights (OHCHR), 2009. *Rule-of-Law Tools for Post-Conflict States: Amnesties, HR/PUB/09/1*, New York and Geneva: United Nations.

Office of the High Commissioner for Human Rights (OHCHR), 'Spain: The State must assume a leadership role and engage more actively to respond to the demands of the relatives of the disappeared', Press Release, Madrid, 30 September 2013. www.ohchr.org/ (last accessed January 2014).

UNDP Human Development Reports, http://hdr.undp.org/en/reports/global/hdr2002/

UN World Development Report (WDR) (2011), *Conflict, Security and Development*, New York: United Nations.

Special Rapporteur on the promotion of truth, justice, reparation and guarantees of non-recurrence. Doc. A/HRC/21/46, 9 August 2012.

INDEX

8 May 1945 as liberation day 218–219, 240–241
20+ generation 12, 35, 36–37, 66–67, 402
anti-terror laws in West Germany 212
East Germany 203–204
Germany 262–263
Spain 267, 268, 304–305, 309
Turkey 363, 377, 386–387
West Germany 203

accountability 17–18, 79–82
Germany post-war, lack of in 120–121
international institutions 27
Spain, lack of in 274
acknowledgement of wrongdoings as TJ category 108109t. 4.1
Action Reconciliation Service 202
actor specific assessment 18–20
Adenauer, K. 130, 136, 141–142, 146, 155–156, 164, 168
Aguilar, P. 21, 63, 329
Aiken, N.T. 101
Aksoy, M. 388
Allied atrocities 140–141
Almond, G.A. 91, 178
American Jewish Committee 168
amnesties 61–63, 69, 86–88, 110
East Germany 237
Spain 271, 282, 283, 284, 288–289, 337
West Germany 133–135, 142–143, 165, 172
Amnesty International 321, 328
anti-Semitism

as continuing post-war in Germany 125, 149–150, 167, 168–169
in other countries 182
Antidemokratisches Denken in der Weimarer Republik (Sontheimer) 201–202
apologies for Nazi regime 207–208
resistance to 156–157
Armenian Church 374–375
Armenian Genocide 344–347, 357–359, 366–367, 372–375, 378–379, 380, 381, 389
artists/writers, past revisited by 149
assassination attempt against Hitler 165–166, 218
Association for the Dealing with Memory and History *(Asociación para la Recuperación de la Memoria Histórica)* (ARMH) 310–311
Atatürk, K. 346, 347, 348
Auschwitz Trials 1963–65 60, 172–174, 176–177, 178
authoritarian regimes
characteristics of 3
civil society 4, 11–12, 43–44
delegitimisation of previous regimes 65
regime change 2
return to 12
steps towards democracy 3
TJ measures in 44, 45, 61, 402
TJ measures leading to 59–60
transitional justice, use of for 1, *see also* Turkey
autocratic regimes
bias in use of TJ measures 35
types of 4
Aznar, J.M. 318–319

454   INDEX